More praise from across the nation for the JobBank series:

"One of the better publishers of employment almanacs is Adams Media Corporation ... publisher of *The Metropolitan New York JobBank* and similarly named directories of employers in Texas, Boston, Chicago, Northern and Southern California, and Washington DC. A good buy...."

> *-Wall Street Journal's*
> *National Business Employment Weekly*

"*JobBank* books are all devoted to specific job markets. This is helpful if you are thinking about working in cities like San Antonio, Washington, Boston, or states such as Tennessee or the Carolinas. You can use them for research, and a particularly useful feature is the inclusion of the type of positions that are commonly offered at the companies listed."

> **-Karen Ronald, Library Director**
> **Wilton Library, Wilton, CT**

"If you are looking for a job ... before you go to the newspapers and the help-wanted ads, listen to Bob Adams, publisher *of The Metropolitan New York JobBank.*"

> **-Tom Brokaw, NBC**

"Since 1985 the Adams *JobBank Series* has proven to be the consummate tool for the efficient job search."

> **-Mel Rappleyea, Human Resources Director**
> **Starbucks Coffee Company**

"Having worked in the Career Services field for 10 years, I know the quality of Adams publications."

> **-Philip Meade, Director of Graduate Career Services**
> **Baruch School of Business (New York NY)**

"I read through the 'Basics of Job Winning' and 'Resumes' sections [in *The Dallas-Fort Worth JobBank*] and found them to be very informative, with some positive tips for the job searcher. I believe the strategies outlined will bring success to any determined candidate."

> **-Camilla Norder, Professional Recruiter**
> **Presbyterian Hospital of Dallas**

"The ultimate in a superior series of job hunt directories."

> **-Cornell University Career Center's**
> *Where to Start*

"Help on the job hunt ... Anyone who is job-hunting in the New York area can find a lot of useful ideas in a new paperback called *The Metropolitan New York JobBank*...."

-Angela Taylor, *New York Times*

"A timely book for Chicago job hunters follows books from the same publisher that were well received in New York and Boston ... [*The Chicago JobBank* is] a fine tool for job hunters...."

-Clarence Peterson, *Chicago Tribune*

"Because our listing is seen by people across the nation, it generates lots for resumes for us. We encourage unsolicited resumes. We'll always be listed [in *The Chicago JobBank*] as long as I'm in this career."

-Tom Fitzpatrick, Director of Human Resources
Merchandise Mart Properties, Inc.

"Job hunting is never fun, but this book can ease the ordeal ...[*The Los Angeles JobBank*] will help allay fears, build confidence, and avoid wheel-spinning."

-Robert W. Ross, *Los Angeles Times*

"*The Seattle JobBank* is an essential resource for job hunters."

-Gil Lopez, Staffing Team Manager
Battelle Pacific Northwest Laboratories

"*The Phoenix JobBank* is a first-class publication. The information provided is useful and current."

-Lyndon Denton
Director of Human Resources and Materials Management
Apache Nitrogen Products, Inc.

"*The Florida JobBank* is an invaluable job-search reference tool. It provides the most up-to-date information and contact names available for companies in Florida. I should know – it worked for me!"

-Rhonda Cody, Human Resources Consultant
Aetna Life and Casualty

"I read through the 'Basics of Job Winning' and 'Resumes' sections [in *The Dallas-Fort Worth JobBank*] and found them to be very informative, with some positive tips for the job searcher. I believe the strategies outlined will bring success to any determined candidate."

-Camilla Norder, Professional Recruiter
Presbyterian Hospital of Dallas

"Through *The Dallas-Fort Worth JobBank,* we've been able to attract high-quality candidates for several positions."

-Rob Bertino, Southern States Sales Manager
CompuServe

What makes the
JobBank series
the nation's premier
line of employment guides?

With vital employment information on thousands of employers across the nation, the JobBank series is the most comprehensive and authoritative set of career directories available today.

Each book in the series provides information on **dozens of different industries** in a given city or area, with the primary employer listings providing contact information, telephone and fax numbers, e-mail addresses, Websites, a summary of the firm's business, internships, and in many cases descriptions of the firm's typical professional job categories.

All of the reference information in the JobBank series is as up-to-date and accurate as possible. Every year, the entire database is thoroughly researched and verified by mail and by telephone. Adams Media Corporation publishes **more local employment guides more often** than any other publisher of career directories.

The JobBank series offers **20 regional titles**, from Boston to San Francisco. All of the information is organized geographically, because most people look for jobs in specific areas of the country.

A condensed, but thorough, review of the entire job search process is presented in the chapter **The Basics of Job Winning**, a feature that has received many compliments from career counselors. In addition, each JobBank directory includes a section on **resumes and cover letters** the *New York Times* has acclaimed as "excellent."

The JobBank series gives job hunters the most comprehensive, timely, and accurate career information, organized and indexed to facilitate your job search. An entire career reference library, JobBank books are designed to help you find optimal employment in any market.

Top career publications from Adams Media

The JobBank Series:
each JobBank book is $17.95

The Atlanta JobBank, 15th Ed.
The Austin/San Antonio JobBank, 4th Ed.
The Boston JobBank, 20th Ed.
The Carolina JobBank, 7th Ed.
The Chicago JobBank, 19th Ed.
The Colorado JobBank, 13th Ed.
The Connecticut JobBank, 3rd Ed.
The Dallas-Fort Worth JobBank, 14th Ed.
The Florida JobBank, 16th Ed.
The Houston JobBank, 12th Ed.
The Los Angeles JobBank, 17th Ed.
The New Jersey JobBank, 3rd Ed.
The Metropolitan New York JobBank, 19th Ed.
The Ohio JobBank, 11th Ed.
The Greater Philadelphia JobBank, 14th Ed.
The Phoenix JobBank, 9th Ed.
The San Francisco Bay Area JobBank, 17th Ed.
The Seattle JobBank, 13th Ed.
The Virginia JobBank, 4th Ed.
The Metropolitan Washington DC JobBank, 16th Ed.

The National JobBank, 2006
(Covers the entire U.S.: $475.00 hc)

Other Career Titles:
The Adams Businesses You Can Start Almanac ($14.95)
The Adams Cover Letter Almanac ($12.95)
The Adams Internet Job Search Almanac, 6th Ed. ($12.95)
The Adams Job Interview Almanac, 2nd Ed. ($17.95)

The Adams Resume Almanac, 2nd Ed. ($17.95)
Business Etiquette in Brief ($7.95)
College Grad Job Hunter, 5th Ed. ($14.95)
The Complete Resume & Job Search Book for College Students, 2nd Ed. ($12.95)
Cover Letters That Knock 'em Dead, 6th Ed. ($12.95)
The Everything Alternative Careers Book ($14.95)
The Everything Cover Letter Book, 2nd Ed. ($14.95)
The Everything Get-A-Job Book ($12.95)
The Everything Job Interview Book ($14.95)
The Everything Leadership Book ($12.95)
The Everything Managing People Book ($14.95)
The Everything Online Job Search Book ($12.95)
The Everything Practice Interview Book ($12.95)
The Everything Resume Book, 2nd Ed. ($14.95)
The Everything Selling Book ($14.95)
The Everything Start Your Own Business Book ($14.95)
Knock 'em Dead, 2005 ($14.95)
Knock 'em Dead Business Presentations ($12.95)
Knock 'em Dead Management ($14.95)
Market Yourself and Your Career, 2nd Ed. ($12.95)
The New Professional Image ($14.95)
Resume Buzz Words ($9.95)
The Resume Handbook, 4th Ed. ($9.95)
Resumes That Knock 'em Dead, 6th Ed. ($12.95)
The Road to CEO ($10.95)
The 250 Job Interview Questions You'll Most Likely Be Asked ($9.95)

19th Edition

THE **Metropolitan New York JobBank**

adams
media

Published by Adams Media, an F+W Publications Company
57 Littlefield Street, Avon, MA 02322 U.S.A.
www.adamsmedia.com

ISBN: 1-59337-443-7
ISSN: 1098-979X
Manufactured in USA

Because addresses and telephone numbers of smaller companies change rapidly, we recommend you call each company and verify the information before mailing to the employers listed in this book. Mass mailings are not recommended.

While the publisher has made every reasonable effort to obtain and verify accurate information, occasional errors are possible due to the magnitude of the data. Should you discover an error, or if a company is missing, please write the editors at the above address so that we may update future editions.

"This publication is designed to provide accurate and authoritative information with regard to the subject matter covered. It is sold with the understanding that the publisher is not engaged in rendering legal, accounting, or other professional advice. If legal advice or other expert assistance is required, the services of a competent professional person should be sought."
--From a *Declaration of Principles* jointly adopted by a Committee of the American Bar Association and a Committee of Publishers and Associations

This book is available on standing order and at quantity discounts for bulk purchases. For information, call 800/872-5627 (in Massachusetts, 508/427-7100).

TABLE OF CONTENTS

- Physical Fitness Facilities
- Professional Sports Clubs; Sporting and Recreational Camps
- Public Golf Courses and Racing and Track Operations
- Theatrical Producers and Services

Automotive/93
- Automotive Repair Shops
- Automotive Stampings
- Industrial Vehicles and Moving Equipment
- Motor Vehicles and Equipment
- Travel Trailers and Campers

Banking, Savings and Loans, & Other Depository Institutions/95
- Banks
- Bank Holding Companies and Associations
- Lending Firms/Financial Services Institutions

Biotechnology, Pharmaceuticals, and Scientific R&D/104
- Clinical Labs
- Lab Equipment Manufacturers
- Pharmaceutical Manufacturers and Distributors

Business Services and Non-Scientific Research/121
- Adjustment and Collection Services
- Cleaning, Maintenance, and Pest Control Services
- Credit Reporting Services
- Detective, Guard, and Armored Car Services/Security Systems Services
- Miscellaneous Equipment Rental and Leasing
- Secretarial and Court Reporting Services

Charities and Social Services/131
- Social and Human Service Agencies
- Job Training and Vocational Rehabilitation Services
- Nonprofit Organizations

Chemicals, Rubber, and Plastics/139
- Adhesives, Detergents, Inks, Paints, Soaps, Varnishes
- Agricultural Chemicals and Fertilizers
- Carbon and Graphite Products
- Chemical Engineering Firms
- Industrial Gases

Communications: Telecommunications and Broadcasting/147
- Cable/Pay Television Services
- Communications Equipment
- Radio and Television Broadcasting Stations
- Telephone, Telegraph, and Other Message Communications

Computer Hardware, Software, and Services/156
- Computer Components and Hardware Manufacturers
- Consultants and Computer Training Companies
- Internet and Online Service Providers
- Networking and Systems Services
- Repair Services/Rental and Leasing
- Resellers, Wholesalers, and Distributors
- Software Developers/Programming Services

Educational Services/176
- Business/Secretarial/Data Processing Schools

Manufacturing: Miscellaneous Industrial/279
- Ball and Roller Bearings
- Commercial Furniture and Fixtures
- Fans, Blowers, and Purification Equipment
- Industrial Machinery and Equipment
- Motors and Generators/Compressors and Engine Parts
- Vending Machines

Mining, Gas, Petroleum, Energy Related/291
- Anthracite, Coal, and Ore Mining
- Mining Machinery and Equipment
- Oil and Gas Field Services
- Petroleum and Natural Gas

Paper and Wood Products/294
- Forest and Wood Products and Services
- Lumber and Wood Wholesale
- Millwork, Plywood, and Structural Members
- Paper and Wood Mills

Printing and Publishing/297
- Book, Newspaper, and Periodical Publishers
- Commercial Photographers
- Commercial Printing Services
- Graphic Designers

Real Estate/318
- Land Subdividers and Developers
- Real Estate Agents, Managers, and Operators
- Real Estate Investment Trusts

Retail/322

Stone, Clay, Glass, and Concrete Products/331
- Cement, Tile, Sand, and Gravel
- Crushed and Broken Stone
- Glass and Glass Products
- Mineral Products

Transportation and Travel/333
- Air, Railroad, and Water Transportation Services
- Courier Services
- Local and Interurban Passenger Transit
- Ship Building and Repair
- Transportation Equipment
- Travel Agencies
- Trucking
- Warehousing and Storage

Utilities: Electric, Gas, and Water/339

Miscellaneous Wholesaling/342
- Exporters and Importers

SECTION FOUR: INDUSTRY ASSOCIATIONS

Associations by Industry/345

SECTION FIVE: INDEX

Index of Primary Employers/401

HOW TO USE THIS BOOK

Right now, you hold in your hands one of the most effective job-hunting tools available anywhere. In *The Metropolitan New York JobBank*, you will find valuable information to help you launch or continue a rewarding career. But before you open to the book's employer listings and start calling about current job openings, take a few minutes to learn how best to use the resources presented in *The Metropolitan New York JobBank*.

The Metropolitan New York JobBank will help you to stand out from other jobseekers. While many people looking for a new job rely solely on newspaper help-wanted ads, this book offers you a much more effective job-search method - - direct contact. The direct contact method has been proven twice as effective as scanning the help-wanted ads. Instead of waiting for employers to come looking for you, you'll be far more effective going to them. While many of your competitors will use trial and error methods in trying to set up interviews, you'll learn not only how to get interviews, but what to expect once you've got them.

In the next few pages, we'll take you through each section of the book so you'll be prepared to get a jump-start on your competition.

Basics of Job Winning

Preparation. Strategy. Time management. These are three of the most important elements of a successful job search. *Basics of Job Winning* helps you address these and all the other elements needed to find the right job.

One of your first priorities should be to define your personal career objectives. What qualities make a job desirable to you? Creativity? High pay? Prestige? Use *Basics of Job Winning* to weigh these questions. Then use the rest of the chapter to design a strategy to find a job that matches your criteria.

In *Basics of Job Winning,* you'll learn which job-hunting techniques work, and which don't. We've reviewed the pros and cons of mass mailings, help-wanted ads, and direct contact. We'll show you how to develop and approach contacts in your field; how to research a prospective employer; and how to use that information to get an interview and the job.

Also included in *Basics of Job Winning*: interview dress code and etiquette, the "do's and don'ts" of interviewing, sample interview questions, and more. We also deal with some of the unique problems faced by those jobseekers who are currently employed, those who have lost a job, and college students conducting their first job search.

Resumes and Cover Letters

The approach you take to writing your resume and cover letter can often mean the difference between getting an interview and never being noticed. In this section, we discuss different formats, as well as what to put on (and what to leave off) your resume. We review the benefits and drawbacks of professional resume writers, and the importance of a follow-up letter. Also included in this section are sample resumes and cover letters which you can use as models.

The Employer Listings

Employers are listed alphabetically by industry. When a company does business under a person's name, like "John Smith & Co.," the company is usually listed by the surname's spelling (in this case "S"). Exceptions occur when a company's name is widely recognized, like "JCPenney" or "Howard Johnson Motor Lodge." In those cases, the company's first name is the key ("J" and "H" respectively).

The Metropolitan New York JobBank covers a very wide range of industries. Each company profile is assigned to one of the industry chapters listed below.

Accounting and Management Consulting
Advertising, Marketing, and Public
    Relations
Aerospace
Apparel, Fashion, and Textiles
Architecture, Construction, and Engineering
Arts, Entertainment, Sports, and Recreation
Automotive
Banking/Savings and Loans
Biotechnology, Pharmaceuticals, and
    Scientific R&D
Business Services and Non-Scientific
    Research
Charities and Social Services
Chemicals/Rubber and Plastics
Communications: Telecommunications and
    Broadcasting
Computer Hardware, Software, and
    Services
Educational Services
Electronic/Industrial Electrical Equipment
    and Components

Environmental and Waste Management
    Services
Fabricated/Primary Metals and Products
Financial Services
Food and Beverages/Agriculture
Government
Health Care: Services, Equipment, and
    Products
Hotels and Restaurants
Insurance
Legal Services
Manufacturing: Miscellaneous Consumer
Manufacturing: Miscellaneous Industrial
Mining/Gas/Petroleum/Energy Related
Paper and Wood Products
Printing and Publishing
Real Estate
Retail
Stone, Clay, Glass, and Concrete Products
Transportation/Travel
Utilities: Electric/Gas/Water
Miscellaneous Wholesaling

Many of the company listings offer detailed company profiles. In addition to company names, addresses, and phone numbers, these listings also include contact names or hiring departments, and descriptions of each company's products and/or services. Many of these listings also feature a variety of additional information including:

Positions advertised - A list of open positions the company was advertising at the time our research was conducted. Note: Keep in mind that *The Metropolitan New York JobBank* is a directory of major employers in the area, not a directory of openings currently available. Positions listed in this book that were advertised at the time research was conducted may no longer be open. Many of the companies listed will be hiring, others will not. However, since most professional job openings are filled without the placement of help-wanted ads, contacting the employers in this book directly is still a more effective method than browsing the Sunday papers.

Special programs - Does the company offer training programs, internships, or apprenticeships? These programs can be important to first time jobseekers and college students looking for practical work experience. Many employer profiles will include information on these programs.

Parent company - If an employer is a subsidiary of a larger company, the name of that parent company will often be listed here. Use this information to supplement your company research before contacting the employer.

Number of employees - The number of workers a company employs.

Company listings may also include information on other U.S. locations and any stock exchanges the firm may be listed on.

A note on all employer listings that appear in *The Metropolitan New York JobBank*: This book is intended as a starting point. It is not intended to replace any effort that you, the jobseeker, should devote to your job hunt. Keep in mind that while a great deal of effort has been put into collecting and verifying the company profiles provided in this book, addresses and contact names change regularly. Inevitably, some contact names listed herein have changed even before you read this. We recommend you contact a company before mailing your resume to ensure nothing has changed.

Industry Associations

This section includes a select list of professional and trade associations organized by industry. Many of these associations can provide employment advice and job-search help, offer magazines that cover the industry, and provide additional information or directories that may supplement the employer listings in this book.

Index of Primary Employers

The Metropolitan New York JobBank index is listed alphabetically by company name.

THE JOB SEARCH

THE BASICS OF JOB WINNING: A CONDENSED REVIEW

This chapter is divided into four sections. The first section explains the fundamentals that every jobseeker should know, especially first-time jobseekers. The next three sections deal with special situations faced by specific types of jobseekers: those who are currently employed, those who have lost a job, and college students.

THE BASICS:
Things Everyone Needs to Know

Career Planning

The first step to finding your ideal job is to clearly define your objectives. This is better known as career planning (or life planning if you wish to emphasize the importance of combining the two). Career planning has become a field of study in and of itself.

If you are thinking of choosing or switching careers, we particularly emphasize two things. First, choose a career where you will enjoy most of the day-to-day tasks. This sounds obvious, but most of us have at some point found the idea of a glamour industry or prestigious job title attractive without thinking of the key consideration: Would we enjoy performing the *everyday* tasks the position entails?

The second key consideration is that you are not merely choosing a career, but also a lifestyle. Career counselors indicate that one of the most common problems people encounter in jobseeking is that they fail to consider how well-suited they are for a particular position or career. For example, some people, attracted to management consulting by good salaries, early responsibility, and high-level corporate exposure, do not adapt well to the long hours, heavy travel demands, and constant pressure to produce. Be sure to ask yourself how you might adapt to the day-to-day duties and working environment that a specific position entails. Then ask yourself how you might adapt to the demands of that career or industry as a whole.

Choosing Your Strategy

Assuming that you've established your career objectives, the next step of the job search is to develop a strategy. If you don't take the time to develop a plan, you may find yourself going in circles after several weeks of randomly searching for opportunities that always seem just beyond your reach.

The most common jobseeking techniques are:

- following up on help-wanted advertisements (in the newspaper or online)
- using employment services
- relying on personal contacts
- contacting employers directly (the Direct Contact method)

Each of these approaches can lead to better jobs. However, the Direct Contact method boasts twice the success rate of the others. So unless you have specific reasons to employ other strategies, Direct Contact should form the foundation of your job search.

If you choose to use other methods as well, try to expend at least half your energy on Direct Contact. Millions of other jobseekers have already proven that Direct Contact has been twice as effective in obtaining employment, so why not follow in their footsteps?

Setting Your Schedule

Okay, so now that you've targeted a strategy it's time to work out the details of your job search. The most important detail is setting up a schedule. Of course, since job searches aren't something most people do regularly, it may be hard to estimate how long each step will take. Nonetheless, it is important to have a plan so that you can monitor your progress.

When outlining your job search schedule, have a realistic time frame in mind. If you will be job-searching full-time, your search could take at least two months or more. If you can only devote part-time effort, it will probably take at least four months.

You probably know a few people who seem to spend their whole lives searching for a better job in their spare time. Don't be one of them. If you are presently working and don't feel like devoting a lot of energy to jobseeking right now, then wait. Focus on enjoying your present position, performing your best on the job, and storing up energy for when you are really ready to begin your job search.

> **The first step in beginning your job search is to clearly define your objectives.**

Those of you who are currently unemployed should remember that *job-hunting is tough work, both physically and emotionally*. It is also intellectually demanding work that requires you to be at your best. So don't tire yourself out by working on your job campaign around the clock. At the same time, be sure to discipline yourself. The most logical way to manage your time while looking for a job is to keep your regular working hours.

If you are searching full-time and have decided to choose several different strategies, we recommend that you divide up each week, designating some time for each method. By trying several approaches at once, you can evaluate how promising each seems and alter your schedule accordingly. Keep in mind that the *majority of openings are filled without being advertised*. Remember also that positions advertised on the Internet are just as likely to already be filled as those found in the newspaper!

If you are searching part-time and decide to try several different contact methods, we recommend that you try them sequentially. You simply won't have enough time to put a meaningful amount of effort into more than one method at once. Estimate the length of your job search, and then allocate so many weeks or months for each contact method, beginning with Direct Contact. The purpose of setting this schedule is not to rush you to your goal but to help you periodically evaluate your progress.

The Direct Contact Method

Once you have scheduled your time, you are ready to begin your search in earnest. Beginning with the Direct Contact method, the first step is to develop a checklist for categorizing the types of firms for which you'd like to work. You might categorize firms by product line, size, customer type (such as industrial or consumer), growth prospects, or geographical location. Keep in mind, the shorter the list the easier it will be to locate a company that is right for you.

Next you will want to use this *JobBank* book to assemble your list of potential employers. Choose firms where *you* are most likely to be able to find a job. Try matching your skills with those that a specific job demands. Consider where your skills might be in demand, the degree of competition for employment, and the employment outlook at each company.

Separate your prospect list into three groups. The first 25 percent will be your primary target group, the next 25 percent will be your secondary group, and the remaining names will be your reserve group.

After you form your prospect list, begin working on your resume. Refer to the Resumes and Cover Letters section following this chapter for more information.

Once your resume is complete, begin researching your first batch of prospective employers. You will want to determine whether you would be happy working at the firms you are researching and to get a better idea of what their employment needs might be. You also need to obtain enough information to sound highly informed about the company during phone conversations and in mail correspondence. But don't go all out on your research yet! You probably won't be able to arrange interviews with some of these firms, so save your big research effort until you start to arrange interviews. Nevertheless, you should plan to spend several hours researching each firm. Do your research in batches to save time and energy. Start with this book, and find out what you can about each of the firms in your primary target group. For answers to specific questions, contact any pertinent professional associations that may be able to help you learn more about an employer. Read industry publications looking for articles on the firm. (Addresses of associations and names of important publications are listed after each section of employer listings in this book.) Then look up the company on the Internet or try additional resources at your local library. Keep organized, and maintain a folder on each firm.

> **The more you know about a company, the more likely you are to catch an interviewer's eye. (You'll also face fewer surprises once you get the job!)**

Information to look for includes: company size; president, CEO, or owner's name; when the company was established; what each division does; and benefits that are important to you. An abundance of company information can now be found electronically, through the World Wide Web or commercial online services. Researching companies online is a convenient means of obtaining information quickly and easily. If you have access to the Internet, you can search from your home at any time of day.

You may search a particular company's Website for current information that may be otherwise unavailable in print. In fact, many companies that maintain a site update their information daily. In addition, you may also search articles written about the company online. Today, most of the nation's largest newspapers, magazines, trade publications, and regional business periodicals have online versions of their publications. To find additional resources, use a search engine like Yahoo! or Alta Vista and type in the keyword "companies" or "employers."

If you discover something that really disturbs you about the firm (they are about to close their only local office), or if you discover that your chances of getting a job there are practically nil (they have just instituted a hiring freeze), then cross them off your prospect list. If possible, supplement your research efforts by contacting individuals who know the firm well. Ideally you should make an informal contact with someone at that particular firm, but often a direct competitor or a major customer will be able to supply you with just as much information. At the very least, try to obtain whatever printed information the company has available -- not just annual reports, but product brochures, company profiles, or catalogs. This information is often available on the Internet.

Getting the Interview

Now it is time to make Direct Contact with the goal of arranging interviews. If you have read any books on job-searching, you may have noticed that most of these books tell you to avoid the human resources office like the plague. It is said that the human resources office never hires people; they screen candidates. Unfortunately, this is often the case. If you can identify the appropriate manager with the authority to hire you, you should try to contact that person directly.

The obvious means of initiating Direct Contact are:

- Mail (postal or electronic)
- Phone calls

Mail contact is a good choice if you have not been in the job market for a while. You can take your time to prepare a letter, say exactly what you want, and of course include your resume. Remember that employers receive many resumes every day. Don't be surprised if you do not get a response to your inquiry, *and don't spend weeks waiting for responses that may never come.* If you do send a letter, follow it up (or precede it) with a phone call. This will increase your impact, and because of the initial research you did, will underscore both your familiarity with and your interest in the firm. Bear in mind that your goal is to make your name a familiar one with prospective employers, so that when a position becomes available, your resume will be one of the first the hiring manager seeks out.

DEVELOPING YOUR CONTACTS: NETWORKING

Some career counselors feel that the best route to a better job is through somebody you already know or through somebody to whom you can be introduced. These counselors recommend that you build your contact base beyond your current acquaintances by asking each one to introduce you, or refer you, to additional people in your field of interest.

The theory goes like this: You might start with 15 personal contacts, each of whom introduces you to three additional people, for a total of 45 additional contacts. Then each of these people introduces you to three additional people, which adds 135 additional contacts. Theoretically, you will soon know every person in the industry.

Of course, developing your personal contacts does not work quite as smoothly as the theory suggests because some people will not be able to introduce you to anyone. The further you stray from your initial contact base, the weaker your references may be. So, if you do try developing your own contacts, try to begin with as many people that you know personally as you can. Dig into your personal phone book and your holiday greeting card list and locate old classmates from school. Be particularly sure to approach people who perform your personal business such as your lawyer, accountant, banker, doctor, stockbroker, and insurance agent. These people develop a very broad contact base due to the nature of their professions.

If you send a fax, always follow with a hard copy of your resume and cover letter in the mail. Often, through no fault of your own, a fax will come through illegibly and employers do not often have time to let candidates know.

Another alternative is to make a "cover call." Your cover call should be just like your cover letter: concise. Your first statement should interest the employer in you. Then try to subtly mention your familiarity with the firm. Don't be overbearing; keep your introduction to three sentences or less. Be pleasant, self-confident, and relaxed. This will greatly increase the chances of the person at the other end of the line developing the conversation. But don't press. If you are asked to follow up with "something in the mail," this signals the conversation's natural end. Don't try to prolong the conversation once it has ended, and don't ask what they want to receive in the mail. Always send your resume and a highly personalized follow-up letter, reminding the addressee of the phone conversation. *Always* include a cover letter if you are asked to send a resume, and treat your resume and cover letter as a total package. Gear your letter toward the specific position you are applying for and prove why you would be a "good match" for the position.

> **Always include a cover letter if you are asked to send a resume.**

Unless you are in telephone sales, making smooth and relaxed cover calls will probably not come easily. Practice them on your own, and then with your friends or relatives.

DON'T BOTHER WITH MASS MAILINGS OR BARRAGES OF PHONE CALLS

Direct Contact does not mean burying every firm within a hundred miles with mail and phone calls. Mass mailings rarely work in the job hunt. This also applies to those letters that are personalized -- but dehumanized -- on an automatic typewriter or computer. Don't waste your time or money on such a project; you will fool no one but yourself.

The worst part of sending out mass mailings, or making unplanned phone calls to companies you have not researched, is that you are likely to be remembered as someone with little genuine interest in the firm, who lacks sincerity -- somebody that nobody wants to hire.

If you obtain an interview as a result of a telephone conversation, be sure to send a thank-you note reiterating the points you made during the conversation. You will appear more professional and increase your impact. However, unless specifically requested, don't mail your resume once an interview has been arranged. Take it with you to the interview instead.

You should never show up to seek a professional position without an appointment. Even if you are somehow lucky enough to obtain an interview, you will appear so unprofessional that you will not be seriously considered.

HELP WANTED ADVERTISEMENTS

Only a small fraction of professional job openings are advertised. Yet the majority of jobseekers -- and quite a few people not in the job market -- spend a lot of time studying the help wanted ads. As a result, the competition for advertised openings is often very severe.

A moderate-sized employer told us about their experience advertising in the help wanted section of a major Sunday newspaper:

It was a disaster. We had over 500 responses from this relatively small ad in just one week. We have only two phone lines in this office and one was totally knocked out. We'll never advertise for professional help again.

If you insist on following up on help wanted ads, then research a firm before you reply to an ad. Preliminary research might help to separate you from all of the other professionals responding to that ad, many of whom will have only a passing interest in the opportunity. It will also give you insight about a particular firm, to help you determine if it is potentially a good match. That said, your chances of obtaining a job through the want ads are still much smaller than they are with the Direct Contact method.

Preparing for the Interview

As each interview is arranged, begin your in-depth research. You should arrive at an interview knowing the company upside-down and inside-out. You need to know the company's products, types of customers, subsidiaries, parent company, principal locations, rank in the industry, sales and profit trends, type of ownership, size, current plans, and much more. By this time you have probably narrowed your job search to one industry. Even if you haven't, you should still be familiar with common industry terms, the trends in the firm's industry, the firm's principal competitors and their relative performance, and the direction in which the industry leaders are headed.

Dig into every resource you can! Surf the Internet. Read the company literature, the trade press, the business press, and if the company is public, call your stockbroker (if you have one) and ask for additional information. If possible, speak to someone at the firm before the

> **You should arrive at an interview knowing the company upside-down and inside-out.**

interview, or if not, speak to someone at a competing firm. The more time you spend, the better. Even if you feel extremely pressed for time, you should set aside several hours for pre-interview research.

If you have been out of the job market for some time, don't be surprised if you find yourself tense during your first few interviews. It will probably happen every time you re-enter the market, not just when you seek your first job after getting out of school.

Tension is natural during an interview, but knowing you have done a thorough research job should put you more at ease. Make a list of questions that you think might be asked in each interview. Think out your answers carefully and practice them with a friend. Tape record your responses to the problem questions. (*See also in this chapter: Informational Interviews.*) If you feel particularly unsure of your interviewing skills, arrange your first interviews at firms you are not as interested in. (But remember it is common courtesy to seem enthusiastic about the possibility of working for any firm at which you interview.) Practice again on your own after these first few interviews. Go over the difficult questions that you were asked.

Take some time to really think about how you will convey your work history. Present "bad experiences" as "learning experiences." Instead of saying "I hated my position as a salesperson because I had to bother people on the phone," say "I realized that cold-calling was not my strong suit. Though I love working with people, I decided my talents would be best used in a more face-to-face atmosphere." Always find some sort of lesson from previous jobs, as they all have one.

Interview Attire

How important is the proper dress for a job interview? Buying a complete wardrobe, donning new shoes, and having your hair styled every morning are not enough to guarantee you a career position as an investment banker. But on the other hand, if you can't find a clean, conservative suit or won't take the time to wash your hair, then you are just wasting your time by interviewing at all.

Personal grooming is as important as finding appropriate clothes for a job interview. Careful grooming indicates both a sense of thoroughness and self-confidence. This is not the time to make a statement -- take out the extra earrings and avoid any garish hair colors not found in nature. Women should not wear excessive makeup, and both men and women should refrain from wearing any perfume or cologne (it only takes a small spritz to leave an allergic interviewer with a fit of sneezing and a bad impression of your meeting). Men should be freshly shaven, even if the interview is late in the day, and men with long hair should have it pulled back and neat.

Men applying for any professional position should wear a suit, preferably in a conservative color such as navy or charcoal gray. It is easy to get away with wearing the same dark suit to consecutive interviews at the same company; just be sure to wear a different shirt and tie for each interview.

Women should also wear a business suit. Professionalism still dictates a suit with a skirt, rather than slacks, as proper interview garb for women. This is usually true even at companies where pants are acceptable attire for female employees. As much as you may disagree with this guideline, the more prudent time to fight this standard is after you land the job.

The final selection of candidates for a job opening won't be determined by dress, of course. However, inappropriate dress can quickly eliminate a first-round candidate. So while you shouldn't spend a fortune on a new wardrobe, you should be sure that your clothes are appropriate. The key is to dress at least as or slightly more formally and conservatively than the position would suggest.

What to Bring

Be complete. Everyone needs a watch, a pen, and a notepad. Finally, a briefcase or a leather-bound folder (containing extra, *unfolded*, copies of your resume) will help complete the look of professionalism.

Sometimes the interviewer will be running behind schedule. Don't be upset, be sympathetic. There is often pressure to interview a lot of candidates and to quickly fill a demanding position. So be sure to come to your interview with good reading material to keep yourself occupied and relaxed.

The Interview

The very beginning of the interview is the most important part because it determines the tone for the rest of it. Those first few moments are especially crucial. Do you smile when you meet? Do you establish enough eye contact, but not too much? Do you walk into the office with a self-assured and confident stride? Do you shake hands firmly? Do you make small talk easily without being garrulous? It is human nature to judge people by that first impression, so make sure it is a good one. But most of all, try to be yourself.

BE PREPARED:
Some Common Interview Questions

Tell me about yourself.

Why did you leave your last job?

What excites you in your current job?

Where would you like to be in five years?

How much overtime are you willing to work?

What would your previous/present employer tell me about you?

Tell me about a difficult situation that you
faced at your previous/present job.

What are your greatest strengths?

What are your weaknesses?

Describe a work situation where you took initiative
and went beyond your normal responsibilities.

Why should we hire you?

Often the interviewer will begin, after the small talk, by telling you about the company, the division, the department, or perhaps, the position. Because of your detailed research, the information about the company should be repetitive for you, and the interviewer would probably like nothing better than to avoid this regurgitation of the company biography. So if you can do so tactfully, indicate to the interviewer that you are very familiar with the firm. If he or she seems intent on providing you with background information, despite your hints, then acquiesce.

But be sure to remain attentive. If you can manage to generate a brief discussion of the company or the industry at this point, without being forceful, great. It will help to further build rapport, underscore your interest, and increase your impact.

> **The interviewer's job is to find a reason to turn you down; your job is to not provide that reason.**
>
> -John L. LaFevre, author, *How You Really Get Hired*
>
> Reprinted from the 1989/90 *CPC Annual,* with permission of the National Association of Colleges and Employers (formerly College Placement Council, Inc.), copyright holder.

Soon (if it didn't begin that way) the interviewer will begin the questions, many of which you will have already practiced. This period of the interview usually falls into one of two categories (or somewhere in between): either a structured interview, where the interviewer has a prescribed set of questions to ask; or an unstructured interview, where the interviewer will ask only leading questions to get you to talk about yourself, your experiences, and your goals. Try to sense as quickly as possible in which direction the interviewer wishes to proceed. This will make the interviewer feel more relaxed and in control of the situation.

Remember to keep attuned to the interviewer and make the length of your answers appropriate to the situation. If you are really unsure as to how detailed a response the interviewer is seeking, then ask.

As the interview progresses, the interviewer will probably mention some of the most important responsibilities of the position. If applicable, draw parallels between your experience and the demands of the position as detailed by the interviewer. Describe your past experience in the same manner that you do on your resume: emphasizing results and achievements and not merely describing activities. But don't exaggerate. Be on the level about your abilities.

The first interview is often the toughest, where many candidates are screened out. If you are interviewing for a very competitive position, you will have to make an impression that will last. Focus on a few of your greatest strengths that are relevant to the position. Develop these points carefully, state them again in different words, and then try to summarize them briefly at the end of the interview.

Often the interviewer will pause toward the end and ask if you have any questions. Particularly in a structured interview, this might be the one chance to really show your knowledge of and interest in the firm. Have a list prepared of specific questions that are of real interest to you. Let your questions subtly show your research and your knowledge of the firm's activities. It is wise to have an extensive list of questions, as several of them may be answered during the interview.

Do not turn your opportunity to ask questions into an interrogation. Avoid reading directly from your list of questions, and ask questions that you are fairly certain the interviewer can answer (remember how you feel when you cannot answer a question during an interview).

Even if you are unable to determine the salary range beforehand, do not ask about it during the first interview. You can always ask later. Above all, don't ask about fringe benefits until you have been offered a position. (Then be sure to get all the details.)

Try not to be negative about anything during the interview, particularly any past employer or any previous job. Be cheerful. Everyone likes to work with someone who seems to be happy. Even if you detest your current/former job or manager, do not make disparaging comments. The interviewer may construe this as a sign of a potential attitude problem and not consider you a strong candidate.

Don't let a tough question throw you off base. If you don't know the answer to a question, simply say so -- do not apologize. Just smile. Nobody can answer every question -- particularly some of the questions that are asked in job interviews.

Before your first interview, you may be able to determine how many rounds of interviews there usually are for positions at your level. (Of course it may differ quite a bit even within the different levels of one firm.) Usually you can count on attending at least two or three interviews, although some firms are known to give a minimum of six interviews for all professional positions. While you should be more relaxed as you return for subsequent interviews, the pressure will be on. The more prepared you are, the better.

Depending on what information you are able to obtain, you might want to vary your strategy quite a bit from interview to interview. For instance, if the first interview is a screening interview, then be sure a few of your strengths really stand out. On the other hand, if later interviews are primarily with people who are in a position to veto your hiring, but not to push it forward, then you should primarily focus on building rapport as opposed to reiterating and developing your key strengths.

If it looks as though your skills and background do not match the position the interviewer was hoping to fill, ask him or her if there is another division or subsidiary that perhaps could profit from your talents.

After the Interview

Write a follow-up letter immediately after the interview, while it is still fresh in the interviewer's mind (see the sample follow-up letter format found in the Resumes and Cover Letters chapter). Not only is this a thank-you, but it also gives you the chance to provide the interviewer with any details you may have forgotten (as long as they can be tactfully added in). If you haven't heard back from the interviewer within a week of sending your thank-you letter, call to stress your continued interest in the firm and the position. If you lost any points during the interview for any reason, this letter can help you regain footing. Be polite and make sure to stress your continued interest and competency to fill the position. Just don't forget to proofread it thoroughly. If you are unsure of the spelling of the interviewer's name, call the receptionist and ask.

THE BALANCING ACT:
Looking for a New Job While Currently Employed

For those of you who are still employed, job-searching will be particularly tiring because it must be done in addition to your normal work responsibilities. So don't overwork yourself to the point where you show up to interviews looking exhausted or start to slip behind at your current job. On the other hand, don't be tempted to quit your present job! The long hours are worth it. Searching for a job while you have one puts you in a position of strength.

Making Contact

If you must be at your office during the business day, then you have additional problems to deal with. How can you work interviews into the business day? And if you work in an open office, how can you even call to set up interviews? Obviously, you should keep up the effort and the appearances on your present job. So maximize your use of the lunch hour, early mornings, and late afternoons for calling. If you keep trying, you'll be surprised how often you will be able to reach the executive you are trying to contact during your out-of-office hours. You can catch people as early as 8 a.m. and as late as 6 p.m. on frequent occasions.

Scheduling Interviews

Your inability to interview at any time other than lunch just might work to your advantage. If you can, try to set up as many interviews as possible for your lunch hour. This will go a long way to creating a relaxed atmosphere. But be sure the interviews don't stray too far from the agenda on hand.

Lunchtime interviews are much easier to obtain if you have substantial career experience. People with less experience will often find no alternative to taking time off for interviews. If you have to take time off, you have to take time off. But try to do this as little as possible. Try to take the whole day off in order to avoid being blatantly obvious about your job search, and try to schedule two to three interviews for the same day. (It is very difficult to maintain an optimum level of energy at more than three interviews in one day.) Explain to the interviewer why you might have to juggle your interview schedule; he/she should honor the respect you're showing your current employer by minimizing your days off and will probably appreciate the fact that another prospective employer is interested in you.

> **Try calling as early as 8 a.m. and as late as 6 p.m. You'll be surprised how often you will be able to reach the executive you want during these times of the day.**

References

What do you tell an interviewer who asks for references from your current employer? Just say that while you are happy to have your former employers contacted, you are trying to keep your job search confidential and would rather that your current employer not be contacted until you have been given a firm offer.

IF YOU'RE FIRED OR LAID OFF:
Picking Yourself Up and Dusting Yourself Off

If you've been fired or laid off, you are not the first and will not be the last to go through this traumatic experience. In today's changing economy, thousands of professionals lose their jobs every year. Even if you were terminated with just cause, do not lose heart. Remember, being fired is not a reflection on you as a person. It is usually a reflection of your company's staffing needs and its perception of your recent job performance and attitude. And if you were not performing up to par or enjoying your work, then you will probably be better off at another company anyway.

> ## Be prepared for the question "Why were you fired?" during job interviews.

A thorough job search could take months, so be sure to negotiate a reasonable severance package, if possible, and determine to what benefits, such as health insurance, you are still legally entitled. Also, register for unemployment compensation immediately. Don't be surprised to find other professionals collecting unemployment compensation -- it is for everyone who has lost their job.

Don't start your job search with a flurry of unplanned activity. Start by choosing a strategy and working out a plan. Now is not the time for major changes in your life. If possible, remain in the same career and in the same geographical location, at least until you have been working again for a while. On the other hand, if the only industry for which you are trained is leaving, or is severely depressed in your area, then you should give prompt consideration to moving or switching careers.

Avoid mentioning you were fired when arranging interviews, but be prepared for the question "Why were you fired?" during an interview. If you were laid off as a result of downsizing, briefly explain, being sure to reinforce that your job loss was not due to performance. If you were in fact fired, be honest, but try to detail the reason as favorably as possible and portray what you have learned from your mistakes. If you are confident one of your past managers will give you a good reference, tell the interviewer to contact that person. Do not to speak negatively of your past employer and try not to sound particularly worried about your status of being temporarily unemployed.

Finally, don't spend too much time reflecting on why you were let go or how you might have avoided it. Think positively, look to the future, and be sure to follow a careful plan during your job search.

THE COLLEGE STUDENT:
Conducting Your First Job Search

While you will be able to apply many of the basics covered earlier in this chapter to your job search, there are some situations unique to the college student's job search.

THE GPA QUESTION

You are interviewing for the job of your dreams. Everything is going well: You've established a good rapport, the interviewer seems impressed with your qualifications, and you're almost positive the job is yours. Then you're asked about your GPA, which is pitifully low. Do you tell the truth and watch your dream job fly out the window?

Never lie about your GPA (they may request your transcript, and no company will hire a liar). You can, however, explain if there is a reason you don't feel your grades reflect your abilities, and mention any other impressive statistics. For example, if you have a high GPA in your major, or in the last few semesters (as opposed to your cumulative college career), you can use that fact to your advantage.

Perhaps the biggest problem college students face is lack of experience. Many schools have internship programs designed to give students exposure to the field of their choice, as well as the opportunity to make valuable contacts. Check out your school's career services department to see what internships are available. If your school does not have a formal internship program, or if there are no available internships that appeal to you, try contacting local businesses and offering your services. Often, businesses will be more than willing to have an extra pair of hands (especially if those hands are unpaid!) for a day or two each week. Or try contacting school alumni to see if you can "shadow" them for a few days, and see what their daily duties are like.

Informational Interviews

Although many jobseekers do not do this, it can be extremely helpful to arrange an informational interview with a college alumnus or someone else who works in your desired industry. You interview them about their job, their company, and their industry with questions you have prepared in advance. This can be done over the phone but is usually done in person. This will provide you with a contact in the industry who may give you more valuable information -- or perhaps even a job opportunity -- in the future. Always follow up with a thank you letter that includes your contact information.

The goal is to try to begin building experience and establishing contacts as early as possible in your college career.

What do you do if, for whatever reason, you weren't able to get experience directly related to your desired career? First, look at your previous jobs and see if there's anything you can highlight. Did you supervise or train other employees? Did you reorganize the accounting system, or boost productivity in some way? Accomplishments like these demonstrate leadership, responsibility, and innovation -- qualities that most companies look for in employees. And don't forget volunteer activities and school clubs, which can also showcase these traits.

On-Campus Recruiting

Companies will often send recruiters to interview on-site at various colleges. This gives students a chance to interview with companies that may not have interviewed them otherwise. This is particularly true if a company schedules "open" interviews, in which the only screening process is who is first in line at the sign-ups. Of course, since many more applicants gain interviews in this format, this also means that many more people are rejected. The on-campus interview is generally a screening interview, to see if it is worth the company's time to invite you in for a second interview. So do everything possible to make yourself stand out from the crowd.

The first step, of course, is to check out any and all information your school's career center has on the company. If the information seems out of date, check out the company on the Internet or call the company's headquarters and ask for any printed information.

Many companies will host an informational meeting for interviewees, often the evening before interviews are scheduled to take place. DO NOT MISS THIS MEETING. The recruiter will almost certainly ask if you attended. Make an effort to stay after the meeting and talk with the company's representatives. Not only does this give you an opportunity to find out more information about both the company and the position, it also makes you stand out in the recruiter's mind. If there's a particular company that you had your heart set on, but you weren't able to get an interview with them, attend the information session anyway. You may be able to persuade the recruiter to squeeze you into the schedule. (Or you may discover that the company really isn't the right fit for you after all.)

Try to check out the interview site beforehand. Some colleges may conduct "mock" interviews that take place in one of the standard interview rooms. Or you may be able to convince a career counselor (or even a custodian) to let you sneak a peek during off-hours. Either way, having an idea of the room's setup will help you to mentally prepare.

Arrive at least 15 minutes early to the interview. The recruiter may be ahead of schedule, and might meet you early. But don't be surprised if previous interviews have run over, resulting in your 30-minute slot being reduced to 20 minutes (or less). Don't complain or appear anxious; just use the time you do have as efficiently as possible to showcase the reasons *you* are the ideal candidate. Staying calm and composed in these situations will work to your advantage.

LAST WORDS

A parting word of advice. Again and again during your job search you will face rejection. You will be rejected when you apply for interviews. You will be rejected after interviews. For every job offer you finally receive, you probably will have been rejected many times. Don't let rejections slow you down. Keep reminding yourself that the sooner you go out, start your job search, and get those rejections flowing in, the closer you will be to obtaining the job you want.

RESUMES AND COVER LETTERS

When filling a position, an employer will often have 100-plus applicants, but time to interview only a handful of the most promising ones. As a result, he or she will reject most applicants after only briefly skimming their resumes.

Unless you have phoned and talked to the employer -- which you should do whenever you can -- you will be chosen or rejected for an interview entirely on the basis of your resume and cover letter. *Your cover letter must catch the employer's attention, and your resume must hold it.* (But remember -- a resume is no substitute for a job search campaign. *You* must seek a job. Your resume is only one tool, albeit a critical one.)

RESUME FORMAT:
Mechanics of a First Impression

The Basics

Employers dislike long resumes, so unless you have an unusually strong background with many years of experience and a diversity of outstanding achievements, keep your resume length to one page. If you must squeeze in more information than would otherwise fit, try using a smaller typeface or changing the margins. Watch also for "widows" at the end of paragraphs. You can often free up some space if you can shorten the information enough to get rid of those single words taking up an entire line. Another tactic that works with some word processing programs is to decrease the font size of your paragraph returns and changing the spacing between lines.

Print your resume on standard 8 1/2" x 11" paper. Since recruiters often get resumes in batches of hundreds, a smaller-sized resume may be lost in the pile. Oversized resumes are likely to get crumpled at the edges, and won't fit easily in their files.

First impressions matter, so make sure the recruiter's first impression of your resume is a good one. Never hand-write your resume (or cover letter)! Print your resume on quality paper that has weight and texture, in a conservative color such as white, ivory, or pale gray. Good resume paper is easy to find at many stores that sell stationery or office products. It is even available at some drug stores. Use *matching* paper and envelopes for both your resume and cover letter. One hiring manager at a major magazine throws out all resumes that arrive on paper that differs in color from the envelope!

Do not buy paper with images of clouds and rainbows in the background or anything that looks like casual stationery that you would send to your favorite aunt. Do not spray perfume or cologne on your resume. Do not include your picture with your resume unless you have a specific and appropriate reason to do so.

Another tip: Do a test print of your resume (and cover letter), to make sure the watermark is on the same side as the text so that you can read it. Also make sure it is right-side up. As trivial as this may sound, some recruiters check for this! One recruiter at a law firm in New Hampshire sheepishly admitted this is the first thing he checks. *"I open each envelope and check the watermarks on the resume and cover letter. Those candidates that have it wrong go into a different pile."*

Getting it on Paper

Modern photocomposition typesetting gives you the clearest, sharpest image, a wide variety of type styles, and effects such as italics, bold-facing, and book-like justified margins. It is also too expensive for many jobseekers. The quality of today's laser printers means that a computer-generated resume can look just as impressive as one that has been professionally typeset.

A computer with a word processing or desktop publishing program is the most common way to generate your resume. This allows you the flexibility to make changes almost instantly and to store different drafts on disk. Word processing and desktop publishing programs also offer many different fonts to choose from, each taking up different amounts of space. (It is generally best to stay between 9-point and 12-point font size.) Many other options are also available, such as bold-facing or italicizing for emphasis and the ability to change and manipulate spacing. It is generally recommended to leave the right-hand margin unjustified as this keeps the spacing between the text even and therefore easier to read. It is not wrong to justify both margins of text, but if possible try it both ways before you decide.

For a resume on paper, the end result will be largely determined by the quality of the printer you use. Laser printers will generally provide the best quality. Do not use a dot matrix printer.

Many companies now use scanning equipment to screen the resumes they receive, and certain paper, fonts, and other features are more compatible with this technology. White paper is preferable, as well as a standard font such as Courier or Helvetica. You should use at least a 10-point font, and avoid bolding, italics, underlining, borders, boxes, or graphics.

Household typewriters and office typewriters with nylon or other cloth ribbons are *not* good enough for typing your resume. If you don't have access to a quality word processing program, hire a professional with the resources to prepare your resume for you. Keep in mind that businesses such as Kinko's (open 24 hours) provide access to computers with quality printers.

Don't make your copies on an office photocopier. Only the human resources office may see the resume you mail. Everyone else may see only a copy of it, and copies of copies quickly become unreadable. Furthermore, sending photocopies of your resume or cover letter is completely unprofessional. Either print out each copy individually, or take your resume to a professional copy shop, which will generally offer professionally-maintained, extra-high-quality photocopiers and charge fairly reasonable prices. You want your resume to represent you with the look of polished quality.

Proof with Care

Whether you typed it or paid to have it produced professionally, mistakes on resumes are not only embarrassing, but will usually remove you from consideration (particularly if something obvious such as your name is misspelled). No matter how much you paid someone else to type, write, or typeset your resume, *you* lose if there is a mistake. So proofread it as carefully as possible. Get a friend to help you. Read your draft aloud as your friend checks the proof copy. Then have your friend read aloud while you check. Next, read it letter by letter to check spelling and punctuation.

If you are having it typed or typeset by a resume service or a printer, and you don't have time to proof it, pay for it and take it home. Proof it there and bring it back later to get it corrected and printed.

If you wrote your resume with a word processing program, use the built-in spell checker to double-check for spelling errors. Keep in mind that a spell checker will not find errors such as "to" for "two" or "wok" for "work." Many spell check programs do not recognize missing or misused punctuation, nor are they set to check the spelling of capitalized words. It's important that you still proofread your resume to check for grammatical mistakes and other problems, even after it has been spellchecked. If you find mistakes, do not make edits in pen or pencil or use white-out to fix them on the final copy!

Electronic Resumes

As companies rely increasingly on emerging technologies to find qualified candidates for job openings, you may opt to create an electronic resume in order to remain competitive in today's job market. Why is this important? Companies today sometimes request that resumes be submitted by e-mail, and many hiring managers regularly check online resume databases for candidates to fill unadvertised job openings. Other companies enlist the services of electronic employment database services, which charge jobseekers a nominal fee to have their resumes posted to the database to be viewed by potential employers. Still other companies use their own automated applicant tracking systems, in which case your resume is fed through a scanner that sends the image to a computer that "reads" your resume, looking for keywords, and files it accordingly in its database.

Whether you're posting your resume online, e-mailing it directly to an employer, sending it to an electronic employment database, or sending it to a company you suspect uses an automated applicant tracking system, you must create some form of electronic resume to take advantage of the technology. Don't panic! An electronic resume is simply a modified version of your conventional resume. An electronic resume is one that is sparsely formatted, but filled with keywords and important facts.

In order to post your resume to the Internet -- either to an online resume database or through direct e-mail to an employer -- you will need to change the way your resume is formatted. Instead of a Word, WordPerfect, or other word processing document, save your resume as a plain text, DOS, or ASCII file. These three terms are basically interchangeable, and describe text at its simplest, most basic level, without the formatting such as boldface or italics that most jobseekers use to make their resumes look more interesting. If you use e-mail, you'll notice that all of your messages are written and received in this format. First, you should remove all formatting from your resume including boldface, italics, underlining, bullets, differing font sizes, and graphics. Then, convert and save your resume as a plain text file. Most word processing programs have a "save as" feature that allows you to save files in different formats. Here, you should choose "text only" or "plain text."

Another option is to create a resume in HTML (hypertext markup language), the text formatting language used to publish information on the World Wide Web. However, the real usefulness of HTML resumes is still being explored. Most of the major online databases do not accept HTML resumes, and the vast majority of companies only accept plain text resumes through their e-mail.

Finally, if you simply wish to send your resume to an electronic employment database or a company that uses an automated applicant tracking system, there is no need to convert your resume to a plain text file. The only change you need to make is to organize the information in your resume by keywords. Employers are likely to do keyword searches for information, such as degree held or knowledge of particular types of software. Therefore, using the right keywords or key phrases in your resume is critical to its ultimate success. Keywords are usually nouns or short phrases that the computer searches for which refer to experience, training, skills, and abilities. For example, let's say an employer searches an employment database for a sales representative with the following criteria:

BS/BA
exceeded quota
cold calls
high energy
willing to travel

Even if you have the right qualifications, neglecting to use these keywords would result in the computer passing over your resume. Although there is no way to know for sure which keywords employers are most likely to search for, you can make educated guesses by checking the help-wanted ads or online job postings for your type of job. You should also arrange keywords in a keyword summary, a paragraph listing your qualifications that immediately follows your name and address (see sample letter in this chapter). In addition, choose a nondecorative font with clear, distinct characters, such as Helvetica or Times. It is more difficult for a scanner to accurately pick up the more unusual fonts. Boldface and all capital letters are best used only for major section headings, such as "Experience" and "Education." It is also best to avoid using italics or underlining, since this can cause the letters to bleed into one another.

Types of Resumes

The most common resume formats are the functional resume, the chronological resume, and the combination resume. (Examples can be found at the end of this chapter.) A functional resume focuses on skills and de-emphasizes job titles, employers, etc. A functional resume is best if you have been out of the work force for a long time or are changing careers. It is also good if you want to highlight specific skills and strengths, especially if all of your work experience has been at one company. This format can also be a good choice if you are just out of school or have no experience in your desired field.

Choose a chronological format if you are currently working or were working recently, and if your most recent experiences relate to your desired field. Use reverse chronological order and include dates. To a recruiter your last job and your latest schooling are the most important, so put the last first and list the rest going back in time.

A combination resume is perhaps the most common. This resume simply combines elements of the functional and chronological resume formats. This is used by many jobseekers with a solid track record who find elements of both types useful.

Organization

Your name, phone number, e-mail address (if you have one), and a complete mailing address should be at the top of your resume. Try to make your name stand out by using a slightly larger font size or all capital letters. Be sure to spell out everything. Never abbreviate St. for Street or Rd. for Road. If you are a college student, you should also put your home address and phone number at the top. Change your message on your answering machine if necessary – RUSH blaring in the background or your sorority sisters screaming may not come across well to all recruiters. If you think you may be moving within six months then include a second address and phone number of a trusted friend or relative who can reach you no matter where you are.

Remember that employers will keep your resume on file and may contact you months later if a position opens that fits your qualifications. All too often, candidates are unreachable because they have moved and had not previously provided enough contact options on their resume.

Next, list your experience, then your education. If you are a recent graduate, list your education first, unless your experience is more important than your education. (For example, if you have just graduated from a teaching school, have some business experience, and are applying for a job in business, you would list your business experience first.)

Keep everything easy to find. Put the dates of your employment and education on the left of the page. Put the names of the companies you worked for and the schools you attended a few spaces to the right of the dates. Put the city and state, or the city and country, where you studied or worked to the right of the page.

The important thing is simply to break up the text in some logical way that makes your resume visually attractive and easy to scan, so experiment to see which layout works best for your resume. However you set it up, *stay consistent*. Inconsistencies in fonts, spacing, or tenses will make your resume look sloppy. Also, be sure to use tabs to keep your information vertically lined up, rather than the less precise space bar.

RESUME CONTENT:
Say it with Style
Sell Yourself

You are selling your skills and accomplishments in your resume, so it is important to inventory yourself and know yourself. If you have achieved something, say so. Put it in the best possible light, but avoid subjective statements, such as "I am a hard worker" or "I get along well with my coworkers." Just stick to the facts.

While you shouldn't hold back or be modest, don't exaggerate your achievements to the point of misrepresentation. <u>Be honest</u>. Many companies will immediately drop an applicant from consideration (or fire a current employee) upon discovering inaccurate or untrue information on a resume or other application material.

Write down the important (and pertinent) things you have done, but do it in as few words as possible. Your resume will be scanned, not read, and short, concise phrases are much more effective than long-winded sentences. Avoid the use of "I" when emphasizing your accomplishments. Instead, use brief phrases beginning with action verbs.

While some technical terms will be unavoidable, you should try to avoid excessive "technicalese." Keep in mind that the first person to see your resume may be a human resources person who won't necessarily know all the jargon -- and how can they be impressed by something they don't understand?

Keep it Brief

Also, try to hold your paragraphs to six lines or less. If you have more than six lines of information about one job or school, put it in two or more paragraphs.

A short resume will be examined more carefully. Remember: Your resume usually has between eight and 45 seconds to catch an employer's eye. So make every second count.

Job Objective

A functional resume may require a job objective to give it focus. One or two sentences describing the job you are seeking can clarify in what capacity your skills will be best put to use. Be sure that your stated objective is in line with the position you're applying for.

Examples:

> An entry-level editorial assistant position in the publishing industry.
> A senior management position with a telecommunications firm.

Don't include a job objective on a chronological resume unless your previous work experiences are <u>completely</u> unrelated to the position for which you're applying. The presence of an overly specific job objective might eliminate you from consideration for other positions that a recruiter feels are a better match for your qualifications. But even if you don't put an objective on paper, having a career goal in mind as you write can help give your resume a solid sense of direction.

USE ACTION VERBS

How you write your resume is just as important as *what* you write. In describing previous work experiences, the strongest resumes use short phrases beginning with action verbs. Below are a few you may want to use. (This list is not all-inclusive.)

achieved	developed	integrated	purchased
administered	devised	interpreted	reduced
advised	directed	interviewed	regulated
arranged	distributed	launched	represented
assisted	established	managed	resolved
attained	evaluated	marketed	restored
budgeted	examined	mediated	restructured
built	executed	monitored	revised
calculated	expanded	negotiated	scheduled
collaborated	expedited	obtained	selected
collected	facilitated	operated	served
compiled	formulated	ordered	sold
completed	founded	organized	solved
computed	generated	participated	streamlined
conducted	headed	performed	studied
consolidated	identified	planned	supervised
constructed	implemented	prepared	supplied
consulted	improved	presented	supported
controlled	increased	processed	tested
coordinated	initiated	produced	trained
created	installed	proposed	updated
determined	instructed	published	wrote

Some jobseekers may choose to include both "Relevant Experience" and "Additional Experience" sections. This can be useful, as it allows the jobseeker to place more emphasis on certain experiences and to de-emphasize others.

Emphasize continued experience in a particular job area or continued interest in a particular industry. De-emphasize irrelevant positions. It is okay to include one opening line providing a general description of each company you've worked at. Delete positions that you held for less than four months (unless you are a very recent college grad or still in school). Stress your <u>results</u> and your achievements, elaborating on how you contributed in your previous jobs. Did you increase sales, reduce costs, improve a product, implement a new program? Were you promoted? Use specific numbers (i.e., quantities, percentages, dollar amounts) whenever possible.

Education

Keep it brief if you have more than two years of career experience. Elaborate more if you have less experience. If you are a recent college graduate, you may choose to include any high school activities that are directly relevant to your career. If you've been out of school for a while you don't need to list your education prior to college.

Mention degrees received and any honors or special awards. Note individual courses or projects you participated in that might be relevant for employers. For example, if you are an English major applying for a position as a business writer, be sure to mention any business or economics courses. Previous experience such as Editor-in-Chief of the school newspaper would be relevant as well.

If you are uploading your resume to an online job hunting site such as CareerCity.com, action verbs are still important, but the key words or key nouns that a computer would search for become more important. For example, if you're seeking an accounting position, key nouns that a computer would search for such as "Lotus 1-2-3" or "CPA" or "payroll" become very important.

Highlight Impressive Skills

Be sure to mention any computer skills you may have. You may wish to include a section entitled "Additional Skills" or "Computer Skills," in which you list any software programs you know. An additional skills section is also an ideal place to mention fluency in a foreign language.

Personal Data

This section is optional, but if you choose to include it, keep it brief. A one-word mention of hobbies such as fishing, chess, baseball, cooking, etc., can give the person who will interview you a good way to open up the conversation.

Team sports experience is looked at favorably. It doesn't hurt to include activities that are somewhat unusual (fencing, Akido, '70s music) or that somehow relate to the position or the company to which you're applying. For instance, it would be worth noting if you are a member of a professional organization in your industry of interest. Never include information about your age, alias, date of birth, health, physical characteristics, marital status, religious affiliation, or political/moral beliefs.

References

The most that is needed is the sentence "References available upon request" at the bottom of your resume. If you choose to leave it out, that's fine. This line is not really necessary. It is understood that references will most likely be asked for and provided by you later on in the interviewing process. Do not actually send references with your resume and cover letter unless specifically requested.

HIRING A RESUME WRITER:
Is it the Right Choice for You?

If you write reasonably well, it is to your advantage to write your own resume. Writing your resume forces you to review your experiences and figure out how to explain your accomplishments in clear, brief phrases. This will help you when you explain your work to interviewers. It is also easier to tailor your resume to each position you're applying for when you have put it together yourself.

If you write your resume, everything will be in your own words; it will sound like you. It will say what you want it to say. If you are a good writer, know yourself well, and have a good idea of which parts of your background employers are looking for, you should be able to write your own resume better than someone else. If you decide to write your resume yourself, have as many people as possible review and proofread it. Welcome objective opinions and other perspectives.

When to Get Help

If you have difficulty writing in "resume style" (which is quite unlike normal written language), if you are unsure which parts of your background to emphasize, or if you think your resume would make your case better if it did not follow one of the standard forms outlined either here or in a book on resumes, then you should consider having it professionally written.

Even some professional resume writers we know have had their resumes written with the help of fellow professionals. They sought the help of someone who could be objective about their background, as well as provide an experienced sounding board to help focus their thoughts.

If You Hire a Pro

The best way to choose a writer is by reputation: the recommendation of a friend, a personnel director, your school placement officer, or someone else knowledgeable in the field.

Important questions:
· "How long have you been writing resumes?"
· "If I'm not satisfied with what you write, will you go over it with me and change it?"
· "Do you charge by the hour or a flat rate?"

There is no sure relation between price and quality, except that you are unlikely to get a good writer for less than $50 for an uncomplicated resume and you shouldn't have to pay more than $300 unless your experience is very extensive or complicated. There will be additional charges for printing. Assume nothing no matter how much you pay. It is your career at stake if there are mistakes on your resume!

Few resume services will give you a firm price over the phone, simply because some resumes are too complicated and take too long to do for a predetermined price. Some services will quote you a price that applies to almost all of their customers. Once you decide to use a specific writer, you should insist on a firm price quote *before* engaging their services. Also, find out how expensive minor changes will be.

COVER LETTERS:
Quick, Clear, and Concise

Always mail a cover letter with your resume. In a cover letter you can show an interest in the company that you can't show in a resume. You can also point out one or two of your skills or accomplishments the company can put to good use.

Make it Personal

The more personal you can get, the better, so long as you keep it professional. If someone known to the person you are writing has recommended that you contact the company, get permission to include his/her name in the letter. If you can get the name of a person to send the letter to, address it directly to that person (after first calling the company to verify the spelling of the person's name, correct title, and mailing address). Be sure to put the person's name and title on both the letter and the envelope. This will ensure that your letter will get through to the proper person, even if a new person now occupies this position. It will not always be possible to get the name of a person. Always strive to get at least a title.

Be sure to mention something about why you have an interest in the company -- *so many candidates apply for jobs with no apparent knowledge of what the company does!* This conveys the message that they just want any job.

Type cover letters in full. Don't try the cheap and easy ways, like using a computer mail merge program or photocopying the body of your letter and typing in the inside address and salutation. You will give the impression that you are mailing to a host of companies and have no particular interest in any one.

Print your cover letter on the same color and same high-quality paper as your resume.

Cover letter basic format

<u>Paragraph 1:</u> State what the position is that you are seeking. It is not always necessary to state how you found out about the position -- often you will apply without knowing that a position is open.

<u>Paragraph 2:</u> Include what you know about the company and why you are interested in working there. Mention any prior contact with the company or someone known to the hiring person if relevant. Briefly state your qualifications and what you can offer. (Do not talk about what you cannot do).

<u>Paragraph 3:</u> Close with your phone number and where/when you can be reached. Make a request for an interview. State when you will follow up by phone (or mail or e-mail if the ad requests no phone calls). Do not wait long -- generally five working days. If you say you're going to follow up, then actually do it! This phone call can get your resume noticed when it might otherwise sit in a stack of 225 other resumes.

Cover letter do's and don'ts

- *Do* keep your cover letter brief and to the point.
- *Do* be sure it is error-free.
- *Do* accentuate what you can offer the company, not what you hope to gain.

- *Do* be sure your phone number and address is on your cover letter just in case it gets separated from your resume (this happens!).
- *Do* check the watermark by holding the paper up to a light -- be sure it is facing forward so it is readable -- on the same side as the text, and right-side up.
- *Do* sign your cover letter (or type your name if you are sending it electronically). Blue or black ink are both fine. Do not use red ink.
- *Don't* just repeat information verbatim from your resume.
- *Don't* overuse the personal pronoun "I."
- *Don't* send a generic cover letter -- show your personal knowledge of and interest in that particular company.

THANK YOU LETTERS:
Another Way to Stand Out

As mentioned earlier, *always* send a thank you letter after an interview (see the sample later in this section). So few candidates do this and it is yet another way for you to stand out. Be sure to mention something specific from the interview and restate your interest in the company and the position.

It is generally acceptable to handwrite your thank you letter on a generic thank you card (but *never* a postcard). Make sure handwritten notes are neat and legible. However, if you are in doubt, typing your letter is always the safe bet. If you met with several people it is fine to send them each an individual thank you letter. Call the company if you need to check on the correct spelling of their names.

Remember to:
- Keep it short.
- Proofread it carefully.
- Send it *promptly*.

FUNCTIONAL RESUME

C.J. RAVENCLAW
129 Pennsylvania Avenue
Washington DC 20500
202/555-6652
e-mail: ravenclaw@dcpress.net

Objective
A position as a graphic designer commensurate with my acquired skills and expertise.

Summary
Extensive experience in plate making, separations, color matching, background definition, printing, mechanicals, color corrections, and personnel supervision. A highly motivated manager and effective communicator. Proven ability to:

- **Create Commercial Graphics**
- **Produce Embossed Drawings**
- **Color Separate**
- **Control Quality**
- **Resolve Printing Problems**
- **Analyze Customer Satisfaction**

Qualifications
Printing:
Knowledgeable in black and white as well as color printing. Excellent judgment in determining acceptability of color reproduction through comparison with original. Proficient at producing four- or five-color corrections on all media, as well as restyling previously reproduced four-color artwork.

Customer Relations:
Routinely work closely with customers to ensure specifications are met. Capable of striking a balance between technical printing capabilities and need for customer satisfaction through entire production process.

Specialties:
Practiced at creating silk screen overlays for a multitude of processes including velo bind, GBC bind, and perfect bind. Creative design and timely preparation of posters, flyers, and personalized stationery.

Personnel Supervision:
Skillful at fostering atmosphere that encourages highly talented artists to balance high-level creativity with maximum production. Consistently beat production deadlines. Instruct new employees, apprentices, and students in both artistry and technical operations.

Experience
Graphic Arts Professor, Ohio State University, Columbus OH (1998-2002).
Manager, Design Graphics, Washington DC (2003-present).

Education
Massachusetts Conservatory of Art, Ph.D. 1996
University of Massachusetts, B.A. 1994

CHRONOLOGICAL RESUME

HARRY SEABORN
557 Shoreline Drive
Seattle, WA 98404
(206) 555-6584
e-mail: hseaborn@centco.com

EXPERIENCE

THE CENTER COMPANY   Seattle, WA
Systems Programmer   2002-present
  • Develop and maintain customer accounting and order tracking
  database using a Visual Basic front end and SQL server.
  • Plan and implement migration of company wide transition from
  mainframe-based dumb terminals to a true client server environment
  using Windows NT Workstation and Server.
  • Oversee general local and wide area network administration
  including the development of a variety of intranet modules to
  improve internal company communication and planning across
  divisions.

INFO TECH, INC.   Seattle, WA
Technical Manager   1996-2002
  • Designed and managed the implementation of a network providing
  the legal community with a direct line to Supreme Court cases
  across the Internet using SQL Server and a variety of Internet tools.
  • Developed a system to make the entire library catalog available on
  line using PERL scripts and SQL.
  • Used Visual Basic and Microsoft Access to create a registration
  system for university registrar.

EDUCATION

SALEM STATE UNIVERSITY   Salem, OR
        M.S. in Computer Science.   1999
        B.S. in Computer Science.   1997

COMPUTER SKILLS

  • Programming Languages: Visual Basic, Java, C++, SQL, PERL
  • Software: SQL Server, Internet Information Server, Oracle
  • Operating Systems: Windows NT, UNIX, Linux

FUNCTIONAL RESUME

Donna Hermione Moss
703 Wizard's Way
Chicago, IL 60601
(312) 555-8841
e-mail: donna@cowfire.com

OBJECTIVE:
To contribute over five years of experience in promotion, communications, and administration to an entry-level position in advertising.

SUMMARY OF QUALIFICATIONS:
- Performed advertising duties for small business.
- Experience in business writing and communications skills.
- General knowledge of office management.
- Demonstrated ability to work well with others, in both supervisory and support staff roles.
- Type 75 words per minute.

SELECTED ACHIEVEMENTS AND RESULTS:
Promotion:
Composing, editing, and proofreading correspondence and public relations materials for own catering service. Large-scale mailings.

Communication:
Instruction; curriculum and lesson planning; student evaluation; parent-teacher conferences; development of educational materials. Training and supervising clerks.

Computer Skills:
Proficient in MS Word, Lotus 1-2-3, Excel, and Filemaker Pro.

Administration:
Record-keeping and file maintenance. Data processing and computer operations, accounts receivable, accounts payable, inventory control, and customer relations. Scheduling, office management, and telephone reception.

PROFESSIONAL HISTORY:
Teacher; Self-Employed (owner of catering service); Floor Manager; Administrative Assistant; Accounting Clerk.

EDUCATION:
Beloit College, Beloit, WI, BA in Education, 1997

CHRONOLOGICAL RESUME

PERCY ZIEGLER
16 Josiah Court
Marlborough CT 06447
203/555-9641 (h)
203/555-8176, x14 (w)

EDUCATION

Keene State College, Keene NH
Bachelor of Arts in Elementary Education, 2003
- Graduated *magna cum laude*
- English minor
- Kappa Delta Pi member, inducted 2001

EXPERIENCE
September 2003-
Present

Elmer T. Thienes Elementary School, Marlborough CT
Part-time Kindergarten Teacher
- Instruct kindergartners in reading, spelling, language   arts, and music.
- Participate in the selection of textbooks and learning aids.
- Organize and supervise class field trips and coordinate in-class presentations.

Summers
2000-2002

Keene YMCA, Youth Division, Keene NH
Child-care Counselor
- Oversaw summer program for low-income youth.
- Budgeted and coordinated special events and field trips, working with Program Director to initiate variations in the program.
- Served as Youth Advocate in cooperation with social worker to address the social needs and problems of participants.

Spring 2002

Wheelock Elementary School, Keene NH
Student Teacher
- Taught third-grade class in all elementary subjects.
- Designed and implemented a two-week unit on Native Americans.
- Assisted in revision of third-grade curriculum.

Fall 2001

Child Development Center, Keene NH
Daycare Worker
- Supervised preschool children on the playground and during art activities.
- Created a "Wishbone Corner," where children could quietly look at books or take a voluntary "time-out."

ADDITIONAL INTERESTS

Martial arts, Pokemon, politics, reading, skiing, writing.

ELECTRONIC RESUME

GRIFFIN DORE
69 Dursley Drive
Cambridge, MA 02138
(617) 555-5555

KEYWORD SUMMARY

Senior financial manager with over ten years experience in Accounting and Systems Management, Budgeting, Forecasting, Cost Containment, Financial Reporting, and International Accounting. MBA in Management. Proficient in Lotus, Excel, Solomon, and Windows.

EXPERIENCE

COLWELL CORPORATION, Wellesley, MA
Director of Accounting and Budgets, 1995 to present
   Direct staff of twenty in General Ledger, Accounts Payable, Accounts Receivable, and International Accounting.
   Facilitate month-end closing process with parent company and auditors.
   Implemented team-oriented cross-training program within accounting group, resulting in timely month-end closings and increased productivity of key accounting staff.
   Developed and implemented a strategy for Sales and Use Tax Compliance in all fifty states.
   Prepare monthly financial statements and analyses.

FRANKLIN AND DELANEY COMPANY, Melrose, MA
Senior Accountant, 1993-1996
   Managed Accounts Payable, General Ledger, transaction processing, and financial reporting. Supervised staff of five.

Staff Accountant, 1991-1993
   Managed Accounts Payable, including vouchering, cash disbursements, and bank reconciliation.
   Wrote and issued policies.
   Maintained supporting schedules used during year-end audits.
   Trained new employees.

EDUCATION

MBA in Management, Northeastern University, Boston, MA, 1995
BS in Accounting, Boston College, Boston, MA, 1991

ASSOCIATIONS

National Association of Accountants

GENERAL MODEL
FOR A COVER LETTER

Your mailing address
Date

Contact's name
Contact's title
Company
Company's mailing address

Dear Mr./Ms. _____:

Immediately explain why your background makes you the best candidate for the position that you are applying for. Describe what prompted you to write (want ad, article you read about the company, networking contact, etc.). Keep the first paragraph short and hard-hitting.

Detail what you could contribute to this company. Show how your qualifications will benefit this firm. Describe your interest in the corporation. Subtly emphasizing your knowledge about this firm and your familiarity with the industry will set you apart from other candidates. Remember to keep this letter short; few recruiters will read a cover letter longer than half a page.

If possible, your closing paragraph should request specific action on the part of the reader. Include your phone number and the hours when you can be reached. Mention that if you do not hear from the reader by a specific date, you will follow up with a phone call. Lastly, thank the reader for their time, consideration, etc.

Sincerely,

(signature)

Your full name (typed)

Enclosure (use this if there are other materials, such as your resume,
            that are included in the same envelope)

SAMPLE COVER LETTER

16 Josiah Court
Marlborough CT 06447
January 16, 2006

Ms. Leona Malfoy
Assistant Principal
Laningham Elementary School
43 Mayflower Drive
Keene NH 03431

Dear Ms. Malfoy:

Toby Potter recently informed me of a possible opening for a third grade teacher at Laningham Elementary School. With my experience instructing third-graders, both in schools and in summer programs, I feel I would be an ideal candidate for the position. Please accept this letter and the enclosed resume as my application.

Laningham's educational philosophy that every child can learn and succeed interests me, since it mirrors my own. My current position at Elmer T. Thienes Elementary has reinforced this philosophy, heightening my awareness of the different styles and paces of learning and increasing my sensitivity toward special needs children. Furthermore, as a direct result of my student teaching experience at Wheelock Elementary School, I am comfortable, confident, and knowledgeable working with third-graders.

I look forward to discussing the position and my qualifications for it in more detail. I can be reached at 203/555-9641 evenings or 203/555-8176, x14 weekdays. If I do not hear from you before Tuesday of next week, I will call to see if we can schedule a time to meet. Thank you for your time and consideration.

Sincerely,

Percy Ziegler

Percy Ziegler

Enclosure

GENERAL MODEL FOR A
THANK YOU/FOLLOW-UP LETTER

Your mailing address
Date

Contact's name
Contact's title
Company
Company's mailing address

Dear Mr./Ms._____:

Remind the interviewer of the reason (i.e., a specific opening, an informational interview, etc.) you were interviewed, as well as the date. Thank him/her for the interview, and try to personalize your thanks by mentioning some specific aspect of the interview.

Confirm your interest in the organization (and in the opening, if you were interviewing for a particular position). Use specifics to re-emphasize that you have researched the firm in detail and have considered how you would fit into the company and the position. This is a good time to say anything you wish you had said in the initial meeting. Be sure to keep this letter brief; a half page is plenty.

If appropriate, close with a suggestion for further action, such as a desire to have an additional interview, if possible. Mention your phone number and the hours you can be reached. Alternatively, you may prefer to mention that you will follow up with a phone call in several days. Once again, thank the person for meeting with you, and state that you would be happy to provide any additional information about your qualifications.

Sincerely,

(signature)

Your full name (typed)

PRIMARY EMPLOYERS

ACCOUNTING & MANAGEMENT CONSULTING

**You can expect to find the following types of companies
in this section:**
Consulting and Research Firms • Industrial Accounting Firms • Management
Services • Public Accounting Firms • Tax Preparation Companies

AON CONSULTING
125 Chubb Avenue, Lyndhurst NJ 07071. 201/460-6854. **Contact:** Human Resources. **World Wide Web address:** http://www.aonconsulting.com. **Description:** An international human resources consulting and benefits brokerage firm providing integrated advisory and support services in retirement planning, health care management, organizational effectiveness, compensation, human resources-related communications, and information technologies. **Corporate headquarters location:** Chicago IL.

CT CORPORATION SYSTEM
111 Eighth Avenue, 13th Floor, New York NY 10011. 212/894-8940. **Fax:** 212/894-8710. **Contact:** Human Resources. **E-mail address:** info@ctadvantage.com. **World Wide Web address:** http://www.ctcorporation.com. **Description:** C.T. Corporation provides research and accounting services for attorneys. **Positions advertised include:** Staff Accountant; Service Team Leader; Internal Support Analyst; Accounts Receivable Maintenance Clerk; Associate Customer Specialist; Quality Assurance Professional; Receptionist; Project Manager; Desktop Support Analyst; Information Technology Manager; Senior Product Manager; Associate Customer Specialist; Operations Process Management Director; Licensing Support Specialist. **Parent company:** Wolters Kluwer U.S. **Number of employees:** 1,100.

DELOITTE & TOUCHE
10 Westport Road, P.O. Box 820, Wilton CT 06897-0820. 203/761-3000. **Fax:** 203/761-3062. **Contact:** Human Resources. **World Wide Web address:** http://www.us.deloitte.com. **Description:** An international firm of certified public accountants providing professional accounting, auditing, tax, and management consulting services to widely diversified clients. The company has a specialized program consisting of national industry groups and functional groups that cross industry lines. Groups are involved in various disciplines including accounting, auditing, taxation management advisory services, small and growing businesses, mergers and acquisitions, and computer applications. **Positions advertised include:** Administrator; Administrative Compliance Auditor; Administrative Project Specialist; Administrative U.S. National. **Special programs:** Internships. **Corporate headquarters location:** This location. **Other U.S. locations:** Nationwide. **Parent company:** Deloitte Touche Tohmatsu International. **Number of employees worldwide:** 95,000.

DELOITTE & TOUCHE
2 Hilton Court, P.O. Box 319, Parsippany NJ 07054-0319. 973/683-7000. **Fax:** 973/683-7459. **Contact:** Human Resources Department. **World Wide Web address:** http://www.us.deloitte.com. **Description:** An international firm of certified public accountants providing professional accounting, auditing, tax, and management consulting services to widely diversified clients. The company has a specialized program consisting of national industry groups and functional groups that cross industry lines. Groups are involved in various disciplines including accounting, auditing, taxation management advisory services, small and growing businesses, mergers and acquisitions, and computer applications. **Positions advertised include:** Accountant. **Corporate headquarters location:** Wilton CT.

Other U.S. locations: Nationwide. **Parent company:** Deloitte Touche Tohmatsu International is a global leader with nearly 90,000 employees in over 130 countries.

DELOITTE TOUCHE TOHMATSU
dba DELOITTE & TOUCHE LLP
1633 Broadway, New York NY 10019-6754. 212/492-4000. **Fax:** 212/492-3990. **Contact:** Human Resources. **World Wide Web address:** http://www.deloitte.com. **Description:** An international auditing partnership of certified public accountants providing professional accounting, auditing, tax, and management consulting services to widely diversified clients from offices in 140 countries. The company has a specialized program consisting of national industry groups and functional groups that cross industy lines. Groups are involved in various disciplines including accounting, auditing, taxation management advisory services, small and growing businesses, mergers and acquisitions, and computer applications. **NOTE:** Apply online. **Positions advertised include:** Senior Industry Knowledge Manager; Administrative Assistant; Administrative Floater; Executive Assistant; Scheduling Manager; Information Technology Recruiting Manager; Tax Recruiting Manager; Client Advisory Associate; Business Development Manager; Relationship Development Manager; Assurance & Compliance Consultant. **Corporate headquarters location:** This location. **Other locations:** Worldwide. **Subsidiaries include:** Deloitte Consulting. **Chairman:** Piet Hoogendoorn. **Annual sales/revenues:** $12.5 billion. **Number of employees:** 98,000.

AG EDWARDS & SONS
2960 Post Road, Southport CT 06890. 203/255-6881. **Contact:** Human Resources. **World Wide Web address:** http://www.agedwards.com. **Description:** An investment firm offering bonds, money market accounts, mutual funds, IRAs, annuities, estate planning, and related services. **Corporate headquarters location:** St. Louis MO. **Other U.S. locations:** Nationwide. **Listed on:** New York Stock Exchange. **Stock exchange symbol:** AGE. **CEO:** Robert L. Bagby. **Number of employees nationwide:** 15,400.

ERNST & YOUNG LLP
125 Chubb Avenue, Lyndhurst NJ 07071. 201/872-2200. **Contact:** Human Resources. **World Wide Web address:** http://www.ey.com. **Description:** A certified public accounting firm that also provides management consulting services. Services include data processing, financial modeling, financial feasibility studies, production planning and inventory management, management sciences, health care planning, human resources, cost accounting, and budgeting systems. **Positions advertised include:** Strategic Sourcing Analyst; Balance Sheet Analyst Manager; Infrastructure Engineer; Assistant Coordinator; Software Development Specialist; Production Analyst; Help Desk Analyst; Client Services Assistant; Project Account Manager; Executive Coordinator; Financial Analyst; Information Technology Technologist; Financial Application Support. **Corporate headquarters location:** New York NY.

ERNST & YOUNG INTERNATIONAL
dba ERNST & YOUNG LLP
5 Times Square, New York NY 10036-6530. 212/773-3000. **Fax:** 212/773-6350. **Contact:** Human Resources. **World Wide Web address:** http://www.ey.com. **Description:** A certified public accounting partnership that also provides accounting and management consulting services. Services include data processing, financial modeling, financial feasibility studies, production planning and inventory management, management sciences, health care planning, human resources, cost accounting, and budgeting systems. **Positions advertised include:** Financial Assistant; Financial Researcher; Bilingual Japanese Administrative Assistant; risk Management Senior Manager; Technology &

Security Risk Services Senior; Structured Finance Advisory Services Manager; Risk Management Services Senior; Knowledge Resources Manager; On-Call Advisory Services Senior; Credit Risk Management Advisor. **Corporate headquarters location:** This location. **Other locations:** Worldwide. **Chairman:** James (Jim) S. Turley. **Annual sales/revenues:** $10.1 billion. **Number of employees:** 110,000.

FIND/SVP, INC.
625 Sixth Avenue, 2nd Floor, New York NY 10011-2020. 212/645-4500. **Fax:** 212/463-6232. **Contact:** Clodagh Whelan, Human Resources. **E-mail address:** careers@findsvp.com. **World Wide Web address:** http://www.findsvp.com. **Description:** Provides business and management consulting, research, and advisory services. The company also offers seminars, conferences, and publications. Founded in 1969. **Positions advertised include:** Industrial Products and Services Director; Corporate Sales Representative; Business Development Manager; Healthcare Team Consultant; Business Consultant; Associate Consultant. **Corporate headquarters location:** This location. **Other locations:** Nationwide. **Listed on:** Over The Counter. **Stock exchange symbol:** FSVP. **Chairman:** Martin E. Franklin. **Annual sales/revenues:** $22 million. **Number of employees:** 169.

JACKSON HEWITT INC.
7 Sylvan Way, Parsippany NJ 07054. 973/496-1040. **Contact:** Human Resources. **World Wide Web address:** http://www.jacksonhewitt.com. **Description:** A full-service company specializing in computerized tax preparation and electronic filing. The foundation of Jackson Hewitt's tax service is Hewtax, a proprietary software program. The company offers a number of filing options including SuperFast Refund, through which customers receive a refund anticipation loan within one to two days of filing; Accelerated Check Refund, which allows Jackson Hewitt to set up a bank account for the IRS to deposit the taxpayer's refund; and a standard electronically filed return. The company also operates a travel agency, Campbell Travel. **Positions advertised include:** Accountant; Corporate Communications Manager; Accounting Director; Vehicle Damage Claim Director; Commercial Marketing Associate; Administrative Assistant; Project Manager; Desktop Support Manager; Receptionist; Database Developer; File Clerk; Director of Security. **NOTE:** Search for current positions by location online.

KPMG
3 Chestnut Ridge Road, Montvale NJ 07645. 201/307-7000. **Contact:** Human Resources. **World Wide Web address:** http://www.kpmgcareers.com. **Description:** KPMG delivers a wide range of value-added assurance, tax, and consulting services. **Corporate headquarters location:** This location. **Other U.S. locations:** Nationwide. **Operations at this facility include:** This location houses the company's administrative offices. **Parent company:** KPMG International is a leader among professional services firms engaged in capturing, managing, assessing, and delivering information to create knowledge that will help its clients maximize shareholder value.

KPMG
345 Park Avenue, New York NY 10154. 212/909-5000. **Contact:** Human Resources. **World Wide Web address:** http://www.kpmgcareers.com. **Description:** KPMG delivers a wide range of value-added assurance, tax, and consulting services including legal and management services. **Positions advertised include:** Senior Associate; Recruiter; Pharmaceutical Regulatory Manager; Associate Pharmaceutical Regulator; Senior Associate Manager; Project Manager; Senior Internal Auditor; Insurance Practice Auditor; Duplicating Operator; Tax Manager; Quantitative Analyst. **Corporate headquarters location:** Montvale NJ. **Other U.S. locations:** Nationwide. **Parent company:**

KPMG International is a professional services firm with more than 85,000 employees worldwide including 6,500 partners and 60,000 professionals, serving clients in 844 cities throughout 155 countries. KPMG International is a leader among professional services firms engaged in capturing, managing, assessing, and delivering information to create knowledge that will help its clients maximize shareholder value. **Number of employees at this location:** 1300.

MERCER HUMAN RESOURCE CONSULTING
601 Merritt 7, Norwalk CT 06856. 203/229-6000. **Contact:** Human Resources. **World Wide Web address:** http://www.mercer.com. **Description:** One of the world's largest actuarial and human resources management consulting firms, providing advice to organizations on all aspects of employee relations. Services include retirement, health and welfare, performance and rewards, communication, investment, human resources administration, risk, finance and insurance, and health care provider consulting. **Corporate headquarters location:** New York NY. **Other U.S. locations:** Nationwide. **International locations:** Worldwide.

PRICEWATERHOUSECOOPERS
300 Atlantic Street, Stamford CT 06901. 203/539-3000. **Contact:** Sue Cohen, Human Resources. **World Wide Web address:** http://www.pricewaterhousecoopers.com. **Description:** One of the largest certified public accounting firms in the world. PricewaterhouseCoopers provides public accounting, business advisory, management consulting, and taxation services. **Corporate headquarters location:** New York NY. **Other U.S. locations:** Nationwide.

PRICEWATERHOUSECOOPERS
1301 Avenue of the Americas, New York NY 10019. 646/471-4000. **Contact:** Human Resources. **World Wide Web address:** http://www.pwcglobal.com. **Description:** One of the largest certified public accounting firms in the world. PricewaterhouseCoopers provides public accounting, business advisory, management consulting, and taxation services. **NOTE:** Interested job seekers may apply online. **Positions advertised include:** BCS Senior Associate; Asset Advisory Associate; ISG Manager; Special Situations Associate; Insurance Manager; Senior Operational Effectiveness Associate; Executive Assistant to the Chairman; Corporate Treasury Technology Associate; Treasury and Finance Associate; OGC Secretariat Associate; Change and Learning Solutions Manager. **Corporate headquarters location:** This location. **Other U.S. locations:** Nationwide. **International locations:** Worldwide. **Chairman:** Andrew Ratcliffe. **Sales/revenue:** Over $13 billion. **Number of employees worldwide:** 125,000.

TOWERS PERRIN
100 Summit Lake Drive, Valhalla NY 10595. 914/745-4000. **Contact:** Human Resources. **World Wide Web address:** http://www.towersperrin.com. **Description:** A management consulting firm. **Corporate headquarters location:** New York NY. **Operations at this facility include:** Administration; Regional Headquarters; Research and Development; Service.

TOWERS PERRIN
335 Madison Avenue, New York NY 10017-4605. 212/309-3400. **Contact:** Recruiting Coordinator. **World Wide Web address:** http://www.towersperrin.com. **Description:** A management consulting firm. **Corporate headquarters location:** This location.

ADVERTISING, MARKETING, AND PUBLIC RELATIONS

You can expect to find the following types of companies
in this section:
Advertising Agencies • Direct Mail Marketers • Market Research Firms • Public
Relations Firms

ASSOCIATED MERCHANDISING CORPORATION (AMC)
500 Seventh Avenue, New York NY 10018. 212/819-6600. **Fax:** 212/819-6701.
Contact: Personnel. **World Wide Web address:** http://www.theamc.com.
Description: Performs retail product development and international apparel
sourcing services for retail clients operating 53 offices worldwide. Founded in
1916. **Positions advertised include:** Commercial Artist; Customer Service
Representative; Product Manager. **Corporate headquarters location:** This
location. **Other locations:** Worldwide. **Parent company:** Target Corporation
(Minneapolis MN). **President/CEO:** Richard J. Kuzmich. **Number of employees:**
1,200.

BBDO WORLDWIDE INC.
1285 Avenue of the Americas, New York NY 10019. 212/459-5000. **Fax:**
212/459-6645. **Recorded jobline:** 212/459-5627. **Contact:** Human Resources
Department. **E-mail address:** nyhrmanagerrecruiting@bbdo.com. **World Wide
Web address:** http://www.bbdo.com. **Description:** Operates a worldwide
network of advertising agencies in 300 offices in 45 countries with related
businesses in public relations, direct marketing, sales promotion, graphic design,
graphic arts, and printing. BBDO Worldwide operates 83 subsidiaries, affiliates,
and associates in advertising and related operations. Since 1891. **Positions
advertised include:** Assistant Media Planner; Assistant National TV Buyer;
Corporate Computer Systems Manager; Media Supervisor; National TV Buyer;
Media Planner; Assistant Account Executive; Budget Coordinator; Systems
Engineer; Administrative Assistant; Accounting Clerk; Finance Manager; Control
Coordinator; Print Estimator; Art Director; Copy Editor; Audio-Visual Technician;
Business Affairs Manager; Media Producer; Traffic Coordinator. **Special
programs:** Interships. **Corporate headquarters location:** This location. **Other
U.S. locations:** Nationwide. **International locations:** Worldwide. **Subsidiaries
include:** BBDO Detroit. **Parent company:** Omnicom Group Inc. (New York NY).
Chairman/CEO: Allen Rosenshine. **Annual sales/revenues:** $1.6 billion.
Number of employees worldwide: 16,600.

BATES USA
498 Seventh Avenue, New York NY 10018. 212/297-7000. **Fax:** 212/297-8888.
Contact: Human Resources. **E-mail address:** hr@batesww.com. **World Wide
Web address:** http://www.batesusa.com. **Description:** One of the largest
advertising and public relations agencies in the United States. **Positions
advertised include:** Account Manager; Account Planner; Creative Designer;
Media Specialist. **Corporate headquarters location:** This location. **Other
locations:** Worldwide.

BOZELL WORLDWIDE
40 West 23rd Street, New York NY 10010. 212/727-5000. **Fax:** 212/463-8419.
Contact: Human Resources. **E-mail address:** bozellhr@newyork.bozell.com.
World Wide Web address: http://www.bozell.com. **Description:** A full-service
advertising agency. Bozell also offers public relations services such as corporate
relations, marketing support, employee relations, financial relations, government
affairs, and community relations. **Corporate headquarters location:** This
location. **Other U.S. locations:** Nationwide. **International locations:** Worldwide.

BURSON-MARSTELLER

230 Park Avenue South, New York NY 10003. 212/614-4141. **Fax:** 212/598-6999. **Contact:** Kay Fynmore, Human Resources Director. **E-mail address:** kay_fynmore@nyc.bm.com. **World Wide Web address:** http://www.bm.com. **Description:** A full-service public relations agency with 75 offices in 34 countries. Founded in 1953. **Positions advertised include:** Public Relations Specialist. **Special programs:** Internships. **Corporate headquarters location:** This location. **Other U.S. locations:** Los Angeles CA; Sacramento CA; San Diego CA; San Francisco CA; Washington DC; Miami FL; Chicago IL; Pittsburgh PA; Dallas TX. **Subsidiaries include:** Cohn & Wolfe, Public Relations. **Parent company:** WPP Group PLC (London, United Kingdom). **Founding Chairman:** Harold Burson. **Annual sales/revenues:** $175 million. **Number of employees at this location:** 340. **Number of employees worldwide:** 1,600.

CLIENTLOGIC

230 Brighton Road, Clifton NJ 07012. 973/778-5588. **Fax:** 973/778-7485. **Contact:** Human Resources. **E-mail address:** cliftonjobs@clientlogic.com. **World Wide Web address:** http://www.clientlogic.com. **Description:** A direct marketing firm. **Corporate headquarters location:** Nashville TN. **Other area locations:** Weehawken NJ. **Parent company:** Onex Corporation.

DDB WORLDWIDE COMMUNICATIONS GROUP, INC.

437 Madison Avenue, New York NY 10022. 212/415-2000. **Fax:** 212/415-3414. **Contact:** James Best, Chief People Officer. **World Wide Web address:** http://www.ddb.com. **Description:** A full-service, international advertising agency operating 200 offices in 100 countries. **Positions advertised include:** Advertising Executive; Media Specialist. **Special programs:** Internships. **Corporate headquarters location:** This location. **Other U.S. locations:** Los Angeles CA; Chicago IL. **Parent company:** Omnicom Group, Inc. (also at this location). **Chairman:** Keith L. Reinhard. **Annual sales/revenues:** $1.2 billion. **Number of employees:** 11,900.

DIRECT MEDIA, INC.

200 Pemberwick Road, Greenwich CT 06830. 203/532-1000. **Contact:** Human Resources. **World Wide Web address:** http://www.directmedia.com. **Description:** Provides direct marketing services such as list management and brokerage. **Positions advertised include:** Copywriter; Package Insert Coordinator; Insert Media Sales Specialist; List Management Account Executive. **Corporate headquarters location:** This location. **Other U.S. locations:** Conway AR; Walnut Creek CA; Schaumburg IL; Merriam KS; Port Chester NY. **International locations:** Toronto, Ontario. **Number of employees worldwide:** 300.

DOREMUS & COMPANY, INC.

200 Varick Street, 11th Floor, New York NY 10014. 212/366-3000. **Fax:** 212/366-3060. **Contact:** Kristin Mooney, Human Resources Director. **E-mail address:** careers@doremus.com. **World Wide Web address:** http://www.doremus.com. **Description:** An agency specializing in corporate and financial advertising. Founded in 1903. **NOTE:** Entry-level positions are offered. **Special programs:** Internships. **Corporate headquarters location:** This location. **Other U.S. locations:** San Francisco CA. **International locations:** London, England; Tokyo, Japan; Frankfurt, Germany; Hong Kong, China. **Parent company:** Omnicom Group Inc. (New York NY). **Annual sales/revenues:** $43.5 million. **Number of employees:** 190

FCB WORLDWIDE

100 West 33rd Street, New York NY 10001. 212/885-3000. **Fax:** 212/885-2803. **Contact:** Director of Personnel. **E-mail address:** careersny@fcb.com. **World

Wide Web address: http://www.fcb.com. **Description:** An international advertising agency. FCB/LKP offers additional services including direct marketing, design and production of sales promotion programs; market and product research; package design; and trademark and trade name development. The company operates offices throughout Europe, Asia, and Latin America. **Corporate headquarters location:** This location. **International locations:** Worldwide. **Parent company:** Foote, Cone & Belding Communications.

FRANKEL
Greenwich Office Park, Building 5, Greenwich CT 06831. 203/862-6000. **Contact:** Human Resources. **World Wide Web address:** http://www.frankel.com. **Description:** Provides marketing services in the promotion, direct, interactive, brand communications, sports/entertainment, and consulting areas. **Corporate headquarters location:** This location. **Other U.S. locations:** Atlanta GA; Troy MI; Minnetonka MN; Parsippany NJ.

GARTNER, INC.
56 Top Gallant Road, Stamford CT 06904. 203/964-0096. **Fax:** 203/316-6436. **Contact:** Human Resources. **World Wide Web address:** http://www.gartner.com. **Description:** Gartner, Inc. is a market research and consulting firm providing strategic decision support. **Special programs:** Internships. **Corporate headquarters location:** This location. **Other U.S. locations:** San Jose CA. **International locations:** Australia; Japan; United Kingdom. **Operations at this facility include:** Research and Development; Sales. **Listed on:** NASDAQ. **Stock exchange symbol:** IT.

GOTHAM INC.
100 Fifth Avenue, New York NY 10011. 212/414-7000. **Contact:** Patti Ransom, Director Human Resources. **E-mail address:** jobs@gothaminc.com. **World Wide Web address:** http://www.gothaminc.com. **Description:** Specializes in creating start-up brands with an emphasis on fashion and beauty advertising. Founded in 1994. **CEO:** Stone Roberts.

GREY GLOBAL GROUP
777 Third Avenue, New York NY 10017. 212/546-2000. **Contact:** Human Resources: **E-mail address:** careers@grey.com. **World Wide Web address:** http://www.greyglobal.com. **Description:** An international advertising agency operating in 83 countries.

HILL AND KNOWLTON INC.
466 Lexington Avenue, 3rd Floor, New York NY 10017. 212/885-0300. **Fax:** 212/885-0570. **Contact:** Human Resources Department. **World Wide Web address:** http://www.hillandknowlton.com. **Description:** One of the largest public relations/public affairs counseling firms in the world. **NOTE:** Human Resources phone: 212/885-0547. **Positions advertised include:** Senior Account Executive; Healthcare Pharmaceutical Account Representative; Bilingual Spanish/English Accountant; Controller. **Corporate headquarters location:** This location. **Other U.S. locations:** San Francisco CA; Washington DC. **International locations:** Worldwide. **Subsidiaries include:** The Wexler Group. **Parent company:** WPP Group plc (London, United Kingdom). **Chairman/CEO:** Paul Taaffe. **Annual sales/revenues:** $325 million. **Number of employees:** 1,117.

IMS HEALTH
100 Campus Road, Totowa NJ 07512. 973/790-0700. **Contact:** Human Resources. **World Wide Web address:** http://www.ims-health.com. **Description:** Conducts market research on the health care industry for pharmaceutical companies. **NOTE:** Apply online. **Positions advertised include:** Account Manager; Account Service Representative; Database Analyst; Revenue Analyst. **Special programs:** Internships. **Corporate headquarters location:**

Plymouth Meeting PA. **Parent company:** Dun & Bradstreet. **Number of employees at this location:** 400.

IMEDIA, INC.
745 US Highway 202/206, Bridgewater NJ, 08807. 908/725-7500. **Fax:** 908-725-7501. **Contact:** Personnel. **E-mail address:** careers@imedia.com. **World Wide Web address:** http://www.imedianet.com. **Description:** Provides public relations and technological consulting services for large companies.

THE INTERPUBLIC GROUP OF COMPANIES, INC.
1271 Avenue of the Americas, 44th Floor, New York NY 10020. 212/399-8000. **Fax:** 212/399-8130. **Contact:** Doris Weil, Director of Corporate Human Resources. **E-mail address:** hr@interpublic.com. **World Wide Web address:** http://www.interpublic.com. **Description:** An advertising agency doing business in 130 countries worldwide. The company plans, creates, and implements advertising campaigns in various media through either its own subsidiaries or contracts with local agencies. Other activities include publishing, market research, public relations, product development, and sales promotion. Interpublic's international business groups include McCann-Erickson WorldGroup and The Lowe Group. **Corporate headquarters location:** This location. **Subsidiaries/affiliates include:** Advanced Marketing Services; Deutsch, Inc.; DeVries Public Relations; Draft Worldwide; FutureBrand Worldwide; Hill Holliday; Jack Morton Worldwide Inc.; McCann Relationship Marketing Partners Worldwide; McCann-Erickson WorldGroup; Modem Media, Inc.; Mullen Advertising Inc.; NFO WorldGroup, Inc.; Octagon; Temerlin McClain; Weber Shandwick Worldwide. **Listed on:** New York Stock Exchange. **Stock exchange symbol:** IPG. **Chairman/President/CEO:** David A. Bell. **Annual sales/revenues:** $6.2 billion. **Number of employees:** 52,000.

THE KAPLAN THALER GROUP, LTD.
World Wide Plaza, 825 Eighth Avenue, 34th Floor, New York NY 10019-7498. 212/474-5000. **Fax:** 212/474-5036. **Contact:** Human Resources. **E-mail address:** kaplanthalergroup@kaplanthaler.com. **World Wide Web address:** http://www.kaplanthaler.com. **Description:** A national advertising agency. **Corporate headquarters location:** This location. **Other U.S. locations:** Nationwide. **International locations:** Worldwide. **Parent company:** Publicis (Paris, France). **President/CEO:** Linda Kaplan Thaler. **Annual sales/revenues:** $15 million. **Number of employees:** 48.

KATZ MEDIA GROUP, INC.
125 West 55th Street, 21st Floor, New York NY 10019-5366. 212/424-6000. **Fax:** 212/424-6110. **Contact:** Human Resources. **World Wide Web address:** http://www.katz-media.com. **Description:** An advertising agency with 21 regional offices nationwide. **Positions advertised include:** Sales Assistant; Supervisor/Sales Manager's Assistant; Research Analyst. **Corporate headquarters location:** This location. **Parent company:** Clear Channel Communications (San Antonio TX). **Subsidiaries include:** National Cable Communications; Christal Suburban Radio. **Listed on:** New York Stock Exchange. **Stock exchange symbol:** CCU. **CEO:** Stuart (Stu) O. Olds.

LOWE
One Dag Hammarskjold Plaza, New York NY 10017. 212/605-8000. **Contact:** Human Resources. **E-mail address:** info@loweworldwide.com. **World Wide Web address:** http://www.loweworldwide.com. **Description:** An advertising agency.

LYONS LAVEY NICKEL SWIFT INC.
220 East 42nd Street, 3rd Floor, New York NY 10017. 212/771-3000. **Fax:** 212/771-3016. **Contact:** Human Resources Manager. **E-mail address:**

jobs@hmcny.com. **World Wide Web address:** http://www.llns.com. **Description:** An advertising agency for pharmaceutical firms. Founded in 1972. **NOTE:** Entry-level positions are offered. **Positions advertised include:** Vice President Supervisor Aricept; Traffic Coordinator; Account Supervisor; Account Assistant; Media Coordinator; Medical Information Specialist; Medical Editor.

MBI, INC.
47 Richards Avenue, Norwalk CT 06857. 203/853-2000. **Contact:** Human Resources. **World Wide Web address:** http://www.mbi-inc.com. **Description:** MBI is a direct marketing firm for collectibles including coin and stamp sets, porcelain dolls, porcelain plates, and die-cast vehicles. **Positions advertised include:** General Manager. **Special programs:** Internships. **Corporate headquarters location:** This location. **Number of employees at this location:** 700.

MARKETING CORPORATION OF AMERICA
372 Danbury Road, Wilton CT 06897. 203/210-2600. **Contact:** Human Resources. **E-mail address:** careers@mcofa.com. **World Wide Web address:** http://www.mcofa.com. **Description:** A consulting firm. **Other U.S. locations:** San Francisco CA; Minneapolis MN; New York NY.

McCANN-ERICKSON WORLDWIDE
750 Third Avenue, New York NY 10017. 212/697-6000. **Contact:** Human Resources. **World Wide Web address:** http://www.mccann.com. **Description:** An advertising agency with operations in 130 countries. **Corporate headquarters location:** This location. **Other U.S. locations:** Atlanta GA; Chicago IL; Louisville KY; Houston TX; Seattle WA. **International locations:** Worldwide. **Parent company:** The Interpublic Group of Companies, Inc.

ARNOLD McGRATH WORLDWIDE
110 Fifth Avenue, New York NY 10011. 212/463-1000. **Fax:** 212/463-1628. **Contact:** Chris Martin, Director of Human Resources. **E-mail address:** cmartin@arnny.com. **World Wide Web address:** http://www.arnny.com. **Description:** An advertising agency. Founded in 1980. **Special programs:** Internships; Apprenticeships; Training. **Corporate headquarters location:** This location.

THE MEDICUS GROUP
1675 Broadway, New York NY 10019-5809. 212/468-3100. **Fax:** 212/468-3208. **Contact:** Emilie Schaum, Director of Human Resources. **World Wide Web address:** http://www.medicusgroup.com. **Description:** Markets a wide range of pharmaceutical and consumer health products and services to health care professionals, patients, and consumers. Services include advertising and promotions, direct-to-consumer marketing, interactive media, medical education, public relations, publication planning, and sales training. Founded in 1972. **Special programs:** Internships. **Office hours:** Monday - Friday, 9:00 a.m. - 5:00 p.m. **Corporate headquarters location:** This location. **International locations:** Worldwide. **Parent company:** Publicis. **Chairman/CEO:** Glenn DeSimone.

MICKELBERRY COMMUNICATIONS
405 Park Avenue, Suite 1003, New York NY 10022. 212/832-0303. **Contact:** Human Resources. **World Wide Web address:** http://www.mickelberry.com. **Description:** A holding company for three marketing companies and a commercial printing group. **Parent company:** Union Capital Corporation.

MILLWARD BROWN
501 Kingshighway East, Fairfield CT 06825. 203/335-5222. **Fax:** 203/256-5470. **Contact** Human Resources. **World Wide Web address:** http://www.millwardbrown.com. **Description:** Provides research-based marketing

consultancy to assist clients in building profitable brands and e-brands and in providing service. **President:** Eileen Campbell.

MOKRYNSKI & ASSOCIATES
401 Hackensack Avenue, 2nd Floor, Hackensack NJ 07601. 201/488-5656. **Contact:** Human Resources. **World Wide Web address:** http://www.mokrynski.com. **Description:** A direct mailing company that manages, acquires, and sells mailing lists for client companies.

MOSS DRAGOTI
437 Madison Avenue, New York NY 10022. 212/415-2900. **Contact:** Director of Human Resources. **World Wide Web address:** http://www.ddb.com. **Description:** An advertising agency. **Parent company:** DDB Worldwide.

ERIC MOWER AND ASSOCIATES
500 Plum Street, Syracuse NY 13204. 315/466-1000. **Contact:** Human Resources. **E-mail address:** hrrecruiter@eric.mower.com. **World Wide Web address:** http://www.mower.com. **Description:** An advertising agency. **Other area locations:** Buffalo NY; Rochester NY. **Annual sales/revenues:** More than $100 million. **Number of employees at this location:** 150.

NFO WORLDGROUP, INC.
2 Pickwick Plaza, 3rd Floor, Greenwich CT 06830. 203/629-8888. **Contact:** Human Resources. **World Wide Web address:** http://www.nfow.com. **Description:** Provides custom and syndicated market research services, primarily using a proprietary panel of prerecruited consumer households throughout the country. NFO also offers Internet-based custom marketing research. **NOTE:** Send resumes to 2700 Oregon Road, Northwood OH 43619. **Corporate headquarters location:** Canton OH. **International locations:** Worldwide. **Subsidiaries include:** Advanced Marketing Solutions, Inc. (CT) provides custom computer software systems used by clients to quickly access and analyze complex business and consumer information; Payment Systems, Inc. (FL) is a leading supplier of information to the financial services industry in the United States. **Parent company:** The Interpublic Group of Companies, Inc. **Listed on:** New York Stock Exchange. **Stock exchange symbol:** IPG. **Number of employees worldwide:** 15,000.

THE NPD GROUP, INC.
900 West Shore Road, Port Washington NY 11050. 516/625-0700. **Fax:** 516/625-4866. **Contact:** Human Resources Department. **E-mail address:** recruit99@npd.com. **World Wide Web address:** http://www.npd.com. **Description:** A market research firm offering a full line of custom and syndicated consumer research services including point-of-sale computerized audits, purchase panels, mail panels, telephone research, mathematical modeling, and consulting. Industries covered include consumer packaged goods, apparel, toys, electronics, automotive, sports, books, and food consumption. **Positions advertised include:** Account Manager; Analytic Director; Director of Retail Business Development; Director of Client Development; Manager of Financial Reporting/Analysis; Marketing Coordinator; Research Manager; Senior Account Manager; Technical Specialist; Vice President of Client Development. **Special programs:** Internships. **Corporate headquarters location:** This location. **Other area locations:** New York NY. **Other U.S. locations:** Chicago IL; Hyattsville MD; Greensboro NC; Cincinnati OH; Houston TX. **International locations:** Worldwide. **Number of employees nationwide:** 800.

NIELSEN MEDIA RESEARCH COMPANY
7700 Broadway, New York NY 10003-9595. 646/654-8300. **Contact:** Josh Lax, Human Resources. **World Wide Web address:** http://www.nielsenmedia.com. **Description:** Nielsen Media Research measures television show audience sizes

and provides this information to broadcast networks and advertising agencies. **NOTE:** Interested job seekers may apply online for specific positions or for general consideration. **Positions advertised include:** Staff Assistant; National Accounts Manager; Meeting and Event Manager; Media Field Interviewer; Executive Staff Assistant; Director of Marketing and Communications; Associate Analyst; Bilingual Technical Field Representative. **Corporate headquarters location:** This location. **Other U.S. locations:** Los Angeles CA; San Francisco CA; Dallas TX; Atlanta GA; Chicago IL; Dunedin FL. **Number of employees at this location:** 195. **Number of employees nationwide:** 3,500.

OGILVY & MATHER
309 West 49th Street, New York NY 10019. 212/237-6000. **Recorded jobline:** 212/237-5627. **Contact:** Human Resources. **World Wide Web address:** http://www.ogilvy.com. **Description:** An advertising agency. **Other U.S. locations:** Nationwide. **International locations:** Worldwide. **Parent company:** WPP Group plc.

PETRY MEDIA CORPORATION
dba BLAIR TELEVISION, INC.
3 East 54th Street, New York NY 10022. 212/230-5900. **Fax:** 212/230-5843. **Contact:** Human Resources Staffing. **World Wide Web address:** http://www.petrymedia.com/blair. **Description:** Provides the media industry with national sales, marketing, and research services. The company's subsidiaries represent 250 TV stations and provides services to advertising agencies and spot TV advertisers. **Positions advertised include:** Sales Assistant; Research Analyst; Sales Associate; Account Executive. **Special programs:** Internships. **Corporate headquarters location:** This location. **Other U.S. locations:** Nationwide. **Subsidiaries include:** Blair Television, Incorporated; Petry Television Incorporated. **Operations at this facility include:** Administration; Research and Development; Sales. **Number of employees at this location:** 250. **Number of employees nationwide:** 500.

POSTERLOID CORPORATION
4862 36th Street, Long Island City NY 11101. 718/729-1050. **Contact:** Human Resources. **World Wide Web address:** http://www.polyvision.com. **Description:** Manufactures and markets indoor menu board display systems for the fast-food and convenience store industries and changeable magnetic display signage used primarily by banks to display interest rates and other information. These displays are custom manufactured for ceiling hanging or for window or counter displays. **Corporate headquarters location:** New York NY. **Parent company:** Alpine Group, Incorpoated is active in the defense and commercial electronics and telecommunications wire and cable industries through subsidiaries, Alpine Polyvision, Incorporated and DNE Technologies, Incorporated, both of which operate out of CT, and Superior TeleTec Incorporated in Atlanta GA. **Listed on:** New York Stock Exchange. **Stock exchange symbol:** AGI. **President:** Robert Sudack. **Number of employees at this location:** 55.

PUBLISHERS CLEARING HOUSE
382 Channel Drive, Port Washington NY 11050. 516/883-5432. **Contact:** Human Resources. **World Wide Web address:** http://www.pch.com. **Description:** A direct mail marketing company. Publishers Clearing House is one of the largest sources of new magazine subscribers. The company also conducts continuing research to develop effective promotions for other products and services. **Corporate headquarters location:** This location. **Subsidiaries include:** Campus Subscriptions. **CEO:** Robin B. Smith. **Sales/revenue:** Approximately $400 million. **Number of employees nationwide:** 465.

RUDER-FINN, INC.

301 East 57th Street, New York NY 10022. 212/593-6400. **Fax:** 212/593-6397. **Contact:** Human Resources. **E-mail address:** careers@ruderfinn.com. **World Wide Web address:** http://www.ruderfinn.com. **Description:** Offers a wide range of services in the public relations field. **Special programs:** Executive Training Program. **Corporate headquarters location:** This location. **Other U.S. locations:** Los Angeles CA; San Francisco CA; Chicago IL; Washington DC. **International locations:** China; France; Israel; Singapore; United Kingdom.

SAATCHI & SAATCHI ADVERTISING

375 Hudson Street, New York NY 10014. 212/463-2304. **Contact:** Human Resources. **World Wide Web address:** http://www.saatchi-saatchi.com. **Description:** An advertising agency. **Company slogan:** Nothing is impossible. **Office hours:** Monday - Friday, 9:00 a.m. - 5:00 p.m. **Corporate headquarters location:** This location. **Other U.S. locations:** Nationwide. **International locations:** Worldwide. **Number of employees at this location:** 500.

SAATCHI & SAATCHI ROWLAND

255 Woodcliff Drive, Suite 200, Fairport NY 14450-4219. 585/249-6100. **Contact:** Human Resources. **E-mail address:** ksavoca@saatchibiz.com. **World Wide Web address:** http://www.saatchibiz.com. **Description:** A full-service, integrated advertising agency. **Corporate headquarters location:** New York NY. **Other area locations:** Rochester NY. **Other U.S. locations:** Wilmington DE. **International locations:** Switzerland; United Kingdom; China; France; Australia. **Parent company:** Saatchi & Saatchi plc. **President:** Christine Withers.

SUDLER & HENNESSEY INC.

230 Park Avenue South, New York NY 10003-1566. 212/614-4100. **Contact:** Roger Gilmore, Human Resources. **E-mail address:** roger_Gilmore@nyc.sudler.com. **World Wide Web address:** http://www.sudler.com. **Description:** An advertising agency. **NOTE:** Available positions can also be viewed at http://www.hotjobs.com. **Corporate headquarters location:** This location.

TBWA/CHIAT/DAY

488 Madison Avenue, 7th Floor, New York NY 10022. 212/804-1000. **Fax:** 212/804-1200. **Contact:** Human Resources. **E-mail address:** resumes@tbwachiat.com. **World Wide Web address:** http://www.tbwachiat.com. **Description:** An advertising agency.

VIACOM OUTDOOR

405 Lexington Avenue, 14th Floor, New York NY 10174. 212/297-6400. **Contact:** Human Resources. **World Wide Web address:** http://www.viacomoutdoor.com. **Description:** An advertising agency specializing in the design of billboards and posters. **Special programs:** Internships. **Other U.S. locations:** Nationwide. **Operations at this facility include:** Administration; Divisional Headquarters; Financial Offices; Marketing; Research and Development; Sales; Service.

J. WALTER THOMPSON COMPANY

466 Lexington Avenue, New York NY 10017. 212/210-7000. **Contact:** Human Resources. **E-mail address:** nygetajob@jwt.com. **World Wide Web address:** http://www.jwt.com. **Description:** A full-service advertising agency. **Positions advertised include:** Administrative Assistant; Financial Analyst. **Corporate headquarters location:** This location. **Other U.S. locations:** Nationwide. **International locations:** Worldwide. **Parent company:** WPP Group. **Listed on:** NASDAQ. **Stock exchange symbol:** WPPGY.

JANE WESMAN PUBLIC RELATIONS, INC.
322 Eighth Avenue, Suite 1702, New York NY 10001. 212/620-4080. **Fax:** 212/620-0370. **Contact:** Human Resources. **E-mail address:** jane@wesmanpr.com. **World Wide Web address:** http://www.wesmanpr.com. **Description:** Provides book publicity services including press kits, author tours, radio and print publicity, and media training. **Corporate headquarters location:** This location.

YOUNG & RUBICAM, INC.
285 Madison Avenue, 9th Floor, New York NY 10017. 212/210-3000. **Fax:** 212/210-5007. **Contact:** Human Resources. **World Wide Web address:** http://www.yandr.com. **Description:** An international advertising agency. The company operates through three divisions: Young & Rubicam International; Marsteller Inc., a worldwide leader in business-to-business and consumer advertising; and Young & Rubicam USA, with 14 consumer advertising agencies operating through four regional groups, and five specialized advertising and marketing agencies. **Special programs:** Internships. **Corporate headquarters location:** This location. **Other U.S. locations:** Nationwide.

AEROSPACE

You can expect to find the following types of companies in this section:
Aerospace Products and Services • Aircraft Equipment and Parts

---

AEROFLEX INCORPORATED
35 South Service Road, Plainview NY 11807. 516/694-6700. **Fax:** 516/694-4823. **Contact:** Bridget DiFalco, Human Resources Director. **World Wide Web address:** http://www.aeroflex.com. **Description:** Manufactures custom-designed hybrid microcircuits for use in applications including electrical systems used in aircraft maintenance, flight and navigational systems, sonar systems, satellite experimentation systems, missile firing systems, power supply systems, computer testing systems, television camera and radio receiver systems, and other applications using miniaturized components. Founded in 1937. **Positions advertised include:** Avionics Technical and Business Development Manager; PXI Marketing Engineer; Technical Writer; Customer Liaison Officer; Production Planner; Principle Product Engineer. **Corporate headquarters location:** This location. **Subsidiaries include:** IFR Systems, Inc. **Listed on:** NASDAQ. **Stock exchange symbol:** ARXX. **Chairman/CEO:** Harvey R. Blau. **Annual sales/revenues:** $202 million. **Number of employees:** 2,030.

ALGONQUIN PARTS INC.
667 Connecticut Avenue, Norwalk CT 06854. 203/838-6548. **Contact:** Human Resources. **World Wide Web address:** http://www.algonquinparts.com. **Description:** Manufactures aircraft parts including frames, wing ribs, bulkheads, hinges, doors, flap tracks, and other related components. Founded in 1938

BREEZE-EASTERN
700 Liberty Avenue, Union NJ 07083. 908/686-4000. **Fax:** 908/686-4279. **Contact:** Ed Chestnut, Director of Human Resources. **E-mail address:** echestnut@breeze-eastern.com. **World Wide Web address:** http://www.breeze-eastern.com. **Description:** Designs, develops, manufactures, and services sophisticated lifting and restraining products, principally helicopter rescue hoist and cargo hook systems; winches and hoists for aircraft and weapon systems; and aircraft cargo tie-down systems. **Positions advertised include:** Product Support Vice President; Assistant Supervisor Overhaul & Repair; Mechanical Design Engineer. **Corporate headquarters location:** This location. **Parent company:** TransTechnology designs, manufactures, sells, and distributes specialty fasteners through several other subsidiaries including: Breeze Industrial Products (Saltsburg PA) manufactures a complete line of standard and specialty gear-driven band fasteners in high-grade stainless steel for use in highly-engineered applications; The Palnut Company (Mountainside NJ) manufactures light- and heavy-duty single and multithread specialty fasteners; Industrial Retaining Ring (Irvington NJ) manufactures a variety of retaining rings made of carbon steel, stainless steel, and beryllium copper; The Seeger Group (Somerville NJ) manufactures retaining clips, circlips, spring pins, and similar components.

CPI AEROSTRUCTURES, INC.
200-A Executive Drive, Edgewood NY 11717. 631/586-5200. **Fax:** 631/586-5814. **Contact:** Personnel Manager. **World Wide Web address:** http://www.cpiaero.com. **Description:** Engaged in contract production of structural aircraft parts and subassemblies for the commercial and military sectors of the aircraft industry. The company also provides engineering, technical, and program management services. **Corporate headquarters**

location: This location. **Listed on:** American Stock Exchange. **Stock exchange symbol:** CVU. **Chairman:** Arthur August. **Annual sales/revenues:** $24 million. **Number of employees:** 50.

DASSAULT FALCON JET CORPORATION

Teterboro Airport, P.O. Box 2000, South Hackensack NJ 07606. 201/262-0800. **Physical address:** Teterboro Airport, 200 Riser Road, Little Ferry NJ 07643. **Contact:** Human Resources. **E-mail address:** resumes@falconjet.com. **World Wide Web address:** http://www.falconjet.com. **Description:** Manufactures and sells a line of two- and three-engine business aircraft. Dassault Falcon Jet also operates international jet aircraft service and maintenance centers (Falcon Jet Service Centers), engaged in the service, repair, and maintenance of a wide range of jet aircraft engines, airframes, avionics, instruments, and accessories. **Positions advertised include:** Warranty Analyst Associate; Avionics Help Desk Associate; Avionics Specifications Coordinator; Service Parts Accounts Director; Field Service Representative; System Administrator; Public Relations Manager; Receptionist; Repair Agent; Technical Help Desk Clerk. **Parent company:** Dassault Aviation.

ELLANEF MANUFACTURING CORPORATION

9711 50th Avenue, Corona NY 11368. 718/699-4000. **Fax:** 718/592-0722. **Contact:** Human Resources. **E-mail address:** henry.david@ellanef.com. **World Wide Web address:** http://www.ellanef.com. **Description:** Manufactures a wide range of aircraft components for major aerospace OEMs and airlines operating nationwide. **Parent company:** Magellan Aerospace Corporation (Mississauga, Ontario, Canada). **Operations at this facility include:** Manufacturing. **Number of employees at this location:** 500.

GOODRICH CORPORATION
MOTION CONTROLS DIVISION

197 Ridgedale Avenue, Cedar Knolls NJ 07927. 973/267-4500. **Contact:** Human Resources. **World Wide Web address:** http://www.goodrich.com. **Description:** Manufactures aircraft systems and components and provides services for the aerospace industry worldwide. **Positions advertised include:** Electrical Engineer. **NOTE:** For employment information contact: Human Resources, Goodrich Corporation, 100 Panton Road, Vergennes VT 05491. 802/877-2911. **Parent company:** Goodrich Company. **Listed on:** New York Stock Exchange. **Stock exchange symbol:** GR.

HONEYWELL
DEFENSE AND AVIONICS SYSTEMS

699 Route 46 East, Teterboro NJ 07608. 201/288-2000. **Contact:** Human Resources. **World Wide Web address:** http://www.honeywell.com. **Description:** Honeywell is engaged in the research, development, manufacture, and sale of advanced technology products and services in the fields of chemicals, electronics, automation, and controls. The company's major businesses are home and building automation and control, performance polymers and chemicals, industrial automation and control, space and aviation systems, and defense and marine systems. **Operations at this facility include:** This location develops and manufactures advanced aerospace products under government contract including instrumentation for air and guidance systems. **Listed on:** New York Stock Exchange. **Stock exchange symbol:** HON.

K&F INDUSTRIES INC.

600 Third Avenue, 27th Floor, New York NY 10016. 212/297-0900. **Fax:** 212/867-1182. **Contact:** Lisa Jones, VP for Human Resources. **Description:** A holding company for two divisions that manufacture aircraft braking systems. **Subsidiaries include:** Aircraft Braking Systems Corporation; Engineered

Fabrics. **Chairman/CEO:** Bernard L. Schwartz. **Annual sales/revenues:** $355 million. **Number of employees:** 1,404

LYNTON AVIATION
3 Airport Road, Morristown Municipal Airport, Morristown NJ 07960-4624. 973/292-9000. **Fax:** 973/539-6657. **Contact:** Sue Lemen, Human Resources Director. **Description:** Performs aviation services including the management, charter, maintenance, and refueling of corporate helicopters and fixed-wing aircraft, and helicopter support services for industrial and utility applications. Lynton Group also provides aircraft sales and brokerage services worldwide. **Corporate headquarters location:** This location.

NORTHROP GRUMMAN CORPORATION
1 Grumman Road West, Bethpage NY 11714. 516/575-0574. **Contact:** Human Resources. **World Wide Web address:** http://www.northgrum.com. **Description:** Manufactures military aircraft, commercial aircraft parts, and electronic systems. Northrop Grumman manufactures the B-2 Spirit Stealth Bomber, as well as parts for the F/A-18 and the 747, and radar equipment. Other operations include computer systems development for management and scientific applications. **NOTE:** Online applications are available. **Positions advertised include:** Structural Analysis Engineer; Avionics Systems Design and Integration Engineer; Aero Design and Analysis Engineer; Engineering Liaison; Pilot; Software Engineer; Program Manager; Purchasing Price Analyst; Strategic Planner; Administrative Assistant; Business Analyst Manager; Subcontract Administrator; Web Applications Technical Leader. **Corporate headquarters location:** Los Angeles CA. **Listed on:** New York Stock Exchange. **Stock exchange symbol:** NOC. **President/CEO/Director:** Ronald D. Sugar. **Sales/revenue:** $17 billion. **Number of employees worldwide:** Over 117,000.

R-V METAL FABRICATING INC.
20 Sand Park Road, Cedar Grove NJ 07009. 973/239-8100. **Fax:** 973/239-2323. **Contact:** Linda Calderio, Customer Service or Human Resources. **E-mail address:** lcalderio@rvmetal.com. **World Wide Web address:** http://www.rvmetal.com. **Description:** Supplies fabricated sheet metal detail parts and assemblies for primarily the aerospace industry.

SMITHS AEROSPACE
110 Algonquin Parkway, Whippany NJ 07981. 973/428-9898. **Fax:** 973//884-2277. **Contact:** Human Resources. **E-mail address:** aerospace@jobpositive.com. **World Wide Web address:** http://www.smiths-aerospace.com. **Description:** Engineers and manufactures electro-mechanical actuation control systems for the aerospace and commercial industries. **Positions advertised include:** Lead Project Engineer. **Parent company:** Smiths Group. **Operations at this facility include:** Divisional Headquarters; Manufacturing; Research and Development; Sales. **Number of employees at this location:** 250.

STELLEX MONITOR AEROSPACE CORPORATION
1000 New Horizons Boulevard, Amityville NY 11701-1181. 631/957-2300. **Contact:** Richard Dallari, Human Resources. **E-mail address:** dallari@monair.com. **World Wide Web address:** http://www.monair.com. **Description:** Manufactures precision structural aerospace parts and assemblies for commercial and military aircraft. **Parent company:** Stellex Aerostructures, Inc.

APPAREL, FASHION, AND TEXTILES

You can expect to find the following types of companies in this section:
Broadwoven Fabric Mills • Knitting Mills • Yarn and Thread Mills • Curtains and Draperies • Footwear • Nonwoven Fabrics • Textile Goods and Finishing

ABERDEEN SPORTSWEAR, INC.
350 Fifth Avenue, Suite 2828, New York NY 10118. 212/244-5100. **Fax:** 212/629-4298. **Contact:** Joel Stolz, Controller. **Description:** Manufactures a line of sport jackets. **Corporate headquarters location:** This location. **Other locations:** Trenton NJ. **President/CEO:** Harold I. Berk.

AMERICAN TROUSER, INC.
350 Fifth Avenue, Suite 3200, New York NY 10118. 212/244-0900. **Fax:** 2121/695-3796. **Contact:** Human Resources. **World Wide Web address:** http://www.american-trouser.com. **Description:** American Trouser manufactures men's pants. **Corporate headquarters location:** Columbus MS. **Operations at this facility include:** Sales; Administration.

ARIS INDUSTRIES, INC.
463 Seventh Avenue, New York NY 10018. 646/473-4200. **Fax:** 646/473-4242. **Contact:** Human Resources. **Description:** Engaged in the licensing and sale of men's and young men's sportswear and outerwear, as well as ladies' sportswear. **Annual sales/revenues:** $19.4 million. **Number of employees:** 71.

BEACON LOOMS, INC.
411 Alfred Avenue, Teaneck NJ 07666. 201/833-1600. **Contact:** Human Resources Department. **E-mail address:** contact@beaconlooms.com. **World Wide Web address:** http://www.beaconlooms.com. **Description:** Produces a wide range of textiles, primarily for sale to retailers. **Corporate headquarters location:** This location. **Other U.S. locations:** Englewood NJ.

BEST MANUFACTURING, INC.
1633 Broadway, 18th Floor, New York NY 10019-6708. 212/974-1100. **Fax:** 212/262-9840. **Contact:** Human Resources. **World Wide Web address:** http://www.bestmfg.com. **Description:** A manufacturer of textiles and washable service apparel. Founded in 1914. **Positions advertised include:** Customer Service Representative. **Corporate headquarters location:** This location. **Other U.S. locations:** Nationwide. **Operations at this facility include:** Administration. **Number of employees at this location:** 85. **Number of employees nationwide:** 1,100.

CHF INDUSTRIES, INC.
One Park Avenue, 9th Floor, New York NY 10016. 212/951-7800. **Contact:** Human Resources. **World Wide Web address:** http://www.chfindustries.com. **Description:** Engaged in the production, export, and import of home fashion products including comforters, curtains, towels, and other textile goods. **Corporate headquarters location:** This location. **Other locations:** Charlotte NC; Chicago IL; Dallas TX; Fall River MA; Kaufman TX; Loris SC; Clinton SC. **Number of employees:** 1,200.

CELANESE ACETATE TEXTILES
3 Park Avenue, 37th Floor, New York NY 10016. 212/251-8000. **Fax:** 212/251-8037. **Contact:** Ellen Sweeney. **E-mail address:** ellen.sweeney@celaneseacetate.com. **World Wide Web address:**

http://www.celanese.com. **Description:** Manufactures acetate products including acetate yarn and Micro Safe fiber. Primary customers include the apparel, furnishings, and industrial markets. **NOTE:** Jobseekers are requested to use the company's Online Application Tool. For questions regarding the Champs trainee program contact: Nadia Soliz, Celanese Chemicals, 1601 West LBJ Freeway, Dallas TX 75234-6034; by phone: 361/242-4312; by e-mail: nsoliz@celanese.com. **Special programs:** Internships; Champs Training Program. **Parent company:** Celanese AG (Kronberg im Taunus, Germany) is an industrial chemical company.

BERNARD CHAUS, INC.
dba JOSEPHINE CHAUS, INC.
530 Seventh Avenue, 18th Floor, New York NY 10018. 212/354-1280. **Fax:** 201/863-6307. **Contact:** Human Resources Director. **World Wide Web address:** http://www.bernardchaus.com. **Description:** Designs, manufactures, and markets women's apparel. Career casual sportswear is marketed under the Chaus, Chaus Woman, and Chaus Petite labels and blouses are marketed under the Josephine label. Weekend casual sportswear bears the Chaus Sport and Chaus Jeanswear labels. Dresses are marketed under the Chaus Dresses, Chaus Woman Dresses, and Chaus Petite Dresses labels. Founded in 1976. **Listed on:** Over The Counter. **Stock exchange symbol:** CHBD. **Chairwoman/CEO:** Josephine Chaus. **Annual sales/revenues:** $145.5 million. **Number of employees:** 242.

CONCORD FABRICS INC.
462 Seventh Avenue, New York NY 10018. 212/760-0300. **Fax:** 212/563-3746. **Contact:** Human Resources Manager. **World Wide Web address:** http://www.concordfabrics.com. **Description:** Designs, develops, and manufactures woven and knitted fabrics for sale to manufacturers and retailers. Concord Fabrics is one of the nation's largest independent textile converters. **Positions advertised include:** Designer. **Special programs:** Internships. **Corporate headquarters location:** This location. **Subsidiaries include:** Andover Fabrics; Mackower UK. **Chairman:** Alvin Weinstein. **Annual sales/revenues:** $50 million. **Number of employees:** 100.

NEIL COOPER LLC
436 Ferry Street, Newark NJ 07105. 973/274-0066. **Contact:** Controller. **Description:** Imports and manufactures men's and boys' leather and cloth coats and jackets in the moderate-to-high price range. The company sells coats to department stores and private label distributors, and distributes products worldwide.

CROSCILL, INC.
dba CROSCILL HOME FASHIONS
261 Fifth Avenue, 25th Floor, New York NY 10016. 212/689-7222. **Fax:** 252/431-0470. **Contact:** Human Resources. **E-mail address:** jobapps@croscill.com. **World Wide Web address:** http://www.croscill.com. **Description:** Manufactures curtains, draperies, and other textile products at five manufacturing plants in North Carolina. Founded in 1945. **NOTE:** Resumes should be sent to: P.O. Box 930, Durham NC 27702. **subsidiaries include:** Royal Home Fashions. **Annual sales/revenues:** $309 million. **Number of employees:** 1,500.

CYGNE DESIGNS INC.
1410 Broadway, Suite 1002, New York NY 10018. 212/997-7767. **Fax:** 212/245-7724. **Contact:** Office Manager. **Description:** Cygne Designs is a private-label designer, merchandiser, and manufacturer of women's apparel, serving retailers including Ann Taylor, The Limited Stores, Express, Lane Bryant, Victoria's Secret Stores, Lerner, and Casual Corner. The company's products include a broad range of woven and knit career, casual, and intimate women's apparel. **Listed**

on: Over The Counter. **Stock exchange symbol:** CYDS. **Chairman/CEO:** Bernard M. Manuel. **Annual sales/revenues:** $41 million. **Number of employees:** 1,441.

DAN RIVER INC.
1325 Avenue of the Americas, New York NY 10019. 212/554-5555. **Contact:** Human Resources. **World Wide Web address:** http://www.danriver.com. **Description:** Manufactures and markets textile products for the home fashions and apparel fabrics markets including a coordinated line of home fashions consisting of packaged bedroom furnishings such as comforters, sheets, pillowcases, shams, bedskirts, decorative pillows, and draperies. The company also manufactures a broad range of woven and knit cotton and cotton-blend apparel fabrics, and is a domestic supplier of men's dress shirt fabrics, primarily oxford and pinpoint oxford cloth. **NOTE:** Resumes should be sent to the company's headquarters: LuAnn Long, Manager of Recruiting, Dan River Inc., P.O. Box 261, Danville VA 24543; phone: 434/799-7044; email: luanne.long@danriver.com. **Positions advertised include:** Administrative Manager; Clerical Supervisor; Customer Service Representative; Merchandiser; Product Manager; Sales Manager. **Corporate headquarters location:** Danville VA. **Other U.S. locations:** Nationwide. **Subsidiaries include:** Dan River Factory Stores, Inc. operates 12 factory outlet stores in the Midwest and the Southeast. **Operations at this facility include:** Sales and Marketing headquarters. **Listed on:** New York Stock Exchange. **Stock exchange symbol:** DRF. **Annual sales/revenues:** $613 million. **Number of employees at this location:** 90. **Number of employees nationwide:** 7,000.

DANSKIN, INC.
530 Seventh Avenue, Floor M1, New York NY 10018. 212/764-4630. **Fax:** 212/764-7265. **Contact:** Human Resources. **E-mail address:** hr_new_york@danskin.com. **World Wide Web address:** http://www.danskin.com. **Description:** Danskin designs, manufactures, and markets several brands of women's activewear, dancewear, tights, and sheer hosiery. Brand names include Danskin, Dance France, Round-the-Clock, Givenchy, and Anne Klein. The company operates two manufacturing facilites and retail operations nationwide. **Positions advertised include:** Account Executive. **Corporate headquarters location:** This location. **Other U.S. locations:** Grenada MS; York PA. **Subsidiaries include:** Pennaco (Grenada MS). **Listed on:** Over The Counter. **Stock exchange symbol:** DANS. **Chairman:** Donald Schupak. **Annual sales/revenues:** $82 million. **Number of employees:** 1,000.

DARLINGTON FABRICS CORPORATION
1359 Broadway, Suite 1404, New York NY 10018. 212/279-7733. **Contact:** Human Resources. **World Wide Web address:** http://www.darlingfabrics.com. **Description:** Darlington Fabrics Corporation is a wide-warp knit elastic knitting company. **NOTE:** Resumes should be sent to: Human Resources, 36 Beach Street, Westerly RI 02891. 401/596-2816. **Parent company:** Moore Corporation Limited (Mississuga, Ontario, Canada). **Operations at this facility include:** Sales office.

DONNKENNY, INC.
1411 Broadway, 10th Floor, New York NY 10018. 212/790-3900. **Contact:** Human Resources. **Description:** A sportswear manufacturer. Three distinct and expanding divisions make up Donnkenny: Donnkenny Classics, Mickey & Co., and Lewis Frimel/Flirts. **Corporate headquarters location:** This location. **Subsidiaries include:** Donnkenny Apparel, Inc. **Listed on:** Over The Counter. **Stock exchange symbol:** DKNY. **Annual sales/revenues:** $107 million. **Number of employees:** 203.

FAB INDUSTRIES, INC.
200 Madison Avenue, 7th Floor, New York NY 10016. 212/592-2700. **Fax:** 212/689-6929. **Contact:** Ms. Marsha Cohen, Office Manager. **E-mail address:** fabindus@mindspring.com. **World Wide Web address:** http://www.fab-industries.com. **Description:** Fab Industries is a manufacturer of knitted textile fabrics, laces, and related finished home products, as well as polyurethane coated fabrics. The company markets its products to the apparel, home furnishings, industrial, retail, and other specialty markets. Fab operates eight manufacturing plants at five locations in North Carolina and New York with sales offices in New York and Los Angeles. **Corporate headquarters location:** This location. **Other locations:** NC; CA. **Subsidiaries include:** Gem Urethane. **Listed on:** American Stock Exchange. **Stock exchange symbol:** FIT. **Number of employees nationwide:** 1,800. **Chariman/CEO:** Samson Bitensky. **Annual sales/revenues:** $63 million. **Number of employees:** 620.

VICTOR FORSTMANN, INC.
dba THE FORSTMANN COMPANY
498 Seventh Avenue, 15th Floor, New York NY 10018-6791. 212/642-6900. **Fax:** 212/642-6870. **Contact:** Administrative Assistant. **World Wide Web address:** http://www.forstmann.com. **Description:** Designs, manufactures, and markets woolen, worsted, and other fabrics primarily used in the production of brand-name and private label apparel for men and women, as well as specialty fabrics for use in billiard and gaming tables, sports caps, and career uniforms from two manufacturing plants in Dublin, Georgia. Since 1563. **Corporate headquarters location:** Dublin GA. **Operations at this facility include:** Sales, Credit & Marketing Office. **Number of employees:** 800.

G-III APPAREL GROUP, LTD.
512 Seventh Avenue, New York NY 10018-4202. 212/403-0500. **Fax:** 212/403-0551. **Contact:** Human Resources. **World Wide Web address:** http://www.g-iii.com. **Description:** G-III Apparel Group, Ltd. designs, manufactures, imports, and markets an extensive range of apparel including coats, jackets, pants, skirts, and other sportswear items under its G-III, Siena, Siena Studio, Colebrook and Co., Kenneth Cole, and Nine West labels, and under private retail and licensed labels. The company also manufactures and markets a full line of women's leather apparel in junior, miss, and half sizes; and an outerwear line of men's leather apparel at a wide range of retail sales prices. The company's products also include textile outerwear, woolen coats, and sportswear. **Corporate headquarters location:** This location. **Subsidiaries include:** Cole Haan; G-III; Jones New York; Kenneth Cole; Nine West. **Listed on:** NASDAQ. **Stock exchange symbol:** GIII. **Annual sales/revenues:** $203 million. **Number of employees:** 344.

GALEY & LORD, INC.
980 Avenue of the Americas, 4th Floor, New York NY 10018-5401. 212/465-3000. **Fax:** 212/465-3024. **Contact:** William Odalen, Human Resources. **World Wide Web address:** http://www.gnlpromo.com. **Description:** Galey & Lord is a leading manufacturer and marketer of apparel fabric sold to clothing manufacturers. The company is a major producer of wrinkle-free cotton fabrics for uniforms and for sportswear manufacturers and printed fabrics for the home. Galey & Lord also manufactures denim. **NOTE:** Direct calls in Spanish to 212/465-3088. **Corporate headquarters location:** This location. **Other U.S. locations:** Greensboro NC. **Subsidiaries include:** G&L Service Company provides marketing services for Galey & Lord. Galey & Lord Home Fashion Fabrics manufactures and distributes fabrics used in home decorating and furnishing. Klopman International is a supplier of fabrics used in career wear. Swift Denim manufactures and distributes a wide variety of denim products. **Listed on:** Over The Counter. **Stock exchange symbol:** GYLDQ.

Chairman/President/CEO: Arthur C. Wiener. **Annual sales/revenues:** $667 million. **Number of employees:** 5,390.

GARAN, INCORPORATED
350 Fifth Avenue, 19th Floor, New York NY 10118. 212/563-2000. **Fax:** 212/971-2250. **Contact:** Jodi Schad, Personnel Manager. **Description:** Garan designs, manufactures, and sells apparel for children, women, and men. Products include shirts, sweatshirts, sweaters, trousers, skirts, shorts, and overalls. Trade names, trademarks, and licensed names include Garanimals, Garan by Marita, Bobbie Brooks, Garan Mountain Lion, Long Gone, Team Rated, National Football League, National Basketball Association, National Hockey League, Major League Baseball, and Disney. Founded in 1941. **Corporate headquarters location:** This location. **Subsidiaries include:** Geranimals. **Parent company:** Berkshire Hathaway (Omaha NE). **Chairman/CEO:** Seymour Lichtenstein. **Annual sales/revenues:** $257 million. **Number of employees:** 5,100.

S. GOLDBERG & COMPANY, INC.
20 East Broadway, Hackensack NJ 07601. 201/342-1200. **Contact:** Personnel Manager. **Description:** Manufactures house slippers. **Corporate headquarters location:** This location. **Operations at this facility include:** Manufacturing.

JLM COUTURE, INC.
525 Seventh Avenue, Suite 1703, New York NY 10018. 212/921-7058. **Fax:** 212/921-7608. **Contact:** Human Resources. **World Wide Web address:** http://www.jlmcouture.com. **Description:** Designs, manufactures, and markets bridal gowns, bridesmaid gowns, veils, and related accessories for department stores, bridal boutiques, and sells through several Websites. **Listed on:** NASDAQ. **Stock exchange symbol:** JLMC. **Chairman:** Daniel M. Sullivan. **Annual sales/revenues:** $25 million. **Number of employees:** 70.

JACLYN, INC.
5801 Jefferson Street, West New York NJ 07093. 201/868-9400. **Contact:** Eric Gailing. **E-mail address:** eric.gailing@jaclyninc.com. **World Wide Web address:** http://www.jaclyninc.com. **Description:** Designs, manufactures, and sells women's and children's handbag fashions, accessories, specialty items, and ready-to-wear apparel. **Corporate headquarters location:** This location. **Operations at this facility include:** Administration; Manufacturing; Research and Development; Sales; Service.

JORDACHE ENTERPRISES
1400 Broadway, Fifth Floor, New York NY 10018. 212/944-1330. **Fax:** 212/239-0063. **Contact:** Becky Diaz, Human Resources Manager. **World Wide Web address:** http://www.jordache.com. **Description:** Manufactures and distributes designer jeans, fashion apparel products, and accessories for the youth market. Licensed products include luggage, eyeglasses, shoes, and purses and the company manufactures Gasoline and FUBU jeans. **Listed on:** Privately held. **Chairman/CEO:** Joseph (Joe) Nakash.

KENNETH COLE PRODUCTIONS
603 West 50th Street, New York NY 10019. 212/265-1500. **Fax:** 212/830-7422. **Contact:** Human Resources. **E-mail address:** nyjobs@kennethcole.com. **World Wide Web address:** http://www.kencole.com. **Description:** Manufactures men's and women's shoes, bags, scarves, watches, belts, and other accessories. **Positions advertised include:** Retail Store Manager; General Manager. **Corporate headquarters location:** This location. **Listed on:** New York Stock Exchange. **Stock exchange symbol:** KCP. **Chairman/CEO:** Kenneth D. Cole. **Annual sales/revenues:** $433 million. **Number of employees:** 1,800.

THE LESLIE FAY COMPANIES, INC.
1412 Broadway, 3rd Floor, New York NY 10018. 212/221-4000. **Fax:** 212/221-4245. **Contact:** Human Resources. **Description:** Engaged in the design, manufacture, and sale of a diversified line of women's dresses, sportswear, blouses, and intimate apparel and sells under several brands including Leslie Fay, Joan Leslie, David Warren, and Trio New York to specialty and department stores. **Corporate headquarters location:** This location. **Parent company:** Three Cities Research. **Chairman:** John J. Pomerantz. **Annual sales/revenues:** $170 million.

LIZ CLAIBORNE, INC.
1441 Broadway, New York NY 10018. 212/354-4900. **Fax:** 212/626-3416. **Contact:** Human Resources. **E-mail address:** staffing@liz.com. **World Wide Web address:** http://www.lizclaiborne.com. **Description:** Liz Claiborne is comprised of 18 apparel and accessories divisions and several licenses. Products are sold under the company brand names and private labels. **Positions advertised include:** Knit Specialist Technician; Woven Designer; Associate Handbag Designer; Menswear Designer; Sigrid Olsen Handbag Designer; Senior Colorist; Junior Color Coordinator; Monet Jewelry Designer; Lucky Accessories Designer; Menswear Dress Shirt Designer; Senior Fabric Research & Development Associate; Latin America Account Executive; Senior Japan Account Executive; Sales Manager; Product Development Engineer; Merchandiser; Planner; Retail Analyst; Production Costing Specialist; Fabric Purchaser; Corporate Communications Manager; LizEdge Program Assistant. **Special programs:** Internships. **Corporate headquarters location:** This location. **Subsidiaries include:** Ellen Tracy, Inc. **Listed on:** New York Stock Exchange. **Stock exchange symbol:** LIZ. **Chairman/CEO:** Paul R. Charron. **Annual sales/revenues:** $3.7 billion. **Number of employees worldwide:** 12,000.

J.B. MARTIN COMPANY
10 East 53rd Street, Suite 3100, New York NY 10022. 212/421-2020. **Contact:** David Budd, Director of Sales. **World Wide Web address:** http://www.jbmartin.com. **Description:** Manufactures high-end velvet specializing in woven velvets for the apparel and home furnishings industries and high-spec industrial applications. Founded in 1893. **Corporate headquarters location:** This location. **Other locations:** SC. **International locations:** Mexico.

MILLIKEN & COMPANY
1045 Sixth Avenue, New York NY 10018. 212/819-4200. **Contact:** Human Resources. **World Wide Web address:** http://www.milliken.com. **Description:** Milliken & Company is one of the world's largest privately held textile and chemical companies. Milliken ranked #16 in FORTUNE's 2004 "100 Best Companies to Work For." **Corporate headquarters location:** Spartanburg SC. **Number of employees worldwide:** 10,000.

MOVIE STAR, INC.
1115 Broadway, New York NY 10010. 212/684-3400. **Contact:** Human Resources Department. **World Wide Web address:** http://www.moviestarinc.com. **Description:** A diversified apparel manufacturer. The company operates through three divisions. The largest division, Sanmark, designs, manufactures, and sells private label sleepwear, robes, loungewear, leisurewear, daywear, and undergarments to mass merchants, as well as to national and regional chains. Cinema Etoile is also an intimate apparel producer. The Irwin B. Schwabe division produces private label work and leisure shirts for chain stores and mail order catalogs as well as shirts that are sold under the Private Property brand name. The 25 Movie Star factory stores carry an assortment of merchandise, some of which is supplied by the three manufacturing divisions, as well as sportswear and accessories. **Corporate**

headquarters location: This location. **Other U.S. locations:** GA; MI. **Listed on:** American Stock Exchange. **Stock exchange symbol:** MSI.

NATIONAL SPINNING COMPANY INC.
111 West 40th Street, 28th Floor, New York NY 10018. 212/382-6400. **Contact:** Human Resources Director. **World Wide Web address:** http://www.natspin.com. **Description:** Engaged in the manufacturing, marketing, and distribution of yarn products to knitwear manufacturers. The company also produces hand-knitting yarn and rug kits for distribution to retail chains throughout the United States. **Corporate headquarters location:** This location.

PAXAR
105 Corporate Park Drive, White Plains NY 10604. 914/697-6800. **Fax:** 914/697-6894. **Contact:** Personnel. **World Wide Web address:** http://www.paxar.com. **Description:** Manufactures various types of labels for retailers and apparel manufacturers. Alkahn offers a complete line of products including care labels, specialty weaves, and printed items. **Company slogan:** From Concept to Checkout. **Corporate headquarters location:** This location. **Other U.S. locations:** CA; IL; NC; GA. **International locations:** Hong Kong; Canada; Mexico; England.

PHILLIPS-VAN HEUSEN CORPORATION
1001 Frontier Road, Suite 100, Bridgewater NJ 08807-2955. 908/685-0050. **Contact:** Human Resources Department. **E-mail address:** hr@pvh.com. **World Wide Web address:** http://www.pvh.com. **Description:** Engaged in the manufacture, wholesale, and retail of men's and women's apparel. **NOTE:** Search for current up-to-date opportunities online. **Positions advertised include:** Administrative Assistant; Office Service Manager; Receptionist; Design Director; Product Development Director; Designer; Technical Designer; Graphic Artist; Design Assistant; CAD Operator; Merchandise Coordinator; Warehouse Manager; Picking Supervisor; Shipping Supervisor; Traffic Manager; Traffic Assistant; Assistant Controller; Financial Analyst. **Corporate headquarters location:** New York NY. **Other U.S. locations:** AL. **Listed on:** New York Stock Exchange. **Stock exchange symbol:** PVH. **Number of employees nationwide:** 14,000.

PHILLIPS-VAN HEUSEN CORPORATION
200 Madison Avenue, 10th Floor, New York NY 10016-3908. 212/381-3500. **Contact:** Manager of Human Resources. **E-mail address:** hr@pvh.com. **World Wide Web address:** http://www.pvh.com. **Description:** Manufactures, wholesales, and retails men's and women's apparel. **Corporate headquarters location:** This location. **Other U.S. locations:** Nationwide. **Listed on:** New York Stock Exchange. **Stock exchange symbol:** PVH. **Number of employees worldwide:** 9000.

PLAYTEX APPAREL, INC.
700 Fairfield Avenue, Stamford CT 06902. 203/356-8000. **Contact:** Dawn Cross, Vice President of Personnel. **World Wide Web address:** http://www.playtexnet.com. **Description:** Manufactures women's intimate apparel. **Parent company:** Sara Lee Corporation.

POLO RALPH LAUREN
650 Madison Avenue, New York NY 10022. 212/318-7000. **Fax:** 212/318-7200. **Contact:** Human Resources Department. **E-mail address:** jobs@poloralphlauren.com. **World Wide Web address:** http://www.polo.com. **Description:** Polo Ralph Lauren manufactures clothing and shoes for women and men. **Corporate headquarters location:** This location. **Operations at this facility include:** This location is an administrative office. **Listed on:** New York

Stock Exchange. **Stock exchange symbol:** RL. **CEO/Chairman:** Ralph Lauren. **Sales/revenue:** $1.7 billion. **Number of employees nationwide:** Over 10,000.

SALANT CORPORATION
1114 Avenue of the Americas, 36th Floor, New York NY 10036. 212/221-7500. **Contact:** Human Resources. **World Wide Web address:** http://www.prnewswire.com. **Description:** Designs, manufactures, imports, and markets a broad line of men's, children's, and women's apparel and accessories to retailers. Menswear is the company's largest sales category, with a focus on sportswear, dress shirts, neckwear, slacks, and jeans marketed under the Perry Ellis, J.J. Farmer, Thomson, John Henry, Gant, Manhattan, AXXA, Liberty of London, UNICEF, Peanuts, and Save the Children brand names. The company's children's brands include Joe Boxer, Dr. Denton, Power Rangers, certain Disney characters, and OshKosh B'Gosh. Women's wear includes sportswear marketed under the Made in the Shade brand name. The company's products are sold through department and specialty stores, major discounters, and mass volume retailers. Salant operates six domestic manufacturing facilities and five distribution centers. **Corporate headquarters location:** This location. **CEO/Chairman:** Michael Setola. **Listed on:** New York Stock Exchange. **Stock exchange symbol:** SLT. **Number of employees worldwide:** Over 4,000.

F. SCHUMACHER & COMPANY
79 Madison Avenue, New York NY 10016. 212/213-7900. **Contact:** Director of Employment. **World Wide Web address:** http://www.fschumacher.com. **Description:** A textile wholesaler specializing in rug and fabric trading. **Corporate headquarters location:** This location. **Other U.S. locations:** Nationwide. **President/CEO:** Gerald Puschel.

SETON COMPANY
849 Broadway, Newark NJ 07104. 973/485-4800. **Contact:** Human Resources. **E-mail address:** hr@setonco.com. **World Wide Web address:** http://www.setonleather.com. **Description:** Company operations are conducted primarily through two business segments. The Leather Division's operations include tanning, finishing, and distributing whole-hide cattle leathers for the automotive and furniture upholstery industries, cattle hide side leathers for footwear, handbag, and other markets, and cattle products for collagen, rawhide pet items, and other applications. The Chemicals and Coated Products Division is engaged in the manufacture and distribution of epoxy and urethane chemicals, specialty leather finishes, industrial and medical tapes, foams, films, and laminates. Other manufacturing facilities are located in Wilmington DE (epoxy, urethane chemicals, leather finishes); Toledo OH (cattle hide processing); Malvern PA (industrial coated products); and Saxton PA (cutting of finished leathers). **Corporate headquarters location:** This location. **Subsidiaries include:** Radel Leather Manufacturing Company; Seton Leather Company.

SPRINGS INDUSTRIES, INC.
104 West 40th Street, New York NY 10018. 212/556-6000. **Contact:** Human Resources. **E-mail address:** springsjobs@springs.com. **World Wide Web address:** http://www.springs.com. **Description:** Produces a wide range of finished apparel fabrics, consumer fashion fabrics, and retail and specialty fabrics. **Special programs:** Production Management Program. **Corporate headquarters location:** Fort Mills SC. **Other U.S. locations:** Nationwide. **International locations:** Canada; Mexico. **Operations at this facility include:** Divisional Headquarters; Regional Headquarters; Sales. **CEO/Chairman:** Crandall Bowles. **Number of employees worldwide:** 17,000.

TOTE ISOTONER INC.
420 Fifth Avenue, 3rd Floor, New York NY 10018. 212/944-1129. **Contact:** Human Resources. **World Wide Web address:** http://www.isotoner.com.

Description: Produces a wide range of gloves and related accessories including nationally distributed Isotoner products.

THE WARNACO GROUP, INC.
90 Park Avenue, New York NY 10016. 212/661-1300. **Contact:** Human Resources Department. **Description:** A manufacturer, designer, and marketer of women's intimate apparel, men's wear, and men's accessories under brand names including Calvin Klein, Fruit of the Loom, Warner's, Olga, and Chaps by Ralph Lauren. Warnaco markets its products through a chain of 48 retail outlets, as well as department stores and mass merchandisers in North America and Europe. **Corporate headquarters location:** This location.

WEST POINT STEVENS, INC.
1185 Avenue of the Americas, New York NY 10036. 212/930-2050. **Contact:** Human Resources. **World Wide Web address:** http://www.westpointstevens.com. **Description:** A major worldwide marketing and manufacturing organization. The company's core products are fabrics made from both natural and man-made fibers and yarns for a broad range of end uses including products for the home and apparel. **Corporate headquarters location:** This location. **Operations at this facility include:** Administration; Design; Marketing; Sales; Service. **Number of employees at this location:** 250. **Number of employees nationwide:** 19,000.

ARCHITECTURE, CONSTRUCTION, AND ENGINEERING

**You can expect to find the following types of companies
in this section:**
Architectural and Engineering Services • Civil and Mechanical Engineering Firms
• Construction Products, Manufacturers, and Wholesalers • General
Contractors/Specialized Trade Contractors

ABB INC.
P.O. Box 5308, Norwalk CT 06856-5308. 203/750-2200. **Physical address:** 501 Merritt Seven, Norwalk CT 06851. **Fax:** 203/750-2263. **Contact:** Human Resources. **World Wide Web address:** http://www.abb.com/us. **Description:** Provides engineering, construction, and sales support services as part of a worldwide engineering firm. Internationally, the company operates in five business segments: oil field equipment and services; power systems; engineering and construction; process equipment; and industrial products. **Corporate headquarters location:** This location. **Other U.S. locations:** Nationwide. **International locations:** Worldwide. **Subsidiaries include:** ABB Lumus Global Inc., Bloomfield NJ; ABB Simcon, Broomfield NJ. **Parent company:** ABB Asea Brown Boveri Ltd. (Baden, Switzerland.) **Number of employees worldwide:** 220,000.

ABB INC.
P.O. Box 6005, North Brunswick NJ 08902. **Physical Address:** 1460 Livingstone Avenue, North Brunswick NJ 08902-6005. 732/932-6000. **Contact:** Human Resources Manager. **World Wide Web address:** http://www.abb.com/us. **Description:** Provides engineering, construction, and sales support services as part of a worldwide engineering firm. Internationally, the company operates through the following business segments: oil field equipment and services; power systems; engineering and construction; process equipment; and industrial products. **Corporate headquarters location:** Norwalk CT. **Other U.S. locations:** New York NY. **Subsidiaries include:** ABB Lumus Global Inc. (Bloomfield NJ); ABB Simcom (Bloomfield NJ); ABB Susa (also at this location). **Parent company:** ABB AG (Baden, Switzerland). **Number of employees worldwide:** 220,000.

ABB LUMMUS GLOBAL INC.
1515 Broad Street, Bloomfield NJ 07003. 973/893-1515. **Fax:** 973/893-2000. **Contact:** Human Resources. **World Wide Web address:** http://www.abb.com/us. **Description:** An engineering firm serving power plants, chemical plants, and petrochemical and oil refineries, as well as other industries such as aviation and storage. **Parent company:** ABB Inc. (Norwalk CT) provides engineering, construction, and sales support services as part of the worldwide engineering firm. Another subsidiary, ABB Simcon (Bloomfield NJ), specializes in chemical engineering. Internationally, the company operates in five business segments: oil field equipment and services, power systems, engineering and construction, process equipment, and industrial products.

AMEC
1633 Broadway, 24th Floor, New York NY 10019. 212/484-0300. **Fax:** 212/484-0580. **Contact:** Human Resources. **World Wide Web address:** http://www.amec.com. **Description:** One of the largest construction management companies in the world offering a wide range of services including construction management, contracting program management, consulting, and design and construction. Founded in 1936. **Special programs:** Internships. **Corporate headquarters location:** London, United Kingdom. **Subsidiaries include:** AMEC

Construction Management, Inc.; Spie S.A. **Operations at this facility include:** Divisional Headquarters; Regional Headquarters. **Listed on:** London Stock Exchange. **Stock exchange symbol:** AMEC. **Annual sales/revenues:** $5 billion. **Number of employees at this location:** 140. **Number of employees nationwide:** 500. **Number of employees worldwide:** 45,000.

ACME ARCHITECTURAL PRODUCTS, INC.
dba ACME STEEL PARTITION COMPANY, INC.
513 Porter Avenue, Brooklyn NY 11222. 718/384-7800. **Contact:** Human Resources. **World Wide Web address:** http://www.acmesteel.com. **Description:** The company manufactures commercial interior products including hollow metal steel doors and frames, steel and glass partitions, toilet partitions, and office panels and furniture, as well as distributing builder's hardware and architectural wood doors.

AMERICAN STANDARD COMPANIES INC.
P.O. Box 6820, Piscataway NJ 08854. 732/980-6000. **Physical address:** One Centennial Avenue, Piscataway NJ 08855. **Contact:** Human Resources. **World Wide Web address:** http://www.americanstandard.com. **Description:** A global, diversified manufacturer. The company's operations are comprised of four segments: air conditioning products, plumbing products, automotive products, and medical systems. The air conditioning products segment (through subsidiary The Trane Company) develops and manufactures Trane and American Standard air conditioning equipment for use in central air conditioning systems for commercial, institutional, and residential buildings. The plumbing products segment develops and manufactures American Standard, Ideal Standard, Porcher, Armitage Shanks, Dolomite, and Standard bathroom and kitchen fixtures and fittings. The automotive products segment develops and manufactures truck, bus, and utility vehicle braking and control systems under the WABCO and Perrot brands. The medical systems segment manufactures Copalis, DiaSorin, and Pylori-Chek medical diagnostic products and systems for a variety of diseases including HIV, osteoporosis, and renal disease. **Corporate headquarters location:** This location. **International locations:** Worldwide. **Listed on:** New York Stock Exchange. **Stock exchange symbol:** ASD. **Chairman/CEO:** Frederic M. Poses. **Number of employees worldwide:** 57,000.

AMMANN AND WHITNEY
96 Morton Street, New York NY 10014-3326. 212/462-8500. **Contact:** Ruth Darvie, Director of Human Resources. **E-mail address:** rdarvie@ammann-whitney.com. **World Wide Web address:** http://www.ammann-whitney.com. **Description:** An engineering firm specializing in structural, civil, architectural, mechanical and electrical engineering, as well as construction inspection services. **Positions advertised include:** Resident Engineer; Construction Inspector; Office Engineer; Senior Architect; Architect; Site Civil Engineer; Structural Drafter; Computer-aided Design Operator; Senior Structural Engineer; Construction Engineer; Design Engineer;. **Other U.S. locations:** Wethersfield CT; Washington DC; Boston MA; Hoboken NJ; Philadelphia PA; Richmond VA.

ARROW GROUP INDUSTRIES, INC.
1680 Route 23 North, P.O. Box 928, Wayne NJ 07474-0928. 973/696-6900. **Fax:** 973/696-8539. **Contact:** Joanne Trezza, Human Resources Director. **E-mail address:** assist@arrowsheds.com. **World Wide Web address:** http://www.sheds.com. **Description:** Manufactures steel storage buildings. **Corporate headquarters location:** This location. **Other U.S. locations:** Breese IL. **Listed on:** Privately held. **Number of employees at this location:** 115. **Number of employees nationwide:** 330.

BARHAM-McBRIDE COMPANY INC.
80 Park Plaza Newark NJ 07102. 973/430-5640. **Contact:** Human Resources. **World Wide Web address:** http://www.pseg.com. **Description:** Mechanical contractors for the architecture and construction industries. **Parent company:** PSEG.

THE LOUIS BERGER GROUP, INC.
100 Halsted Street, East Orange NJ 07018. 973/678-1960. **Fax:** 973/676-0532. **Contact:** Ms. Terry Williams, Human Resources Manager. **E-mail address:** recruiter@louisberger.com. **World Wide Web address:** http://www.louisberger.com. **Description:** A diversified consulting firm. The company provides cultural, environmental, and transportation-related engineering and planning services in the United States. Louis Berger also aids in urban and rural development projects in Africa, Asia, Latin America, and the Middle East. This location also hires seasonally. Founded in 1940. **NOTE:** Entry-level positions and part-time jobs are offered. **Positions advertised include:** Proposal Coordinator; Office Administrator; Corporate Security Director; Security Manager; Transportation Engineer; Cost Engineer; Engineer; Project Management & Accounting Assistant; Traffic Engineer; Air Quality Control Specialist; Geologist; Industrial Hygienist. **Special programs:** Summer Jobs. **Office hours:** Monday - Friday, 8:30 a.m. - 5:15 p.m. **Corporate headquarters location:** This location. **Other U.S. locations:** Washington DC; Chicago IL; Needham MA; Las Vegas NV. **International locations:** Worldwide. **Listed on:** Privately held. **President:** Derish Wolff. **Information Systems Manager:** Michael Stern. **Annual sales/revenues:** More than $100 million. **Number of employees at this location:** 270. **Number of employees nationwide:** 900. **Number of employees worldwide:** 2,000.

J. BROWN/LMC GROUP
1010 Washington Boulevard, 8th Floor, Stamford CT 06901. 203/352-0600. **Contact:** Human Resources. **World Wide Web address:** http://www.jbrown.com. **Description:** An international engineering and construction firm serving the plastics, pharmaceutical, food, biotechnology, chemical, oil, and gas industries. **Other U.S. locations:** San Francisco CA; Chicago IL; Cincinnati OH. **Number of employees nationwide:** 185.

BURNS AND ROE ENTERPRISES, INC.
800 Kinderkamack Road, Oradell NJ 07649. 201/265-2000. **Contact:** Human Resources. **World Wide Web address:** http://www.roe.com. **Description:** Engaged in construction, engineering, maintenance, and operation services. The company specializes in the design and engineering of complex facilities. **Special programs:** Internships. **Positions advertised include:** Principal Nuclear Engineer; Vendor Document Programmer; Utilities Supervisor Services. **Corporate headquarters location:** This location. **Listed on:** Privately held. **Number of employees at this location:** 600. **Number of employees nationwide:** 1,200. **Number of employees worldwide:** 1,250.

C/S GROUP
3 Werner Way, Lebanon NJ 08833. 908/236-0800. **Fax:** 908/236-0604. **Contact:** Susan Kizies, Director of Human Resources. **E-mail address:** careerops@c-sgroup.com. **World Wide Web address:** http://www.c-sgroup.com. **Description:** Manufactures building materials including wall protection products, sun controls, and fire vents. Founded in 1948. **NOTE:** Entry-level positions and part-time jobs are offered. **Positions advertised include:** Database Analyst Programmer. **Corporate headquarters location:** This location. **Other U.S. locations:** Garden Grove CA; Muncy PA. **International locations:** France; Spain; United Kingdom. **Listed on:** Privately held. **Annual sales/revenues:** More than $100 million.

CENTEX HOMES
500 Craig Road, Manalapan NJ 07726. 732/780-1800. **Contact:** Human Resources. **World Wide Web address:** http://www.centexhomes.com. **Description:** Centex Homes designs, constructs, and sells homes nationwide. **Other U.S. locations:** Nationwide. **Parent company:** Centex Corporation. **Listed on:** New York Stock Exchange. **Stock exchange symbol:** CTX.

CLAYTON BRICK
2 Porete Avenue, North Arlington NJ 07032. 201/998-7600. **Contact:** Human Resources. **World Wide Web address:** http://www.claytonco.com. **Description:** Engaged in precast concrete panel construction and installation. **NOTE:** For employment information contact the central Clayton Companies office: P.O. Box 3015, 515 Lakewood-New Egypt Road, Lakewood NJ 08701, 732/363-1995, or contact Wayne Tart at 732/905-3156 or by e-mail at waynetart@netscape.com.

DREW INDUSTRIES INCORPORATED
200 Mamaroneck Avenue, Suite 301, White Plains NY 10601. 914/428-9098. **Fax:** 914/428-4581. **Contact:** Human Resources. **World Wide Web address:** http://www.drewindustries.com. **Description:** Drew Industries is the holding company of Kinro, Inc. Kinro is one of the leading producers of aluminum and vinyl windows for manufactured homes, and windows and doors for recreational vehicles. Kinro has nine domestic manufacturing plants. **Corporate headquarters location:** This location. **Subsidiaries include:** Lippert Components, Inc.; Kinro, Inc. **Listed on:** American Stock Exchange. **Stock exchange symbol:** DW. **Annual sales/revenues:** $325 million. **Number of employees:** 2,800.

EDWARDS AND KELCEY INC.
P.O. Box 1936, 299 Madison Avenue, Morristown NJ 07962-1936. 973/267-8830. **Contact:** Harry P. Daley, Human Resources Director. **World Wide Web address:** http://www.ekcorp.com. **Description:** A consulting, engineering, planning, and communications organization whose range of services includes location and economic feasibility studies; valuations and appraisals; cost analyses; computer technology; marketing studies; traffic and transportation studies; soils and foundation analyses; environmental impact studies; master planning; structural surveys; and preliminary and final designs. Services also include preparation of contract documents and observation of construction operations for public transit systems, terminals, railroads, bus depots, parking garages, airports, ports, highways, streets, bridges, tunnels, traffic control systems, military facilities, communications systems, storm and sanitary sewers, water supply and distribution, flood control, and land development. Founded in 1946. **NOTE:** Entry-level positions are offered. **Positions advertised include:** Industrial Electrician. **Special programs:** Internships. **Corporate headquarters location:** This location. **Other U.S. locations:** Atlanta GA; Chicago IL; Baltimore MD; Boston MA; Minneapolis MN; Manchester NH; New York NY; Saratoga Springs NY; Cincinnati OH; Chadds Ford PA; West Chester PA; Providence RI; Dallas TX; Houston TX; Leesburg VA; Milwaukee WI. **International locations:** Puerto Rico. **Operations at this facility include:** Administration; Divisional Headquarters. **Listed on:** Privately held. **Annual sales/revenues:** More than $100 million. **Number of employees at this location:** 200. **Number of employees nationwide:** 730.

FM GLOBAL.
400 Interpace Parkway, Building C, 3rd Floor, Parsippany NJ 07054-1196. 973/402-2200. **Contact:** District Office. **World Wide Web address:** http://www.fmglobal.com. **Description:** A loss control services organization. The company helps owner company policyholders to protect their properties and occupancies from damage caused by fire, wind, flood, and explosion; boiler, pressure vessel, and machinery accidents; and many other insured hazards.

Corporate headquarters location: Johnston RI. **Other U.S. locations:** Nationwide. **International locations:** Worldwide.

GAF MATERIALS CORPORATION
1361 Alps Road, Wayne NJ 07470. 973/628-3000. **Toll-free phone:** 800/766-3411. **Contact:** Human Resources. **E-mail address:** employment@gaf.com. **World Wide Web address:** http://www.gaf.com. **Description:** Manufactures roofing materials. **Operations at this facility include:** Administration; Manufacturing.

INDUSTRIAL ACOUSTICS COMPANY, INC.
1160 Commerce Avenue, Bronx NY 10462. 718/430-4541. **Fax:** 718/430-4766. **Contact:** Michele Pisani, Human Resources Department. **E-mail address:** hr@industrialacoustics.com. **World Wide Web address:** http://www.industrialacoustics.com. **Description:** IAC is an international company with engineering and manufacturing capabilities serving the architectural, air conditioning, industrial, medical and life sciences, power plant, and military/commercial aviation markets. The company develops and markets noise control products, turnkey systems for air conditioning and air handling units, jet engine aircraft hush-house test facilities, detention cells, acoustical ceilings for correctional institutions, and other special purpose ceilings. Founded in 1949. **Positions advertised include:** Project Engineer; Auto Cad Drafter/Designer. **Corporate headquarters location:** This location. **International locations:** Germany; United Kingdom. **President/CEO:** Robert E. Schmitt. **Annual sales/revenues:** $100 million. **Number of employees:** 300.

KSW MECHANICAL SERVICES
3716 23rd Street, Long Island City NY 11101. 718/361-6500. **Fax:** 718/784-1943. **Contact:** Human Resources. **Description:** A mechanical contracting firm engaged in the installation of heating, ventilation, and air conditioning systems in commercial buildings. **Corporate headquarters location:** This location. **Listed on:** Over The Counter. **Stock exchange symbol:** KSWW. **Chairman/CEO:** Floyd Warkol. **Annual sales/revenues:** $50 million. **Number of employees:** 45.

MELARD MANUFACTURING CORPORATION
2 Paulison Avenue, Passaic NJ 07055-5703. 973/472-8888. **Contact:** Personnel. **World Wide Web address:** http://www.masco.com. **Description:** Manufactures a broad range of hardware products including bath accessories and plumbing equipment. **Positions advertised include:** Assistant Controller. **Corporate headquarters location:** This location. **Parent company:** Masco Corporation.

JOS. L. MUSCARELLE, INC.
99 West Essex Street, Route 17, Maywood NJ 07607. 201/845-8100. **Contact:** Joseph Muscarelle, Jr., President. **Description:** Engaged in construction and real estate development.

PARAMOUNT ELECTRONICS COMPANY
57 Willoughby Street, Brooklyn NY 11201. 718/237-8730. **Contact:** Human Resources. **Description:** Provides contract drafting services. **Corporate headquarters location:** This location.

PARSONS BRINCKERHOFF INC.
One Penn Plaza, New York NY 10119. 212/465-5000. **Contact:** Joe Alberti, Personnel. **E-mail address:** careeres@pbworld.com. **World Wide Web address:** http://www.pbworld.com. **Description:** Provides total engineering and construction management services, including the development of major bridges, tunnels, highways, marine facilities, buildings, industrial complexes, and railroads. Founded in 1885. **Corporate headquarters location:** This location. **International locations:** Worldwide. **Subsidiaries include:** Parsons

Brinckerhoff Construction Services; Parsons Brinckerhoff Development Corporation; Parsons Brinckerhoff International; Parsons Brinckerhoff Quade & Douglas. **President/CEO:** Thomas J. O'Neill. **Sales/revenue:** Approximately $1.4 billion. **Number of employees worldwide:** Over 9,000.

PATENT CONSTRUCTION SYSTEMS
One Mack Centre Drive, Paramus NJ 07652. 201/986-1290. **Fax:** 201/261-5544. **Contact:** Human Resources and Labor Relations. **E-mail address:** jobs@pcshd.com. **World Wide Web address:** http://www.pcshd.com. **Description:** Manufactures and markets scaffolding as well as concrete forming and shoring products. Founded in 1909. **Positions advertised include:** Sales Representative. **Parent company:** Harsco Corporation.

ALBERT PEARLMAN, INC.
60 East 42nd Street, Suite 1041, New York NY 10165. 212/687-5055. **Fax:** 212/687-6228. **Contact:** Human Resources. **E-mail address:** randyp@albertpearlman.com. **World Wide Web address:** http://www.albertpearlman.com. **Description:** The largest painting contractor in New York City. **Corporate headquarters location:** This location. **Other locations:** Hackensack, NJ; Long Island, NY.

PIONEER INDUSTRIES
171 South Newman Street, Hackensack NJ 07601. 201/933-1900. **Contact:** Personnel Director. **World Wide Web address:** http://www.pioneer-industries.com. **Description:** Produces industrial doors, fireproof and theft-proof doors, and other sheet metal specialties. **Corporate headquarters location:** Bloomfield Hills MI. **Parent company:** Core Industries. **Operations at this facility include:** Manufacturing.

SCHIAVONE CONSTRUCTION CO.
150 Meadowlands Parkway, 3rd Floor, Secaucus NJ 07094. 201/867-5070. **Contact:** Recruiting. **Description:** A heavy construction firm engaged in large-scale projects such as highways, tunnels, and bridges. Clients include city, state, and federal governments.

SLANT/FIN CORPORATION
100 Forest Drive, Greenvale NY 11548. 516/484-2600. **Contact:** Human Resources. **E-mail address:** info@slantfin.com. **World Wide Web address:** http://www.slantfin.com. **Description:** Engaged in the manufacture and sale of heating and cooling equipment for both domestic and foreign markets. **Corporate headquarters location:** This location. **International locations:** Canada. **Number of employees worldwide:** 600.

SLATTERY SKANSKA INC.
16-16 Whitestone Expressway, Whitestone NY 11357. 718/767-2600. **Fax:** 718/767-2668. **Contact:** Larry Bolyard, Director of Human Resources Department. **E-mail address:** larry.bolyard@slattery.skanska.com. **World Wide Web address:** http://www.slatteryskanska.com. **Description:** A heavy construction firm engaged in large-scale projects such as mass transit, sewage treatment plants, highways, bridges, and tunnels. **Positions advertised include:** Estimator; Superintendent; Project Engineer. **Office hours:** Monday - Friday, 8:00 a.m. - 4:30 p.m. **Corporate headquarters location:** This location. **Parent company:** Skanska USA. **Operations at this facility include:** Administration. **Number of employees at this location:** 1,000.

STROBER BROTHERS, INC.
Pier 3, Furman Street, Brooklyn NY 11201. 718/875-9700. **Fax:** 718/246-3080. **Contact:** Human Resources. **World Wide Web address:** http://www.strober.com. **Description:** Strober Organization, Inc. is a supplier of

building materials to professional building contractors in the residential, commercial, and renovation construction markets. The company operates 10 building centers across four states, offering a broad selection of gypsum wallboard and other drywall products, lumber, roofing, insulation and acoustical materials, plywood, siding products, metal specialties, hardware and tools, waterproofing, masonry, and steel decking products. The building centers also offer a full spectrum of millwork. Founded in 1912. **Corporate headquarters location:** This location.

TESTWELL LABORATORIES, INC.
47 Hudson Street, Ossining NY 10562. 914/762-9000. **Fax:** 914/762-9638. **Contact:** Personnel Director. **World Wide Web address:** http://www.testwelllabs.com. **Description:** Provides construction materials and environmental testing, inspection, and consulting services for the construction, environmental, and real estate industries. **Corporate headquarters location:** This location. **Other area locations:** Albany NY. **Other U.S. locations:** Miami FL; Mays Landing NJ. **Operations at this facility include:** Administration; Regional Headquarters; Sales; Service. **Number of employees at this location:** 90. **Number of employees nationwide:** 400.

TURNER CORPORATION
375 Hudson Street, New York NY 10014. 212/229-6000. **Contact:** Human Resources. **World Wide Web address:** http://www.turnerconstruction.com. **Description:** A holding company involved in construction, general building, contract management, and real estate development. **Corporate headquarters location:** This location. **Subsidiaries include:** Turner Construction Company; Turner Medical Building Services.

WELSBACH ELECTRIC CORPORATION
P.O. Box 560252, 111-01 14th Avenue, College Point NY 11356-0252. 718/670-7900. **Contact:** Personnel. **World Wide Web address:** http://www.welsbachelectric.com. **Description:** An electrical contractor engaged in the installation and maintenance of streetlights and traffic signals. **Corporate headquarters location:** This location. **Parent company:** EMCOR Group, Inc. **Listed on:** New York Stock Exchange. **Stock exchange symbol:** EME. **President:** Fred Goodman.

ARTS, ENTERTAINMENT, SPORTS, AND RECREATION

You can expect to find the following types of companies in this section:
Botanical and Zoological Gardens • Entertainment Groups • Motion Picture and Video Tape Production and Distribution • Museums and Art Galleries • Physical Fitness Facilities • Professional Sports Clubs; Sporting and Recreational Camps • Public Golf Courses and Racing and Track Operations • Theatrical Producers and Services

A&E TELEVISION NETWORKS
235 East 45th Street, New York NY 10017. 212/210-1400. **Fax:** 212/907-9402. **Contact:** Human Resources. **World Wide Web address:** http://www.aande.com/corporate. **Description:** A joint venture of The Hearst Corporation, ABC, Inc., and NBC, the company is a media corporation that provides magazine and book publishing services, distributes home videos, and operates Websites and the A&E and History Channel cable stations. **NOTE:** The company prefers resumes to be faxed to the above number along with the position to which applying and salary requirements. **Positions advertised include:** Affiliate Sales Administration Manager; Inventory Analyst; Legal & Business Affairs Assistant; Traffic Services Assistant; Account Executive. **Corporate headquarters location:** This location. **Subsidiaries include:** The History Channel; Biography Channel; History Channel International; Genealogy.com; Military.com; Mysteries.com.

AMERIC DISC
11 Oval Drive, Islandia NY 11749. 631/234-0200. **Contact:** Human Resources. **World Wide Web address:** http://www.americdisc.com. **Description:** Americ Disc is one of the nation's leading independent multimedia manufacturing companies offering CD-audio and CD-ROM mastering and replication; videocassette and audiocassette duplication; laser video disc recording; off-line and online video editing; motion picture film processing; film-to-tape and tape-to-film transfers; and finishing, packaging, warehousing, and fulfillment services. **Corporate headquarters location:** Quebec, Canada. **Other area locations:** Forest Hills NY; Nesconset NY. **Other locations:** Worldwide.

THE AMERICAN KENNEL CLUB
260 Madison Avenue, 4th Floor, New York NY 10016. 212/696-8200. **Recorded jobline:** 919/816-3896. **Contact:** Vicki Lane Rees, Human Resources Director. **World Wide Web address:** http://www.akc.org. **Description:** An independent, nonprofit organization devoted to the advancement of purebred dogs. The American Kennel Club adopts and enforces rules and regulations governing dog shows, obedience trials, and field trials, and fosters and encourages interest in the health and welfare of purebred dogs. The club also offers a wide range of books and magazines for national distribution. Founded in 1884. **NOTE:** Entry-level positions are offered. Resumes should be sent to: AKC Human Resources Department, P.O. Box 37905, Raleigh NC 27627-7905; or fax: 919/816-4282. **Positions advertised include:** Computer Support Specialist; Administrative Assistant; Desktop Publishing Specialist; Editorial Assistant. **Office hours:** Monday - Friday, 8:30 a.m. - 4:15 p.m. **Corporate headquarters location:** This location. **Other U.S. locations:** Raleigh NC. **Listed on:** Privately held, Not-for-Profit company. **President/CEO:** Al Cheaure. **Number of employees at this location:** 75. **Number of employees nationwide:** 450.

AMERICAN MUSEUM OF NATURAL HISTORY
Central Park West at 79th Street, New York NY 10024-5192. 212/769-5000. **Contact:** Human Resources. **World Wide Web address:** http://www.amnh.org. **Description:** A museum of anthropology, astronomy, mineralogy, and zoology. The museum has a research library and 38 exhibition halls and offers educational and research programs. The museum also publishes several in-house and nationally distributed magazines based on research conducted there. Founded in 1869. **Corporate headquarters location:** This location.

AMERICAN SYMPHONY ORCHESTRA LEAGUE
33 West 60th Street, 5th Floor, New York NY 10023. 212/262-5161. **Fax:** 212/262-5198. **Contact:** Hilary Field, Human Resources Assistant. **E-mail address:** hfield@symphony.org or hr@symphony.org. **World Wide Web address:** http://www.symphony.org. **Description:** A national service organization for America's professional, symphony, chamber, youth, and college orchestras. Founded in 1942. **Positions advertised include:** Executive Assistant to the President; Secretary to the Board of Directors. **Office hours:** Monday - Friday, 9:00 a.m. - 5:30 p.m. **Other U.S. locations:** Washington DC.

APOLLO THEATRE
253 West 125th Street, New York NY 10027. 212/531-5300. **Fax:** 212/749-2743. **Contact:** Human Resources. **World Wide Web address:** http://www.apollotheater.com. **Description:** A nonprofit performing arts theater with performances year-round. **Parent company:** The Apollo Theater Foundation, Inc.

ARISTA RECORDS
6 West 57th Street, 2nd Floor, New York NY 10019. 212/489-7400. **Fax:** 212/830-2107. **Contact:** Human Resources. **World Wide Web address:** http://www.arista.com. **Description:** Provides sales, promotional, and artist and repertoire activities for Arista Records and its contracted artists. Founded in 1974. **Corporate headquarters location:** This location. **Parent company:** BMG Entertainment. **Operations at this facility include:** Corporate Administration; Sales.

ASCENT MEDIA EAST
235 Pegasus Avenue, Northvale NJ 07647. 201/767-3800. **Contact:** Human Resources. **World Wide Web address:** http://www.apvi.com. **Description:** Services include post-production work and audio and video restoration for a variety of networks including the Children's Television Network (CTW). **Corporate headquarters location:** New York NY. **Parent company:** International Post Ltd. provides a wide range of post-production services, primarily to the television advertising industry, and distributes television programming to the international market through its operating subsidiaries. Other subsidiaries of the parent company include Big Picture/Even Time Limited; Cabana; Manhattan Transfer, Inc.; and The Post Edge, Inc. The company's services include creative editorial services, film-to-tape transfer, electronic video editing, computer-generated graphics, duplication, and audio services, all in multiple standards and formats, as well as network playback operations. The company's services are provided in the New York metropolitan area and South Florida.

BROADWAY VIDEO INC.
1619 Broadway, 10th Floor, New York NY 10019. 212/265-7600. **Contact:** Vice President of Operations. **E-mail address:** info@broawayvideo.com. **World Wide Web address:** http://www.broadwayvideo.com. **Description:** An entertainment production company offering editing, design, sound, and related services for all types of media. **Corporate headquarters location:** This location. **Founder:** Mr. Lorne Michaels.

BROOKLYN ACADEMY OF MUSIC
30 Lafayette Avenue, Brooklyn NY 11217. 718/636-4111. **Fax:** 718/636-4179. **Contact:** Sarah Weinstein, Director of Human Resources. **E-mail address:** hrresumes@bam.org. **World Wide Web address:** http://www.bam.org. **Description:** A nonprofit arts showcase offering dance, opera, and theatrical performances, as well as performances by the Brooklyn Philharmonic Orchestra. Founded in 1859. **NOTE:** Job openings can be found at the stage door located at 116 St. Felix Street. **Positions advertised include:** Marketing Intern; Summer Concerts Intern; BA Mart Internship; Membership Coordinator; Director Human Resources; Marketing Manager E-media. **Special programs:** Internships.

BROOKLYN BOTANIC GARDEN
1000 Washington Avenue, Brooklyn NY 11225-1099. 718/623-7200. **Fax:** 718/622-7826. **Contact:** Director of Human Resources Department. **E-mail address:** personnel@bbg.org. **World Wide Web address:** http://www.bbg.org. **Description:** Exhibits over 10,000 plants in the Steinhardt Conservatory. Brooklyn Botanic Garden also offers programs teaching hands-on gardening to children ages three to 17. Brooklyn Botanic Garden offers special events such as the Cherry Blossom Festival, student art exhibitions, tours of the Japanese Hill-and-Pond Garden, and the Annual Spring Plant Sale. Founded in 1910. **Positions advertised include:** Grants Writer; Education Coordinator; Gardening Instructor; Vice President of Horticulture; Arborist; Maintainer; Security Guard.

CNBC
MSNBC
One Msnbc Plaza, Secaucus NJ 07094. 201/735-2622. **Fax:** 201/346-6506. **Contact:** Personnel. **World Wide Web address:** http://www.msnbc.com. **Description:** Operates all-news networks offering current business and finance news. CNBC and MSNBC are both updated 24 hours a day, seven days a week. **Positions advertised include:** Multimedia Producer; Interactive Producer. **NOTE:** CNBC's website is http://moneycentral.msn.com/investor/home.asp. **Corporate headquarters location:** This location. **Parent company:** NBC.

CINE MAGNETICS VIDEO & DIGITAL LABORATORIES
100 Business Park Drive, Armonk NY 10504-1750. 914/273-7500. **Fax:** 914/273-7575. **Contact:** Human Resources. **E-mail address:** cminfo@cinemagnetics.com. **World Wide Web address:** http://www.cinemagnetics.com. **Description:** Cine Magnetics is involved in video and film duplication and photo finishing. **Corporate headquarters location:** This location. **Other U.S. locations:** Studio City CA.

CITY CENTER OF MUSIC AND DRAMA INC. (CCMD)
70 Lincoln Center Plaza, 4th Floor, New York NY 10023-6580. 212/870-4266. **Fax:** 212/870-4286. **Contact:** Cynthia Herzegovitch, Human Resources Administrator. **Description:** Organizational and management offices for the nonprofit cultural organization with activities that include plays, ballets, and operas. The center operates the New York State Theater, the New York City Opera, the New York Ballet, and City Center Special Productions. **Positions advertised include:** Clerical Supervisor. **Corporate headquarters location:** This location. **Operations at this facility include:** Administration. **Number of employees:** 2,000.

CLEAR CHANNEL ENTERTAINMENT
220 West 42nd Street, New York NY 10036. 917/421-4000. **Fax:** 917/421-5673. **Contact:** Human Resources. **World Wide Web address:** http://www.cc.com. **Description:** This subsidiary of Clear Channel Communications produces and promotes live entertainment by booking 135 venues worldwide averaging 29,000 events annually. **Positions advertised include:** Legal and Business Affairs

Assistant; Booking Specialist; Event Associate; Promotions Assistant; Finance Assistant. **Corporate headquarters location:** This location. **Parent company:** Clear Channel Communications, Inc. (San Antonio TX). **Chairman/CEO:** Brian Becker. **Annual sales/revenues:** $2.5 billion.

THE CLOISTERS
Fort Tryon Park, New York NY 10040. 212/923-3700. **Contact:** Assistant Museum Educator. **World Wide Web address:** http://www.metmuseum.org. **Description:** A museum devoted to the art of medieval Europe. The collection includes architectural fragments, sculptures, frescoes, illuminated manuscripts, tapestries, stained glass, and paintings. Established in 1938. **Special programs:** Internships. **Parent company:** The Metropolitan Museum of Art.

COMEDY CENTRAL
1775 Broadway, 9th Floor, New York NY 10019. 212/767-8600. **Contact:** Human Resources. **World Wide Web address:** http://www.comedycentral.com. **Description:** Operator of the Comedy Central cable television network, which produces such shows as The Daily Show and South Park. **NOTE:** The company's stated policy is to not accept postal mail for any reason – apply online through the company Website. However, resumes for production positions will not be considered without reels/tapes. **Positions advertised include:** Writer; Producer; Sales Operations Analyst. **Special programs:** Internships. **Parent company:** Comedy Central is a joint venture between Viacom, Inc., and Time Warner Entertainment Company.

COURTROOM TELEVISION NETWORK LLC
600 Third Avenue, 2nd Floor, New York NY 10016. 212/973-2800. **Fax:** 240/337-8569. **Contact:** Human Resources. **World Wide Web address:** http://www.courttv.com. **Description:** Court TV is a cable television network providing coverage of publicized legal battles and couret proceedings. **Positions advertised include:** Copy Editor; Administrative Assistant; Junior Web Designer; Senior Staff Writer; Production Assistant; Executive Director. **Corporate headquarters location:** This location. **Parent company:** Turner Broadcasting System, Inc. (Atlanta GA).

DUART FILM AND VIDEO
245 West 55th Street, New York NY 10019. 212/757-4580. **Contact:** Supervisor. **World Wide Web address:** http://www.duart.com. **Description:** Involved in motion picture services and television broadcasting.

4KIDS ENTERTAINMENT, INC.
1414 Avenue of the Americas, New York NY 10019. 212/758-7666. **Fax:** 212/980-0933. **Contact:** John Gansley, Human Resources. **World Wide Web address:** http://www.4kidsentertainmentinc.com. **Description:** A vertically integrated merchandising and entertainment company. 4Kids Entertainment is involved in merchandise licensing, toy design, and TV, movie, and music production. **Positions advertised include:** Sales Clerk; Marketing Specialist; Legal Assistant; Accountant; Graphic Designer. **Corporate headquarters location:** This location. **International locations:** London, United Kingdom. **Subsidiaries include:** 4Kids Entertainment International Limited; 4Kids Entertainment Licensing, Inc.; 4Kids Entertainment Home Video, Inc.; 4Kids Productions Inc.; 4Kids Ad Sales, Inc.; Leisure Concepts UK; Leisure Concepts, Inc.; 4Kids Technology, Inc.; The Summit Media Group, Inc.; Websites 4 Kids, Inc.; 4Kids Entertainment Music, Inc. **Listed on:** New York Stock Exchange. **Stock exchange symbol:** KDE. **Chairman/CEO:** Alfred (Al) R. Kahn. **Annual sales/revenues:** $53 million. **Number of employees:** 188.

HBO (HOME BOX OFFICE)
1100 Avenue of the Americas, New York NY 10036. 212/512-1000. **Contact:** Shelley Fischel, Human Resources Director. **World Wide Web address:** http://www.hbo.com. **Description:** Operates HBO, HBO HDTV, and Cinemax, television networks dedicated to movies. Divisions of HBO include: MoreMAX, ThrillerMAX, and ActionMAX. **Positions advertised include:** Financial Operations and Reporting Assistant; Production Coordinator; Attorney; Product Development and Production Supervisor; Financial Analyst; Legal Contract Administrator; Executive Assistant; Compressionist; Writer; Producer. **Other U.S. locations:** Los Angeles CA. **Parent company:** AOL Time Warner Inc. **Chairman/CEO:** Chris Albrecht. **Annual sales/revenues:** $2.5 billion. **Number of employees:** 2,000.

THE HUDSON RIVER MUSEUM OF WESTCHESTER
ANDRUS PLANETARIUM
511 Warburton Avenue, Yonkers NY 10701. 914/963-4550. **Contact:** Human Resources. **World Wide Web address:** http://www.hrm.org. **Description:** A museum of art, history, and science. Collections include 19th-century fine and decorative arts, and 19th- and 20th-century paintings. Andrus Planetarium is the only public planetarium in Westchester County.

LINCOLN CENTER FOR THE ARTS, INC.
NEW YORK CITY BALLET
70 Lincoln Center Plaza, New York NY 10023. 212/875-5255. **Fax:** 212/875-5185. **Contact:** Stacy Tonkas, Human Resources Director. **E-mail address:** humanresources@lincolncenter.org. **World Wide Web address:** http://www.lincolncenter.org. **Description:** An international center for the performing arts presenting live performances of opera, ballet, music, theater, dance, circus, and puppetry. **Positions advertised include:** Institutional Giving Director; Publicist; Human Resources Assistant; Customer Service Representative. **Executive Director:** Scott Noppe-Brandon. **Annual sales/revenues:** $25 million.

MGM/UNITED ARTISTS
ORION PICTURES CORPORATION
1350 Avenue of the Americas, 24th Floor, New York NY 10019. 212/708-0300. **Fax:** 212/708-0377. **Contact:** Human Resources. **World Wide Web address:** http://www.mgm.com. **Description:** Metro-Goldwyn-Mayer Inc. is one of the nation's largest film distribution companies. **Special programs:** Internships. **Corporate headquarters location:** Santa Monica CA. **Subsidiaries include:** MGM Pictures; Movielink, LLC; United Artists Corporation. **Operations at this facility include:** Administration; Sales; Service. **Listed on:** New York Stock Exchange. **Stock exchange symbol:** MGM. **Chairman/CEO:** Alex Yemenidjian. **Annual sales/revenues:** $1.65 billion. **Number of employees at this location:** 250. **Number of employees nationwide:** 1,150.

MADISON SQUARE GARDEN, L.P.
2 Penn Plaza, 16th Floor, New York NY 10121. 212/465-6000. **Fax:** 212/465-6026. **Recorded jobline:** 212/465-6335. **Contact:** Human Resources. **E-mail address:** msghr@thegarden.com. **World Wide Web address:** http://www.thegarden.com. **Description:** Operates sports and entertainment events in the Arena, Rotunda, and Paramount Theatre. Professional sports teams include the NBA's New York Knicks, the WNBA's New York Liberty, and the NHL's New York Rangers. Madison Square Garden also operates the MSG Network (one of the nation's oldest regional cable television sports networks). In addition, Madison Square Garden operates its own restaurants, catering, fast food, and merchandise divisions. **NOTE:** Seasonal and part-time jobs are offered. **Positions advertised include:** Accountant; Marketing Representative; Financial Analyst; Advertising Clerk; Graphic Designer. **Special programs:**

Internships. **Internship information:** Madison Square Garden has a college internship program that runs during the fall, spring, and summer semesters. For application information, call 212/465-6258. **Corporate headquarters location:** This location. **Parent company:** Regional Programming Partners. **Listed on:** Privately held. **Chairman:** James L. Dolan. **Annual sales/revenues:** $790 million.

THE METROPOLITAN MUSEUM OF ART

1000 Fifth Avenue, New York NY 10028-0198. 212/535-7710. **Fax:** 212/472-2764. **Contact:** Employment Office. **E-mail address:** employoppty@metmuseum.org. **World Wide Web address:** http://www.metmuseum.org. **Description:** A museum containing one of the most extensive art collections in the world. Permanent exhibits range from ancient art to modern art. Operations include conservation and curatorial departments, education services, libraries, concerts and lectures, internships, fellowships, publications and reproductions, and exhibitions. The museum also operates The Cloisters in Fort Tryon Park.

THE METROPOLITAN OPERA ASSOCIATION, INC.

Lincoln Center, New York NY 10023. 212/362-6000. **Fax:** 212/870-7405. **Contact:** Lisa Fuld, Human Resources Associate. **E-mail address:** resumes@mail.metopera.org. **World Wide Web address:** http://www.metopera.org. **Description:** The Opera produces approximately 25 operas per year, tours internationally, and performs free outdoor concerts in New York area parks. Founded in 1883. **NOTE:** Entry-level positions, part-time jobs, and second and third shifts are offered.

MOUNTAIN CREEK

200 Route 94, Vernon NJ 07462. 973/827-2000. **Contact:** Human Resources. **World Wide Web address:** http://www.mountaincreek.com. **Description:** Operates as a water amusement park in the summer and a ski resort in the winter.

MULTIMEDIA TUTORIAL SERVICES, INC.

205 Kings Highway, Brooklyn NY 11223. 718/234-0404. **Contact:** Human Resources. **Description:** Produces and markets tutorial education programs, primarily in videotape and also CD-ROM formats, for use by adults and children in homes, work, schools, libraries, and other locales. Principal products consist of a series of 92 videotapes and supplemental materials on mathematics and an interactive, audio-visual, CD-ROM based system for language instruction. The company's videotapes include colorful computer graphics and real life vignettes. **Corporate headquarters location:** This location.

MUSEUM OF MODERN ART

11 West 53rd Street, New York NY 10019. 212/708-9400. **Fax:** 212/333-1107. **Contact:** Human Resources Manager. **E-mail address:** jobs@moma.org. **World Wide Web address:** http://www.moma.org. **Description:** Houses one of the world's foremost collections of modern art. **Special programs:** Internships. **Corporate headquarters location:** This location. **Number of employees at this location:** 550.

NYS THEATRE INSTITUTE

37 First Street, Troy NY 12180. 518/274-3200. **Fax:** 518/274-3815. **Contact:** Arlene Leff, Intern Program Director. **World Wide Web address:** http://www.nysti.org. **Description:** A professional resident theater company that specializes in theater for family audiences with a strong arts and education approach. **Special programs:** Internships.

NEW JERSEY SHAKESPEARE FESTIVAL

36 Madison Avenue, Madison NJ 07940. 973/408-3278. **Fax:** 973/408-3361. **Contact:** Joseph Discher, Artistic Associate. **E-mail address:** njsf@njshakespeare.org. **World Wide Web address:** http://www.njshakespeare.org. **Description:** A nonprofit professional theater devoted to producing the works of Shakespeare and other classic masterworks. Founded in 1962. **NOTE:** Entry-level positions are offered. **Positions advertised include:** Box Office Associate; Casting Internship; Sales Manager; Assistant Production Manager; Scenic Charge Artist. **Special programs:** Internships; Apprenticeships; Training.

NEW JERSEY SPORTS & EXPOSITION AUTHORITY

50 Route 120, East Rutherford NJ 07073. 201/935-8500. **Recorded jobline:** 201/460-4265. **Contact:** Gina Klein, Director of Human Resources. **E-mail address:** hr@njsea.com. **World Wide Web address:** http://www.njsea.com. **Description:** A state-appointed agency responsible for coordinating and running sports and entertainment activities at the Meadowlands Sports Complex, which includes Meadowlands Racetrack (harness and thoroughbred racing, as well as other events), Giants Stadium (New York Giants, New York Jets, concerts, and other events), and Continental Airlines Arena (New Jersey Nets, New Jersey Devils, tennis, track, concerts, and other events). **Corporate headquarters location:** This location.

NEW LINE CINEMA

888 Seventh Avenue, 19th Floor, New York NY 10106. 212/649-4900. **Contact:** Human Resources. **World Wide Web address:** http://www.newline.com. **Description:** Produces and distributes low-budget theatrical motion pictures (generally action/adventure and comedy films targeted at the younger market). The company also acquires distribution rights to films produced by others, and has agreements with distributors in ancillary markets such as home video, pay television, and free television. **Positions advertised include:** Music & Development Assistant; Contract Accounting Assistant. **Special programs:** Internships. **Parent company:** AOL Time Warner, Incorporated.

THE NEW YORK BOTANICAL GARDEN

200th Street & Southern Boulevard, Bronx NY 10458-5126. 718/817-8700. **Contact:** Human Resources. **E-mail address:** hr@nybg.org. **World Wide Web address:** http://www.nybg.org. **Description:** An internationally recognized center for botanical research offering 47 gardens and plant collections. The New York Botanical Garden is dedicated to environmental education and the conservation of plant diversity. Founded in 1891. **Positions advertised include:** Associate Vice President for Development; Director of the Plant Research Laboratory; Institutional Database Administrator; Project Manager; Manager of Public and School Programs; Director of Horticulture for Public Programs; Associate Rose Garden Curator; Gardener for Public Programs; Administrative Assistant; Assistant Gardener; Research Assistant; Herbarium Assistant; Office Assistant; Gate Attendant. **Special programs:** Internships. **Corporate headquarters location:** This location. **Operations at this facility include:** Education; Research and Development.

THE NEW YORK RACING ASSOCIATION

P.O. Box 90, Jamaica NY 11417. 718/641-4700. **Contact:** Human Resources. **World Wide Web address:** http://www.nyracing.com. **Description:** A state-franchised, nonprofit racing association that owns, operates, and manages three horseracing tracks: Aqueduct, Belmont Park, and Saratoga, where pari-mutuel wagering is conducted. These facilities are the site of some of America's most prestigious stakes races: The Wood Memorial, and The Belmont and Travers Stakes.

NEW YORK SHAKESPEARE FESTIVAL
425 Lafayette Street, New York NY 10003. 212/539-8500. **Contact:** General Manager. **Description:** A nonprofit organization involved in many productions: year-round on-Broadway, off-Broadway, on tour around the country, television specials of theatrical works, free Shakespearean productions in Central Park each summer, and the development of new works.

OXYGEN MEDIA, INC.
75 9th Avenue, 7th Floor, New York City NY 10011. 212/651-2000. **Contact:** Human Resources. **E-mail address:** jobs@oxygen.com. **World Wide Web address:** http://www.oxygen.com. **Description:** Produces and broadcasts television programs and Websites geared toward women viewers. **Positions advertised include:** Junior Accountant. **CEO/Chairman:** Geraldine Laybourne. **Number of employees at this location:** 450.

PPI ENTERTAINMENT
88 St. Francis Street, Newark NJ 07105. 973/344-4214. **Contact:** Personnel. **World Wide Web address:** http://www.peterpan.com. **Description:** Manufactures and distributes records, tapes, videos, and CD-ROMs. **Corporate headquarters location:** This location. **Listed on:** Privately held.

PARAMOUNT CENTER FOR THE ARTS
1008 Brown Street, Peekskill NY 10566. 914/739-2333. **Contact:** Human Resources. **E-mail address:** info@paramountcenter.org. **World Wide Web address:** http://www.paramountcenter.org. **Description:** A former vaudeville house revived as a performing arts facility offering programs in music, theater, film, and dance. **Office hours:** Monday – Friday, 10:00 a.m. – 6:00 p.m., Saturday, 12:00 p.m. – 4:00 p.m.

PRO-FITNESS HEALTHSOUTH
40 Richards Avenue, Norwalk CT 06854. 203/853-6478. **Contact:** Human Resources. **Description:** Pro-Fitness manages a chain of fitness centers. **Operations at this facility include:** This location houses administrative offices.

RADIO CITY ENTERTAINMENT
1260 Avenue of the Americas, New York NY 10020. 212/247-4777. **Contact:** Human Resources. **World Wide Web address:** http://www.radiocity.com. **Description:** A diversified entertainment production company. **NOTE:** Resumes may be mailed to the Human Resources Department, 2 Penn Plaza, New York NY 10121. **Special programs:** Internships. **Corporate headquarters location:** This location. **Parent company:** Madison Square Garden, L.P.

ROUNDABOUT THEATRE COMPANY, INC.
231 West 39th Street, Suite 1200, New York NY 10018. 212/719-9393. **Fax:** 212/869-8817. **Contact:** Human Resources Department. **E-mail address:** jobs@roundabouttheatre.org. **World Wide Web address:** http://www.roundabouttheatre.org. **Description:** A theater presenting revivals of classic plays. Founded in 1965. **Positions advertised include:** Ticket Services Representative; Tele-Sales Representative. **Special programs:** Internships. **Number of employees at this location:** 50.

SHOWTIME NETWORKS INC.
1633 Broadway, New York NY 10019. 212/708-1600. **Contact:** Human Resources. **World Wide Web address:** http://www.mtv.com. **Description:** Operates a number of premium cable networks including SHOWTIME, SHO2, SHO3, Showtime Extreme, Showtime Beyond, The Movie Channel, The Movie Channel 2, Sundance, and FLIX. **Corporate headquarters location:** This location. **Parent company:** Viacom International Incorporated. **Listed on:** New York Stock Exchange. **Stock exchange symbol:** VIA.

SHUBERT ORGANIZATION, INC.
234 West 44th Street, 7th Floor, New York NY 10036. 212/944-3700. **Contact:** Human Resources. **World Wide Wedb address:** http://www.shubertorg.com. **Description:** Owns 16 Broadway theatres, the National Theatre in Washington DC, and the Shubert Theatre in Los Angeles CA. The Shubert Organization also produces plays. **Corporate headquarters location:** This location. **Operations at this facility include:** Administration; Sales. **President:** Phillip Smith. **Sales/revenue:** $325 million. **Number of employees nationwide:** 1,450.

SONY PICTURES ENTERTAINMENT
550 Madison Avenue, 7th Floor, New York NY 10022. 212/833-8500. **Fax:** 212/833-6249. **Contact:** Kathleen Alvarez, Human Resources Supervisor. **World Wide Web address:** http://www.sonypictures.com. **Description:** Sony Pictures is involved in motion pictures, television, theatrical exhibitions, and studio facilities and technology. The motion picture business distributes movies produced by Columbia TriStar Pictures. The television business, which encompasses Columbia TriStar Television, Columbia TriStar Television Distribution, and Columbia TriStar International Television, is involved with numerous cable channels and distributes and syndicates television programs such as *Days of Our Lives* and *Dawson's Creek*. Loews Cineplex Entertainment operates state-of-the-art theaters in 385 locations with 2,926 screens in 15 states. Sony Pictures Imageworks specializes in motion picture special effects and production planning through revisualization sequences. **Positions advertised include:** Administrative Assistant; Publicity Breaks Coordinator. **Special programs:** Internships. **Internship information:** Sony Pictures Entertainment offers various fall, spring, and summer internships in its Manhattan and Inwood, Long Island offices. Students must be available to work 15 to 21 hours per week. Majors in film, communications, management, and marketing are a plus, but all majors are welcome. Applicants must have basic office experience, excellent writing skills, and good interpersonal skills. Most internships are for academic credit, but some offer pay or a weekly stipend. **Office hours:** Monday – Friday, 9:00 a.m. – 5:00 p.m. **Corporate headquarters location:** Culver City CA. **Parent company:** Sony Corporation of America. **Operations at this facility include:** Administration; Sales. **Listed on:** New York Stock Exchange. **CEO/Chairman:** John Calley. **Sales/revenue:** $4.8 billion. **Stock exchange symbol:** SNE. **Number of employees at this location:** 100.

SOUTH STREET SEAPORT MUSEUM
207 Front Street, New York NY 10038. 212/748-8600. **Fax:** 212/748-8610. **Contact:** Director of Human Resources Department. **World Wide Web address:** http://www.southstseaport.org. **Description:** A maritime history museum. Through educational programs, exhibitions, and the preservation of buildings and ships, the museum interprets the role of the seaport in the development of the city, state, and nation. Founded in 1967. **Special programs:** Internships.

STATEN ISLAND INSTITUTE OF ARTS AND SCIENCES
75 Stuyvesant Place, Staten Island NY 10301. 718/727-1135. **Fax:** 718/273-5683. **Contact:** Human Resources. **Description:** An organization that focuses on Staten Island and its people with strong collections in arts and sciences. Founded in 1881.

TRANS-LUX CORPORATION
110 Richards Avenue, Norwalk CT 06854. 203/853-4321. **Contact:** Human Resources. **World Wide Web address:** http://www.trans-lux.com. **Description:** Designs, produces, leases, sells, and services large-scale, multicolor, real-time electronic information displays for both indoor and outdoor use. These displays are used primarily in applications for the financial, banking, gaming, corporate, retail, health care, transportation, and sports markets. The company also owns

an expanding chain of movie theaters in the western region of the United States and owns real estate in the United States and Canada. **Positions advertised include:** Controller. **Corporate headquarters location:** This location. **International locations:** Australia; Canada. **Subsidiaries include:** Trans-Lux Fair-Play; Trans-Lux Sports; Trans-Lux West. **Listed on:** American Stock Exchange. **Stock exchange symbol:** TLX.

USA INTERACTIVE
152 West 57th Street, New York NY 10019. 212/314-7300. **Contact:** Human Resources. **World Wide Web address:** http://www.usainteractive.com. **Description:** An e-commerce and entertainment company operating one of the nation's largest cable television networks. **Corporate headquarters location:** This location.

UNIVERSAL MUSIC GROUP
825 Eighth Avenue, 28th Floor, New York NY 10019. 212/333-8000. **Contact:** Human Resources. **World Wide Web address:** http://www.universalstudios.com/music. **Description:** Produces and markets popular and classical records and is active in the areas of film development, production, and distribution, as well as event television, video theater, merchandising, touring, and music publishing. **Subsidiaries include:** MCA; Universal Concerts. **Parent company:** The Seagram Company Ltd.

WARNER BROS. INC.
1325 Avenue of the Americas, 31st Floor, New York NY 10019. 212/636-5000. **Contact:** Department of Human Resources. **World Wide Web address:** http://www.warnerbros.com. **Description:** Offices of the diversified entertainment company. **Parent company:** AOL Time Warner. **Listed on:** New York Stock Exchange. **Stock exchange symbol:** AOL.

WILDLIFE CONSERVATION SOCIETY (WCS)
BRONX ZOO
2300 Southern Boulevard, Bronx NY 10460. 718/220-5100. **Fax:** 718/220-2464. **Contact:** Mariam Benitez, Human Resources Director. **E-mail address:** hr@wcs.org. **World Wide Web address:** http://www.wcs.org/home/zoos/bronxzoo. **Description:** Operates the Aquarium for Wildlife Conservation, the Bronx Zoo, the Central Park Wildlife Center, the Prospect Park Wildlife Center, and the Queens Wildlife Center. Wildlife Conservation Society (WCS) also manages the St. Catherine Wildlife Survival Center off the coast of Georgia and nearly 300 international field projects in over 50 nations. Additionally, WCS conducts environmental education programs at local, national, and international levels. **Office hours:** Monday - Friday, 9:00 a.m. - 5:00 p.m.

WILLIAM MORRIS AGENCY, INC.
1325 6th Avenue, New York NY 10019. 212/903-1110. **Fax:** 212/903-1474. **Contact:** Human Resources. **World Wide Web address:** http://www.wma.com. **Description:** One of the largest talent and literary agencies in the world. Founded in 1898. **Positions advertised include:** Agent Trainee. **Special programs:** Training. **Corporate headquarters location:** Beverly Hills CA. **Other U.S. locations:** Nashville TN. **Operations at this facility include:** Regional Headquarters. **Number of employees at this location:** 200. **Number of employees nationwide:** 700. **Number of employees worldwide:** 750.

WORLD WRESTLING FEDERATION ENTERTAINMENT, INC.
1241 East Main Street, P.O. Box 3857, Stamford CT 06902. 203/352-8600. **Contact:** Human Resources. **World Wide Web address:** http://www.wwe.com. **Description:** Develops and markets television programming and pay-per-view broadcasting for the World Wrestling Federation. The company also produces

and manages live wrestling events. **Positions advertised include:** Director of Internal Audit; Director of Job Notification. **Special Programs:** Internships. **Corporate headquarters location:** This location.

YONKERS RACEWAY
810 Central Park Avenue, Yonkers NY 10704. 914/968-4200. **Fax:** 914/968-1121. **Contact:** Anita Tripo, Director of Personnel. **World Wide Web address:** http://www.yonkersraceway.com. **Description:** Operates a major harness racing facility, as well as a convention and meeting facility. **Corporate headquarters location:** This location.

AUTOMOTIVE

You can expect to find the following types of companies in this section:
Automotive Repair Shops • Automotive Stampings • Industrial Vehicles and Moving Equipment • Motor Vehicles and Equipment • Travel Trailers and Campers

---

ARLEN CORPORATION
505 Eighth Avenue, Suite 300, New York NY 10018. 212/736-8100. **Contact:** Human Resources. **Description:** Manufactures and distributes steering wheels, physical security devices, interior accessories, and composite plastic and acrylic molded styling accessories for the automotive aftermarket and for automotive and marine original equipment manufacturers. The company also manufactures and distributes metal trim and accessories for the light-truck and sport-utility market.

AUDIOVOX CORPORATION
150 Marcus Boulevard, Hauppauge NY 11788. 631/231-7750. **Fax:** 631/231-2968. **Contact:** Human Resources. **E-mail address:** employment@audiovox.com. **World Wide Web address:** http://www.audiovox.com. **Description:** Engaged in the sale and distribution of a variety of automotive electronic components including car radios, speakers, alarm systems, and cellular phones. **Positions advertised include:** Returns Clerk; Parts Clerk; Warehouse Clerk; Assembler; Project Engineers; Security Products Project Engineer; Video Products Project Engineer. **Special programs:** Internships. **Corporate headquarters location:** This location. **Other U.S. locations:** CA; FL; GA; IL; KY; LA; NC; OH; PA; SC; TN; VA. **Subsidiaries include:** Quintex Mobile Communications. **Operations at this facility include:** Administration; Divisional Headquarters; Regional Headquarters; Research and Development; Sales; Service. **Listed on:** NASDAQ. **Stock exchange symbol:** VOXXE. **Number of employees at this location:** 350. **Number of employees nationwide:** 1,000.

BMW OF NORTH AMERICA, INC.
P.O. Box 964, Hewitt NJ 07461. 201/307-4000. **Physical address:** 300 Chestnut Ridge Road, Woodcliff Lake NJ 07675. **Contact:** Employment Manager. **E-mail address:** bmwna@hreasy.com. **World Wide Web address:** http://www.bmwusa.com. **Description:** BMW of North America is responsible for U.S. marketing operations for BMW's extensive line of motorcycles and automobiles. **Parent company:** BMW-Bayerische Motoren Werke AG (Munich, Germany).

FORD MOTOR COMPANY
698 U.S. Highway 46, Teterboro NJ 07608. 201/288-9421. **Contact:** Human Resources Manager. **World Wide Web address:** http://www.ford.com/careercenter. **Description:** Ford is engaged in the manufacture, assembly, and sale of cars, trucks, and related parts and accessories. Ford is also one of the largest providers of financial services in the United States. The company's two core businesses are the Automotive Group and the Financial Services Group (Ford Credit, The Associates, USL Capital, and First Nationwide). Ford is also engaged in a number of other businesses, including electronics, glass, electrical and fuel-handling products, plastics, climate control systems, automotive service and replacement parts, vehicle leasing and rental, and land development. **Corporate headquarters location:** Dearborn MI. **Operations at this facility include:** This location is a parts

distribution center. **Listed on:** New York Stock Exchange. **Stock exchange symbol:** F.

KEM MANUFACTURING COMPANY INC.

18-35 River Road, Fair Lawn NJ 07410. 201/796-8000. **Toll-free phone:** 800/536-5366. **Fax:** 201/796-3277. **Contact:** Personnel. **World Wide Web address:** http://www.kemparts.com. **Description:** Manufactures and markets a wide range of products for distribution to the automotive aftermarket. KEM also produces Perfect Part, a complete general service line. **Corporate headquarters location:** This location. **Operations at this facility include:** Manufacturing.

MERCEDES-BENZ USA, LLC

1 Mercedes Drive, Montvale NJ 07645. 201/573-0600. **Fax:** 201/573-6791. **Contact:** Human Resources. **E-mail address:** careers@mbusa.com. **World Wide Web address:** http://www.mercedesbenzcareers.com. **Description:** An importer of the complete line of Mercedes-Benz automobiles and related components. Mercedes-Benz of North America distributes Mercedes products to dealers throughout the United States. **Corporate headquarters location:** This location. **Parent company:** DaimlerChrysler. **Operations at this facility include:** Administration. **Number of employees nationwide:** 1,500.

MERIDIAN AUTOMOTIVE SYSTEMS, INC.

203 North Street, Canandaigua NY 14424-1096. 585/394-3680. **Contact:** Personnel. **World Wide Web address:** http://www.meridianautosystems.com. **Description:** Manufactures interior trim panels for the automotive industry, as well as blowmolded and injection molded plastic components for cars and trucks. **Company slogan:** Where Solutions Take Shape. **Corporate headquarters location:** Dearborn MI. **Other U.S. locations:** Nationwide. **International locations:** Worldwide. **Annual sales/revenues:** $977. **Number of employees:** 5,900.

STANDARD MOTOR PRODUCTS INC.

37-18 Northern Boulevard, Long Island City NY 11101. 718/392-0200. **Contact:** Recruiting. **World Wide Web address:** http://www.smpcorp.com. **Description:** Engaged primarily in the manufacture of electrical and fuel system automotive replacement parts sold internationally under the Standard Blue Streak, Hygrade, Champ, and Four Seasons brand names. Products include ignition parts, automotive wire and cable parts, carburetor parts and kits, general service auto parts (radio antennas, gasoline cans, brooms and brushes, polishing cloths, fuses, and other auto accessories), and automotive heating and air conditioning systems. **Corporate headquarters location:** This location. **International locations:** Canada; Hong Kong; Puerto Rico. **Listed on:** New York Stock Exchange. **Stock exchange symbol:** SMP. **Number of employees worldwide:** 3,500.

VOLVO CARS OF NORTH AMERICA, INC.

7 Volvo Drive, Rockleigh NJ 07647. 201/768-7300. **Contact:** Human Resources. **World Wide Web address:** http://www.volvo.com. **Description:** Supports the sale and service of Volvo automobiles and related parts and accessories for approximately 400 dealers. **Corporate headquarters location:** This location.

BANKING, SAVINGS & LOANS, AND OTHER DEPOSITORY INSTITUTIONS

You can expect to find the following types of companies in this section:
Banks • Bank Holding Companies and Associations • Lending Firms/Financial Services Institutions

---

APPLE BANK FOR SAVINGS
122 East 42nd Street, New York NY 10168. 212/224-6400. **Toll-free phone:** 800/722-6888. **Fax:** 212/224-6592. **Contact:** Human Resources. **World Wide Web address:** http://www.theapplebank.com. **Description:** Operates a full-service savings bank serving New York City, Long Island, and Westchester with a total of 46 branches. Founded in 1836. **NOTE:** Entry-level positions are offered. **Positions advertised include:** Mortgage Underwriter; Bank Teller; Assistant Manager; Customer Service Representative. **Corporate headquarters location:** This location. **Other locations:** Greater New York City metropolitan area. **Number of employees at this location:** 900.

ASTORIA FEDERAL SAVINGS BANK
1150 Franklin Avenue, Garden City NY 11530. 516/746-0700. **Contact:** Human Resources. **E-mail address:** hr@astoriafederal.com. **World Wide Web address:** http://www.astoriafederal.com. **Description:** Provides a full range of banking and related financial services. **NOTE:** Hiring is conducted through the parent company. Interested jobseekers should address all inquiries to Manager of Human Resources, Astoria Financial Corporation, One Astoria Federal Plaza, Lake Success NY 11042-1085. **Positions advertised include:** Assistant Bank Office Manager; Teller. **Parent company:** Astoria Federal Savings & Loan Association (Lake Success NY).

ASTORIA FEDERAL SAVINGS BANK
451 Fifth Avenue, Brooklyn NY 11215. 718/965-7500. **Contact:** Human Resources Department. **E-mail address:** hr@astoriafederal.com. **World Wide Web address:** http://www.astoriafederal.com. **Description:** A savings bank offering a complete range of traditional banking and mortgage services. **NOTE:** Hiring is conducted through the parent company. Interested jobseekers should address all inquiries to Manager of Human Resources, Astoria Financial Corporation, One Astoria Federal Plaza, Lake Success NY 11042-1085. **Positions advertised include:** Assistant Bank Office Manager; Teller. **Parent company:** Astoria Federal Savings & Loan Association (Lake Success NY).

ASTORIA FINANCIAL CORPORATION
ASTORIA FEDERAL SAVINGS & LOAN ASSOCIATION
One Astoria Federal Plaza, Lake Success NY 11042-1085. 516/327-3000. **Toll-free phone:** 800/ASTORIA. **Fax:** 516/327-7610. **Contact:** Recruiting. **E-mail address:** hr@astoriafederal.com. **World Wide Web address:** http://www.astoriafederal.com. **Description:** AFC is the holding company for the Astoria Federal Savings and Loan Association operating 100 branches in the New York City metropolitan region as well as originating mortgages in the Northeast. The company offers complete banking services including offering CDs; checking, savings, and money market accounts; and NOW accounts. Founded in 1888. **NOTE:** See website for employment open house schedules. **Positions advertised include:** Internal Auditor; Assistant Banking Office Manager; Bank Office Manager; Personal Banker; Teller; Operations Supervisor; Telephone Banking Specialist. **Corporate headquarters location:** This location.

Subsidiaries include: A.F. Insurance Agency; Astoria Federal Savings & Loan Association. **Listed on:** NASDAQ; New York Stock Exchange. **Stock exchange symbol:** ASFC; AF. **Chairman/President/CEO:** George L. Engelke, Jr. **Annual sales/revenues:** $1.4 billion. **Number of employees at this location:** 400. **Number of employees nationwide:** 2,000.

BANK OF AMERICA
New Fairfield Shopping Center, Route 37 & 39, New Fairfield CT 06812. 203/746-2596. **Contact:** Maureen Foley, Human Resources. **World Wide Web address:** http://www.bankofamerica.com. **Description:** A full-service banking institution. Along with general banking services, Bank of America performs services such as accounting, auditing, marketing, business development, insurance, operational, tax, investment, and personnel administration. **Corporate headquarters location:** Charlotte NC. **Parent company:** Bank of America. **Listed on:** New York Stock Exchange. **Stock exchange symbol:** BAC.

BANK OF AMERICA
69 State Street, Albany, NY 12207. 518/447-4300. **Fax:** 518/626-2554. **Contact:** Human Resources. **World Wide Web address:** http://www.bankofamerica.com. **Description:** The bank provides commercial and consumer banking services to individuals, corporations, institutions, and governments of the Genesee, Finger Lakes, Southern Tier, and western regions of upstate New York. **NOTE:** Applications accepted online through the company Website. **Positions advertised include:** Emerging Markets/Outside Loan Officer; Applications Development Analyst; Infrastructure Specialist; Senior Relation Manager; Large Government Account Officer; Associate Staff Auditor; Technical Project Analyst; Infrastructure Engineer. **Corporate headquarters location:** Charlotte NC. **Other U.S. locations:** Nationwide.

BANK OF AMERICA
29 Broadway, New York NY 10004. 212/563-7625. **Contact:** Human Resources. **World Wide Web address:** http://www.bankofamerica.com. **Description:** A nationwide securities brokerage firm serving retail customers and institutional investors. **Positions advertised include:** Personal Financial Consultant; Investment Center Manager. **Other U.S. locations:** Nationwide.

BANK OF NEW YORK
385 Rifle Camp Road, West Paterson NJ 07424. 973/357-7405. **Contact:** Personnel. **World Wide Web address:** http://www.bankofny.com. **Description:** A bank that serves individuals, corporations, foreign and domestic banks, governments, and other institutions through banking offices in New York City and foreign branches, representative offices, subsidiaries, and affiliates. **Positions advertised include:** Teller; Training & Development Specialist; Personal Banking Representative. **Corporate headquarters location:** New York NY. **Parent company:** Bank of New York Company, Inc. **Listed on:** New York Stock Exchange. **Stock exchange symbol:** BK. **Number of employees nationwide:** 12,000.

BANK OF NEW YORK
101 Barclay Street, Floor 1-E, New York NY 10286. 212/815-4984. **Contact:** Human Resources. **World Wide Web address:** http://www.bankofny.com. **Description:** A bank that serves individuals, corporations, foreign and domestic banks, governments, and other institutions through banking offices in New York City and foreign branches, representative offices, subsidiaries, and affiliates. **Corporate headquarters location:** New York NY. **Parent company:** The Bank of New York Company, Inc. (New York NY). **Number of employees nationwide:** 12,000.

BANK OF NEW YORK
One Wall Street, 13th Floor, New York NY 10286. 212/635-6790. **Fax:** 212/809-9528. **Contact:** Human Resources. **World Wide Web address:** http://www.bankofny.com. **Description:** A bank that serves individuals, corporations, foreign and domestic banks, governments, and other institutions through banking offices in New York City and foreign branches, representative offices, subsidiaries, and affiliates. **Special programs:** Internships. **Corporate headquarters location:** This location. **Parent company:** Bank of New York Company, Inc. (also at this location). **Number of employees nationwide:** 12,000.

BANK OF TOKYO MITSUBISHI
1251 Sixth Avenue, New York NY 10020-1104. 212/782-4000. **Fax:** 782-6415. **Contact:** Human Resources. **World Wide Web address:** http://www.btmny.com. **Description:** One of the 50 largest commercial banks in the United States. The company operates five offices throughout the New York metropolitan area, as well as in London and the Bahamas. **Corporate headquarters location:** This location. **Parent company:** The Bank of Tokyo Ltd. (Tokyo, Japan).

BARCLAYS BANK PLC
222 Broadway, 10th Floor, New York NY 10038. 212/412-4000. **Contact:** Human Resources. **World Wide Web address:** http://www.barclays.com. **Description:** An international banking institution with more than 5,000 offices in 60 countries including most international trade centers. International banking services include commercial loans, foreign exchange services, drafts and money transfers, foreign collections, leasing, stock and security custodial services, and economic information and publications. Barclays Bank also operates a global investment bank through its BZW Group subsidiary. **Parent company:** Barclays plc (London, United Kingdom). **Corporate headquarters location:** London, United Kingdom. **Other U.S. locations:** San Francisco CA.

BRIDGE BANCORP, INC.
dba BRIDGEHAMPTON NATIONAL BANK
2200 Montauk Highway, P.O. Box 3005, Bridgehampton NY 11932-3005. 631/537-1001 ext. 297. **Contact:** Deborah McGrory, Human Resources Officer. **E-mail address:** dmcgror@bridgenb.com. **World Wide Web address:** http://www.bridgenb.com. **Description:** A bank holding company engaged in commercial banking through wholly owned subsidiary Bridgehampton National Bank operating full-service banking offices located on Eastern Long Island, as well as a residential mortgage and loan center. Founded in 1910. **Positions advertised include:** Credit Analyst; Loan and Credit Assistant; Loan Representative; Customer Service Representative; Teller; Accounts Payable Staff Accountant; Electrical Delivery Systems Assistant. **Listed on:** Over The Counter. **Stock exchange symbol:** BDGE. **Annual sales/revenues:** $26.5 million. **Number of employees:** 115.

CITIBANK (NEW YORK STATE)
One EAB Plaza, Uniondale NY 11555. 516/627-3999. **Contact:** Human Resources. **World Wide Web address:** http://www.citibank.com. **Description:** A full-service commercial bank offering a range of services through more than 80 branch banking offices in metropolitan New York and Long Island. **Positions advertised include:** Wire & Proof Clerk; Consumer Markets Group Relationship Manager; Loan Administrator; Senior Unit Manager; Financial Associate; Teller; Sales Relationship Manager; Financial Center Operations Manager; Financial Executive; Mortgage Specialist; Client Financial Analyst; Business Banking Officer; Financial Center Manager; Branch Manager; Small Business Manager. **Parent company:** Citigroup, Inc. (New York NY).

CITIBANK, N.A.
399 Park Avenue, New York NY 10043-0001. 212/559-1000. **Contact:** Search and Staffing. **World Wide Web address:** http://www.citibank.com. **Description:** Operates a global, full-service consumer franchise encompassing branch banking, credit and charge cards, and private banking. In branch banking, Citibank services almost 20 million accounts in 41 countries and territories. In global card products, Citibank is one of the world's largest bankcard and charge card issuers. In addition, Citibank issues and services approximately 5 million private-label cards for department stores and retail outlets. Citibank Private Bank offices in 31 countries and territories provide a full-range of wealth management services and serve as a window that gives clients access to the full range of Citibank's global capabilities. **Positions advertised include:** Financial Associate; Teller; Financial Center Manager; Branch Manager; Business Banking Officer; Litigation Support Specialist; Service Officer. **Parent company:** Citigroup, Inc. (New York NY).

DIME COMMUNITY BANCSHARES, INC.
dba SAVINGS BANK OF WILLIAMSBURGH
209 Havemeyer Street, Brooklyn NY 11211. 718/782-6200 ext. 8308. **Fax:** 718/486-8793. **Contact:** Human Resources. **World Wide Web address:** http://www.dimewill.com. **Description:** Through its main subsidiary, the company operates a full-service bank with 20 branches serving the Bronx, Brooklyn, Queens, and Nassau County offering deposit options including CDs, savings, checking, NOW, and money market accounts as well as mortgages. **Subsidiaries include:** Havemeyer Investments; Dime Savings Bank of Williamsburg. **Listed on:** NASDAQ. **Stock exchange symbol:** DCOM. **Chairman/CEO:** Vincent F. Palagiano. **Annual sales/revenues:** $200 million. **Number of employees:** 365.

EMIGRANT SAVINGS BANK
5 East 42nd Street, New York NY 10017. 212/850-4000. **Fax:** 212/850-4372. **Contact:** Human Resources. **E-mail address:** employment@emigrant.com. **World Wide Web address:** http://www.emigrant.com. **Description:** Offers a wide range of traditional banking services. Emigrant Savings Bank has 36 branches in Manhattan, Brooklyn, and Queens, as well as in Nassau, Suffolk, and Westchester Counties. Founded in 1850. **Positions advertised include:** Teller. **NOTE:** Human Resources phone: 212/850-4888. **Corporate headquarters location:** This location. **Other locations:** Throughout New York metropolitan area. **Subsidiaries/affiliates include:** Emigrant Mortgage Company; Emigrant Funding Corporation; American Property Financing, Inc.; Emigrant Business Credit Corporation. **Parent company:** Emigrant Bancorp (also at this location).

FIRST OF LONG ISLAND CORPORATION
30 Glen Head Road, Glen Head NY 11545-1411. 516/671-4900. **Fax:** 516/671-3971. **Contact:** Debra Ryan, Human Resources. **E-mail address:** humres@optonline.net. **World Wide Web address:** http://www.fnbli.com. **Description:** First of Long Island Corporation is the holding company for First National Bank of Long Island, a full-service commercial bank that provides a broad range of financial services to individual, professional, corporate, institutional, and government customers through its 20 branches in Nassau and Suffolk counties. **Subsidiaries include:** First National Bank of Long Island; First of Long Island Agency sells insurance, primarily fixed-annuity products. Founded in 1927. **Listed on:** NASDAQ. **Stock exchange symbol:** FLIC. **Chairman/President/CEO/Director:** J. William Johnson. **Annual sales/revenues:** $42.5 million. **Number of employees:** 187.

GREATER COMMUNITY BANCORP
2 Sears Drive, Paramus NJ 07653. 973/942-1111. **Contact:** Human Resources. **World Wide Web address:** http://www.greatercommunity.com. **Description:** A holding company. **Subsidiaries include:** Greater Community Bank conducts general commercial and retail banking. **Listed on:** NASDAQ. **Stock exchange symbol:** GFLS.

GREENPOINT FINANCIAL CORP.
90 Park Avenue, New York NY 10016-1303. 212/834-1000. **Fax:** 212/834-1404. **Contact:** Human Resources. **World Wide Web address:** http://www.greenpoint.com. **Description:** A holding company operating 80 bank branches in the New York metropolitan area through its main subsidiary, GreenPoint Bank. The bank offers full-service banking products including consumer and insurance services in New York and services mortgages nationwide as well as offering real estate loans to low-income customers. **Positions advertised include:** Assistant Branch Manager; Branch Manager; Business Banking Specialist; Customer Service Representative; Building Services Maintenance Person; Sales Representative; Senior Business Banking Specialist; Senior Risk Analyst; Portfolio Originations Analyst. **Other area locations:** Albertson NY; Brooklyn NY; Great Neck NY; Hicksville NY; Kew Gardens NY; Ridgewood NY; Sunnyside NY. **Corporate headquarters location:** This location. **Subsidiaries include:** GreenPoint Bank; GreenPoint Mortgage Funding; GreenPoint Community Development. **Listed on:** New York Stock Exchange. **Stock exchange symbol:** GPT. **Chairman/CEO:** Thomas S. Johnson. **Annual sales/revenues:** $1.8 billion. **Number of employees:** 4,755.

HSBC BANK USA
452 Fifth Avenue, 12th Floor, New York NY 10018. 212/525-5000. **Fax:** 877/525-7575. **Recorded jobline:** 888/HRHELP4 (888/474-3574). **Contact:** HR Resourcing. **World Wide Web address:** http://www.us.hsbc.com. **Description:** A full-service bank with 400 branches in New York and operations in California, Pennsylvania, Florida, and Panama offering personal, commercial, and both residential and commercial mortgages and loans. The bank's investment products include mutual funds, wealth management services, a discount brokerage, and insurance. **Positions advertised include:** Senior Collateral Examination Officer; Senior Information Technology Audit Officer; Branch Customer Service Representative; Branch Manager; Consumer Banker; Personal Banking Officer. **Corporate headquarters location:** This location. **Other area locations:** Statewide. **locations:** CA; PA; FL. **International locations:** Panama. **Parent company:** HSBC Holdings plc. (London, United Kingdom). **Chairman:** Sir John R. H. Bond. **Annual sales/revenues:** $4.9 billion. **Number of employees:** 14,000.

HUDSON CITY SAVINGS BANK
West 80 Century Road, Paramus NJ 07652. 201/967-1900. **Fax:** 201/967-0332. **Contact:** Human Resources. **World Wide Web address:** http://www.hudsoncitysavingsbank.com. **Description:** Operates a full-service mutual savings bank with 80 branches in Bergen, Burlington, Camden, Essex, Gloucester, Hudson, Middlesex, Monmouth, Morris, Ocean, Passaic, and Union Counties. Hudson City Savings Bank provides a wide range of traditional banking services, as well as other financial services including IRAs. **Positions advertised include:** Teller; Clerk.

HUDSON UNITED BANK
1500 Route 202, Harding Township NJ 07920. 973/425-3000. **Contact:** Human Resources. **E-mail address:** career@hudsonunitedbank.com. **World Wide Web address:** http://www.hudsonunitedbank.com. **Description:** A full-service bank. **Positions advertised include:** Branch Manager; Sales Associate; Assistant Branch Manager; Administrative Assistant; Call Center Representative; Branch

Sales Manager; Teller; Marketing Representative. **NOTE:** Positions posted on Monster.com. Please send resumes to 1000 MacArthur Boulevard, Mahwah NJ 07430. **Corporate headquarters location:** This location.

INDEPENDENCE COMMUNITY BANK
7500 Fifth Avenue, Brooklyn NY 11209. 718/745-6100. **Contact:** Human Resources Director. **World Wide Web address:** http://www.icbny.com. **Description:** A savings bank that offers a wide range of traditional banking services as well as specialized financial services, loans, and insurance services through 70 full-service branches serving the New York City metropolitan region. **Positions advertised include:** Assistant Branch Manager; Customer Service Representative. **Corporate headquarters location:** Brooklyn NY. **Other locations:** Brooklyn NY; Queens NY; Long Island NY; New Jersey. **Listed on:** NASDAQ. **Stock exchange symbol:** ICBC. **Chairman:** Charles J. Hamm. **Annual sales/revenues:** $550 million. **Number of employees:** 1,373.

INDEPENDENCE COMMUNITY BANK CORP.
195 Montague Street, Brooklyn NY 11201. 718/722-5300. **Fax:** 718/722-5319. **Contact:** Human Resources Director. **World Wide Web address:** http://www.icbny.com. **Description:** A savings bank that offers a wide range of traditional banking services as well as specialized financial services, loans, and insurance services through 70 full-service branches serving the New York City metropolitan region. **Positions advertised include:** Assistant Branch Manager; Branch Manager; Customer Service Representative; Head Teller; Safe Deposit Attendant; Teller; Mortgage Loan Processor; Mortgage Servicer; Levy and Subpoena Representative. **Corporate headquarters location:** This location. **Other locations:** Brooklyn NY; Queens NY; Long Island NY; New Jersey. **Listed on:** NASDAQ. **Stock exchange symbol:** ICBC. **Chairman:** Charles J. Hamm. **Annual sales/revenues:** $550 million. **Number of employees:** 1,373.

INTERCHANGE BANK
Park 80 West/Plaza 2, Saddle Brook NJ 07663. 201/703-2265. **Fax:** 201/703-5291. **Contact:** Human Resources. **E-mail address:** humanresources@interchangebank.com. **World Wide Web address:** http://www.interchangebank.com. **Description:** A full-service bank with locations throughout Bergen County. **Positions advertised include:** Administrative Assistant; Assistant Branch Manager; Business Development Officer; Commercial Lender; Customer Services Representative; General Auditor; Investment Advisor;; Loan Operations Manager; Loan Service Associate; Mortgage Originator; Claims Specialist; Retail Branch Manager; Teller. **Parent company:** Interchange Financial Services Corporation. **Listed on:** NASDAQ. **Stock exchange symbol:** IFCJ.

LEUCADIA NATIONAL CORPORATION
315 Park Avenue South, New York NY 10010. 212/460-1900. **Fax:** 212/598-4869. **Contact:** Laura E. Ulbrandt, Human Resources. **Description:** Leucadia National is a diversified holding company with subsidiaries with interests in over 30 companies involved in the insurance, manufacturing, banking, investments, and real estate industries. The insurance business offers property, casualty, and life insurance nationwide. **Corporate headquarters location:** This location. **Subsidiaries include:** Allcity Insurance; American Investment Bank, N.A.; American Investment Financial; Charter, CPL; Empire Insurance Group; Intramerica; MK Gold Company. **Listed on:** New York Stock Exchange. **Stock exchange symbol:** LUK. **Chairman:** Iam M. Cumming. **Annual sales/revenues:** $297 million. **Number of employees:** 1,066.

M&T BANK
350 Park Avenue, 5th Floor, New York NY 10022. 212/350-2000. **Contact:** Human Resources Department. **World Wide Web address:**

http://www.mandtbank.com. **Description:** A full-service savings bank providing cooperative apartment loans, home improvement loans, mortgage loans, pension plans, retirement accounts, life insurance, student loans, and other traditional banking services. **Positions advertised include:** Senior Commercial Real Estate Representative; Account Representative; Branch Sales Associate; Assistant Branch Manager; Property Manager; Branch Manager. **Corporate headquarters location:** Buffalo NY. **Listed on:** New York Stock Exchange. **Stock exchange symbol:** MTB. **Chairman/President/CEO:** Robert G. Wilmers. **Annual sales/revenues:** $2.3 billion. **Number of employees:** 9,197.

NORTH FORK BANCORPORATION, INC.
NORTH FORK BANK
275 Broad Hollow Road, Melville NY 11747. 631/844-1000. **Contact:** Human Resources. **World Wide Web address:** http://www.northforkbank.com. **Description:** A commercial bank holding company. The principal subsidiary, North Fork Bank (also at this location), is one of the largest independent commercial banks headquartered on Long Island. **Corporate headquarters location:** This location. **Listed on:** New York Stock Exchange. **Stock exchange symbol:** NFB. **President/CEO/Chairman:** John Adams Kanas.

PNC BANK
P.O. Box 6000, Bridgewater NJ 08807. 908/429-2200. **Physical address:** 1130 Route 22 East, Bridgewater NJ 08807. **Fax:** 908/707-8329. **Contact:** Human Resources Department. **World Wide Web address:** http://www.pncbank.com. **Description:** Operates a full-service commercial bank offering a wide range of traditional banking, trust, and other financial services. **Corporate headquarters location:** This location.

PATRIOT NATIONAL BANK
900 Bedford Street, Stamford CT 06901. 203/324-7500. **Fax:** 203/316-2983. **Contact:** Human Resources. **World Wide Web address:** http://www.pnbdirectonline.com. **Description:** A full-service banking institution offering a broad range of consumer and commercial banking services. Founded in 1994. **Corporate headquarters location:** This location. **Other area locations:** Greenwich CT; Norwalk CT; Old Greenwich CT.

RIDGEWOOD SAVINGS BANK
71-02 Forest Avenue, Ridgewood NY 11385. 718/240-4800. **Contact:** Human Resources Representative. **World Wide Web address:** http://www.ridgewoodbank.com. **Description:** A full-service savings bank. **Corporate headquarters location:** This location. **Other area locations:** Statewide. **Operations at this facility include:** Administration; Service. **Number of employees at this location:** 550.

ROSLYN SAVINGS BANK
One Jericho North Plaza, Jericho NY 11753. 516/942-6000. **Contact:** Human Resources. **World Wide Web address:** http://www.roslyn.com. **Description:** Operates a full-service mutual savings bank. Roslyn Savings offers a full range of commercial and savings bank services through 12 offices including locations in Brooklyn, Queens, Deer Park, and Nassau County. Founded in 1895. **Corporate headquarters location:** This location. **Parent company:** Roslyn Bancorp Inc. **Listed on:** NASDAQ. **Stock exchange symbol:** RSLN.

THE ROYAL BANK OF CANADA
165 Broadway, New York NY 10006. 212/428-6200. **Contact:** Human Resources. **World Wide Web address:** http://www.royalbank.com. **Description:** One of North America's largest banks. **Parent company:** RBC Financial Group. **Listed on:** New York Stock Exchange. **Stock exchange symbol:** RY. **President/CEO:** Gordon M. Nixon.

STERLING NATIONAL BANK & TRUST COMPANY
148 West 37th Street, New York NY 10018. 212/760-9610. **Fax:** 212/490-8852. **Contact:** Human Resources. **E-mail address:** hrresumes@sterlingbancorp.com. **World Wide Web address:** http://www.sterlingbancorp.com. **Description:** A full-service commercial bank offering a complete range of corporate and individual services. **Corporate headquarters location:** This location. **Parent company:** Sterling Bancorp. **Listed on:** New York Stock Exchange. **Stock exchange symbol:** STL.

SUFFOLK BANCORP
P.O. Box 9000, 6 West Second Street, Riverhead NY 11901. 631/727-2700. **Contact:** Human Resources. **E-mail address:** info@scnb.com. **World Wide Web address:** http://www.suffolkbancorp.com. **Description:** Suffolk Bancorp is engaged in the commercial banking business through its subsidiary, Suffolk County National Bank. The bank is one of the largest independent banks headquartered on Long Island. Founded in 1890. **Subsidiaries include:** Island Computer Corporation.

TD WATERHOUSE SECURITIES, INC.
100 Wall Street, New York NY 10005. 212/806-3500. **Contact:** Human Resources. **E-mail address:** careers@tdwaterhouse.com. **World Wide Web address:** http://www.tdwaterhouse.com. **Description:** TD Waterhouse Securities, Inc. provides brokerage and banking services for individuals that manage their own investments and financial affairs. **Positions advertised include:** Surveillance Manager; Institutional Sales Representative; Credit Analyst; Investment Consultant. **Corporate headquarters location:** This location. **Other U.S. locations:** Nationwide. **Parent company:** TD Waterhouse Investor Services. **Operations at this facility include:** Administration; Divisional Headquarters; Regional Headquarters; Service. **Listed on:** New York Stock Exchange. **Number of employees at this location:** 250. **Number of employees nationwide:** 800.

TRUST COMPANY BANK
35 Journal Square, Jersey City NJ 07306. 973/442-9131. **Toll-free phone:** 800/233-BANK. **Contact:** Human Resources. **E-mail address:** humanresources@tcofnj.com. **World Wide Web address:** http://www.tcofnj.com. **Description:** A bank serving New Jersey. **Company Slogan:** The bank with heart since 1896. **Positions advertised include:** Teller. **Office hours:** Monday – Friday, 8:00 a.m. – 5:30 p.m. **Listed on:** NASDAQ. **Stock Exchange Symbol:** TCNJ. **President:** Alan Wilzig.

U.S. FEDERAL RESERVE BANK OF NEW YORK
33 Liberty Street, New York NY 10045-0001. 212/720-5000. **Contact:** Human Resources. **World Wide Web address:** http://www.ny.frb.org. **Description:** One of 12 regional Federal Reserve banks that, along with the Federal Reserve Board in Washington DC and the Federal Open Market Committee, comprise the Federal Reserve System, the nation's central bank. Responsibilities include monetary policy, banking supervision and regulation, and processing payments. **Special programs:** Internships. **Other U.S. locations:** San Francisco CA; Washington DC; Atlanta GA; Chicago IL; Boston MA; Minneapolis MN; Kansas City MO; St. Louis MO; Cleveland OH; Philadelphia PA; Dallas TX; Richmond VA. **Operations at this facility include:** Administration; Regional Headquarters; Research and Development. **Number of employees at this location:** 3,200.

VALLEY NATIONAL BANK
1455 Valley Road, Wayne NJ 07470. 973/696-4020. **Contact:** Peter Verbout, Director of Human Resources. **World Wide Web address:** http://www.valleynationalbank.com. **Description:** Operates a commercial bank

offering a wide range of traditional banking services. **Positions advertised include:** Business Development Officer. **Corporate headquarters location:** This location. **Parent company:** Valley National Bancorp.

WACHOVIA BANK

One Maple Street, Summit NJ 07901. 908/277-7750. **Contact:** Human Resources. **World Wide Web address:** http://www.wachovia.com. **Description:** Wachovia is one of the nation's largest bank holding companies with subsidiaries that operate over 4,500 ATM's and over 1,330 full-service bank branches in the south Atlantic states. These subsidiaries provide retail banking, retail investment, and commercial banking services. The corporation provides other financial services including mortgage banking, home equity lending, leasing, insurance, and securities brokerage services. **Subsidiaries include:** CoreStates Financial Corporation; The Money Store, Inc. **Operations at this facility include:** Regional Headquarters. **Listed on:** New York Stock Exchange. **Stock exchange symbol:** WB. **Number of employees worldwide:** 87,000.

WACHOVIA BANK

120 Albany Street Plaza, New Brunswick NJ 08901. 732/843-4200. **Contact:** Human Resources. **World Wide Web address:** http://www.wachovia.com. **Description:** Wachovia is one of the nation's largest bank holding companies with subsidiaries that operate over 4,500 ATM's, and over 1,330 full-service bank branches in the south Atlantic states. These subsidiaries provide retail banking, retail investment, and commercial banking services. The corporation provides other financial services including mortgage banking, home equity lending, leasing, insurance, and securities brokerage services from more than 222 branch locations. **Listed on:** New York Stock Exchange. **Positions advertised include:** Loss Specialist; Cons Credit Decision Maker. **Stock exchange symbol:** WB. **Number of employees worldwide:** 87,000.

WACHOVIA CORPORATION

245 Main Street, White Plains NY 10601. 914/682-7416. **Recorded jobline:** 800/FUNHIRE. **Contact:** Human Resources. **World Wide Web address:** http://www.wachovia.com. **Description:** A bank. **Parent company:** Wachovia Corporation is one of the nation's largest bank holding companies with subsidiaries operating over 1,330 full-service bank branches in the south Atlantic states. **Corporate headquarters location:** Charlotte NC. **Listed on:** New York Stock Exchange. **Stock exchange symbol:** WB.

WASHINGTON MUTUAL, INC.

49 East Franklin Avenue, Hempstead NY 11550. 516/489-4801. **Contact:** Human Resources. **World Wide Web address:** http://www.wamu.com. **Description:** Washington Mutual, Inc. is a financial services company that, through its subsidiaries, engages in the following lines of business: consumer banking, mortgage banking, commercial banking, financial services and consumer finance. **Positions advertised include:** Project Coordinator; Loan Coordinator; Project Analyst; Mortgage Underwriter; Mortgage Loan Coordinator. **Corporate headquarters location:** Seattle WA. **Listed on:** New York Stock Exchange. **Stock exchange symbol:** WM.

WEBSTER BANK

2 National Place, Danbury CT 06810. 203/730-6366. **Contact:** Human Resources. **World Wide Web address:** http://www.websterbank.com. **Description:** Webster Bank is primarily involved in attracting deposits from the general public and investing these funds in mortgage loans for the purchase, construction, and refinancing of one- to four-family homes. Webster Bank also provides commercial banking services to businesses. **Corporate headquarters location:** Waterbury CT. **Parent company:** Webster Financial Corporation. **Listed on:** NASDAQ. **Stock exchange symbol:** WBST.

BIOTECHNOLOGY, PHARMACEUTICALS, AND SCIENTIFIC R&D

You can expect to find the following types of companies in this section:
Clinical Labs • Lab Equipment Manufacturers • Pharmaceutical Manufacturers and Distributors

---

ALPHARMA INC.
One Executive Drive, Fort Lee NJ 07024. 201/947-7774. **Toll-free phone:** 800/645-4216. **Fax:** 201/947-6145. **Contact:** Human Resources. **World Wide Web address:** http://www.alpharma.com. **Description:** A multinational pharmaceutical company that develops, manufactures, and markets specialty generic and proprietary human pharmaceuticals and animal health products. The U.S. Pharmaceuticals Division is a market leader in liquid pharmaceuticals and a prescription market leader in creams and ointments. The International Pharmaceuticals Division manufactures generic pharmaceuticals and OTC products. Other divisions include the Animal Health Division, which manufactures and markets antibiotics and other feed additives for the poultry and swine industries; the Aquatic Animal Health Division, which serves the aquaculture industry and is a manufacturer and marketer of vaccines for farmed fish; and the Fine Chemicals Division, which is a basic producer of specialty bulk antibiotics. **Corporate headquarters location:** This location. **Listed on:** New York Stock Exchange. **Stock exchange symbol:** ALO.

ALTEON INC.
170 Williams Drive, Ramsey NJ 07446. 201/934-5000. **Fax:** 201/934-0090. **Contact:** Human Resources Director. **E-mail address:** careers@alteon.com. **World Wide Web address:** http://www.alteonpharma.com. **Description:** A pharmaceutical company engaged in the discovery and development of novel therapeutic and diagnostic products for treating complications associated with diabetes and aging. **Positions advertised include:** Clinical Research Associate; Clinical Team Manager; Regulatory & Quality Assurance Manager. **Listed on:** American Stock Exchange. **Stock exchange symbol:** ALT.

AMERICAN STANDARDS TESTING BUREAU INC.
P.O. Box 583, New York NY 10274-0583. 212/943-3160. **Physical address:** 40 Water Street, New York NY 10004. **Toll-free phone:** 800/221-5170. **Fax:** 212/825-2250. **Contact:** John Zimmerman, Director, Professional Staffing. **Description:** Offers lab consulting and forensic services to the government and various industries. The company specializes in biotechnology, environmental sciences, forensics, engineering, failure analysis, and products liability. **Positions advertised include:** Aerospace Engineer; Biomedical Engineer; Chemical Engineer; Clerical Supervisor; Chemist; Environmental Engineer. **Corporate headquarters location:** This location. **Other U.S. locations:** Nationwide. **Operations at this facility include:** Administration; Divisional Headquarters; Research and Development; Sales. **Annual sales/revenues:** $50 million. **Number of employees at this location:** 430.

APPLERA CORPORATION
301 Merritt Seven, Norwalk CT 06856. 203/840-2000. **Toll-free phone:** 800/761-5381. **Fax:** 203/840-2410. **Contact:** Human Resources. **World Wide Web address:** http://www.applera.com. **Description:** A worldwide leader in the development, manufacture, and distribution of analytical and life science systems used in environmental technology, pharmaceuticals, biotechnology, chemicals,

plastics, food, agriculture, and scientific research. Founded in 1937. **Positions advertised include:** Financial Analyst; Associate Benefits Administrator; Design Specialist; Travel Specialist. **Corporate headquarters location:** This location. **Subsidiaries include:** Applied Biosystems; Celera Genomics; Celera Diagnostics. **Listed on:** New York Stock Exchange. **Stock exchange symbol:** ABI.

AVENTIS PHARMACEUTICALS
200-400 Crossing Boulevard, Bridgewater NJ 08807. 908/304-7000. **Contact:** Human Resources. **World Wide Web address:** http://www.aventispharma-us.com. **Description:** An international pharmaceutical company working with respiratory, cardiac, and osteopathic medications. **Positions advertised include:** Animal Care Technician; Associate Chemist; Associate Scientist; Epidemiologist; Global Change Coordinator; Global Program Manager; Manager. **Operations at this facility include:** Marketing; Research and Development.

BASF CORPORATION
KNOLL PHARMACEUTICALS
100 Campus Drive, Florham Park NJ 07932. 973/245-6000. **Fax:** 973/245-6002. **Contact:** Liz Roman, Director of Human Resources. **World Wide Web address:** http://www.basf.com. **Description:** BASF Corporation is an international chemical products organization, doing business in five operating groups: Chemicals; Coatings and Colorants; Consumer Products and Life Sciences; Fiber Products; and Polymers. **Positions advertised include:** Quality Assurance Plant Specialist; Product Manager; Regulatory Supervisor; Business Process Optimization Manager; Technical Service Representative. **Corporate headquarters location:** This location. **Operations at this facility include:** This location serves as the U.S. headquarters and houses management offices and the pharmaceutical division, Knoll Pharmaceuticals. **Listed on:** New York Stock Exchange. **Stock exchange symbol:** BF. **Number of employees worldwide:** 125,000.

BARR LABORATORIES, INC.
2 Quaker Road, P.O. Box 2900, Pomona NY 10970-0519. 845/362-1100. **Fax:** 845/362-2774. **Contact:** Human Resources. **World Wide Web address:** http://www.barrlabs.com. **Description:** Barr Laboratories is a leading independent developer, manufacturer, and marketer of off-patent pharmaceuticals. **Positions advertised include:** R&D Documentation Specialist; Senior Validation Engineer; Quality Control Manager; Quality Control Chemist; Technical Group Leader Quality Control; External Auditor. **Corporate headquarters location:** This location. **Other locations:** NJ; OH; PA; OH. **Operations at this facility include:** Development and production laboratories; Administration; Manufacturing; Research & Development; Pharmacy operations. **Listed on:** New York Stock Exchange. **Stock exchange symbol:** BRL. **Chairman/CEO:** Bruce L. Downey. **Annual sales/revenues:** $1.2 billion. **Number of employees:** 1,075.

BERLEX LABORATORIES, INC.
300 Fairfield Road, Wayne NJ 07470. 973/694-4100. **Contact:** Human Resources. **World Wide Web address:** http://www.berlex.com. **Description:** Researches, manufactures, and markets ethical pharmaceutical products in the fields of cardiovascular medicine, endocrinology and fertility control, diagnostic imaging, oncology, and central nervous system disorders. Berlex Laboratories has three strategic units: Berlex Drug Development & Technology (New Jersey), Oncology/Central Nervous System (California), and Berlex Biosciences (California). The company also owns Berlex Drug Development and Technology and operates a national sales force. The sales force, which is divided into three geographic regions, markets the complete line of Berlex products including BETASERON, which is used to treat multiple sclerosis. **Positions advertised**

include: Sales Administrative Assistant; Clinical Supplies Packaging Specialist; Drug Safety Specialist; Facility Systems & Services Specialist. **Corporate headquarters location:** This location. **Parent company:** Schering AG (Germany).

BIO-REFERENCE LABORATORIES
481B Edward H. Ross Drive, Elmwood Park NJ 07407. 201/791-2600. **Contact:** Human Resources. **World Wide Web address:** http://www.bio-referencelabs.com. **Description:** Operates a clinical laboratory. Bio-Reference offers a list of chemical diagnostic tests including blood and urine analysis, blood chemistry, hematology services, serology, radioimmunological analysis, toxicology (including drug screening), Pap smears, tissue pathology (biopsies), and other tissue analyses. Bio-Reference markets its services directly to physicians, hospitals, clinics, and other health facilities. **Corporate headquarters location:** This location. **Listed on:** NASDAQ. **Stock exchange symbol:** BRLI.

BIOSPECIFICS TECHNOLOGIES CORPORATION
35 Wilbur Street, Lynbrook NY 11563. 516/593-7000. **Fax:** 516/593-7039. **Contact:** Human Resources. **World Wide Web address:** http://www.biospecifics.com. **Description:** An industry leader in the production and development of enzyme pharmaceuticals used for wound healing, tissue regeneration, and tissue remodeling. Biospecifics Technologies Corporation produces Collagenase Santyl ointment, an enzyme used for the treatment of chronic wounds and dermal ulcers. **NOTE:** Resumes should be mailed or faxed to the above address. **Positions advertised include:** Clinical Lab Technician. **Office hours:** Monday - Friday, 9:00 a.m. - 5:00 p.m. **Listed on:** NASDAQ. **Stock exchange symbol:** BSTC. **President/CEO:** Edwin H. Wegman. **Annual sales/revenues:** $8.2 million. **Number of employees:** 48.

BOEHRINGER INGELHEIM PHARMACEUTICALS, INC.
900 Old Ridgebury Road, Ridgefield CT 06877. 203/798-9988. **Contact:** Director of Human Resources. **World Wide Web address:** http://www.boehringer-ingelheim.com. **Description:** Involved in the research, development, manufacture, and marketing of pharmaceutical products used to treat cardiovascular, pulmonary, viral, and immunological diseases. **Corporate headquarters location:** Ingelheim, Germany. **Number of employees nationwide:** 5,100.

BRADLEY PHARMACEUTICALS, INC.
383 Route 46 West, Fairfield NJ 07004-2402. 973/882-1505. **Fax:** 973/575-5366. **Contact:** Human Resources. **E-mail address:** personnel@bradpharm.com. **World Wide Web address:** http://www.bradpharm.com. **Description:** Manufactures and markets over-the-counter and prescription pharmaceuticals, and health-related products including nutritional, personal hygiene, and internal medicine brands. Founded in 1985. **Positions advertised include:** Product Manager; Sales Assistant Training Manager; Quality Assurance Director; Pharmaceutical Sales Representative; Telemarketing. **Corporate headquarters location:** This location. **Subsidiaries include:** Doak Dermatologics Company Inc. (Westbury NY); Kenwood Therapeutics. **Listed on:** NASDAQ. **Stock exchange symbol:** BPRX.

BRISTOL-MYERS SQUIBB COMPANY
345 Park Avenue, New York NY 10154-0037. 212/546-4000. **Fax:** 212/546-4020. **Contact:** Stephen E. Bear, Human Resources Director. **World Wide Web address:** http://www.bms.com. **Description:** Manufacturer of pharmaceuticals, medical devices, nonprescription drugs, toiletries, and beauty aids. The company's pharmaceutical products include cardiovascular drugs, anti-infective agents, anticancer agents, AIDS therapy treatments, central nervous system

drugs, diagnostic agents, and other drugs. The company's line of nonprescription products includes formulas, vitamins, analgesics, remedies, and skin care products sold under the brand names Bufferin, Excedrin, Nuprin, and Comtrex. Beauty aids include Clairol and Ultress hair care, Nice 'n Easy hair colorings, hair sprays, gels, and deodorants. **NOTE:** Resumes may be sent to the company's human resources address: Bristol-Myers Squibb Company, P.O. Box 5335, Princeton NY 08543-5335; or by fax to: 609/897-6412. **Positions advertised include:** Chemist. **Corporate headquarters location:** This location. **Subsidiaries include:** ConvaTec; Mead Johnson & Company. **Listed on:** New York Stock Exchange. **Stock exchange symbol:** BMY. **Chairman/CEO:** Peter R. Dolan. **Annual sales/revenues:** $18.1 billion. **Number of employees:** 46,000.

CELGENE CORPORATION
86 Morris Avenue, Summit NJ 07901. 732/271-1001. **Fax:** 732/271-4184. **Contact:** Human Resources. **E-mail address:** jobs@celgene.com. **World Wide Web address:** http://www.celgene.com. **Description:** Engaged in the development and commercialization of a broad range of immunotherapeutic drugs designed to control serious disease states. Celgene also manufactures and sells chiral intermediates, key building blocks in the production of advanced therapeutic compounds and certain agrochemical and food-related products. The focus of Celgene's immunotherapeutics program is the development of small molecule compounds that modulate bodily production of tumor necrosis factor alpha, a hormone-like protein. Elevated levels of this cytokine are believed to cause symptoms associated with several debilitating diseases such as HIV and AIDS-related conditions, sepsis, and inflammatory bowel disease. **NOTE:** Search and apply for positions online. Resumes only accepted for current openings. **Positions advertised include:** Associate Director Clinical Operations; Associate Director QC; Attorney; Manager Sales Operations; Clinical Operations Coordinator; Clinical Pharmacologist; Data Manager; Manager Scientific and Medical Writing; Medical Reviewer; Sr. SAS Programmer; QC Analyst; Product Manager Strategic Marketing. **Corporate headquarters location:** This location. **Listed on:** NASDAQ. **Stock exchange symbol:** CELG.

CELSIS LABORATORY GROUP
165 Fieldcrest Avenue, Edison NJ 08837. 732/346-5100. **Contact:** Human Resources. **E-mail address:** info@celsis.com. **World Wide Web address:** http://www.celsislabs.com. **Description:** An independent testing laboratory specializing in toxicology, microbiology, and analytical chemistry. **Number of employees at this location:** 50.

DARBY GROUP COMPANIES, INC.
865 Merrick Avenue, Westbury NY 11590. 516/683-1800. **Fax:** 516/832-7101. **Contact:** Debra Leff, Human Resources Department. **World Wide Web address:** http://www.darbygroup.com. **Description:** A manufacturer and distributor of over-the-counter drugs, pharmaceuticals, and vitamins operating 12 distribution facilities nationwide. **Corporate headquarters location:** This location. **Other U.S. locations:** Nationwide. **Subsidiaries include:** Dental Division; Medical Division; Burns Veterinary Supply; Darby Corporate Solutions. **Chairman:** Michael Ashkir. **Annual sales/revenues:** $625 million. **Number of employees:** 1,500.

DAXOR CORPORATION
The Empire State Building, 350 Fifth Avenue, Suite 7120, New York NY 10118. 212/244-0555. **Fax:** 212/244-0806. **Contact:** Human Resources. **World Wide Web address:** http://www.daxor.com. **Description:** Promotes the safety of the American Blood Banking System. The company's Idant Division also researches cryobiology for artificial insemination purposes and operates one of the largest sperm banks in the United States. **Subsidiaries include:** IDANT Laboratories.

Listed on: American Stock Exchange. Stock exchange symbol: DXR. Chairman/President/CEO: Joseph Feldschuh. Annual sales/revenues: 2.7 million. Number of employees: 30.

E-Z-EM INC.
717 Main Street, Westbury NY 11590. 516/333-8230. Fax: 516/333-1392. Contact: Human Resources. E-mail address: hr@ezem.com. World Wide Web address: http://www.ezem.com. Description: E-Z-EM is a worldwide producer of barium sulfate contrast systems for use in GI tract X-ray examinations. The company operates in two industry segments: diagnostic products and surgical products. The diagnostic products segment includes both contrast systems, consisting of barium sulfate formulations and related apparatus used in X-ray, CT-scanning, and other imaging examinations; and noncontrast systems, which include interventional radiology products, custom contract pharmaceuticals, gastrointestinal cleansing laxatives, X-ray protection equipment, and immunoassay tests. Corporate headquarters location: This location. Listed on: American Stock Exchange. Stock exchange symbol: EZM. Annual sales/revenues: $122 million. Number of employees: 932.

ELAN
89 Headquarters Plaza #1420, Morristown NJ 07960. 973/272-6755. Fax: 973292/6759. Contact: Human Resources. World Wide Web address: http://www.elan.com. Description: Develops proprietary lipid- and liposome-based pharmaceuticals for the treatment, prevention, and diagnosis of cancer, systemic fungal infections, and inflammatory and vaso-occlusive diseases. Positions advertised include: Senior Scientist; Formulations Manager. Corporate headquarters location: This location.

EMISPHERE TECHNOLOGIES, INC.
765 Old Saw Mill River Road, Tarrytown NY 10591-6751. 914/347-2220. Fax: 914/347-2498. Contact: Barbara Mohl, Human Resources Director. E-mail address: jobs@emisphere.com. World Wide Web address: http://www.emisphere.com. Description: Researches and develops oral drug delivery systems. Positions advertised include: Analytical Research Associate; Drug Delivery Research Associate; Patent Paralegal; Documentation Control Professional; Laboratory Animal Technician. Listed on: NASDAQ. Stock exchange symbol: EMIS. Chairman/CEO: Michael M. Goldberg. Annual sales/revenues: $3.4 million. Number of employees: 241.

ENZO BIOCHEM, INC.
dba ENZO CLINICAL LABS
60 Executive Boulevard, Farmingdale NY 11735. 631/755-5500. Fax: 631/863-0143. Contact: Human Resources. World Wide Web address: http://www.enzo.com. Description: Through its subsidiaries, the company is engaged in the research, development, marketing, and manufacturing of health care products. Enzo's products and services are sold to scientists and medical personnel worldwide. The company has proprietary technologies and expertise in manipulating and modifying genetic material and other biological molecules. Founded in 1976. Positions advertised include: Phlebotomist; Histotechnologist; Grosser. Subsidiaries include: Enzo Therapeutics, Inc. is developing antisense genetic medicines to combat cancer, viral, and other diseases. Enzo Diagnostics, Inc. develops and markets proprietary DNA probe-based products to clinicians and researchers. EnzoLabs, Inc. provides diagnostic testing services to the New York medical community. Corporate headquarters location: This location. Parent company: Enzo Biochem. Listed on: New York Stock Exchange. Stock exchange symbol: ENZ. Chairman/CEO: Elazar Rabbani. Annual sales/revenues: $54 million. Number of employees: 231.

ENZON, INC.
20 Kingsbridge Road, Piscataway NJ 08854-3998. 732/980-4500. **Fax:** 732/980-5911. **Contact:** Human Resources. **E-mail address:** hr@enzon.com. **World Wide Web address:** http://www.enzon.com. **Description:** A biopharmaceutical company that develops advanced therapeutics for life threatening diseases, primarily in the area of oncology. **Positions advertised include:** Human Resources Specialist; Manufacturing Manager; Accounting Manager; Associate Director; Quality Assurance Clerk; Validation Specialist; Application Engineer; Research Associate; Clinical Project Manager; Computer Support Specialist; Clinical Research Assistant. **Office hours:** Monday - Friday, 8:30 a.m. - 5:00 p.m. **Other area locations:** South Plainfield NJ. **Listed on:** NASDAQ. **Stock exchange symbol:** ENZN. **President/CEO:** Peter Tombros. **Annual sales/revenues:** $11 - $20 million. **Number of employees at this location:** 55. **Number of employees nationwide:** 90.

EON LABS, INC.
227-15 North Conduit Avenue, Laurelton NY 11413. 718/276-8600. **Toll-free phone:** 800/526-0225. **Fax:** 718/949-3120. **Contact:** Human Resources. **World Wide Web address:** http://www.eonlabs.com. **Description:** Manufactures both prescription and over-the-counter generic pharmaceuticals. **Positions advertised include:** Quality Control Chemist. **Listed on:** NASDAQ. **Stock exchange symbol:** ELAB. **Chairman:** Thomas Strüngmann. **Annual sales/revenues:** $244 million. **Number of employees:** 324.

FISHER SCIENTIFIC COMPANY
One Reagent Lane, Fair Lawn NJ 07410. 201/796-7100. **Contact:** Michelle Valvano, Personnel Manager. **World Wide Web address:** http://www.fisherscientific.com. **Description:** Fisher Scientific manufactures, distributes, and sells a wide range of products used in industrial and medical laboratories. Products include analytical and measuring instruments, apparatus, and appliances; reagent chemicals and diagnostics; glassware and plasticware; and laboratory furniture. Customers are primarily industrial laboratories, medical and hospital laboratories, and educational and research laboratories. Manufacturing operations are carried out by six operating divisions in 11 U.S. locations. **Positions advertised include:** Accountant; Facilities Manager; Office Manager; Analytical Chemist; Financial Analyst. **Operations at this facility include:** This location produces reagents. **Listed on:** New York Stock Exchange. **Stock exchange symbol:** FSH.

FOREST LABORATORIES, INC.
909 Third Avenue, 24th Floor, New York NY 10022-4731. 212/421-7850. **Fax:** 212/750-9152. **Contact:** Human Resources. **E-mail address:** staffing@frx.com. **World Wide Web address:** http://www.frx.com. **Description:** Develops, manufactures, and sells branded and generic prescription drugs for the treatment of cardiovascular, central nervous system, pulmonary, and women's health problems. In the United States, Forest Laboratories' ethical specialty products and generics are marketed directly by the company's subsidiaries Forest Pharmaceuticals and Inwood Laboratories. In the United Kingdom, Ireland, and certain export markets, Forest Laboratories products are marketed directly by the company's subsidiaries, Pharmax Ltd. and Tosara Group. **Positions advertised include:** Sales Force Automation Analyst; Forecast Analyst; Licensing Secretary; Product Manager; Senior Product Manager; Customer Planning Long Term Care/Government Manager; Customer Planning Analyst; Customer Planning Pharmacy Benefit Manager; Business Development Assistant Director; Respiratory Product Manager; Senior Respiratory Product Manager. **Special programs:** Internships; Co-ops; Summer Jobs. **Office hours:** Monday - Friday, 9:00 a.m. - 5:00 p.m. **Corporate headquarters location:** This location. **Other U.S. locations:** St. Louis MO; Jersey City NJ; Commack NY; Farmingdale NY; Inwood NY; Cincinnati OH. **International locations:** Ireland; United Kingdom.

Subsidiaries include: Forest Pharmaceuticals, Inc.; Inwood Laboratories, Inc.; Pharmax Ltd.; Tosara Group. **Operations at this facility include:** Accounting/Auditing; Administration; Financial Offices; Marketing; Sales. **Listed on:** New York Stock Exchange. **Stock exchange symbol:** FRX. **President:** Howard Solomon. **Annual sales/revenues:** $1.6 billion. **Number of employees at this location:** 350. **Number of employees nationwide:** 3,731.

E. FOUGERA & COMPANY
SAVAGE LABORATORIES
60 Baylis Road, Melville NY 11747. 631/454-6996. **Contact:** Human Resources Manager. **E-mail address:** hr@altanainc.com. **World Wide Web address:** http://www.fougera.com. **Description:** Manufactures various generic pharmaceuticals including multisource topicals and ophthalmics. Products include surgical lubricants, antifungal creams, hydrocortisone ointments, and other generic treatments. **Corporate headquarters location:** This location. **Parent company:** Altana, Inc. (also at this location) also owns Savage Laboratories, which manufactures ethical pharmaceuticals. **Positions advertised include:** Microbiologist; Quality Assurance Monitor; Analytical Services Supervisor.

GLAXOSMITHKLINE CORPORATION
257 Cornelison Avenue, Jersey City NJ 07302. 201/434-3000. **Contact:** Human Resources. **World Wide Web address:** http://www.gsk.com. **Description:** Develops, manufactures, and sells products in four general categories: denture, dental care, oral hygiene, and professional dental products; proprietary products; ethical pharmaceutical products; and household products. Dental-related products include Polident denture cleansers. **Positions advertised include:** Pharmaceutical Sales Representative. **Listed on:** New York Stock Exchange. **Stock exchange symbol:** GSK.

GLAXOSMITHKLINE CORPORATION
65 Industrial South, Clifton NJ 07012. 973/778-9000. **Contact:** Human Resources. **World Wide Web address:** http://www.gsk.com. **Description:** GlaxoSmithKline Corporation is a health care company engaged in the research, development, manufacture, and marketing of ethical pharmaceuticals, animal health products, ethical and proprietary medicines, and eye care products. The company is also engaged in many other aspects of the health care field including the production of medical and electronic instruments. **Positions advertised include:** Warehouse Technician; Validation Engineer; Systems Programmer Analyst; Staff Accountant; Production Technician. **Corporate headquarters location:** Philadelphia PA. **Operations at this facility include:** This location manufactures toothpaste and Massengill products. **Listed on:** New York Stock Exchange. **Stock exchange symbol:** GSK.

GLAXOSMITHKLINE PHARMACEUTICALS
101 Possumtown Road, Piscataway NJ 08854. 732/469-5200. **Contact:** Human Resources Manager. **World Wide Web address:** http://www.gsk.com. **Description:** Manufactures penicillin. **Positions advertised include:** Analytical Chemist; Clinical Operations Project Manager. **Corporate headquarters location:** Philadelphia PA. **Parent company:** GlaxoSmithKline Corporation is health care company engaged in the research, development, manufacture, and marketing of ethical pharmaceuticals, animal health products, ethical and proprietary medicines, and eye care products. **Listed on:** New York Stock Exchange. **Stock exchange symbol:** GSK.

HI-TECH PHARMACAL CO., INC.
369 Bayview Avenue, Amityville NY 11701. 631/789-8228. **Fax:** 631/789-8429. **Contact:** Carole Wood, Human Resources Manager. **World Wide Web address:** http://www.hitechpharm.com. **Description:** Develops, manufactures,

and markets prescription and generic liquid and semi-solid drugs, as well as nutritional products. Hi-Tech Pharmacal manufactures more than 100 generic products marketed under the company's own brand names. **Subsidiaries include:** Health Care Products manufactures branded items marketed under the H-T, Sooth-It, and Diabetic Tussin brands. **Listed on:** NASDAQ. **Stock exchange symbol:** HITK. **Chairman:** Bernard Seltzer. **Annual sales/revenues:** $33 million. **Number of employees:** 164.

HOFFMANN-LA ROCHE INC.
340 Kingsland Street, Nutley NJ 07110-0119. 973/235-5000. **Contact:** Director of Staffing. **World Wide Web address:** http://www.rocheusa.com. **Description:** An international health care organization that develops and manufactures pharmaceuticals, diagnostics, and vitamins. **NOTE:** Entry-level positions, part-time jobs, and second and third shifts are offered. **Positions advertised include:** Accounting Systems Developer; Administrative Assistant; Animal Resource Technician; Associate Clinical Director; Clinical Director; Clinical Liaison; Education Team Leader. **Corporate headquarters location:** This location. **Other U.S. locations:** Nationwide. **International locations:** Worldwide. **Subsidiaries include:** Roche Biomedical Laboratories; Roche Diagnostics (ethical pharmaceuticals); Roche Vitamins Inc. **Parent company:** F. Hoffmann-La Roche Ltd. **Operations at this facility include:** Divisional Headquarters. **Listed on:** Privately held. **Annual sales/revenues:** More than $100 million. **Number of employees at this location:** 6,000. **Number of employees nationwide:** 20,000. **Number of employees worldwide:** 80,000.

HUNTINGDON LIFE SCIENCES
P.O. Box 2360, Mettlers Road, East Millstone NJ 08875. 732/873-2550. **Fax:** 732/873-3992. **Contact:** Human Resources. **E-mail address:** careers@princeton.huntingdon.com. **World Wide Web address:** http://www.huntingdon.com. **Description:** Provides contract biological safety (toxicological) testing services on a worldwide basis through two laboratories in the United States and the United Kingdom. The toxicology divisions of Huntington Life Sciences conduct studies designed to test pharmaceutical products, biologicals, chemical compounds, and other substances in order to produce the data required to identify, quantify, and evaluate the risks to humans and the environment resulting from the manufacture or use of these substances. These divisions also perform analytical and metabolic chemistry services. Huntington Life Sciences also performs clinical trials of new and existing pharmaceutical and biotechnology products and medical devices. The company is engaged in the clinical development process including analytical chemistry, evaluation of clinical data, data processing, biostatistical analysis, and the preparation of supporting documentation for compliance with regulatory requirements. Founded in 1952. **NOTE:** Entry-level positions, part-time jobs, and second and third shifts are offered. **Positions advertised include:** Bioanalytical Scientist and Analyst; Animal Lab Technician; Associate Research Scientist; Necropsy Technician. **Special programs:** Summer Jobs. **Office hours:** Monday - Friday, 8:30 a.m. - 5:00 p.m. **Corporate headquarters location:** Cambridgeshire, England. **Parent company:** Huntingdon Life Sciences, Ltd. **President:** Alan Staple. **Annual sales/revenues:** $51 - $100 million. **Number of employees at this location:** 200. **Number of employees worldwide:** 1,500.

IMCLONE SYSTEMS INC.
180 Varick Street, 6th Floor, New York NY 10014-4606. 212/645-1405. **Fax:** 212/645-2054. **Contact:** Human Resources Director. **World Wide Web address:** http://www.imclone.com. **Description:** Engaged primarily in the research and development of therapeutic products for the treatment of cancer and cancer-related diseases. **Positions advertised include:** Chemistry Research Associate; Chemistry Research Scientist; Modeling Chemistry Senior Scientist; Facilities Worker; Immunology Research Associate; Immunology

Scientist; Immunology Senior Scientist; Intellectual Property Law Clerk; Molecular & Cell Biology Senior Scientist. **Corporate headquarters location:** This location. **Other locations:** Somerville NJ. **Listed on:** NASDAQ. **Stock exchange symbol:** IMCLE. **Annual sales/revenues:** $33 million. **Number of employees:** 400.

IMMUNOMEDICS, INC.
300 American Road, Morris Plains NJ 07950. 973/605-8200. **Fax:** 973/605-8282. **Contact:** Human Resources. **E-mail address:** hr@immunomedics.com. **World Wide Web address:** http://www.immunomedics.com. **Description:** Manufactures products to treat and detect infectious diseases and cancer. Products include LeukoScan, a diagnostic imaging tool that can scan for cancers such as osteomyelitis. **Positions advertised include:** Clinical Research Associate. **Listed on:** NASDAQ. **Stock exchange symbol:** IMMU.

IVAX PHARMACEUTICALS INC.
140 LeGrand Avenue, Northvale NJ 07647. 201/767-1700. **Fax:** 201/767-1700. **Contact:** Personnel. **World Wide Web address:** http://www.ivaxpharmaceuticals.com. **Description:** Produces ethical pharmaceuticals for the cardiovascular, nervous, digestive, and respiratory systems. **Corporate headquarters location:** Miami FL.

LABORATORY CORPORATION OF AMERICA (LABCORP)
116 Millburn Avenue, Suite 211, Millburn NJ 07041. 973/912-8617. **Contact:** Human Resources. **World Wide Web address:** http://www.labcorp.com. **Description:** The company is one of the nation's leading clinical laboratory companies, providing services primarily to physicians, hospitals, clinics, nursing homes, and other clinical labs nationwide. LabCorp performs tests on blood, urine, and other body fluids and tissue, aiding the diagnosis of disease. **NOTE:** Direct employment correspondence to: LabCorp Human Resources, 309 East Davis Street, Burlington NC 27215. **Corporate headquarters location:** Burlington NC. **Operations at this facility include:** This location is a blood-drawing facility.

LIFECELL CORPORATION
One Millennium Way, Branchburg NJ 08876. 908/947-1100. **Fax:** 908/947-1200. **Contact:** Human Resources. **E-mail address:** hr@lifecell.com. **World Wide Web address:** http://www.lifecell.com. **Description:** Designs, manufactures, and produces products dealing with skin grafts for burn patients and with the preservation of transfusable blood platelets (blood cells that control clotting). LifeCell's main product, AlloDerm, removes the cells in allograft skin (from a cadaveric donor) that the patient's own immune system would normally reject. This technology enables the AlloDerm to become populated with the patient's own skin cells and blood vessels. Founded in 1986. **Listed on:** NASDAQ. **Stock exchange symbol:** LIFC.

MERCK & COMPANY, INC.
126 East Lincoln Avenue, P.O. Box 2000, Rahway NJ 07065. 732/594-4000. **Contact:** Human Resources. **World Wide Web address:** http://www.merck.com. **Description:** A worldwide organization engaged in discovering, developing, producing, and marketing products for health care and the maintenance of the environment. Products include human and animal pharmaceuticals and chemicals sold to the health care, oil exploration, food processing, textile, paper, and other industries. Merck also runs an ethical drug mail-order marketing business. **Positions advertised include:** Staff Biologist; Associate Director; Hospital Sales Representative; Facilities Director; Spectroscoptist; Chemist. **NOTE:** Applicants should indicate position of interest. **Corporate headquarters location:** Whitehouse Station NJ. **Other U.S. locations:** Albany GA; Montvale

NJ; Whitehouse Station NJ; Wilson NC; West Point PA; Elkton VA. **Listed on:** New York Stock Exchange. **Stock exchange symbol:** MRK.

MERCK & COMPANY, INC.

P.O. Box 100, One Merck Drive, Whitehouse Station NJ 08889-0100. 908/423-1000. **Contact:** Human Resources. **World Wide Web address:** http://www.merck.com. **Description:** A worldwide organization engaged in discovering, developing, producing, and marketing products for health care and the maintenance of the environment. Products include human and animal pharmaceuticals and chemicals sold to the health care, oil exploration, food processing, textile, paper, and other industries. Merck also runs an ethical drug mail-order marketing business. **Corporate headquarters location:** This location. **Other U.S. locations:** Albany GA; Montvale NJ; Rahway NJ; Wilson NC; West Point PA; Elkton VA. **Listed on:** New York Stock Exchange. **Stock exchange symbol:** MRK.

NAPP TECHNOLOGIES

401 Hackensack Avenue, Hackensack NJ 07601. 201/843-4664. **Fax:** 201/843-4737. **Contact:** Personnel. **E-mail address:** tom.smith@napptech.com. **World Wide Web address:** http://www.napptech.com. **Description:** Produces bulk pharmaceuticals, cosmetic raw materials, and fine chemicals. **Corporate headquarters location:** This location.

NOVARTIS PHARMACEUTICALS CORPORATION

556 Morris Avenue, Summit NJ 07901. 908/277-5000. **Contact:** Human Resources. **World Wide Web address:** http://www.novartis.com. **Description:** Novartis Pharmaceuticals Corporation is one of the largest life science companies in the world. The company has three major divisions: health care, agribusiness, and nutrition. The health care division specializes in pharmaceuticals, both proprietary and generic, and ophthalmic health care. The agribusiness division is involved in seed technology, animal health, and crop protection. The nutrition sector includes medical, health, and infant nutrition. **Positions advertised include:** Communications Associate; Communications Operations Representative; Finance Business Administration Services Representative; Human Resources; Information Technologist Representative; Pharmaceutical Operations Representative; Sales Associate; State Government Affairs Representative; Transportation Tissue Engineer. **NOTE:** Resumes should be sent to Human Resources, Novartis Pharmaceuticals Corporation, 59 Route 10, East Hanover NJ 07936. **Corporate headquarters location:** East Hanover NJ. **Operations at this facility include:** This location manufactures pharmaceuticals.

NOVARTIS PHARMACEUTICALS CORPORATION

59 Route 10, East Hanover NJ 07936. 973/503-7500. **Contact:** Human Resources. **World Wide Web address:** http://www.novartis.com. **Description:** Novartis Pharmaceuticals Corporation is one of the largest life science companies in the world. The company has three major divisions: health care, agribusiness, and nutrition. The health care division specializes in pharmaceuticals, both proprietary and generic, and ophthalmic health care. The agribusiness division is involved in seed technology, animal health, and crop protection. The nutrition sector includes medical, health, and infant nutrition. **Corporate headquarters location:** This location. **Other area locations:** Summit NJ. **Operations at this facility include:** This location houses administrative offices and Novartis Pharmaceuticals' primary research facility.

NOVO NORDISK OF NORTH AMERICA

405 Lexington Avenue, Suite 6400, New York NY 10174. 212/878-6600. **Contact:** Human Resources Department. **World Wide Web address:** http://www.novonordisk.com. **Description:** A holding company whose divisions

produce insulin, industrial enzymes, and other drugs and bioindustrial items. The Health Care Group is the diabetes care division that develops and manufactures insulin and delivery systems related to the treatment of diabetes. The Biopharmaceuticals division develops, produces, and markets products for the treatment of coagulation and other blood disorders as well as growth disorders. The Bioindustrial division consists of detergents, providing enzymes to the detergent industry. **NOTE:** Human Resources is located at 100 Overlook Center, Suite 200, Princeton NJ 08540. 609/987-5800. Jobseekers may apply for positions online. **Positions advertised include:** Managed Care Account Executive; Pharmaceutical Sales Representative. **Other U.S. locations:** Davis CA; Clayton NC; Franklinton NC; Princeton NJ; Seattle WA. **Parent company:** Novo Nordisk A/S (Baysvaerd, Denmark). **Operations at this facility include:** This location is the corporate service office for North America. **Listed on:** New York Stock Exchange. **Stock exchange symbol:** NVO. **President:** Martin Soeters. **Number of employees at this location:** 25. **Number of employees nationwide:** 1,000. **Number of employees worldwide:** 13,000.

OSI PHARMACEUTICALS, INC.
58 South Service Road, Suite 110, Melville NY 11747. 631/962-2000. **Fax:** 631/752-3880. **Contact:** Human Resources. **E-mail address:** employment@osip.com. **World Wide Web address:** http://www.osip.com. **Description:** A biopharmaceutical company utilizing proprietary technologies to discover and develop products for the treatment and diagnosis of human diseases. The company conducts a full range of drug discovery activities from target identification through clinical candidates for its own products and in collaborations and co-ventures with other major pharmaceutical companies. **NOTE:** Jobseekers may apply for positions online. **Positions advertised include:** Purchasing Specialist. **Corporate headquarters location:** This location. **Other area locations:** Farmingdale NY; Uniondale NY. **Other U.S. locations:** Boulder CO. **International locations:** England. **Listed on:** NASDAQ. **Stock exchange symbol:** OSIP. **President:** Dr. Colin Goddard.

ORGANON INC.
375 Mount Pleasant Avenue, West Orange NJ 07052. 973/325-4500. **Toll-free phone:** 800/241-8812. **Fax:** 973/669-6144. **Contact:** Human Resources. **E-mail address:** wohr@organon-usa.com. **World Wide Web address:** http://www.organon-usa.com. **Description:** A worldwide leader in pharmaceutical research and development in the fields of reproductive medicine, anesthesiology, central nervous system disorders, thrombosis, and immunology. **NOTE:** Entry-level positions and part-time jobs are offered. **Positions advertised include:** Pharmaceutical Scientist. **Special programs:** Internships; Summer Jobs. **Office hours:** Monday - Friday, 8:00 a.m. - 4:30 p.m. **Corporate headquarters location:** This location. **Parent company:** Akzo Nobel. **Annual sales/revenues:** More than $100 million. **Number of employees at this location:** 1,200.

ORTHO-McNEIL PHARMACEUTICAL
1000 Route 202 North, P.O. Box 300, Raritan NJ 08869-0602. 908/218-6000. **Contact:** Human Resources. **World Wide Web address:** http://www.ortho-mcneil.com. **Description:** Develops and sells pharmaceutical products including women's health, infectious disease, and wound healing products. **Positions advertised include:** National Account Manager; Clinical Research Associate. **NOTE:** All hiring is done out of the corporate offices. Resumes should be sent to Johnson & Johnson Recruiting Services, Employment Management Center, Room JH-215, 501 George Street, New Brunswick NJ 08906-6597. **Parent company:** Johnson & Johnson (New Brunswick NJ).

OSTEOTECH INC.
51 James Way, Eatontown NJ 07724. 732/542-2800. **Fax:** 732/542-9312. **Contact:** Human Resources. **E-mail address:** hr@osteotech.com. **World Wide**

Web address: http://www.osteotech.com. **Description:** Processes human bone and connective tissue for transplantation and develops and manufactures biomaterial and device systems for musculoskeletal surgery. Osteotech is a leader in volume and quality of tissue processing for the American Red Cross and the Musculoskeletal Tissue Foundation. Founded in 1986. **NOTE:** Entry-level positions and second and third shifts are offered. **Company slogan:** Innovators in musculoskeletal tissue science. **Positions advertised include:** Clinical Research Technician; Clinical Research Associate; Auditor Associate; Processing Technology. **Special programs:** Training. **Office hours:** Monday - Friday, 8:00 a.m. - 5:00 p.m. **Corporate headquarters location:** This location. **Other U.S. locations:** Nationwide. **International locations:** The Netherlands. **Listed on:** NASDAQ. **Stock exchange symbol:** OSTE. **President:** Richard Bauer. **Annual sales/revenues:** $21 - $50 million. **Number of employees at this location:** 180. **Number of employees nationwide:** 200. **Number of employees worldwide:** 225.

PDK LABS INC.
145 Ricefield Lane, Hauppauge NY 11788. 631/273-2630. **Contact:** Human Resources. **E-mail address:** info@pdklabs.com. **World Wide Web address:** http://www.pdklabs.com. **Description:** PDK Labs manufactures and distributes over-the-counter pharmaceutical products and vitamins. The company's line of products primarily consists of nonprescription caffeine products, pain relievers, decongestants, diet aids, and a broad line of vitamins, nutritional supplements, and cosmetics. The company markets its products through direct mail, regional distributors, and private label manufacturing.

PFIZER
201 Tabor Road, Morris Plains NJ 07950. 973/385-2000. **Contact:** Corporate Human Resources. **World Wide Web address:** http://www.pfizer.com. **Description:** A leading pharmaceutical company that distributes products concerning cardiovascular health, central nervous system disorders, infectious diseases, and women's health worldwide. The company's brand-name products include Benadryl, Ben Gay, Cortizone, Desitin, Halls, Listerine, Sudafed, Viagra, and Zantac 75. **Positions advertised include:** Executive Assistant; Buyer; Scientist; Regional Area Manager; Maintenance Craft Worker; Financial Analyst; Administrative Associate; Marketing Communications Manager; Business Development Manager; Associate Director; Data Management Specialist; Meteorologist; Scientist Chemistry Project Team Leader.

PFIZER
100 Route 206 North, Peapack NJ 07977. 908/901-8000. **Contact:** Human Resources. **World Wide Web address:** http://www.pfizer.com. **Description:** Pfizer manufactures and markets agricultural products, performance chemicals used in consumer products, prescription pharmaceuticals, and food ingredients. **Corporate headquarters location:** This location. **Operations at this facility include:** This location houses administrative offices. **Number of employees worldwide:** 60,000.

PHARMACEUTICAL FORMULATIONS, INC.
P.O. Box 1904, 460 Plainfield Avenue, Edison NJ 08818-1904. 732/985-7100. **Fax:** 732/819-3330. **Contact:** Human Resources. **E-mail address:** pfiresumes@pfiotc.com. **World Wide Web address:** http://www.pfiotc.com. **Description:** Manufactures and distributes over-the-counter, solid-dosage pharmaceutical products in tablet, caplet, and capsule forms. **Corporate headquarters location:** This location. **Operations at this facility include:** Administration; Manufacturing; Research and Development; Sales; Service. **Number of employees at this location:** 320.

PRECISION PHARMA
155 Duryea Road, Melville NY 11747. 631/752-7314. **Fax:** 631/845-6367. **Contact:** Human Resources. **E-mail address:** hr@precisionpharma.com. **World Wide Web address:** http://www.precisionpharma.com. **Description:** Precision Pharma is a leader in the field of pathogen inactivation of blood products. The company's technologies are designed to address the risk of viral contamination of blood products. Founded in 1995. **Positions advertised include:** Fractionation Technician; Mechanic. **Corporate headquarters location:** This location. **President/CEO:** James A. Moose.

QMED, INC.
25 Christopher Way, Eatontown NJ 07724. 732/544-5544. **Fax:** 732/544-5404. **Contact:** Human Resources. **E-mail address:** jobs@qmedinc.com. **World Wide Web address:** http://www.qmedinc.com. **Description:** Designs, manufactures, and markets testing devices that enable medical professionals to perform minimally invasive diagnostic procedures for certain illnesses, such as silent myocardial ischemia, venous blood flow insufficiencies, and diabetic neuropathy. **Positions advertised include:** Licensed Practical Nurse; Patient Education Nurse; Help Desk Manager; Information Technology Developer; Registered Nurse; Operations Program Analyst; Accounting Manager; Medical Assistant; Customer Service Specialist; Account Manager. **Listed on:** NASDAQ. **Stock exchange symbol:** QEKG.

QUEST DIAGNOSTICS INCORPORATED
One Malcolm Avenue, Teterboro NJ 07608. 201/393-5000. **Fax:** 201/462-4715. **Contact:** Personnel. **World Wide Web address:** http://www.questdiagnostics.com. **Description:** One of the largest clinical laboratories in North America, providing a broad range of clinical laboratory services to health care clients that include physicians, hospitals, clinics, dialysis centers, pharmaceutical companies, and corporations. The company offers and performs tests on blood, urine, and other bodily fluids and tissues to provide information for health and well-being. **Positions advertised include:** Technologist; Histotechnologist; Assistant Administrator; Phlebotomy Service Representative; Pathologist Representative; Group Leader; Field Operations Manager; Customer Service Representative; Dispatcher; Imaging Clerk. **Corporate headquarters location:** This location. **Other U.S. locations:** Nationwide. **Listed on:** New York Stock Exchange. **Stock exchange symbol:** DGX.

QUEST DIAGNOSTICS INCORPORATED
575 Underhill Boulevard, Syosset NY 11791. 516/677-3800. **Fax:** 516/677-4015. **Contact:** Jamie Drumerhauser, Human Resources. **World Wide Web address:** http://www.questdiagnostics.com. **Description:** Quest Diagnostics is one of the largest clinical laboratories in North America, providing a broad range of clinical laboratory services to health care clients that include physicians, hospitals, clinics, dialysis centers, pharmaceutical companies, and corporations. The company offers and performs tests on blood, urine, and other bodily fluids and tissues to provide information for health and well-being. **NOTE:** Online applications are available. **Positions advertised include:** Laboratory Manager; District Sales Manager; Billing Supervisor; **Corporate headquarters location:** Teterboro NJ. **Other U.S. locations:** Nationwide. **International locations:** Worldwide. **Operations at this facility include:** This location is a clinical laboratory. **Listed on:** New York Stock Exchange. **Stock exchange symbol:** DGX. **Sales/revenue:** Over $4 billion. **Number of employees worldwide:** 33,400.

REGENERON PHARMACEUTICALS, INC.
777 Old Saw Mill River Road, Suite 10, Tarrytown NY 10591. 914/345-7400. **Fax:** 914/345-7790. **Contact:** Human Resources. **E-mail address:**

jobs@regeneron.com. **World Wide Web address:** http://www.regeneron.com. **Description:** A research company that develops pharmaceuticals to treat neurological, oncological, inflammatory, allergic, and bone disorders as well as muscle atrophy. **Positions advertised include:** Senior Director; Medical Program Coordinator; Endocrinologist; Biostatistician; Assay Development Associate Director; Quality Auditor; Eye Angiogenesis; Bioreactor Development Associate Director; Cell Line and Process Development Research Associate. **Special programs:** Internships. **Corporate headquarters location:** This location. **Other area locations:** Rensselaer NY. **Listed on:** NASDAQ. **Stock exchange symbol:** REGN.

ROCHE VITAMINS INC.
45 Waterview Boulevard, Parsippany NJ 07054-1298. 973/257-1063. **Fax:** 800/526-0189. **Contact:** Human Resources. **E-mail address:** michael-j.malecki@dsm.com. **World Wide Web address:** http://www.roche-vitamins.com. **Description:** A pharmaceutical company that manufactures pharmaceutical drugs, diagnostic kits, and vitamins for dietary, pharmaceutical, and cosmetic use. **Corporate headquarters location:** This location.

SGS U.S. TESTING COMPANY INC.
291 Fairfield Avenue, Fairfield NJ 07004. 973/575-5252. **Toll-free phone:** 800/777-8378. **Fax:** 973/575-1071. **Contact:** Personnel. **E-mail address:** hrustc@yahoo.com. **World Wide Web address:** http://www.ustesting.sgsna.com. **Description:** An independent laboratory specializing in the testing of a variety of industrial and consumer products. Services include biological, chemical, engineering/materials, environmental, electrical, paper/packaging, textiles, certification programs, and inspections. **Positions advertised include:** Account Executive, Outside Sales. **Corporate headquarters location:** This location. **Other U.S. locations:** Los Angeles CA; Tulsa OK. **Parent company:** SGS North America. **Operations at this facility include:** Administration; Sales; Service.

SAVIENT PHARMACEUTICALS, INC.
One Tower Center 14th Floor, East Brunswick NJ 08816. 732/418-9300. **Fax:** 732/418-9235. **Contact:** Human Resources. **E-mail address:** hr@btgc.com. **World Wide Web address:** http://www.savientpharma.com. **Description:** Develops, manufactures, and markets novel therapeutic products. The company specializes in preclinical studies, research and development, and biotechnology derived products. **Positions advertised include:** Area Manager; Controller; Sales Manager; Director of Marketing. **Corporate headquarters location:** This location. **International locations:** Rehovot, Israel.

SCHERING-PLOUGH CORPORATION
2000 Galloping Hill Road, Kenilworth NJ 07033. 908/298-4000. **Contact:** Human Resources Department. **World Wide Web address:** http://www.schering-plough.com. **Description:** Engaged in the discovery, development, manufacture, and marketing of pharmaceutical and consumer products. Pharmaceutical products include prescription drugs, over-the-counter medicines, eye care products, and animal health products promoted to the medical and allied health professions. The consumer products group consists of proprietary medicines, toiletries, cosmetics, and foot care products. Brand names include Coricidin, Maybelline, Claritin, Coppertone, and Dr. Scholl's. **Positions advertised include:** Associate Manager; Compliance Manager; Computer Systems Validation Specialist; Mechanical Supervisor; Porter; Premium Buyer; CAD Operator; Validation Engineer; Computer Systems Administrator; Staff Validation Specialist; Publishing Technician; Medical Writer. **Note:** Current positions are updated on the website. **Corporate headquarters location:** This location. **Other area locations:** Statewide. **International locations:** Worldwide.

SCHERING-PLOUGH CORPORATION

One Giralda Farms, Madison NJ 07940-1000. 973/822-7000. **Contact:** Human Resources Department. **World Wide Web address:** http://www.schering-plough.com. **Description:** Engaged in the discovery, development, manufacture, and marketing of pharmaceutical and consumer products. Pharmaceutical products include prescription drugs, over-the-counter medicines, eye care products, and animal health products. The consumer products group consists of proprietary medicines, toiletries, cosmetics, and foot care products. Brand names include Coricidin, Maybelline, Claritin, Coppertone, and Dr. Scholl's. **Positions advertised include:** Associate Manager; Compliance Manager; Computer Systems Validation Specialist; Mechanical Supervisor; Porter; Premium Buyer; CAD Operator; Validation Engineer; Computer Systems Administrator; Staff Validation Specialist; Publishing Technician; Medical Writer. **Note:** Current positions are updated on the website. **Corporate headquarters location:** Kenilworth NJ. **Other area locations:** Statewide. **International locations:** Worldwide.

SCIENTIFIC INDUSTRIES, INC.

70 Orville Drive, Bohemia NY 11716. 631/567-4700. **Toll-free phone:** 888/850-6208. **Contact:** Personnel. **World Wide Web address:** http://www.scientificindustries.com. **Description:** Manufactures and markets laboratory equipment including vortex mixers and miscellaneous laboratory apparatuses including timers, rotators, and pumps. The company develops and sells computerized control and data logging systems for sterilizers and autoclaves. Scientific Industries' products are used by hospital laboratories, clinics, research laboratories, pharmaceutical manufacturers, and medical device manufacturers. **Office hours:** Monday – Friday, 9:00 a.m. – 5:00 p.m. **Corporate headquarters location:** This location. **Listed on:** NASDAQ. **Stock exchange symbol:** SCND. **President/CEO:** Helena Santos.

STERIS-ISOMEDIX SERVICES

23 Elizabeth Drive, Chester NY 10918. 845/469-4087. **Contact:** Human Resources. **World Wide Web address:** http://www.steris.com/isomedix. **Description:** Provides contract sterilization services to manufacturers of prepackaged health care and consumer products.

SYNAPTIC PHARMACEUTICAL CORPORATION

215 College Road, Paramus NJ 07652. 201/261-1331. **Contact:** Human Resources. **World Wide Web address:** http://www.synapticcorp.com. **Description:** Synaptic Pharmaceutical Corporation researches and develops pharmaceuticals. Founded in 1987. **NOTE:** For current job postings and on-line contact information, see the above Website. Part-time jobs are offered. **Positions advertised include:** Scientist. **Corporate headquarters location:** This location. **Operations at this facility include:** This location houses administrative offices and is not involved in the manufacturing process. **Listed on:** NASDAQ. **Stock exchange symbol:** SNAP. **Number of employees at this location:** 130.

TEVA PHARMACEUTICALS USA

18-01 River Road, Fair Lawn NJ 07410. 201/703-2553. **Fax:** 201/703-9491. **Contact:** Human Resources. **World Wide Web address:** http://www.tevapharmusa.com. **Description:** Manufactures and markets generic pharmaceuticals. The company focuses on therapeutic medicines for the analgesic, cardiovascular, dermatological, and anti-inflammatory markets. **Corporate headquarters location:** This location. **Other area locations:** Elmwood Park NJ; Fairfield NJ; Paterson NJ; Waldwick NJ. **Other U.S. locations:** Mexico MO. **Number of employees nationwide:** 790.

UNDERWRITERS LABORATORIES INC.
1285 Walt Whitman Road, Melville NY 11747-3801. 631/271-6200. **Fax:** 631/271-8259. **Contact:** Employment Coordinator. **E-mail address:** melville@us.ul.com. **World Wide Web address:** http://www.ul.com. **Description:** An independent, nonprofit organization that specializes in product safety testing and certification worldwide. **Special programs:** Summer Jobs. **Corporate headquarters location:** Northbrook IL. **Other U.S. locations:** Santa Clara CA; Research Triangle Park NC; Camas WA. **Number of employees at this location:** 800. **Number of employees worldwide:** 4,000.

UNIGENE LABORATORIES, INC.
110 Little Falls Road, Fairfield NJ 07004. 973/882-0860. **Fax:** 973/227-6088. **Contact:** Human Resources. **World Wide Web address:** http://www.unigene.com. **Description:** A biopharmaceutical research and manufacturing company that has developed a patented method to produce calcitonin, a leading drug for treating osteoporosis. Founded in 1980. **Corporate headquarters location:** This location. **Other U.S. locations:** Boonton NJ. **Listed on:** NASDAQ. **Stock exchange symbol:** UGNE. **President:** Warren P. Levy, Ph.D. **Annual sales/revenues:** $5 - $10 million. **Number of employees at this location:** 65.

UNILEVER HOME & PERSONAL CARE USA
45 River Road, Edgewater NJ 07020. 201/943-7100. **Contact:** Human Resources. **World Wide Web address:** http://www.unilever.com. **Description:** Researches and develops household and personal care products. **Corporate headquarters location:** Greenwich CT. **Annual sales/revenues:** More than $100 million. **Number of employees at this location:** 500.

WATSON PHARMACEUTICALS, INC.
131 West Street, Danbury CT 06810. 203/744-7200. **Contact:** Human Resources. **World Wide Web address:** http://www.watsonpharm.com. **Description:** Manufactures generic prescription drugs. **Corporate headquarters location:** Corona CA. **Other U.S. locations:** Nationwide. **Parent company:** Watson Pharmaceuticals. **Listed on:** New York Stock Exchange. **Stock exchange symbol:** WPI. **Number of employees at this location:** 85.

WATSON PHARMACEUTICALS, INC.
360 Mount Kemble Avenue, Morristown NJ 07962. 973/355-8300. **Contact:** Human Resources. **World Wide Web address:** http://www.watsonpharm.com. **Description:** Manufactures generic drugs. **Positions advertised include:** Meeting & Travel Services Manager; System Analyst Developer; Associate Director Regulatory Affairs; Sales Automation Manager; Accountant; Administrative Assistant; Analytics & Sales Information Director. **Corporate headquarters location:** This location. **Listed on:** New York Stock Exchange. **Stock exchange symbol:** WPI. **Number of employees nationwide:** 1,500.

WATSON PHARMACEUTICALS, INC.
33 Ralph Avenue, P.O. Box 30, Copiague NY 11726-1297. 631/842-8383. **Contact:** Personnel Director. **World Wide Web address:** http://www.watsonpharm.com. **Description:** Manufactures brand-name and generic pharmaceuticals in the areas of dermatology, women's health, neuropsychiatry, and primary care. **Positions advertised include:** Scientist; Chemist; Documentation Coordinator; Validation Engineer; Training Manager; Scheduler; Packaging Manager.

WYETH CORPORATION
5 Giralda Farms, Madison NJ 07940. 973/660-5000. **Contact:** Human Resources. **World Wide Web address:** http://www.wyeth.com. **Description:** Manufactures and markets prescription drugs and medical supplies, packaged

medicines, food products, household products, and housewares. Each division operates through one or more of Wyeth Corporation's subsidiaries. Prescription Drugs and Medical Supplies operates through: Wyeth-Ayerst Laboratories (produces ethical pharmaceuticals, biologicals, nutritional products, over-the-counter antacids, vitamins, and sunburn remedies); Fort Dodge Animal Health (veterinary pharmaceuticals and biologicals); Sherwood Medical (medical devices, diagnostic instruments, test kits, and bacteria identification systems); and Corometrics Medical Systems (medical electronic instrumentation for obstetrics and neonatology). The Packaged Medicines segment operates through Whitehall-Robins Healthcare (produces analgesics, cold remedies, and other packaged medicines). The Food Products segment operates through American Home Foods (canned pasta, canned vegetables, specialty foods, mustard, and popcorn). The Household Products and Housewares segment operates through: Boyle-Midway (cleaners, insecticides, air fresheners, waxes, polishes, and other items for home, appliance, and apparel care); Dupli-Color Products (touch-up, refinishing, and other car care and shop-use products); Ekco Products (food containers, commercial baking pans, industrial coatings, food-handling systems, foilware, and plasticware); Ekco Housewares (cookware, cutlery, kitchen tools, tableware and accessories, and padlocks); and Prestige Group (cookware, cutlery, kitchen tools, carpet sweepers, and pressure cookers). **Positions advertised include:** Administrative Assistant; Regional Manager; Clinical Research Associate; Executive Assistant; Manager of Information Management; Project Manager; Human Resources Assistant; Forecasting Analyst; Trade Promotion Manager; Category Manager. **Corporate headquarters location:** This location. **Number of employees worldwide:** 53,000.

WYETH
401 North Middletown Road, Pearl River NY 10965-1299. 845/732-5000. **Contact:** Personnel Director. **World Wide Web address:** http://www.wyeth.com. **Description:** Manufactures both prescription and nonprescription pharmaceutical and hospital products including pharmaceuticals for the treatment of infectious diseases, mental illness, cancer, arthritis, skin disorders, glaucoma, tuberculosis, and other diseases; adult and pediatric vaccines; vitamin, multivitamin, and mineral products; and Davis & Geck surgical sutures, wound closure devices, and other hospital products. **Listed on:** New York Stock Exchange. **Stock exchange symbol:** WYE.

BUSINESS SERVICES & NON-SCIENTIFIC RESEARCH

You can expect to find the following types of companies in this section:
Adjustment and Collection Services • Cleaning, Maintenance, and Pest Control Services • Credit Reporting Services • Detective, Guard, and Armored Car Services • Security Systems Services • Miscellaneous Equipment Rental and Leasing • Secretarial and Court Reporting Services

---

ADT SECURITY SERVICES
21 Northfield Avenue, Edison NJ 08837. 732/225-0047. **Contact:** Personnel. **World Wide Web address:** http://www.adt.com. **Description:** Services more than 15,000 burglar, fire, and other alarm systems. ADT Security Services also manufactures a variety of alarms and monitoring equipment for use in alarm service operations and for sale to commercial and industrial users. **Positions advertised include:** Data Entry Processor. **Corporate headquarters location:** Boca Raton FL. **Other U.S. locations:** Orlando FL; St. Petersburg FL; Tampa FL; Atlanta GA; Baltimore MD; Rockville MD. **Parent company:** Tyco Fire & Security.

ADT SECURITY SERVICES
335 West 16th Street, New York NY 10011. 646/336-2300. **Contact:** Human Resources. **World Wide Web address:** http://www.adt.com. **Description:** Designs, programs, markets, and installs protective systems to safeguard life and property from hazards such as burglary, hold-up, and fire. ADT Security Services has over 180,000 customers in the United States, Canada, and Western Europe. Founded in 1874. **Positions advertised include:** Commercial Sales Representative. **Corporate headquarters location:** Boca Raton FL. **Parent company:** Tyco International Ltd. **Listed on:** New York Stock Exchange. **Stock exchange symbol:** TYC.

ADECCO SA
175 Broad Hollow Road, Melville NY 11747. 631/844-7800. **Fax:** 631/844-7022. **Contact:** Human Resources. **World Wide Web address:** http://www.adecco.com. **Description:** Provides a wide variety of job search and placement services, from temporary placements to executive recruitment. **Corporate headquarters location:** Zurich, Switzerland. **Other locations:** Worldwide. **Subsidiaries include:** Lee Hecht Harrison. **Operations at this facility include:** North American headquarters. **Listed on:** New York Stock Exchange; Swiss Exchange. **Stock exchange symbol:** ADO; ADEN. **Annual sales/revenues:** $18 million. **Number of employees worldwide:** 700,000.

ALLIED SECURITY, INC.
14 East 39th Street, 2nd Floor, New York NY 10016. 212/532-1744. **Fax:** 212/689-7521. **Contact:** Human Resources. **World Wide Web address:** http://www.alliedsecurity.com. **Description:** A full-service corporate security firm that provides contract guard services, electronic security, and investigative services. **Positions advertised include:** Security Guard. **Corporate headquarters location:** King of Prussia PA. **Other area locations:** Albany NY; Hudson NY; Mineola NY; Yonkers NY. **Other U.S. locations:** Nationwide. **Subsidiaries/Affiliates include:** Spectaguard Inc. **Parent company:** MacAndrews & Forbes. **Operations at this facility include:** Divisional Office. **Annual sales/revenues:** $500 million. **Number of employees:** 19,000.

AMERICAN CLAIMS EVALUATION, INC.
One Jericho Plaza, 3rd Floor, Wing B, Jericho NY 11753. 516/938-8000. **Fax:** 516/938-0405. **Contact:** Gary J. Knauer, CFO, Treasurer, Secretary, & Human Resources VP. **Description:** American Claims Evaluation, Inc. provides a full range of vocational rehabilitation and disability management services through its wholly owned subsidiaries. The company is a health care cost containment services company that verifies the accuracy of hospital bills submitted to its clients for payment. Such clients include commercial health insurance companies, third-party administrators, health maintenance organizations, and self-insured corporate clients. **Corporate headquarters location:** This location. **Subsidiaries include:** RPM Rehabilitation & Associates, Inc. **Listed on:** NASDAQ. **Stock exchange symbol:** AMCE. **Chairman/President/CEO:** Gary Gelman. **Annual sales/revenues:** $1.3 million. **Number of employees:** 22.

AMERICAN STUDENT LIST COMPANY, LLC
330 Old Country Road, Mineola NY 11501-4143. 516/248-6100. **Fax:** 516/248-6364. **Contact:** Human Resources. **World Wide Web address:** http://www.americanstudentlist.com. **Description:** A leading provider of direct marketing information of preschool children and students from elementary schools, high schools, colleges, and post-graduate schools throughout the United States. Lists are rented primarily to various colleges, educational institutions, financial institutions, magazine publishers, and national organizations. Lists are available for all geographic areas of the United States and are provided to customers in the form of mailing labels, magnetic tape, or computer diskettes. **Other U.S. locations:** Boca Raton FL. **Parent company:** Havas Advertising (Levallois-Perret Cedex, France).

AUTOMATIC DATA PROCESSING (ADP)
99 Jefferson Road, P.O. Box 450, Parsippany NJ 07054. 973/739-3000. **Contact:** Human Resources. **World Wide Web address:** http://www.adp.com. **Description:** One of the world's largest providers of computerized transaction processing, data communications, and information services. ADP pays over 18 million U.S. employees. The company provides payroll processing, payroll tax filing, job costing, labor distribution, automated bill payment, management reports, unemployment compensation management, human resource information, and benefits administration support to over 300,000 businesses. **Special programs:** Internships. **Corporate headquarters location:** Roseland NJ. **Operations at this facility include:** Divisional Headquarters; Research and Development. **Listed on:** New York Stock Exchange. **Stock exchange symbol:** ADP. **Annual sales/revenues:** More than $100 million. **Number of employees nationwide:** 25,000.

AUTOMATIC DATA PROCESSING (ADP)
One ADP Boulevard, Roseland NJ 07068. 973/974-5000. **Contact:** Human Resources. **World Wide Web address:** http://www.adp.com. **Description:** ADP is one of the world's largest providers of computerized transaction processing, data communications, and information services. ADP pays over 18 million U.S. employees. The company provides payroll processing, payroll tax filing, job costing, labor distribution, automated bill payment, management reports, unemployment compensation management, human resource information, and benefits administration support to over 300,000 businesses. **Corporate headquarters location:** This location. **Operations at this facility include:** This location houses administrative offices. **Listed on:** New York Stock Exchange. **Stock exchange symbol:** ADP. **Annual sales/revenues:** More than $100 million. **Number of employees nationwide:** 25,000.

BAX GLOBAL
896 Frelinghuysen Avenue, Newark NJ 07114. 973/954-2000. **Fax:** 973/954-2030. **Contact:** Human Resources. **World Wide Web address:**

http://www.baxglobal.com. **Description:** Bax Global offers business-to-business freight delivery through a worldwide network of offices in 124 countries, with 155 offices in the U.S. **Other area locations:** Secaucus NJ. **Other U.S. locations:** Nationwide. **International locations:** Worldwide.

BISYS GROUP, INC.
2091 Springdale Road, Cherry Hill NJ 08003. 824/424-0150. **Contact:** Human Resources. **World Wide Web address:** http://www.bisys.com. **Description:** A national, third-party provider of computing, administrative, and marketing support services to financial organizations. Services are offered through three major business units: Information Services, Loan Services, and Investment Services. The company derives a majority of its revenues from services provided through a single integrated software product, TOTAL PLUS, which includes comprehensive loan and deposit administration; branch automation and electronic banking services; operations and new business systems support; and accounting, financial management, and regulatory reporting services. **Positions advertised include:** Computer Operator; Conversion Analyst; Relationship Manager; Client Services Representative. **NOTE:** Resumes may be submitted on-line at the above Website. Job postings are listed by location in the "Careers" section. **Listed on:** New York Stock Exchange. **Stock exchange symbol:** BSG.

BRINKS INC
481 New Jersey Railroad Avenue, Newark NJ 07114. 973/824-0778. **Fax:** 973/824-1396. **Contact:** Human Resources. **World Wide Web address:** www.brinksinc.com. **Description:** An armored security service specializing in transporting currency. **Corporate headquarters location:** Dallas TX.

BRINKS INC
652 Kent Avenue, Brooklyn NY 11211. 718-643-3200. **Contact:** Personnel. **World Wide Web address:** http://www.brinksinc.com. **Description:** An armored security service specializing in transporting currency. **Other U.S. locations:** Nationwide.

CT CORPORATION SYSTEM
111 Eighth Avenue, 13th Floor, New York NY 10011. 212/590-9009. **Fax:** 212/894-8710. **Contact:** Human Resources. **E-mail address:** info@ctadvantage.com. **World Wide Web address:** http://www.ctcorporation.com. **Description:** C.T. Corporation provides research and accounting services for attorneys. **Positions advertised include:** Staff Accountant; Service Team Leader; Internal Support Analyst; Accounts Receivable Maintenance Clerk; Associate Customer Specialist; Quality Assurance Professional; Receptionist; Project Manager; Desktop Support Analyst; Information Technology Manager; Senior Product Manager; Associate Customer Specialist; Operations Process Management Director; Licensing Support Specialist. **Parent company:** Wolters Kluwer U.S. **Number of employees:** 1,100.

CASCADE LINEN SERVICES
835 Myrtle Avenue, Brooklyn NY 11206. 718/963-9600. **Contact:** Human Resources. **Description:** Provides commercial linen supply and rental services for hotels, restaurants, and medical institutions. **Corporate headquarters location:** This location.

CENDANT CORPORATION
One Campus Drive, Parsippany NJ 07054-0642. 973/428-9700. **Fax:** 973/496-5966. **Contact:** Human Resources. **E-mail address:** cendant.jobs@cendant.com. **World Wide Web address**: http://www.cendant.com. **Description:** Provides a wide range of business services including dining services, hotel franchise management, mortgage

programs, and timeshare exchanges. Cendant Corporation's Real Estate Division offers employee relocation and mortgage services through Century 21, Coldwell Banker, ERA, Cendant Mortgage, and Cendant Mobility. The Travel Division provides car rentals, vehicle management services, and vacation timeshares through brand names including Avia, Days Inn, Howard Johnson, Ramada, Travelodge, and Super 8. The Membership Division offers travel, shopping, auto, dining, and other financial services through Travelers Advantage, Shoppers Advantage, Auto Vantage, Welcome Wagon, Netmarket, North American Outdoor Group, and PrivacyGuard. **Positions advertised include;** Commercial Marketing Associate; Mortgage Processor; Staff Accountant; Financial Analyst; International Treasury Manager; Marketing Manager; Executive Assistant; Regional Business Consultant; Staff Accountant; Director; Finance Manager; Administrative Assistant; Marketing Communications Manager. **Corporate headquarters location:** New York NY. **Listed on:** New York Stock Exchange. **Stock exchange symbol:** CD. **President/CEO:** Henry Silverman. **Number of employees at this location:** 1,100. **Number of employees worldwide:** 28,000.

CENDANT CORPORATION
9 West 57th Street, 37th Floor, New York NY 10019. 212/413-1800. **Fax:** 212/413-1918. **Contact:** Terence P. Conley, Human Resources. **World Wide Web address:** http://www.cendant.com. **Description:** Provides a wide range of business services including dining services, hotel franchise management, mortgage programs, and timeshare exchanges. Cendant Corporation's Real Estate Division offers employee relocation and mortgage services through Century 21, Coldwell Banker, ERA, Cendant Mortgage, and Cendant Mobility. The Travel Division provides car rentals, vehicle management services, and vacation timeshares through brand names including Avia, Days Inn, Howard Johnson, Ramada, Travelodge, and Super 8. The Membership Division offers travel, shopping, auto, dining, and other financial services through Travelers Advantage, Shoppers Advantage, Auto Vantage, Welcome Wagon, Netmarket, North American Outdoor Group, and PrivacyGuard. Founded in 1997. **NOTE:** Paper resumes are no longer accepted. **Positions advertised include:** International Relocation Consultant; Partner Marketing Manager; Hotel Manager; Field Auditor. **Corporate headquarters location:** This location. **Subsidiaries include:** Avis Group Holdings, Inc.; Budget Group, Inc.; Century 21 Real Estate Corporation; Coldwell Banker Real Estate Corporation; Days Inn Worldwide Inc.; Fairfield Resorts, Inc.; Galileo International, Inc.; Howard Johnson International Inc.; Jackson Hewitt Inc.; NRT Incorporated; PHH Arval; Ramada Franchise Systems Inc.; Super 8 Motels, Inc.; Travelodge Hotels, Inc.; Trendwest Resorts, Inc. **Listed on:** New York Stock Exchange. **Stock exchange symbol:** CD. **Chairman/President/CEO:** Henry R. Silverman. **Annual sales/revenues:** $14 billion. **Number of employees worldwide:** 85,000.

COLIN SERVICE SYSTEMS, INC.
One Brockway Place, White Plains NY 10601. 914/328-0800. **Fax:** 914/328-3385. **Contact:** Judy Archer, Human Resources Director. **World Wide Web address:** http://www.colin.com. **Description:** A housekeeping and mechanical maintenance company providing administrative, safety, and training services for commercial clients covering 10 states from six regional offices specializing in cleaning services. **Positions advertised include:** Customer Service Representative; Environmental Engineer; Custodian; Housekeeper. **Corporate headquarters location:** This location. **President:** Richard Marteo. **Annual sales/revenues:** $100 million. **Number of employees:** 4,000.

COMPUTER OUTSOURCING SERVICES, INC. (COSI)
2 Christie Heights Street, Leonia NJ 07605. 201/840-4753. **Fax:** 201/363-9675. **Contact:** Human Resources. **World Wide Web address:** http://www.cosi-us.com. **Description:** Provides payroll, data processing, and tax filing services to companies in book publishing, apparel, direct response marketing, and other

industries. **Corporate headquarters location:** This location. **Listed on:** NASDAQ. **Stock exchange symbol:** COSI.

CYBERDATA, INC.
20 Max Avenue, Hicksville NY 11801. 516/942-8000. **Fax:** 516/942-0800. **Contact:** Job Opportunities Department. **E-mail address:** jobs@cyberdata.com. **World Wide Web address:** http://www.cyberdata.com. **Description:** Provides an array of information-based services for client companies including information management, storage, and dissemination. CyberData, Inc. offers a mass fax service through a large number of modems. **Positions advertised include:** Computer Programmer; Sales Representative.

DICE INC.
3 Park Avenue, 33rd Floor, New York NY 10016. 212/725-6550. **Fax:** 212/725-6559. **Contact:** Jeff Deese, Human Resources Director. **World Wide Web address:** http://www.dice.com. **Description:** Provides online services to IT companies and operates a job board Website for technology professionals. The technical resources offered include hundreds of technical books, a retail store, and information on the newest technologies. Founded in 1994. **NOTE:** Mail Resumes to: Human Resources, 4101 NW Urbandale Drive, Urbandale IA 50322. **Corporate headquarters location:** This location. **Other locations:** Urbandale IA; Alpharetta GA; Augustine FL. **Subsidiaries include:** MeasureUp; dice.com. **Listed on:** Over The Counter. **Stock exchange symbol:** DICEQ. **Chairman/President/CEO/Director:** Scot W. Melland. **Annual sales/revenues:** $56 million. **Number of employees:** 153.

DUN & BRADSTREET
One Diamond Hill Road, Murray Hill NJ 07974. 908/665-5000. **Contact:** Human Resources. **World Wide Web address:** http://www.dnb.com. **Description:** A holding company. **Positions advertised include:** Automotive Solutions Leader; Product Strategy Leader; Channel Management Leader; Communications Consultant; MBA Project Leader & Recruiter; Administrative Assistant Sales; Teleweb Leader; Global Marketing & Promotions Leader; New Customer Acquisitions Manager; Sales Support Coordinator; Marketing Coordinator; Financial Analyst; Director Marketing Strategy; Product Marketing Manager; Program Manager; Communications Executive Assistant; Principal Consultant; Human Resources Director. **Subsidiaries include:** Dun & Bradstreet, Inc. provides information to the business community about other companies including data on credit and marketing. Moody's Investor Services provides ratings and other financial market information to assist individuals and companies in assessing investment opportunities. **Listed on:** New York Stock Exchange. **Stock exchange symbol:** DNB. **Number of employees worldwide:** 12,000.

EMCOR GROUP, INC.
301 Merritt Seven, 6th Floor, Norwalk CT 06851. 203/849-7800. **Contact:** Elissa Hall, Human Resources. **World Wide Web address:** http://www.emcorgroup.com. **Description:** Emcor is a diversified business services company engaged primarily in developing, integrating, and maintaining electrical and mechanical systems for the commercial construction industry. In addition to electrical and mechanical construction services, the company also provides complete facilities management services across a number of market sectors, including healthcare, hotels/hospitality, education, government/public, transportation, water/wastewater, pharmaceutical, and others. **Positions advertised include:** Desktop Support Specialist. **Corporate headquarters location:** This location. **Other U.S. locations:** Nationwide. **International locations:** Worldwide. **Listed on:** New York Stock Exchange. **Stock exchange symbol:** EME.

ESQUIRE DEPOSITION SERVICES
216 East 45th Street, 8th Floor, New York NY 10017. 212/687-8010. **Fax:** 212/557-2153. **Contact:** Human Resources. **World Wide Web address:** http://www.esquiredeposition.com. **Description:** A court reporting firm using state-of-the-art technology to provide printed and computerized transcripts, video recordings of testimony from depositions, and speech recognition systems to the legal profession primarily in metropolitan New York City and Southern California. The company's technologies include real-time transcription, interactive real-time transcription, full-text search and retrieval programs, compressed transcripts, and multimedia technology systems. **Parent company:** The Hobart West Group. **Annual sales/revenues:** $200 million.

THE GREAT BRIDAL EXPO GROUP INC.
510 Montauk Highway, P.O. Box 337, West Islip NY 11795. 631/669-1200. **Fax:** 631/669-1680. **Contact:** Human Resources Department. **E-mail address:** info@greatbridalexpo.com. **World Wide Web address:** http://www.greatbridalexpo.com. **Description:** Produces and presents trade-show expositions in major cities in the United States. These expositions introduce prospective brides and grooms and their families to products and services they may need to plan their weddings, honeymoons, and homes.

GUARDIAN CLEANING INDUSTRIES
170 Varick Street, 3rd Floor, New York NY 10013. 212/645-9500. **Contact:** Human Resources. **World Wide Web address:** http://www.guardian.baweb.com. **Description:** An industrial/commercial maintenance firm providing cleaning and exterminating services.

HEALTH MANAGEMENT SYSTEMS, INC.
401 Park Avenue South, New York NY 10016. 212/685-4545. **Fax:** 212/889-8776. **Contact:** Lewis D. Levetown, Director Human Resources. **E-mail address:** recruit@hmsy.com. **World Wide Web address:** http://www.hmsy.com. **Description:** The company works with government health agencies, Medicaid, and Medicare to recover overpaid healthcare expenses from providers by supplying information management services and software. HMS provides financial systems and consulting, retroactive insurance claims reprocessing, data processing, and third-party liability recovery services. **Corporate headquarters location:** This location. **Other U.S. locations:** Nationwide. **Affiliates include:** Accordis. **Parent company:** HMS Holdings Corp. (also at this location). **Chairman/CEO:** William (Bill) F. Miller III. **Annual sales/revenues:** $59 million. **Number of employees:** 433.

HEALTHPLEX, INC.
60 Charles Lindbergh Boulevard, Uniondale NY 11553-3608. 516/794-3000. **Fax:** 516/794-3186. **Contact:** Human Resources. **World Wide Web address:** http://www.healthplex.com. **Description:** Provides administrative services, primarily claims processing and related electronic data processing services. **Subsidiaries include:** Dentcare Delivery Systems, Inc.; International Healthcare Services, Inc.; OASYS Corporation. **Annual sales/revenues:** $21 million. **Number of employees:** 140.

HOUSEHOLD INTERNATIONAL
200 Somerset Corporate Boulevard, Bridgewater NJ 08807. 908/203-2100. **Contact:** Personnel. **World Wide Web address:** http://www.household.com/corp/index.jsp. **Description:** Provides data processing services for the insurance and banking industries. **Positions advertised include:** Account Executive, Beneficial.

INTERPOOL, INC.
633 Third Avenue, 27th Floor, New York NY 10017. 212/916-3261. **Contact:** Human Resources. **World Wide Web address:** http://www.interpool.com. **Description:** Leases containers and chassis, primarily to container shipping lines. The company is one of the world's leading lessors of intermodal dry cargo containers and one of the largest lessors of intermodal container chassis in the United States. Founded in 1968. **Corporate headquarters location:** Princeton NJ. **International locations:** Worldwide. **Subsidiaries include:** Interpool Limited conducts the international container leasing business. **Listed on:** New York Stock Exchange. **Stock exchange symbol:** IPX. **Annual sales/revenues:** $300 million. **Number of employees:** 200.

KEANE
39 Old Ridgebury Road, Suite 8, Danbury CT 06810-5108. 203/744-8877. **Fax:** 203/794-1176. **Contact:** Human Resources. **E-mail address:** info.ct@keane.com. **World Wide Web address:** http://www.keane.com. **Description:** Keane collaborates with Global 2000 and government agencies to produce software to help the agencies business strategies. **Positions advertised include:** Managing Director. **Corporate headquarters location:** Boston MA. **Other area locations:** Rocky Hill CT. **Other U.S. locations:** Nationwide. **International locations:** Coventry, England; London, England; New Delhi, India; Hyderabad, India. **Listen on:** American Stock Exchange. **Stock Exchange Symbol:** KEA.

LOOMIS FARGO & COMPANY
701 Kingstand Avenue, Lyndhurst NJ 07071. 201/939-2700. **Fax:** 201/939-1934. **Contact:** Personnel. **World Wide Web address:** http://www.loomisfargo.com. **Description:** An armored security service specializing in transporting currency. **NOTE:** Applications will not be mailed to jobseekers. They must be picked up in person. **Other U.S. locations:** Nationwide.

JOHN C. MANDEL SECURITY BUREAU INC.
611 Jackson Avenue, Bronx NY 10455. 718/402-5002. **Fax:** 718/402-5004. **Contact:** Personnel Department. **World Wide Web address:** http://www.johncmandel.com. **Description:** Provides security services through armed and unarmed guards on an around-the-clock basis throughout the New York City metropolitan area. Clients range from private housing developments and projects to a wide range of commercial and industrial customers. **Corporate headquarters location:** This location. **Other locations:** Amenia NY; Brooklyn NY.

GREG MANNING AUCTIONS, INC.
775 Passaic Avenue, West Caldwell NJ 07006. 973/882-0004. **Fax:** 973/882-3499. **Contact:** Personnel. **E-mail address:** info@gregmanning.com. **World Wide Web address:** http://www.gregmanning.com. **Description:** Conducts public auctions of rare stamps, stamp collections, and stocks. Items included in the auctions are rare stamps; sports trading cards and sports memorabilia; rare glassware and pottery; pre-Colombian art objects; Egyptian, Middle Eastern, and Far Eastern antiquities; and rare coins. **Corporate headquarters location:** This location. **Listed on:** NASDAQ. **Stock exchange symbol:** GMAI.

MERCER HUMAN RESOURCE CONSULTING
1166 Avenue of the Americas, New York NY 10036. 212/345-7000. **Fax:** 212/345-7414. **Contact:** National Recruiting Coordinator. **World Wide Web address:** http://www.mercerhr.com. **Description:** An actuarial and human resources management consulting firm with 140 offices in 40 countries worldwide. The company offers advice to organizations on all aspects of employee/management relationships. Services include retirement, health and welfare, performance and rewards, communication, investment, human

resources administration, risk, finance and insurance, and health care provider consulting. **Positions advertised include:** Actuarial Analyst; Actuarial Consultant; Administrative Assistant; Compensation Analyst; Consultant; Administrative Assistant Floater; Senior Consultant. **Corporate headquarters location:** This location. **Other U.S. locations:** Nationwide. **International locations:** Worldwide. **Parent company:** Marsh & McLennan Companies, Inc. **Number of employees:** 13,000.

NASSAU LIBRARY SYSTEM
900 Jerusalem Avenue, Uniondale NY 11553. 516/292-8920. **Fax:** 516/481-4777. **Contact:** Jan Heinlein, Personnel. **E-mail address:** heinlein@nassaulibrary.org. **World Wide Web address:** http://www.nassaulibrary.org. **Description:** An association of autonomous local public libraries and a central service center, with 54 libraries in the system. The system office supports local library service through a wide range of supplementary and complementary services, collections, specialized staff, and professional programming; provides effective and economical centralized services; initiates legislation beneficial to library service; and develops, promotes, and maintains standards of library service within Nassau County. The system also provides extensive technical services to member libraries. **Corporate headquarters location:** This location.

ONESOURCE FACILITY SERVICES
429 West 53rd Street, New York NY 10019. 212/408-6200. **Contact:** Human Resources. **World Wide Web address:** http://www.2onesource.com. **Description:** Provides a variety of services including janitorial, landscaping, and pest control to public institutions, retail stores, schools, industrial facilities, and commercial buildings. **Corporate headquarters location:** Atlanta GA.

REED BUSINESS INFORMATION
360 Park Avenue South, New York NY 10014. 646/746-6400. **Fax:** 646/746-7433. **Contact:** Director of Human Resources. **World Wide Web address:** http://www.reedbusiness.com. **Description:** Reed Business Information is a leading business-to-business magazine publisher with more than 80 specialty publications serving 16 major service and industry sectors including media, electronics, research and technology, computers, food service, and manufacturing. **Corporate headquarters location:** This location. **Other U.S. locations:** Nationwide. **International locations:** Worldwide. **Parent company:** Reed Elsevier Group plc. **Operations at this facility include:** This location publishes several magazine titles including *Broadcasting & Cable*, *Childbirth*, *Daily Variety*, *Graphic Arts Monthly*, *Library Journal*, *Modern Bride*, *Motor Boat*, and *Publishers Weekly*. **Listed on:** New York Stock Exchange. **Stock exchange symbol:** ENL; RUK. **Number of employees at this location:** 500. **Number of employees worldwide:** 12,000.

RESEARCH INTERNATIONAL
3 Landmark Square, Fourth Floor, Stamford CT 06901. 203/358-0900. **Fax:** 312/787-4156. **Contact:** Human Resources. **E-mail address:** greatjobs@research-int.com. **World Wide Web address:** http://www.research-int.com. **Description:** A company specializing in custom market research. Company teams up with clients and coaches them on making their own companies thrive. **Positions advertised include:** Senior Research Manager. **Other U.S. locations:** Nationwide. **International locations:** Worldwide.

RIOT MANHATTAN
545 Fifth Avenue, 5th Floor, New York NY 10017. 212/907-1200. **Fax:** 212/907-1201. **Contact:** Human Resources. **E-mail address:** info@rioting.com. **World Wide Web address:** http://www.riotmanhattan.com. **Description:** Provides post

production and creative services. **Corporate headquarters location:** This location.

SANBORN MAP COMPANY
629 Fifth Avenue, Pelham NY 10803. 914/738-1649. **Fax:** 914/738-1680. **Contact:** General Manager. **E-mail address:** pelham@sanborn.com. **World Wide Web address:** http://www.sanbornmap.com. **Description:** A mapping and geographical information service, Sanborn Map Company is a data source for AM/FM, GIS, and environmental investigations. Sanborn's operations are organized through three units: Mapping, Custom Databases, and Environmental Data Services. Mapping involves building footprint maps showing street addresses and building details based on actual field inspections. Sanborn's Environmental Data Services operation uses an archive of maps dating back to 1867 to show building and land use including underground tanks and pipes, types of material stored, and owners and occupants of properties. The company's Custom Databases operation produces databases and designed digital map files based on Sanborn's existing map collection and its current field survey services. Information collected from the field survey services include land and building uses, housing unit counts, building vacancy status, building construction details, and building condition. **Corporate headquarters location:** This location. **Other area locations:** Rochester NY. **Other U.S. locations:** Chesterfield MO; San Antonio TX; Columbus OH; Colorado Springs CO; Charlotte NC. **Operations at this facility include:** Administration; Manufacturing; Research and Development; Sales. **CEO:** Pankaj Desai. **Number of employees at this location:** 35.

SCIENCE MANAGEMENT LLC
SMC CONSULTING
745 Routes 202/206, Bridgewater NJ 08807. 908/722-0300. **Fax:** 908/722-0421. **Contact:** Personnel. **E-mail address:** info@smcmgmt.com. **World Wide Web address:** http://www.smcmgmt.com. **Description:** Works with IBM to provide disaster recovery services to large corporations. SMC Consulting (also at this location) provides management consulting services. **Corporate headquarters location:** This location.

SUFFOLK COOPERATIVE LIBRARY SYSTEM
627 North Sunrise Service Road, Bellport NY 11713. 631/286-1600. **Contact:** Dorothy Curto, Human Resources Specialist. **World Wide Web address:** http://www.suffolk.lib.ny.us. **Description:** A county-chartered library association that provides a variety of support services to the 52 libraries comprising the Suffolk County library system. **Corporate headquarters location:** This location.

TEAM STAFF, INC.
300 Atrium Drive, Somerset NJ 08873. 732/748-1700. **Toll-free phone:** 800/565-8303. **Fax:** 732/748-3220. **Contact:** Human Resources. **E-mail address:** peo@teamstaff.com. **World Wide Web address:** http://www.teamstaff.com. **Description:** A full-line provider of human resource management services to employers in a wide variety of industries. Services include professional employer organization (employee leasing) services, placement of temporary and permanent staffing, and payroll and payroll tax service preparation. **Corporate headquarters location:** This location.

TEMCO SERVICE INDUSTRIES INC.
One Park Avenue, 1st Floor, New York NY 10016. 212/889-6353. **Contact:** Human Resources. **Description:** Offers a wide variety of maintenance, security, and related services through a workforce directed by a network of experienced managers. The company operates in the following areas: Building Maintenance Services; Engineering Maintenance Services; Extermination and Security Services; and Incineration and Heat Recovery Systems. **Corporate**

headquarters location: This location. **International locations:** Belgium. **Operations at this facility include:** Administration; Sales; Service.

WESTCHESTER LIBRARY SYSTEM
410 Saw Mill River Road, Ardsley NY 10502. 914/674-3600. **Fax:** 914/674-4185. **Contact:** Personnel. **World Wide Web address:** http://www.wls.lib.ny.us. **Description:** Provides a wide range of buying, distribution, and other support services to the 38 member libraries in the Westchester County library system. **Corporate headquarters location:** This location.

WINFIELD SECURITY
35 West 35th Street, New York NY 10001. 212/947-3700. **Contact:** Human Resources. **World Wide Web address:** http://www.winfieldsecurity.com. **Description:** Provides security guard services for office buildings, schools, businesses, and manufacturers. **Corporate headquarters location:** This location. **Other area locations:** Bronx NY; Brooklyn NY; Queens NY. **Other U.S. locations:** Bloomfield NJ.

WINSTON RESOURCES, INC.
535 Fifth Avenue, Suite 701, New York NY 10017. 212/557-5000. **Contact:** Human Resources. **Description:** Winston Resources is a network of recruiting companies. Winston Resources has seven owned offices and 21 offices licensed or franchised under various names. Businesses include a wide range of industries. Founded in 1967. **Corporate headquarters location:** This location.

WUNDERMAN
285 Madison Avenue, New York NY 10017. 212/941-3000. **Contact:** Careers. **World Wide Web address:** http://www.wunderman.com. **Description:** Provides communications and database technologies for the marketing industry through the company's international research and development marketing lab. **Positions advertised include:** Chief of Staff; Assistant Account Executive; Account Executive. **International locations:** Worldwide.

CHARITIES AND SOCIAL SERVICES

You can expect to find the following types of companies in this section:
Social and Human Service Agencies • Job Training and Vocational Rehabilitation Services • Nonprofit Organizations

---

ALCOHOLICS ANONYMOUS (A.A.)
P.O. Box 459, Grand Central Station, New York NY 10163. 212/870-3400. **Physical address:** 475 Riverside Drive, 11th Floor, New York NY 10115. **Contact:** Human Resources. **World Wide Web address:** http://www.alcoholics-anonymous.org. **Description:** Alcoholics Anonymous (A.A.) is a fellowship of men and women who share their experiences with each other so that they may work on their common problems and help others to recover from alcoholism. A.A. consists of 89,000 local groups in 141 countries. Founded in 1935. **Corporate headquarters location:** This location. **Subsidiaries include:** A.A. World Services, Inc. operates at this location with 100 employees coordinating with local groups, with A.A. groups in treatment and correctional facilities, and with members and groups overseas. A.A. literature is prepared, published, and distributed through this office. The A.A. Grapevine, Inc. publishes the *A.A. Grapevine,* the fellowship's monthly international journal. The magazine has a circulation of about 119,000 in the United States, Canada, and other countries. A.A. Grapevine, Inc. also produces a selection of cassette tapes and anthologies of magazine articles.

AMERICAN FOUNDATION FOR THE BLIND
11 Penn Plaza, Suite 300, New York NY 10001. 212/502-7600. **Toll-free phone:** 800/AFB-LINE. **Fax:** 212/502-7777. **Contact:** Kelly Bleach, Director of Personnel. **E-mail address:** afbinfo@afb.net. **World Wide Web address:** http://www.afb.org. **Description:** A nonprofit organization. The American Foundation for the Blind (AFB) is a leading national resource for people who are blind or visually impaired, the organizations that serve them, and the general public. AFB operates through four primary areas of activity: development, collection, and dissemination of information; identification, analysis, and resolution of critical issues; education of the public and policymakers on the needs and capabilities of people who are blind or visually impaired; and production and distribution of talking books and other audio materials. Founded in 1921.

AMERICAN RED CROSS
203 West Jersey Street, Elizabeth NJ 07202. 908/353-2500. **Contact:** Human Resources. **World Wide Web address:** http://www.redcross.org. **Description:** A humanitarian organization that aids disaster victims, gathers blood for crisis distribution, trains individuals to respond to emergencies, educates individuals on various diseases, and raises funds for other charities. **Other U.S. locations:** Nationwide.

AMERICAN SOCIETY FOR THE PREVENTION OF CRUELTY TO ANIMALS
424 East 92nd Street, New York NY 10128. 212/876-7700. **Fax:** 212/876-0014. **Contact:** Human Resources. **E-mail address:** hr@aspca.org. **World Wide Web address:** http://www.aspca.org. **Description:** The society is involved in six primary areas: animals as pets; humane education; animals for sport and entertainment; experimentation on animals; animal industries; and protection of wild animals and endangered species. Founded in 1866. **NOTE:** Human Resources phone: 212/876-0014. **Positions advertised include:** Director of

Medicine; Veterinarian; Custodian; Executive Assistant to COO; Assistant Director; Animal Behavior Counselor.

THE ARC OF BERGEN AND PASSAIC COUNTIES, INC.
223 Moore Street, Hackensack NJ 07601. 201/343-0322. **Fax:** 201/343-0401. **Contact:** Human Resources. **E-mail address:** arcbpc@aol.com. **World Wide Web address:** http://www.arcbergenpassaic.org. **Description:** A nonprofit organization that works with mentally disabled people to improve their quality of life.

BEDFORD STUYVESANT RESTORATION CORPORATION
1368 Fulton Street, Brooklyn NY 11216-2630. 718/636-6900. **Fax:** 718/636-0511. **Contact:** Human Resources. **E-mail address:** info@restorationplaza.org. **World Wide Web address:** http://www.restorationplaza.org. **Description:** A nonprofit community development corporations promoting the economic revitalization of the Bedford Stuyvesant section of Brooklyn since 1967.

THE BOYS' CLUB OF NEW YORK (BCNY)
287 East 10th Street, New York NY 10009. 212/677-1109. **Contact:** Hiring. **World Wide Web address:** http://www.bcny.org. **Description:** Provides a variety of services to young men in the New York City area. BCNY's educational program has helped hundreds of young men to attend leading prep schools and colleges, offering support and counseling to help them succeed. BCNY's job training program offers teenage members their first work experience in top-flight New York companies. The club offers a year-round program serving boys between 6 and 17 years old. Founded in 1876. **Corporate headquarters location:** This location.

CATHOLIC CHARITIES OF THE DIOCESE OF BROOKLYN & QUEENS
191 Joralemon Street, Brooklyn NY 11201. 718/722-6002. **Fax:** 718/722-6096. **Contact:** Sister Ellen Patricia Finn. **World Wide Web address:** http://www.ccbq.org. **Description:** A network of private social service organizations that provides food, shelter, and clothing to disadvantaged individuals. **Positions advertised include:** Social Worker; Case Aid; Staff Psychiatrist; Service Clinician; Case Manager; Social Service Assistant; Driver; Administrative Assistant; Program Coordinator. **Other locations:** Brooklyn NY; Queens NY.

CHILDREN'S AID SOCIETY
105 East 22nd Street, New York NY 10010. 212/949-4800. **Contact:** Human Resources Manager. **E-mail address:** jobs@childrensaidsociety.org. **World Wide Web address:** http://www.childrensaidsociety.org. **Description:** Provides early, intensive, and long-term support to thousands of city children and their families through various programs and services including medical and dental care, foster care, group homes, adoption, homemakers, emergency assistance, food distribution, Head Start, tutoring, mentors, community centers, community schools, counseling, court diversion programs, camps, sports, arts, dance, theater, chorus, internships, jobs, teen pregnancy prevention, leadership projects, college and prep/college scholarships, and services to the homeless. Founded in 1853. **NOTE:** Jobseekers may submit an application online. **Positions advertised include:** Accounts Payable Supervisor; Purchasing Manager; Clinical Nurse Administrator; Summer Camp Group Leader; Lifeguard; Social Worker; Medical Receptionist; Senior Social Worker; Gym/Recreation Specialist; Nutritionist; Nurse; Head Teacher; Violence Prevention Coordinator; Center Director; Family Services Director; Foster Care Social Worker; Homefinding Supervisor; Substance Abuse Specialist; Education Coordinator. **Corporate headquarters location:** This location. **Other locations:** Throughout the New York City metropolitan area. **Operations at this facility include:** Administration; Regional Headquarters.

CHILDREN'S VILLAGE

Westmore Hall, 1st Floor, Dobbs Ferry NY 10522. 914/693-0600 ext. 1214. **Fax:** 914/674-4512. **Contact:** Human Resources Department. **E-mail address:** recruiter@childrensvillage.org. **World Wide Web address:** http://www.childrensvillage.org. **Description:** A nonprofit organization that operates a residential treatment center for emotionally disturbed children. **Positions advertised include:** Social Worker; Assistant Director; Registered Nurse; Financial Analyst; Administrative Assistant; Child Care Worker; Sociotherapist; Cyber Café Supervisor. **Corporate headquarters location:** This location. **Other locations:** Harlem NY.

COMMUNITY ACTION COMMITTEE OF DANBURY

66 North Street, Danbury CT 06810. 203/744-4700. **Contact:** Human Resources. **Description:** A nonprofit organization that provides daycare, heating assistance, Head Start programs, counseling, bill payment assistance, and rental assistance services to low-income families.

COMMUNITY COUNSELING SERVICES COMPANY

461 Fifth Avenue, New York NY 10117. 212/695-1175. **Fax:** 212/967-6451. **Contact:** Human Resources Department. **E-mail address:** careers@ccsfundraising.com. **World Wide Web address:** http://www.ccsfundraising.com. **Description:** A nationwide fundraising company that organizes campaigns for nonprofit clients. **Positions advertised include:** Capital Campaign Director.

COMMUNITY SERVICE SOCIETY OF NEW YORK

105 East 22nd Street, New York NY 10010. 212/254-8900. **Fax:** 212/614-5336. **Contact:** Personnel Manager. **E-mail address:** cssemployment@cssny.org. **World Wide Web address:** http://www.cssny.org. **Description:** A nonprofit, social advocacy organization that conducts policy analysis and research, provides training and technical assistance to strengthen community-based organizations, and develops service programs that respond to the complex problems faced by the poor in New York City. **Positions advertised include:** Volunteer Program Coordinator; Training Manager; Program Manager; Program Specialist; Contract Coordinator; Experience Corps Program Coordinator.

THE FORD FOUNDATION

320 East 43rd Street, New York NY 10017. 212/573-5000. **Fax:** 212/351-3677. **Contact:** Human Resources. **World Wide Web address:** http://www.fordfound.org. **Description:** One of the largest philanthropic organizations in the United States. This private, nonprofit institution donates funds for educational, developmental, research, and experimental efforts designed to produce significant advances in a wide range of social problems. The company also operates several overseas field offices in Asia, Latin America, the Middle East, and Africa. **Corporate headquarters location:** This location. **Other locations:** Worldwide.

FOSTER HOME SERVICES
JEWISH CHILD CARE ASSOCIATION

120 Wall Street, 12th Floor, New York NY 10005. 212/425-3333. **Fax:** 212/652-4731. **Contact:** Human Resources. **World Wide Web address:** http://www.jewishchildcareny.org. **Description:** Provides social services for children including the placement of abused children in foster homes, as well as training programs for future foster parents. Founded in 1822. **NOTE:** See website for a current listing of job openings with detailed application information. **Positions advertised include:** Registered Nurse; Social Worker; Residential Milieu Counselor; Recruiter/Trainer. **Corporate headquarters location:** This location. **Operations at this facility include:** Administration; Service.

GIRL SCOUTS OF THE UNITED STATES OF AMERICA
420 Fifth Avenue, New York NY 10018-2798. 212/852-8000. **Toll-free phone:** 800/GSU-SA4U. **Fax:** 212/852-6514. **Contact:** Staffing Department. **World Wide Web address:** http://www.girlscouts.org. **Description:** Girl Scouts is a non-profit national scouting organization for girls. **Positions advertised include:** Inventory Management Director; Adult Development & Instructional Design Consultant. **Corporate headquarters location:** This location. **Chairperson:** Cynthia Bramlett Thompson. **Annual sales/revenues:** 41.6 million. **Number of employees:** 480.

HENRY STREET SETTLEMENT
265 Henry Street, New York NY 10002. 212/766-9200. **Contact:** Human Resources. **World Wide Web address:** http://www.henrystreet.org. **Description:** Provides various social services including daycare, home care, housekeeping, Meals on Wheels, work training for 16- to 21-year-olds, after-school homework help, shelter for battered women, and care for pregnant teenagers. **Positions advertised include:** Shelter Director; Case Manager; Mental Health Care Social Worker; Information Systems Technician; Support Specialist; ESOL Instructor; Residence Assistant; Accounting Manager; Program Director; Training Coordinator; Youth Counselor; Parent Advocate Coordinator; Case Manager; Parent Advocate; Office Assistant; Case Manager; Docent Opportunity; Housekeeper; Job Developer.

HOPE HOUSE
19-21 Belmont Avenue, Dover NJ 07801. 973/361-5555. **Fax:** 973/361-5290. **Contact:** Human Resources. **E-mail address:** information@hopehousenj.org. **World Wide Web address:** http://www.hopehouse.com. **Description:** A nonprofit organization that provides AIDS outpatient, substance abuse, and family counseling; does house cleaning for the elderly; and performs household chores for home-bound individuals. Hope House also operates a 40-bed residential facility for children and adolescents. **Positions advertised include:** Executive Director; Counselor. **NOTE:** Send resume to the following address attention Human Resources. Hope House, P.O. Box 851, Dover NJ, 07801. Fax resume to: 973/361-6586.

HOPES
124 Grand Street, Hoboken NJ 07030. 201/656-3711. **Contact:** Human Resources. **Description:** A nonprofit organization funded by the state of New Jersey that sponsors programs such as Head Start and a medical transportation program for senior citizens.

JEWISH COMMUNITY CENTER ASSOCIATION
15 East 26th Street, 10th Floor, New York NY 10010-1579. 212/532-4949. **Fax:** 212/481-4174. **Contact:** C. Carlson, Personnel Manager. **E-mail address:** info@jcca.org. **World Wide Web address:** http://www.jcca.org. **Description:** The nonprofit, national coordinating body for the Jewish Community Center movement in North America. The association has more than 50 area locations and serves as the continental coordinating body for the Jewish Community Center Movement in North America associated with over 275 JCCs, YM-YWHAs and camps operating over 500 sites in the U.S. and Canada. **Corporate headquarters location:** This location. **Other locations:** Nationwide. **International locations:** Israel.

JUST ONE BREAK, INC.
120 Wall Street, 20th Floor, New York NY 10005. 212/785-7300. **Fax:** 212/785-4513. **Contact:** Recruiter. **E-mail address:** jobs@justonebreak.com. **World Wide Web address:** http://www.justonebreak.com. **Description:** A nonprofit

organization that helps people with disabilities find employment. Founded in 1947.

LIGHTHOUSE INTERNATIONAL

111 East 59th Street, New York NY 10022-1202. 212/821-9200. **Toll-free phone:** 800/829-0500. **Fax:** 212/821-9708. **Recorded jobline:** 212/821-9419. **Contact:** Nicole Ruderman, Recruiting Coordinator. **E-mail address:** nruderman@lighthouse.org. **World Wide Web address:** http://www.lighthouse.org. **Description:** Enables people who are blind or partially blind to lead independent lives through education, research, information, career and social services, and vision rehabilitation. Lighthouse International serves more than 5,000 persons. **Positions advertised include:** School Nurse; Vision Rehabilitation Assistant; Administrative Coordinator; Job Coach. **Special programs:** Internships. **Other area locations:** Brooklyn NY; Poughkeepsie NY; Queens NY; White Plains NY. **Number of employees at this location:** 305. **Number of employees nationwide:** 375.

LITTLE FLOWER CHILDREN'S SERVICES OF NEW YORK

186 Joralemon Street, Brooklyn NY 11201. 718/875-3500. **Fax:** 718/625-6102. **Contact:** Human Resources. **E-mail address:** jobs@lfchild.org. **World Wide Web address:** http://www.littleflowerny.org. **Description:** Provides foster care and adoption services, group homes, residential treatment units, shelter cottages, intermediate care facilities for mentally handicapped children, and therapeutic foster boarding homes. Little Flower Children's Services cares for approximately 2,600 children annually. **Positions advertised include:** Caseworker; Youth Counselor; Direct Care Worker; Registered Nurse; Licensed Practical Nurse; Secretary; Clerk; Maintenance Worker; Grounds Keeper; Kitchen Worker; Driver. **Corporate headquarters location:** Wading River NY. **Other locations:** Queens NY. **Number of employees:** 650.

LITTLE FLOWER CHILDREN'S SERVICES OF NEW YORK

2450 North Wading River Road, Wading River NY 11792. 631/929-6200 ext. 157. **Fax:** 631/929-6121. **Contact:** Human Resources. **E-mail address:** jobs@lfchild.org. **World Wide Web address:** http://www.littleflowerny.org. **Description:** Provides adoption and foster care services, foster homes for individuals who are mentally handicapped, intermediate care facilities, residential treatment facilities, and therapeutic foster boarding homes. Little Flower Children's Services cares for more than 2,600 children annually. **Positions advertised include:** Caseworker; Youth Counselor; Direct Care Worker; Registered Nurse; Licensed Practical Nurse; Secretary; Clerk; Maintenance Worker; Grounds Keeper; Kitchen Worker; Driver. **Special programs:** Internships. **Corporate headquarters location:** This location. **Other locations:** Brooklyn NY; Queens NY. **Number of employees:** 650.

LOWER WEST SIDE HOUSEHOLD SERVICES CORPORATION

250 West 57th Street, Suite 1511, New York NY 10107-1511. 212/307-7107. **Fax:** 212/956-2308. **Contact:** Brenda Franklin, Assistant Program Manager. **E-mail address:** contact@homecareny.org. **World Wide Web address:** http://www.homecareny.org. **Description:** A nonprofit company that provides home health care services to the elderly, infants, toddlers, and adults living in the five boroughs of New York City and Westchester County. Services include nursing, custodial care, nutrition, social work, and arrangements for medical equipment. The agency also provides free custodial care for individuals and families infected with HIV/AIDS. **NOTE:** Second and thirds shifts are offered. Founded in 1969. **Positions advertised include:** Service Coordinator; Data Entry Clerk; Home Health Aide; Licensed Practical Nurse; Occupational Therapist; Physical Therapist; Social Worker; Speech-Language Pathologist. **Special programs:** Training. **Office hours:** Monday - Friday, 8:00 a.m. - 5:00

p.m. **Corporate headquarters location:** This location. **Other U.S. locations:** Scarsdale NY. **Number of employees at this location:** 250.

MARCH OF DIMES BIRTH DEFECTS FOUNDATION
1275 Mamaroneck Avenue, White Plains NY 10605. 914/428-7100. **Fax:** 914/997-4479. **Contact:** Mary Jane Scott, Human Resources. **E-mail address:** recruiter@marchofdimes.com. **World Wide Web address:** http://www.marchofdimes.org. **Description:** A private foundation operating the Campaign for Healthier Babies, which includes programs of research, community service, education, and advocacy. Birth defects are the primary focus of March of Dimes research efforts. The foundation's 55 chapters across the country work with their communities to determine and meet the needs of women, children, and families. Through specially designed programs, women are provided with access to prenatal care. Founded in 1938 by President Franklin Roosevelt to prevent polio. **Positions advertised include:** Assistant Design Director; Senior Designer; Program Quality Improvement Manager; External Program Grants Manager; Director of Program Services. **Corporate headquarters location:** This location. **Other U.S. locations:** Nationwide. **Chairman:** Gary D. Forsee. **Annual sales/revenues:** $218 million.

MARYKNOLL FATHERS AND BROTHERS
P.O. Box 302, Maryknoll NY 10545. 914/941-7590. **Contact:** Human Resources. **World Wide Web address:** http://www.home.maryknoll.org. **Description:** Maryknoll Fathers and Brothers is an international order of religious missionaries. Founded in 1911. **Special programs:** Summer Jobs. **Corporate headquarters location:** This location. **Other locations:** Chicago IL; Los Angeles CA; Minneapolis MN; New York NY; Ossining NY; Washington DC.

NEW YORK STATE COALITION AGAINST DOMESTIC VIOLENCE
350 New Scotland Avenue, Albany NY 12208. 518/482-5465. **Contact:** Sherry Frohman, Executive Director of Human Resources. **Description:** An organization providing support and services to battered women and their children. **Parent company:** National Coalition Against Domestic Violence is a nonprofit public education and advocacy organization and a coalition of direct service programs, currently composed of 33 member organizations offering services to battered women and their children. Activities of the coalition include public education and advocacy; technical assistance to member groups; information and technical assistance to public agencies and legislative committees; and professional training for law enforcement and human service workers. In addition, the coalition staff prepares policy statements and offers assistance and expertise in the preparation of protocols and practices for a wide variety of public and private entities.

SAVE THE CHILDREN
54 Wilton Road, Westport CT 06880. 203/221-4000. **Toll-free phone:** 800/728-3843. **Contact:** Personnel. **World Wide Web address:** http://www.savethechildren.org. **Description:** A nonprofit organization that works to raise funds for disadvantaged children worldwide. **Positions advertised include:** Marketing Manager; Outbound Call Center Representative; Deputy Director of Education; Education Specialist; Program Specialist; Family Planning/Reproductive Health Advisor; AVP Planning, Monitoring and Evaluation. **Corporate headquarters location:** This location.

TECHNOSERVE INC.
49 Day Street, Norwalk CT 06854. 203/852-0377. **Fax:** 203/838-6717. **Contact:** Stacey Daves-Ohlin, Director of Human Resources. **World Wide Web address:** http://www.technoserve.org. **Description:** A private, nonprofit development aid organization that works with low-income people and development institutions in Africa, Latin America, and Eastern Europe to help establish or strengthen self-

help enterprises. **NOTE:** See website for details on positions. All applicants should be fluent in French; only senior level applicants should apply. **Positions advertised include:** Trade Specialist; Agribusiness Specialist; Finance Specialist; Business Specialist Service Provider. **Special programs:** Internships. **Corporate headquarters location:** This location. **Other U.S. locations:** Washington DC. **Number of employees at this location:** 25. **Number of employees nationwide:** 220.

U.S. FUNDS FOR UNICEF
333 East 38th Street, 6th Floor, New York NY 10016. 212/686-5522. **Contact:** Employment Manager. **World Wide Web address:** http://www.unicefusa.org. **Description:** Organized for educational and charitable purposes, U.S. Funds for UNICEF aims to increase awareness of the needs of children around the world. **Special programs:** Internships. **Corporate headquarters location:** This location. **Other U.S. locations:** Los Angeles CA; Washington DC; Atlanta GA; Chicago IL; Boston MA; Houston TX. **Operations at this facility include:** Administration; Divisional Headquarters. **Listed on:** Privately held. **Number of employees at this location:** 100.

UNITED CEREBRAL PALSY ASSOCIATIONS OF NEW YORK STATE
330 West 34th Street, 14th Floor, New York NY 10001. 212/947-5770. **Fax:** 212/594-4538. **Contact:** Human Resources Department. **E-mail address:** info@cerebralpalsynys.org. **World Wide Web address:** http://www.cerebralpalsynys.org. **Description:** A nonprofit health care organization that provides services to persons with developmental disabilities. **Special programs:** Internships. **Corporate headquarters location:** Washington DC. **Other area locations:** Bronx NY; Brooklyn NY; Queens NY; Staten Island NY. **Operations at this facility include:** Administration; Divisional Headquarters. **Annual sales/revenues:** $51 - $100 million. **Number of employees at this location:** 1,700.

UNITED WAY OF NEW YORK CITY
2 Park Avenue South, 2nd Floor, New York NY 10016-1601. 212/251-2500. **Contact:** Human Resources. **World Wide Web address:** http://www.uwnyc.org. **Description:** A nonprofit organization that offers referral and crisis intervention services for pregnant women and parents.

UNITED WAY OF STAMFORD
62 Palmers Hill Road, Stamford CT 06902. 203/348-7711. **Contact:** Human Resources. **World Wide Web address:** http://www.unitedway.org. **Description:** A nonprofit organization that offers referral and crisis intervention services for pregnant women and parents. **Other U.S. locations:** Nationwide.

URBAN LEAGUE OF HUDSON COUNTY
253 Martin Luther King Jr. Drive, Jersey City NJ 07305. 201/451-8888. **Contact:** Human Resources. **World Wide Web address:** http://www.urbanleaguehudsonnj.org. **Description:** A nonprofit organization that sponsors a variety of social programs including employment services and parenting programs.

WESTCHESTER COMMUNITY OPPORTUNITY PROGRAM
2269 Saw Mill River Road, Building 3, Suite G-16, Elmsford NY 10523-3833. 914/592-5600. **Contact:** Personnel. **Description:** A county-sponsored, nonprofit social services agency operating through numerous community action programs that provides clinical services, employment training programs, energy programs, and a wide range of other community services. **Corporate headquarters location:** This location.

YWCA
610 Lexington Avenue, New York NY 10022. 212/755-4500. **Fax:** 212/838-1279.
Contact: Human Resources. **E-mail address:** info@ywcanyc.org. **World Wide
Web address:** http://www.ywcanyc.org. **Description:** Provides counseling,
physical fitness activities, a shelter, and daycare facilities for women and their
children. **Corporate headquarters location:** This location. **Other U.S.
locations:** Nationwide.

CHEMICALS, RUBBER, AND PLASTICS

You can expect to find the following types of companies in this section:
Adhesives, Detergents, Inks, Paints, Soaps, Varnishes • Agricultural Chemicals and Fertilizers • Carbon and Graphite Products • Chemical Engineering Firms • Industrial Gases

---

ACETO CORPORATION
One Hollow Lane, Suite 201, Lake Success NY 11042-1215. 516/627-6000. **Fax:** 516/627-6093. **Contact:** Kevin Carraher, Human Resources Director. **E-mail address:** hr@aceto.com. **World Wide Web address:** http://www.aceto.com. **Description:** Manufactures chemicals for a wide variety of uses in agricultural markets, color producing industries, and pharmaceutical and health care industries. The chemicals are used to synthesize colors used in photography, textiles, plastics, paints, and printing inks. In the pharmaceutical industry, the company supplies bulk pharmaceuticals and specialty chemicals for use as raw materials to synthesize pharmaceuticals and antibiotics. Aceto also manufactures plastics, surface coatings, and other specialty performance chemicals including antioxidants for plastics, adhesion promoters for automotive finishes, and catalysts for use in the manufacture of certain resins. Founded in 1947. **Corporate headquarters location:** This location. **Other locations:** Worldwide. **Listed on:** NASDAQ. **Stock exchange symbol:** ACET. **Chairman/President/CEO:** Leonard S. Schwartz. **Annual sales/revenue:** $229 million. **Number of employees:** 240.

ASHLAND SPECIALTY CHEMICAL COMPANY
One Drew Plaza, Boonton NJ 07005. 973/263-7600. **Fax:** 973/263-4487. **Contact:** Personnel. **World Wide Web address:** http://www.ashchem.com. **Description:** This location supplies specialty chemicals and services to the international maritime industry and other industrial markets worldwide. Through its industrial chemical sector, the Drew Division also manufactures and markets products for water management and fuel treatment, as well as specialized chemicals for major industries. The Ameroid Marine Division provides chemical and sealing products and applications technology for these products to the maritime industry. Ashland Chemical Company provides shipboard technical service for more than 15,000 vessels in more than 140 ports around the world. **Positions advertised include:** Water Treatment Technical Sales Representative; Office Services Assistant; Office Typist. **Corporate headquarters location:** Dublin OH. **Parent company:** Ashland Inc. **Listed on:** New York Stock Exchange. **Stock exchange symbol:** ASH.

BALCHEM CORPORATION
2007 NY State Route 284, P.O. Box 175, Slate Hill NY 10973-0175. 845/355-5300. **Fax:** 845/355-6314. **Contact:** Human Resources. **E-mail address:** bcphr@balchem.com. **World Wide Web address:** http://www.balchem.com. **Description:** A leader in the manufacturing and marketing of encapsulated food ingredients for a variety of industries. The company is also a leading supplier of ethylene oxide, a packaging sterilant. Founded in 1967. **NOTE:** Resumes should be sent to the company's headquarters location to the attention of: JoAnne Fernandez, Balchem Corporation, P.O. Box 600, New Hampton NY 10958; or by fax: 845/326-5734; or to the above e-mail address. **Positions advertised include:** Senior Research Scientist; Western Regional Technical Sales Representative; Applications Specialist. **Corporate headquarters location:** New Hampton NY. **Other locations:** Green Pond SC; New Hampton NY; Verona MO. **Subsidiaries include:** BCP Ingredients, Inc; ARC Specialty Products.

Operations at this facility include: Manufacturing. **Listed on:** American Stock Exchange. **Stock exchange symbol:** BCP. **President/CEO/CFO/Director:** Dino A. Rossi. **Annual sales/revenues:** $60 million. **Number of employees nationwide:** 220.

BOC GASES
575 Mountain Avenue, Murray Hill NJ 07974. 908/464-8100. **Fax:** 410/749-4073. **Contact:** Corporate Personnel. **World Wide Web address:** http://www.boc.com/gases. **Description:** BOC Gases manufactures industrial, electronic, and medical gases; and cryogenic equipment. **Corporate headquarters location:** This location. **Other U.S. locations:** Nationwide.

BENJAMIN MOORE & COMPANY
51 Chestnut Ridge Road, Montvale NJ 07645. 201/573-9600. **Fax:** 201/573-6631. **Contact:** Personnel. **World Wide Web address:** http://www.benjaminmoore.com. **Description:** Manufactures paints, varnishes, and other coatings. **Positions advertised include:** Cost Planning & Analysis Manager; Tax Accountant; Financial Analyst; Accounts Receivable Assistant; Benefits Administrator; Human Resources Information Systems Consultant; Color Marketing Manager; Business to Business Marketing Manager; Associate Project Manager; Manager of Retail Advertising; Retail Store Design Manager; Retail Regional Manager. **Corporate headquarters location:** This location. **Other U.S. locations:** Nationwide. **Operations at this facility include:** Administration; Research and Development; Sales; Service. **Listed on:** Privately held. **Number of employees at this location:** 175. **Number of employees nationwide:** 1,800.

CAMBREX CORPORATION
One Meadowlands Plaza, East Rutherford NJ 07073-2150. 201/804-3000. **Fax:** 201/804-9852. **Contact:** Melissa Lesko, Professional Staffing Department. **E-mail address:** human.resources@cambrex.com. **World Wide Web address:** http://www.cambrex.com. **Description:** Manufactures and markets products and provides services to the life sciences industries. Cambrex Corporation operates in four segments: Human Health; Biotechnology; Animal Health and Agriculture; and Specialty Products. Founded in 1981. **NOTE:** Apply online. **Positions advertised include:** Staff Accountant; Internal Auditor; Employee Benefits Manager; Payroll Specialist; Network Engineer; Corporate Counsel. **Office hours:** Monday - Friday, 8:30 a.m. - 5:00 p.m. **Corporate headquarters location:** This location.

CHEMETALL OAKITE
50 Valley Road, Berkeley Heights NJ 07922. 908/464-6900. **Contact:** Suzanne Watson, Recruiter. **E-mail address:** resumes@oakite.com. **World Wide Web address:** http://www.oakite.com. **Description:** Manufactures and markets specialty chemical products used primarily for industrial cleaning, metal conditioning, and surface preparation. **NOTE:** Resumes must be submitted in Microsoft Word, Word Perfect, or Microsoft Publisher format. **Corporate headquarters location:** This location. **Other U.S. locations:** Nationwide. **International locations:** Canada

CIBA SPECIALTY CHEMICALS
540 White Plains Road, Tarrytown NY 10591-9005. 914/785-2000. **Fax:** 914/785-2183. **Contact:** Loretta Czernecki, Human Resources Manager. **E-mail address:** Loretta.cznecki@cibasc.com or careers@cibasc.com. **World Wide Web address:** http://www.cibasc.com. **Description:** Ciba manufactures specialty chemicals through five divisions: additives, colors, consumer care, performance polymers, and water treatments. **NOTE:** Human Resources phone: 914/785-3828. **Corporate headquarters location:** Basel, Switzerland. **Operations at this facility include:** NAFTA regional headquarters. Coating

Effects and Plastic Additives business segment headquarters, marketing, and technical operations. Research & Development center for new product development, analytical and technical service support for Ciba's light stabilizer, antioxidant, process chemicals, imaging/coating additives, process/lubricant additives, and water/paper treatment businesses. **Listed on:** New York Stock Exchange. **Stock exchange symbol:** CSB. **Annual sales/revenues:** $5 billion. **Number of employees nationwide:** 3,000. **Number of employees worldwide:** 19,000.

COLORITE WATERWORKS
COLORITE POLYMERS
101 Railroad Avenue, Ridgefield NJ 07657. 201/941-2900. **Toll-free phone:** 800/631-1577. **Fax:** 201/941-2665. **Contact:** Human Resources. **E-mail address:** info@coloritepolymers.com. **World Wide Web address:** http://www.tekni-plex.com/companies/colorpoly.html. **Description:** Manufactures plastic garden hoses. Colorite Polymers (also at this location) manufactures PVC compounds. **Parent company:** Tekni-Plex Inc.

CREST FOAM INDUSTRIES, INC.
100 Carol Place, Moonachie NJ 07074. 201/807-0809. **Fax:** 201/807-1113. **Contact:** Human Resources. **E-mail address:** info@crestfoam.com. **World Wide Web address:** http://www.crestfoam.com. **Description:** Manufactures reticulated and specialty foam for a wide variety of industries such as aerospace, electronics, and medical.

DAICOLOR-POPE INC.
33 Sixth Avenue, Paterson NJ 07524. 973/278-5170. **Contact:** Human Resources. **Description:** Manufactures pigments used by printing companies to produce inks.

DEGUSSA CORPORATION
P.O. Box 677, 379 Interpace Parkway, Parsippany NJ 07054-0677. 973/541-8000. **Fax:** 973/541-8013. **Contact:** Personnel. **World Wide Web address:** http://www.degussa-nafta.com/internet/dh-us/. **Description:** Manufactures specialty chemicals, polymers, colorants, additives, and raw materials for the coatings industry. **Special programs:** Internships; Co-ops. **Corporate headquarters location:** This location. **Other U.S. locations:** Theodore AL; Pleasanton CA; Piscataway NJ; Lockland OH. **Parent company:** Degussa AG. **Operations at this facility include:** Divisional Headquarters; Regional Headquarters. **Annual sales/revenues:** More than $100 million. **Number of employees at this location:** 350. **Number of employees nationwide:** 875.

DOW CHEMICAL COMPANY
39 Old Ridgebury Road, Danbury CT 06817. 203/794-2000. **Contact:** Human Resources. **World Wide Web address:** http://www.dow.com. **Description:** Dow Chemical Corporation is a science and technology company providing chemical, plastic, and agricultural products and services to consumer markets. **Parent Company:** The Dow Chemical Company.

FAIRMOUNT CHEMICAL COMPANY, INC.
117 Blanchard Street, Newark NJ 07105. 973/344-5790. **Toll-free phone:** 800/872-9999. **Fax:** 973/690-5298. **Contact:** Human Resources. **Description:** Manufactures and distributes chemical intermediates for the imaging industry; hydrazine salts and derivatives; additives used in the manufacture of plastics; and specialty chemicals, primarily pharmaceutical intermediates.

GENERAL CHEMICAL CORPORATION
90 East Halsey Road, Parsippany NJ 07054. 973/515-0900. **Contact:** Human Resources. **E-mail address:** hrinfor@genchem.com. **World Wide Web**

address: http://www.genchem.com. **Description:** Manufactures inorganic chemicals and soda ash. **Positions advertised include:** Office Manager; Network Technician. **Corporate headquarters location:** This location. **Other U.S. locations:** Claymont DE; Syracuse NY; Pittsburgh PA; Green River WY. **Parent company:** The General Chemical Group Inc. (Hampton NH). **Operations at this facility include:** Administration; Manufacturing; Sales; Service. **Number of employees at this location:** 180. **Number of employees nationwide:** 2,000.

HONEYWELL
101 Columbia Road, Morristown NJ 07962-1057. 973/455-2000. **Contact:** Human Resources Director. **World Wide Web address:** http://www.honeywell.com. **Description:** Honeywell is engaged in the research, development, manufacture, and sale of advanced technology products and services in the fields of chemicals, electronics, automation, and controls. The company's major businesses are home and building automation and control, performance polymers and chemicals, industrial automation and control, space and aviation systems, and defense and marine systems. **Corporate headquarters location:** This location. **Listed on:** New York Stock Exchange. **Stock exchange symbol:** HON.

IFF
1040 Broad Street, Shrewsbury NJ 07702. 732/578-6700. **Contact:** Staffing. **E-mail address:** staffing.manager@iff.com. **World Wide Web address:** http://www.iff.com. **Description:** Manufactures and distributes flavors and fragrances for use in foods, beverages, detergents, cosmetics, and other personal care items. **Positions advertised include:** Research Scientist. **Other U.S. locations:** Nationwide. **International locations:** Worldwide. **Listed on:** NASDAQ. **Stock exchange symbol:** IFF.

INTERNATIONAL FLAVORS & FRAGRANCES INC.
521 West 57th Street, New York NY 10019-2960. 212/765-5500. **Fax:** 212/708-7132. **Contact:** Human Resources. **E-mail address:** staffing.manager@iff.com. **World Wide Web address:** http://www.iff.com. **Description:** Creates and manufactures flavors and fragrances used by other manufacturers in a wide variety of consumer products. Fragrance products are sold principally to manufacturers of perfumes, cosmetics, personal care items, soaps, detergents, air fresheners, and household products. Flavor products are sold principally to manufacturers of dairy, meat, processed foods, beverages, pharmaceuticals, snacks, baked goods, confectioneries, tobacco products, oral care products, and animal foods. **Corporate headquarters location:** This location. **Other U.S. locations:** Hazlet NJ; South Brunswick NJ; Union Beach NJ. **Subsidiaries include:** Bush Booke Allen, Inc. **Operations at this facility include:** Administration; Regional Headquarters; Sales; Service. **Listed on:** New York Stock Exchange. **Stock exchange symbol:** IFF. **Chairman/CEO:** Richard A. Goldstein. **Annual sales/revenues:** $1.8 billion. **Number of employees:** 5,728.

INTERNATIONAL SPECIALTY PRODUCTS
1361 Alps Road, Wayne NJ 07470. 973/628-4000. **Contact:** Human Resources. **E-mail address:** jobs2@ispcorp.com. **World Wide Web address:** http://www.ispcorp.com. **Description:** Manufactures specialty chemicals and building materials. Chemicals include high-pressure acetylene derivatives, industrial organic and inorganic chemicals, GAF filter systems, and GAF mineral products. Building materials include prepared roofing, roll roofing, built-up roofing systems, and single-ply roofing. **Corporate headquarters location:** This location. **Listed on:** New York Stock Exchange. **Stock exchange symbol:** ISP. **Number of employees at this location:** 700. **Number of employees nationwide:** 4,300.

KING INDUSTRIES INC.

P.O. Box 588, Norwalk CT 06852. 203/866-5551. **Toll-free phone:** 800/431-7900. **Physical address:** Science Road, Norwalk CT 06852. **Contact:** Human Resources. **World Wide Web address:** http://www.kingindustries.com. **Description:** A chemical plant that produces additives for coatings and lubricants.

KOHL & MADDEN PRINTING INK CORP.

222 Bridge Plaza South, Suite 701, Fort Lee NJ 07024. 201/886-1203. **Toll-free phone:** 800/793-0022. **Contact:** Human Resources Manager. **World Wide Web address:** http://www.kohlmadden.com. **Description:** Produces printing inks, compounds, and varnishes. **Corporate headquarters location:** This location. **Parent company:** Sun Chemical Corporation. **Operations at this facility include:** Administration; Divisional Headquarters; Sales. **Listed on:** Privately held. **Number of employees at this location:** 25. **Number of employees nationwide:** 450.

MILLENNIUM CHEMICALS, INC.

230 Half Mile Road, Red Bank NJ 07701. 732/933-5000. **Contact:** Human Resources. **E-mail address:** careers@millenniumchem.com. **World Wide Web address:** http://www.millenniumchem.com. **Description:** Produces a range of chemical products including detergents and fragrances. **Corporate headquarters location:** This location. **Subsidiaries include:** Millennium Petrochemicals Inc. **Listed on:** New York Stock Exchange. **Stock exchange symbol:** MCH.

NATIONAL STARCH AND CHEMICAL COMPANY

10 Finderne Avenue, P.O. Box 6500, Bridgewater NJ 08807. 908/685-5000. **Toll-free phone:** 800/366-4031. **Fax:** 908/685-6956. **Contact:** Human Resources. **E-mail address:** nstarch.jobs@nstarch.com. **World Wide Web address:** http://www.nationalstarch.com. **Description:** Manufactures industrial chemicals including adhesives, resins, starches, and specialty chemicals for the packaging, textile, paper, food, furniture, electronic materials, and automotive markets. **NOTE:** Entry-level positions are offered. **Positions advertised include:** Administrative Coordinator; Chemist Nutritional Application Specialist; Global Network Technology Manager; Human Resources Technology Support Manager; Principal Chemist; Research Associate; Chemist; Technical Services Technician. **Special programs:** Internships; Co-ops. **Corporate headquarters location:** This location. **Other U.S. locations:** Nationwide. **International locations:** Worldwide. **Parent company:** The ICI Group. **Annual sales/revenues:** More than $100 million. **Number of employees nationwide:** 8,500. **Number of employees worldwide:** 10,000.

OLIN CORPORATION

501 Merritt Seven, Norwalk CT 06856. 203/750-3000. **Fax:** 203/495-8625. **Contact:** Human Resources. **World Wide Web address:** http://www.olin.com. **Description:** Produces copper alloys, ammunition, and chlorine and caustic soda. **Positions advertised include:** Lab Technician; Research Scientist/Engineer. **Corporate headquarters location:** This location. **Other U.S. locations:** Nationwide. **Listed on:** New York Stock Exchange. **Stock exchange symbol:** OLN. **Number of employees nationwide:** 6,700.

PVC CONTAINER CORPORATION

2 Industrial Way West, Eatontown NJ 07724-2202. 732/542-0060. **Toll-free phone:** 800/975-2784. **Fax:** 732/544-8007. **Contact:** Personnel. **E-mail address:** mpelich@pvcc.com. **World Wide Web address:** http://www.novapakcorp.com. **Description:** Designs and manufactures plastic bottles and polyvinyl chloride compounds. **Positions advertised include:**

Quality Engineer; South East Regional Sales Manager; Machine Operator; Plastics Lab Technician.

PRAXAIR TECHNOLOGY, INC.
39 Old Ridgebury Road, Danbury CT 06810. 203/837-2000. **Contact:** Barbara Harris, Vice President of Personnel. **World Wide Web address:** http://www.praxair.com. **Description:** Praxair produces gases and gas production equipment for customers in the aerospace, chemicals, electronics, food processing, health care, glass, metal fabrication, petroleum, primary metals, pulp, and paper industries. Praxair also coats customer-supplied parts and equipment with metallic and ceramic coatings for the textile, aircraft engine, paper, petrochemical, metals, and printing industries. **Positions advertised include:** Administrative Specialist; Inside Sales Representative. **Corporate headquarters location:** This location. **International locations:** Worldwide. **Listed on:** New York Stock Exchange. **Stock exchange symbol:** PX.

RED DEVIL, INC.
2400 Vauxhall Road, Union NJ 07083. 908/688-6900. **Fax:** 908/688-8872. **Contact:** Maria Janeira, Director of Human Resources. **World Wide Web address:** http://www.reddevil.com. **Description:** Manufactures and distributes paint sundries; hand tools; and a full-line of caulks, sealants, and adhesives for home and professional use. **Corporate headquarters location:** This location. **Number of employees at this location:** 150. **Number of employees nationwide:** 250.

REEDY INTERNATIONAL
25 East Front Street, Suite 200, Key Port NJ 07735. 732/264-1777. **Fax:** 732/264-1189. **Contact:** Human Resources. **E-mail address:** info@readyintl.com. **World Wide Web address:** http://www.reedyintl.com. **Description:** Produces chemical components for items such as Styrofoam and car parts.

SAINT-GOBAIN PERFORMANCE PLASTICS
150 Dey Road, Wayne NJ 07470. 973/696-4700. **Contact:** Anne Ginestre, Human Resources Manager. **World Wide Web address:** http://www.nortonplastics.com. **Description:** Manufactures a wide range of plastic products and shapes including pipes, rods, sheet, tape, rectangular stock, insulated wire, and coaxial cable core; finished plastic products such as laboratory wire; and nylon products such as rods, tubes, slabs, and custom castings. **Special programs:** Internships.

SIKA CORPORATION
P.O. Box 297, 201 Polito Avenue, Lyndhurst NJ 07071. 201/933-8800. **Fax:** 201/933-6166. **Contact:** Personnel. **E-mail address:** resume@sika-corp.com. **World Wide Web address:** http://www.sikausa.com. **Description:** Manufactures specialty chemicals including sealants and adhesives for the construction and transportation industries. Founded in 1937. **Positions advertised include:** Area Sales Manager; Area Transportation Manager; Chemist; Sales Representative. **NOTE:** Search website for updated job listings. **Corporate headquarters location:** This location. **Parent company:** Sika Finanz AG. **Operations at this facility include:** Administration; Manufacturing; Regional Headquarters; Research and Development; Sales; Service. **Listed on:** Privately held. **Annual sales/revenues:** More than $100 million. **Number of employees at this location:** 200. **Number of employees nationwide:** 700.

STAR-GLO INDUSTRIES L.L.C.
2 Carlton Avenue, East Rutherford NJ 07073. 201/939-6162. **Fax:** 201/939-4054. **Contact:** Personnel. **World Wide Web address:** http://www.starglo.com. **Description:** Manufactures precision-molded rubber and plastic parts, often

bonded to metal. Sales are made primarily to original equipment manufacturers in the business machine and computer, welding, food packaging equipment, chemical, and aerospace industries. **Corporate headquarters location:** This location.

STEPAN COMPANY
100 West Hunter Avenue, Maywood NJ 07607. 201/845-3030. **Contact:** Human Resources. **E-mail address:** stepanhr@stepan.com. **World Wide Web address:** http://www.stepan.com. **Description:** Produces specialty chemicals and food additives. **Corporate headquarters location:** Northfield IL. **Operations at this facility include:** Administration; Manufacturing; Research and Development; Sales. **Listed on:** New York Stock Exchange. **Stock exchange symbol:** SCL. **Number of employees at this location:** 100. **Number of employees nationwide:** 1,300.

SULZER-METCO INC.
1101 Prospect Avenue, Westbury NY 11590-0201. 516/334-1300. **Contact:** Human Resources. **E-mail address:** hr-us@sulzermetco.com. **World Wide Web address:** http://www.sulzermetco.com. **Description:** Develops a thermal spray coating process that is used on industrial surfaces to increase resistance. **Positions advertised include:** Technical Engineer. **International locations:** Germany; the Netherlands; Switzerland.

SUPERIOR PRINTING INK COMPANY, INC.
70 Bethune Street, New York NY 10014-1768. 212/741-3600. **Contact:** Human Resources. **World Wide Web address:** http://www.superiorink.com. **Description:** Manufactures inks and pigments used in lithographic and other printing processes.

TICONA
86-90 Morris Avenue, Summit NJ 07901. 908/598-4000. **Fax:** 908/598-4165. **Contact:** Human Resources. **World Wide Web address:** http://www.ticona.com. **Description:** Produces and markets chemicals and manufactured fibers for industrial and textile uses. **Parent company:** Hoechst Group.

USA DETERGENTS
1735 Jersey Avenue, North Brunswick NJ 08902. 732/828-1800. **Fax:** 732/246-7733. **Contact:** Human Resources. **Description:** Manufactures laundry detergents, household cleaners, and scented candles.

UNIFLEX, INC.
383 West John Street, Hicksville NY 11802. 516/932-2000. **Contact:** Human Resources. **World Wide Web address:** http://www.uniflexinc.com. **Description:** Designs, manufactures, and markets a broad line of customized plastic packaging for sales and advertising promotions; clear bags for apparel and soft goods manufacturers; and specialized, recyclable bags and other products for use in hospitals, medical laboratories, and emergency care centers. Medical products include patented, disposable bags for the safe handling of specimens, and general purpose bags for personal belongings. Specialty advertising products include handle bags, drawstring bags, tote bags, and litter bags. The Haran Packaging Division manufactures and markets custom flexible plastic for the health care, food, financial, and other markets. Tamper-evident security bags are sold to banks, retailers, casino operations, stockbrokers, and courier firms that have security concerns for cash and other valuables. **Corporate headquarters location:** This location. **Other area locations:** Westbury NY. **Other U.S. locations:** Albuquerque NM. **Subsidiaries include:** The Cycle Plastics produces and markets jumbo flexible loop handle bags, double drawstring bags, and reclosable, resealable, Trac-Loc bags. These products are

sold to retailers, cosmetics firms, food packing companies, and medical/health care supply firms.

UNILEVER CORPORATION

390 Park Avenue, New York NY 10022. 212/888-1260. **Contact:** Human Resources. **World Wide Web address:** http://www.unilever.com. **Description:** An international consumer products firm manufacturing a wide range of soaps, toiletries, and foods. **Corporate headquarters location:** This location. **Parent company:** Unilever NV (Netherlands). **Listed on:** New York Stock Exchange. **Stock exchange symbol:** UN.

COMMUNICATIONS: TELECOMMUNICATIONS AND BROADCASTING

You can expect to find the following types of companies in this section:
Cable/Pay Television Services • Communications Equipment • Radio and Television Broadcasting Stations • Telephone, Telegraph, and Other Message Communications

---

ABC, INC.
77 West 66th Street, New York NY 10023. 212/456-7777. **Contact:** Human Resources. **World Wide Web address:** http://www.abc.go.com. **Description:** Engaged in television and radio broadcasting, providing cable television service to subscribers, and specialized newspaper publishing. Broadcasting operations include ABC Television Network Group, the Broadcast Group, the Cable and International Broadcast Group, and the Multimedia Group. In addition to its network operation, the Broadcasting segment consists of 8 network-affiliated television stations, 10 radio stations, cable television systems providing service to subscribers in 16 states, and the developing of multimedia video-by-wire business. Publishing operations consist of 8 daily newspapers, 78 weekly newspapers, 63 shopping guides, and other specialized publications. **Positions advertised include:** Senior Promotions Manager; Manager of Sales Administration; Copy Editor; Manager of Network Promotions; Communications Manager; Retail Manager; Learning Editor. **Parent company:** The Walt Disney Company.

ACTV INC.
1270 Avenue of the Americas, New York NY 10020. 212/217-1600. **Contact:** Human Resources. **E-mail address:** jobs@actv.com. **World Wide Web address:** http://www.actv.com. **Description:** Engaged in individual television programming. The company's primary markets are in-home entertainment and education. **Corporate headquarters location:** This location. **Other U.S. locations:** San Francisco CA; Lexington MA. **Operations at this facility include:** Administration; Production; Research and Development; Sales; Service. **Listed on:** NASDAQ. **Stock exchange symbol:** IATV. **Annual sales/revenues:** $13.7 million. **Number of employees:** 143.

AT&T CORPORATION
295 North Maple Avenue, Basking Ridge NJ 07920. 908/221-6035. **Contact:** Human Resources. **World Wide Web address:** http://www.att.com. **Description:** AT&T is a major long-distance telephone company that provides domestic and international voice and data communications and management services, telecommunications products, and leasing and financial services. The company manufactures data communications products, computer products, switching and transmission equipment, and components. **NOTE:** Please send resumes to the resume scanning center at 1200 Peachtree Street, Room 7075, Promenade 1, Atlanta GA 30309. **Positions advertised include:** Telecommunications Analyst. **Corporate headquarters location:** New York NY. **Other U.S. locations:** Nationwide. **Subsidiaries include:** AT&T Capital Corporation offers financing and leases and provides consumer credit through its AT&T Universal credit card. **Listed on:** New York Stock Exchange. **Stock exchange symbol:** T.

ARCH WIRELESS

80 East Ridgewood Avenue, Paramus NJ 07652. 201/265-1130. **Contact:** Human Resources. **World Wide Web address:** http://www.arch.com. **Description:** A telecommunications service company providing a wide variety of specialized data- and message-processing and communications services. The company operates a nationwide computer-controlled network that electronically receives, processes, and transmits record and data communications. Arch Wireless also operates a radio paging business. **Positions advertised include:** Outside Sales Representative; Sales Executive.

BERGER BROWN COMMUNICATIONS

215 Ridgedale Avenue, Florham Park NJ 07932. 973/410-0500. **Fax:** 973/410-0600. **Contact:** Human Resources. **E-mail address:** bb.info@bergerbrown.com. **World Wide Web address:** http://www.bergerbrown.com. **Description:** A nationally recognized public relations & advertising firm. **Positions advertised include:** Publicist.

CBS BROADCASTING INC.

51 West 52nd Street, 19th Floor, New York NY 10019. 212/975-4321. **Contact:** Human Resources Department. **E-mail address:** cbsrecruitment@cbs.com. **World Wide Web address:** http://www.cbs.com. **Description:** A broad-based entertainment and communications company that operates one of the country's major commercial television networks and two nationwide radio networks. **Positions advertised include:** Audio/Video Broadcast Engineer; Executive Assistant; Affiliate System Engineering Manager; Human Resources Coordinator. **Special programs:** Internships. **Internship information:** The company offers unpaid, full-time, summer internship positions for students. **Corporate headquarters location:** This location. **Parent company:** Viacom Inc. (New York NY).

CNN NEWS GROUP (CABLE NEWS NETWORK)

5 Penn Plaza, 20th Floor, New York NY 10001. 212/714-7800. **Contact:** Human Resources. **World Wide Web address:** http://www.cnn.com. **Description:** A cable news network. CNN has 43 bureaus worldwide and provides 24-hour news programming worldwide. Programming includes international, domestic, and business news; sports; weather; special reports; and topical programming. **NOTE:** Current job openings are listed at http://www.turnerjobs.com. **Corporate headquarters location:** Atlanta GA. **Other locations:** Worldwide. **Parent company:** Turner Broadcasting Systems, Inc. (Atlanta GA). **Number of employees:** 4,000.

CABLEVISION SYSTEMS CORPORATION

1111 Stewart Avenue, Bethpage NY 11714. 516/803-2300. **Fax:** 516/803-3065. **Contact:** Human Resources. **E-mail address:** careers@cablevision.com. **World Wide Web address:** http://www.cablevision.com. **Description:** Owns and operates cable television systems serving customers in the New York metropolitan region. **Positions advertised include:** Customer Relations Coordinator; Field Telecommunications Technician; Cablevision Sales Representative; Outbound Telephone Sales Representative. **Special programs:** Internships. **Corporate headquarters location:** This location. **Other locations:** Statewide. **Subsidiaries include:** CCG Holdings, Inc.; Rainbow Media Holdings, Inc.; Clearview Cinema Group; Lightpath; Madison Square Garden; New York Knickerbockers; New York Rangers; The Wiz; Radio City Music Hall; New York Liberty. **Operations at this facility include:** Administration. **Listed on:** New York Stock Exchange. **Stock exchange symbol:** CVC. **Chairman:** Charles F. Dolan. **Annual sales/revenues:** $4 billion. **Number of employees at this location:** 700. **Number of employees nationwide:** 21,000.

COGNITRONICS CORPORATION
3 Corporate Drive, Danbury CT 06810. 203/830-3400. **Contact:** Janet Freund, Director of Human Resources. **World Wide Web address:** http://www.cognitronics.com. **Description:** Designs, manufactures, and markets voice processing systems. Products include passive announcers, which are used by telephone operating companies to inform callers about network conditions or procedures; intelligent announcers, which are primarily used by telephone companies to provide voice announcements in connection with custom calling features, such as selective call forwarding and caller originator trace; interactive voice response; audiotex, a UNIX-based voice processing platform; and call processing, automated attendant, and audiotex systems. **Corporate headquarters location:** This location. **Subsidiaries include:** Dacon Electronics, Private Legal Counsel. **Listed on:** American Stock Exchange. **Stock exchange symbol:** CGN. **Number of employees nationwide:** 80.

COMTECH TELECOMMUNICATIONS CORPORATION
105 Baylis Road, Melville NY 11747-3833. 631/777-8900. **Fax:** 631/777-8877. **Contact:** Human Resources. **E-mail address:** jobs@comtechpst.com. **World Wide Web address:** http://www.comtechtel.com. **Description:** Manufactures and markets high-tech microwave and telecommunications products and systems including antennas, frequency converters, and VSAT transceivers and modems. Products are used worldwide in satellite, tropospheric scatter, and wireless communications systems. The company also manufactures high-power amplifiers that are used to test electronic systems for electromagnetic compatibility and susceptibility; for defense systems; and for high power testing of electronic components and systems. Comtech, through its subsidiaries, offers products to customers including domestic and foreign common carriers and telephone companies, defense contractors, medical and automotive suppliers, oil companies, private and wireless networks, broadcasters, utilities, and government entities. **Corporate headquarters location:** This location. **Subsidiaries include:** Comtech Antenna Systems; Comtech EF Data; Comtech Mobile Datacom; Comtech PST; Comtech Systems. **Operations at this facility include:** Comtech PST Corporation; Corporate Administration. **Listed on:** NASDAQ. **Stock exchange symbol:** CMTL. **Chairman/President/CEO:** Fred V. Kornberg. **Annual sales/revenues:** $119 million. **Number of employees:** 626.

COMVERSE TECHNOLOGY INC.
170 Crossways Park Drive, Woodbury NY 11797-2048. 516/677-7200. **Fax:** 516/677-7355. **Contact:** Human Resources. **E-mail address:** resumes@comverse.com. **World Wide Web address:** http://www.cmvt.com. **Description:** Manufactures, markets, and supports specialized telecommunications systems for multimedia communications and information processing applications. The company's systems are used in a broad range of applications by fixed and wireless telephone network operators, government agencies, financial institutions, and other public and commercial organizations worldwide. Products include AUDIODISK, which is a multimedia digital monitoring system; and the ULTRA series, which is a variety of multimedia recording systems. **Corporate headquarters location:** This location. **Other U.S. locations:** Nationwide. **International locations:** Worldwide. **Subsidiaries include:** Comverse Network Systems; Comverse Infosys; Ulticom, Inc.; Starhome; Verint Systems Inc.; and Startel. **Listed on:** NASDAQ. **Stock exchange symbol:** CMVT. **Chairman:** Kobi Alexander. **Annual sales/revenues:** $736 million. **Number of employees:** 5,650.

COPYTELE, INC.
900 Walt Whitman Road, Suite 203C, Melville NY 11747. 631/549-5900. **Fax:** 631/549-5974. **Contact:** Anne Rotondo, Corporate Secretary. **World Wide Web address:** http://www.copytele.com. **Description:** Designs, develops, and markets encryption products, multifunctional telecommunications products, high-

resolution flat panel displays, and specialty printers. **Listed on:** Over The Counter. **Stock exchange symbol:** COPY. **Chairman/CEO:** Denis A. Krusos. **Annual sales/revenues:** $5 million. **Number of employees:** 48.

COX RADIO, INC.
444 Westport Avenue, 3rd Floor, Norwalk CT 06851. 203/845-3630. **Fax:** 203/845-3097. **Contact:** Human Resources. **World Wide Web address:** http://www.coxradio.com. **Description:** Owns and operates more than 15 radio stations. **Corporate headquarters location:** Atlanta GA. **Listed on:** New York Stock Exchange. **Stock exchange symbol:** CXR.

CRESCENT TELEPHONE COMPANY
6 Nevada Drive, Building C, Lake Success NY 11042. 516/326-0517. **Fax:** 516/437-0807. **Contact:** Human Resources Department. **Description:** Provides telecommunication services for operator-assisted and long-distance telephone calls.

DHB INDUSTRIES, INC.
400 Post Avenue, Suite 303, Westbury NY 11590. 516/997-1155 **Fax:** 516/997-1144. **Contact:** Human Resources. **World Wide Web address:** http://www.dhbt.com. **Description:** DHB Industries is a diversified holding company operating in two divisions: DHB Armor Group and DHB Sports Group. Through its subsidiaries, the Armor Group develops, manufactures, and distributes technically advanced bullet resistant garments, bullet-proof vests, bomb projectile blankets, and body armor from materials such as Kevlar and other related ballistic accessories for the military and law enforcement. The Sports Group manufactures and distributes protective athletic apparel and equipment including pads and braces as well as other therapy products. **Subsidiaries include:** Protective Apparel Corporation of America manufactures and distributes bullet-, bomb-, and projectile-resistant garments; NDL Products manufactures and distributes protective sports apparel and fitness products and related items; Intelligent Data Corporation develops sophisticated telecommunications systems for remote document signature and authentication; Zydacron designs and manufactures video teleconferencing codecs; Darwin Molecular Corporation develops novel drugs to treat cancer and AIDS; Point Blank Body Armor; Point Blank International; Dr. Bone Savers. **Corporate headquarters location:** This location. **Listed on:** American Stock Exchange. **Stock exchange symbol:** DHB. **Chairman/CEO:** David H. Brooks. **Annual sales/revenues:** $130 million. **Number of employees:** 500.

FOX NEWS NETWORK, LLC
dba FOX NEWS CHANNEL
1211 Avenue of the Americas, New York NY 10036. 212/301-3000. **Fax:** 212/301-8588. **Contact:** Department of Human Resources. **E-mail address:** resume@foxnews.com. **World Wide Web address:** http://www.foxnews.com. **Description:** A cable news company operating international television news network. **Corporate headquarters location:** This location. **Parent company:** Fox Entertainment Group Inc.

GRANITE BROADCASTING CORPORATION
767 Third Avenue, 34th Floor, New York NY 10017. 212/826-2530. **Fax:** 212/826-2858. **Contact:** Dolores Perez, Personnel Manager. **World Wide Web address:** http://www.granitetv.com. **Description:** Granite Broadcasting Corporation owns and operates eight network-affiliated television stations in California, Illinois, Indiana, Michigan, Minnesota, New York, and Washington. **Corporate headquarters location:** This location. **Subsidiaries include:** KBJR-TV/NBC; KBWB-TV/WB; KSEE-TV/NBC; WDWB-TV/WB; WEEK-TV/NBC; WKBW-TV/ABC; WPTA-TV/ABC; WTVH-TV/CBS. **Listed on:** NASDAQ. **Stock**

exchange symbol: GBTVK. **Chairman/CEO:** W. Con Cornwall. **Annual sales/revenues:** $135 million. **Number of employees:** 732.

HEARST-ARGYLE TELEVISION, INC.
888 Seventh Avenue, 27th Floor, New York NY 10106. 212/887-6800. **Fax:** 212/887-6835. **Contact:** Personnel. **World Wide Web address:** http://www.hearstargyle.com. **Description:** Owns and manages 27 network affiliated television stations nationwide and manages two radio stations. The company's television stations comprise one of the largest non-network-owned television station groups. Hearst-Argyle Television, Inc.'s television stations include: 10 NBC affiliates, 12 ABC affiliated stations, two CBS affiliates, and a WB affiliate, as well as managing a UPN affiliate and an independent station. The company is involved in television production and syndication through a joint venture with NBC Enterprises and through a partnership with Internet Broadcasting Systems, Inc. is involved in convergence of local TV broadcasts and the Internet. **Corporate headquarters location:** This location. **Subsidiaries include:** Hearst-Argyle Television Productions. **Listed on:** New York Stock Exchange. **Stock exchange symbol:** HTV. **Chairman:** Victor F. Ganzi. **Annual sales/revenues:** $721 million. **Number of employees:** 3,179.

INTEL CORPORATION
1515 Route 10, Parsippany NJ 07054. 973/993-3000. **Contact:** Human Resources. **World Wide Web address:** http://www.intel.com. **Description:** This Intel Corporation business offers computer telephony services that provide telephone network access to computer terminals. **Other U.S. locations:** Nationwide. **International locations:** Worldwide. **Listed on:** NASDAQ. **Stock exchange symbol:** INTC.

KING WORLD PRODUCTIONS
1700 Broadway, 33rd Floor, New York NY 10019. 212/315-4000. **Fax:** 212/582-9255. **Contact:** Human Resources. **E-mail address:** kwjobs@kinigworld.com. **World Wide Web address:** http://www.kingworld.com. **Description:** A broadcasting company engaged in the syndication of television. **Parent company:** CBS Enterprises.

KROLL DIRECT MARKETING
101 Morgan Lane, Suite 120, Plainsboro NJ 08536. 609/275-2900. **Fax:** 609/275-6606. **Contact:** Personnel Manager. **World Wide Web address:** http://www.krolldirect.com. **Description:** A telemarketing company.

L-3 COMMUNICATIONS HOLDINGS, INC.
600 Third Avenue, New York NY 10016. 212/697-1111. **Fax:** 212/867-5249 **Contact:** Human Resources. **World Wide Web address:** http://www.l-3com.com. **Description:** Manufactures secure and specialized products for satellite, avionics, and marine communications including the black box flight recorders used on aircraft for both military and commercial industries. **Positions advertised include:** Criminal Justice Specialist; Contracting Support; Fusion System Analyst. **Corporate headquarters location:** This location. **Other locations:** Nationwide. **Listed on:** New York Stock Exchange. **Stock exchange symbol:** LLL. **Annual sales/revenues:** $4 billion. **Number of employees:** 25,000.

LORAL SPACE & COMMUNICATIONS LTD.
600 Third Avenue, 38th Floor, New York NY 10016. 212/697-1105. **Fax:** 212/338-5662. **Contact:** Human Resources. **World Wide Web address:** http://www.loral.com. **Description:** The company is engaged in the production of satellites specializing in communications and weather satellites. Through its subsidiaries Loral offers satellite-based telephone service, broadcasting and private data communications, and delivers Internet content. **Positions**

advertised include: Finance Officer; Accountant; Communications Assistant; Human Resources Associate; Legal Counselor. **Corporate headquarters location:** This location. **Other U.S. locations:** Bedminster NJ; Palo Alto CA; Washington DC. **Subsidiaries include:** Loral CyberStar, Inc.; Loral Skynet; SatMex; Globalstar; Space Systems/Loral. **Listed on:** New York Stock Exchange. **Stock exchange symbol:** LOR. **Chairman/CEO:** Bernard L. Schwartz. **Annual sales/revenues:** $1 billion. **Number of employees nationwide:** 2800.

LUCENT TECHNOLOGIES INC.
67 Whippany Road, Whippany NJ 07981. 973/386-3000. **Contact:** Employment Manager. **World Wide Web address:** http://www.lucent.com. **Description:** Manufactures communications products including switching, transmission, fiber-optic cable, wireless systems, and operations systems to fulfill the needs of telephone companies and other communications services providers. **Positions advertised include:** Accounting Policy Manager; Internal Audit Manager; Government Solutions Director; Recruiter; Transaction Manager; Corporate Counsel; Government Recruiter; Global Sales Manager; Client Manager; Manager; Conference Planner. **Corporate headquarters location:** This location.

LUCENT TECHNOLOGIES INC.
283 King George Road, Room B2C36, Warren NJ 07059. 908/559-5000. **Contact:** Human Resources. **World Wide Web address:** http://www.lucent.com. **Description:** This location is a research and development center. Overall, Lucent Technologies Inc. manufactures communications products including switching, transmission, fiber-optic cable, wireless systems, and operations systems to fulfill the needs of telephone companies and other communications services providers. **Positions advertised include:** Business Management Intern; Director of Human Resources for Managed Services. **Special programs:** Summer Jobs. **Corporate headquarters location:** Murray Hill NJ.

LUCENT TECHNOLOGIES INC.
5 Penn Plaza, 10th Floor, New York NY 10001. 212/290-5900. **Contact:** Human Resources. **World Wide Web address:** http://www.lucent.com. **Description:** Manufactures communications products including switching, transmission, fiber-optic cable, wireless systems, and operations systems, to supply the needs of telephone companies and other communications services providers. **NOTE:** Interested jobseekers should send resumes to Lucent Technologies, Inc., 600 Mountain Avenue, Murray Hill NJ 07974. **Corporate headquarters location:** Murray Hill NJ. **Subsidiaries include:** Bell Laboratories. **Listed on:** New York Stock Exchange. **Stock exchange symbol:** LU. **Annual sales/revenues:** $12.3 billion. **Number of employees:** 47,000.

LYNCH INTERACTIVE CORPORATION
401 Theodore Fremd Avenue, Rye NY 10580. 914/921-8821. **Fax:** 914/921-6410. **Contact:** Human Resources. **E-mail address:** rdolan@lynchinteractivecorp.com. **World Wide Web address:** http://www.lynchinteractivecorp.com. **Description:** A holding company with subsidiaries involved in multimedia services and manufacturing. **NOTE:** Human Resources phone: 914/921-7601. **Subsidiaries include:** Telecommunications operations consist of six exchange companies: Western New Mexico Telephone Company (NM); Inter-Community Telephone Company (ND); Cuba City Telephone Exchange Company (WI); Belmont Telephone Company (WI); Bretton Woods Telephone Company (NH); and J.B.N. Telephone Company, Inc. (KS). Services offered include local network, network access, and long distance. Lynch Entertainment Corporation and Lombardo Communications are the general partners of Coronet Communications Company, which owns a CBS-affiliated television station (WHBF-TV) serving Rock Island and Moline IL, and Davenport and Bettendorf IA. Capital Communications Corporation operates WOI-TV, an

ABC affiliate broadcasting to Des Moines IA. The Morgan Group Inc. (IN), Lynch Corporation's only service subsidiary, provides services to the manufactured housing and recreational vehicle industries. Lynch Manufacturing Corporation and its subsidiary, Lynch Machinery-Miller Hydro, Inc. (GA), manufacture glass-forming machines and packaging machinery, as well as replacement parts for each. M-tron Industries, Inc. (SD) manufactures, imports, and distributes quartz crystal products and clock oscillator modules used for clocking digital circuits, precision time base references, and frequency- and time-related circuits. Safety Railway Service Corporation and its subsidiary, Entoleter, Inc. (CT), produce various capital equipment including granulators, air scrubbers, and shredders. **Corporate headquarters location:** This location. **Listed on:** American Stock Exchange. **Stock exchange symbol:** LIC. **Chairman:** Frederic V. Salerno. **Annual sales/revenues:** $86 million. **Number of employees nationwide:** 600.

NBC (NATIONAL BROADCASTING COMPANY, INC.)
30 Rockefeller Plaza, New York NY 10112. 212/664-4444. **Fax:** 212/664-4426. **Contact:** Human Resources. **World Wide Web address:** http://www.nbc.com. **Description:** A national television broadcasting communications firm. Founded in 1926. **NOTE:** Interested job seekers may apply online. **Positions advertised include:** Sales Planner Supervisor. **Special programs:** Internships. **Corporate headquarters location:** This location. **Subsidiaries include:** CNBC; Bravo; Telemundo. **Parent company:** NBC Universal. **Listed on:** New York Stock Exchange. **Stock exchange symbol:** GE.

NEXTEL COMMUNICATIONS
2 Industrial Road, Fairfield NJ 07004. 973/276-0283. **Contact:** Human Resources. **World Wide Web address:** http://www.nextel.com. **Description:** Nextel Communications is engaged in the specialized mobile radio (SMR) wireless communications business. These services permit the company's customers to dispatch fleets of vehicles and place calls using their two-way mobile radios to or from any telephone in North America through interconnection with the public switched telephone network. Nextel Communications also sells and rents two-way mobile radio equipment and provides related installation, repair, and maintenance services. **Corporate headquarters location:** Reston VA. **Operations at this facility include:** This location provides customer service for cellular phones. **Listed on:** NASDAQ. **Stock exchange symbol:** NXTL.

NICE SYSTEMS INC.
116 John Street, Suite 1601, New York NY 10038. 646/836-6900. **Contact:** Human Resources. **World Wide Web address:** http://www.nice.com. **Description:** Develops, designs, manufactures, markets, and services digital voice recording systems. The company's products are used in a variety of telemarketing applications. **NOTE:** Jobseekers may apply for positions online. **Other U.S. locations:** Denver CO; Herndon VA. **Corporate headquarters location:** Rutherford NJ. **International locations:** Israel; England; France; Germany; Hong Kong. **Listed on:** NASDAQ. **Stock exchange symbol:** NICE. **Sales/revenue:** $127 million.

PETRY MEDIA CORPORATION
dba BLAIR TELEVISION, INC.
3 East 54th Street, New York NY 10022. 212/230-5900. **Fax:** 212/230-5843. **Contact:** Human Resources Staffing. **World Wide Web address:** http://www.petrymedia.com/blair. **Description:** Provides the media industry with national sales, marketing, and research services. The company's subsidiaries represent 250 TV stations and provides services to advertising agencies and spot TV advertisers. **Positions advertised include:** Sales Assistant; Research Analyst; Sales Associate; Account Executive. **Special programs:** Internships. **Corporate headquarters location:** This location. **Other U.S. locations:** Nationwide. **Subsidiaries include:** Blair Television, Incorporated; Petry

Television Incorporated. **Operations at this facility include:** Administration; Research and Development; Sales. **Number of employees at this location:** 250. **Number of employees nationwide:** 500.

PORTA SYSTEMS CORPORATION

6851 Jericho Turnpike, Syosset NY 11791. 516/364-9300. **Fax:** 516/682-4636. **Contact:** Personnel. **E-mail address:** cu-sales@portasystems.com. **World Wide Web address:** http://www.portasystems.com. **Description:** Designs, manufactures, and markets telecommunications equipment, software, and systems to customers worldwide. Products are used for the connection, testing, management, and security of telecommunications and computer networks and systems. Porta Systems Corporation is comprised of three operating divisions: Operations Support Systems (OSS); Connection/Protection; and Signal Processing. **Corporate headquarters location:** This location. **International locations:** Mexico; Chile; England; Poland; the Philippines; China. **Operations at this facility include:** Administration; Manufacturing; Research and Development; Sales. **Listed on:** American Stock Exchange. **Stock exchange symbol:** PSI.

RFL ELECTRONICS INC.

353 Powerville Road, Boonton Township NJ 07005-9151. 973/334-3100. **Fax:** 973/334-3863. **Contact:** Human Resources. **E-mail address:** hrmanager@rflelect.com. **World Wide Web address:** http://www.rflelect.com. **Description:** Designs and manufactures a wide range of telecommunication and teleprotection products for the electric, water, gas, and telephone utilities; railroads; mines; pipelines; airlines; oil drilling and refining firms; private contractors; OEMs; and government agencies. **Positions advertised include:** Senior Software Engineer; Order Entry Administrator.

ROANWELL CORPORATION

2564 Park Avenue, Bronx NY 10451. 718/401-0288. **Toll-free phone:** 866/929-3301. **Fax:** 718/401-0663. **Contact:** Human Resources. **World Wide Web address:** http://www.roanwellcorp.com. **Description:** Manufactures terminal voice communication equipment. **Corporate headquarters location:** This location.

TELCORDIA TECHNOLOGIES

One Telcordia Drive, Piscataway NJ 08854. 732/699-2000. **Contact:** Human Resources. **World Wide Web address:** http://www.telcordia.com. **Description:** Develops, provides, and maintains telecommunications information networking software, and professional services for businesses, governments, and telecommunications carriers. **Positions advertised include:** Applied Research; Business Processing Consultant; Corporate Marketing Communication; Contract Management; Systems Engineer; Accounting Representative; Human Resources Representative; Product Manager; Account Executive; Finance Representative; Applied Research Representative.

VERIZON COMMUNICATIONS

540 Broad Street, Newark NJ 07101. 973/649-9900. **Contact:** Human Resources. **World Wide Web address:** http://www.verizon.com. **Description:** A full-service communications services provider. Verizon offers residential local and long distance telephone services and Internet access; wireless service plans, cellular phones, and data services; a full-line of business services including Internet access, data services, and telecommunications equipment and services; and government network solutions including Internet access, data services, telecommunications equipment and services, and enhanced communications services. **Positions advertised include:** Strategic Account Manager. **Corporate headquarters location:** New York NY. **Listed on:** New York Stock Exchange. **Stock exchange symbol:** VZ.

VIACOM INC.
1515 Broadway, 31st Floor, New York NY 10036. 212/258-6000. **Contact:** Human Resources. **World Wide Web address:** http://www.viacom.com. **Description:** A diversified entertainment and communications company with operations in four principal segments: Networks, Entertainment, Cable Television, and Broadcasting. Viacom Networks operates three advertiser-supported basic cable television program services: MTV (Music Television including MTV Europe and MTV Latino), VH-1/Video Hits One, and Nickelodeon/Nick at Nite; and three premium subscription television services: SHOWTIME, The Movie Channel, and FLIX. Viacom Entertainment distributes television series, feature films, made-for-television movies, miniseries, and movies for prime time broadcast network television; acquires and distributes television series for initial exhibition on a first-run basis; and develops, produces, distributes, and markets interactive software for multimedia markets. Viacom Cable Television owns and operates cable television systems in California, the Pacific Northwest, and the Midwest. Viacom Broadcasting owns and operates five network-affiliated television stations and 14 radio stations. **Corporate headquarters location:** This location. **Listed on:** New York Stock Exchange. **Stock exchange symbol:** VIA.

WESTERN UNION CORPORATION
436 Forest Avenue, Paramus NJ 07652. 201/261-4641. **Contact:** Personnel. **World Wide Web address:** http://www.westernunion.com. **Description:** Provides telecommunications systems and services to businesses, government agencies, and consumers. The company operates a nationwide communications network that includes Westar satellites in orbit. **Positions advertised include:** Account Executive.

WORLD WRESTLING FEDERATION ENTERTAINMENT, INC.
1241 East Main Street, P.O. Box 3857, Stamford CT 06902. 203/352-8600. **Contact:** Human Resources. **World Wide Web address:** http://www.wwe.com. **Description:** Develops and markets television programming and pay-per-view broadcasting for the World Wrestling Federation. The company also produces and manages live wrestling events. **Positions advertised include:** Director of Internal Audit; Director of Job Notification. **Special Programs:** Internships. **Corporate headquarters location:** This location.

COMPUTER HARDWARE, SOFTWARE, AND SERVICES

You can expect to find the following types of companies in this section:
Computer Components and Hardware Manufacturers • Consultants and Computer Training Companies • Internet and Online Service Providers • Networking and Systems Services • Repair Services/Rental and Leasing • Resellers, Wholesalers, and Distributors • Software Developers/Programming Services • Web Technologies

ACI
90 Woodbridge Center Drive, Suite 400, Woodbridge NJ 07095. 732/602-0200. **Contact:** Personnel. **World Wide Web address:** http://www.aci.com. **Description:** Provides systems integration services. **Positions advertised include:** Analyst; Help Desk Associate; Unix Administrator; DBA; Project Manager; Technical Writer; Quality Assurance Tester; Developer; Java Programmer.

AM BEST COMPANY
1 AMbest Road, Oldwick NJ 08858. 908/439-2200. **Fax:** 908/439-3027. **Contact:** Human Resources. **E-mail address:** hr@ambest.com. **World Wide Web address:** http://www.ambest.com. **Description:** Manufactures products including software, CD-ROMs, and diskette support products for the insurance industry. **Positions advertised include:** Tax Analyst; Customer Service Representative; Financial Analyst; Editorial Assistant; Sales Analyst. **Corporate headquarters location:** This location.

AMI (ADVANCED MEDIA INC.)
80 Orville Drive, Bohemia NY 11716. 631/244-1616. **Fax:** 631/244-3209. **Contact:** Office Manager. **World Wide Web address:** http://www.advancedmedia.com. **Description:** Provides professional multimedia development products, services, and proprietary technologies to corporate accounts. AMI's services include Website designing and redesigning. **Listed on:** Over The Counter. **Stock exchange symbol:** AVMJ. **Annual sales/revenues:** $1.26 million. **Number of employees:** 7.

AXS-ONE INC.
301 Route 17 North, 12th Floor, Rutherford NJ 07070. 201/935-3400. **Toll-free phone:** 800/828-7660. **Fax:** 201/935-8482. **Contact:** Human Resources. **E-mail address:** careers@axsone.com. **World Wide Web address:** http://www.axsone.com. **Description:** Develops and markets various financial software products. **Positions advertised include:** Senior Consultant.

ACCENTURE
5 Spring Street, Murray Hill NJ 07974. 908/898-5000. **Contact:** Human Resources. **World Wide Web address:** http://www.accenture.com. **Description:** A management and technology consulting firm. Accenture offers a wide range of services including business re-engineering; customer service system consulting; data system design and implementation; Internet sales systems research and design; and strategic planning. **Number of employees nationwide:** 5,600.

AFFINITI GROUP
106 Apple Street, Suite 110, Tinton Falls NJ 07724. 732-747-9600. **Contact:** Human Resources. **E-mail address:** careers@affinitigroup.com. **World Wide Web address:** http://www.affinitigroup.com. **Description:** Provides systems

integration and software development services. **Positions advertised include:** Sales Representative; Programmer; Unix System Administrator; Technical Support Representative; Network Engineer; Traffic Coordinator.

AJILON SERVICES INC.
625 Madison Avenue, New York NY 10022. 212/224-0220. **Contact:** Human Resources. **World Wide Web address:** http://www.ajilon.com. **Description:** Offers computer consulting services, staffing services, project support, and end user services with 450 offices in 17 countries. **Corporate headquarters location:** Towson MD. **Other U.S. locations:** Worldwide.

ANALYSTS INTERNATIONAL CORPORATION (AIC)
111 Wood Avenue South, Iselin NJ 08830. 732/906-0100. **Fax:** 732/906-8808. **Contact:** Human Resources. **World Wide Web address:** http://www.analysts.com. **Description:** AiC is an international computer consulting firm. The company assists clients in analyzing, designing, and developing systems in a variety of industries using different programming languages and software. **Corporate headquarters location:** Minneapolis MN.

ANALYSTS INTERNATIONAL CORPORATION
7 Penn Plaza, Suite 300, New York NY 10001. 212/465-1660. **Fax:** 212/465-1724. **Contact:** Recruiter. **World Wide Web address:** http://www.analysts.com. **Description:** AIC is an international computer consulting firm. The company assists clients in developing systems in a variety of industries using different programming languages and software. **Corporate headquarters location:** Minneapolis MN. **Other U.S. locations:** Nationwide. **International locations:** Cambridge, England; Toronto, Canada. **Listed on:** NASDAQ. **Stock exchange symbol:** ANLY. **Annual sales/revenues:** $426 million. **Number of employees:** 3,200.

ANSOFT CORPORATION
669 River Drive, Suite 200, Elmwood Park NJ 07407-1361. 201/796-2003. **Contact:** Human Resources. **E-mail address:** jobs@ansoft.com. **World Wide Web address:** http://www.ansoft.com. **Description:** Develops and distributes circuit design software. **NOTE:** Send resumes and cover letters to: 4 Station Square, Suite 200, Pittsburgh PA 15219-1119. 412/261-3200. **Positions advertised include:** Customer Support Engineer; Marketing Engineer; Software Engineer; Technical Writer; Research & Development Engineer. **Corporate headquarters location:** Pittsburgh PA.

ASPECT COMPUTER CORPORATION
19 World's Fair Drive, Somerset NJ 08873. 732/563-1304. **Contact:** Human Resources. **World Wide Web address:** http://www.aspectcom.com. **Description:** Manufactures computers.

AUTHENTIDATE HOLDING CORPORATION
2 World Financial Center, 225 Liberty Street, 43rd Floor, New York NY 10281. 212/329-1100. **Fax:** 212/329-1101. **Contact:** Human Resources. **World Wide Web address:** http://www.authentidate.com. **Description:** The company's main subsidiary, AuthentiDate, Inc., is engaged in the manufacture and distribution of document imaging systems, computer systems and related peripheral equipment, components, and accessories and network and Internet services. **Corporate headquarters location:** Schenectady NY. **Subsidiaries include:** AuthentiDate, Inc.; Computer Professionals International; DocSTAR; Authentidate Sports Edition; Trac Medical Solutions, Inc.; DJS Marketing Group, Inc.; WebCMN, Inc. **Listed on:** NASDAQ. **Stock exchange symbol:** ADAT. **President/CEO:** John H. Botti. **Annual sales/revenues:** $16 million. **Number of employees:** 41.

BANCTEC SYSTEMS, INC.
888 Veterans Memorial Highway, Suite 515, Hauppauge NY 11788. 631/234-5353. **Contact:** Human Resources. **E-mail address:** jobs@banctec.com. **World Wide Web address:** http://www.banctec.com. **Description:** BancTec is engaged in systems integration and specializes in document management solutions. The company also provides network support services and develops image management software. Founded in 1972. **NOTE:** Resumes should be sent to P.O. Box 660204, Dallas TX 75266-0204. **Corporate headquarters location:** Dallas TX. **Other locations:** Worldwide. **Number of employees worldwide:** 4,000.

BLUEBIRD AUTO RENTAL SYSTEMS INC.
200 Mineral Springs Drive, Dover NJ 07801. 973/560-0080. **Contact:** Human Resources. **E-mail address:** info@barsnet.com. **World Wide Web address:** http://www.barsnet.com. **Description:** Designs computer applications for automobile rental agencies.

CAM GRAPHICS COMPANY INC.
206 New Highway, Amityville NY 11701. 631/842-3400. **Fax:** 631/842-1005. **Contact:** Human Resources. **E-mail address:** info@camgraphics.com. **World Wide Web address:** http://www.camgraphics.com. **Description:** CAM Graphics Company supplies businesses and manufacturers with assorted memory-related devices.

CAPGEMINI U.S.
100 Walnut Avenue, Clark NJ 07066. 732/669-6000. **Fax:** 732/669-6205. **Contact:** Human Resources. **World Wide Web address:** http://www.us.capgemini.com. **Description:** A leading provider of information technology consulting services with offices nationwide. **Positions advertised include:** Human Resources Manager; Administrative Assistant; Government Solutions Manager; Sales Executive; Sales Associate; Pharmacist Manager. **Other U.S. locations:** Nationwide.

CAPGEMINI U.S.
5 Times Square, 9th Floor, New York NY 10036. 917/934-8000. **Fax:** 917/934-8001. **Contact:** Human Resources. **World Wide Web address:** http://www.us.capgemini.com. **Description:** Provider of management consulting services including business strategy, operations, and people and information management. Services include systems integration; application design, development, and documentation; systems conversions and migrations; and information technology consulting. **NOTE:** Jobseekers are encouraged to apply online. **Positions advertised include:** Oracle Planner; Graphic Designer; JD Edwards Planner; Patient Financial Services Manager; Supply Chain Health Manager; Health Information Manager; Health Revenue Manager; Tech Direct Sales Executive; Business Transformation Manager; Campus Health Providers Consultant; Clinical Health Integrator. **Corporate headquarters location:** This location. **Other U.S. locations:** Nationwide. **International locations:** Worldwide. **Parent company:** Cap Gemini Ernst & Young (Paris, France). **Annual sales/revenues:** $2.6 billion. **Number of employees:** 10,000.

CHERRYROAD TECHNOLOGIES INC.
199 Cherry Hill Road, Parsippany NJ 07054. 973/402-7802. **Contact:** Human Resources. **World Wide Web address:** http://www.cherryroad.com. **Description:** A computer information technology company that provides comprehensive systems integration and consulting services that maximize enterprise performance for private and public sector as well as federal clients. **NOTE:** Job searches may search for jobs and submit resumes online. **Positions advertised include:** Management Consultant; PeopleSoft Practice Manager;

PeopleSoft Technical Consultants; Practice Manager. **Corporate headquarters location:** This location. **Other U.S. locations:** Nationwide.

CIBER, INC.
7 Ridgedale Avenue, Cedar Knolls NJ 07927. 973/267-0088. **Fax:** 973/267-8675. **Contact:** Human Resources. **World Wide Web address:** http://www.ciber.com. **Description:** A leading systems integrator. The company's services include computer network design, installation, and administration; helpdesk support; technical education; cabling and telecommunications sales and service; computer product sales and services; and Internet services. Clients include many small and mid-range companies, national and global *Fortune* 1000 companies, and large government agencies. Founded in 1984. **Positions advertised include:** Educational Sales Consultant. **Corporate headquarters location:** This location. **Other U.S. locations:** NY; PA. **Listed on:** New York Stock Exchange. **Stock exchange symbol:** CBR. **Annual sales/revenues:** More than $100 million.

CIBER, INC.
252 Fernwood Avenue, Edison NJ 08837. 732/225-1700. **Fax:** 732/225-1973. **Contact:** Human Resources. **World Wide Web address:** http://www.ciber.com. **Description:** Provides consulting for client/server development, mainframe and legacy systems, industry-specific analysis, application-specific analysis, and network development.

CLARION OFFICE SUPPLIES INC.
101 East Main Street, Little Falls NJ 07424. 973/785-8383. **Contact:** Human Resources. **World Wide Web address:** http://www.clarionofficesupply.com. **Description:** Distributes a wide variety of office supplies including computer hardware. Clarion Office Supplies provides individuals and businesses with most major brands of CPUs and monitors.

COMMVAULT SYSTEMS
2 Crescent Place, P.O. Box 900, Oceanport NJ 07757-0900. 732/870-4000. **Contact:** Human Resources. **E-mail address:** employment@commvault.com. **World Wide Web address:** http://www.commvault.com. **Description:** Develops and sells software for businesses with computer backup systems. **Positions advertised include:** Inside Sales Representative; Product Marketing Manager; Systems Tester. **Corporate headquarters location:** This location.

COMPUTER ASSOCIATES INTERNATIONAL, INC.
1351 Washington Boulevard, Suite 800, Stamford CT 06902. 203/352-6800. **Toll-free phone:** 800/243-9462. **Fax:** 203/937-3015. **Contact:** Human Resources. **World Wide Web address:** http://www.ca.com. **Description:** Computer Associates International is one of the world's leading developers of client/server and distributed computing software. The company develops, markets, and supports enterprise management, database and applications development, business applications, and consumer software products for a broad range of mainframe, midrange, and desktop computers. Computer Associates International serves major business, government, research, and educational organizations. **Positions advertised include:** Sales Executive; Customer Relationship Manager. **Corporate headquarters location:** Islandia NY. **Other U.S. locations:** Nationwide. **Listed on:** New York Stock Exchange. **Stock exchange symbol:** CA. **Annual sales/revenues:** More than $100 million.

COMPUTER ASSOCIATES INTERNATIONAL, INC.
Route 206 and Orchard Road, Princeton NJ 08543. 908/874-9000. **Fax:** 908/874-9420. **Contact:** Hiring Manager. **E-mail address:** joinca@ca.com. **World Wide Web address:** http://www.cai.com. **Description:** One of the world's leading developers of client/server and distributed computing software. The

company develops, markets, and supports enterprise management, database and applications development, business applications, and consumer software products for a broad range of mainframe, midrange, and desktop computers. Computer Associates International serves major business, government, research, and educational organizations. Founded in 1976. **Positions advertised include:** Consultant; Database Management Administrator. **NOTE:** Search for positions online. Mail resumes to: CAI Inc., One Computer Associates Plaza, Islandia NY 11749. **Corporate headquarters location:** Islandia NY. **Other U.S. locations:** Nationwide. **Listed on:** New York Stock Exchange. **Stock exchange symbol:** CA. **Annual sales/revenues:** More than $100 million.

COMPUTER ASSOCIATES INTERNATIONAL, INC.
2 Executive Drive, Fort Lee NJ 07024. 201/592-0009. **Contact:** Hiring Manager. **E-mail address:** joinca@ca.com. **World Wide Web address:** http://www.cai.com. **Description:** Computer Associates International is one of the world's leading developers of client/server and distributed computing software. The company develops, markets, and supports enterprise management, database and applications development, business applications, and consumer software products for a broad range of mainframe, midrange, and desktop computers. Computer Associates International serves major business, government, research, and educational organizations. Founded in 1976. **NOTE:** Mail resumes to: CAI Inc., One Computer Associates Plaza, Islandia NY 11749. **Corporate headquarters location:** Islandia NY. **Other U.S. locations:** Nationwide. **Operations at this facility include:** This location sells software, offers technical support, and is home to the marketing department. **Listed on:** New York Stock Exchange. **Stock exchange symbol:** CA. **Annual sales/revenues:** More than $100 million.

COMPUTER ASSOCIATES INTERNATIONAL, INC.
One Computer Associates Plaza, Islandia NY 11749. 631/342-5224. **Fax:** 631/342-5329. **Contact:** Global Recruiting Department. **E-mail address:** joinca@ca.com. **World Wide Web address:** http://www.ca.com. **Description:** A developer of client/server and computer software, the company develops, markets, and supports enterprise management, database and applications development, business applications, and consumer software products for a broad range of mainframe, midrange, and desktop computers. Computer Associates International serves major business, government, research, and educational organizations. Founded in 1976. **Positions advertised include:** Account Manager; Accountant; Assistant Teacher; Business Development Owner; Business Manager; Channel Marketing Manager; Channel Program Manager; Collections Representative; Contract Representative; Database Manager; Product Management Director; Sales Accountant; Finance Manager; Procurement Coordinator; Unicenter Product Manager; Project Manager; Proposal Specialist; Quality Assurance Engineer; Regional Legal Manager; Sales Specialist; Software Engineer. **Special programs:** Internships. **Corporate headquarters location:** This location. **Other U.S. locations:** Nationwide. **Subsidiaries include:** ACCPAC International, Inc. **Operations at this facility include:** Administration; Research and Development; Sales. **Listed on:** New York Stock Exchange. **Stock exchange symbol:** CA. **Chairman/President/CEO:** Sanjay Kumar. **Annual sales/revenues:** $3 billion. **Number of employees at this location:** 2,500. **Number of employees worldwide:** 16,600.

COMPUTER HORIZONS CORPORATION
49 Old Bloomfield Avenue, Mountain Lakes NJ 07046-1495. 973/299-4000. **Toll-free phone:** 800/321-2421. **Fax:** 973/402-7986. **Contact:** Human Resources. **E-mail address:** info@computerhorizons.com. **World Wide Web address:** http://www.computerhorizons.com. **Description:** A full-service technology solutions company offering contract staffing, outsourcing, re-engineering,

migration, downsizing support, and network management. Founded in 1969. **Corporate headquarters location:** This location. **Other U.S. locations:** Nationwide. **Subsidiaries include:** Birla Horizons International Ltd.; Horizons Consulting, Inc.; Strategic Outsourcing Services, Inc.; Unified Systems Solutions, Inc. **Listed on:** NASDAQ. **Stock exchange symbol:** CHRZ. **Number of employees nationwide:** 1,500.

COMPUTER HORIZONS CORPORATION
747 Third Avenue, 15th Floor, New York NY 10017. 212/371-9600. **Toll-free phone:** 800/321-2421. **Fax:** 973/402-7986. **Contact:** Recruiting. **E-mail address:** info@computerhorizons.com. **World Wide Web address:** http://www.computerhorizons.com. **Description:** A full-service technology solutions company offering contract staffing, outsourcing, re-engineering, migration, downsizing support, and network management. The company has a worldwide network of 33 offices. Founded in 1969. **Positions advertised include:** Systems Analyst. **Corporate headquarters location:** Mountain Lakes NJ. **Other U.S. locations:** Nationwide. **Subsidiaries include:** Birla Horizons International Ltd.; Horizons Consulting, Inc.; Strategic Outsourcing Services, Inc.; Unified Systems Solutions, Inc. **Listed on:** NASDAQ. **Stock exchange symbol:** CHRZ. **Annual sales/revenues:** $279 million. **Number of employees nationwide:** 1,500. **Number of employees worldwide:** 2,800

CORPORATE DISK COMPANY
1800 Bloomsbury Avenue, Ocean City NJ 07712. 732/431-5300. **Contact:** Controller. **World Wide Web address:** http://www.disk.com. **Description:** Provides a broad range of integrated software and information distribution options in multiple formats on disk, in print, and online to many industries including the technology, insurance, financial services, pharmaceutical, publishing, government, and transportation communities. **NOTE:** Resumes should be sent to Human Resources, Corporate Disk Company, 1226 Michael Drive, Wood Dale IL 60191.

CYBER DIGITAL, INC.
400 Oser Avenue, Suite 1650, Hauppauge NY 11788-3641. 631/231-1200. **Fax:** 631/231-1446. **Contact:** Personnel. **E-mail address:** cybd@cyberdigitalinc.com. **World Wide Web address:** http://www.cyberdigitalinc.com. **Description:** Cyber Digital designs, develops, manufactures, and markets digital switching and networking systems that enable simultaneous communication of voice and data to a large number of users. The company's systems are based on its proprietary software technology that permits the modem-less transmission of data between a variety of incompatible and dissimilar end user equipment including computers, printers, workstations, and data terminals over standard telephone lines. **Corporate headquarters location:** This location. **Listed on:** Over The Counter. **Stock exchange symbol:** CYBD.

CYBERCHRON CORPORATION
P.O. Box 160, 2700 Route 9, Cold Spring NY 10516. 845/265-3700 ext. 243. **Fax:** 845/265-2909. **Contact:** Ms. Gerry Maroulis, Human Resources. **E-mail address:** gmaroulis@cyberchron.com. **World Wide Web address:** http://www.cyberchron.com. **Description:** Cyberchron manufactures computers that are made to withstand environmental extremes. The U.S. military is one user of Cyberchron's products as well as foreign defense departments. **NOTE:** Human Resources telephone extension: x243. **Positions advertised include:** Regional Sales Representative.

DRS TECHNOLOGIES
5 Sylvan Way, Suite 60, Parsippany NJ 07054. 973/898-1500. **Fax:** 973/898-4730. **Contact:** Ann Carcione, Human Resources. **World Wide Web address:** http://www.drs.com. **Description:** A producer of magnetic recording heads for

162 /The Metropolitan New York JobBank

the information processing industry. **Positions advertised include:** Advertising & Media Manager. **Corporate headquarters location:** This location.

DATA SYSTEMS & SOFTWARE INC.
200 Route 17 South, Mahwah NJ 07430. 201/529-2026. **Fax:** 201/529-3163. **Contact:** Human Resources. **E-mail address:** ir@dssinc.com. **World Wide Web address:** http://www.dssiinc.com. **Description:** A leading provider of consulting and development services for computer software and systems to high-technology companies in Israel and the United States, principally in the area of embedded real-time systems.

DATATECH INDUSTRIES INC.
23 Madison Road, Fairfield NJ 07004. 973/808-4000. **Contact:** Human Resources. **Description:** Specializes in installing mainframes and networking hardware for businesses.

DENDRITE INTERNATIONAL, INC.
1200 Mount Kemble Avenue, Morristown NJ 07960. 973/425-1200. **Fax:** 973/425-2100. **Contact:** Personnel. **World Wide Web address:** http://www.dendrite.com. **Description:** Develops software and provides consulting services aimed at optimizing the sales force effectiveness of pharmaceutical and consumer packaged goods companies. **Positions advertised include:** Bilingual CSR; Production Control Programmer. **Corporate headquarters location:** This location. **International locations:** Worldwide. **Listed on:** NASDAQ. **Stock exchange symbol:** DRTE. **Annual sales/revenues:** More than $100 million.

DESIGN STRATEGY CORPORATION
600 Third Avenue, 25th Floor, New York NY 10016. 212/370-0000. **Fax:** 212/949-3648. **Contact:** Human Resources. **World Wide Web address:** http://www.designstrategy.com. **Description:** Develops and markets inventory control software. **Positions advertised include:** SAS Programmer/Analyst; Network Engineer; Egenera Systems Administrator. **Corporate headquarters location:** This location. **Other locations:** Upper Marlboro MD; Cranford NJ.

DESKTOP ENGINEERING INTERNATIONAL, INC.
172 Broadway, Woodcliff Lake NJ 07677. 201/505-9200. **Toll-free phone:** 800/888-8680. **Fax:** 201/505-1566. **Contact:** Human Resources. **E-mail address:** information@deiusa.com. **World Wide Web address:** http://www.deiusa.com. **Description:** Designs and manufactures software for use in mechanical and structural engineering industries.

DIRECT INSITE CORPORATION
80 Orville Drive, Suite 100, Bohemia NY 11716. 631/244-1500. **Fax:** 631/563-8085. **Contact:** Human Resources. **World Wide Web address:** http://www.directinsite.com. **Description:** Direct Insite Corp. designs, markets, and supports information delivery software products including end user data access tools for personal computers and client/server environments, and systems management software products for corporate mainframe data centers. Products include dbExpress, which offers methods of searching, organizing, analyzing, and utilizing information contained in databases; systems management software products, which improve mainframe system performance, reduce hardware expenditures, and enhance the reliability and availability of the data processing environment; client/server products, which develop client/server relational database administration and programmer productivity tools. **Corporate headquarters location:** This location. **Subsidiaries include:** d.b.Express; Account Management Systems. **Listed on:** NASDAQ. **Stock exchange symbol:** DIRI. **Chairman/CEO:** James A. Cannavino. **Annual sales/revenues:** $4 million. **Number of employees:** 65.

EDS
25 Hanover Road, 3rd Floor, Florham Park NJ 07932-1424. 973/301-7502. **Contact:** Human Resources. **World Wide Web address:** http://www.eds.com. **Description:** Provides integrated hardware, software, and network solutions to *Fortune* 500 companies. EDS focuses primarily on international corporations in the service, wholesale, distribution, and transportation industries. **Listed on:** New York Stock Exchange. **Stock exchange symbol:** EDS.

E.F.L.S.
545 Eighth Avenue, Suite 401, New York NY 10018. 212/868-1126. **Fax:** 212/714-1453. **Contact:** Human Resources. **World Wide Web address:** http://www.efls.net. **Description:** Provides telephone and messaging services as well as computer consulting services for Macintosh systems.

ELECTROGRAPH SYSTEMS INC.
40 Marcus Boulevard, Hauppauge NY 11788. 631/436-5050. **Fax:** 631/436-5075. **Contact:** Human Resources. **World Wide Web address:** http://www.electrograph.com. **Description:** Distributes microcomputer peripherals, components, and accessories throughout the East Coast of the United States. Electrograph Systems distributes national brand names such as Mitsubishi, Sony, Hitachi, Magnavox, Toshiba, and Idex. The company's products include monitors, printers, large-screen televisions, CD-ROMs, computer video products, optical storage products, notebook computers, and personal computers. Founded in 1982. **Other U.S. locations:** Garden Grove CA; Madeira Beach FL; Woodridge IL; Olathe KS; Timonium MD; Plano TX. **Parent company:** Manchester Technologies, Inc. (also at this location).

FDS INTERNATIONAL
18 West Ridgewood Avenue, Paramus NJ 07652. 201/670-1300. **Fax:** 201/670-0400. **Contact:** Human Resources Department. **E-mail address:** jobs@fdsinternational.com. **World Wide Web address:** http://www.fdsinternational.com. **Description:** Develops transportation and custom brokerage software.

FUJITSU CONSULTING
333 Thornall Street, Edison NJ 08837. 732/549-4100. **Fax:** 732/549-2375. **Contact:** Recruiting Administrator. **World Wide Web address:** http://consulting.fujitsu.com. **Description:** Provides computer consulting services including outsourcing solutions and systems integration. **Positions advertised include:** Consultant. **Corporate headquarters location:** This location. **Parent company:** Fujitsu Limited. **Number of employees worldwide:** 8,000.

FUJITSU CORPORATION
85 Challenger Road, 3rd Floor, Ridgefield Park NJ 07660. 201/229-4400. **Contact:** Human Resources. **World Wide Web address:** http://www.fujitsu.com. **Description:** This location is engaged in sales, service, and support. Overall, Amdahl designs, develops, manufactures, markets, and services large-scale, high-performance, general purpose computer systems including both hardware and software. Customers are primarily large corporations, government agencies, and large universities with high-volume data processing requirements. Amdahl markets more than 470 different systems. **Positions advertised include:** Field Operations Installer; Field Operations Engineer; Area Sales Manager. **NOTE:** Mail employment correspondence to: 1250 East Arques Avenue, Sunnyvale CA 94088. **Corporate headquarters location:** Sunnyvale CA.

GLOBE MANUFACTURING SALES, INC.
1159 U.S. Route 22, Mountainside NJ 07092. 908/232-7301. **Fax:** 908/232-0179. **Contact:** Personnel. **World Wide Web address:** http://www.globebrackets.com.

Description: Manufactures computer brackets that hold computer chips and other plastic parts. **Parent company:** AK Stamping Company, Inc.

HAUPPAUGE DIGITAL INC.
dba HAUPPAUGE COMPUTER WORKS INC.
91 Cabot Court, Hauppauge NY 11788. 631/434-1600. **Fax:** 631/434-3198. **Contact:** Cheryl Willins, Human Resources Manager. **World Wide Web address:** http://www.hauppauge.com. **Description:** Manufactures PC circuit boards that allow viewers to use computers to watch TV, videoconference, and watch VCRs or camcorders as well as boards that allow for radio and Internet broadcasting. **Corporate headquarters location:** This location. **Other locations:** Worldwide. **Listed on:** NASDAQ. **Stock exchange symbol:** HAUP. **Chairman/CEO:** Kenneth H. Plotkin. **Annual sales/revenues:** $43 million. **Number of employees:** 107.

HRSOFT, INC.
10 Madison Avenue, 3rd Floor, Morristown NJ 07962. 973/984-6334. **Toll-free phone:** 800/437-6781. **Fax:** 973/984-5427. **Contact:** Human Resources. **E-mail address:** jobinfo@hrsoft.com. **World Wide Web address:** http://www.hrsoft.com. **Description:** Develops and provides human resource-related business software and services.

HYPERION SOLUTIONS
900 Long Ridge Road, Stamford CT 06902. 203/703-3000. **Fax:** 203/322-3904. **Contact:** Human Resources. **World Wide Web address:** http://www.hyperion.com. **Description:** Hyperion Solutions develops, markets, and supports a family of network-based business information software products for large multidivision or multilocation companies worldwide. The product line provides executives, managers, and analysts with the capability to collect, process, access, and analyze critical business information in a timely manner, using networked personal computers. **Positions advertised include:** Compensation Manager; Financial Applications Instructor; Partner Technical Account Manager; Administrative Assistant; Performance Engineer; Software Engineer. **Special programs:** Internships. **Corporate headquarters location:** Sunnyvale CA. **Other U.S. locations:** Nationwide. **Operations at this facility include:** Administration; Divisional Headquarters; Regional Headquarters; Research and Development; Sales; Service. **Listed on:** NASDAQ. **Stock exchange symbol:** HYSL. **Number of employees worldwide:** 2,300.

IBM CORPORATION
1551 South Washington Avenue, 3rd Floor, Piscataway NJ 08854. 732/926-2000. **Recorded jobline:** 800/964-4473. **Contact:** IBM Staffing Services Center. **World Wide Web address:** http://www.ibm.com. **Description:** IBM develops, manufactures, and markets advanced information processing products including computers and microelectronic technology, software, networking systems, and information technology-related services. IBM operates in the United States, Canada, Europe, Middle East, Africa, Latin America, and Asia Pacific. **NOTE:** Jobseekers should send a resume to IBM Staffing Services Center, 1DPA/051, 3808 Six Forks Road, Raleigh NC 27609. **Corporate headquarters location:** Armonk NY. **Operations at this facility include:** This location is a marketing office. **Subsidiaries include:** IBM Credit Corporation; IBM Instruments, Inc.; IBM World Trade Corporation. **Number of employees at this location:** 100.

IDT CORPORATION
520 Broad Street, Newark NJ 07102. 973/438-1000. **Toll-free phone:** 800/CAL-LIDT. **Contact:** Human Resources Manager. **World Wide Web address:** http://www.idt.net. **Description:** An Internet access provider that offers dial-up services, Web hosting, and e-mail by phone. Founded in 1990. **NOTE:** Entry-level positions, part-time jobs, and second and third shifts are offered. **Special**

programs: Internships; Apprenticeships; Summer Jobs. **Corporate headquarters location:** This location. **Other U.S. locations:** Nationwide. **International locations:** London, England; Mexico City, Mexico. **Subsidiaries include:** Amerimax; Net2Phone; Union Telecard Alliances. **Listed on:** NASDAQ. **Stock exchange symbol:** IDTC. **Founder:** Howard Jonas. **Annual sales/revenues:** More than $100 million. **Number of employees at this location:** 1,000. **Number of employees nationwide:** 1,200. **Number of employees worldwide:** 1,500.

IPC INFORMATION SYSTEMS
516 West 19th Street, New York NY 10011. 212/367-3600. **Contact:** Manager of Human Resources. **World Wide Web address:** http://www.ipc.com. **Description:** IPC Information Systems provides network communications solutions for the financial industry. Through its Information Transport Systems (ITS) business, the company provides its customers with voice, data, and video solutions through the design, integration, implementation, and support of local and wide area networks. ITS solutions incorporate the latest technology and are supported by a team of systems engineers. Founded in 1973. **Corporate headquarters location:** New York NY. **International locations:** Asia; Europe. **Number of employees at this location:** 70. **Number of employees nationwide:** 775.

IPC INFORMATION SYSTEMS
Wall Street Plaza, 88 Pine Street, New York NY 10005. 212/825-9060. **Fax:** 212/344-5106. **Contact:** Human Resources. **World Wide Web address:** http://www.ipc.com. **Description:** Provides network communications solutions for the financial industry. Through its Information Transport Systems (ITS) business, the company provides its customers with voice, data, and video solutions through the design, integration, implementation, and support of local and wide area networks. ITS solutions incorporate the latest technology and are supported by a team of systems engineers. Founded in 1973. **Corporate headquarters location:** This location. **International locations:** Asia; Europe. **Number of employees nationwide:** 775.

ITT INDUSTRIES
4 West Red Oak Lane, White Plains NY 10604. 914/641-2021. **Fax:** 914/696-2965. **Contact:** Katherine Campbell, Human Resources. **E-mail address:** Katherine.Campbell@itt.com. **World Wide Web address:** http://www.ittind.com. **Description:** A multinational company with operations divided into four business segments: fluid technology; defense electronics; motion and flow control; and electronic components; as well as providing maintenance services for its products. **Corporate headquarters location:** This location. **Other locations:** Worldwide. **Listed on:** New York Stock Exchange. **Stock exchange symbol:** ITT. **Subsidiaries include:** ITT Defense Electronics & Services. **Chairman/President/CEO:** Louis J. Giuliano. **Annual sales/revenues:** $5 billion. **Number of employees:** 38,000.

ITT INDUSTRIES
AEROSPACE/COMMUNICATIONS DIVISION
100 Kingsland Road, Clifton NJ 07014. 973/284-0123. **Contact:** Human Resources. **World Wide Web address:** http://www.ittind.com. **Description:** Designs and engineers software for satellite communications under government contracts.

IKEGAMI ELECTRONICS INC.
37 Brook Avenue, Maywood NJ 07607. 201/368-9171. **Fax:** 201/569-1626. **Contact:** Human Resources. **World Wide Web address:** http://www.ikegami.com. **Description:** Manufactures and sells computer and

broadcast monitors. **Positions advertised include:** Broadcast Field Service Engineer.

INFORMATION BUILDERS INC.
Two Penn Plaza, New York NY 10121-2898. 212/736-4433. **Fax:** 212/239-6674. **Contact:** Lila Goldberg, Human Resources Director. **E-mail address:** employment_opportunities@ibi.com. **World Wide Web address:** http://www.ibi.com. **Description:** A software development firm. Products include FOCUS, EDA, and SmartMart software for various platforms. **NOTE:** Jobseekers may see http://www.hotjobs.com for a listing of current openings with detailed application information. **Positions advertised include:** WebFOCUS Technical Specialist; MVS Systems Programmer; Network Operating Systems Analyst; XML Programmer; Sales Engineer; Software Engineer; Inside Sales Representative; Software Sales Representative; Direct Marketing Manager; Administrator; Senior Administratorp Business Development Analyst; Senior Implementation Manager; Project Manager; WebFOCUS Team Leader. **Corporate headquarters location:** This location. **Other U.S. locations:** Nationwide. **President:** Gerald D. Cohen. **Annual sales/revenues:** $300 million. **Number of employees:** 1,800.

INNODATA CORPORATION
North American Solutions Center, 3 University Plaza Drive, Hackensack NJ 07601. 201/488-1200. **Contact:** Human Resources. **E-mail address:** careers@innodata-isogen.com. **World Wide Web address:** http://www.innodata.com. **Description:** A worldwide electronic publishing company specializing in data conversion for CD-ROM, print, and online database publishers. The company also offers medical transcription services to health care providers through its Statline Division. **Positions advertised include:** Business Development Executive. **Corporate headquarters location:** Brooklyn NY. **Listed on:** NASDAQ. **Stock exchange symbol:** INOD.

INSTRUCTIVISION, INC.
P.O. Box 2004, 16 Chapin Road, Pine Brook NJ 07058. 973/575-9992. **Toll-free phone:** 888/551-5144. **Fax:** 973/575-9134. **Contact:** Human Resources. **World Wide Web address:** http://www.instructivision.com. **Description:** Develops video production and education software. Instructivision also operates a full-service video production facility encompassing a production stage, an interformat digital editing suite, offline editing, 3-D animation, and audio recording equipment.

INTERNATIONAL BUSINESS MACHINES CORPORATION (IBM)
New Orchard Road, Armonk NY 10504. 914/499-1900. **Fax:** 914/765-7382. **Recorded jobline:** 800/796-9876. **Contact:** IBM Staffing Services Center. **World Wide Web address:** http://www.ibm.com. **Description:** A developer, manufacturer, and marketer of advanced information processing products including computers and microelectronic technology, software, networking systems, and information technology-related services. **Positions advertised include:** Executive Assistant; Business Controls Advisor; EOL Administrator Analyst; Human Capital Analyst; Sales Operation Specialist; SAP Conversion Analyst; SAP Security Analyst; Senior Tax Specialist; Tax Supplemental Specialist; Treasury Operations Manager. **Corporate headquarters location:** Armonk NY. **Other locations:** Worldwide. **Subsidiaries include:** Hitachi Global Storage Technologies; IBM Canada Ltd.; IBM Credit Corporation; IBM Global Services; IBM Instruments, Inc.; IBM Software; IBM World Trade Corporation; International Business Machines – Microelectronics; Lotus Development Corporation; Tivoli Software. **Listed on:** New York Stock Exchange. **Stock exchange symbol:** IBM. **Chairman/President/CEO:** Samuel J. Palmisano. **Annual sales/revenues:** $81.2 billion. **Number of employees:** 315,889.

INTERNET COMMERCE CORPORATION
805 Third Avenue, 9th Floor, New York NY 10022. 212/271-7640. **Fax:** 212/271-8580. **Contact:** Claire Schank, Human Resources Manager. **E-mail address:** hr@icc.net. **World Wide Web address:** http://www.icc.net. **Description:** Manufactures computer systems that enable protection, retrieval, and monitoring of digital information use. **Corporate headquarters location:** This location. **Other area locations:** Setauket NY. **Listed on:** NASDAQ. **Stock exchange symbol:** ICCA. **Chairman:** Charles C. Johnston. **Number of employees:** 115.

INVESTMENT TECHNOLOGY GROUP, INC.
380 Madison Avenue, 4th Floor, New York NY 10017. 212/588-4000. **Toll-free phone:** 800/215-4484. **Fax:** 212/444-6295. **Contact:** Human Resources. **E-mail address:** itg_hr@itginc.com. **World Wide Web address:** http://www.itginc.com. **Description:** Provides automated securities trade execution and analysis services to institutional equity investors. ITG's two main services are POSIT, one of the largest automated stock crossing systems operated during trading hours, and QuantEX, a proprietary software to enhance customers' trading efficiencies, access to market liquidity, and portfolio analysis capabilities. **NOTE:** Human resources phone number is 617/692-6700. **Corporate headquarters location:** This location. **Other U.S. locations:** Los Angeles CA; Boston MA. **International locations:** Dublin, Ireland; Toronto, Canada; Melbourne, Australia; Hong Kong, China. **Subsidiaries include:** Hoenig Group Inc. **Listed on:** New York Stock Exchange. **Stock exchange symbol:** ITG. **Chairman:** Raymond L. Killian Jr. **Annual sales/revenues:** $388 million. **Number of employees:** 635.

ION NETWORKS INC.
1551 South Washington Avenue, Piscataway NJ 08854. 732/529-0100. **Contact:** Human Resources. **E-mail address:** resumes@ion-networks.com. **World Wide Web address:** http://www.ion-networks.com. **Description:** Develops and markets software and hardware for computer security. **Corporate headquarters location:** This location. **International locations:** Belgium; United Kingdom. **Listed on:** NASDAQ. **Stock exchange symbol:** IONN.

ITOX
8 Elkins Road, East Brunswick NJ 08816. 732/390-2815. **Toll-free phone:** 888/200-ITOX (4869). **Fax:** 7322/390-2817. **Contact:** Human Resources. **E-mail address:** sales@itox.com. **World Wide Web address:** http://www.itox.com. **Description:** Manufactures computer components including graphics accelerator boards, motherboards, and sound cards for commercial and industrial systems.

JCC USA
Crossroads Corporate Center, One International Boulevard, Suite 400, Mahwah NJ 07495. 201/512-8835. **Contact:** Human Resources. **E-mail address:** feedbackeast@jccusa.com. **World Wide Web address:** http://www.jccusa.com. **Description:** Manufactures and sells computer terminals with various display screens.

JUNO ONLINE SERVICES, INC.
1540 Broadway, 27th Floor, New York NY 10036. 212/597-9000. **Contact:** Human Resources. **World Wide Web address:** http://www.juno.com. **Description:** A leading Internet access provider offering a variety of online services. Founded in 1996. **Positions advertised include:** Corporate Systems Administrator; Project Manager, Quality Assurance Engineer. **Special programs:** Internships. **Office hours:** Monday - Friday, 9:00 a.m. - 6:00 p.m. **Parent company:** United Online, Inc. **Corporate headquarters location:** Westlake Village CA. **Listed on:** NASDAQ. **Stock exchange symbol:** UNTD.

KANTEK INC.
3460 Hampton Road, Oceanside NY 11572. 516/594-4600. **Fax:** 516/594-1555. **Contact:** Human Resources Department. **E-mail address:** info@kantek.com. **World Wide Web address:** http://www.kantek.com. **Description:** Manufactures glare reduction screens for computer monitors as well as other computer and desk accessories. Founded in 1982. **NOTE:** Human Resources phone: 516/593-3212.

KEANE, INC.
100 Walnut Avenue, Suite 202, Clark NJ 07066. 732/396-4321. **Contact:** Human Resources. **World Wide Web address:** http://www.keane.com. **Description:** Keane offers businesses a variety of computer consulting services. Keane also develops, markets, and manages software for its clients and assists in project management. **Positions advertised include:** Project Manager; Programming Analyst; Mainframe Programming Analyst. **Corporate headquarters location:** Boston MA. **Other U.S. locations:** Nationwide. **Operations at this facility include:** This location designs, develops, and manages software for corporations and health care facilities. **Listed on:** American Stock Exchange. **Stock exchange symbol:** KEA. **Number of employees worldwide:** 7,800.

KEANE, INC.
525 Seventh Avenue, New York NY 10018-4901. 212/677-8800. **Fax:** 212/677-9654. **Contact:** Human Resources. **E-mail address:** careers.nyc@keane.com. **World Wide Web address:** http://www.keane.com. **Description:** Keane develops, markets, and manages software for its clients and assists in project management as well as offering computer consulting services. Founded in 1965. **Company slogan:** We Get IT Done. **Positions advertised include:** Programmer Analyst; Systems Analyst; Service Delivery Manager; Application Specialist; Database Administrator; Project Manager; Business Analyst. **Corporate headquarters location:** Boston MA. **Other U.S. locations:** Nationwide. **Operations at this facility include:** Divisional Headquarters **Listed on:** American Stock Exchange. **Stock exchange symbol:** KEA. **Annual sales/revenues:** $873 million. **Number of employees:** 7,800.

LSI COMPUTER SYSTEMS INC.
1235 Walt Whitman Road, Melville NY 11747-3010. 631/271-0400. **Fax:** 631/271-0405. **Contact:** Human Resources. **E-mail address:** hr@lsicsi.com. **World Wide Web address:** http://www.lsicsi.com. **Description:** Manufactures integrated circuits and microchips. Founded in 1969. **Positions advertised include:** Integrated Circuit Design Engineer; Integrated Circuit Layout Designer; Test Engineer.

MDY ADVANCED TECHNOLOGIES
21-00 Route 208 South, Fair Lawn NJ 07410. 201/797-6676. **Fax:** 201/797-6852. **Contact:** Human Resources. **E-mail address:** jobs@mdy.com. **World Wide Web address:** http://www.mdy.com. **Description:** Provides computer networking and record management services. **Positions advertised include:** New York Account Executive; Sales Accountant Executive Inside Sales; Telemarketing Representative.

MAINTECH
39 Paterson Avenue, Wallington NJ 07057. 973/614-1700. **Toll-free phone:** 800/426-8324. **Contact:** Personnel. **World Wide Web address:** http://www.maintech.com. **Description:** Provides on-site computer maintenance services.

MAINTECH
560 Lexington Avenue, 15th Floor, New York NY 10020. 212/704-2400. **Fax:** 212/944-1639. **Contact:** Jan Ferrer or Louise Ross. **E-mail address:**

jferrer@voltdelta.com or lross@voltdelta.com. **World Wide Web address:** http://www.maintech.com. **Description:** Provides on-site computer maintenance services. **Corporate headquarters location:** Wallington NJ. **Other locations:** Orange CA. **Parent company:** Volt Delta Resources (also at this location).

MANCHESTER TECHNOLOGIES, INC.
160 Oser Avenue, Hauppauge NY 11788-3711. 631/435-1199. **Fax:** 631/951-7913. **Contact:** Human Resources. **E-mail address:** cdinow@mecnet.com or staffing@mecnet.com. **World Wide Web address:** http://www.mecnet.com. **Description:** A network integrator and reseller of computer systems, software, and peripherals. Manchester also services and maintains computer systems, manages networks, distributes peripherals, and offers temporary IT staffing. Founded in 1973. **NOTE:** Human Resources phone: 631/951-7065. **Positions advertised include:** Purchasing Clerk; Customer Service Representative. **Subsidiaries include:** Coastal Office Products; Electrograph Systems; ManTech Computer Services; Donovan Consulting Group; eTrack Solutions. **Listed on:** NASDAQ. **Stock exchange symbol:** MANC. **Chairman/President/CEO:** Barry R. Steinberg. **Annual sales/revenues:** $262 million. **Number of employees:** 348.

MERCATOR SOFTWARE
45 Danbury Road, Wilton CT 06897-0840. 203/761-0208. **Fax:** 203/762-9677. **Contact:** Human Resources. **E-mail address:** hr@mercator.com. **World Wide Web address:** http://www.mercator.com. **Description:** Develops electronic data interchange software (EDI) software that helps businesses become e-businesses. **Corporate headquarters location:** This location. **Other U.S. locations:** Boca Raton FL; Bannockburn IL; New York NY; Reston VA. **International locations:** Ontario, Canada.

MERCURY INTERACTIVE CORPORATION
317 Madison Avenue, 10th Floor, New York NY 10017-5201. 212/687-4646. **Contact:** Jeff Loehr, Director of Human Resources. **World Wide Web address:** http://www.mercury.com/us. **Description:** Mercury Interactive is a provider of automated software quality tools for enterprise applications testing. The company's products are used to isolate software and system errors prior to application deployment. **Corporate headquarters location:** Sunnyvale CA. **Other U.S. locations:** Nationwide. **International locations:** Worldwide. **Subsidiaries include:** Freshwater Software, Inc. **Listed on:** NASDAQ. **Stock exchange symbol:** MERQ. **Chairman/President/CEO:** Amnon Landon. **Annual sales/revenue:** $400 million. **Number of employees:** 1,822.

MOBIUS MANAGEMENT SYSTEMS, INC.
120 Old Post Road, Rye NY 10580. 914/921-7200. **Fax:** 914/921-1360. **Contact:** Human Resources. **E-mail address:** staffing@mobius.com. **World Wide Web address:** http://www.mobius.com. **Description:** Develops and sells business-related software products including a report distribution program and an automated balance program. **Positions advertised include:** Customer Support Representative; Quality Assurance Analyst; Quality Assurance Software Developer; Software Engineer; Project Manager; Business Systems Analyst; Senior Technical Writer. **Other U.S. locations:** Nationwide. **Listed on:** NASDAQ. **Stock exchange symbol:** MOBI. **Chairman/President/CEO:** Mitchell Gross. **Annual sales/revenues:** $68 million. **Number of employees:** 408.

MOTOROLA, INC.
85 Harristown Road, Glenrock NJ 07452. 201/447-7500. **Contact:** Human Resources. **World Wide Web address:** http://www.motorola.com. **Description:** A leading supplier of corporate networking solutions including data, voice, and video interfaces. Motorola also provides platform software and Internet connectivity services.

MUZE INC.
304 Hudson Street, 8th Floor, New York NY 10013. 212/824-0300. **Fax:** 212/824-0422. **Contact:** Jeanne Petras, Director of Personnel. **E-mail address:** humanresource@muze.com. **World Wide Web address:** http://www.muze.com. **Description:** Muze is a multimedia company that develops software for touch-screen, point-of-sales terminals that allow users access to a musical database. **Positions advertised include:** MS Access Database Coordinator; In-house Legal Counsel; E-Commerce Developer; Java/XML Developer. **Special programs:** Internships. **Corporate headquarters location:** This location. **International locations:** United Kingdom. **Parent company:** MetroMedia. **Operations at this facility include:** Administration; Manufacturing; Research and Development; Sales; Service. **Number of employees at this location:** 120.

NETWORK SPECIALISTS INC.
dba NSI SOFTWARE
Baker Waterfront Plaza, 2 Hudson Place, Suite 700, Hoboken NJ 07030. 201/656-2121. **Toll-free phone:** 800/775-4674. **Fax:** 201/656-3865. **Contact:** Human Resources. **E-mail address:** info@nsisoftware.com. **World Wide Web address:** http://www.nsisw.com. **Description:** Develops network performance and fault-tolerant software tools. Products are compatible with Novell NetWare, Microsoft Windows NT, and UNIX. **Positions advertised include:** HP Overlay Sales Executive; Product Manager; Software Developer; Implementation Systems Engineer.

NEXTSOURCE
120 east 56th Street, 12th Floor, New York NY 10022. 212/736-5870. **Toll-free phone:** 800/727-6583. **Fax:** 212/736-9046. **Contact:** Human Resources. **World Wide Web address:** http://www.nextsource.com. **Description:** Develops and offers instructor-led and computer-based personal computer training programs and provides consulting services, primarily to large businesses and public sector organizations. The company's instructor-led training programs include a wide range of introductory and advanced classes in operating systems including MS/DOS, Microsoft Windows, and Macintosh systems; word processing; spreadsheets; databases; communications; executive overviews; integrated software packages; computer graphics; and desktop publishing. The company's computer-based training programs include offerings on Lotus Notes, CC Mail, Microsoft Office, and Lotus Smartsuite. The consulting division provides computer personnel on a temporary basis. **Parent company:** Formula Systems, Limited. **Listed on:** NASDAQ. **Stock exchange symbol:** FORTY. **President/CEO:** Joseph Musacchio. **Sales/revenue:** Over $700 million.

OM TECHNOLOGIES
140 Broadway, 25th Floor, New York NY 10005. 646/428-2800. **Contact:** Human Resources. **World Wide Web address:** http://www.om.com. **Description:** OM Technologies develops software for the securities and brokerage industries. **Corporate headquarters location:** Stockholm, Sweden. **International locations:** Worldwide. **Listed on:** Stockholmsborsen. **Stock exchange symbol:** OM. **Number of employees worldwide:** Over 16,000.

ORACLE CORPORATION
517 Route 1 South, Iselin NJ 08830. 732/636-2000. **Contact:** Human Resources. **World Wide Web address:** http://www.oracle.com. **Description:** Oracle Corporation designs and manufactures database and information management software for businesses and provides consulting services. **Corporate headquarters location:** Redwood Shores CA. **Other U.S. locations:** Nationwide. **Operations at this facility include:** This location designs and manufactures business software programs for small companies. **Listed on:**

NASDAQ. **Stock exchange symbol:** ORCL. **Number of employees worldwide:** 42,000.

ORACLE CORPORATION
560 White Plains Road, Tarrytown NY 10591. 914/524-1600. **Contact:** Human Resources. **E-mail address:** resumes_us@oracle.com. **World Wide Web address:** http://www.oracle.com. **Description:** Designs and manufactures database and information management software for business and provides consulting services. **NOTE:** Resumes should be submitted online or sent to Human Resources, 500 Oracle Parkway, Redwood Shores CA 94065. **Corporate headquarters location:** Redwood Shores CA. **Other U.S. locations:** Nationwide. **International locations:** Worldwide. **Listed on:** NASDAQ. **Stock exchange symbol:** ORCL. **CEO/Chairman:** Lawrence J. Ellison. **Number of employees worldwide:** 43,000.

PNY TECHNOLOGIES, INC.
299 Webro Road, Parsippany NJ 07054. 973/515-9700. **Toll-free phone:** 800/234-4597. **Fax:** 973/560-5283. **Contact:** Human Resources. **E-mail address:** hr@pny.com. **World Wide Web address:** http://www.pny.com. **Description:** Manufactures and designs computer memory products. Founded in 1985. **NOTE:** Entry-level positions are offered. **Positions advertised include:** Buyer; End of the Line Inspector; Memory Marketing Manager; Test Technician; Traffic Coordinator. **Corporate headquarters location:** This location. **Listed on:** Privately held. **Annual sales/revenues:** More than $100 million. **Number of employees at this location:** 250. **Number of employees nationwide:** 320. **Number of employees worldwide:** 420.

PARAGON COMPUTER PROFESSIONALS INC.
20 Commerce Drive, Suite 226, Cranford NJ 07016. 908/709-6767. **Toll-free phone:** 800/462-5582. **Contact:** Human Resources Administrative Assistant. **World Wide Web address:** http://www.paracomp.com. **Description:** Offers computer consulting services to a variety of businesses. **Positions advertised include:** E-business Strategist; E-business Architect; Infrastructure Architect; Project Manager; Lead Developer; Interface Developer; Client Side Developer; Server Side Developer; Legacy Integration; Database Administrator; Business Systems Analyst; Systems Analyst; Quality Analyst. **Corporate headquarters location:** This location.

PENCOM SYSTEMS INC.
40 Fulton Street, 18th Floor, New York NY 10038-1850. 212/513-7777. **Fax:** 212/227-1854. **Contact:** Tom Morgan, Recruiting. **E-mail address:** career@pencom.com. **World Wide Web address:** http://www.pencom.com. **Description:** Provides computer consulting services including open systems management and software consulting. **NOTE:** Resumes submitted via e-mail must be formatted in HTML, Microsoft Word, or plain text. **Positions advertised include:** Research Associate; Toxicologist; Regulatory Affairs Associate; Quality Assurance Engineer; Project Manager; Pharmacist; Pharmaceutical Sales Representative; Microbiologist; Clinical Researcher; Clinical Database Designer; Biostatistician; **Corporate headquarters location:** This location. **Other U.S. locations:** Santa Clara CA; Boston MA; Ruston VA; Chicago IL; Livingston NJ.

PRAXAIR MRC
542 Route 303, Orangeburg NY 10962. 845/398-8307. **Contact:** Human Resources Department. **World Wide Web address:** http://www.praxairmrc.com. **Description:** Designs and manufactures thin-film coating and etching systems used in the manufacture of integrated circuits for sale to the semiconductor, computer, and telecommunications industries. The company also processes and fabricates ultra-high-purity metals and metal alloys, principally for thin-film purposes. Praxair MRC's thin-film technology products are also used in

nonelectronic applications such as protective coatings for corrosion and wear resistance in razor blades and various automotive products. The company operates in three segments: Sputtering Equipment, Associated Target Materials, and Other High-Purity Materials. **Special programs:** Internships. **Corporate headquarters location:** This location. **International locations:** France; Korea; Taiwan. **Parent company:** Praxair, Incorporated. **Listed on:** New York Stock Exchange. **Stock exchange symbol:** PX. **Number of employees at this worldwide:** Over 250.

PRINCETON INFORMATION
399 Thornall Street, 4th Floor, Edison NJ 08837-2246. 732/906-5660. **Contact:** Human Resources. **E-mail address:** newjersey@princetoninformation.com. **World Wide Web address:** http://www.princetoninformation.com. **Description:** Offers computer consulting services. **Positions advertised include:** Developer.

QUALITY SOFTWARE SYSTEMS INC.
200 Centennial Avenue, Suite 110, Piscataway NJ 08854. 732/885-1919. **Fax:** 732-885-1872. **Contact:** Human Resources. **E-mail address:** emtrojanello@qssi-wns.com. **World Wide Web address:** http://www.qssi-wns.com. **Description:** Develops software to aid in warehouse management and development. **Positions advertised include:** Sales; Implementation Consultant.

RARITAN COMPUTER INC.
400 Cottontail Lane, Somerset NJ 08873. 732/764-4600. **Fax:** 732/764-8887. **Contact:** Human Resources. **E-mail address:** hr@raritan.com. **World Wide Web address:** http://www.raritan.com. **Description:** Designs and manufactures a line of products for sharing PCs and peripherals. Products include MasterConsole, a keyboard/video/mouse switch; CompuSwitch, a KVM switch allowing central control for up to four PCs; and Guardian, a virtual keyboard and mouse device that emulates keyboard and mouse signals. Founded in 1985. **Positions advertised include:** Software Group Consultant; System Tester; Software Engineer; Assistant Controller; Network Communication Director; Marketing Communication Launch Manager; Material Planner; Product Marketing Manager; Product Manager; Sales Engineer; Business Marketing Manager; Technical Support Representative; National Account Manager; Territory Sales Manager. **Corporate headquarters location:** This location. **Number of employees at this location:** 40. **Number of employees nationwide:** 100.

ROYALBLUE TECHNOLOGIES INC.
17 State Street, 42nd Floor, New York NY 10004-1501. 212/269-9000. **Contact:** Human Resources. **E-mail address:** resumes@royalblue.com. **World Wide Web address:** http://www.royalblue.com. **Description:** Develops software for the NASDAQ stock exchange. **Positions advertised include:** Technical Support Supervisor; Visual Basic Developer; Software Designer/Developer; Graduate Developer; Data Implementation Consultant; First-line Support Analyst. **International locations:** China; France; Japan; United Kingdom. **Number of employees worldwide:** Over 400.

SPHERION
9 Polito Avenue, 9th Floor, Lyndhurst NJ 07071. 201/392-0800. **Contact:** Human Resources. **World Wide Web address:** http://www.spherion.com. **Description:** A nationwide computer outsourcing service company, providing short-run supplemental and long-term contractual support for computer operations, communications operations, PC help desks, local area networks, computer programming, and technology training. The company's computer services are provided from offices strategically located throughout the United States. The company also provides the expertise for meeting applications and systems development objectives within information systems organizations. Capabilities extend beyond evaluating computer software and hardware to providing

technically qualified professionals for any task in the systems development life cycle -- from conception through feasibility analysis, system design, programming, testing, implementation, and full systems maintenance and support. **Positions advertised include:** Dispatcher. **Corporate headquarters location:** Fort Lauderdale FL. **Other U.S. locations:** Nationwide. **International locations:** Worldwide. **Listed on:** New York Stock Exchange. **Stock exchange symbol:** SFN.

STANDARD MICROSYSTEMS CORPORATION

80 Arkay Drive, P.O. Box 18047, Hauppauge NY 11788. 631/435-6000. **Fax:** 631/435-0373. **Contact:** Human Resources. **E-mail address:** jobsny@smsc.com. **World Wide Web address:** http://www.smsc.com. **Description:** This location houses the VLSI circuit design and LAN hub and switch engineering centers, marketing, customer support, and wafer fabrication, as well as operations and administrative staff. The company's Component Products Division supplies MOS/VLSI circuits for personal computers and embedded control systems. These include input/output devices for disk drive control, communications interface, power management and other PC motherboard functions, Ethernet and Fast Ethernet controllers for local area network applications, and ARCNET controllers for embedded networking applications. The System Products Division provides a broad range of networking solutions for scaling, managing, and controlling LANs. Its products include network adapters, hubs, switches, and network management software. This division has an installed base of over 12 million nodes. Standard Microsystems uses internally developed integrated circuits. Founded in 1971. **Positions advertised include:** Design Engineer; Product Engineer; Design Automation Engineer. **Special programs:** Internships. **Corporate headquarters location:** This location. **Other U.S. locations:** Irvine CA; San Jose CA; Danvers MA; Austin TX. **International locations:** Worldwide. **Listed on:** NASDAQ. **Stock exchange symbol:** SMSC. **Annual sales/revenues:** More than $100 million. **Number of employees at this location:** 500. **Number of employees worldwide:** 800.

STORAGE ENGINE, INC.

One Sheila Drive, Tinton Falls NJ 07724. 732/747-6995. **Fax:** 732/747-6542. **Contact:** Human Resources. **E-mail address:** hr@storageengine.com. **World Wide Web address:** http://www.eccs.com. **Description:** Designs and configures computer systems. Storage Engine's mass storage enhancement products include RAID (Redundant Array of Independent Disks) products and technology; external disk, optical, and tape systems; internal disk and tape storage devices; and RAM. The company also provides related technical services. **Corporate headquarters location:** This location.

SUN MICROSYSTEMS, INC.

400 Atrium Drive, Somerset NJ 08873. 732/469-1000. **Contact:** Human Resources. **World Wide Web address:** http://www.sun.com. **Description:** Sun Microsystems produces high-performance computer systems, workstations, servers, CPUs, peripherals, and operating systems software. The company developed its own microprocessor called SPARC. **Positions advertised include;** Systems Engineer. **Note:** Submit resume online. **Corporate headquarters location:** Palo Alto CA. **Operations at this facility include:** This location is a sales office. **Subsidiaries include:** Forte Software Inc. manufactures enterprise application integration software. **Listed on:** NASDAQ. **Stock exchange symbol:** SUNW.

SUNBURST TECHNOLOGY

101 Castleton Street, Suite 201, Pleasantville NY 10570. 914/747-3310. **Contact:** Human Resources. **E-mail address:** hr-us@sunburst.com. **World Wide Web address:** http://www.sunburst.com. **Description:** Develops and

markets educational videos and software. **Special programs:** Internships. **Office hours:** Monday - Friday, 8:00 a.m. - 5:00 p.m. **Corporate headquarters location:** This location. **Annual sales/revenues:** $21 - $50 million. **Number of employees at this location:** 150.

SYMBOL TECHNOLOGIES INC.
One Symbol Plaza, Holtsville NY 11742-1300. 631/738-2400. **Contact:** Human Resources. **E-mail address:** jobopps@symbol.com. **World Wide Web address:** http://www.symbol.com. **Description:** Symbol Technologies designs, manufactures, and markets integrated products based on barcode laser scanning, hand-held computing, and wireless LANs. **Positions advertised include:** Senior Manager. **Corporate headquarters location:** Costa Mesa CA. **Operations at this facility include:** This location manufactures barcode and data capture equipment. **Listed on:** New York Stock Exchange. **Stock exchange symbol:** SBL.

SYNCSORT
50 Tice Boulevard, Woodcliff Lake NJ 07677. 201/930-8200. **Fax:** 201/930-8281. **Contact:** Human Resources. **World Wide Web address:** http://www.syncsort.com. **Description:** Develops operating systems software for businesses. **NOTE:** Submit resume online. **Positions advertised include:** Software Designer; Software Developer; Sales Representative.

SYSTEMAX INC.
11 Harbor Park Drive, Port Washington NY 11050. 516/608-7000. **Fax:** 516/608-7111. **Contact:** Human Resources. **E-mail address:** recruiting@systemax.com. **World Wide Web address:** http://www.systemax.com. **Description:** A direct marketer of brand-name and private-label computer, office, and industrial products targeting mid-range and major corporate accounts, small office/home customers, and value-added resellers. Founded in 1949. **Positions advertised include:** Inside Sales Representative. **Special programs:** Internships; Summer Jobs. **Corporate headquarters location:** This location. **Other U.S. locations:** CA; FL; GA; IL; NJ; NC; OH. **Subsidiaries include:** Global Computer Supplies; Midwest Micro Corp.; Misco America, Inc.; Misco Canada Inc.; TigerDirect Inc. **Listed on:** New York Stock Exchange. **Stock exchange symbol:** SYX. **Annual sales/revenues:** More than $100 million. **Number of employees at this location:** 500. **Number of employees nationwide:** 2,000. **Number of employees worldwide:** 4,000.

TSR INC.
400 Oser Avenue, Suite 150, Hauppauge NY 11788. 631/231-0333. **Contact:** Recruiter. **World Wide Web address:** http://www.tsrconsulting.com. **Description:** Provides computer consulting services. **Positions advertised include:** Data Analyst; Senior Developer Programmer/Analyst; Senior Business Analyst; Rational Administrator; Centura/Oracle Developer. **Corporate headquarters location:** This location. **Listed on:** NASDAQ. **Stock exchange symbol:** TSRI.

TRACK DATA
56 Pine Street, New York NY 10005. 212/943-4555. **Contact:** Human Resources. **World Wide Web address:** http://www.trackdata.com. **Description:** Electronically provides trading information, news, and third-party database services on stocks, bonds, commodities, and other securities through its Dial/Data service. The company's AIQ Systems division produces expert systems software for individual and professional investors. **Listed on:** NASDAQ. **Stock exchange symbol:** TRAC.

VESON INC.
29 Broadway, Suite 1002, New York NY 10006. 212/422-0300. **Contact:** Michael Veson, Manager. **World Wide Web address:** http://www.veson.com. **Description:** Develops computer software for the shipping industry.

WEN TECHNOLOGY CORPORATION
999 Central Park Avenue, Yonkers NY 10704. 914/376-5435. **Fax:** 914/376-7092. **Contact:** Human Resources. **E-mail address:** info@wentech.com. **World Wide Web address:** http://www.wentech.com. **Description:** Manufactures computer monitors and displays. **Corporate headquarters location:** This location. **Annual sales/revenues:** $51 - $100 million. **Number of employees at this location:** 40.

EDUCATIONAL SERVICES

You can expect to find the following types of companies in this section:
Business/Secretarial/Data Processing Schools •
Colleges/Universities/Professional Schools • Community Colleges/Technical
Schools/Vocational Schools • Elementary and Secondary Schools • Preschool
and Child Daycare Services

AFS INTERCULTURAL PROGRAMS, INC.
71 West 23rd Street, 17th Floor, New York NY 10010. 212/807-8686. **Fax:** 212/807-1001. **Contact:** Human Resources. **E-mail address:** jobs@afs.org. **World Wide Web address:** http://www.afs.org. **Description:** An international exchange organization that provides intercultural learning opportunities for high school students, families, and teachers. The agency operates programs in approximately 55 countries via an international network of volunteers. **Positions advertised include:** Youth Ambassadors Program Coordinator; Development Associate; Admissions Advisor; Administrative Assistant; Regional Coordinator. **Other locations:** Worldwide.

ALS INTERNATIONAL
18 John Street, Suite 300, New York NY 10038. 212/766-4111. **Toll-free phone:** 800/788-0450. **Fax:** 212/349-0964. **Contact:** Human Resources Supervisor. **E-mail address:** hr@alsintl.com. **World Wide Web address:** http://www.alsintl.com. **Description:** A translation and interpreting company serving a worldwide, diversified clientele. **Positions advertised include:** Language Specialist; Translator; On-site Technician; Studio Engineer; Software Engineer/Programmer.

ADELPHI UNIVERSITY
One South Avenue, 2 Levermore Hall, Garden City NY 11530. 516/877-3220. **Toll-free phone:** 800/ADELPHI. **Fax:** 516/877-4970. **Contact:** Lisa S Araujo, Assistant Vice President Human Resources & Labor Relations. **E-mail address:** humanres@adelphi.edu. **World Wide Web address:** http://www.adelphi.edu. **Description:** A private university with approximately 7,000 undergraduate and graduate students enrolled. Founded in 1896. **NOTE:** Entry-level positions are offered. Human Resources phone: 516/877-3224. **Positions advertised include:** Administrative Assistant; Secretary; Teacher/Professor. **Corporate headquarters location:** This location. **Number of employees at this location:** 1,300.

AMERICAN INSTITUTE FOR FOREIGN STUDY (AIFS)
River Plaza, 9 West Broad Street, Stamford CT 06902. 203/399-5000. **Toll-free phone:** 800/727-2437. **Contact:** Human Resources. **World Wide Web address:** http://www.aifs.org. **Description:** Engaged in the placement of au pairs in American homes, as well as the placement of American students in study programs abroad.

BARNARD COLLEGE
3009 Broadway, New York NY 10027-6598. 212/854-2551. **Fax:** 212/854-2454. **Contact:** Employment Manager. **World Wide Web address:** http://www.barnard.edu. **Description:** An independent college of liberal arts and sciences for women, affiliated with Columbia University. Barnard College has an enrollment of approximately 2,200 undergraduates from more than 40 countries. Barnard offers approximately 50 majors in the humanities, social sciences, arts, and natural sciences. Double- and joint-degree programs with Columbia

(dentistry, engineering, international and public policy, law, and administration), Juilliard, and the Jewish Theological Seminary are offered. Founded in 1889. **Positions advertised include:** Psychological Counselor; Web/Oracle Programmer; Teacher; Housekeeping and Custodial Services Manager; Student Health Services Director; Room Reservation Specialist; Administrative Assistant; Assistant to the Director; English Poetry Lecturer; Philosophy Lecturer; Migration and Diaspora Studies Lecturer; Dance Department Chairperson; Anthropology Lecturer; Asian and Middle Eastern Cultures Lecturer; Biology Lab Associate; Biology Lecturer; Economics Lecturer; Assistant Physics Professor; Architecture & Urban Studies Lecturer; Art History Lecturer; Sociology Lecturer; Slavic Professor; Spanish Professor; Theater Professor; Security Guard.

BARUCH COLLEGE
THE CITY UNIVERSITY OF NEW YORK (CUNY)
One Bernard Baruch Way, Box D-0202, New York NY 10010. 212/802-2740. **Fax:** 212/802-2745. **Contact:** Human Resources. **World Wide Web address:** http://www.baruch.cuny.edu. **Description:** A college offering undergraduate and graduate programs through its School of Business, School of Liberal Arts and Sciences, and School of Public Affairs. **Positions advertised include:** Accountancy Instructor; Black & Hispanic Studies Instructor; Career Counseling Instructor; Communication Studies Instructor; Computer Information Systems Instructor; Economics & Finance Instructor; English Instructor; Fine and Performing Arts Instructor; History Instructor; Law Instructor; Management Instructor; Marketing Instructor; Mathematics Instructor; Modern Languages Instructor; Comparative Literature Instructor; Natural Sciences Instructor; Philosophy Instructor; Political Science Instructor; Psychology Instructor; Public Affairs Instructor; Sociology and Anthropology Instructor; Statistics Instructor; Computer Information Systems Assistant Instructor; College Assistant; Continuing and Professional Studies Instructor; CUNY Custodial Assistant; CUNY Office Assistant. **Other area locations:** Bronx NY; Brooklyn NY; Flushing NY; Jamaica NY; Staten Island NY. **Operations at this facility include:** Administration; Research and Development; Service. **Number of employees at this location:** 1,800.

BERGEN COMMUNITY COLLEGE
400 Paramus Road, Paramus NJ 07652-1595. 201/447-7442. **Fax:** 201/251-4987. **Contact:** Human Resources. **World Wide Web address:** http://www.bergen.cc.nj.us. **Description:** A community college enrolling over 12,000 students. The college offers associate degrees in arts, sciences, and applied sciences. **Positions advertised include:** Director of Human Resources; Financial Aide Assistant. **NOTE:** Search for updated jobs at website. Send resumes to above address.

BLOOMFIELD COLLEGE
467 Franklin Street, Bloomfield NJ 07003. 973/748-9000. **Fax:** 973/743-3998. **Contact:** Human Resources. **World Wide Web address:** http://www.bloomfield.edu. **Description:** A private four year college with ties to the Presbyterian Church offering bachelors and bachelor of science degrees. **Positions advertised include:** Admissions Counselor; New Business Development Manager.

THE CITY COLLEGE OF NEW YORK
THE CITY UNIVERSITY OF NEW YORK (CUNY)
Convent Avenue at 138th Street, New York NY 10031. 212/650-7000. **Contact:** Human Resources Department. **World Wide Web address:** http://www.ccny.cuny.edu. **Description:** A public, coeducational college offering both undergraduate and graduate programs of study in a wide variety of disciplines. **Positions advertised include:** Associate Architecture Professor; Education Teacher; Assistant Physics Professor; Economics Professor; Medical

178 /The Metropolitan New York JobBank

Lecturer; Associate Film & Video Production Professor; Advertising & Public Relations Professor; Film & Video Full Professor; Associate Biomedical Engineering Professor; Administrative Coordinator; Associate Biology Professor; Medical School Research Assistant; Medical School Postdoctoral Fellow; Postdoctoral Research Associate – Laser Institute; Chemistry Research Associate; Asian Studies Assistant Professor; Information Systems Assistant; Custodial Assistant; Office Assistant; Maintenance Worker. **Other area locations:** Bronx NY; Brooklyn NY; Flushing NY; Jamaica NY; Staten Island NY.

COLUMBIA UNIVERSITY
2960 Broadway, New York NY 10027. 212/854-1754. **Contact:** Department of Human Resources. **World Wide Web address:** http://www.columbia.edu. **Description:** A private university comprised of 15 schools and 71 academic departments and divisions. The university is affiliated with Barnard College, Teachers College, and Union Theological Seminary. There are approximately 20,000 students enrolled at the university including 11,800 graduate and professional, 5,600 undergraduate, and 2,500 nondegree students. Founded in 1754. **NOTE:** Interested jobseekers are strongly encouraged to apply online via the company Website, but may send Scannable resumes to: Columbia University, P.O. Box 920, Burlington MA 01803. **Positions advertised include:** Facilities Porter; Computer Science Technology Director; Library Assistant; Financial Services Assistant; Earth Institute Associate Director; Facilities Handy Person; Real Estate Building Superintendent; Financial Assistant; Administrative Assistant; Law School Development Assistant; Earth Institute Research Analyst; Facilities Groundskeeper; HelpDesk Support Specialist; Law School Director; School of Business Associate Director; Allumni Relations Manager; Facilities Project Manager; Security Officer; Heavy Cleaner; First Cook; Bibliographic Assistant; Dining Retail Worker;

DOWLING COLLEGE
150 Idle Hour Boulevard, Oakdale NY 11769-1999. 631/244-3020. **Fax:** 631/589-6123. **Contact:** Bridget Carroll, Human Resources. **E-mail address:** carrollb@dowling.edu. **World Wide Web address:** http://www.dowling.edu. **Description:** Dowling College is an independent, comprehensive, coeducational college. The college serves approximately 6,000 full- and part-time students, offering undergraduate programs leading to bachelor of arts, bachelor of science, and bachelor of business administration degrees. Graduate program degrees include master of science in reading and special education, master of business administration, and master of education with the following concentrations: elementary education, secondary education, special education, life-span special services, and reading. Founded in 1968. **Positions advertised include:** Adjunct Business Professor; Director of Institutional Research and Assessment; Security Officer; Clerk; Enrollment Services Associate. **Corporate headquarters location:** This location. **Number of employees at this location:** 900.

FASHION INSTITUTE OF TECHNOLOGY
7th Avenue at 27th Street, New York NY 10001-5992. 212/217-7999. **Contact:** Human Resources. **World Wide Web address:** http://www.fitnyc.suny.edu. **Description:** A fashion institute offering degrees in art and design or business and technology.

FLIGHTSAFETY INTERNATIONAL, INC.
Marine Air Terminal, LaGuardia Airport, Flushing NY 11371. 718/565-4100. **Fax:** 718/565-4169. **Contact:** Personnel. **E-mail address:** jobs@flightsafety.com. **World Wide Web address:** http://www.flightsafety.com. **Description:** FlightSafety International provides high-technology training to operators of aircraft and ships from 42 training centers in North America and Europe. Total training systems are used including the company's 200 simulators and training devices, computer-based training, and professional instructors. The company's

worldwide clients include corporations, airlines, the military, and government agencies. Founded in 1951. **Positions advertised include:** Pilot Simulator Instructor; Flight Engineer Instructor. **Corporate headquarters location:** This location. **Other U.S. locations:** Nationwide. **International locations:** Canada; France; United Kingdom. **Subsidiaries include:** FlightSafety Boeing Training International; MarineSafety International. **Parent company:** Berkshire Hathaway (Omaha NE). **Number of employees worldwide:** 2,000.

FORDHAM UNIVERSITY
441 East Fordham Road, Bronx NY 10458. 718/817-1000. **Contact:** Human Resources Department. **World Wide Web address:** http://www.fordham.edu. **Description:** A private, Jesuit university offering bachelor's and master's degrees from three campuses and 11 schools. **Positions advertised include:** Public Affairs Assistant; Assistant Director of Student Financial Services; Media Relations Specialist; Custodial Services Supervisor; Security Duty Supervisor; Resident Director; Wellness Center Coordinator; Underwriting Sales Representative; Duplicating Coordinator; Financial Services Representative; Admissions Clerk; Government Documents Clerk; Serials Clerk; Executive Secretary; Secretary; On-Campus Recruitment Assistant; Enrollment Services Representative; Weekend Evening Supervisor. **Special programs:** Internships.

HOFSTRA UNIVERSITY
205 Hofstra University, Human Resources Center, Hempstead NY 11549-1000. 516/463-6600. **Contact:** Human Resources Department. **World Wide Web address:** http://www.hofstra.edu. **Description:** A private, four-year university offering both undergraduate and graduate degree programs. The university enrolls over 12,800 students. **Positions advertised include:** Financial Aid Counselor; Assistant Cheerleading Coach; Assistant Director for the Annual Fund; Manager of Telecommunications; Director of Financial Aid; Honors College Dean; Associate Professor of Print Journalism; Education Lecturer; Assistant Sedimentology/Field Geology Professor; Associate Professor of Broadcast Journalism; Associate Dean of Library and Information Services; Assistant Business Professor; Associate Policy Studies Professor.

HUNTER COLLEGE
THE CITY UNIVERSITY OF NEW YORK (CUNY)
695 Park Avenue, East Building, 1502, New York NY 10021. 212/772-4451. **Fax:** 212/650-3889. **Contact:** Robert McGarry, Director of Human Resources. **E-mail address:** jobs@hccs.hunter.cuny.edu. **World Wide Web address:** http://www.hunter.cuny.edu. **Description:** One of the largest coeducational colleges of CUNY. Hunter College offers undergraduate and graduate programs in arts and sciences, education, health sciences, nursing, and social work. Founded in 1870. **NOTE:** Resumes can be mailed to 71 East 94th Street, New York NY 10128. **Positions advertised include:** Associate Nursing Professor; Associate Special Education Professor; Associate Education Professor; Head Librarian; Health Professions Library Instructor; Assistant to the Chair of Biological Sciences; Director of Alumni Relations; Director of Development, Major and Planned Gifts; College Assistant; CUNY Office Assistant; CUNY Administrative Assistant; College Security Specialist; Custodial Assistant. **Other area locations:** Bronx NY; Brooklyn NY; Flushing NY; Jamaica NY; Staten Island NY.

IONA COLLEGE
715 North Avenue, New Rochelle NY 10801. 914/633-2000. **Contact:** Rosemary Bartolomeo, Manager of Employment. **E-mail address:** rbartolomeo@iona.edu. **World Wide Web address:** http://www.iona.edu. **Description:** A four-year Catholic college offering bachelor's and master's degree programs. Founded in 1940. **NOTE:** Employment Manager phone: 914/633-2496, fax: 914/637-7732. Faculty applicants should contact the Dean's Office in the School of Arts &

Sciences or the Hagan School of Business. **Positions advertised include:** Facilities Custodian; Library Document Delivery Assistant; Career Services Associate Director; Business School Academic Advisor; Director of Libraries.

JOHN JAY COLLEGE OF CRIMINAL JUSTICE
THE CITY UNIVERSITY OF NEW YORK (CUNY)
899 Tenth Avenue, New York NY 10019. 212/237-8000. **Contact:** Donald J. Gray, Director of Human Resources Department. **E-mail address:** dgray@jjay.cuny.edu. **World Wide Web address:** http://www.jjay.cuny.edu. **Description:** A college with undergraduate and graduate programs of study concentrating in criminal justice. **Positions advertised include:** Assistant Organic Chemistry Professor; Associate African-American Studies Professor; LSAT and GRE Preparation Instructor; Biochemist; Molecular Biologist; Forensic Chemistry Criminologist; CUNY Office Assistant.

KATHARINE GIBBS SCHOOLS INC.
50 West 40th Street, 1st Floor, New York NY 10138-1347. 212/867-9300. **Contact:** President. **World Wide Web address:** http://www.katharinegibbs.com. **Description:** One of the nation's foremost business instruction schools. **Corporate headquarters location:** Piscataway NJ. **Other U.S. locations:** MA; CT; PA; RI; VA.

KEAN UNIVERSITY
1000 Morris Avenue, Union NJ 07083. 908/527-2150. **Contact:** Human Resources. **World Wide Web address:** http://www.kean.edu. **Description:** A university offering more than 60 programs of study for graduates and undergraduates. The university has an enrollment of over 12,000 students. Founded in 1855.

LEHMAN COLLEGE
THE CITY UNIVERSITY OF NEW YORK (CUNY)
250 Bedford Park Boulevard West, Shuster Hall, Room 230, Bronx NY 10468. 718/960-8181. **Contact:** Personnel Office. **World Wide Web address:** http://www.lehman.cuny.edu. **Description:** A public coeducational liberal arts college offering over 90 undergraduate and graduate programs. **NOTE:** Personnel phone: 718/960-8181.

LINDAMOOD-BELL
2777 Summer Street, Stamford CT 06905. 203/355-0044. **Toll-free phone:** 800/300-1818. **Contact:** Human Resources. **World Wide Web address:** http://www.lindamoodbell.com. **Description:** A learning-enhancing organization. Runs process-based educational programs. Reaches students from those with severe learning disabilities to those who are extremely gifted. **NOTE:** Part time positions offered. **Positions advertised include:** Clinician. **Special programs:** Seasonal work. **Corporate headquarters location:** San Luis Obispo CA. **Other U.S. locations:** Nationwide. **International locations:** London, England.

LONG ISLAND UNIVERSITY
C.W. Post Campus, 720 Northern Boulevard, Brookville NY 11548-1326. 516/299-2000. **Contact:** Human Resources. **World Wide Web address:** http://www.liunet.edu. **Description:** A university offering undergraduate and graduate programs of study. The university's programs of study are offered through its six schools: College of Liberal Arts & Sciences; School of Education; College of Management; School of Health Professions; School of Visual & Performing Arts; and the Palmer School of Library & Information Sciences. **Positions advertised include:** Assistant Mathematics Professor. **Special programs:** Internships. **Corporate headquarters location:** This location. **Other area locations:** Brentwood NY; Brooklyn NY; Greenvale NY; Southampton NY.

Operations at this facility include: Administration. **Number of employees:** 4,328.

MERCY COLLEGE
Verrazzano Hall, 555 Broadway, Dobbs Ferry NY 10522. 914/674-7318. **Fax:** 914/674-7578. **Contact:** Theresa Morgan, Human Resources Director. **E-mail address:** hr@mercy.edu. **World Wide Web address:** http://www.mercynet.edu. **Description:** A private commuter college offering a wide range of undergraduate, graduate, associate, and certificate programs.

MONMOUTH UNIVERSITY
400 Cedar Avenue, West Long Branch NJ 07764-1898. 732/571-3400. **Recorded jobline:** 732/571-3513. **Contact:** Human Resources. **E-mail address:** mujobs@monmouth.edu. World **Wide Web address:** http://www.monmouth.edu. **Description:** A private four-year university offering 26 undergraduate programs & many graduate & certificate degrees. **Positions advertised include:** Assistant Dean of Advising; Head Coach; Director of Tennis; Assistant Director of Residential Life; Assistant to the Dean; Electrician.

MONMOUTH UNIVERSITY
400 Cedar Avenue, West Long Branch NJ 07764-1898. 732/571-3470. **Recorded jobline**: 732/571-3513. **Contact:** Human Resources. **E-mail address:** mujobs@monmouth.edu. **World Wide Web address:** http://www.monmouth.edu. **Description:** A private four-year university offering 26 undergraduate programs & many graduate & certificate degrees. **Positions advertised include:** Assistant Dean of Advising; Head Coach; Director of Tennis; Assistant Director of Residential Life; Assistant to the Dean; Electrician.

MONTCLAIR STATE UNIVERSITY
One Normal Avenue, Box CO 316, Upper Montclair NJ 07043. 973/655-4398. **Fax:** 973/655-7210. **Contact:** Division of Human Resources. **E-mail address:** hr@mail.monclair.edu. **World Wide Web address:** http://www.montclair.edu. **Description:** A state university with an enrollment of 13,500. The university offers over 70 programs of study. The university is located about 30 minutes south of New York City **Positions advertised include:** Adjunct Instructor; Admissions Counselor; Assistant Director; Assistant Professor; Contract Administrator; Project Coordinator; Project Director; Department Chair Person; Mail Clerk; Head Coach; Pro Award Officer. **NOTE:** E-mail applications can only be accepted in text format in Microsoft Word or Adobe Acrobat.

NASSAU COMMUNITY COLLEGE
One Education Drive, 8th Floor, Room 820,, Garden City NY 11530. 516/572-7211. **Contact:** Beverly Harrison, Associate Vice President Human Resources. **E-mail address:** harrisb@ncc.edu. **World Wide Web address:** http://www.sunynassau.edu. **Description:** A two-year college that is part of the State University of New York educational system. **Special programs:** Internships. **Number of employees at this location:** 2,500.

NEW JERSEY CITY UNIVERSITY
2039 Kennedy Boulevard, Hepburn Hall 105, Jersey City NJ 07305. 201/200-2335. **Fax:** 201/200-2219. **Contact:** Robert Piaskowsky, Director of Human Resources. **World Wide Web address:** http://www.njcu.edu. **Description:** A state university with approximately 10,000 students enrolled in undergraduate, graduate, and continuing education programs. **Positions advertised include:** Director; Dean of Students; Assistant Dean; Nurse; Criminal Justice Professor; Fitness Exercise Specialist; Information Technology Specialist; Health Science Professor; Business Administration; Special Education; Learning Disabilities Teachers Consultant; Early Childhood Education; Education Technology;

Elementary Technology; Literacy Education; Speech Language Specialist; Therapeutic Services Supervisor; Typist Clerk.

NEW JERSEY INSTITUTE OF TECHNOLOGY
323 Martin Luther King Jr. Boulevard, Cullimore Hall, Room 211, Newark NJ 07102. 973/596-3140. **Fax:** 973/642-4056. **Contact:** Human Resources. **World Wide Web address:** http://www.njit.edu. **Description:** A technical institute of higher learning offering undergraduate and graduate degrees in engineering, architecture, liberal arts/sciences, management, and education. **Positions advertised include:** Academic Advisor; Academic Coordinator; Accounts Payable Clerk; Administrative Assistant; Assistant Physical Education Specialist; Assistant Theatre Technician; Assistant Trainer; Associate Dean; Control Specialist; Academic Computing Director; University Information Systems Director; University Learning Director; Facility Engineer; HVAC Mechanic; Library Assistant; Provost; Receptionist; Security Officer; Recycler.

NEW YORK INSTITUTE OF TECHNOLOGY
P.O. Box 8000, Old Westbury NY 11568-8000. 516/686-7667. **Fax:** 516/686-7929. **Contact:** Human Resources. **E-mail address:** humanresources@nyit.edu. **World Wide Web address:** http://www.nyit.edu. **Description:** A technical university offering associate, bachelor's, and master's degree programs in health and life sciences, architecture, arts/sciences, education, technology, and management. **Positions advertised include:** Senior Technician; Assistant to the Dean; Office Assistant; Refund Coordinator; Cleaner; Assistant Fine Arts Professor; Academic Clinical Coordinator; Director of Major Gifts; Associate Director of Admissions and Operations; Associate Registrar; Dean of Students.

NEW YORK UNIVERSITY
7 East 12th Street, Main Floor, New York NY 10003-4475. 212/998-1250. **Fax:** 212/995-4229. **Contact:** Personnel Department. **World Wide Web address:** http://www.nyu.edu/hr. **Description:** A state university. **NOTE:** Interested job seekers may apply online. The University no longer accepts faxed or e-mailed resumes. **Positions advertised include:** Math Department Manager; Associate Director of Career Counseling and Placement; Administrative Aide; Administrative Assistant; Security Officer; Senior Medical Records Assistant; Senior Clinical Aide; X-Ray Technician; Director of Advisement; Administrative Secretary; Admissions Officer; Director of Theatrical Production; Junior Collector; Financial Analyst; Administrator of Alumni and Internship Services; Facilities Coordinator; Dental Hygienist; Chief Information Officer. **Office hours:** Monday – Friday, 9:00 a.m. – 4:00 p.m.

PACE UNIVERSITY
One Pace Plaza, New York NY 10038-1598. 212/346-1200. **Contact:** Human Resources. **World Wide Web address:** http://www.pace.edu. **Description:** A university with three campus locations and an enrollment of nearly 14,000 students. Founded in 1906. **Positions advertised include:** Secretary; Administrative Assistant; Admissions Recruiter; Evening Program Coordinator; Assistant Vice-President of Marketing and Communications; Tutor; International Student Advisor; Coordinator of Support Services for Online Teaching and Learning; Courseware Designer; Director of Funded Research Administration; Assistant Dean of Students. **Other area locations:** Pleasantville NY; White Plains NY.

PRINCETON REVIEW INC.
265A Post Road West, Westport CT 06880. 203/226-2662. **Contact:** Human Resources. **World Wide Web address:** http://www.princetonreview.com. **Description:** Offers a variety of review and test preparation courses for students taking exams such as the SAT, GRE, LMAT, LSAT, and GMAT. **Corporate**

headquarters location: New York NY. **Listed on:** NASDAQ. **Stock exchange symbol:** REVU.

QUEENS COLLEGE
THE CITY UNIVERSITY OF NEW YORK (CUNY)
65-30 Kissena Boulevard, Flushing NY 11367-1597. 718/997-4455. **Fax:** 718/997-5799. **Contact:** Human Resources Department. **World Wide Web address:** http://www.qc.edu. **Description:** A liberal arts commuter college. Founded in 1937. **Special programs:** Tuition Assistance Program.

RUTGERS STATE UNIVERSITY OF NEW JERSEY
56 Bevier Road, Piscataway NJ 08854. 732/445-3020. **Fax:** 732/445-3087. **Contact:** Personnel Department. **E-mail address:** info@hr.Rutgers.edu. **World Wide Web address:** http://www.rutgers.edu. **Description:** A four-year, state university offering undergraduate and graduate programs in a wide variety of disciplines. **Positions advertised include:** Administrative Director; Administrative Assistant; Area Director; Assistant to the Dean; Director Athletics; Editorial Media Specialist; Unit Computing Specialist. **Other U.S. locations:** Camden NJ; Newark NJ.

RUTGERS STATE UNIVERSITY OF NEW JERSEY
UNIVERSITY COLLEGE-NEWARK
249 University Avenue, Room 202, Newark NJ 07102. 973/353-5500. **Contact:** Irma Mendoza, Human Resources. **E-mail address:** angelis@newark.rutgers.edu. **World Wide Web address:** http://www.rutgers.edu. **Description:** A campus of the state university. **Positions advertised include:** Administrative Director; Administrative Assistant; Area Director; Assistant to the Dean; Director Athletics; Editorial Media Specialist; Unit Computing Specialist. **Other U.S. locations:** Brunswick NJ; Camden NJ.

SACRED HEART UNIVERSITY
5151 Park Avenue, Fairfield CT 06825-1000. 203/371-7999. **Fax:** 203/365-7527. **Contact:** Human Resources. **E-mail address:** resumehr@sacredheart.edu. **World Wide Web address:** http://www.sacredheart.edu. **Description:** One of the largest Catholic universities in the New England area. Sacred Heart University offers programs through the College of Arts & Sciences, the College of Business, the College of Education & Health Professions, and the University College. Founded in 1963. **Positions advertised include:** Cleaning Supervisor; Director of Bands; Director of Major and Planned Gifts; Graduate Residence Hall Director; Programmer Analyst; Public Safety Officer.

ST. JOHN'S UNIVERSITY
8000 Utopia Parkway, Jamaica NY 11439. 718/990-6161. **Contact:** Human Resources. **E-mail address:** employment@stjohns.edu. **World Wide Web address:** http://www.stjohns.edu. **Description:** A private, four-year university. St. John's University offers bachelor's and master's degrees. Founded in 1870.

SARAH LAWRENCE COLLEGE
One Mead Way, Bronxville NY 10708. 914/395-2315. **Fax:** 914/395-2669. **Contact:** Human Resources. **E-mail address:** admin@slc.edu. **World Wide Web address:** http://www.slc.edu. **Description:** Sarah Lawrence College is a four-year, liberal arts college that emphasizes independent study through undergraduate and graduate programs. **Positions advertised include:** Assistant to the Dean of Graduate Studies; Center for Continuing Education Director; Planned Giving Officer; Cognitive Developmental Psychology Professor.

SCORE! LEARNING, INC.
Goodwives Shopping Center, 25 Old Kings Highway North, Suite 43, Darien CT 06820. 203/656-1455. **Toll-free phone:** 800/49SCORE. **Contact:** Human

Resources. **E-mail address:** score@trm.brassring,com. **World Wide Web address:** http://www.escore.com. **Description:** Provides learning programs for children. Founded in 1992. **NOTE:** Apply online or send resume to SCORE! Recruiting, 343 Winter Street, Waltham MA 02451. **Positions advertised include:** Assistant Director. **Corporate headquarters location:** Oakland CA. **Other area locations:** Westport CT. **Other U.S. locations:** Nationwide. **Parent company:** Kaplan Inc., The Washington Post Company.

SETON HALL UNIVERSITY
400 South Orange Avenue, Stafford Hall, South Orange NJ 07079. 973/761-9178. **Fax:** 973/761-9007. **Contact:** Aisha Agee, Human Resources Specialist. **E-mail address:** ageeaiash@shu.edu. **World Wide Web address:** http://www.shu.edu. **Description:** A Catholic university offering a wide range of undergraduate and graduate programs. **Positions advertised include:** Secretary; Assistant Psychology Professor; Assistant Professor of Philosophy; Assistant Professor of Spanish; Physiologist.

STATE UNIVERSITY OF NEW YORK AT STONY BROOK
390 Administration, Stony Brook NY 11794-0751. 631/689-6151. **Fax:** 631/632-1351. **Recorded jobline:** 631/632-9222. **Contact:** Rebecca West, Human Resources. **World Wide Web address:** http://www.sunysb.edu/hr. **Description:** A state university that offers bachelor's, master's, and doctoral degrees. The university has over 17,000 students enrolled. Founded in 1957.

STATE UNIVERSITY OF NEW YORK DOWNSTATE MEDICAL CENTER UNIVERSITY HOSPITAL AND HEALTH SCIENCE CENTER AT BROOKLYN
151 East 34th Street, Room 103, Brooklyn NY 11203. 718/270-1000. **Physical address:** 450 Clarkson Avenue, Brooklyn NY 11203. **Fax:** 718/270-1815. **Contact:** Human Resources. **Wide Web address:** http://www.hscbklyn.edu. **Description:** An academic medical center that includes colleges of medicine, nursing, and health-related professions and a school of graduate studies as well as University Hospital of Brooklyn.

TASA (TOUCHSTONE APPLIED SCIENCE ASSOCIATES, INC.)
P.O. Box 382, 4 Hardscrabble Heights, Brewster NY 10509-0382. 845/277-8100. **Fax:** 845/277-3548. **Contact:** Human Resources. **E-mail address:** tasa@tasa.com. **World Wide Web address:** http://www.tasa.com. **Description:** TASA designs, develops, publishes, and distributes educational tests, instructional materials, and microcomputer software to elementary and secondary schools, colleges, and universities. The educational tests, known as Primary, Standard, and Advanced Degrees of Reading Power tests and Degrees of Word Meaning tests, are components on the company's Degrees of Literacy Power program. **Corporate headquarters location:** This location.

WESTERN CONNECTICUT STATE UNIVERSITY
181 White Street, Danbury CT 06810. 203/837-8210. **Contact:** Human Resources. **World Wide Web address:** http://www.wcsu.edu. **Description:** A four-year state university offering the Ancell School of Business, the School of Arts & Sciences, and the School of Professional Studies.

WILLIAM PATERSON UNIVERSITY OF NEW JERSEY
358 Hamburg Turnpike, College Hall-Room 150, Wayne NJ 07470. 973/720-2723. **Fax:** 973/720-2090. **Contact:** Human Resources. **World Wide Web address:** http://www.wpunj.edu. **Description:** A public university with approximately 9,000 students. Programs include liberal arts, nursing, sciences, English, history, and music. **Positions advertised include:** Assistant Director of Financial Aide; Assistant Director of Counsel; Associate Director Career Development Center; Director of the Honors College; Grant Writer; Accounting Manager.

ELECTRONIC/INDUSTRIAL ELECTRICAL EQUIPMENT AND COMPONENTS

You can expect to find the following types of companies in this section:
Electronic Machines and Systems • Semiconductor Manufacturers

---

ADEMCO GROUP
(ALARM DEVICE MANUFACTURING COMPANY)
165 Eileen Way, Syosset NY 11791. 516/921-6704. **Fax:** 516/364-5344. **Contact:** Human Resources Department. **E-mail address:** opportunities@ademco.com. **World Wide Web address:** http://www.ademco.com/ademco. **Description:** Ademco manufactures alarm and security products. Products include smoke detectors, glass break detectors, and other home invasion alarms. Ademco's automated manufacturing facility processes more than 4 million printed circuit boards per year. The company also runs a quality service laboratory that conducts UL certified testing. Founded in 1929. **Positions advertised include:** Marketing Service Representative; Group Leader; Security & Fire Manager; Director of National Accounts; Contracts Manager; Sales Representative. **International locations:** Worldwide. **Corporate headquarters location:** This location. **Parent company:** Honeywell International. **Subsidiaries include:** ADEMCO Video Systems.

ADVANCED TECHNOLOGY MATERIALS, INC. (ATMI)
7 Commerce Drive, Danbury CT 06810. 203/794-1100. **Fax:** 203/792-8040. **Contact:** Human Resources Manager. **World Wide Web address:** http://www.atmi.com. **Description:** A developer of semiconductor materials and devices. ATMI specializes in chemical vapor deposition and thin-film technology, synthesis of organometallic reagents, wide bandgap semiconductor substrates and devices, and both absorption- and combustion-based air pollution abatement equipment. **Positions advertised include:** Inventory Analyst; Human Resources Administrator; Manufacturing Supervisor; Financial Analyst; Research Scientist. **Corporate headquarters location:** This location. **Other U.S. locations:** Phoenix AZ; San Jose CA. **Subsidiaries include:** EcoSys manufactures environmental equipment for the semiconductor industry. **Operations at this facility include:** Manufacturing; Research and Development. **Listed on:** NASDAQ. **Stock exchange symbol:** ATMI. **Annual sales/revenues:** $21 - $50 million. **Number of employees at this location:** 120. **Number of employees nationwide:** 225.

AGILENT TECHNOLOGIES
550 Clark Drive, Netcong NJ 07857. 973/448-9177. **Contact:** Employment Office. **World Wide Web address:** http://www.agilent.com. **Description:** Designs and manufactures test, measurement, and monitoring instruments, systems, and solutions. The company also designs and manufactures semiconductor and optical components. Agilent Technologies serves the communications, electronics, life sciences and health care industries. Founded in 1999. **Positions advertised include:** Field Technology Support Specialist. **NOTE:** Send employment correspondence to: Resume Processing Center, 89 Davis Road, Suite 160, Orinda CA 94563. **Corporate headquarters location:** Palo Alto CA. **Other U.S. locations:** Nationwide. **International locations:** Worldwide. **Listed on:** New York Stock Exchange. **Stock exchange symbol:** A. **Number of employees worldwide:** 46,000.

ALPHA WIRE COMPANY
711 Lidgerwood Avenue, Elizabeth NJ 07207. 908/925-8000. **Toll-free phone:** 800/52A-LPHA. **Fax:** 908/925-6923. **Contact:** Human Resources. **E-mail address:** info@alphawire.com. **World Wide Web address:** http://www.alphawire.com. **Description:** An international distributor of high-tech and high-reliability wire, cable, tubing, and connector products including communications and control cables, shrinkable and nonshrinkable tubing and insulation, instrumentation cables, flat cable and connectors, coaxial and data cables, plenum cable, and hook-up wire used for electrical and electronic equipment. Products are sold to a network of distributors and OEMs. Founded in 1922. **Positions advertised include:** District Sales Manager. **NOTE:** Entry-level positions and part-time jobs are offered. **Special programs:** Internships. **Office hours:** Monday - Friday, 8:00 a.m. - 8:00 p.m. **Corporate headquarters location:** St. Louis MO. **Other U.S. locations:** Nationwide. **International locations:** Worldwide. **Operations at this facility include:** Administration; Research and Development; Sales; Service. **General Manager:** Brian O'Connell. **Purchasing Manager:** Ben Ochinegro. **Annual sales/revenues:** $51 - $100 million. **Number of employees at this location:** 120. **Number of employees nationwide:** 180. **Number of employees worldwide:** 185.

AMERICAN GAS & CHEMICAL COMPANY LTD.
220 Pegasus Avenue, Northvale NJ 07647. 201/767-7300. **Toll-free phone:** 800/288-3647. **Fax:** 201/767-1741. **Contact:** Human Resources Department. **E-mail address:** hr@amgas.com. **World Wide Web address:** http://www.amgas.com. **Description:** Manufactures electronic chemical and gas leak detectors. **Corporate headquarters location:** This location. **Operations at this facility include:** Administration; Manufacturing; Research and Development; Sales. **Listed on:** Privately held. **Number of employees at this location:** 125.

AMERICAN MEDICAL ALERT CORPORATION
3265 Lawson Boulevard, P.O. Box 40, Oceanside NY 11572. 516/536-5850. **Toll-free phone:** 800/286-2622. **Fax:** 516/536-5276. **Contact:** Human Resources. **E-mail address:** info@amac.com. **World Wide Web address:** http://www.amacalert.com. **Description:** A manufacturer and distributor of the Personal Emergency Response System for the home health industry. The Personal Emergency Response System is an in-home safety device used by the chronically ill or physically impaired allowing them to communicate with emergency care providers using digital-wireless technology. Founded in 1981. **NOTE:** Entry-level positions are offered. **Positions advertised include:** Administrative Assistant; Sales Representative. **Corporate headquarters location:** This location. **Other U.S. locations:** Parker CO; Decatur GA; Tinley Park IL. **Operations at this facility include:** Administration; Sales; Service. **Listed on:** NASDAQ. **Stock exchange symbol:** AMAC. **Annual sales/revenues:** $14 million. **Number of employees:** 183

AMERICAN TECHNICAL CERAMICS CORPORATION (ATC)
One Norden Lane, Huntington Station NY 11746. 631/622-4700. **Fax:** 631/622-4673. **Contact:** Susan McNally, Human Resources. **E-mail address:** hr@atceramics.com. **World Wide Web address:** http://www.atceramics.com. **Description:** American Technical Ceramics Corporation (ATC) is a high-technology firm engaged in the design, development, and manufacture of ceramic and porcelain capacitors. ATC's processing technology creates high-performance capacitors for critical applications in both the commercial and military markets including missile systems, satellite broadcasting equipment, mobile telephones, medical electronics, and aircraft radar and navigation systems. **NOTE:** Human Resources phone: 631/622-4774. **Positions advertised include:** Metals Engineer; Process Engineer. **Corporate headquarters location:** This location. **Other U.S. locations:** Jacksonville FL.

International locations: Worldwide. **Listed on:** American Stock Exchange. **Stock exchange symbol:** AMK. **President/CEO/Director:** Victor Insetta. **Annual sales/revenues:** $49.6 million. **Number of employees:** 479.

AMPHENOL CORPORATION
One Kennedy Avenue, Danbury CT 06810. 203/743-9272. **Contact:** Human Resources. **World Wide Web address:** http://www.amphenolrf.com. **NOTE:** Submit resume online. **Description:** Manufactures coaxial connectors and cable assemblies. **Corporate headquarters location:** Wallingford CT. **Other U.S. locations:** Hamden CT. **Listed on:** New York Stock Exchange. **Stock exchange symbol:** APH. **Number of employees nationwide:** 3,070.

ANDREA ELECTRONICS CORPORATION
45 Melville Park Road, Melville NY 11747. 631/719-1800. **Fax:** 631/719-1950. **Contact:** Heather Hinkley, Human Resources Manager. **World Wide Web address:** http://www.andreaelectronics.com. **Description:** Andrea Electronics Corporation designs, develops, and produces electronic audio systems, intercommunication systems, and related equipment for military and industrial companies. **Corporate headquarters location:** This location. **Other locations:** UT. **International locations:** Hong Kong; Israel. **Listed on:** American Stock Exchange. **Stock exchange symbol:** AND. **Chairman:** Douglas J. Andrea. **Annual sales/revenues:** $10 million. **Number of employees:** 88.

ARIES ELECTRONICS
P.O. Box 130, 62A Trenton Ave., Frenchtown NJ 08825. 908/996-6841. **Fax:** 908/996-3891. **Contact:** Personnel. **E-mail address:** info@arieselec.com. **World Wide Web address:** http://www.arieselec.com. **Description:** Manufactures a wide variety of electronic components including pin grid array footprints, ZIF and test sockets, cable assemblies, DIP/SIP sockets/headers, display sockets, programming devices, and switches.

AROTECH CORPORATION
250 West 57th Street, Suite 310, New York NY 10107. 212/258-3222. **Fax:** 212/258-3281. **Contact:** Human Resources. **E-mail address:** info@arotech.com. **World Wide Web address:** http://www.arotech.com. **Description:** Formerly Electric Fuel Corporation, Arotech, through its subsidiaries is engaged in training simulators for military and law enforcement applications; ceramic armor and ballistic glass for military and passenger vehicles; and zinc-air batteries and fuel cells for military, homeland security, electric vehicle, lifejacket, and safety device products. Founded in 1990. **Corporate headquarters location:** This location. **Subsidiaries include:** IES Interactive Training; M.D.T. Protective Industries; Electric Fuel Batteries. **Listed on:** NASDAQ. **Stock exchange symbol:** ARTX. **Chairman/CEO:** Robert S. Ehrlich. **Annual sales/revenues:** $6.4 million. **Number of employees:** 127.

ARROW ELECTRONICS, INC.
dba ARROW/ZEUS ELECTRONICS
2900 Westchester Avenue, Suite 401, Purchase NY 10577-2508. 914/701-7400. **Fax:** 914/701-4283. **Contact:** Human Resources Department. **World Wide Web address:** http://www.arrow.com. **Description:** Arrow Electronics distributes electronic components and computer products including semiconductors, computer peripherals, passive components, and interconnect products from over 600 suppliers to over 150,000 manufacturers with 225 sales offices and 20 distribution centers in 39 countries. The Arrow/Zeus division specializes in supplying electronic components to military and aerospace contractors with parts and solutions tailored to specific needs. **Positions advertised include:** Marketing Specialist; Sales Representative. **Corporate headquarters location:** Melville NY. **Other locations:** Brookhaven NY. **Subsidiaries/Affiliates include:** Microtronica; Marubun/Arrow; Spoerle; Sasco Semiconductor; CCI Electronique.

Operations at this facility include: Sales. **Listed on:** New York Stock Exchange. **Stock exchange symbol:** ARW. **Annual sales:** $7.4 billion. **Number of employees at this location:** 65. **Number of employees worldwide:** 11,700.

ASTREX, INC.
205 Express Street, Plainview NY 11803. 516/433-1700. **Toll-free phone:** 800/633-6360. **Fax:** 516/433-1796. **Contact:** Victoria Gagliardo, Human Resources. **World Wide Web address:** http://www.astrex.net. **Description:** Distributes electronic components used to connect, control, regulate, or store electricity in equipment. Products assembled and sold by Astrex include connectors, relays, switches, and LEDs. Founded in 1960. **Positions advertised include:** Inside Sales Representative; Strategic Account Manager; Credit Manager; Customer Service Representative; Sales Representative. **Corporate headquarters location:** This location. **Other U.S. locations:** Nationwide. **Annual sales/revenues:** $17 million. **Number of employees at this location:** 30. **Number of employees nationwide:** 60.

AVNET, INC.
390 Rabro Drive, Hauppauge NY 11788. 631/582-8638. **Contact:** Human Resources. **E-mail address:** talent.acquisition@avnet.com. **World Wide Web address:** http://www.avnet.com. **Description:** One of the nation's largest distributors of electronic components and computer products for industrial and military customers. The company also manufactures and distributes other electronic, electrical, and video communications products. **NOTE:** Resumes must be sent to Avnet, Inc., Human Resources, 2211 South 47th Street, Phoenix AZ 85034. Resumes can be faxed to 602/643-4670. **Corporate headquarters location:** Phoenix AZ. **Other locations:** Worldwide. **Subsidiaries include:** Avnet Applied Computing; Avnet Direct; Avnet Electronics Marketing; Avnet Hall-Mark; Avnet Computer Marketing Avnet Enterprise Solutions. **Listed on:** New York Stock Exchange. **Stock exchange symbol:** AVT. **Annual sales/revenues:** $8.9 billion. **Number of employees:** 11,000.

BAE SYSTEMS
One Hazelteen Way, Greenlawn NY 11740. 631/261-7000. **Contact:** Human Resources. **World Wide Web address:** http://www.baesystems.com. **Description:** Designs, develops, and manufactures information electronics systems that acquire, protect, enhance, communicate, and display information for the defense and technically related markets. **NOTE:** Applications may be done on-line. **Positions advertised include:** Material Clerk; Legal Counsel/Attorney; Antenna Design Engineering Manger; Engineering Manager; Radio Frequency Systems Department Engineer; Senior Technical/Antenna Staff Member; Staff Contract Administrator; Senior Electro-Optic Systems Engineer; Senior Servo Systems Engineer; Digital Servo Systems Engineer; Reliability & Maintainability Engineer; Principal Electromagnetic Interference Engineer; Principal Systems Engineer; Truck Driver; Senior Staff Engineer; Business Development Director; Staff Project Engineer; Senior Electronic Assembler; Citation Project Engineer; Micro-Electronic Assembler. **Corporate headquarters location:** Hampshire, United Kingdom. **Other area locations:** Johnson City NY; Syosset NY; Yonkers NY. **Other U.S. locations:** Nationwide. **International locations:** Worldwide. **Subsidiaries include:** Airbus S.A.S.; Saab AB. **Operations at this facility include:** BAE's Advanced Systems Division. **Listed on:** Over The Counter. **Stock exchange symbol:** BAESY. **Annual sales/revenues:** $13.1 billion. **Number of employees at this location:** 925. **Number of employees nationwide:** 22,000. **Number of employees worldwide:** 70,100.

BAE SYSTEMS
One Ridge Hill, Mail Stop 9, Yonkers NY 10710-5598. 914/964-2500. **Fax:** 914/964-3913. **Contact:** Human Resources Department. **World Wide Web address:** http://www.baesystems.com. **Description:** Designs, manufactures,

and sells flight simulators, weapon systems, tactical air defense systems, small arms, and training devices for the U.S. government, as well as commercial and international customers. BAE Systems also develops simulation-based devices for the entertainment industry. The company also provides a variety of simulator-related training services at customer-owned facilities, its Tampa training center, and the British Aerospace-owned Dulles training facility. BAE Systems conducts business through its three primary operating segments: Training Devices, Training Services, and Systems Management. **Positions advertised include:** Program Manager; Calibration Lab Technician. **Corporate headquarters location:** Hampshire, United Kingdom. **Other area locations:** Greenlawn NY; Johnson City NY; Syosset NY. **Other U.S. locations:** Nationwide. **International locations:** Worldwide. **Subsidiaries include:** Airbus S.A.S.; Saab AB. **Operations at this facility include:** BAE's Information & Electronic Warfare Systems Division. **Listed on:** Over The Counter. **Stock exchange symbol:** BAESY. **Annual sales/revenues:** $13.1 billion. **Number of employees at this location:** 925. **Number of employees nationwide:** 22,000. **Number of employees worldwide:** 70,100.

BEL FUSE INC.
206 Van Vorst Street, Jersey City NJ 07302. 201/432-0463. **Fax:** 201/432-9542. **Contact:** Personnel Department. **World Wide Web address:** http://www.belfuse.com. **Description:** Designs, manufactures, and sells products used in local area networking, telecommunications, business equipment, and consumer electronic applications. Magnetic components manufactured by the company fall into four major groups: pulse transformers; delay lines, filters, and AC/DC converters; power transformers, line chokes, and coils; and packaged modules. The company manufactures miniature and micro fuses for supplementary circuit protection. Bel Fuse sells its products to approximately 550 customers throughout North America, Western Europe, and the Far East. **Other U.S. locations:** CA; IN. **International locations:** France; Hong Kong; Macau. **Listed on:** NASDAQ. **Stock exchange symbol:** BELF.

BLONDER TONGUE LABORATORIES, INC.
One Jake Brown Road, Old Bridge NJ 08857-1000. 732/679-4000. **Fax:** 732/679-4353. **Contact:** Human Resources. **E-mail address:** employment@blondertongue.com. **World Wide Web address:** http://www.blondertongue.com. **Description:** Designs and manufactures signal processing equipment for the television industry. Products are used for satellite communications, master antennae systems (MATV), and other systems using RF technology. **Corporate headquarters location:** This location. **Operations at this facility include:** Administration; Divisional Headquarters; Manufacturing; Regional Headquarters; Research and Development; Sales; Service. **Listed on:** American Stock Exchange. **Stock exchange symbol:** BDR. **Annual sales/revenues:** $51 - $100 million. **Number of employees at this location:** 500.

CHYRON CORPORATION
5 Hub Drive, Department WWW, Farmingdale NY 11735. 631/845-2000. **Fax:** 631/845-2090. **Contact:** Human Resources. **E-mail address:** careers@chyron.com. **World Wide Web address:** http://www.chyron.com. **Description:** Designs, manufactures, and markets worldwide digital equipment, software, systems, and solutions that facilitate the production and enhance the presentation of live and programmed television content. Chyron also provides comprehensive solutions that address the management and routing of video and data signals prior to transmission. **NOTE:** Entry-level positions are offered. Jobseekers may apply online. **Positions advertised include:** Test Engineer. **Special programs:** Internships. **Corporate headquarters location:** This location. **International locations:** Reading, United Kingdom (Chyron Pro-Bel). **Operations at this facility include:** Chyron Graphics – Manufacturing;

Corporate Administration; Research and Development; Sales; Service. **Listed on:** Over The Counter. **Stock exchange symbol:** CYRO. **Chairman/President/CEO:** Michael I. Wellesley-Wesley. **Annual sales/revenues:** $46 million. **Number of employees:** 200.

CONTINENTAL CONNECTOR COMPANY

53 La France Avenue, Bloomfield NJ 07003. 973/429-8500. **Contact:** Personnel. **World Wide Web address:** http://www.continentalconnector.com. **Description:** Continental Connector Corporation is engaged in the development, manufacture, and sale of a broad line of multiprecision rack and panel circuit connectors. Manufacturing operations consist primarily of the processing and assembly of plated metals, receptacles, and plugs of various types designed and molded from thermosetting molding compounds and other precision connector parts. **Corporate headquarters location:** Las Vegas NV. **Operations at this facility include:** This location manufactures circuit connectors. **Parent company:** ASC Group Inc.

COOPER WIRING DEVICES

45-31 Court Square, Long Island City NY 11101. 718/937-8000. **Contact:** Human Resources. **E-mail address:** jobs@cooperwiringdevices.com. **World Wide Web address:** http://www.cooperwiringdevices.com. **Description:** Manufactures electrical wiring devices. **Positions advertised include:** Customer Service Supervisor. **Corporate headquarters location:** This location. **Parent company:** Cooper Industries (Houston TX).

DRS PHOTRONICS

133 Bauer Drive, Oakland NJ 07436. 201/337-3800. **Fax:** 201/337-4775. **Contact:** Human Resources. **World Wide Web address:** http://www.drs.com. **Description:** Designs, manufactures, and markets high-technology electronic products used to process, display, and store information for the U.S. Department of Defense, international defense departments, other U.S. prime defense contractors, and industrial corporations. The company's advanced signal processing, display, data storage, trainer, emulation, and electro-optical systems are utilized in numerous applications for military use and for the disk drive and television broadcast industries. Founded in 1968.

DATA DELAY DEVICES, INC.

3 Mount Prospect Avenue, Clifton NJ 07013. 973/773-2299. **Fax:** 973/773-9672. **Contact:** Human Resources. **World Wide Web address:** http://www.datadelay.com. **Description:** Manufactures analog and digital delay lines. The company's products are used by computer, telecommunications, and aerospace firms, as well as the military.

DATA DEVICE CORPORATION

105 Wilbur Place, Bohemia NY 11716. 631/567-5600. **Fax:** 631/567-6357. **Contact:** Ada Villanuvea, Human Resources Supervisor. **World Wide Web address:** http://www.ddc-web.com. **Description:** A manufacturer of high-performance microelectronic components and data conversion products for military, aerospace, and industrial applications for distribution in North America and Europe. **Positions advertised include:** Material Control Stock Clerk; Sales/Marketing Manager. **Special programs:** Internships. **Corporate headquarters location:** This location. **Subsidiaries/affiliates include:** ILC Dover, Inc. **Parent company:** ILC Industries, Inc. (also at this location). **Operations at this facility include:** Manufacturing; Research and Development.

DEL GLOBAL TECHNOLOGIES CORPORATION

One Commerce Park, Valhalla NY 10595. 914/686-3600. **Fax:** 914/686-5424. **Contact:** Human Resources. **World Wide Web address:** http://www.delglobaltech.com. **Description:** Del Global Technologies

Corporation is comprised of five operations that are engaged in the design, manufacture, and distribution of electronic components, assemblies, and systems for medical, industrial, and defense markets. Products are sold throughout the world to a broad range of OEM customers, distributors, radiologists, and defense agencies. The Dynarad subsidiary manufactures and markets mobile medical imaging systems, mammography equipment, portable dental X-ray units, and advanced neonatal imaging systems. Del Medical Systems markets medical diagnostic products on a worldwide basis. The Power Conversion Division provides standard and custom high-voltage power supplies, transformers, and custom low-voltage power supplies. The Bertan subsidiary designs and manufactures precision high-voltage power supplies and high-voltage instrumentation. The RFI subsidiary designs and manufactures electronic noise suppression filters, high-voltage capacitors, pulse transformers, and specialty magnetics. **Positions advertised include:** Manufacturing Technician; Quality Engineer; Electrical Engineer. **Listed on:** Over The Counter. **Stock exchange symbol:** DGTC. **President/CEO/Director:** Samuel E. Park. **Annual sales/revenues:** $101 million. **Number of employees:** 540.

DEUTSCH RELAYS INC.
55 Engineers Road, Hauppauge NY 11788. 631/342-1700. **Fax:** 631/342-9455. **Contact:** Diane Goerz, Human Resources Manager. **E-mail address:** info@deutschrelays.com. **World Wide Web address:** http://www.deutschrelays.com. **Description:** Manufactures and designs miniature electronic relays, electro-mechanical hermetically sealed relays, time delay devices, and mating sockets for use in harsh environments.

THE DEWEY ELECTRONICS CORPORATION
27 Muller Road, Oakland NJ 07436. 201/337-4700. **Toll-free phone:** 800/888-8680. **Fax:** 201/337-3976. **Contact:** Carol Grofsik, Director of Personnel Administration. **E-mail address:** dewey@deweyelectronics.com. **World Wide Web address:** http://www.deweyelectronics.com. **Description:** Develops, designs, engineers, and manufactures electronics systems for military and civilian customers. **Corporate headquarters location:** This location.

DIONICS, INC.
65 Rushmore Street, Westbury NY 11590. 516/997-7474. **Fax:** 516/997-7479. **Contact:** Human Resources. **World Wide Web address:** http://www.dionics-usa.com. **Description:** The company designs, manufactures, and sells silicon semiconductor electronic products as individual discrete components, multicomponent integrated circuits, and multicomponent hybrid circuits.

EDO CORPORATION
ELECTRONIC SYSTEMS GROUP
455 Commack Road, Deer Park NY 11729-4591. 631/595-5000. **Fax:** 631/595-6517. **Contact:** Human Resources. **E-mail address:** employment@nycedo.com. **World Wide Web address:** http://www.edocorp.com. **Description:** Engaged in the engineering and manufacturing of electronic systems including defensive avionics, ATC radar, satellite communications systems, and components. **Corporate headquarters location:** New York NY. **Subsidiaries include:** Advanced Engineering & Research Associates, Inc.; Combat Systems; Electro-Ceramic Products; Fiber Science; Marine and Aircraft Systems; Specialty Plastics; Technology Services and Analysis. **Operations at this facility include:** Administration; Manufacturing Divisions – Antenna Products & Technologies, Sensors & Force Protection, Space & Communications Products, Defense Programs and Technologies; Research and Development. **Listed on:** New York Stock Exchange. **Stock exchange symbol:** EDO. **Annual sales/revenues:** $329 million. **Number of employees:** 2,000.

EMCORE CORPORATION
145 Belmont Drive, Somerset NJ 08873. 732/271-9090. **Contact:** Human Resources. **World Wide Web address:** http://www.emcore.com. **Description:** Manufactures semiconductors through the metal organic chemical vapor deposition production system. **NOTE:** Entry-level positions and second and third shifts are offered. **Special programs:** Training; Co-ops. **Office hours:** Monday - Friday, 8:00 a.m. - 5:00 p.m. **Corporate headquarters location:** This location. **Listed on:** NASDAQ. **Stock exchange symbol:** EMKR. **Annual sales/revenues:** $21 - $50 million.

EVENTIDE, INC.
One Alsan Way, Little Ferry NJ 07643. 201/641-1200. **Contact:** Human Resources Department. **E-mail address:** catbert@eventide.com. **World Wide Web address:** http://www.eventide.com. **Description:** Manufactures electronic harmonizers. **Positions advertised include:** Hardware/Software Engineer.

FIRECOM, INC.
39-27 59th Street, Woodside NY 11377. 718/899-6100. **Fax:** 718/899-1932. **Contact:** Human Resources. **E-mail address:** info@firecominc.com. **World Wide Web address:** http://www.firecominc.com. **Description:** Designs, manufactures, and distributes fire alarm and communication systems used for safety in large commercial buildings, primarily in the metropolitan New York area. Founded in 1963. **Corporate headquarters location:** This location. **Subsidiaries include:** Commercial Radio-Sound Corp. (NY); Fire Controls, Inc. (NY). **Chairman/President/CEO:** Paul Mendez. **Number of employees at this location:** 120.

FREQUENCY ELECTRONICS, INC.
55 Charles Lindbergh Boulevard, Mitchel Field NY 11553. 516/794-4500. **Fax:** 516-794-4340. **Contact:** Human Resources Department. **E-mail address:** hr@freqelec.com. **World Wide Web address:** http://www.freqelec.com. **Description:** A manufacturer of products used to synchronize voice, data, and video transmissions in wireless communications systems for ground-based stations and commercial satellites. **Positions advertised include:** Sr. RF Design Engineer; Crystal Engineer; Sr. Technician; Material Control Planner/Administrator; Reliability Engineer. **Number of employees at this location:** 250.

INTERNATIONAL MICROWAVE CORPORATION
25 Van Zant Street, Suite 11A, Norwalk CT 06855. 203/857-4222. **Contact:** Human Resources. **World Wide Web address:** http://www.imcwireless.com. **Description:** Engaged in the manufacture and repair of microwave radios. **Corporate headquarters location:** This location. **Other U.S. locations:** Nationwide. **Listed on:** Privately held. **Number of employees at this location:** 35.

JACO ELECTRONICS, INC.
145 Oser Avenue, Hauppauge NY 11788. 631/273-5500. **Toll-free phone:** 800/645-5112. **Fax:** 631/273-5799. **Contact:** Diane Eckhoff, Personnel Director. **E-mail address:** deckhoff@jacoelect.com. **World Wide Web address:** http://www.jacoelectronics.com. **Description:** Jaco Electronics distributes electronic components to original equipment manufacturers, which include semiconductors, transistors, diodes, capacitors, and resistors as well as offering inventory, manufacturing and computer configuration services. **NOTE:** Personnel phone extension: x3095. **Positions advertised include:** Regional Display Sales Manager. **Subsidiaries include:** Nexus Custom Electronics, Inc. a contract manufacturer of printed circuit board. **Listed on:** NASDAQ. **Stock exchange symbol:** JACO. **Chairman/President/Treasurer:** Joel H. Girsky. **Annual sales/revenues:** $194 million. **Number of employees:** 363.

KEARFOTT GUIDANCE & NAVIGATION CORPORATION
150 Totowa Road, Mail Code HWA01, Wayne NJ 07474. 973/785-6459. **Fax:** 973/785-6255. **Contact:** Personnel. **E-mail address:** humanresources@kearfott.com. **World Wide Web address:** http://www.kearfott.com. **Description:** Manufactures precision electromechanical and electronic components used to generate, sense, control, and display motion such as synchros, resolvers, cant angle sensors, and servo motors. Founded in 1917. **Corporate headquarters location:** This location. **Parent company:** Astronautics Corporation of America. **Listed on:** Privately held. **Number of employees at this location:** 1,300.

KULITE SEMICONDUCTOR PRODUCTS
One Willow Tree Road, Leonia NJ 07605. 201/461-0900. **Contact:** Karen Birdsall, Human Resources Manager. **E-mail address:** karen@kulite.com. **World Wide Web address:** http://www.kulite.com. **Description:** Manufactures computerized metering systems for medical applications and for use in aircraft. Sales offices are located throughout the United States. **Corporate headquarters location:** This location.

L-3 GOVERNMENT SOLUTIONS INC
25 Van Zant Street, Suite 11A, Norwalk CT 06855. 203/857-4222. **Contact:** Human Resources. **World Wide Web address:** http://www.imcwireless.com. **Description:** Engaged in the manufacture and repair of microwave radios. **Corporate headquarters location:** Chantilly VA. **Other U.S. locations:** Nationwide. **Listed on:** Privately held. **Number of employees at this location:** 35.

LG ELECTRONICS USA, INC.
1000 Sylvan Avenue, Englewood Cliffs NJ 07632. 800/243-0000. **Contact:** Human Resources. **World Wide Web address:** http://www.us.lge.com. **Description:** The North American wireless division of LGE, a business unit of LG Electronics, a global manufacturer of electronics products. **Positions advertised include:** Accounts Payable Coordinator; Business Development Manager; Credit Analyst; Field Quality Manager; Inside Sales Coordinator; Junior Industrial Designer; National Account Manager; Planning Assistant Manager; Senior Financial Analyst; Western Sales Director. **Corporate headquarters location:** Seoul, Korea.

LSI COMPUTER SYSTEMS INC.
1235 Walt Whitman Road, Melville NY 11747-3010. 631/271-0400. **Fax:** 631/271-0405. **Contact:** Roberta Williams, Human Resources Manager. **E-mail address:** hr@lsicsi.com. **World Wide Web address:** http://www.lsicsi.com. **Description:** Manufactures integrated circuits and microchips. Founded in 1969. **Positions advertised include:** Integrated Circuit Design Engineer; Integrated Circuit Layout Designer; Test Engineer.

LAMBDA EMI
405 Essex Road, Neptune NJ 07753. 732/922-9300. **Contact:** Human Resources. **World Wide Web address:** http://www.lambda-emi.com. **Description:** Manufactures DC power supplies. **Parent company:** Lambda Electronics.

THE LECROY CORPORATION
700 Chestnut Ridge Road, Chestnut Ridge NY 10977-6499. 845/425-2000. **Fax:** 845/578-4461. **Contact:** Corporate Staffing. **E-mail address:** hrweb@lecroy.com. **World Wide Web address:** http://www.lecroy.com. **Description:** The LeCroy Corporation is a leading manufacturer of digital oscilloscopes and related products for the electronics, computer, and

communications markets. Founded in 1964. **Positions advertised include:** Corporate Accounting Manager; Sales Engineer; Field Engineer; Layout Technician; Mechanical Design Engineer; Program Manager. **Corporate headquarters location:** This location. **International locations:** Geneva, Switzerland. **Listed on:** NASDAQ. **Stock exchange symbol:** LCRY. **Annual sales/revenues:** $111.5 million. **Number of employees at this location:** 190. **Number of employees worldwide:** 407.

LEVITON MANUFACTURING CO. INC.
59-25 Little Neck Parkway, Little Neck NY 11362-2591. 718/229-4040. **Fax:** 800/832-9538. **Contact:** Mark Fogel, Director of Human Resources. **E-mail address:** careers@leviton.com. **World Wide Web address:** http://www.leviton.com. **Description:** A family-owned manufacturer of electronic components and electrical wiring devices. Leviton produces more than 80,000 variations of light switches, sockets, and plugs for both consumer and industrial customers. Products are used in small appliances, lamps, and similar products. Founded in 1906. **Positions advertised include:** Inside Sales Representative; Director of Business Systems; Data Entry Operator; Demand Analyst; Test Engineer; Accounts Payable Clerk; Cost Estimator; Graphic Artist; Marketing Service Coordinator; Technical Service Representative. **Corporate headquarters location:** This location. **Other U.S. locations:** Atlanta GA; Chicago IL; Coffeyville KS; Sparks NV; Pawtucket RI; Bothell WA. **International locations:** Canada; Mexico. **Subsidiaries include:** American Insulated Wire; Electricord Company; Leviton Telcom. **President/CEO:** Harold Leviton. **Annual sales/revenues:** $350 million.

MERRIMAC INDUSTRIES, INC.
41 Fairfield Place, West Caldwell NJ 07006. 973/575-1300. **Fax:** 973/882-5984. **Contact:** Human Resources. **E-mail address:** hrdept@merrimacind.com. **World Wide Web address:** http://www.merrimacind.com. **Description:** An international manufacturer of high-reliability signal-processing components. Products include IF-baseband components (used by electronics and military electronics OEMs); RF-microwave components (for military electronics and fiber optics users); high-reliability space and missile products (electronic components used in military satellite and missile programs); integrated microwave products (for the military and commercial communications markets); and satellite reception products (products for the CATV and satellite master antenna systems). **Corporate headquarters location:** This location. **Operations at this facility include:** Administration; Manufacturing; Research and Development; Sales.

MICROWAVE DISTRIBUTORS COMPANY
500 Johnson Avenue, Suite A, Bohemia NY 11716-2675. 631/589-8000. **Fax:** 631/589-8167. **Contact:** Personnel. **World Wide Web address:** http://www.microwavedistributors.com. **Description:** A distributor of microwave and RF components. **Corporate headquarters location:** This location.

MYERS POWER PRODUCTS INC.
P.O. Box 893, Somerville NJ 08876. **Physical address:** 80 Readington Road, Somerville NJ 08876. **Toll-free phone:** 888/222-2287. **Fax:** 908/526-6866. **Contact:** Personnel. **World Wide Web address:** http://www.myerscpi.com. **Description:** Manufactures frequency converters and uninterrupted power supplies.

NCT GROUP, INC.
20 Ketchum Street, Westport CT 06880. 203/226-4447. **Fax:** 203/348-4106. **Contact:** Human Resources. **World Wide Web address:** http://www.nct-active.com. **Description:** Designs and manufactures electronic products that reduce noise and vibration. **Office hours:** Monday - Friday, 9:00 a.m. - 5:00 p.m.

Corporate headquarters location: This location. **International locations:** Cambridge, England.

NAPCO SECURITY GROUP
333 Bayview Avenue, Amityville NY 11701. 631/842-9400. **Fax:** 631/8429137. **Contact:** Human Resources. **World Wide Web address:** http://www.napcosecurity.com. **Description:** Manufactures electronic security equipment. The company's products are used in residential, commercial, institutional, and industrial installations. **Corporate headquarters location:** This location. **International locations:** England. **Subsidiaries include:** Alarm Lock manufactures and distributes a variety of door security hardware. **Listed on:** NASDAQ. **Stock exchange symbol:** NSSC. **Chairman:** Richard Soloway. **Sales/revenue:** $54 million. **Number of employees worldwide:** 800.

NOISE COM
25 Eastmans Road, Parsippany NJ 07054. 201/261-8797. **Fax:** 201/261-8339. **Contact:** Human Resources. **E-mail address:** jobs@noisecom.com. **World Wide Web address:** http://www.noisecom.com. **Description:** Manufactures test equipment for the wireless telecommunications industry. **Parent company:** Wireless Telecom Group. **Listed on:** American Stock Exchange. **Stock exchange symbol:** WTT.

NORTHROP GRUMMAN NORDEN SYSTEMS
P.O. Box 5300, Norwalk CT 06856. 203/852-5000. **Physical address:** 10 Norden Place, Norwalk CT 06856. **Contact:** Jane Nelson, Personnel Director. **World Wide Web address:** http://www.northgrum.com. **Description:** Northrop Grumman manufactures military aircraft, commercial aircraft parts, radar equipment, and electronic systems. Northrop Grumman has developed the B-2 Stealth Bomber, as well as parts for the F/A-18 and the 747. **Positions advertised include:** Electronics Engineer; Software Engineer. **Corporate headquarters location:** Los Angeles CA. **Operations at this facility include:** This location designs, develops, and manufactures advanced command, control, and communications systems; avionics systems; and data processing systems for military applications. **Listed on:** New York Stock Exchange. **Stock exchange symbol:** NOC.

OKONITE COMPANY
102 Hilltop Road, P.O. Box 340, Ramsey NJ 07446. 201/825-0300. **Fax:** 201/825-2672. **Contact:** Paulette Vita, Personnel Manager. **World Wide Web address:** http://www.okonite.com. **Description:** Manufactures power cable for large-scale users. **Corporate headquarters location:** This location. **Other area locations:** Passaic NJ; Paterson NJ.

ORBIT INTERNATIONAL CORPORATION
80 Cabot Court, Hauppauge NY 11788. 631/435-8300. **Contact:** Lynn Cooper, Human Resources Manager. **E-mail address:** lcooper@orbitintl.com. **World Wide Web address:** http://www.orbitintl.com. **Description:** Manufactures electronic devices for the aerospace industry. Founded in 1957. **Special programs:** Summer Jobs. **Corporate headquarters location:** This location. **Subsidiaries include:** Behlman Electronics, Inc., through its military division, designs and manufactures power conversion devices and electronic products for measurement and display. The commercial products division of Behlman produces distortion-free commercial power units and low-noise, uninterruptable power sources. **Listed on:** NASDAQ. **Stock exchange symbol:** ORBT. **Number of employees at this location:** 120.

PANASONIC INDUSTRIAL COMPANY
One Panasonic Way, Mailstop 3A-5, Secaucus NJ 07094. 201/348-7000. **Fax:** 201/392-6007. **Contact:** Kisha Rand-Hudson, Human Resources. **E-mail**

address: hudsonk@panasonic.com. **World Wide Web address:** http://www.panasonic.com. **Description:** Panasonic is one of the world's largest manufacturers of consumer and industrial electronic equipment and components. Brand names include Panasonic, Technics, and Quasar. **Positions advertised include:** Legal Secretary; Category Planning Analyst; Demand Specialist; Marketing Manager; Account Manager; Compensation Analyst; Technical Support Specialist; Product Development Engineer; Programmer; Technical Repair Specialist; Account Manager; Sales Manager; Instructor; Account Executive. **Other U.S. locations:** Nationwide. **Operations at this facility include:** This location houses the U.S. headquarters. **Parent company:** Matsushita Electronics Corporation of America. **Number of employees at this location:** 300. **Number of employees nationwide:** 10,000.

PHELPS DODGE HIGH PERFORMANCE CONDUCTORS
48 Broadway Avenue, Elizabeth NJ 07006. 908/351-3200. **Fax:** 908/351-9475. **Contact:** Marge Engel, Human Resources Manager. **World Wide Web address:** http://www.phelpsdodge.com. **Description:** One of the world's leading suppliers of conductive wire. **Corporate headquarters location:** Inman SC. **Operations at this facility include:** Administration; Manufacturing; Sales. **Number of employees at this location:** 175. **Number of employees nationwide:** 400.

PHILIPS ELECTRONICS NORTH AMERICA CORPORATION
1251 Avenue of the Americas, New York NY 10020. 212/536-0500. **Contact:** Denise Townsen, Supervisor of Human Resources. **World Wide Web address:** http://www.philips.com. **Description:** Philips Electronics North America is a multimarket manufacturing organization with nationwide locations and various subsidiaries, concentrating its efforts primarily in the fields of consumer electronics, consumer products, electrical and electronics components, and professional equipment. **Positions advertised include:** Quality Assurance Analyst; Quality Services Manager; Senior Customer Care Consultant; Senior Trainer. **Office hours:** Monday – Friday, 9:00 a.m. – 5:00 p.m. **Corporate headquarters location:** This location. **Operations at this facility include:** This location provides services including intellectual property, legal, tax, customs, employee benefits, communications and processing, government affairs, manufacturing technology, purchasing, travel, environmental affairs, audit, compensation, training, and development to Philips companies nationwide. **Listed on:** New York Stock Exchange. **Stock exchange symbol:** PHG. **Number of employees at this location:** 230.

PHILIPS RESEARCH
345 Scarborough Road, Briarcliff Manor NY 10510. 914/945-6000. **Fax:** 914/945-6375. **World Wide Web address:** http://www.research.philips.com. **Contact:** Human Resources. **Description:** This location conducts research in microelectronics, High Definition TV (HDTV), medical imaging, lighting, integrated circuit design, software engineering, materials engineering, and manufacturing automation to support Philips' international business interests. **Corporate headquarters location:** This location. **International locations:** Germany; England; the Netherlands; China. **Parent company:** Philips Electronics North America is a multimarket manufacturing organization with nationwide locations and various subsidiaries. The company concentrates its efforts primarily in the fields of consumer electronics, consumer products, electrical and electronics components, and professional equipment. **Listed on:** New York Stock Exchange. **Stock exchange symbol:** PHG. **Number of employees worldwide:** 2,500.

PHOTOCIRCUITS CORPORATION
31 Sea Cliff Avenue, Glen Cove NY 11542. 516/674-1000. **Fax:** 516/609-1080. **Contact:** Human Resources. **E-mail address:** gcrecruiter@photocircuits.com. **World Wide Web address:** http://www.photocircuits.com. **Description:** A

manufacturer of printed circuit boards. **Positions advertised include:** HVAC Mechanic; Maintenance Technician. **Special programs:** Internships. **Corporate headquarters location:** This location. **Other U.S. locations:** Peachtree City GA. **Operations at this facility include:** Administration; Manufacturing; Sales. **Number of employees at this location:** 1,525.

PHOTRONICS INC.
15 Secor Road, Brookfield CT 06804. 203/775-9000. **Contact:** Human Resources. **World Wide Web address:** http://www.photronics.com. **Description:** A leading manufacturer of photomasks used for the manufacture of semiconductors and integrated circuits. **Corporate headquarters location:** This location. **Other U.S. locations:** Phoenix AZ; Milpitas CA; Allen TX; Austin TX. **International locations:** China; Germany; Japan; Korea; Singapore; Taiwan; United Kingdom. **Listed on:** NASDAQ. **Stock exchange symbol:** PLAB.

POWERTECH, INC.
0-02 Fair Lawn Avenue, Fair Lawn NJ 07410. 201/791-5050. **Fax:** 201/791-6805. **Contact:** Human Resources. **World Wide Web address:** http://www.power-tech.com. **Description:** Manufactures silicon power transistors.

RICHARDSON ELECTRONICS
701-1 Koehler Avenue, Ronkonkoma NY 11779. 631/468-3900. **Toll-free phone:** 800/737-6937. **Fax:** 631/468-3950. **Contact:** Sales Manager. **World Wide Web address:** http://www.rell.com. **Description:** An international distributor of electronic components including turn-key microwave generators. **Corporate headquarters location:** La Fox IL. **Other U.S. locations:** Nationwide. **International locations:** Worldwide. **Operations at this facility include:** This location supports industrial, avionics, marine, and scientific products. **Listed on:** NASDAQ. **Stock exchange symbol:** RELL.

SHARP ELECTRONICS CORPORATION
Sharp Plaza, Mahwah NJ 07430. 201/529-8200. **Fax:** 201/529-8425. **Contact:** Human Resources. **World Wide Web address:** www.sharpusa.com. **Description:** An electronics company that produces appliances, office equipment, and entertainment products. **Other U.S. locations:** Camas WA; Memphis TN; Romeoville IL; Huntington Beach CA; Miami FL. **International locations:** Worldwide.

SIEMENS CORPORATION
153 East 53rd Street, 56th Floor, New York NY 10022-4611. 212/258-4000. **Contact:** Human Resources. **World Wide Web address:** http://www.usa.siemens.com. **Description:** Siemens operates internationally through the following groups: power engineering and automation; electrical installations; communications; medical engineering; data systems; and components. **Corporate headquarters location:** This location. **Other U.S. locations:** Nationwide. **Parent company:** Siemens AG (Munich, Germany). **Operations at this facility include:** This location is the United States management and administrative headquarters. **Listed on:** New York Stock Exchange. **Stock exchange symbol:** SI. **President/CEO:** Klaus Kleinfeld. **Sales/revenue:** Over $20 billion. **Number of employees worldwide:** 70,000.

SIGNAL TRANSFORMER COMPANY, INC.
500 Bayview Avenue, Inwood NY 11096-1792. 516/239-5777. **Fax:** 516/239-7208. **Contact:** Human Resources. **World Wide Web address:** http://www.signaltransformer.com. **Description:** Manufactures and distributes transformers for a wide range of applications, from printed circuit board requirements to rectifiers and chokes. **Office hours:** Monday – Friday, 8:00 a.m. – 6:00 p.m. **Corporate headquarters location:** This location. **Parent company:**

Insilco Technologies Group. **Operations at this facility include:** Administration; Manufacturing; Sales.

SPELLMAN HIGH VOLTAGE ELECTRONICS CORPORATION
475 Wireless Boulevard, Hauppauge New York 11788. 631/630-3000. **Fax:** 631-630-3008. **Contact:** Human Resources. **E-mail address:** hr@spellmanhv.com. **World Wide Web address:** http://www.spellmanhv.com. **Description:** A manufacturer of high voltage dc power supplies, X-ray generators, and Monoblock X-ray sources. **Positions advertised include:** Engineering Technician; Test Technician; Electro/Mechanical Inspector; Power Supply Design Engineer.

SYSKA HENNESSY GROUP
11 West 42nd Street, New York NY 10036-2300. 212/921-2300. **Contact:** Human Resources. **E-mail address:** info@syska.com. **World Wide Web address:** http://www.syska.com. **Description:** An electrical engineering company. **Positions advertised include:** Senior Mechanical Engineer.

THERMO ELECTRIC COMPANY, INC.
109 North Fifth Street, Saddle Brook NJ 07663. 201/843-5800. **Fax:** 201/843-4568. **Contact:** Human Resources. **E-mail address:** info@te-direct.com. **World Wide Web address:** http://www.thermo-electric-direct.com. **Description:** An international leader in industrial temperature instrumentation. Thermo Electric Company, Inc. provides solutions for temperature control needs worldwide. Products include temperature sensors, instrumentation, and specialty wire and cable. **Corporate headquarters location:** This location. **Operations at this facility include:** Administration; Manufacturing; Research and Development; Sales; Service. **Listed on:** Privately held. **Number of employees at this location:** 200. **Number of employees nationwide:** 225.

THOMAS ELECTRONICS, INC.
100 Riverview Drive, Wayne NJ 07470. 973/696-5200. **Fax:** 973/696-8298. **Contact:** Personnel. **World Wide Web address:** http://www.thomaselectronics.com. **Description:** Manufactures cathode ray tubes and liquid crystal displays for use by military and industrial OEMs. **Corporate headquarters location:** This location.

VECTRON INTERNATIONAL
P.O. Box 5160, Norwalk CT 06856. 203/853-4433. **Physical address:** 166 Glover Avenue, Norwalk CT 06856. **Fax:** 203/849-1423. **Contact:** Human Resources. **World Wide Web address:** http://www.vectron.com. **Description:** An electrical engineering firm. **Positions advertised include:** Board Designer; Circuit Design Engineer; Manager of Military Sales. **Special programs:** Internships. **Other U.S. locations:** Olathe KS; Hudson NH. **International locations:** Germany. **Parent company:** Dover Corporation. **Listed on:** New York Stock Exchange. **Stock exchange symbol:** DOV. **Number of employees at this location:** 250.

VISHAY INTERTECHNOLOGY, INC.
10 Melville Park Road, Melville NY 11747-3113. 631/847-3000. **Contact:** Human Resources. **World Wide Web address:** http://www.vishay.com. **Description:** Manufactures transistors, transient voltage suppressors, diodes, and rectifiers. **Listed on:** New York Stock Exchange. **Stock exchange symbol:** VSH.

XEROX CORPORATION
P.O. Box 1600, Stamford CT 06904. 203/968-3000. **Physical address:** 800 Long Ridge Road, Stamford CT 06904. **Contact:** Human Resources. **World Wide Web address:** http://www.xerox.com. **Description:** Develops, manufactures, markets, services, and finances information processing products

including copiers, duplicators, scanners, electronic printing systems, word processing systems, personal computers, and computer peripherals. Xerox does business in over 120 countries. Founded in 1906. **Positions advertised include:** Account Executive. **Corporate headquarters location:** This location. **Other U.S. locations:** Nationwide. **Listed on:** New York Stock Exchange. **Stock exchange symbol:** XRX. **Number of employees nationwide:** 90,000.

ENVIRONMENTAL & WASTE MANAGEMENT SERVICES

**You can expect to find the following types of companies
in this section:**
Environmental Engineering Firms • Sanitary Services

ATC ASSOCIATES INC.
104 East 25th Street, 10th Floor, New York NY 10010-2917. 212/353-8280. **Fax:**
212/353-8306. **E-mail address:** atcjobs@atc-enviro.com. **Contact:** Human
Resources. **World Wide Web address:** http://www.atc-enviro.com. **Description:**
An environmental consulting firm operating 65 offices in the U.S. providing
asbestos, lead, water, and soil testing. Founded in 1985. **Positions advertised
include:** Project Manager. **Corporate headquarters location:** Woburn MA.
Other locations: Nationwide. **Number of employees nationwide:** 1,800.

ARCADIS G&M, INC.
88 Duryea Road, Melville NY 11747. 631/249-7600. **Contact:** Human
Resources. **World Wide Web address:** http://www.arcadis-us.com.
Description: A consulting firm that provides environmental and engineering
services. The company focuses on the environmental, building, and infrastructure
markets. Founded in 1888. **NOTE:** Interested jobseekers are encouraged to
apply online. **Positions advertised include:** Engineering Technician. **Special
programs:** Internships. **Corporate headquarters location:** Arnhem,
Netherlands. **Other U.S. locations:** Nationwide. **Listed on:** NASDAQ. **Stock
exchange symbol:** ARCAF. **Annual sales/revenues:** $502 million. **Number of
employees worldwide:** 8,000.

BROOKS LABORATORIES
9 Isaac Street, Norwalk CT 06850. 203/853-9792. **Contact:** Human Resources.
World Wide Web address: http://www.brookslabs.com. **Description:** An
environmental consulting firm and laboratory engaged in water testing, lead
inspection, and air quality testing. **Positions advertised include:** Chemist.

CLEAN HARBORS, INC.
3 Sutton Place, Edison NJ 08817. 732/248-1997. **Toll-free phone:** 800/782-
8805. **Fax:** 732/248-4414. **Contact:** Human Resources. **World Wide Web
address:** http://www.cleanharbors.com. **Description:** Clean Harbors, Inc.,
through its subsidiaries, provides comprehensive environmental services in 35
states in the Northeast, Midwest, Central, and Mid-Atlantic regions. Clean
Harbors provides a wide range of hazardous waste management and
environmental support services to a diversified customer base from over 40
locations. The company's hazardous waste management services include
treatment, storage, recycling, transportation, risk analysis, site assessment,
laboratory analysis, site closure, and disposal of hazardous materials through
environmentally • sound methods including incineration. Environmental
remediation services include emergency response, surface remediation,
groundwater restoration, industrial maintenance, and facility decontamination.
Positions advertised include: Class B Driver; Field Technician; Class A Driver;
Field Service Foreman; Pack Chemist; Apollo Chemist. **NOTE:** See Website for
current job opportunities and contact information. **Corporate headquarters
location:** Braintree MA. **Other U.S. locations:** Nationwide. **Number of
employees nationwide:** 1,400.

COMMODORE APPLIED TECHNOLOGIES, INC.
150 East 58th Street, Suite 3238, New York NY 10155-0035. 212/308-5800. **Fax:**
212/753-0731. **Contact:** Human Resources. **World Wide Web address:**

http://www.commodore.com. **Description:** Develops technologies to destroy PCBs, chemical weapons, dioxins, and pesticides. Commodore Applied Technologies also salvages and resells cross-contaminated CFCs, and acquires and cleans up environmentally distressed properties. **Corporate headquarters location:** Alexandria VA. **Subsidiaries include:** Commodore Advanced Sciences, Inc.; Commodore Separation Technologies, Inc.; Commodore Solution Technologies, Inc.; Teledyne-Commodore LLC. **Listed on:** Over The Counter. **Stock exchange symbol:** CXII. **Annual sales/revenues:** $10 million.

COVANTA ENERGY GROUP
40 Lane Road, Fairfield NJ 07007. 973/882-9000. **Contact:** Human Resources. **World Wide Web address:** http://www.covantaenergy.com. **Description:** Develops waste-to-energy facilities nationwide through its subsidiaries and provides hazardous waste disposal and recycling services. **Positions advertised include:** Auxiliary Operator; Maintenance Mechanic. **Number of employees at this location:** 310.

EARTH TECH
One World Financial Center, New York NY 10281. 212/798-8500. **Fax:** 212/798-8501. **Contact:** Human Resources. **World Wide Web address:** http://www.earthtech.com. **Description:** An engineering consulting firm specializing in water, environmental, transportation, and construction. **Parent company:** Tyco International Ltd.

GROUNDWATER AND ENVIRONMENTAL SERVICES, INC. (GES)
P.O. Box 1750, Wall NJ 07719. 732/919-0100. **Physical address:** 1340 Campus Parkway, Wall NJ 07719. **Fax:** 732/919-0916. **Contact:** Human Resources. **E-mail address:** resume@gesonline.com. **World Wide Web address:** http://www.gesonline.com. **Description:** An environmental engineering firm specializing in groundwater remediation. Founded in 1985. **Positions advertised include:** Business Developmental Manager; Geologist; Scientist; Hydrogeologist; Environmental Engineer; Project Manager; Well Driller.

HAMON RESEARCH-COTTRELL
58 East Main Street, Somerville NJ 08876. 908/685-4000. **Contact:** Human Resources. **E-mail address:** info.hcorp@hamonusa.com. **World Wide Web address:** http://www.hamon-researchcottrell.com. **Description:** An environmental treatment and services company that provides a comprehensive range of services and technologies directed at controlling air pollution; protecting the integrity of the nation's water resources; providing services in support of the management and remediation of hazardous waste; and providing services for the operations, maintenance, and management of treatment facilities. **Office hours:** Monday - Friday, 8:00 a.m. - 5:00 p.m. **Parent company:** Hamon Group.

HANDEX ENVIRONMENTAL
500 Campus Drive, Morganville NJ 07751. 732/536-8500. **Contact:** Human Resources. **World Wide Web address:** http://www.handex.com. **Description:** Provides environmental remediation and educational services including comprehensive solutions to contamination of groundwater and soil resulting from leaking underground storage tanks; petroleum distribution systems; refineries; heavy industrial plants; chemical, aerospace, and pharmaceutical facilities; airports; auto and truck fleet facilities; and related contamination sources. **Positions advertised include:** Professional Engineer; Filler Press Field Engineer; Permits Coordinator; Staff Hydrologist; General Manager.

HATCH MOTT MACDONALD, INC.
27 Bleeker Street, Millburn NJ 07041. 973/379-3400. **Toll-free phone:** 800/832-3272. **Fax:** 973/912-3354. **Contact:** Personnel. **E-mail address:** hr@hatchmott.com. **World Wide Web address:** http://www.killam.com.

Description: An infrastructure engineering, environmental, and industrial process consulting firm that serves both public and private sectors. The company operates within a wide range of areas providing architectural, environmental, outsourcing, transportation engineering, and water resource management services. Founded in 1937. **Positions advertised include:** Asbestos Inspector; Assistant Resident Engineer; Business Development Manager, Environment; Civil Engineer, Water; Civil Engineer, Environmental; Environmental Geologist; Project Manager. **Special programs:** Internships. **Internship information:** Internships are offered May through September, as well as during December and January. **Corporate headquarters location:** This location. **Other area locations:** Cape May Court House NJ; Freehold NJ; Hackensack NJ; Randolph NJ; Toms River NJ; Whitehouse NJ. **Other U.S. locations:** Nationwide. **Subsidiaries include:** BAC Killam, Inc.; Carlan Killam Consulting Group, Inc.; E3-Killam, Inc.; Killam Associates - New England; Killam Management & Operational Services, Inc.

HUDSON TECHNOLOGIES, INC.
275 North Middletown Road, Pearl River NY 10965. 845/735-6000. **Fax:** 845/512-6070. **Contact:** Michele Chazen, Human Resources Manager. **World Wide Web address:** http://www.hudsontech.com. **Description:** Hudson provides services for the recovery and reclamation of refrigerants in response to the requirements of the United States Clean Air Act from 13 locations. The company's services consist of removing used refrigerants from air conditioning and refrigeration systems and transferring them into cylinders for collection. Hudson's reclamation services consist of cleaning used refrigerants to remove impurities and contaminants and returning them to their original purity standards. Founded in 1991. **Corporate headquarters location:** This location. **Other locations:** Nationwide. **Listed on:** NASDAQ. **Stock exchange symbol:** HDSN. **Chairman/CEO:** Kevin J. Zugibe. **Annual sales/revenues:** $20 million. **Number of employees:** 102.

MIDCO RESIDENTIAL SERVICES
11 Harmich Road, South Plainfield NJ 07080. 908/561-8380. **Contact:** Human Resources. **Description:** Provides integrated solid waste management services to residential customers concentrated in the Midwestern and mid-South regions of the United States and in Costa Rica.

MORETRENCH AMERICAN CORPORATION
P.O. Box 316, 100 Stickle Avenue, Rockaway NJ 07866. 973/627-2100. **Fax:** 973/627-3950. **Contact:** Personnel. **E-mail address:** lobrzut@mtac.com. **NOTE:** E-mail resume for current information about positions available. **World Wide Web address:** http://www.moretrench.com. **Description:** A nationwide engineering and contracting firm specializing in groundwater control and hazardous waste removal. **Corporate headquarters location:** This location.

RECOVERY TECHNOLOGIES GROUP
7000 Boulevard East, Guttenberg NJ 07093. 201/854-7777. **Fax:** 201/854-1771. **Contact:** Office Manager. **E-mail address:** contactus@rtginc.com. **World Wide Web address:** http://www.rtginc.com. **Description:** Develops and owns waste-to-energy facilities that provide a means of disposal of nonhazardous municipal solid waste. **Corporate headquarters location:** This location.

FABRICATED METAL PRODUCTS AND PRIMARY METALS

You can expect to find the following types of companies in this section:
Aluminum and Copper Foundries • Die-Castings • Iron and Steel Foundries • Steel Works, Blast Furnaces, and Rolling Mills

ALPHA METALS, INC.
600 Route 440, Jersey City NJ 07304. 201/434-6778. **Fax:** 201/434-7508. **Contact:** Human Resources. **World Wide Web address:** http://www.alphametals.com. **Description:** Manufactures specialized alloys, chemicals, and instrumentation for soldering applications used by electronics OEMs throughout the world. The company's consumer division manufactures solders for plumbing and hobbyists. **Positions advertised include:** Human Resources Coordinator; Operations Coordinator.

ATLANTIC METAL PRODUCTS, INC.
21 Fadem Road, Springfield NJ 07081. 973/379-6200. **Contact:** Personnel. **World Wide Web address:** http://www.atlanticmetal.com. **Description:** Manufactures custom precision sheet metal parts for the computer and office equipment industries. **Corporate headquarters location:** This location. **Other U.S. locations:** Hillside NJ.

DAYTON T. BROWN INC.
1175 Church Street, Bohemia NY 11716. 631/589-6300. **Toll-free phone:** 800/232-6300. **Fax:** 631/589-0046. **Contact:** Angela Chewening, Human Resources Representative. **World Wide Web address:** http://www.daytontbrown.com. **Description:** Engaged in sheet metal fabrication. Dayton T. Brown also offers engineering and testing services for industrial and commercial companies. **Positions advertised include:** Senior Business Development Manager; Metallurgical Technician; Electromagnetic Interference/Electromagnetic Compatibility Technician; Production Manager. **Corporate headquarters location:** This location.

HUGO NEU SCHNITZER EAST
One Jersey Avenue, Jersey City NJ 07302. 201/333-4300. **Contact:** Barney Marsh-Gessner, Personnel Manager. **E-mail address:** humanresources@hugoneu.com. **World Wide Web address:** http://www.hugoneu.com. **Description:** A metals recycling firm, engaged primarily in the purchase, sale, and export of scrap metal. **Corporate headquarters location:** This location.

KNOX ENTERPRISES
33 Riverside Avenue, 5th Floor, Westport CT 06880. 203/226-6288. **Contact:** Human Resources. **World Wide Web address:** http://www.knoxandco.com. **Description:** A holding company. **Corporate headquarters location:** This location. **Subsidiaries include:** Jackburn Manufacturing, Inc. (PA) manufactures fabricated steel parts; Setterstix Corporation (DE) manufactures rolled paper products for the confectionery and health care industries. **Number of employees nationwide:** 145.

METEX CORPORATION
970 New Durham Road, Edison NJ 08817. 732/287-0800. **Fax:** 732/248-8739. **Contact:** Human Resources. **E-mail address:** hr@metexcorp.com. **World Wide**

Web address: http://www.metexcorp.com. **Description:** Manufactures and sells knitted wire mesh and products made from these materials. The company designs and manufactures knitted wire products and components through its Technical Products Division. Products are used in applications that include adverse environment protective materials used primarily as high-temperature gaskets; seals; shock and vibration isolators; noise reduction elements and shrouds; and phase separation devices used as air, liquid, and solid filtering devices. Metex is also an OEM for the automobile industry, supplying automobile manufacturers with exhaust seals and components for use in exhaust emission control devices. **Positions advertised include:** Sales Manager. **NOTE:** Search and apply for jobs directly online. **Corporate headquarters location:** Great Neck NJ. **Parent company:** United Capital Corporation. **Operations at this facility include:** Administration; Manufacturing; Research and Development; Sales. **Number of employees at this location:** 380.

NIAGARA CORPORATION
667 Madison Avenue, 11th Floor, New York NY 10021. 212/317-1000. **Contact:** Human Resources. **Description:** Manufactures, processes, and distributes cold drawn steel bars. Niagara Corporation sells its products primarily to steel service centers in the United States and Canada. Founded in 1993. **Corporate headquarters location:** This location. **Subsidiaries include:** LaSalle Steel Company (Griffith IN; Hammond IN); Niagara LaSalle Corporation (Buffalo NY, Chattanooga TN, Midlothian TX). **Listed on:** NASDAQ. **Stock exchange symbol:** NIAG. **President/CEO:** Michael J. Scharf. **Sales/revenue:** Approximately $200 million. **Number of employees nationwide:** 1,125.

STURM, RUGER & COMPANY INC.
One Lacey Place, Southport CT 06890. 203/259-7843. **Contact:** Human Resources Department. **World Wide Web address:** http://www.ruger-firearms.com. **Description:** Designs, manufactures, and sells pistols, revolvers, rifles, and shotguns for a variety of sporting purposes. The company also manufactures and markets various models of police revolvers, pistols, rifles, and selective firearms for law enforcement agencies and military establishments. **Corporate headquarters location:** This location. **Subsidiaries include:** Pine Tree Castings (Newport NH) produces both chrome and stainless ferrous investment castings; Ruger Investment Casting (Prescott AZ) produces aluminum, ferrous, and titanium commercial investment castings as well as components for the company's firearm production; Uni-Cast (Manchester NH) produces a wide variety of complex parts primarily for defense-related products.

TIFFEN COMPANY
90 Oser Avenue, Hauppauge NY 11788-3886. 631/273-2500. **Fax:** 631/273-2557. **Contact:** Human Resources. **World Wide Web address:** http://www.tiffen.com. **Description:** Engaged in sheet metal fabrication used to manufacture photographic-related products and accessories.

TINNERMAN PALNUT ENGINEERED PRODUCTS
152 Glen Road, Mountainside NJ 07092. 908/233-3300. **Fax:** 908/233-6566. **Contact:** Human Resources Manager. **E-mail address:** careers@tinnermanpalnut.com. **World Wide Web address:** http://www.palnut.com. **Description:** Manufactures light- and heavy-duty single and multithread specialty fasteners. **Positions advertised include:** Sales Engineer; Manufacturing Engineer; Global Sourcing Analyst; Product Engineer. **Corporate headquarters location:** Brunswick OH.

U.S. CAN COMPANY
669 River Drive, Suite 340, Elmwood Park NJ 07407. 201/794-4441. **Contact:** Human Resources. **World Wide Web address:** http://www.uscanco.com. **Description:** Manufactures a wide range of steel container products. Principal

clients include paint and ink manufacturers. **Corporate headquarters location:** Oak Brook IL. **Operations at this facility include:** Manufacturing.

FINANCIAL SERVICES

**You can expect to find the following types of companies
in this section:**
Consumer Financing and Credit Agencies • Investment Specialists • Mortgage
Bankers and Loan Brokers • Security and Commodity Brokers, Dealers, and
Exchanges

ALLIANCE CAPITAL MANAGEMENT L.P.
1345 Avenue of the Americas, New York NY 10105. 212/969-1000. **Fax:** 212/969-2229. **Contact:** Human Resources. **World Wide Web address:** http://www.alliancecapital.com. **Description:** Alliance Capital Management manages mutual funds for corporations and individual investors operating 36 offices in 19 countries. **Positions advertised include:** Fixed Income Software Developer; Applications Support Specialist. **Corporate headquarters location:** This location. **Other locations:** Worldwide. **Chairman/CEO:** Bruce W. Calvert. **Annual sales/revenues:** $2.75 billion. **Number of employees worldwide:** 4,200.

AMBAC FINANCIAL GROUP INC.
One State Street Plaza, 15th Floor, New York NY 10004. 212/668-0340. **Fax:** 212/509-9190. **Contact:** Gregg Bienstock, Human Resources. **World Wide Web address:** http://www.ambac.com. **Description:** AMBAC Inc. is a holding company that provides, through its affiliates, financial guarantee insurance, financial services, and health care information services to both public and private clients worldwide. **Positions advertised include:** Underwriter; Financial Services Specialist; Legal Counselor; Risk Management Associate; Investment Manager; Operations Manager; Internal Auditor; Information Technology Specialist. **Corporate headquarters location:** This location. **Other locations:** London, England; Tokyo, Japan; Sydney, Australia. **Subsidiaries include:** Ambac Assurance; Cadre Financial; Ambac Indemnity Corporation, a leading financial guarantee insurance company; Ambac Capital Management, Inc., a provider of municipal investment contracts; Ambac Financial Services, L.P., a provider of interest rate swaps to municipalities; HCIA Inc., a health care information company. **Listed on:** New York Stock Exchange. **Stock exchange symbol:** ABK. **Chairman/CEO:** Phillip B. Lassiter. **Annual sales/revenues:** $740.5 million. **Number of employees:** 370.

AMERICAN EXPRESS COMPANY
822 Lexington Avenue, New York NY 10021. 212/640-2000. **Contact:** Ursula F. Fairbairn, Staffing Department. **World Wide Web address:** http://www.americanexpress.com. **Description:** American Express Company is a diversified travel and financial services company. Founded in 1850. **NOTE:** Applicants are encouraged to use the company's online Resume Builder to create a resume profile account to apply to positions as well as using the automated Job Search Agent. **Positions advertised include:** Travel Support Counselor; Senior Marketing Manager; Corp Services Operations Team Leader; Senior Risk Management Manager; Purchasing/Training Manager; Acquisition Manager; Senior Marketing Manager; Cardmember Cross-Sell Senior Manager; Account Management Representative; Contracts Manager; Treasury Manager; Interactive Education Manager; Senior Customer Information Manager; Senior Marketing Manager; Training & Syndication Manager; Special Security Agent; Senior Prospect Marketing Capabilities/Information Manager; Executive Assistant; Information & Analysis Manager; Business Development Manager; Receptionist; Senior Product Development Manager; Senior Marketing Analyst; Finance Manager; Creative Services Manager; Commodities Manager; Sales

Effectiveness Manager; Business Planning & Financial Analysis Manager; Administrative Assistant; Customer Information Manager; New Industry Development Vice President; Interactive Marketing Manager; Assistant Style Editor. **Corporate headquarters location:** This location. **Other U.S. locations:** Nationwide. **International locations:** Worldwide. **Subsidiaries include:** American Express Publishing Corporation; American Express Sharepeople; American Express Tax and Business Services Inc.; American Express Travel Related Services offers consumers the Personal, Gold, and Platinum Cards, as well as revolving credit products such as Optima Cards, which allow customers to extend payments. Other products include the American Express Corporate Card, which helps businesses manage their travel and entertainment expenditures; and the Corporate Purchasing Card, which helps businesses manage their expenditures on supplies, equipment, and services. American Express Travel Related Services also offers American Express Traveler's Cheques and travel services including trip planning, reservations, ticketing, and management information. American Express Financial Advisors provides a variety of financial products and services to help individuals, businesses, and institutions meet their financial goals. American Express Financial Advisors has a staff of more than 8,000 in the United States and offers products and services that include financial planning; annuities; mutual funds; insurance; investment certificates; and institutional investment advisory trust, tax preparation, and retail securities brokerage services. **Listed on:** New York Stock Exchange. **Stock exchange symbol:** AXP. **Chairman/CEO:** Kenneth I. Chenault. **Annual sales/revenues:** $24 billion. **Number of employees at this location:** 5,000. **Number of employees nationwide:** 84,400.

AMERICAN STOCK EXCHANGE LLC
86 Trinity Place, New York NY 10006. 212/306-1215. **Fax:** 212/306-1218. **Contact:** Catherine M. Casey, Senior Vice President of Human Resources. **E-mail address:** career@amex.com. **World Wide Web address:** http://www.amex.com. **Description:** One of the nation's largest stock exchanges, the American Stock Exchange is one of the only primary marketplaces for both stocks and derivative securities. The American Stock Exchange also handles surveillance, legal, and regulatory functions that are related to the stock exchange. **NOTE:** Human Resources phone: 212/306-1239. **Positions advertised include:** Assistant General Counsel; Chief Sales Officer; Business Strategy and Equity Order Flow Vice President; Exchange Traded Funds Analyst; Exchange Traded Funds Marketing Specialist; Building Operations Manager; Compliance Analyst; Financial Analyst; Public Relations Specialist. **Special programs:** Internships. **Parent company:** NASD (District of Columbia). **Chairman/CEO:** Salvatore F. Sodano. **Annual sales/revenues:** $287 million. **Number of employees at this location:** 700.

ATALANTA SOSNOFF CAPITAL CORPORATIOn
101 Park Avenue, 6th Floor, New York NY 10178-0002. 212/867-5000. **Fax:** 212/922-1820. **Contact:** Human Resources Director. **E-mail address:** ksk@atalantasosnoff.com. **World Wide Web address:** http://www.atalantasosnoff.com. **Description:** Atalanta Sosnoff Capital Corporation providfes discretionary investment management and brokerage services. **Corporate headquarters location:** This location. **Other locations:** Cardiff CA. **Listed on:** New York Stock Exchange. **Stock exchange symbol:** ATL. **Chairman/CEO:** Martin T. Sosnoff. **Annual sales/revenues:** $15.4 million. **Number of employees:** 46.

BEAR, STEARNS & COMPANY, INC.
115 South Jefferson Road, Whippany NJ 07981. 973/793-2600. **Fax:** 973/793-2040. **Contact:** Managing Director of Personnel. **World Wide Web address:** http://www.bearstearns.com. **Description:** An investment banking, securities trading, and brokerage firm engaged in corporate finance, mergers, and

acquisitions; institutional equities and fixed income sales and trading; individual investor services; asset management; and correspondent clearing. **Corporate headquarters location:** New York NY. **Parent company:** The Bear Stearns Companies Inc. is a leading worldwide investment banking, securities trading, and brokerage firm. **Listed on:** New York Stock Exchange. **Stock exchange symbol:** BSC.

BEAR, STEARNS & COMPANY, INC.
THE BEAR STEARNS COMPANIES INC.
383 Madison Avenue, 30th Floor, New York NY 10179. 212/272-2000. **Fax:** 2212/272-4785. **Contact:** Human Resources. **World Wide Web address:** http://www.bearstearns.com. **Description:** A leading worldwide investment banking, securities trading, and brokerage firm. **NOTE:** The company does not accept hard copy resumes and requests that resumes be submitted online via the company Website. **Corporate headquarters location:** This location. **Other U.S. locations:** Nationwide. **International locations:** Worldwide. **Subsidiaries include:** Bear, Stearns & Company, Inc. is an investment banking and brokerage firm; Bear, Stearns Securities Corporation provides professional and correspondent clearing services including securities lending; Custodial Trust Company provides master trust, custody, and government securities services; Bear Sterns Asset Management Inc. provides financial management services; Global Clearing Services. **Listed on:** New York Stock Exchange. **Stock exchange symbol:** BSC. **Chairman/CEO:** James E. Cayne. **Annual sales/revenues:** $6.9 billion. **Number of employees nationwide:** 10,600.

SANFORD C. BERNSTEIN & CO., LLC
dba BERNSTEIN INVESTMENT RESEARCH & MANAGEMENT
1345 Avenue of the Americas, New York NY 10105. 212/486-5800. **Fax:** 212/756-4455. **Contact:** Human Resources. **E-mail address:** resumes@bernstein.com. **World Wide Web address:** http://www.bernstein.com. **Description:** An investment management research company that conducts research on specific companies and provides investment-banking services for both private and institutional clients. **Positions advertised include:** Financial Advisor. **Corporate headquarters location:** This location. **Other U.S. locations:** Nationwide. **Parent company:** Alliance Capital Management L.P. (also at this location).

BROWN BROTHERS HARRIMAN & COMPANY
140 Broadway, New York NY 10005. 212/483-1818. **Fax:** 212/493-8545. **Contact:** Human Resources. **E-mail address:** jobs@bbh.com. **World Wide Web address:** http://www.bbh.com. **Description:** Operating some 40 partnerships and 16 offices in seven countries worldwide, the company provides commercial banking, brokerage, and investment advisory services. Founded in 1818. **Positions advertised include:** Human Resources Assistant; Domestic Banking Officer; Event Planner; Operations Specialist; Relationship Manager. **Corporate headquarters location:** This location. **Other locations:** Boston MA; Jersey City NJ; Palm Beach FL. **Number of employees:** 3,000.

CIT GROUP, INC.
650 CIT Drive, Livingston NJ 07039. 973/740-5000. **Contact:** Personnel Officer. **World Wide Web address:** http://www.citgroup.com. **Description:** A diversified financial services organization that provides flexible funding alternatives, secured business lending, and financial advisory services for corporations, manufacturers, and dealers. Founded in 1908. **Positions advertised include:** Asset Management Specialist; Regional Account Manager; Document Administrator; AVP Financial Systems; Executive Assistant; Internal Audit Manager; Risk Management Vice President; Information Security Specialist; Executive Secretary; Night Shift Operator; Manager; Tax Manager; Underwriter; Accounting Manager; Network Analyst; Information Security Specialist.

Corporate headquarters location: New York NY. **Other U.S. locations:** Nationwide. **International locations:** Worldwide. **Number of employees nationwide:** 2,500.

CIT GROUP, INC.
1211 Avenue of the Americas, 12th Floor, New York NY 10036. 212/382-7000. **Contact:** Human Resources. **World Wide Web address:** http://www.citgroup.com. **Description:** This division provides factoring services to a wide range of customers as a subsidiary of CIT Financial Services. Overall, CIT Group is a diversified financial services organization providing flexible funding alternatives, secured business lending, and financial advisory services for corporations, manufacturers, and dealers. Founded in 1908. **Positions advertised include:** Executive Assistant; Verification Examiner; Collateral Analyst Supervisor; Contracts Associate; Field Examiner; Underwriter; Credit Officer; Attorney; District Sales Manager. **Corporate headquarters location:** This location. **Other locations:** Worldwide. **Subsidiaries include:** Capital Finance; CIT Commercial Finance Group; CIT Equipment Financing; CIT Specialty Finance Group; CIT Structured Finance. **Listed on:** New York Stock Exchange. **Stock exchange symbol:** CIT. **Annual sales/revenues:** $3.5 billion. **Number of employees nationwide:** 2,500.

CAMERON ASSOCIATES
640 Fifth Avenue, 15th Floor, New York NY 10019. 212/245-8800. **Contact:** Human Resources. **E-mail address:** careers@cameronassociates.com. **World Wide Web address:** http://www.cameronassociates.com. **Description:** An investor relations firm providing financial services for public companies. Cameron Associates also offers corporate communications services. **Corporate headquarters location:** Toronto, Canada.

CANTOR FITZGERALD SECURITIES CORPORATION
135 East 57th Street, New York NY 10022. 212/938-5000. **Contact:** Human Resources Department. **World Wide Web address:** http://www.cantor.com. **Description:** An institutional brokerage firm dealing in fixed income securities, equities, derivatives, options, eurobonds, and emerging markets. Founded in 1945. **NOTE:** You may see the website for the appropriate web address for forward resumes. **Positions advertised include:** Computer Programmer. **Special programs:** Summer Internships (you may e-mail internshipopportunities@cantor.com). **Corporate headquarters location:** This location. **Other U.S. locations:** Los Angeles CA; Chicago IL; Boston MA; Dallas TX. **International locations:** Germany; China; England; Italy; France; Japan.

CITIGROUP INC.
399 Park Avenue, New York NY 10043. 212/559-1000. **Fax:** 212/793-3946. **Contact:** Human Resources. **World Wide Web address:** http://www.citigroup.com. **Description:** A holding company offering a wide range of financial services through its subsidiaries. **Positions advertised include:** Financial Analyst; Data Privacy/Information Security Specialist; Administrative Assistant; Data Analyst; Area Sales Manager; GI Analyst & Liaison; Event Planner; Senior Reviewer; Senior Contract Recruiter. **Corporate headquarters location:** This location. **Subsidiaries include:** Citibank; CitiFinancial; Global Corporate & Investment Banking; Primerica Financial Services; Salomon Smith Barney; SSB Citi Asset Management Group; Travelers Life & Annuity; Travelers Property Casualty Corp. **Listed on:** New York Stock Exchange. **Stock exchange symbol:** C. **Chairman/CEO:** Sanford (Sandy) I. Weill. **Annual sales/revenues:** $92.6 billion. **Number of employees:** 255,000.

CREDIT SUISSE FIRST BOSTON CORPORATION
11 Madison Avenue, New York NY 10010-3629. 212/325-2000. **Fax:** 212/325-6665. **Contact:** Recruiting. **World Wide Web address:** http://www.csfb.com.

Description: A diversified financial services firm serving as underwriters, distributors, and investment dealers. **NOTE:** Apply online. **Corporate headquarters location:** This location. **International locations:** Switzerland; United Kingdom. **Parent company:** Credit Suisse Group (Zurich, Switzerland). **Subsidiaries include:** Credit Suisse First Boston (USA), Inc.; Imagyn Medical Technologies, Inc.; Sprout Group. **CEO:** John J. Mack. **Annual sales/revenues:** $13.7 billion. **Number of employees:** 28,415.

CROWN FINANCIAL GROUP
525 Washington Boulevard, P.O. Box 260, Jersey City NJ 07310. 201/459-9500. **Toll-free phone:** 800/888-8118. **Fax:** 201/459-9545. **Contact:** Human Resources. **World Wide Web address:** http://www.crownfin.com. **Description:** Markets and trades approximately 7,300 securities. The company is also an active underwriter of small and mid-sized capitalization debt and equity services.

DEUTSCHE BANK AG
31 West 52nd Street, New York NY 10019. 212/250-2500. **Contact:** Human Resources. **World Wide Web address:** http://www.deutsche-bank.com. **Description:** A merchant investment bank. Deutsche Bank also manages index funds. **Corporate headquarters location:** Frankfurt, Germany. **Subsidiaries include:** DWS Group; Deutsche Bank, S.A.E.; Deutsche Financial Services Corporation; BPT Limited; Coral Eurobet plc; Deutsche Banc Alex, Brown Incorporated; The Laurel Pub Company Limited; Piaggio SpA; RREEF; Taunus Corporation. **Listed on:** New York Stock Exchange. **Stock exchange symbol:** DB. **Annual sales/revenues:** $66.5 billion. **Number of employees:** 95,000.

THE DREYFUS CORPORATION
200 Park Avenue, 7th Floor, New York NY 10166. 212/922-6000. **Fax:** 212/922-7533. **Contact:** Human Resources. **World Wide Web address:** http://www.dreyfus.com. **Description:** A nationwide investment corporation managing over 150 mutual funds. **NOTE:** Entry-level positions are offered. **Positions advertised include:** Associate Financial Analyst; Human Resources Consultant; Regional Wholesaler; Secretary; Fund Wholesaler; Broker-Dealer Channel Wholesaler; Financial Advisor Channel Wholesaler; Portfolio Assistant; Risk Manager and Compliance Team Leader; Executive Secretary; Financial Consultant; Mellon Business Advisor. **Corporate headquarters location:** This location. **Parent company:** Mellon Financial Corporation (Pittsburgh PA).

FIDUCIARY TRUST INTERNATIONAL
600 Fifth Avenue, New York NY 10020. 212/632-3000. **Contact:** Human Resources. **World Wide Web address:** http://www.ftci.com. **Description:** Provides global investment management and custody services for institutional and individual clients with offices in 35 countries. **Positions advertised include:** Human Resources Analyst; Marketing Administrative Assistant; Credit Research Analyst; Legal Administrative Assistant; Futures Associate; Fixed Income Portfolio Analyst. **Parent company:** Franklin Templeton Investments. **Number of employees:** 6,800.

FINANCIAL FEDERAL CORPORATION
733 Third Avenue, 7th Floor, New York NY 10017. 212/599-8000. **Fax:** 212/286-5885. **Contact:** Human Resources Department. **World Wide Web address:** http://www.financialfederal.com. **Description:** Provides financing of leases and capital loans on industrial, commercial, and professional equipment to middle market customers in a variety of industries. Founded in 1989. **Corporate headquarters location:** This location. **Other U.S. locations:** Irvine CA; Lisle IL; Charlotte NC; Teaneck NJ; Houston TX. **Listed on:** New York Stock Exchange. **Stock exchange symbol:** FIF. **Chairman/President/CEO:** Paul R. Sinsheimer. **Annual sales/revenues:** $139 million. **Number of employees nationwide:** 237.

FIRST INVESTORS CORPORATION
95 Wall Street, 23rd Floor, New York NY 10005. 212/858-8000. **Fax:** 212/858-8003. **Contact:** Human Resources. **E-mail address:** hr@firstinvestors.com. **World Wide Web address:** http://www.firstinvestors.com. **Description:** Specializes in the distribution and management of investment programs for individuals and corporations, as well as retirement plans. First Investors operates nationwide and through several area locations in Westchester County, New Jersey, and Long Island. Founded in 1930. **Corporate headquarters location:** This location. **Other locations:** Nationwide. **Subsidiaries include:** First Investors Life Insurance Company; First Investors Federal Savings Bank; First Investors Management Company, Inc.; Administrative Data Management Corp.; SMART Tuition Management Services. **Number of employees:** 1,000.

FIRST MONTAUK FINANCIAL CORPORATION
328 Newman Springs Road, Red Bank NJ 07701. 732/842-4700. **Contact:** Human Resources. **World Wide Web address:** http://www.firstmontauk.com. **Description:** A diversified holding company that provides financial services throughout the United States to individuals, corporations, and institutions. **Subsidiaries include:** First Montauk Securities Corporation is a securities broker/dealer with a nationwide network of more than 300 registered representatives in 90 branch offices serving approximately 25,000 retail and institutional clients. Montauk Insurance Services, Inc. is an insurance agency.

GE CAPITAL CORPORATION
260 Long Ridge Road, Stamford CT 06927. 203/357-4000. **Contact:** Human Resources. **World Wide Web address:** http://www.gecapital.com. **Description:** GE Capital Corporation is one of the largest leasing companies in the United States and Canada, providing financing and related management services to corporate clients through 27 divisions. **NOTE:** Fill out online application at www.gecareers.com. **Corporate headquarters location:** This location. **Parent company:** General Electric Company operates in the following areas: aircraft engines (jet engines, replacement parts, and repair services for commercial, military, executive, and commuter aircraft); appliances; broadcasting (NBC); industrial (lighting products, electrical distribution and control equipment, transportation systems products, electric motors and related products, a broad range of electrical and electronic industrial automation products, and a network of electrical supply houses); materials (plastics, ABS resins, silicones, superabrasives, and laminates); power systems (products for the generation, transmission, and distribution of electricity); technical products and systems (medical systems and equipment, as well as a full range of computer-based information and data interchange services for both internal use and external commercial and industrial customers); and capital services (consumer services, financing, and specialty insurance.)

GILMAN & CIOCIA INC.
1311 Mamaroneck Avenue, Suite 160, White Plains NY 10605. 914/397-4829. **Fax:** 914/997-5461. **Contact:** Victoria O'Hara, Human Resources Director. **E-mail address:** resumes@gilcio.com. **World Wide Web address:** http://www.gilcio.com. **Description:** Provides income tax and financial planning services including insurance, investments, pensions, and estate planning. **Positions advertised include:** Tax Preparer; Financial Planner; Receptionist. **Corporate headquarters location:** This location. **Listed on:** Over The Counter. **Stock exchange symbol:** GTAX. **Chairman:** James Ciocia. **Annual sales/revenues:** $ 106.5 million. **Number of employees:** 819.

GOLDMAN SACHS & COMPANY
85 Broad Street, New York NY 10004. 212/902-1000. **Contact:** Recruiting Department. **World Wide Web address:** http://www.gs.com. **Description:** An investment banking firm. **NOTE:** Interested jobseekers should send resumes to

180 Maiden Lane, 23rd Floor, New York NY 10038. **Corporate headquarters location:** This location. **Other U.S. locations:** Nationwide. **International locations:** Worldwide.

J.B. HANAUER & COMPANY
4 Gatehall Drive, Parsippany NJ 07054. 973/829-1000. **Toll-free phone:** 800/631-1094. **Fax:** 973/829-0565. **Contact:** Human Resources. **World Wide Web address:** http://www.jbh.com. **Description:** A full-service brokerage firm specializing in fixed-income investments. J.B. Hanauer & Company provides a broad range of financial products and services. Founded in 1931. **NOTE:** Entry-level positions are offered. **Special programs:** Internships; Training. **Corporate headquarters location:** This location. **Other U.S. locations:** North Miami FL; Tampa FL; West Palm Beach FL; Princeton NJ; Rye Brook NY; Philadelphia PA. **Listed on:** Privately held. **Annual sales/revenues:** More than $100 million. **Number of employees at this location:** 250. **Number of employees worldwide:** 600.

ING AMERICAS
1325 Avenue of the Americas, New York NY 10019. 646/424-6000. **Contact:** Human Resources. **World Wide Web address:** http://www.ing.com. **Description:** A financial services company offering comprehensive financial products and services including life insurance; fixed and variable annuities; defined contribution retirement plans; and mutual funds as well as other investment and banking services. **Positions advertised include:** Internal Wholesaler. **Corporate headquarters location:** Atlanta GA. **Parent company:** ING Groep (Amsterdam, The Netherlands). **Operations at this facility:** ING U.S. Financial Services. **Number of employees:** 30,000.

INVESTEC ERNST & COMPANY
One Battery Park Plaza, 2nd Floor, New York NY 10004. 212/898-6200. **Contact:** Human Resources. **E-mail address:** info@investec.com. **World Wide Web address:** http://www.investec.com. **Description:** A securities brokerage firm. Investec Ernst & Company is one of the largest financial clearinghouses in New York City, with over 80 correspondents. **NOTE:** Human Resources phone: 212/898-6450. **Corporate headquarters location:** This location. **Other locations:** Chicago IL; New York NY; Rhinebeck NY; Stamford CT; Woodbury NY.

J.P. MORGAN CHASE & COMPANY
270 Park Avenue, New York NY 10017. 212/270-6000. **Fax:** 212/270-2613. **Contact:** John J. Farrell Jr., VP of Human Resources. **World Wide Web address:** http://www.jpmorganchase.com. **Description:** Specializes in global financial services and retail banking. The company's consumer services include credit card; diversified consumer lending; mortgages and home finance; automobile loans; private banking; and asset management services. The bank offers commercial banking services for middle market companies and small business banking. The company is also engaged in global markets; investment banking operations; mergers and acquisition consulting, risk management; treasury and securities services and debt underwriting. **Positions advertised include:** Personal Financial Advisor; Client Associate; Teller; Client Service Delivery Manager; Personal Financial Services Banker; Consumer Banker; Small Business Relationship Manager; Researcher; Programmer; Group Product Manager Vice President; Home Equity Retention Vice President; Credit & Rate Markets Vice President; Credit Portfolio Group Vice President; Senior Product Manager; CFS Enterprise eCommerce Architect; Risk Manager; Junior Structure and Documentation Counsel; Client Associate Manager. **Corporate headquarters location:** This location. **Other locations:** Worldwide. **Subsidiaries include:** J.P. Morgan Private Bank; J.P. Morgan Fleming Asset Management; American Century; Brown & Company Securities Corp.; J.P.

Morgan H&Q; J.P. Morgan Partners; Chase. **Listed on:** New York Stock Exchange. **Stock exchange symbol:** JPM. **Chairman/CEO:** William B. Harrison Jr. **Annual sales/revenues:** $43.4 billion. **Number of employees:** 94,335.

J.P. MORGAN CHASE & COMPANY
60 Wall Street, New York NY 10005. 212/483-2323. **Contact:** John J. Farrell Jr., VP of Human Resources. **World Wide Web address:** http://www.jpmorganchase.com. **Description:** Specializes in global financial services and retail banking. The company's consumer services include credit card; diversified consumer lending; mortgages and home finance; automobile loans; private banking; and asset management services. The bank offers commercial banking services for middle market companies and small business banking. The company is also engaged in global markets; investment banking operations; mergers and acquisition consulting, risk management; treasury and securities services and debt underwriting. **Positions advertised include:** Personal Financial Advisor; Client Associate; Teller; Client Service Delivery Manager; Personal Financial Services Banker; Consumer Banker; Small Business Relationship Manager; Researcher; Programmer; Group Product Manager Vice President; Home Equity Retention Vice President; Credit & Rate Markets Vice President; Credit Portfolio Group Vice President; Senior Product Manager; CFS Enterprise eCommerce Architect; Risk Manager; Junior Structure and Documentation Counsel; Client Associate Manager. **Corporate headquarters location:** New York NY. **Other locations:** Worldwide. **Subsidiaries include:** J.P. Morgan Private Bank; J.P. Morgan Fleming Asset Management; American Century; Brown & Company Securities Corp.; J.P. Morgan H&Q; J.P. Morgan Partners; Chase. **Listed on:** New York Stock Exchange. **Stock exchange symbol:** JPM. **Chairman/CEO:** William B. Harrison Jr. **Annual sales/revenues:** $43.4 billion. **Number of employees:** 94,335.

J.P. MORGAN CHASE & COMPANY
2 Chase Manhattan Plaza, New York NY 10081-6500. 212/270-6000. **Contact:** John J. Farrell Jr., VP of Human Resources. **World Wide Web address:** http://www.jpmorganchase.com. **Description:** Specializes in global financial services and retail banking. The company's consumer services include credit card; diversified consumer lending; mortgages and home finance; automobile loans; private banking; and asset management services. The bank offers commercial banking services for middle market companies and small business banking. The company is also engaged in global markets; investment banking operations; mergers and acquisition consulting, risk management; treasury and securities services and debt underwriting. **Positions advertised include:** Personal Financial Advisor; Client Associate; Teller; Client Service Delivery Manager; Personal Financial Services Banker; Consumer Banker; Small Business Relationship Manager; Researcher; Programmer; Group Product Manager Vice President; Home Equity Retention Vice President; Credit & Rate Markets Vice President; Credit Portfolio Group Vice President; Senior Product Manager; CFS Enterprise eCommerce Architect; Risk Manager; Junior Structure and Documentation Counsel; Client Associate Manager. **Corporate headquarters location:** New York NY. **Other locations:** Worldwide. **Subsidiaries include:** J.P. Morgan Private Bank; J.P. Morgan Fleming Asset Management; American Century; Brown & Company Securities Corp.; J.P. Morgan H&Q; J.P. Morgan Partners; Chase. **Listed on:** New York Stock Exchange. **Stock exchange symbol:** JPM. **Chairman/CEO:** William B. Harrison Jr. **Annual sales/revenues:** $43.4 billion. **Number of employees:** 94,335.

J.P. MORGAN PARTNERS
1221 6th Avenue, 39th & 40th Floors, New York City NY 10020-1080. 212/899-3400. **Fax:** 212/899-3401. **Contact:** Human Resources. **World Wide Web address:** http://www.jpmorganpartners.com. **Description:** Provides equity and other financial services.

JEFFERIES & COMPANY, INC.
Metro Center, One Station Place, 3 North, Stamford CT 06902. 203/708-5800. **Contact:** Human Resources. **E-mail address:** Eastcoastrecruiting@jefco.com. **World Wide Web address:** http://www.jefco.com. **Description:** Jefferies & Company is engaged in equity, convertible debt and taxable fixed income securities brokerage and trading, and corporate finance. Jefferies is one of the leading national firms engaged in the distribution and trading of blocks of equity securities and conducts such activities primarily in the third market, which refers to transactions in listed equity securities taking place away from national securities exchanges. Founded in 1962. **Corporate headquarters location:** New York NY. **Other U.S. locations:** Nationwide. **International locations:** Worldwide. **Listed on:** New York Stock Exchange. **Stock exchange symbol:** JEF. **Number of employees worldwide:** 1,600.

JEFFERIES & COMPANY, INC.
51 JFK Parkway, 3rd Floor, Short Hills NJ 07078. 973/912-2900. **Fax:** 310/971-1066. **Contact:** See NOTE. **World Wide Web address:** http://www.jefco.com. **Description:** Engaged in equity, convertible debt and taxable fixed income securities brokerage and trading, and corporate finance. Jefferies & Company is one of the leading national firms engaged in the distribution and trading of blocks of equity securities and conducts such activities primarily in the third market, which refers to transactions in listed equity securities effected away from national securities exchanges. Founded in 1962. **NOTE:** Fax or email resumes for non-banking opportunities to Mel Locke (310/914-1066; mlocke@jefco.com), and for banking opportunities to Eastcoastrecruiting@jefco.com. **Parent company:** Jefferies Group, Inc. is a holding company which, through Jefferies & Company and its three other primary subsidiaries, Investment Technology Group, Inc., Jefferies International Limited, and Jefferies Pacific Limited, is engaged in securities brokerage and trading, corporate finance, and other financial services.

JEFFERIES GROUP, INC.
dba JEFFERIES & COMPANY, INC.
520 Madison Avenue, 12th Floor, New York NY 10022. 212/284-2300. **Fax:** 310/914-1066. **Contact:** See NOTE. **World Wide Web address:** http://www.jefco.com. **Description:** An investment banking firm providing banking, research, and merger consulting services to small and mid-sized business. Through the Jefferies & Company subsidiary the firm is engaged in equity, convertible debt, and taxable fixed income securities as well as brokering off-exchange trades for institutional investors and underwrites stock offerings specializing in high-yield junk bonds. **NOTE:** Fax or e-mail resumes for non-banking opportunities to Mel Locke (310/914-1066; mlocke@jefco.com), and for banking opportunities to Eastcoastrecruiting@jeffco.com. **Subsidiaries include:** Jefferies International Limited; Jefferies Pacific Limited; The Europe Company. Founded in 1962. **Corporate headquarters location:** This location. **Other U.S. locations:** Nationwide. **International locations:** Worldwide. **Listed on:** New York Stock Exchange. **Stock exchange symbol:** JEF. **Chairman/CEO:** Richard B. Handler. **Annual sales/revenues:** $755 million.

LEHMAN BROTHERS HOLDINGS
745 Seventh Avenue, New York NY 10019. 212/526-7000. **Contact:** Stephanie Jacobs, Recruiting. **E-mail address:** invbank.associate.us@lehman.com. **World Wide Web address:** http://www.lehman.com. **Description:** An equities trading company engaged in merchant banking and other financial services including underwriting, fixed-income products, and asset management, as well as stock trading, currency, derivatives, and commodities. **Corporate headquarters location:** This location. **Subsidiaries include:** Lehman Brothers Bank, FSB. **Chairman/CEO:** Richard (Dick) S. Fuld Jr. **Annual sales/revenues:** $17 billion. **Number of employees:** 12,343.

LOUIS DREYFUS CORPORATION
20 Westport Road, Wilton CT 06897. 203/761-2000. **Fax:** 203-761-8380. **Contact:** Human Resources. **World Wide Web address:** http://www.louisdreyfus.com. **Description:** A financial company involved in the worldwide trade of agricultural and energy-related commodities. **Special programs:** Internships. **Office hours:** Monday - Friday, 9:00 a.m. - 5:00 p.m. **Other U.S. locations:** Nationwide. **International locations:** Worldwide. **Number of employees nationwide:** 1,200. **Number of employees worldwide:** 7,000.

MERRILL LYNCH & CO., INC.
4 World Financial Center, North Tower, New York NY 10080. 212/449-1000. **Contact:** Human Resources. **World Wide Web address:** http://www.merrilllynch.com. **Description:** One of the largest securities brokerage firms in the United States, Merrill Lynch provides financial services in the following areas: securities, extensive insurance, and real estate and related services. The company also brokers commodity futures, commodity options, and corporate and municipal securities. In addition, Merrill Lynch is engaged in investment banking activities. **NOTE:** Jobseekers are asked to call or see website for specific information on where to mail resumes. **Positions advertised include:** Equity Portfolio Trader; Credit Analyst; Equity Financial Analyst; Managing Directors Administrator; Valuation and Documentation Specialist; Corporate Strategy Analyst; Market Data Project and Service Manager; Problem Management Specialist; Equity Control Group Analyst; Policies and Procedures Analyst; Senior Financial Analyst; Senior Executive Assistant; Distressed Loan Closer; Credit Policy Project Manager. **Corporate headquarters location:** This location. **Other U.S. locations:** Nationwide. **International locations:** Worldwide. **Subsidiaries include:** Merrill Lynch Investment Managers Limited. **Listed on:** New York Stock Exchange. **Stock exchange symbol:** MER. **Chairman/CEO:** Stanley (Stan) O'Neil. **Annual sales/revenues:** $28.3 billion. **Number of employees worldwide:** 50,900.

MORGAN STANLEY DEAN WITTER & COMPANY
One Pickwick Plaza, Greenwich CT 06830. 203/625-4600. **Contact:** Human Resources. **World Wide Web address:** http://www.msdw.com. **Description:** One of the largest investment banking firms in the United States. Services include financing; financial advisory services; real estate services; corporate bond services; equity services; government and money market services; merger and acquisition services; investment research services; investment management services; and individual investor services. **Corporate headquarters location:** New York NY. **Other U.S. locations:** Nationwide.

MORGAN STANLEY DEAN WITTER & COMPANY
1221 Avenue of the Americas, New York NY 10020. 212/762-7100. **Contact:** Human Resources Director. **World Wide Web address:** http://www.msdw.com. **Description:** One of the largest investment banking firms in the United States. Services include financing, financial advisory services, real estate services, corporate bond services, equity services, government and money market services, merger and acquisition services, investment research services, investment management services, and individual investor services. **NOTE:** Resumes should be sent to the corporate headquarters: Human Resources, 1585 Broadway, New York NY 10036. 212/761-4000.

MORGAN STANLEY DEAN WITTER & COMPANY
1585 Broadway, New York NY 10036. 212/761-4000. **Contact:** Human Resources. **World Wide Web address:** http://www.msdw.com. **Description:** One of the largest investment banking firms in the United States. Services include financing, financial advisory services, real estate services, corporate bond services, equity services, government and money market services, merger

and acquisition services, investment research services, investment management services, and individual investor services. **Corporate headquarters location:** This location.

NATIONAL ASSOCIATION OF SECURITIES DEALERS, INC. (NASD)
One Liberty Plaza, 165 Broadway, New York NY 10006. 212/858-4000. **Contact:** Human Resources. **E-mail address:** careers.fr@nasd.com. **World Wide Web address:** http://www.nasd.com. **Description:** The self-regulatory organization of the securities industry, overseeing the over-the-counter market. Working closely with the Securities and Exchange Commission, NASD sets the standards for over the counter securities and market makers, and provides ongoing surveillance of trading activities. NASD also provides key services for its membership and companies, particularly through its cooperative efforts with governmental and other agencies on policies and legislation that affect the investment banking and securities business. **Positions advertised include:** Legal Assistant; Human Resources Manager; Regulatory Policy and Oversight Examiner. **Special programs:** Internships. **Corporate headquarters location:** Washington DC. **Other U.S. locations:** Nationwide. **President/CEO/Chairman:** Robert Glauber. **Sales/revenue:** $1.5 billion. **Number of employees at this location:** 350. **Number of employees nationwide:** 2,500.

NEW YORK STOCK EXCHANGE
11 Wall Street, New York NY 10005. 212/656-2266. **Contact:** Ms. Dale Bernstein, Managing Director of Staffing and Training. **World Wide Web address:** http://www.nyse.com. **Description:** The principal securities trading marketplace in the United States, serving a broad range of industries within and outside of the securities industry. More than 2,500 corporations, accounting for approximately 40 percent of American corporate revenues, are listed on the exchange. The New York Stock Exchange is engaged in a wide range of public affairs and economic research programs. **Positions advertised include:** Confidential Secretary; Director of Listings and Client Service; Administrative Secretary. **Corporate headquarters location:** This location. **Number of employees at this location:** 1,550.

OPPENHEIMER
125 Broad Street, 16th Floor, New York NY 10004. 212/668-8000. **Toll-free phone:** 800/221-5588. **Contact:** Human Resources. **E-mail address:** info@opco.com. **World Wide Web address:** http://www.opco.com. **Description:** A stock brokerage firm with 89 offices nationwide serving corporate clients and individual investors. **Subsidiaries include:** Freedom Investments. **Parent company:** Fahnestock Viner Holdings Inc. (Toronto, Canada).

PARAGON CAPITAL MARKETS
7 Hanover Square, 2nd Floor, New York NY 10004. 212/742-1500. **Contact:** Human Resources. **World Wide Web address:** http://www.paragonmarkets.com. **Description:** A full-service securities brokerage firm offering a diverse range of financial products and services. Founded in 1986. **Corporate headquarters location:** This location. **Other U.S. locations:** Boca Raton FL; Boulder CO. **Operations at this facility include:** Administration; Sales; Service. **Number of employees at this location:** 100. **Number of employees nationwide:** 150.

PERSHING
One Pershing Plaza, 9th Floor, Jersey City NJ 07399. 201/413-2000. **Contact:** Personnel Department. **World Wide Web address:** http://www.pershing.com. **Description:** A securities brokerage firm. **Positions advertised include:** Brokerage Operations Associate; International Clearance Associate; International Clearance Fall Control Associate; International Clearance Trade; Processing Associate; Margin Specialist; Compliance Associate; Account Manager;

International Account Manager; Trainer; Client Services Associate; Graphic Designer; Marketing Manager; Business Analyst; Compliance Specialist. **Parent company:** Donaldson, Lufkin & Jenrette Securities Corporation.

PHIBRO INC.
500 Nyala Farms Road, Westport CT 06880. 203/221-5800. **Contact:** Human Resources. **World Wide Web address:** http://www.phibro.com. **Description:** A commodities trading group that deals with oil, gas, grain, wheat, and cocoa.

PRUDENTIAL SECURITIES INC.
199 Water Street, New York NY 10292. 212/778-1000. **Contact:** Director of Personnel. **World Wide Web address:** http://www.prudential.com. **Description:** An international securities brokerage and investment firm. The company offers clients more than 70 investment products including stocks, options, bonds, commodities, tax-favored investments, and insurance, as well as several specialized financial services. **Corporate headquarters location:** This location. **Other U.S. locations:** Nationwide. **Parent company:** Prudential Financial, Incorporated. **Listed on:** New York Stock Exchange. **Stock exchange symbol:** PRU. **President:** Michael Rice.

RYAN BECK & CO
650 Madison Avenue, 10th Floor, New York NY 10022. 212/407-0500. **Contact:** Staffing Specialist. **E-mail address:** jobs@ryanbeck.com. **World Wide Web address:** http://www.ryanbeck.com. **Description:** Having recently acquired Gruntal & Co. and The GMS Group, Ryan Beck now operates 35 offices in 12 states offering financial services in three distinct areas: capital markets, investment banking, and the private client group. Founded in 1946. **NOTE:** Jobseekers should contact the human resources department at the company's headquarters: Liz Maynor, Staffing Specialist, 220 South Orange Avenue, Livingston NJ 07039; phone: 973/597-5980; fax: 973-597-6408. **Positions advertised include:** Financial Consultant; Sales Associate; Client Services Representative; Operations Specialist; Investment Analyst; Senior Investment Banker. **Corporate headquarters location:** Livingston NJ. **Other U.S. locations:** Nationwide. **Parent company:** BankAtlantic Bancorp, Inc. (Fort Lauderdale FL). **Annual sales/revenues:** $44 million. **Number of employees:** 400.

SG COWEN SECURITIES CORPORATION
1221 Avenue of the Americas, 9th Floor, New York NY 10020. 212/278-6000. **Contact:** Human Resources. **World Wide Web address:** http://www.sgcowen.com. **Description:** An investment banking firm. **Special programs:** Training; Tuition Reimbursement Program; Summer Associate Program. **Corporate headquarters location:** This location. **Other area locations:** Albany NY. **Other U.S. locations:** Chicago IL; Boston MA; Cleveland OH; Dayton OH; Philadelphia PA; Dallas TX; Denver CO; San Francisco CA. **International locations:** Canada; France; Switzerland; United Kingdom. **Parent company:** Societe Generale Group (Paris, France). **Number of employees at this location:** 1,000. **Number of employees nationwide:** 2,300.

SALOMON SMITH BARNEY
1345 6th Avenue, New York NY 10105. 212/586-5505. **Fax:** 212/307-2879. **Contact:** Human Resources. **World Wide Web address:** http://www.salomonsmithbarney.com. **Description:** An international investment banking, market making, and research firm serving corporations, state, local, and foreign governments, central banks, and other financial institutions. **Corporate headquarters location:** This location. **Parent company:** Citigroup. **Listed on:** New York Stock Exchange. **Stock exchange symbol:** C. **Number of employees worldwide:** Over 40,000.

SCHONFELD SECURITIES
650 Madison Avenue, 20th Floor, New York NY 10022. 212/832-0900. **Contact:** Human Resources. **World Wide Web address:** http://www.schonfeld.com. **Description:** A securities trading firm. **Corporate headquarters location:** New York, NY. **Other area locations:** Purchase NY; Brooklyn NY. **Other U.S. locations:** Paramus NJ; Miami Beach FL; Boca Raton FL; Chicago IL; Houston TX; Los Angeles CA. **Parent company:** Schonfeld Group.

SCUDDER INVESTMENTS
345 Park Avenue, New York NY 10154. 212/326-6200. **Contact:** Human Resources. **World Wide Web address:** http://www.scudder.com. **Description:** An investment firm with principal operations in securities brokerage. **Parent company:** Deutsche Asset Management.

TD WATERHOUSE SECURITIES, INC.
100 Wall Street, New York NY 10005. 212/806-3500. **Contact:** Human Resources. **E-mail address:** careers@tdwaterhouse.com. **World Wide Web address:** http://www.tdwaterhouse.com. **Description:** TD Waterhouse Securities, Inc. provides brokerage and banking services for individuals that manage their own investments and financial affairs. **Positions advertised include:** Surveillance Manager; Institutional Sales Representative; Credit Analyst; Investment Consultant. **Corporate headquarters location:** This location. **Other U.S. locations:** Nationwide. **Parent company:** TD Waterhouse Investor Services. **Operations at this facility include:** Administration; Divisional Headquarters; Regional Headquarters; Service. **Listed on:** New York Stock Exchange. **Number of employees at this location:** 250. **Number of employees nationwide:** 800.

THOMSON FINANCIAL
195 Broadway, New York NY 10007. 646/822-2000. **Contact:** Personnel Manager. **World Wide Web address:** http://www.thomsonfinancial.com. **Description:** Provides financial information to the investment industry through its many business units. American Banker/Bond Buyer publishes banking and financial industry information in a variety of publications. Rainmaker Information provides software products to help members of the sales and investment industries.

UBS PAINEWEBBER INC.
1285 Avenue of the Americas, 3rd Floor, New York NY 10019. 212/713-2000. **Contact:** Personnel. **World Wide Web address:** http://www.ubspainewebber.com. **Description:** A full-service securities firm with over 300 offices nationwide. Services include investment banking, asset management, merger and acquisition consulting, municipal securities underwriting, estate planning, retirement programs, and transaction management. Clients include corporations, governments, institutions, and individuals. Founded in 1879. **Corporate headquarters location:** This location. **Other U.S. locations:** Nationwide. **Annual sales/revenues:** More than $100 million.

UBS WARBURG LLC
299 Park Avenue, New York NY 10171-0026. 212/821-3000. **Fax:** 212/821-3285. **Contact:** Human Resources. **World Wide Web address:** http://www.ibb.ubs.com. **Description:** A national investment banking firm serving corporate clients. **Parent company:** UBS AG. **Listed on:** New York Stock Exchange. **Stock exchange symbol:** UBS.

UNITED STATES TRUST COMPANY OF NEW YORK
114 West 47th Street, New York NY 10036. 212/852-1000. **Contact:** Human Resources. **World Wide Web address:** http://www.ustrust.com. **Description:** An

investment management, private banking, and securities services firm. Service categories include investment management; estate and trust administration; financial planning; and corporate trust. **Corporate headquarters location:** This location.

VALUE LINE
220 East 42nd Street, 6th Floor, New York NY 10017. 212/907-1500. **Contact:** Human Resources. **World Wide Web address:** http://www.valueline.com. **Description:** An investment advisory firm. **Positions advertised include:** Junior Security Analyst. **Corporate headquarters location:** This location. **Listed on:** NASDAQ. **Stock exchange symbol:** VALU.

WARWICK GROUP, INC.
70 Main Street, 2nd Floor, New Canaan CT 06840. 203/966-7447. **Contact:** Human Resources. **World Wide Web address:** http://www.warwickgroup.com. **Description:** An investment bank.

WASHINGTON MUTUAL HOME LOANS CENTER
One Garret Mountain Plaza, 3rd Floor, West Paterson NJ 07424. 973/881-2360. **Contact:** Human Resources. **World Wide Web address:** http://www.wamu.com. **Description:** A full-service mortgage banking company that originates, acquires, and services residential mortgage loans. **Positions advertised include:** Assistant Financial Center Manager; Mortgage Sales Assistant; Financial Center Manager. **Corporate headquarters location:** Pittsburgh PA. **Other U.S. locations:** KY; OH. **Parent company:** PNC Financial Services Group. **Operations at this facility include:** Regional Headquarters. **Listed on:** New York Stock Exchange. **Stock exchange symbol:** WM. **Number of employees nationwide:** 6,000.

FOOD AND BEVERAGES/AGRICULTURE

You can expect to find the following types of companies
in this section:
Crop Services and Farm Supplies • Dairy Farms • Food
Manufacturers/Processors and Agricultural Producers • Tobacco Products

ALTRIA GROUP, INC.
120 Park Avenue, New York NY 10017. 212/880-5000. **Contact:** Human Resources Department. **World Wide Web address:** http://www.philipmorris.com. **Description:** A holding company. Its principal wholly-owned subsidiaries are Philip Morris Incorporated (also at this location), Philip Morris U.S.A., Philip Morris International Incorporated, Kraft Foods, Incorporated, and Philip Morris Capital Corporation. In the tobacco industry, Philip Morris U.S.A. and Philip Morris International together form one of the largest international cigarette operations in the world. U.S. brand names include Marlboro, Parliament, Virginia Slims, Benson & Hedges, and Merit. In the food industry, Kraft Foods, Inc. is one of the largest producers of packaged grocery products in North America. Major brands include Jell-O, Post, Kool-Aid, Crystal Light, Entenmann's, Miracle Whip, Stove Top, and Shake 'n Bake. Kraft markets a number of products under the Kraft brand including natural and process cheeses and dry packaged dinners. The Oscar Mayer unit markets processed meats, poultry, lunch combinations, and pickles under the Oscar Mayer, Louis Rich, Lunchables, and Claussen brand names. Kraft is also one of the largest coffee companies with principal brands including Maxwell House, Sanka, Brim, and General Foods International Coffees. Kraft Foods Ingredients Corporation manufactures private-label and industrial food products for sale to other food processing companies. Philip Morris Capital Corporation is engaged in financial services and real estate. **Positions advertised include:** Associate Manager of Security; Field Auditor; Customer Service Administrator; Administrative Assistant. **Special programs:** Summer Internships. **Corporate headquarters location:** This location. **Other area locations:** Rye Brook NY. **Other U.S. locations:** Stamford CT; Richmond VA. **International locations:** Australia; Brazil; Hong Kong; Japan; Switzerland. **Listed on:** New York Stock Exchange. **Stock exchange symbol:** MO. **Number of employees nationwide:** 155,000. **Number of employees worldwide:** 166,000.

ANHEUSER-BUSCH, INC.
200 U.S. Highway 1, Newark NJ 07114. 973/645-7700. **Contact:** Human Resources. **World Wide Web address:** http://www.budweiser.com. **Description:** A leading producer of beer. Beer brands include Budweiser, Michelob, Busch, King Cobra, and O'Doul's (nonalcoholic) beverages. **Corporate headquarters location:** St. Louis MO. **Other U.S. locations:** Los Angeles CA; Jacksonville FL; Tampa FL; Merrimack NH; Baldwinsville NY; Columbus OH; Houston TX; Williamsburg VA. **Parent company:** Anheuser-Busch Companies is a diverse company involved in the entertainment, brewing, baking, and manufacturing industries. The company is one of the largest domestic brewers, operating 13 breweries throughout the United States and distributing through over 900 independent wholesalers. Related businesses include can manufacturing, paper printing, and barley malting. Anheuser-Busch Companies is also one of the largest operators of theme parks in the United States, with locations in Florida, Virginia, Texas, Ohio, and California. Through subsidiary Campbell Taggart Inc., Anheuser-Busch Companies is also one of the largest commercial baking companies in the United States, producing foods under the Colonial brand name, among others. Anheuser-Busch Companies also has

various real estate interests. **Listed on:** New York Stock Exchange. **Stock exchange symbol:** BUD.

BESTFOODS BAKING COMPANY
700 Sylvan Avenue, Englewood Cliffs NJ 07632. 201/894-4000. **Contact:** Corporate Personnel. **World Wide Web address:** http://www.bestfoods.com. **Description:** Bestfoods produces and distributes a variety of food products including soups, sauces, and bouillons; dressings including Hellmann's mayonnaise; starches and syrups; bread spreads including Skippy peanut butter; desserts and baking aids; and pasta. **Corporate headquarters location:** This location. **Operations at this facility include:** This location houses the administrative and marketing offices and is also the world headquarters.

CHEF SOLUTIONS
164 Madison Street, East Rutherford NJ 07073. 973/779-2090. **Fax:** 973/779-7338. **Contact:** Human Resources. **E-mail address:** resumes@chefsolutions.com. **World Wide Web address:** http://www.chefsolutions.com. **Description:** Manufactures and markets a line of food products, primarily salads. **Positions advertised include:** Food Service Worker; Grocer. **Corporate headquarters location:** Wheeling IL. **Operations at this facility include:** Administration; Manufacturing; Research and Development; Sales; Service. **Number of employees at this location:** 200.

DI GIORGIO CORPORATION
WHITE ROSE FOOD
380 Middlesex Avenue, Carteret NJ 07008. 732/541-5555. **Fax:** 732/541-3730. **Contact:** Personnel Director. **World Wide Web address:** http://www.whiterose.com. **Description:** A major area distributor of approximately 850 grocery, dairy, and frozen food items. **Corporate headquarters location:** San Francisco CA. **Other U.S. locations:** Farmingdale NY.

THE FRESH JUICE COMPANY
280 Wilson Avenue, Newark NJ 07105. 973/465-7100. **Contact:** Human Resources. **Description:** Markets and sells frozen and fresh-squeezed Florida orange juice, grapefruit juice, apple juice, and other noncarbonated beverages under the brand name Just Pik't.

FRIENDSHIP DAIRIES, INC.
One Jericho Plaza, Jericho NY 11753-1668. 716/973-3031. **Contact:** Human Resources. **E-mail address:** myfriends@friendshipdairies.com. **World Wide Web address:** http://www.friendshipdairies.com. **Description:** Engaged in the production of dairy products such as cottage cheese, sour cream, and milk. Friendship Dairies distribute their goods nationally. **Corporate headquarters location:** Jericho NY. **Number of employees at this location:** 200.

THE HAIN CELESTIAL GROUP
50 Charles Lindbergh Boulevard, Uniondale NY 11553. 516/237-6200. **Fax:** 516/237-6240. **Contact:** Maureen Paradine, Director of Human Resources. **World Wide Web address:** http://www.hain-celestial.com. **Description:** Formerly the Hain Food Group, the company markets and distributes health, organic, natural, and specialty food and beverage products. Specialty products include kosher foods, low calorie and diet foods and beverages, snack foods, and dietetic foods. **Corporate headquarters location:** This location. **Subsidiaries include:** Celestial Seasonings; Imagine Foods, Inc.; Earth's Best; Garden of Eatin'; Terra Chips; The Good Lunch; West Brae Natural; Westsoy; Yves Veggie Cuisine. **Listed on:** NASDAQ. **Stock exchange symbol:** HAIN. **Chairman/President/CEO:** Irwin D. Simon. **Annual sales/revenues:** $396 million. **Number of employees:** 1,337.

INTERBAKE FOODS, INC.
891 Newark Avenue, Elizabeth NJ 07208-3599. 908/527-7000. **Contact:** Human Resources. **World Wide Web address:** http://www.interbake.com. **Description:** Interbake Foods operates in four business segments: Food Service; Grocery Products; Dairy Products; and Girl Scout Products. The Food Service segment offers a line of more than 160 items including crackers, cookies, tart shells, and other products to institutional customers, such as health care institutions, schools and colleges, and commercial establishments; the Dairy Products segment produces wafers for ice-cream manufacturers; the Grocery Products segment includes a wide range of cookies and crackers; and the Girl Scout Products segment manufactures Girl Scout Cookies. **Operations at this facility include:** This location is a bakery. **Parent company:** General Biscuits of America, Inc. is the American subsidiary of General Biscuit, S.A. (France).

INVERNESS MEDICAL INOVATIONS
500 Halls Mill Road, Freehold NJ 07728. 732/308-3000. **Fax:** 732/761-2837. **Contact:** Human Resources. **E-mail address:** hrresumes@invernessmedical.com. **World Wide Web address:** http://www.invernessmedical.com. **Description:** Manufactures and distributes vitamins, herbs, nonprescription drugs, and nutritional supplements under the brand names Fields of Nature, Pine Brothers throat drops, Rybutol, Nature's Wonder, Synergy Plus, and Liquafil vitamin supplements. **Corporate headquarters location:** This location. **Listed on:** NASDAQ. **Stock exchange symbol:** IVCO.

KRASDALE FOODS INC.
65 West Red Oak Lane, White Plains NY 10604. 914/694-6400. **Fax:** 914/697-5225. **Contact:** Human Resources. **World Wide Web address:** http://www.krasdalefoods.com. **Description:** Engaged in the wholesale distribution of canned goods and other processed food products throughout the tri-state area. Founded in 1908. **Corporate headquarters location:** This location. **Other locations:** Bronx NY. **President/CEO:** Charles A Krasne. **Annual sales/revenues:** $550 million. **Number of employees:** 750.

LINCOLN SNACKS COMPANY
30 Buxton Farm Road, Stamford CT 06905. 203/329-4545. **Contact:** Human Resources. **World Wide Web address:** http://www.lincolnsnacks.com. **Description:** Manufactures and markets caramelized popcorn and glazed popcorn and nut mixes. Brand names include Poppycock, Fiddle Faddle, Screaming Yellow Zonkers, and Golden Gourmet Nuts. **Corporate headquarters location:** This location.

M&M/MARS INC.
800 High Street, Hackettstown NJ 07840. 908/852-1000. **Contact:** Human Resources. **World Wide Web address:** http://www.mmmars.com. **Description:** M&M/Mars produces a variety of candy and snack foods. **Corporate headquarters location:** This location. **Other U.S. locations:** Albany GA; Burr Ridge IL. **Operations at this facility include:** This location houses administrative offices.

MCT DAIRIES, INC.
15 Bleeker Street, Millburn NJ 07041. 973/258-9600. **Toll-free phone:** 877/258-9600. **Fax:** 973/258-9222. **Contact:** Human Resources. **E-mail address:** info@mctdairies,com. **World Wide Web address:** http://www.mctdairies.com. **Description:** Buys and sells cheeses and other industrial dairy products including bulk domestic and imported cheeses, whey powders, dairy flavorings, and buttermilk. **Corporate headquarters location:** This location.

MARATHON ENTERPRISES INC.
66 East Union Avenue, East Rutherford NJ 07073. 201/935-3330. **Contact:** Personnel Manager. **Description:** Manufactures Sabrett brand hot dogs. **Corporate headquarters location:** This location.

MOTT'S INC.
P.O. Box 3800, Stamford CT 06905-0800. 203/968-7500. **Physical address:** 6 High Ridge Park, Stamford CT 06905. **Contact:** Human Resources. **World Wide Web address:** http://www.motts.com. **Description:** A major producer of apple juice, applesauce, and related fruit products. **Positions advertised include:** Human Resources Manager; Trade Spend Analyst, Special Beverages; Master Data Analyst; Cash Application Supervisor; Procurement Category Manager; Procurement Coordinator. **Corporate headquarters location:** This location. **Other U.S. locations:** CT; FL; LA; NJ; NY; PA. **International locations:** Canada; Mexico. **Parent company:** Cadbury Schwepps plc (London, England.) **Listed on:** New York Stock Exchange. **Stock exchange symbol:** CSG.

NABISCO FAIR LAWN BAKERY
22-11 State Route 208, Fair Lawn NJ 07410. 201/794-4000. **Contact:** Personnel. **World Wide Web address:** http://www.kraftfoods.com/careers. **Description:** Nabisco is one of the largest consumer foods operations in the country. The company markets a broad line of cookie and cracker products including brand names such as Oreo, Ritz, Premium, Teddy Grahams, Chips Ahoy!, and Wheat Thins. The company operates 10 cake and cookie bakeries, a flourmill, and a cheese plant. The bakeries produce over 1 billion pounds of finished products each year. Over 150 biscuit brands reach the consumer via one of the industry's largest distribution networks. **Operations at this facility include:** This location is a bakery. **Parent company:** Kraft Foods. **Listed on:** New York Stock Exchange. **Stock exchange symbol:** KFT. **Number of employees at this location:** 1,200.

NABISCO GROUP HOLDINGS
7 Campus Drive, P.O. Box 311, Parsippany NJ 07054-0311. 973/682-5000. **Contact:** Human Resources. **World Wide Web address:** http://www.kraft.com. **Description:** Nabisco is one of the largest consumer foods operations in the country. The company markets a broad line of cookie and cracker products including brand names such as Oreo, Ritz, Premium, Teddy Grahams, Chips Ahoy!, and Wheat Thins. The company operates 10 cake and cookie bakeries, a flourmill, and a cheese plant. The bakeries produce over 1 billion pounds of finished products each year. Over 150 biscuit brands reach the consumer via one of the industry's largest distribution networks. **Operations at this facility include:** This location houses administrative offices. **Parent company:** Kraft Foods. **Listed on:** New York Stock Exchange. **Stock exchange symbol:** KFT. **Annual sales/revenues:** More than $100 million.

NABISCO INC.
100 DeForest Avenue, East Hanover NJ 07936. 973/503-2000. **Contact:** Staffing Center. **World Wide Web address:** http://www.kraft.com. **Description:** One of the largest consumer foods operations in the country. The company markets a broad line of cookie and cracker products including brand names such as Oreo, Ritz, Premium, Teddy Grahams, Chips Ahoy!, and Wheat Thins. The company operates 10 cake and cookie bakeries, a flourmill, and a cheese plant. The bakeries produce over 1 billion pounds of finished products each year. Over 150 biscuit brands reach the consumer via one of the industry's largest distribution networks. **Special programs:** Internships. **Corporate headquarters location:** Northfield IL. **Parent company:** Kraft Foods. **Listed on:** New York Stock Exchange. **Stock exchange symbol:** KFT.

224 /The Metropolitan New York JobBank

NEW HUNTINGTON TOWN HOUSE INC.
124 East Jericho Turnpike, Huntington Station NY 11746. 631/427-8485.
Contact: Vice President. **World Wide Web address:**
http://www.newhuntingtontownhouse.com. **Description:** A general service
catering company specializing in weddings, organizational functions, bar
mitzvahs, anniversaries, and special parties through over 25 area locations
including the New York City area. **Corporate headquarters location:** This
location.

PEPPERIDGE FARM INC.
595 Westport Avenue, Norwalk CT 06851. 203/846-7000. **Fax:** 203/846-7033.
Contact: Dan Zimmerman, Director of Human Resources. **World Wide Web
address:** http://www.cambpellsoup.com. **Description:** Manufactures and
distributes a range of fresh and frozen baked goods and confections including
bread, cookies, cakes, pastries, and crackers. **Special programs:** Internships.
Corporate headquarters location: This location. **Parent company:** Campbell
Soup Company (Camden NJ). **Listed on:** New York Stock Exchange. **Stock
exchange symbol:** CPB. **Annual sales/revenues:** More than $100 million.
Number of employees at this location: 280. **Number of employees
nationwide:** 4,700.

PEPSI-COLA BOTTLING GROUP, INC.
One Pepsi Way, Somers NY 10589-2201. 914/767-6000. **Contact:** Human
Resources. **World Wide Web address:** http://www.pbg.com. **Description:**
Manufactures and distributes Pepsi-Cola beverages. **Listed on:** New York Stock
Exchange. **NOTE:** Jobseekers may see http://www.pbgjobs.com for employment
opportunities. **Positions advertised include:** Unix Administrator; Powerbuilder
Programmer; A/R Workflow Specialist; Java Programmer; Java Developer; Tax
and Financial Applications Support; Project Leader; Power PreSell Specialist;
Senior Analyst; NIS Specialist. **Corporate headquarters location:** This location.
Other U.S. locations: Nationwide. **Stock exchange symbol:** PBG. **President:**
Eric J. Foss. **Sales/revenue:** Over $9 billion. **Number of employees
worldwide:** 65,000.

PEPSICO, INC.
700 Anderson Hill Road, Purchase NY 10577. 914/253-2000. **Contact:** Staffing
Director. **World Wide Web address:** http://www.pepsico.com. **Description:**
Operates on a worldwide basis within four companies which include Frito-Lay
Company, Pepsi-Cola Company, The Quaker Oats Company, and Tropicana
Products, Inc. Pepsi-Cola Company primarily markets its brands worldwide and
manufactures concentrates for its brands for sale to franchised bottlers
worldwide. The segment also operates bottling plants and distribution facilities
located in the United States and key international markets. **NOTE:** Interested job
seekers may apply online. **Positions advertised include:** Data Analyst;
Corporate IT Auditor; Domestic Audit Manager; Corporate Auditor; Treasury
Operations Analyst; Legal Assistant; **Corporate headquarters location:** This
location. **Other U.S. locations:** Nationwide. **International locations:** Canada;
Mexico; United Kingdom. **Listed on:** New York Stock Exchange; also, the
Amsterdam, Chicago, Swiss, and Tokyo Stock Exchanges. **Stock exchange
symbol:** PEP. **CEO/Chairman:** Steve Reinemund. **Sales/revenue:** $25 billion.
Number of employees worldwide: Over 142,000.

PHILIP MORRIS INTERNATIONAL INC.
800 Westchester Avenue, Port Chester NY 10573. 914/335-5000. **Contact:**
Human Resources. **World Wide Web address:** http://www.philipmorris.com.
Description: In the tobacco industry, Philip Morris U.S.A. and Philip Morris
International together form one of the largest international cigarette operations in
the world. U.S. brand names include Marlboro, Parliament, Virginia Slims,
Benson & Hedges, and Merit. **Corporate headquarters location:** This location.

International locations: Worldwide. **Parent company:** Altria Group, Incorporated. **Listed on:** New York Stock Exchange. **Stock exchange symbol:** MO. **Sales/revenue:** Approximately $28 billion. **Number of employees worldwide:** 40,000.

POLAND SPRINGS OF AMERICA
170 West Commercial Avenue, Moonachie NJ 07074. 201/531-2044. **Contact:** Human Resources. **World Wide Web address:** http://www.polandspring.com. **Description:** Distributes bottled spring and distilled drinking water for home and industrial use. The company also provides water coolers, microwave ovens, and similar equipment for installation in commercial and industrial locations. **Parent company:** Perrier Group of America (Greenwich CT).

RECKITT BENCKISER
Morris Corporate Center IV, 399 Interpace Parkway, Parsippany NJ 07054-0225. 973/404-2600. **Contact:** Staffing Supervisor. **E-mail address:** human.resources@reckitt.com. **World Wide Web address:** http://www.reckitt.com. **Description:** Manufactures cleaning and specialty food products including the brand names Easy-Off oven cleaner, French's mustard, Lysol, and Woolite detergent.

REITMAN INDUSTRIES
10 Patton Drive, West Caldwell NJ 07006. 973/228-5100. **Contact:** Human Resources. **World Wide Web address:** http://www.rrmarketing.com. **Description:** Engaged in the wholesale importation and distribution of liquors and wines. **Corporate headquarters location:** This location.

SARA LEE COFFEE AND TEA
500 Mamaroneck Avenue, 5th floor, Harrison NY 10528. 914/670-3300. **Contact:** Personnel. **E-mail address:** recruiting@saralee.com. **World Wide Web address:** http://www.saralee.com. **Description:** Produces a nationally distributed brand of premium coffee. The company also operates a chain of cafes and drive-thru restaurants. **Corporate headquarters location:** Chicago IL. **Other U.S. locations:** Nationwide. **Subsidiaries include:** Cain's Coffee Company; Greenwich Mills Company. **Parent company:** Sara Lee Corporation. **Operations at this facility include:** Administration; Divisional Headquarters; Sales. **Listed on:** New York Stock Exchange. **Stock exchange symbol:** SLE.

SCHIEFFELIN & SOMERSET COMPANY
2 Park Avenue, 17th Floor, New York NY 10016. 212/251-8200. **Fax:** 212/251-8384. **Contact:** Human Resources. **E-mail address:** hrstaffing@schieffelin-somerset.com. **World Wide Web address:** http://www.schieffelin.com. **Description:** Sells and markets premium alcoholic beverages. **NOTE:** Resumes are requested to be in Microsoft Word format. **Corporate headquarters location:** This location. **Other U.S. locations:** CA; FL; IL; NJ; TX; GA. **Parent company:** MoetHennessyLouisVuitton/Diageo. **Operations at this facility include:** Administration; Sales. **Listed on:** NASDAQ/NYSE. **Stock exchange symbol:** LVMHY/DEO. **Number of employees at this location:** 100. **Number of employees nationwide:** 200.

TOPPS COMPANY
One Whitehall Street, New York NY 10004. 212/376-0300. **Contact:** Human Resources. **World Wide Web address:** http://www.topps.com. **Description:** Internationally manufactures and markets a variety of chewing gum, candy, and other similar products. Topps also licenses its technology and trademarks and sells its chewing gum base and flavors to other overseas manufacturers. The company is best known for its internationally registered trademark Bazooka and its perennial Topps Baseball Bubble Gum picture cards. Topps is a leading marketer, under exclusive licenses, of collectible picture cards, albums, and

stickers for baseball, football, and hockey. The company is also a leading producer and distributor of cards and stickers featuring pictures of popular motion picture, television, and cartoon characters, also under exclusive licenses. **Corporate headquarters location:** This location. **Other U.S. locations:** Duryea PA. **International locations:** Ireland. **Listed on:** NASDAQ. **Stock exchange symbol:** TOPP.

TRADER JOE'S
186 Columbia Turnpike, Florham Park NJ 07932. 973/514-1511. **Contact:** Human Resources, **E-mail address:** midatjobs@traderjoes.com. **World Wide Web address:** http://www.traderjoes.com. **Description:** A grocery store offering a variety of unique items and having a wide selection of fine wines. **Positions advertised include:** Grocery Store Supervisor. **Other area locations:** Marlton; Wayne; Westfield; Westwood.

TUSCAN DAIRY FARM
750 Union Avenue, Union NJ 07083. 908/686-1500. **Contact:** Human Resources. **Description:** Produces and distributes milk and related products throughout northern New Jersey and adjacent areas. **Corporate headquarters location:** This location.

UST INC.
100 West Putnam Avenue, Greenwich CT 06830. 203/661-1100. **Fax:** 203/622-3493. **Contact:** Human Resources. **World Wide Web address:** http://www.ustinc.com. **Description:** A holding company whose subsidiaries produce and market moist, smokeless tobacco products. **Positions advertised include:** Auditor; Senior Auditor; Senior Buyer; Brand Manager; Manager, Consumer Research; Sales Representative; Senior Brand Manager. **Special programs:** Internships. **Corporate headquarters location:** This location. **Subsidiaries include:** International Wine & Spirits Ltd.; U.S. Smokeless Tobacco Company. **Operations at this facility include:** Administration; Divisional Headquarters. **Listed on:** New York Stock Exchange. **Stock exchange symbol:** UST. **Number of employees at this location:** 500.

UNILEVER FOODS
800 Sylvan Avenue, Englewood Cliffs NJ 07632. 201/567-8000. **Contact:** Personnel Administrator. **World Wide Web address:** http://www.unileverna.com. **Description:** An international consumer products firm manufacturing a wide range of soaps, toiletries, and foods. **Other U.S. locations:** Flemington NJ.

UNITED DISTILLERS & VINTNERS NORTH AMERICA, INC.
6 Landmark Square, 6th Floor, Stamford CT 06901. 203/323-3311. **Contact:** Human Resources. **Description:** A manufacturer and distributor of alcoholic beverages including Johnnie Walker, Smirnoff, Tanqueray, Jose Cuervo, Malibu, and Bailey's.

WAKEFERN FOOD CORPORATION
600 York Street, Elizabeth NJ 07207. 908/527-3300. **Contact:** Human Resources. **World Wide Web address:** http://www.shoprite.com. **Description:** Operates a retailer-owned, nonprofit food cooperative. The company provides purchasing, warehousing, and distribution services to various grocery retailers throughout the metropolitan area. Many products are distributed under the Shop-Rite name. **Special programs:** Internships.

WEGMANS
724 Route 202 South, Bridgewater NJ, 08807. 908/243-9600. **Fax:** 609/243-0349. **Contact:** Human Resources. **E-mail address:** employment@wegmans.com. **World Wide Web Address:** http://www.wegmans.com. **Description:** Operates grocery stores in New York,

Pennsylvania, New Jersey, and Virginia. **Positions advertised include:** Seafood Manager; Service Desk Associate; Producer Associate; Meat Associate; Deli Associate; Bakery Associate; Grocery Associate; Overnight Associate; Dairy Associate. **NOTE:** Mail resumes to: 29 Emmons Drive Suite 630, Princeton NJ, 03540, or apply online. **Number of employees nationwide:** 32,000.

GEORGE WESTON BAKERIES, INC.
10 Hamilton Avenue, Greenwich CT 06830. 203/531-2000. **Contact:** Human Resources. **World Wide Web address:** http://www.georgewestonfoods.com.au. **Description:** An Australian-based food manufacturer.

GEORGE WESTON BAKERIES, INC.
55 Paradise Lane, Bayshore NY 11706. 631/273-6000. **Contact:** Human Resources. **World Wide Web address:** http://www.gwbakerires.com. **Description:** Produces and distributes a variety of food products including soups, sauces, and bouillons; dressings including Hellmann's mayonnaise; starches and syrups; bread spreads including Skippy peanut butter; desserts and baking aids; and pasta. **Corporate headquarters location:** This location.

GOVERNMENT

You can expect to find the following types of companies in this section:
Courts • Executive, Legislative, and General Government • Public Agencies (Firefighters, Military, Police) • United States Postal Service

---

DANBURY, CITY OF
City Hall, 155 Deer Hill Avenue, Danbury CT 06810. 203/797-4500. **Contact:** Human Resources. **World Wide Web address:** http://www.ci.danbury.ct.us. **Description:** The administrative offices for the City of Danbury.

ECONOMIC OPPORTUNITY COUNCIL OF SUFFOLK
475 East Main Street, Suite 206, Patchogue NY 11772. 631/289-2124. **Fax:** 631/289-2178. **Contact:** Songhi Scott, CFO/Human Resources. **E-mail address:** eoc@eoc-suffolk.com. **World Wide Web address:** http://www.eoc-suffolk.com. **Description:** A county agency responsible for various social programs in Suffolk County. The council provides counseling in energy conservation, outreach, summer work, health and education, housing, and employment training. **Special programs:** Internships. **Number of employees at this location:** 10. **Number of employees nationwide:** 50.

NEW JERSEY DEPARTMENT OF TRANSPORTATION
REGION 3 CONSTRUCTION
100 Daniels Way, Freehold NJ 07728. 732/409-3263. **Contact:** Human Resources. **Description:** Designs, builds, and maintains roads and highways throughout the state of New Jersey.

NEW JERSEY TURNPIKE AUTHORITY
P.O. Box 1121, New Brunswick NJ 08903. 732/247-0900. **Contact:** Human Resources. **World Wide Web address:** http://www.state.nj.us/turnpike. **Description:** A state mandated, unsubsidized organization responsible for construction, maintenance, repair, and operation on New Jersey Turnpike projects.

U.S. ENVIRONMENTAL PROTECTION AGENCY (EPA)
290 Broadway, 28th Floor, New York NY 10007. 212/637-3000. **Contact:** Human Resources. **World Wide Web address:** http://www.epa.gov. **Description:** The EPA is dedicated to improving and preserving the quality of the environment, both nationally and globally, and protecting human health and the productivity of natural resources. The agency is committed to ensuring that federal environmental laws are implemented and enforced effectively; U.S. policy, both foreign and domestic, encourages the integration of economic development and environmental protection so that economic growth can be sustained over the long term; and public and private decisions affecting energy, transportation, agriculture, industry, international trade, and natural resources fully integrate considerations of environmental quality. Founded in 1970. **Special programs:** Internships. **Corporate headquarters location:** Washington DC. **Other U.S. locations:** San Francisco CA; Denver CO; Atlanta GA; Chicago IL; Kansas City KS; Boston MA; Philadelphia PA; Dallas TX; Seattle WA. **Number of employees nationwide:** 19,000.

U.S. POSTAL SERVICE
16 Washington Street, Norwalk CT 06856. 203/854-4747. **Contact:** Human Resources. **World Wide Web address:** http://www.usps.com. **Description:** Main post office for the city of Norwalk. **NOTE:** Jobseekers must apply in person.

U.S. POSTAL SERVICE
46 Grove Street, Passaic NJ 07055. 973/779-0277. **Contact:** Human Resources. **World Wide Web address:** http://www.usps.com. **Description:** A post office for the city of Passaic.

U.S. POSTAL SERVICE
NEW JERSEY INTERNATIONAL BULK MAIL
80 County Road, Jersey City NJ 07097-9998. 201/714-6390. **Contact:** Human Resources. **Description:** A United States Post Office that processes foreign, military, and general bulk mail for distribution throughout the world.

HEALTH CARE SERVICES, EQUIPMENT, AND PRODUCTS

You can expect to find the following types of companies in this section:
Dental Labs and Equipment • Home Health Care Agencies • Hospitals and Medical Centers • Medical Equipment Manufacturers and Wholesalers • Offices and Clinics of Health Practitioners • Residential Treatment Centers/Nursing Homes • Veterinary Services

AFP IMAGING CORPORATION
250 Clearbrook Road, Elmsford NY 10523. 914/592-6100. **Fax:** 914/592-6148. **Contact:** Human Resources Manager. **E-mail address:** afp@afpimaging.com. **World Wide Web address:** http://www.afpimaging.com. **Description:** Provides medical equipment utilized by radiologists, cardiologists, and other medical professionals for generating, recording, processing, and viewing hard copy diagnostic images. The company's products are applied in medical diagnostics X-ray inspection. Products are marketed under the AFP, DENT-X, and SENS-A-RAY 2000 brand names. **International locations:** Geilenkirchen, Germany. **Listed on:** Over The Counter. **Stock exchange symbol:** AFPC. **Chairman:** David Vozick. **Annual sales/revenues:** $24 million. **Number of employees:** 106.

ALL METRO HEALTH CARE
50 Broadway, Lynbrook NY 11563. 516/887-1200. **Toll-free phone:** 800/225-1200. **Fax:** 516/593-2848. **Contact:** Human Resources. **E-mail address:** all-metro@aol.com. **Description:** A home health care provider. Plaza Domestic Agency and Caregivers on Call also operate out of this facility. Founded in 1955. **Positions advertised include:** Certified Nurses Aide; Clerical Supervisor; Home Health Aide; Licensed Practical Nurse; Marketing Manager; Occupational Therapist; Physical Therapist; Registered Nurse. **Office hours:** Sunday - Saturday, 8:30 a.m. - 8:30 p.m. **Corporate headquarters location:** This location. **Other area locations:** Statewide. **Other U.S. locations:** FL; MO; NJ. **Parent company:** All Metro Aids Inc. **Annual sales/revenues:** $50 million. **Number of employees at this location:** 2,000. **Number of employees nationwide:** 5,000.

AMERICUS DENTAL LABS LP
150-15 Hillside Avenue, Jamaica NY 11432. 718/658-6655. **Fax:** 718/657-8389. **Contact:** Human Resources. **E-mail address:** info@americuslab.com. **World Wide Web address:** http://www.americuslab.com. **Description:** A dental lab that manufactures crowns, bridges, and other dental products. **Positions advertised include:** Ceramist; Die Trimmer. **Corporate headquarters location:** This location. **Other locations:** New York NY. **Number of employees:** 150.

ANIMAL MEDICAL CENTER
THE E&M BOBST HOSPITAL
510 East 62nd Street, New York NY 10021. 212/838-8100. **Fax:** 212/758-8157. **Contact:** Human Resources. **E-mail address:** careers@amcny.org. **World Wide Web address:** http://www.amcny.org. **Description:** A full-service, nonprofit animal hospital with a staff of over 80 veterinarians. Founded in 1910. **Positions advertised include:** Staff Accountant; Stockroom Clerk; Pet Outreach Coordinator; Public Relations Administrative Assistant; Receptionist Medical Records; Veterinary Technician.

C.R. BARD, INC.
730 Central Avenue, Murray Hill NJ 07974. 908/277-8000. **Fax:** 908/277-8412. **Contact:** Human Resources. **World Wide Web address:** http://www.crbard.com. **Description:** Manufactures and distributes disposable medical, surgical, diagnostic, and patient care products. Cardiovascular products include angioplastic recanalization devices such as balloon angioplasty catheters, inflation devices, and developmental atherectomy and laser devices; electrophysiology products such as temporary pacing catheters, diagnostic and therapeutic electrodes, and cardiac mapping systems; a cardiopulmonary system; and blood oxygenators, cardiotomy reservoirs, and other products used in open heart surgery. Urological products include Foley catheters, trays, and related urine contract collection systems used extensively in postoperative bladder drainage. Surgical products include wound and chest drainage systems and implantable blood vessel replacements. **Corporate headquarters location:** This location. **Listed on:** New York Stock Exchange. **Stock exchange symbol:** BCR.

BARKSDALE HEALTH CARE SERVICES INC.
BARKSDALE HOME CARE SERVICES CORP.
BARKSDALE SERVICES CORP.
327 Fifth Avenue, Pelham NY 10803. 914/738-5600. **Fax:** 914/738-0658. **Contact:** Rosa K. Barksdale, CEO. **World Wide Web address:** http://www.barksdaleathome.com. **Description:** A home health care agency providing health care services to private homes, hospitals, and institutions in Westchester County and the Bronx NY. **Positions advertised include:** Nurses Aide; Personal Care Aide; Certified Nurses Aide; Medical Social Worker; Live-in Companion; Home Health Aide; Licensed Practical Nurse; Registered Nurse. **Corporate headquarters location:** This location. **Other locations:** Riverdale NY.

BARNERT HOSPITAL
680 Broadway, Paterson NJ 07514. 973/977-6600. **Fax:** 973/279-2924. **Recorded jobline:** 973/977-6824. **Contact:** Human Resources. **World Wide Web address:** http://www.barnerthosp.com. **Description:** A 280-bed hospital. **Positions advertised include:** Nurse Assistant; Unit Clerk; Medical Assistant; Ultrasonographer; Physical Therapist; Laboratory Technician; Medical Technologist; Pharmacy Tech; Independent Living Specialist; Mental Health Clinic; Outpatient Clinician; Resident Counselor; American Sign Language Associate; Maintenance Supervisor; Operator; Mechanic; Patient Biller; Credit Representative; House Keeper; Communications Representative; Registrar. **Special programs:** Internships. **Operations at this facility include:** Administration; Service. **Number of employees at this location:** 1,000.

BAYER DIAGNOSTICS DIVISION
BAYER HEALTHCARE
511 Benedict Avenue, Tarrytown NY 10591-5097. 914/631-8000. **Fax:** 914/333-6536. **Contact:** Kim MacNeil, Human Resources. **E-mail address:** hr.grp@bayer.com or kim.macneil.b@bayer.com. **World Wide Web address:** http://www.bayerdiag.com. **Description:** Develops, manufactures, and sells clinical diagnostic systems. Bayer Diagnostics specializes in critical care, laboratory, and point-of-care testing. **NOTE:** See http://www.monster.com for current job listings. **Positions advertised include:** Reimbursement & Public Affairs Director; Diabetes Sales Specialist; FDA/Regulatory Counselor; Finished Goods Supply Chain Manager; Training Specialist; Senior Training Specialist; Product Engineer; Clinical Account Specialist; Telehelthcare Specialist; Marketing Manager; Multistix PRO Senior Marketing Manager; Service and Support Engineer; Laboratory Automation Engineer; Health Care Professional/Manager; Research Scientist; Staff System Engineer; Senior Financial Analyst; Sales Trainer; National Advertising Division Marketing

Manager; Managed Care Manager; Hemotology Sales Specialist. **Corporate headquarters location:** Pittsburgh PA. **Other area locations:** Middletown NY; Nyack NY. **Other U.S. locations:** IL; LA; MA; OH; PA. **International locations:** Worldwide. **Parent company:** Bayer Corporation (Pittsburgh PA). **Operations at this facility include:** Administration; Divisional Headquarters; Manufacturing; Research and Development; Sales; Service. **Listed on:** New York Stock Exchange. **Stock exchange symbol:** BAY. **Number of employees at this location:** 800. **Number of employees nationwide:** 8,000.

BECTON DICKINSON & COMPANY

One Becton Drive, Franklin Lakes NJ 07417. 201/847-6800. **Contact:** Human Resources. **World Wide Web address:** http://www.bd.com. **Description:** A medical company engaged in the manufacture of health care products, medical instrumentation, diagnostic products, and industrial safety equipment. Major medical equipment product lines include hypodermics, intravenous equipment, operating room products, thermometers, gloves, and specialty needles. The company also offers contract packaging services. Founded in 1896. **Positions advertised include:** Administrative Assistant; Project Leader; Customer Service Associate; Customer Service Representative; Transactional Six Sigma Black Belt; Help Desk Analyst; Product Development Engineer; Cost Analyst; Training Administrator; Project Manager; Rebate Reconciliation Analyst; Corporate Development Manager; Business Analyst; Claims Associate; Data Entry Associate. **Corporate headquarters location:** This location. **Listed on:** New York Stock Exchange. **Stock exchange symbol:** BDX. **Number of employees worldwide:** 18,000.

BETH ISRAEL HEALTH CARE SYSTEM

First Avenue at 16th Street, New York NY 10003. 212/420-2000. **Contact:** Human Resources. **World Wide Web address:** http://www.bethisraelny.org. **Description:** An integrated health care system providing a full continuum of primary, acute, tertiary, and long-term care. The system also operates New York HealthCare/Doctors' Walk In, the Japanese Medical Practice, Schnurmacher Nursing Home of Beth Israel Medical Center, Robert Mapplethorpe Residential Treatment Facility, Phillips Beth Israel School of Nursing, Karpas Health Information Center, and D-O-C-S, a multisite, private, group medical practice in the suburbs. **NOTE:** Resumes should be sent to Human Resources, 555 West 57th Street, New York NY 10019; or faxed to: 212/523-7193. **Positions advertised include:** Registered Dietician; Director of Safety; Cathode Laboratory Expiditer; Senior Credentialing Analyst; Patient Advocate; Medical Biller; Medical Administrative Assistant; Senior Systems Analyst; Cardiovascular Technician; Radiological Technician; Registered Nurse; Cardiology Nurse; Nurse Recruiter. **Corporate headquarters location:** This location. **Other locations:** Throughout the New York City metropolitan region. **Subsidiaries include:** Beth Israel Medical Center; St Luke's-Roosevelt Hospital Center. Long Island College Hospital; New York Eye and Ear Infirmary. **Parent company:** Continuum Health Partners Inc.

BIOSEARCH MEDICAL PRODUCTS, INC.

35A Industrial Parkway, Somerville NJ 08876. 908/722-5000. **Toll-free phone:** 800/326-5976. **Fax:** 908/722-5024. **Contact:** Human Resources. **World Wide Web address:** http://www.biosearch.com. **Description:** Manufactures specialty medical devices for the gastroenterology, endoscopy, urology, and enteral feeding markets. The company's products are sold directly to hospitals and alternative care centers through domestic and international specialty dealers. Founded in 1978. **NOTE:** Entry-level positions are offered. **Special programs:** Training. **Parent company:** Hydromer Inc. **Listed on:** NASDAQ. **Stock exchange symbol:** BMPI. **Annual sales/revenues:** $5 - $10 million. **Number of employees at this location:** 30.

BON SECOURS & CANTERBURY PARTNERSHIP FOR CARE
25 McWilliams Place, Jersey City NJ 07302. 201/418-2065. **Fax:** 201/418-2063. **Contact:** Personnel. **World Wide Web address:** http://www.bonsecoursnj.com. **Description:** Operates two community hospitals: St. Mary Hospital (Hoboken NJ) and St. Francis Hospital (Jersey City NJ). **Positions advertised include:** Assistant Manager; Case Manager; Clinical Nurse Specialist; Coder Analyst; Home Health Care Nurse; Lead Therapist; Occupational Therapist; Receptionist; Registration Associate; Respiratory Therapist; Registered Nurse; Social Worker; X-ray Technologist. **NOTE:** Entry-level positions are offered. **Special programs:** Internships. **Corporate headquarters location:** This location. **Annual sales/revenues:** $11 - $20 million. **Number of employees at this location:** 1,500.

CVS PROCARE
80 Air Park Drive, Ronkonkoma NY 11779. 631/981-0034. **Fax:** 631/981-0722. **Contact:** Human Resources. **World Wide Web address:** http://www.cvsprocare.com. **Description:** A national provider of outpatient drug therapies and a broad array of distribution, case management, and support services to meet the ongoing needs of patients with chronic medical conditions, the health professionals who care for them, and the third-party payers responsible for such care. The company's services include distribution of prescription drug therapies, drug utilization review programs, patient compliance monitoring, psychosocial support services, and assistance in insurance investigation, verification, and reimbursement. **Parent company:** CVS Corporation (Woonsocket RI). **Other U.S. locations:** Nationwide.

CANTEL INDUSTRIES, INC.
Overlook at Great Notch, 150 Clove Road, 9th Floor, Little Falls NJ 07424. 973/890-7220. **Contact:** Human Resources. **World Wide Web address:** http://www.cantelmedical.com. **Description:** A holding company. **Subsidiaries include:** Carson Group Inc. (Canada) markets and distributes medical instruments including flexible and rigid endoscopes; precision instruments including microscopes and image analysis systems; and industrial equipment including remote visual inspection devices, laser distance measurement and thermal imaging products, and online optical inspection and quality assurance systems for specialized industrial applications. Carson also offers a full range of photographic equipment and supplies for amateur and professional photographers. **Listed on:** NASDAQ. **Stock exchange symbol:** CNTL.

CENTER FOR VETERINARY CARE
236 East 75th Street, New York NY 10021. 212/734-7480. **Contact:** Human Resources. **Description:** A full-service animal hospital offering medical and surgical procedures.

COMMUNITY MEDICAL CENTER
99 Highway 37 West, Toms River NJ 08755. 732/240-8000. **Contact:** Human Resources. **E-mail address:** info@sbhcs.com. **World Wide Web address:** http://www.sbhcs.com. **Description:** An affiliate of Saint Barnabus Health Care System, Community Medical Center is a 596-bed, general, short-term care hospital.

CORDIS CORPORATION
45 Technology Drive, Warren NJ 07059. 908/755-8300. **Contact:** Human Resources. **World Wide Web address:** http://www.cordis.com. **Description:** Cordis manufactures medical devices such as catheters to treat cardiovascular diseases. **NOTE:** All hiring is done through the parent company. Resumes should be sent to Johnson & Johnson Recruiting Services, Employment Management Center, Room JH-215, 501 George Street, New Brunswick NJ 08906-6597. **Operations at this facility include:** This location handles

administration, research and development, and quality assurance. **Parent company:** Johnson & Johnson (New Brunswick NJ).

CURATIVE HEALTH SERVICES, INC.
150 Motor Parkway, 4th Floor, Hauppauge NY 11788. 631/232-7000. **Fax:** 631/232-9322. **Contact:** Michelle, LeDell, Director of Human Resources. **World Wide Web address:** http://www.curative.com. **Description:** Curative Health Services primarily manages, on behalf of hospital clients, a nationwide network of wound-care centers. Most of the wound-care centers managed by Curative Health Services are outpatient, although, a small portion are inpatient. The company is also engaged in the research and development of therapeutic products for wound-healing applications. **NOTE:** Jobseekers can see http://www.monster.com for a current the job listing. **Corporate headquarters location:** This location. **Other U.S. locations:** Nationwide. **Listed on:** NASDAQ. **Stock exchange symbol:** CURE. **Chairman:** Joseph L. Feshbach. **Annual sales/revenues:** $139 million. **Number of employees:** 340.

DATASCOPE CORPORATION
14 Phillips Parkway, Montvale NJ 07645. 201/391-8100. **Contact:** Human Resources. **E-mail address:** career_opportunities@datascope.com. **World Wide Web address:** http://www.datascope.com. **Description:** Manufactures cardiac assist systems for hospital use in interventional cardiology and cardiac surgery; and patient monitors for use in the operating room, postanesthesia care, and critical care. Datascope's VasoSeal product rapidly seals femoral arterial punctures after catheterization procedures including coronary angioplasty and angiography. Datascope also manufactures a line of collagen hemostats, which are used to control bleeding during surgery. The company's cardiac assist product is an intra-aortic balloon pumping system used for treating cardiac shock, heart failure, and cardiac arrhythmia. The pump can also be used in various procedures including cardiac surgery and coronary angioplasty. Datascope's patient monitoring products comprise a line of multifunction and stand-alone models that measure a broad range of physiological data including blood oxygen saturation, airway carbon dioxide, ECG, and temperature. **Positions advertised include:** Industrial Engineer; Electro-Mechanical Engineer; Electrical Engineer; Secretary; Lotus Notes Database Developer. **Listed on:** NASDAQ. **Stock exchange symbol:** DSCP.

EBI MEDICAL SYSTEMS, INC.
100 Interpace Parkway, Parsippany NJ 07054. 973/299-9300. **Toll-free phone:** 800/526-2579. **Fax:** 973/402-1396. **Contact:** Department of Human Resources. **E-mail address:** humanresources@ebimed.com. **World Wide Web address:** http://www.ebimedical.com. **Description:** Designs, develops, manufactures, and markets products used primarily by orthopedic medical specialists in both surgical and nonsurgical therapies. Products include electrical bone growth stimulators, orthopedic support devices, spinal fixation devices for spinal fusion, external fixation devices, and cold temperature therapy. Founded in 1977. **NOTE:** Entry-level positions and part-time jobs are offered. **Special programs:** Internships; Training; Summer Jobs. **Corporate headquarters location:** This location. **Other U.S. locations:** OK. **International locations:** Puerto Rico. **Parent company:** Biomet, Inc. **Listed on:** NASDAQ. **Stock exchange symbol:** BMET. **Number of employees at this location:** 360.

ETHICON, INC.
U.S. Route 22, P.O. Box 151, Somerville NJ 08876. 908/218-0707. **Contact:** Human Resources. **World Wide Web address:** http://www.ethiconinc.com. **Description:** Manufactures products for precise wound closure including sutures, ligatures, mechanical wound closure instruments, and related products. The company also makes its own surgical needles and provides needle-suture

combinations to surgeons. **Corporate headquarters location:** This location. **Parent company:** Johnson & Johnson (New Brunswick NJ).

FLUSHING HOSPITAL MEDICAL CENTER
4500 Parsons Boulevard, Flushing NY 11355. 718/670-5000. **Recorded jobline:** 718/670-JOBS. **Contact:** Recruitment Department. **E-mail address:** yng@jhmc.org. **World Wide Web address:** http://www.flushinghospital.org. **Description:** A 428-bed hospital. Flushing Hospital Medical Center is a major teaching affiliate of The Albert Einstein School of Medicine. **NOTE:** Recruitment phone: 718/206-8670. **Number of employees at this location:** 2,400.

FUJI MEDICAL SYSTEMS USA
419 West Avenue, Stamford CT 06902. 203/324-2000. **Contact:** Human Resources. **World Wide Web address:** http://www.fujimed.com. **Description:** Manufactures and distributes X-ray machines, digital imaging systems, and radiography printers for medical offices and hospitals. **Parent company:** Fuji Photo Film Co., Ltd.

GERICARE
5 Odell Plaza, Yonkers NY 10701. 914/476-6500. **Contact:** Human Resources. **World Wide Web address:** http://www.gericaremedicalsupply.com. **Description:** A supplier of pharmaceuticals and related products to long-term care facilities, hospitals, and assisted living communities.

HACKENSACK UNIVERSITY MEDICAL CENTER
30 Prospect Avenue, Hackensack NJ 07601. 201/996-2000. **Contact:** Human Resources. **World Wide Web address:** http://www.humc.net. **Description:** A teaching medical hospital and research center affiliated with the University of Medicine. **Positions advertised include:** Registered Nurse; Licensed Practical Nurse; OB Technician; Case Manager; Social Worker.

HANGER ORTHOPEDIC GROUP, INC.
151 Hempstead Turnpike, West Hempstead NY 11552. 516/481-9670. **Contact:** Human Resources. **World Wide Web address:** http://www.hanger.com. **Description:** A provider of orthotic and prosthetic rehabilitation services with 600 offices in 43 states. **NOTE:** Send resumes to: Sharon King, Recruitment Manager, P.O. Box 406, Alpharetta GA 30009; phone: 800/303-4969; fax: 800/288-5702; e-mail: sking@hanger.com. **Corporate headquarters location:** Bethesda MD. **Other U.S. locations:** Nationwide. **Operations at this facility include:** Hanger Prosthetics & Orthotics East, Inc. **Listed on:** New York Stock Exchange. **Stock exchange symbol:** HGR. **Number of employees nationwide:** 125. **Annual sales/revenues:** $525.5 million. **Number of employees:** 3,083.

HAUSMANN INDUSTRIES
130 Union Street, Northvale NJ 07647. 201/767-0255. **Toll-free phone:** 877/737-3332. **Fax:** 201/767-1369. **Toll-free fax:** 877-737-33322. **Contact:** Human Resources. **E-mail address:** info@hausmann.com. **World Wide Web address:** http://www.hausmann.com. **Description:** Manufactures medical examination tables and physical therapy equipment. **Corporate headquarters location:** This location.

HERON HOME & HEALTH CARE AGENCY
168-30 89th Avenue, Jamaica NY 11432. 718/291-8788. **Fax:** 718/291-8852. **E-mail address:** heron@heronhomecare.com. **World Wide Web address:** http://www.heronhomecare.com. **Contact:** Director. **Description:** A home health care agency providing skilled medical professionals to homebound patients and sells surgical and medical equipment. **Corporate headquarters location:** This location. **Other area locations:** Manhattan NY; Long Island NY.

HOOPER HOLMES, INC.
dba PORTAMEDIC
170 Mount Airy Road, Basking Ridge NJ 07920. 908/766-5000. **Contact:** Manager of Human Resources. **E-mail address:** hres@hooperholmes.com. **World Wide Web address:** http://www.hooperholmes.com. **Description:** Performs health exams for insurance companies. Founded in 1899. **Positions advertised include:** Administrative Assistant. **Office hours:** Monday - Friday, 8:30 a.m. - 5:00 p.m. **Corporate headquarters location:** This location. **Other U.S. locations:** Nationwide. **Operations at this facility include:** Administration; Divisional Headquarters; Research and Development; Sales; Service. **Listed on:** American Stock Exchange. **Stock exchange symbol:** HH. **Annual sales/revenues:** More than $100 million. **Number of employees at this location:** 120. **Number of employees nationwide:** 2,500.

HOWMEDICA OSTEONICS
325 Corporate Drive, Mahwah NJ 07430. 201/825-4900. **Contact:** Human Resources Department. **E-mail address:** hr@howost.com. **World Wide Web address:** http://www.osteonics.com. **Description:** Manufactures medical implants including artificial knees, hips, shoulders, and elbows. **Parent company:** Stryker Corporation.

HUNTERDON DEVELOPMENTAL CENTER
P.O. Box 4003, Clinton NJ 08809-4003. 908/735-4031. **Physical address:** 40 Pittstown Road, Clinton NJ 08060. **Contact:** Human Resources. **Description:** A state-run residential facility for adults with developmental disabilities.

IMPATH INC.
521 West 57th Street, 5th Floor, New York NY 10019. 212/698-0300. **Fax:** 212/258-2137. **Contact:** Human Resources. **E-mail address:** hr@impath.com. **World Wide Web address:** http://www.impath.com. **Description:** Maintains a database of some one million cancer patients' profiles used to assist physicians, pharmaceutical companies, and managed care providers in the diagnosis, prognosis, and treatment of cancer. **NOTE:** Apply online. **Positions advertised include:** Lead Lab Assistant; Lab Assistant; Histology Technician; Senior A/R Manager; Sales Administration Liaison; Accounts Payable Coordinator; Clinical Research Coordinator; Accounts Payable Supervisor; Sales Representative; Regional Sales Representative; Surgical Pathologist. **Corporate headquarters location:** This location. **Other U.S. locations:** AZ; CA; MA; NJ. **Listed on:** NASDAQ. **Stock exchange symbol:** IMPH. **Chairman/CEO:** Carter H. Eckert. **Annual sales/revenues:** $188 million. **Number of employees:** 1,219.

INTEGRAMED AMERICA, INC.
One Manhattanville Road, 3rd Floor, Purchase NY 10577-2133. 914/253-8000. **Fax:** 914/253-8008. **Contact:** Human Resources. **E-mail address:** info@integramed.com. **World Wide Web address:** http://www.integramed.com. **Description:** Manages and provides services to clinical facilities and physician practices that provide assisted reproductive technology (ART) and infertility services. ART services consist of medical, psychological, and financial consultations and administration of the appropriate ART services and techniques. Infertility services provided include diagnostic testing, fertility drug therapy, tubal surgery, and intrauterine insemination. **Corporate headquarters location:** This location. **Other locations:** Nationwide. **Listed on:** NASDAQ. **Stock exchange symbol:** INMD. **Chairman/President/CEO:** Gerarda Canet. **Annual sales/revenues:** $88 million. **Number of employees:** 660.

J & K HEALTHCARE SERVICES INC.
140 Huguenot Street, New Rochelle NY 10801. 914/633-7810. **Fax:** 914/633-7864. **Contact:** Manager. **Description:** A 24-hour, supplemental staffing, private

nursing, and home health care agency offering nursing and personal care services to Westchester County Medicaid recipients.

JACOBI MEDICAL CENTER
1400 Pelham Parkway South, Building 2, Room 101, Bronx NY 10461. 718/918-5000. **Contact:** Barbara Juliano, Manager of Employment & Recruitment. **World Wide Web address:** http://www.ci.nyc.ny.us/html/hhc/jacobi/home.html. **Description:** A major medical center with over 700 beds operating six community-based Family Health Services Clinics and other medical centers throughout New York City. **Special programs:** Internships. **Parent company:** New York Health and Hospitals Corporation. **Operations at this facility include:** Administration; Regional Headquarters; Service. **Annual sales/revenues:** $4.3 billion. **Number of employees at this location:** 5,000. **Number of employees nationwide:** 60,000.

LA WEIGHTLOSS CENTERS
Radisson Hotel, Danbury CT 06811. 203/778-2501. **Toll-free phone:** 800/331-4035. **Contact:** Human Resources. **World Wide Web address:** http://www.laweightloss.com. **Description:** A weight loss center. **Positions advertised include:** Sales Counselor; Bilingual Sales Counselor.

MANHATTAN EYE, EAR & THROAT HOSPITAL
210 East 64th Street, New York NY 10021. 212/838-9200. **Fax:** 212/605-3765. **Contact:** Recruitment Manager. **World Wide Web address:** http://www.meeth.org. **Description:** A nonprofit hospital specializing in problems of the eye, ear, and throat. Founded in 1825. **NOTE:** Entry-level positions are offered. Recruitment phone: 212/605-3708. **Number of employees:** 450.

MARY IMMACULATE HOSPITAL
SAINT VINCENT CATHOLIC MEDICAL CENTERS
152-11 89th Avenue, Jamaica NY 11432. 718/558-2000. **Fax:** 718/558-2304. **Contact:** M. Caravel, Human Resources. **E-mail address:** mcaravello@svcmcny.org. **World Wide Web address:** http://www.svcmc.org. **Description:** One of the medical centers operated by St. Vincent Catholic Medical Centers in the New York area. **Positions advertised include:** Cat Scan Technician; Chief Physicist; Housekeeping Cleaner; Emergency Department Clerk; Radiology Clerk; Health Information Coordinator; Materials Management Coordinator; Mental Health Psychiatric Technician; Operating Room Technician; Patient Care Associate; Pharmacist; Radiological Technologist; Registered Nurse; Respiratory Therapist; Special Procedures Technician; Staff Nurse; Operating Room Nurse.

THE MATHENY SCHOOL AND HOSPITAL
P.O. Box 339, Peapack NJ 07977. 908/234-0011. **Fax:** 908/234-9496. **Contact:** Human Resources. **World Wide Web address:** http://www.matheny.org. **Description:** A licensed hospital and school for people with severe physical disabilities such as cerebral palsy and spina bifida. **NOTE:** Entry-level positions and second and third shifts are offered. **Positions advertised include:** Nurse; Occupational Therapist; Physical Therapist; Social Worker; Speech Therapist; Research Therapist; Rehab Technologist. **Special programs:** Internships; Apprenticeships; Training. **President:** Robert Schonhorn.

MAXIM HEALTHCARE
622 George's Road, North Brunswick NJ 08902. 732/246-1687. **Toll-free phone:** 800/697-2247. **Contact:** Manager. **World Wide Web address:** http://www.maxhealth.com. **Description:** A home health care agency. **Positions advertised include:** Sales Recruiter. **Corporate headquarters location:** Lake Success NY. **Other U.S. locations:** Nationwide. **Number of employees nationwide:** 20,000.

MEDICAL RESOURCES, INC.
125 State Street, Suite 200, Hackensack NJ 07601. 201/488-6230. **Fax:** 201/488-8455. **Contact:** Human Resources. **World Wide Web address:** http://www.mrii.com. **Description:** Owns and manages medical diagnostic imaging centers nationwide. The centers offer magnetic resonance imaging (MRI), computerized tomography (CT), nuclear medicine, mammography, ultrasound, and X-ray. **Positions advertised include:** Data Analyst; Ultrasound Technologist; MRI Technologist; CT Technologist. **Listed on:** NASDAQ. **Stock exchange symbol:** MRII. **Annual sales/revenues:** More than $100 million.

MEDPOINTE INC.
265 Davidson Avenue, Somerset NJ 08873. 732/561-2200. **Contact:** Human Resources. **World Wide Web address:** http://www.medpointe.com. **Description:** A major manufacturer of ethical drugs and consumer products. Health care products include tranquilizers, laxatives, antibacterials, analgesics, decongestants, and cold and cough remedies. The company also manufactures tests for pregnancy, mononucleosis, rubella, and meningitis. Consumer products include Arrid antiperspirants and deodorants, Trojan condoms, hair lotions, and pet care items. **NOTE:** Entry-level positions and second and third shifts are offered. **Corporate headquarters location:** This location. **Other U.S. locations:** Decatur IL. **Number of employees nationwide:** 2,200.

MENNEN MEDICAL INC.
10123 Main Street, Clarence NY 14031. 716/759-6921. **Toll-free phone:** 800/223-2201. **Fax:** 215/322-0199. **Contact:** Human Resources Director. **E-mail address:** humanresources_hr@mennenmedical.com. **World Wide Web address:** http://www.mennenmedical.com. **Description:** Mennen Medical Inc. manufactures and sells heart monitors. **Positions advertised include:** Clinical Education Specialist; Clinical Care Registered Nurse; Medical Equipment Sales Representative. **Parent company:** Charterhouse Group International.

MONMOUTH-OCEAN HOSPITAL SERVICE CORPORATION
4806 Megill Road, Wall Township, Neptune NJ 07753. 732/919-3045. **Fax:** 732-919-2699. **Contact:** Human Resources. **E-mail address:** http://www.jobs@monoc.org. **World Wide Web address:** http://www.monoc.org. **Description:** The Monmouth Ocean Hospital Service Corporation, is a non-profit company consisting of nineteen acute-care hospitals located in Monmouth, Ocean, Atlantic, Begen, Cape May, Hudson, Essex and Union Counties, New Jersey. **NOTE:** Search for open positions online. **Positions advertised include:** Control Center Supervisor; Emergency Medical Dispatcher; Emergency Medical Technician; EMS Supervisor (Clinical/QA); Medical Collector; Paramedic; Registered Nurse. **Number of employees nationwide:** 850.

NATIONAL HOME HEALTH CARE CORPORATION
700 White Plains Road, Suite 275, Scarsdale NY 10583. 914/722-9000. **Fax:** 914/722-9239. **Contact:** Human Resources. **World Wide Web address:** http://www.nhhc.net. **Description:** National Home Health Care, through its subsidiaries, is a national provider of a variety of health related services including home care, general care, nurses, and therapists. **Corporate headquarters location:** This location. **Subsidiaries include:** Health Acquisition Corporation provides home health care services, primarily through certified home health aides and personal care aides in the New York metropolitan area; Brevard Medical Center, Incorporated provides both primary and specialty outpatient medical services in Brevard County FL; First Health, Incorporated provides primary care outpatient medical services in Volusia County FL. **Listed on:** NASDAQ. **Stock exchange symbol:** NHHC. **President/CEO:** Steven Fialkow. **Number of employees nationwide:** 2,200.

NEW CANAAN VETERINARY HOSPITAL
7 Vitti Street, New Canaan CT 06840. 203/966-1627. **Contact:** Human Resources. **E-mail address:** ncvhdoc1@aol.com. **Description:** New Canaan Veterinary Hospital is an animal hospital. Services include radiology, dentistry, electrocardiography, surgery, diagnostic ultrasound, boarding, and kennel services.

THE NEW YORK EYE AND EAR INFIRMARY
310 East 14th Street, Second Avenue, New York NY 10003. 212/979-4000. **Contact:** Human Resources. **World Wide Web address:** http://www.nyee.edu. **Description:** A hospital specializing in ocular and auditory care. Founded in 1820. **NOTE:** To contact Human Resources directly, call 2121/979-4275. **Positions advertised include:** Outpatient Registrar; Medical Records Clerk; Administrative Coordinator; LPN; Registered Nurse; Ancillary Technician; Nursing Assistant; Ophthalmic Technician; Physician Assistant; Social Worker; Security Guard. **Number of employees at this location:** 600.

NEW YORK METHODIST HOSPITAL
506 Sixth Street, Brooklyn NY 11215. 718/768-4305. **Fax:** 718/768-4324. **Contact:** Human Resources. **World Wide Web address:** http://www.nym.org. **Description:** An acute-care teaching hospital affiliated with the Weil Medical College of Cornel University. Founded in 1881. **Positions advertised include:** Food Service Worker; Laundry Worker; Radiation Therapist; Respiratory Therapist; Stationary Engineer; Physician Assistant; Radiologic Technologist; Imaging Technologist; EEG Technician; Lab Supervisor; X-Ray Technician; Senior Accountant; LPN; Registered Nurse; Case Manager; Anesthesia Technician; Nurse Clinical Coordinator. **Operations at this facility include:** Administration; Research and Development. **Number of employees nationwide:** 2,300.

NEW YORK UNIVERSITY MEDICAL CENTER
One Park Avenue, 16th Floor, New York NY 10016. 212/263-1999. **Fax:** 212/404-3897. **Contact:** Recruitment and Staffing Department. **E-mail address:** nyumc-careers@msnyuhealth.org. **World Wide Web address:** http://www.med.nyu.edu. **Description:** A nonprofit medical center engaged in patient care, research, and education. The central component of New York University Medical Center is Tisch Hospital, a 726-bed acute care facility and a major center for specialized procedures in cardiovascular services, neurosurgery, AIDS, cancer treatment, reconstructive surgery, and transplantation. The medical center also includes the Rusk Institute of Rehabilitation Medicine, the Hospital of Joint Diseases, and several medical schools. The Rusk Institute of Rehabilitation Medicine, a 152-bed unit, is one of the world's largest university-affiliated centers for the treatment and training of physically disabled adults and children, as well as for research in rehabilitation medicine. The Hospital of Joint Diseases, with 226 beds, is dedicated solely to neuromusculoskeletal diseases. The School of Medicine, the Post-Graduate Medical School, and the Skirball Institute of Biomolecular Medicine are also part of the medical center. **Positions advertised include:** Assistant Research Scientist; Staff Physical Therapist; Divisional Assistant; Office Assistant; Departmental Assistant; Restricted Funds Manager; Executive Assistant; Assistant Laboratory Technician; Programmer; Receptionist; Network Support Specialist; Nurse Practitioner; Billing Coordinator; Library Assistant; Special Procedure Technician; MRI Specialist; CT Technologist; Business Systems Analyst; Grants Writer. **Special programs:** Internships; Summer Job; Tuition Assistance Program. **Corporate headquarters location:** This location. **Number of employees at this location:** 8,000.

NUTRITION 21
4 Manhattanville Road, Purchase NY 10577-2197. 914/701-4500. **Fax:** 914/696-0860. **Contact:** Human Resources Department. **E-mail address:**

mail@nutrition21.com. **World Wide Web address:** http://www.nutrition21.com. **Description:** Develops and markets nutrition products. The company focuses on products with medical value for consumers concerned with cardiovascular health and diabetes. The company is composed of an Ingredients Division, a Consumer Products Division, and Therapeutic Division. Founded in 1982. **Corporate headquarters location:** This location. **Listed on:** NASDAQ. **Stock exchange symbol:** NXXI. **President/CEO/Director:** Gail Montgomery. **Sales/revenue:** $14.7 million. **Number of employees at this location:** 27.

OCEAN COUNTY VETERINARY HOSPITAL
838 River Avenue, Lakewood NJ 08701. 732/363-7202. **Fax:** 732/370-4176. **Contact:** Human Resources. **World Wide Web address:** http://www.ocvh.com. **Description:** Provides health care services to dogs, cats, and exotic pets including surgery, hospitalization, and diagnostic testing. **Positions advertised include:** Technician; Receptionist.

OVERLOOK HOSPITAL
P.O. Box 220, Summit NJ 07902-0220. 908/522-2241. **Physical address:** 99 Beauvoir Avenue, Summit NJ 07901. **Contact:** Human Resources. **World Wide Web address:** http://www.overlookfoundation.org. **Description:** A part of Atlantic Health Systems, Overlook Hospital is a 490-bed, public hospital with extensive facilities for pediatrics, oncology, cardiology, and same-day surgery.

P.S.A. HEALTHCARE
4900 Route 33, Suite 100, Neptune NJ 07753-6804. 732/938-5550. **Fax:** 732/938-6535. **Contact:** Human Resources. **World Wide Web address:** http://www.psakids.com. **Description:** Provides infusion therapy, nursing, and other home health care services to clients. **Positions advertised include:** Clinical Care Coordinator; Registered Nurse; Field Nurse Recruiter.

PARK EAST ANIMAL HOSPITAL
52 East 64th Street, New York NY 10021. 212/832-8417. **Fax:** 212/355-3620. **Contact:** Vicki Ungar, Office Manager. **World Wide Web address:** http://www.parkeastanimalhospital.com. **Description:** A 24-hour small animal hospital offering medical, nursing, and surgical services for pets. This location also hires seasonally. Founded in 1961. **Special programs:** Internships; Training; Summer Jobs. **Corporate headquarters location:** This location. **President:** Dr. Lewis Berman. **Number of employees at this location:** 25.

PFIZER
235 East 42nd Street, New York NY 10017. 212/573-2323. **Recorded jobline:** 212/733-4150. **Contact:** Employee Resources. **E-mail address:** resumes@pfizer.com. **World Wide Web address:** http://www.pfizer.com. **Description:** A leading pharmaceutical company that distributes products concerning cardiovascular health, central nervous system disorders, infectious diseases, and women's health worldwide. The company's brand-name products include Benadryl, Ben Gay, Cortizone, Desitin, Halls, Listerine, Sudafed, and Zantac 75. **Company slogan:** We're part of the cure. **NOTE:** Interested job seekers may apply online. **Positions advertised include:** Marketing Manager; Conventions Manager; Corporate Philanthropy Programs Manager; Administrative Assistant; Senior Human Resources Manager; Capacity and Inventory Analysis Manager; Supply Chain Manager; Corporate Counsel; Product Manager; Assistant Director of Corporate Media Relations; Regional Medical Research Specialist; Business Technology Manager. **Corporate headquarters location:** This location. **Other U.S. locations:** Nationwide. **International locations:** Worldwide. **Subsidiaries include:** Pfizer Animal Health Group; Pfizer Consumer Products Division; Pfizer Hospital Products Group; Pfizer International; Pfizer Pharmaceutical Group; Pfizer Specialty Chemicals.

Listed on: New York Stock Exchange. **Stock exchange symbol:** PFE. **Number of employees worldwide:** 46,000.

QUANTRONIX
41 Research Way, East Setauket NY 11733. 631/784-6100. **Fax:** 631/784-6101. **Contact:** Human Resources. **E-mail address:** hr@quantronixlasers.com. **World Wide Web address:** http://www.quantronixlasers.com. **Description:** Manufactures laser systems for dental and medical uses. The company also manufactures lasers for industrial purposes. **NOTE:** Interested job seekers may apply online. **Positions advertised include:** High Power Industrial Laser Scientist; Diode-Pumped Laser Engineer; Ultrafast Systems Scientist; Applications Technician; Micro-Electronic Technician; Product Manager; Customer Service Representative; Marketing/Graphic Artist; CNC Operator; Optical Inspection Technician; Buyer; Senior Planner; Stockroom Clerk. **Corporate headquarters location:** This location. **International locations:** Germany; Malaysia; France; India; Japan.

RICHMOND CHILDREN'S CENTER
100 Corporate Drive, Yonkers NY 10701. 914/968-7170. **Contact:** Director of Human Resources. **World Wide Web address:** http://www.richmondgroup.org. **Description:** A nonprofit, intermediate care facility (residential to long-term) for individuals with severe to profound physical and developmental disabilities. Services in the main facility include medical care; recreational services; and physical, language, occupational, and speech therapies. Richmond Children's Center offers other services in the community including case management, early intervention, group homes, and respite programs (for children with special needs who are cared for at home). **Number of employees at this location:** 325.

SACHEM ANIMAL HOSPITAL
227 Union Avenue, Holbrook NY 11741. 631/467-2121. **Contact:** Human Resources. **World Wide Web address:** http://www.sachemanimalhospital.com. **Description:** Sachem Animal Hospital provides general medical and surgical services, dental services, and boarding for domestic and exotic pets. The hospital also specializes in reproduction and infertility services.

ST. CLARE'S HOSPITAL
600 McClellan Street, Schenectady NY 12304. 518/347-5630. **Toll-free phone:** 800/462-1713. **Fax:** 518/347-5522. **Contact:** Peter Jones, Employment Coordinator. **E-mail address:** jobs@stclares.org. **World Wide Web address:** http://www.stclares.org. **Description:** A 200-bed acute care hospital. Founded in 1949. **Positions advertised include:** Registered Nurse; LPN; Clinical Leader; Nursing Supervisor; Supervisor/Educator; Cardiology Technician; Certified Respiratory Therapy Technician; Chaplain; Diet Technician; Medical Technologist; Patient Care Dietician; Pharmacist; Physical Therapy Assistant; Security Officer; Microbiology Technical Specialist; Ultrasound Technologist; Film Librarian; Receptionist; Unit Secretary; Weekend Clerk. **Office hours:** Monday - Friday, 10:00 a.m. - 2:00 p.m. **Corporate headquarters location:** This location. **Operations at this facility include:** Administration. **President/CEO:** Paul Chodkowski. **Number of employees at this location:** 1,150.

ST. LUKE'S-ROOSEVELT HOSPITAL CENTER
1111 Amsterdam Avenue, New York NY 10025. 212/523-4000. **Contact:** Recruitment. **World Wide Web address:** http://www.wehealnewyork.org. **Description:** A 1,315-bed, teaching hospital associated with Columbia University. **NOTE:** Resumes should be sent to Human Resources, 555 West 57th Street, 19th Floor, New York NY 10019 or faxed to: 212/523-7193. **Positions advertised include:** Nurse Practitioner; Neurophysiology Technician; Occupational Therapist; General Accounting Manager; Nurse Supervisor; Registered Dietician; Expeditor; Director of Safety; Patient Advocate; Medical

Biller; Medical Administrative Assistant; Senior Systems Analyst; Nurse Recruiter; Medical Office Coordinator; Nurse Educator; EEG Technician; Senior Financial Analyst; Epilepsy Monitoring Technician. **Special programs:** Internships. **Parent company:** Continuum Health Partners, Inc. **Number of employees at this location:** 6,000.

SAINT BARNABAS HEALTH CARE SYSTEM
368 Lakehurst Road, Suite 203, Toms River NJ 08755. 888/724-7123. **Contact:** Human Resources. **E-mail address:** info@sbhcs.com. **World Wide Web address:** http://www.sbhcscareers.com. **Description:** A health care delivery system that spans the state of New Jersey and includes eight acute care hospitals, nine nursing and rehabilitation centers, three assisted living facilities, geriatric centers, and ambulatory care centers. **NOTE:** Search and apply for positions online. **Positions advertised include:** Administrative Assistant; Case Coordinator; Certified Nursing Assistant (CNA); CM Director of Nursing; Coder; Compliance Associate; Endo Technician; General Clerical; Housekeeper; Licensed Practical Nurse; Payroll Coordinator; Respiratory Therapist; Respiratory Therapy Coordinator; Staff Registered Nurse. **Other area locations:** Statewide.

HENRY SCHEIN, INC.
135 Duryea Road, Melville NY 11747. 631/843-5500. **Fax:** 631/843-5658. **Contact:** Human Resources. **World Wide Web address:** http://www.henryschein.com. **Description:** Manufactures and distributes dental and medical instruments. Henry Schein, Incorporated serves the dental, medical, and veterinary markets. **Positions advertised include:** Associate Financial Analyst; Veterinary Division Telesales Representative; Hyperion Senior Systems Analyst; Credit and Collections Representative. **Corporate headquarters location:** This location. **Other U.S. locations:** Nationwide. **International locations:** Worldwide. **Operations at this facility include:** Sales. **Listed on:** NASDAQ. **Stock exchange symbol:** HSIC. **President/CEO/Chairman:** Stanley M. Bergman. **Sales/revenue:** $2.8 billion. **Number of employees at this location:** 1,000. **Number of employees nationwide:** 1,700.

SIEMENS MEDICAL
186 Wood Avenue South, Iselin NJ 08830. 732/321-4500. **Contact:** Personnel Office. **World Wide Web address:** http://www.siemensmedical.com. **Description:** Develops, manufactures, and sells medical systems including digital X-rays and 3-D ultrasound equipment. Products are used in a variety of areas including cardiology, audiology, surgery, critical care, and oncology. **Positions advertised include:** Advanced Consultant; Business & Product Development Manager; Repair Operating Manager; Technical Competence Center Representative; New Units Vice President. **Corporate headquarters location:** This location.

SOUTH BEACH PSYCHIATRIC CENTER
777 Seaview Avenue, Staten Island NY 10305. 718/667-2726. **Fax:** 718/667-2467. **Contact:** Human Resources. **World Wide Web address:** http://www.omh.state.ny.us. **Description:** South Beach Psychiatric Center is a New York State Office of Mental Health outpatient facility that is organized to deliver comprehensive mental health services to people in West Brooklyn, Staten Island, and New York City. **Positions advertised include:** Licensed Psychologist; Mental Health Therapy Aide; Nurse Administrator; Community Mental Health Nurse; Psychiatrist; Director of Nursing. **Corporate headquarters location:** Albany NY. **Operations at this facility include:** Administration. **Number of employees at this location:** 1,100.

TENDER LOVING CARE/STAFF BUILDERS
1234 Summer Street, 3rd Floor, Stamford CT 06905. 203/327-2680. **Contact:** Office Manager. **World Wide Web address:** http://www.tlcathome.com.

Description: A home health care agency. **Corporate headquarters location:** Lake Success NY. **Other U.S. locations:** Nationwide. **Number of employees nationwide:** 20,000.

TENDER LOVING CARE/STAFF BUILDERS

1983 Marcus Avenue, Suite 200, Lake Success NY 11042. 516/358-1000. **Fax:** 516/358-2465. **Contact:** Human Resources Department. **World Wide Web address:** http://www.tlcathome.com. **Description:** A home health care agency. **Corporate headquarters location:** This location. **Other U.S. locations:** Nationwide. **Operations at this facility include:** Administration. **Number of employees at this location:** 300. **Number of employees nationwide:** 20,000.

TENDER LOVING CARE/STAFF BUILDERS

99 Railroad Station Plaza, Suite 100, Hicksville NY 11801-2898. 516/935-3737. **Contact:** Human Resources. **World Wide Web address:** http://www.tlcathome.com. **Description:** A home health care agency. **Corporate headquarters location:** Lake Success NY. **Other U.S. locations:** Nationwide.

TRINITAS HOSPITAL

18-20 South Broad Street, Elizabeth NJ 07201. 908/994-5325. **Fax:** 908/527-0195. **Contact:** Human Resources. **World Wide Web address:** http://www.trinitashospital.org. **Description:** A hospital providing treatments for a variety of illnesses including cardiovascular diseases and cancer. **Positions advertised include:** Telephone Operator; Receptionist; Secretary; Lead Cashier; Registrar Trainee; Registrar; Insurance Bill Representative; Radiation Therapist; Van Driver; Diet Aide; Medical Technologist; Registered Nurse; Licensed Practical Nurse; Certified Nurses Aide; Occupational Therapist; Physical Therapist; Medical Technologist; Physicist; Mental Health Worker; Fitness Aide.

TRIZETTO GROUP, INC.

1700 Broadway, New York NY 10019. 212/765-8500. **Contact:** Human Resources. **World Wide Web address:** http://www.trizetto.com. **Description:** Develops health management software for insurance agencies and health care providers. **NOTE:** Interested jobseekers should send resumes to 1085 Morris Avenue, Union NJ 07083. **Corporate headquarters location:** Newport Beach CA. **Listed on:** NASDAQ. **Stock exchange symbol:** TZIX.

U.S. SURGICAL

150 Glover Avenue, Norwalk CT 06856. 203/845-1000. **Contact:** Human Resources Department. **World Wide Web address:** http://www.ussurg.com. **Description:** A manufacturer of surgical instruments. **Parent company:** Tyco Healthcare Group LP.

UNIVERSITY HOSPITAL

30 Bergen Street, Building 8, Newark NJ 07107. 973/972-0012. **Recorded jobline:** 973/972-6740. **Contact:** Human Resources. **World Wide Web address:** http://www.theuniversityhospital.com. **Description:** A 466-bed teaching hospital of the University of Medicine and Dentistry of New Jersey. **Positions advertised include:** Transport Customer Service; Principal Lab Assistant; Food Service Worker; Program Support Specialist; Research Associate; Patient Accounts Clerk; Research Teaching Specialist; Advanced Practical Nurse; Management Assistant; Case Management Coordinator.

VITAL SIGNS, INC.

20 Campus Road, Totowa NJ 07512. 973/790-1330. **Toll-free phone:** 800/932-0760. **Fax:** 973/790-4271. **Contact:** Human Resources. **E-mail address:** humanresources@vital-signs.com. **World Wide Web address:** http://www.vital-signs.com. **Description:** Manufactures disposable medical products such as

face masks, manual resuscitators, anesthesia kits, and other respiratory-related critical care products. **Corporate headquarters location:** This location. **Operations at this facility include:** Administration; Manufacturing; Research and Development; Service. **Number of employees at this location:** 350. **Number of employees nationwide:** 450.

WATERVIEW NURSING CARE CENTER
119-15 27th Avenue, Flushing NY 11354. 718/461-5000. **Fax:** 718/321-1984. **Contact:** Personnel. **World Wide Web address:** http://www.healthlistings.com/waterview. **Description:** A 200-bed facility that offers specialized, long-term nursing care to chronically ill individuals of all ages. Waterview's in-house medical staff provides care in areas that include psychiatry, psychotherapy, dentistry, podiatry, otolaryngology, ophthalmology, hematology, urology, neurology, optometry, portable X-rays, and lab work. **Special programs:** Training; Summer Jobs. **Office hours:** Monday - Friday, 9:00 a.m. - 5:00 p.m. **Number of employees at this location:** 280.

WEIGHT WATCHERS INTERNATIONAL INC.
175 Crossways Park West, Woodbury NY 11797. 516/390-1400. **Contact:** Human Resources. **World Wide Web address:** http://www.weightwatchers.com. **Description:** Conducts and supervises franchised weight-control classes in 21 countries, markets packaged products through its food licensees, and publishes the *Weight Watchers* magazine in three countries. **Corporate headquarters location:** This location. **Listed on:** New York Stock Exchange. **Stock exchange symbol:** WTW.

WESTSIDE VETERINARY CENTER
220 West 83rd Street, New York NY 10024. 212/580-1800. **Contact:** Human Resources. **Description:** An animal hospital offering medical, surgical, and dental services.

WOODBRIDGE DEVELOPMENTAL CENTER
Rahway Avenue, P.O. Box 189, Woodbridge NJ 07001. 732/499-5525. **Contact:** Human Resources. **Description:** A residential treatment facility for adolescents and adults with developmental disabilities.

HOTELS AND RESTAURANTS

You can expect to find the following types of companies in this section:
Casinos • Dinner Theaters • Hotel/Motel Operators • Resorts • Restaurants

AS MANAGEMENT
760 Summer Street, Suite 103, Stamford CT 06901. 203/967-4003. **Contact:** Human Resources. **Description:** Manages and operates four restaurants in Massachusetts and Florida under the name Victoria Station.

ARK RESTAURANTS CORPORATION
85 Fifth Avenue, 14th Floor, New York NY 10003. 212/206-8800. **Fax:** 212/206-8845. **Contact:** Marilyn Guy, Personnel Manager. **World Wide Web address:** http://www.arkrestaurants.com. **Description:** Ark Restaurants Corporation and its subsidiaries own, operate, or manage 27 restaurants nationwide. **Corporate headquarters location:** This location. **Listed on:** NASDAQ. **Stock exchange symbol:** ARKR. **Chairman:** Ernest Bogen. **Annual sales/revenues:** $115 million. **Number of employees:** 2,000.

THE CARLYLE HOTEL
35 East 76th Street, New York NY 10021. 212/744-1600. **Fax:** 212/717-4682. **Contact:** Human Resources. **E-mail address:** carlylejobs@rosewoodhotels.com. **World Wide Web address:** http://www.rosewoodhotels.com. **Description:** A luxury hotel offering 180-rooms, three restaurants, and banquet/meeting facilities. **Corporate headquarters location:** This location. **Parent company:** Rosewood Hotels & Resorts.

CHEFS INTERNATIONAL, INC.
62 Broadway, P.O. Box 1332, Point Pleasant Beach NJ 08742. 732/295-0350. **Contact:** Office Manager. **World Wide Web address:** http://www.jackbakerslobstershanty.com. **Description:** Operates eight Lobster Shanty restaurants in New Jersey and Florida. **Corporate headquarters location:** This location.

CLUB HOTEL BY DOUBLETREE
789 Connecticut Avenue, Norwalk CT 06854. 203/853-3477. **Fax:** 203/855-9404. **Contact:** Human Resources. **World Wide Web address:** http://www.doubletree.com. **Description:** A 268-room business hotel operating as part of the Doubletree chain.

COURTYARD BY MARRIOTT
475 White Plains Road, Tarrytown NY 10591. 914/631-1122. **Contact:** General Manager. **World Wide Web address:** http://www.courtyard.com. **Description:** A hotel with 139 guest rooms and two meeting rooms. **Positions advertised include:** Senior Account Executive. **Parent company:** Marriott International, Inc. (Washington DC).

CROWNE PLAZA
66 Hale Avenue, White Plains NY 10601. 914/682-0050. **Toll-free phone:** 800/752-4672. **Fax:** 914/682-0405. **Contact:** Human Resources. **World Wide Web address:** http://www.crowneplaza.com. **Description:** A 401-room hotel with 13 meeting rooms. **Parent company:** Six Continents PLC (London, United Kingdom).

DORAL ARROWWOOD
975 Anderson Hill Road, Rye Brook NY 10573. 914/935-6651. **Fax:** 914/323-1126. **Contact:** Human Resources. **E-mail address:** sgarbo@doralarrowwood.com. **World Wide Web address:** http://www.arrowwood.com. **Description:** A hotel and conference center with 272 guest rooms and 36 meeting rooms.

ESSEX HOUSE
160 Central Park South, New York NY 10019. 212/247-0300. **Fax:** 212/315-1839. **Contact:** Human Resources. **World Wide Web address:** http://www.essexhouse.com. **Description:** Operates a hotel with 597 guest rooms and 150 condominiums. **Parent company:** Starwood Hotels & Resorts Worldwide Inc. (White Plaines NY).

GURNEY'S INN
290 Old Montauk Highway, Montauk NY 11954. 631/668-2345. **Fax:** 631/668-1881. **Contact:** Human Resources. **E-mail address:** hr@gurneys-inn.com. **World Wide Web address:** http://www.gurneys-inn.com. **Description:** Gurney's resort, spa, and convention center offers fine-dining and a full-service, 109-room hotel. **NOTE:** Entry-level positions are offered. Human Resources phone: 631/668-1770. **Positions advertised include:** Hair Stylist; Front Desk Receptionist; Message Therapist; Lifeguard; Weight Room Attendant; Spa Attendant; Porter; Fitness Instructor; Service Desk Attendant; Counter Server. **Special programs:** Internships; Apprenticeships; Summer Jobs. **Office hours:** Monday - Friday, 9:00 a.m. - 5:00 p.m. **Corporate headquarters location:** This location. **Number of employees at this location:** 250.

THE HELMSLEY PARK LANE HOTEL
36 Central Park South, New York NY 10019. 212/371-4000. **Fax:** 212/935-5489. **Contact:** Personnel. **World Wide Web address:** http://www.helmsleyhotels.com. **Description:** Operates a 650-room, luxury hotel with a wide range of lodging, lounge, dining, and meeting rooms. **Parent company:** Helmsley Hotels Group.

HILTON OF HASBROUCK HEIGHTS
650 Terrace Avenue, Hasbrouck Heights NJ 07604. 201/288-6100. **Contact:** Human Resources. **World Wide Web address:** http://www.hilton.com. **Description:** A hotel that provides a wide range of lodging, restaurant, lounge, meeting, and banquet facilities as part of an international chain. **Positions advertised include:** Customer Service Representative; Food and Beverage Service Worker; Hotel/Motel Clerk; Housekeeper. **Operations at this facility include:** Administration.

HILTON PARSIPPANY
One Hilton Court, Parsippany NJ 07054. 973/267-7373. **Fax:** 973/984-6853. **Contact:** Human Resources. **World Wide Web address:** http://www.hilton.com. **Description:** Recently renovated location of the hotel chain. Features a Ruth's Chris Steak House and accessibility to various area attractions.

HILTONS OF WESTCHESTER
699 Westchester Avenue, Rye Brook NY 10573. 914/939-6300. **Fax:** 914/939-7374. **Contact:** Human Resources. **World Wide Web address:** http://www.hilton.com. **Description:** Hiltons of Westchester is comprised of two separate Hilton hotels: a 444-room facility in Rye Brook and a 252-room facility in Tarrytown. Founded in 1919. **NOTE:** Entry-level positions, part-time jobs, and second and third shifts are offered. **Positions advertised include:** Assistant Director of Human Resources. **Corporate headquarters location:** Beverly Hills CA. **Other U.S. locations:** Nationwide. **International locations:** Worldwide.

Parent company: Hilton Hotels Corp. (Beverly Hills CA). **Number of employees at this location:** 500.

HOTEL INTER-CONTINENTAL NEW YORK
111 East 48th Street, New York NY 10017. 212/755-5900. **Contact:** Human Resources. **World Wide Web address:** http://www.interconti.com. **Description:** A hotel with 682 rooms. **Special programs:** Internships. **Number of employees at this location:** 500.

LOEWS CORPORATION
655 Madison Avenue, 7th Floor, New York NY 10021-8087. 212/521-2000. **Fax:** 212/521-2466. **Contact:** Margorie Kouroupos, Human Resources. **E-mail address:** hrrep@newposition.com. **World Wide Web address:** http://www.loews.com. **Description:** A holding company and one of the largest diversified financial corporations in the U.S. with interests in the financial, tobacco, hotel, drilling, and watch industries. **Positions advertised include:** Graphic Designer; Digital Image Librarian; Information Technology Security Specialist; Internal Auditor Assistant; Internal Hotel Auditor Assistant. **Corporate headquarters location:** This location. **Subsidiaries include:** CNA Financial Corporation, which provides insurance services; Carolina Group, and Lorillard, Inc., which produce tobacco products; Loews Hotels Holding Corporation, which owns and operates a nationwide chain of hotels; Diamond Offshore Drilling, Inc., an offshore drilling company; and Bulova Corporation, which distributes watches and clocks. **Listed on:** New York Stock Exchange. **Stock exchange symbol:** LTR. **Co-Chairmen:** Lawrence A. Tisch and Preston (Bob) R. Tisch. **Annual sales/revenues:** $17.5 billion. **Number of employees:** 25,800.

MARRIOTT EASTSIDE
525 Lexington Avenue, New York NY 10017. 212/755-4000. **Toll-free phone:** 800/228-9290. **Fax:** 212/751-3440. **Contact:** Director of Personnel. **World Wide Web address:** http://www.marriotthotels.com. **Description:** Operates a luxury hotel with 652 guest rooms and dining, meeting, and sales function facilities. **Parent company:** Marriott International, Inc. (Washington DC).

THE NEW YORK HELMSLEY HOTEL
212 East 42nd Street, New York NY 10017. 212/490-8900. **Fax:** 212/986-4792. **Contact:** Marilyn O'Brien, Personnel Director. **E-mail address:** general_info@helmsleyhotels.com. **World Wide Web address:** http://www.helmsleyhotels.com. **Description:** Operates a 793-room luxury hotel facility with a wide range of lodging, dining, meeting, and other facilities. **Parent company:** Helmsley Hotels Group.

PARK CENTRAL HOTEL
870 Seventh Avenue, New York NY 10019-4038. 212/247-8000. **Toll-free phone:** 800/346-1359. **Contact:** Human Resources. **World Wide Web address:** http://www.parkcentralny.com. **Description:** A 1,260-room hotel with restaurant, lounge, banquet, convention, and meeting facilities. **Corporate headquarters location:** Hampton NH. **Parent company:** Omni/Donley Hotel Group. **Operations at this facility include:** Sales; Service.

PRIME HOSPITALITY CORPORATION
700 Route 46 East, Fairfield NJ 07007. 973/882-1010. **Contact:** Human Resources. **E-mail address:** recruiter@primehospitality.com. **World Wide Web address:** http://www.primehospitality.com. **Description:** An independent hotel operating company with ownership and management of 86 full- and limited-service hotels in 19 states and one resort hotel in the U.S. Virgin Islands. Hotels typically contain 100 to 200 guest rooms or suites and operate under franchise agreements with national hotel chains or under the company's Wellesley Inns or AmeriSuites trade names. Founded in 1961. **Corporate headquarters location:**

This location. **Other U.S. locations:** Nationwide. **Operations at this facility include:** Administration. **Listed on:** New York Stock Exchange. **Stock exchange symbol:** PDQ. **Annual sales/revenues:** More than $100 million. **Number of employees at this location:** 190. **Number of employees nationwide:** 6,050.

RENAISSANCE WESTCHESTER HOTEL
80 West Red Oak Lane, White Plains NY 10604. 914/694-5400. **Contact:** Human Resources. **World Wide Web address:** http://www.renaissancehotels.com. **Description:** A hotel with 364 guest rooms and 18 meeting rooms. **Parent company:** Marriott International, Incorporated. **Listed on:** New York Stock Exchange. **Stock exchange symbol:** MAR.

RESTAURANT ASSOCIATES CORPORATION
120 West 45th Street, 16th Floor, New York NY 10036. 212/789-8201. **Fax:** 212/613-4695. **Contact:** Manager of Recruitment. **E-mail address:** careers@restaurantassociates.com. **World Wide Web address:** http://www.restaurantassociates.com. **Description:** A broad-based company that operates 60 restaurants in major cities, cultural centers, and leisure attractions along the East Coast. Private food service facilities are also offered to corporations, institutions, and clubs. **NOTE:** To contact Human Resources directly, call 212/789-8201. **Positions advertised include:** Director; Assistant Director; Restaurant Manager; Bar Manager; Beverage Manager; Sous Chef; Controller; Catering Director; Catering Sales Director. **Special programs:** Internships. **Corporate headquarters location:** This location. **Parent company:** Compass Group. **Operations at this facility include:** Divisional Headquarters.

SARA LEE COFFEE AND TEA
500 Mamaroneck Avenue, 5th floor, Harrison NY 10528. 914/670-3300. **Contact:** Personnel. **E-mail address:** recruiting@saralee.com. **World Wide Web address:** http://www.saralee.com. **Description:** Produces a nationally distributed brand of premium coffee. The company also operates a chain of cafes and drive-thru restaurants. **Corporate headquarters location:** Chicago IL. **Other U.S. locations:** Nationwide. **Subsidiaries include:** Cain's Coffee Company; Greenwich Mills Company. **Parent company:** Sara Lee Corporation. **Operations at this facility include:** Administration; Divisional Headquarters; Sales. **Listed on:** New York Stock Exchange. **Stock exchange symbol:** SLE.

SHERATON CROSSROADS
1 International Boulevard, Rt. 17 North, Mahwah NJ 07495. 201/529-1660. **Fax:** 201/529-4709. **Contact:** Human Resources. **World Wide Web address:** http://www.starwoodhotels.com. **Description:** A 227-room hotel, 40 minutes from New York City, offering a view of the Ramapo Valley and 23,000 ft of meeting space capable of accommodating 1,200 people. **Other U.S. locations:** Nationwide.

SHERATON DANBURY
18 Old Ridgebury Road, Danbury CT 06810. 203/794-0600. **Fax:** 203/830-5125. **Contact:** Human Resources. **World Wide Web address:** http://www.starwood.com/sheraton. **Description:** One location of the hotel chain, offering meeting facilities, a business center, two restaurants, and a fitness center. **Positions advertised include:** Catering Sales Manager. **Other U.S. locations:** Nationwide.

STARBUCKS COFFEE
757 Third Avenue, New York NY 10017. 212/715-9884. **Contact:** Human resources. **World Wide Web address:** http://www.starbucks.com. **Description:** A worldwide retail gourmet coffee chain **NOTE:** Retail and corporate positions

are available. **Corporate headquarters location:** Seattle WA **Listed on:** NASDAQ. **Stock exchange symbol:** SBUX.

STARWOOD HOTELS & RESORTS WORLDWIDE, INC.
1111 Westchester Avenue, White Plains NY 10604. 914/640-8100. **Fax:** 914/640-8310. **Contact:** Personnel. **World Wide Web address:** http://www.starwoodhotels.com. **Description:** Manages and operates hotels under the names Westin, Sheraton, Four Points, St. Regis, and others. **Corporate headquarters location:** This location. **Listed on:** New York Stock Exchange. **Stock exchange symbol:** HOT.

TARRYTOWN HOUSE
East Sunnyside Lane, Tarrytown NY 10591. 914/591-8200. **Contact:** Human Resources. **Description:** A historic hotel and conference center with 148 guest rooms, 30 meeting rooms, and eight private dining areas. Founded in 1981. **Special programs:** Internships; Training. **Internship information:** Internships are available year round in sales/marketing, accounting, human resources, operations, and the culinary arts. **Corporate headquarters location:** This location. **Other U.S. locations:** CT; NJ; OR; TX; WA. **International locations:** Canada; France. **Parent company:** Dolce International. **Number of employees at this location:** 235. **Number of employees worldwide:** 2,500.

INSURANCE

You can expect to find the following types of companies in this section:
Commercial and Industrial Property/Casualty Insurers • Health Maintenance Organizations (HMO's) • Medical/Life Insurance Companies

---

AMALGAMATED LIFE INSURANCE COMPANY
730 Broadway, New York NY 10003-9511. 212/473-5700. **Fax:** 212/780-4104. **Contact:** Human Resources Recruiter. **E-mail address:** hr@amalgamatedlife.com. **World Wide Web address:** http://www.amalgamatedlife.com. **Description:** Originally a nonprofit insurance firm specializing in handling claims service and group medical, life, and health maintenance policies for the national textile workers union, in 1992 the company was authorized by the State of New York to sell life, health, and disability insurance commercially outside its traditional non-profit base. The company is an insurance company, a third party administrator, a medical utilization service provider, a computer services company, an insurance brokerage, a union printer, and the administrator of the "Patron Funds" employee benefit plans. Founded in 1944. **Positions advertised include:** Senior Underwriter; Help Desk Coordinator; Property and Casualty Insurance Coordinator; Retiree Programs and Advocacy Coordinator; Sales Executive; Accountant; Technical Writer. **Corporate headquarters location:** This location. **Other locations:** District of Columbia; IL; KY; MA; NH; NJ; NV; NY. **Subsidiaries include:** Alicomp, Inc.; Alicare, Inc.; Amalgamated Agency, Inc.; Alicare Medical Management, Inc. **President/CEO:** Ronald L. Minikes. **Number of employees at this location:** 400. **Number of employees nationwide:** 500.

AMERICAN INTERNATIONAL GROUP, INC.
70 Pine Street, New York NY 10270. 212/770-7000. **Fax:** 212/509-9705. **Contact:** Axel I. Freudmann, Human Resources Director. **E-mail address:** aig.hr@aig.com. **World Wide Web address:** http://www.aig.com. **Description:** American International Group, Inc. (AIG) is a leading U.S.-based international insurance organization and one of the nation's largest underwriters of commercial and industrial coverage. Member companies write property, casualty, marine, life, and financial services insurance in approximately 130 countries and jurisdictions. The company is also engaged in a broad range of financial businesses. AIG's General Insurance operations group is composed of Domestic General-Brokerage, which markets property and casualty insurance products through brokers to large corporate buyers and other commercial customers; Domestic Personal Lines, which is in the business of U.S. personal lines, principally personal auto; and Foreign General, which comprises AIG's overseas property and casualty operations. **NOTE:** The company requests job seekers to post resumes online via the company's Website. **Positions advertised include:** Senior Auditor; Collection Accountant; Staff Auditor; Accountant; Collection Representative; Corporate Comptroller; Senior Business Analyst; Treasury Operations Director; Corporate Receivables Manager; Senior Accountant; Asset Manager; Financial Analyst; Direct Marketing Actuary; Actuarial Analyst. **Subsidiaries include:** 21st Century Insurance Group; AIG Global Investment Group; American General Corporation; American Life Insurance Company; HSB Group, Inc.; International Lease Finance Corporation; John McStay Investment Counsel, L.P.; SunAmerica Inc.; United Guaranty Corporation; AIG International Services; AccessAIG; American International Technology Enterprises; American International Underwriters. **Corporate headquarters location:** This location. **Listed on:** New York Stock Exchange. **Stock exchange symbol:** AIG.

Chairman/CEO: Maurice (Hank) R. Greenberg. **Annual sales/revenues:** $55.5 billion. **Number of employees:** 81,000.

AON CORPORATION
dba AON RISK SERVICES
685 Third Avenue, New York NY 10017. 212/792-9200. **Contact:** Human Resources Department. **World Wide Web address:** http://www.aon.com. **Description:** An insurance brokerage that specializes in property and casualty insurance. **NOTE:** Resumes may be sent to the company's headquarters address: Aon Risk Services, 200 East Randolph Street, 12th Floor, Chicago IL 60601; or fax: 877/860-9251. **Positions advertised include:** Associate Risk Specialist; Surety Analyst; Client Specialist; Production Specialist; Senior Production Specialist; Senior Client Specialist; Account Representative; Financial Analyst; Senior Financial Analyst; Risk Consultant; Assistant Legal Director; Claims Coordinator; Assistant Director; Associate Production Specialist; Associate Client Specialist; Senior Client Specialist; Technical Staff Broker. **Corporate headquarters location:** Chicago IL. **Parent company:** Aon Corporation. **Listed on:** New York Stock Exchange. **Stock exchange symbol:** AOC.

ARISTA INVESTORS CORPORATION
dba ARISTA INSURANCE COMPANY
116 John Street, New York NY 10038. 212/964-2150. **Fax:** 212/608-6473. **Contact:** Peter J. Norton, Human Resources Manager. **Description:** Through its subsidiary, Arista Insurance Company, the company is engaged in the sale and underwriting, as well as acting as a third-party administrator of statutory disability insurance for corporations and other insurance companies. **Listed on:** Over The Counter. **Stock exchange symbol:** ARINA. **Chairman:** Bernard Kooper. **Annual sales/revenues:** $4 million. **Number of employees:** 38.

ATLANTIC MUTUAL COMPANIES
140 Broadway, 33rd Floor, New York NY 10005-1101. 212/943-1800. **Fax:** 212/428-6566. **Contact:** Human Resources Department. **World Wide Web address:** http://www.atlanticmutual.com. **Description:** Operates two multiple-line insurance companies that write property, liability, and marine insurance. **Subsidiaries include:** Atlantic Mutual Insurance Company and its wholly owned subsidiary, Centennial Insurance Company, share the same offices and staff. Services are sold primarily through independent insurance agents and brokers. Another subsidiary is Atlantic Lloyd's Insurance Company of Texas. **Other U.S. locations:** Nationwide. **International locations:** Canada; England. **Chairman/CEO:** Klaus G. Dorfi. **Annual sales/revenues:** $837 million. **Number of employees:** 1,800.

CNA INSURANCE COMPANIES
40 Wall Street, New York NY 10005. 212/440-3000. **Contact:** Human Resources Manager. **World Wide Web address:** http://www.cna.com. **Description:** A property and casualty insurance writer offering commercial and personal policies. Since 1897. **Positions advertised include:** Actuarial Supervisor; Senior Actuarial Analyst; Regulatory Filings Technician; Underwriting Technician; Claims Consultant; Claims Specialist; Workers Compensation Specialist; Medical Case Manager. **Corporate headquarters location:** Chicago IL.

THE CENTRE GROUP
One Chase Manhattan Plaza, New York NY 10005. 212/898-5300. **Fax:** 212/898-5400. **Contact:** Human Resources. **World Wide Web address:** http://www.entercentre.com. **Description:** A reinsurance company that offers finite risk reinsurance, insurance, and financial solutions ranging from workers' compensation and product liability coverage to managed environmental impairment liabilities and post-closure reclamation. **International locations:**

Australia; China; France; Ireland; Switzerland; United Kingdom. **Parent company:** Zurich Financial Services Group.

THE CHUBB GROUP OF INSURANCE COMPANIES
15 Mountain View Road, Warren NJ 07059. 908/903-2000. **Contact:** Human Resources. **World Wide Web address:** http://www.chubb.com. **Description:** A property and casualty insurer with more than 115 offices in 30 countries worldwide. The Chubb Group of Insurance Companies offers a broad range of specialty insurance products and services designed for individuals and businesses, serving industries including high-technology, financial institutions, and general manufacturers. Founded in 1882. **Positions advertised include:** Property Accounting; Statistical Accounting; Investment Accounting; Accounting Systems. **NOTE:** Entry-level positions are offered. **Special programs:** Internships. **Corporate headquarters location:** This location. **Listed on:** New York Stock Exchange. **Stock exchange symbol:** CB. **Annual sales/revenues:** More than $100 million. **Number of employees worldwide:** 11,000.

EMPIRE BLUE CROSS AND BLUE SHIELD
622 3rd Avenue, New York NY 10017. 212/476-1000. **Fax:** 212/476-2343. **Contact:** Staffing Department. **World Wide Web address:** http://www.empireblue.com. **Description:** A nonprofit health insurance company offering coverage that includes comprehensive hospital, medical, prescription drug, and dental plans, as well as programs supplemental to Medicare. **Positions advertised include:** Direct Mail Operations Director; Facilities Management Director; Information Technology Auditing Director; Financial Systems Analyst; Junior Fair Hearing Officer; Lead Underwriter; Project Associate; Account Reporting Project Leader; National Accounts Project Manager; Reporting Project Manager; Secretary; Administrative Assistant; Senior Accountant; Senior Plan Sales Associate; Senior Underwriter; Staff Accountant. **Corporate headquarters location:** This location. **Parent company:** WellChoice, Inc. (also at this location).

FIDELITY NATIONAL TITLE INSURANCE COMPANY OF NEW YORK
2 Park Avenue, Suite 300, New York NY 10016. 212/481-5858. **Contact:** Human Resources. **World Wide Web address:** http://www.fntic.com. **Description:** Provides title insurance and escrow services nationwide. **Parent company:** Fidelity National Financial, Inc. (Santa Barbara CA).

FINANCIAL GUARANTY INSURANCE COMPANY
125 Park Avenue, 6th Floor, New York NY 10017. 212/312-3000. **Toll-free phone:** 800/352-0001. **Fax:** 212/312-3093. **Contact:** Human Resources. **World Wide Web address:** http://www.fgic.com. **Description:** A leading insurer of debt securities. FGIC also guarantees a variety of nonmunicipal structured obligations such as mortgage-backed securities. **Subsidiaries include:** FGIC Securities Purchase; FGIC Capital Market Services Group. **Parent company:** General Electric Capital Corporation (Fairfield CT).

FINANCIAL SECURITY ASSURANCE HOLDINGS LTD./FINANCIAL SECURITY ASSURANCE INC.
350 Park Avenue, New York NY 10022. 212/826-0100. **Fax:** 212/688-3107. **Contact:** Human Resources. **World Wide Web address:** http://www.fsa.com. **Description:** A monoline financial guaranty insurer of municipal bonds and asset-backed securities, including residential mortgage-backed securities. **Other U.S. locations:** San Francisco CA; Dallas TX. **International locations:** Sydney, Australia; Paris, France; Tokyo, Japan; Singapore; Madrid, Spain; London, United Kingdom. **Parent company:** Dexia Group (Brussels, Belgium). **Listed on:** New York Stock Exchange. **Stock exchange symbol:** FSA. **Annual sales/revenues:** $379 million. **Number of employees:** 283.

FIREMAN'S FUND INSURANCE COMPANY
110 Allen Road, Liberty Corner NJ 07938. 908/542-5600. **Contact:** Human Resources. **World Wide Web address:** http://www.the-fund.com. **Description:** A holding company for a group of property/liability insurance companies operating primarily in the United States. **Positions advertised include:** Attorney; Claim Representative; Underwriter/Assistant Underwriter. **Corporate headquarters location:** Novato CA. **Parent company:** Allianz AG.

GAB ROBINS NORTH AMERICA INC.
9 Campus Drive, Suite 7, Parsippany NJ 07054. 973/993-3400. **Fax:** 973/993-3767. **Contact:** Human Resources. **E-mail address:** answers@gabrobins.com. **World Wide Web address:** http://www.gabrobinsna.com. **Description:** Provides adjustment, inspection, appraisal, and claims management services to 15,000 insurance industry customers. Specific services include the settlement of claims following major disasters; appraisal, investigation, and adjustment of auto insurance claims; casualty claims; and fire, marine, life, accident, health, and disability claims. **Corporate headquarters location:** This location. **Parent company:** SGS North America. **Number of employees nationwide:** 3,400.

GARDEN STATE HOSPITALIZATION PLAN
900 U.S. Highway - 9 North, Suite 101, Woodbridge NJ 07095-1096. 732/636-0404. **Fax:** 732/636-6929. **Contact:** Human Resources. **Description:** Provides hospitalization insurance throughout New Jersey. **Corporate headquarters location:** This location.

GEICO (GOVERNMENT EMPLOYEES INSURANCE COMPANY)
750 Woodbury Road, Woodbury NY 11797. 516/496-5208. 800/645-7550 ext.5356. **Fax:** 516/496-5769. **Contact:** Human Resources Department. **E-mail address:** r2jobs@geico.com. **World Wide Web address:** http://www.geico.com. **Description:** A multiple-line property and casualty insurer offering private passenger automobile, homeowners, fire, and extended coverage; professional and comprehensive personal liability; and boat owners insurance. **Positions advertised include:** Auto Damage Adjuster; Claims Examiner; Claims Service Representative; Customer Service Insurance Counselor; Sales Counselor; Telephone Claim Representative. **Corporate headquarters location:** Chevy Chase MD. **Other U.S. locations:** Nationwide. **Parent company:** Berkshire Hathaway (Omaha NE). **Number of employees at this location:** 1,800. **Number of employees nationwide:** 20,000.

GENERAL RE CORPORATION
695 East Main Street, P.O. Box 10351, Stamford CT 06904. 203/328-5000. **Contact:** James Hamilton, Senior Vice President of Human Resources. **World Wide Web address:** http://www.gcre.com. **Description:** Provides property and casualty reinsurance to primary insurers on a direct basis. The company markets reinsurance directly to these insurers through its own sales team. Reinsurance is marketed and underwritten on both a treaty and facultative basis. Treaty marketing efforts are focused on small- to medium-sized regional and specialty property and casualty insurers. **Corporate headquarters location:** This location. **Other U.S. locations:** Nationwide. **International locations:** Worldwide. **Parent company:** Berkshire Hathaway Inc. **Number of employees worldwide:** 2,700.

GENERAL REINSURANCE CORPORATION
One Liberty Plaza, 22nd Floor, New York NY 10006-1433. 212/341-8000. **Fax:** 212/341-8150. **Contact:** Human Resources. **E-mail address:** jfoulds@gcr.com. **World Wide Web address:** http://www.genre.com. **Description:** A holding company for global reinsurance and risk assessment, risk transfer, and risk management operations which provides property and casualty reinsurance to primary insurers on a direct basis. The company markets reinsurance directly to these insurers through its own sales team. Reinsurance is marketed and

underwritten on both a treaty and facultative basis. Treaty marketing efforts are focused on small to medium-sized regional and specialty property and casualty insurers. The company does not underwrite businesses that involve aviation, ocean marine, and professional liability. **Corporate headquarters location:** Stamford CT. **Subsidiaries include:** Gen Re Securities; General Reinsurance; General Star; Genesis; General RE New England Asset Management; Herbert Clough; USAIG; General Cologne Life Re of America; General Cologne Life RE Australia; General Cologne Life RE UK. **Parent company:** Berkshire Hathaway (Omaha NE). **Annual sales/revenues:** $8.4 billion.

GROUP HEALTH INCORPORATED
441 Ninth Avenue, New York NY 10001. 212/615-0000. **Fax:** 212/563-8563. **Contact:** Employment Manager. **World Wide Web address:** http://www.ghi.com. **Description:** One of the largest, nonprofit health services corporations operating throughout New York. The company provides insurance benefits and third-party administrative services. Founded in 1937. **Positions advertised include:** Oracle Database Administrator; Senior Programmer Analyst; Voice Communications Engineer; Claims Supervisor; Marketing Representative; Senior Financial Analyst; Senior Group Underwriter; Large Case Manager; Pre-Certification Nurse. **Corporate headquarters location:** This location. **Other area locations:** Albany NY; Buffalo NY; Garden City NY; Long Island NY; Rochester NY; Syracuse NY; Tarrytown NY. **Subsidiaries include:** GHI HMO. **Operations at this facility include:** Administration; Sales; Service. **Number of employees nationwide:** 2,200.

THE GUARDIAN LIFE INSURANCE COMPANY OF AMERICA
7 Hanover Square, New York NY 10004. 212/598-8000. **Fax:** 212/919-2170. **Contact:** Human Resources. **World Wide Web address:** http://www.guardianlife.com. **Description:** Guardian, a mutual company, specializes in life and disability insurance and also offers retirement programs, and provides HMO, PPO, dental, and vision health plans from 45 locations nationwide. The company offers other financial services in addition to health and live insurance. **Corporate headquarters location:** This location. **Other locations:** Nationwide. **Subsidiaries include:** First Commonwealth, Inc. **President/CEO/Director:** Dennis J. Manning. **Annual sales/revenues:** $7.2 billion. **Number of employees:** 5,500.

HIP HEALTH PLAN OF GREATER NEW YORK
7 West 34th Street, 7th Floor, New York NY 10001-8190. 212/630-5000. **Fax:** 212/630-0060. **Recorded jobline:** 212/630-8300. **Contact:** Human Resources Department – Recruitment. **E-mail address:** career_ops@hipusa.com. **World Wide Web address:** http://www.hipusa.com. **Description:** A health maintenance organization marketing a comprehensive prepaid health plan with care delivered by independent medical groups and coverage provided for hospitalization. **NOTE:** Human Resources phone: 212/630-8510. **Positions advertised include:** Assistant Pharmacy Services Director; Pharmacy Coordinator; Account Specialist; Concurrent Reviewer; Planning Analyst; Claims Examiner; Senior Financial Analyst; Claims Data Analyst; Contract File Associate; In-House Associate; Geriatric Social Worker; Technical Support Analyst; Contractual Rebates Director; Catostrophic Case Manager; Registered Nurse; Prior Approval Nurse; Transplant Case Manager; Secretary; Marketing Associate; Contract Associate; Field Associate; Customer Service Advocate; Database Development Manager; Actuarial Student; Compliance Coordinator; Government Programs Direct Marketing Analyst; Project Manager. **Corporate headquarters location:** This location. **Number of employees at this location:** 1,000.

JEFFERSON INSURANCE GROUP
525 Washington Boulevard, Jersey City NJ 07310. 201/222-8666. **Fax:** 201/222-9161. **Contact:** Supervisor of Recruitment and Training. **World Wide Web**

address: http://www.jeffgroup.com. **Description:** A property and casualty insurance company. Member companies include Jefferson Insurance Company of New York, Monticello Insurance Company, and Jeffco Management Company, Inc. **Corporate headquarters location:** This location. **Parent company:** Allianz (Germany). **Listed on:** Privately held.

JUNIPER GROUP, INC.
111 Great Neck Road, Suite 604, Great Neck NY 11021. 516/829-4670. **Fax:** 516/829-4691. **Contact:** Human Resources. **E-mail address:** info@junipergroup.com. **World Wide Web address:** http://www.junipergroup.com. **Description:** Juniper Group operates in two segments: health care and entertainment. The company's principal revenues are generated from health care, which consists of management for hospitals and health care cost containment for health care payers. The entertainment segment acquires and distributes film rights to various media including home video, pay-per-view, pay television, cable television, networks, ad-hoc networks, and independent syndicated television stations. Founded in 1989. **Corporate headquarters location:** This location. **Subsidiaries include:** Juniper Internet Communications; Juniper Pictures; Nuclear Cardiac Imaging; PartnerCare. **Listed on:** NASDAQ. **Stock exchange symbol:** JUNI. **Chairman/CEO:** Vlado Paul Hreljanovic. **Annual sales/revenues:** $1.2 million. **Number of employees:** 31.

KEMPER INSURANCE COMPANIES
30 Rockefeller Plaza, 12th Floor, New York NY 10112. 646/710-7000. **Contact:** Human Resources. **World Wide Web address:** http://www.kemperinsurance.com. **Description:** Provides a wide range of commercial and personal property/casualty insurance in the United States and foreign markets. **NOTE:** See the website for more detailed application information. **Positions advertised include:** Claim Clerk; Claim Specialist; Claim Analyst; Senior Auditor; Staff Accountant. **Corporate headquarters location:** Long Grove IL. **Other U.S. locations:** Nationwide. **Annual sales/revenues:** $2.85 billion. **Number of employees:** 9,000

LAWYERS TITLE INSURANCE CORPORATION
10 Bank Street, Suite 1120, White Plains NY 10606. 914/682-3900. **Contact:** Human Resources. **World Wide Web address:** http://www.landam.com. **Description:** Provides title insurance and other real estate-related services on commercial and residential transactions in the United States, Canada, the Bahamas, Puerto Rico, and the U.S. Virgin Islands. Lawyers Title Insurance Corporation also provides search and examination services and closing services for a broad-based customer group that includes lenders, developers, real estate brokers, attorneys, and homebuyers. This location covers New Jersey, New York, and Pennsylvania. Founded in 1925. **Positions advertised include:** Project Manager. **Corporate headquarters location:** Richmond VA. **Other U.S. locations:** Pasadena CA; Tampa FL; Chicago IL; Boston MA; Troy MI; Westerville OH; Memphis TN; Dallas TX. **Subsidiaries include:** Datatrace Information Services Company, Inc. (Richmond VA) markets automated public record information for public and private use; Genesis Data Systems, Inc. (Englewood CO) develops and markets computer software tailored specifically to the title industry; and Lawyers Title Exchange Company functions as an intermediary for individual and corporate investors interested in pursuing tax-free property exchanges. **Parent company:** LandAmerica Financial Group, Inc.

LEUCADIA NATIONAL CORPORATION
315 Park Avenue South, New York NY 10010. 212/460-1900. **Fax:** 212/598-4869. **Contact:** Laura E. Albrandt, Human Resources. **Description:** Leucadia National is a diversified holding company with subsidiaries with interests in over 30 companies involved in the insurance, manufacturing, banking, investments,

and real estate industries. The insurance business offers property, casualty, and life insurance nationwide. **Corporate headquarters location:** This location. **Subsidiaries include:** Allcity Insurance; American Investment Bank, N.A.; American Investment Financial; Charter, CPL; Empire Insurance Group; Intramerica; MK Gold Company. **Listed on:** New York Stock Exchange. **Stock exchange symbol:** LUK. **Chairman:** Iam M. Cumming. **Annual sales/revenues:** $297 million. **Number of employees:** 1,066.

LIBERTY INTERNATIONAL UNDERWRITERS INC.
55 Water Street, New York NY 10041. 212/208-4100. **Contact:** Human Resources Manager. **E-mail address:** resume@libertyinternational.com. **World Wide Web address:** http://www.libertyiu.com. **Description:** A property and casualty insurance company with some specialty lines including marine and nonstandard automotive. Founded in 1999. **Positions advertised include:** Strategic Software Architect; Professional Liability Claims Attorney; Claims Adjuster. **Parent company:** Liberty Mutual Insurance Company.

LIBERTY MUTUAL INSURANCE GROUP
1133 Avenue of the Americas, 27th Floor, New York NY 10036. 212/391-7500. **Contact:** Personnel. **World Wide Web address:** http://www.libertymutual.com. **Description:** A full-line insurance firm offering life, medical, and business insurance, as well as investment and retirement plans. **NOTE:** Jobseekers may apply online. **Positions advertised include:** Claims Manager; Legal Office Manager; Service Representative; Sales Representative; Consultant; Customer Service Coordinator; Strategic Software Architect; Professional Liability Claims Attorney; Claims Adjuster. **Special programs:** Internships. **Corporate headquarters location:** Boston MA. **Subsidiaries include:** Colorado Casualty Insurance Company; Liberty Financial. **Operations at this facility include:** Administration; Sales; Service. **Annual sales/revenues:** $14.5 billion. **Number of employees:** 35,000.

MBIA INSURANCE CORPORATION
113 King Street, Armonk NY 10504. 914/273-4545. **Contact:** Human Resources. **World Wide Web address:** http://www.mbia.com. **Description:** A leading insurer of municipal bonds including new issues and bonds traded in the secondary market. The company also guarantees asset-backed transactions offered by financial institutions and provides investment management services for school districts and municipalities. **Positions advertised include:** Public Finance Managing Director; Senior Derivative Analyst. **Corporate headquarters location:** This location. **Other U.S. locations:** New York NY; San Francisco CA. **International locations:** Australia; England; France; Japan; Singapore; Spain. **Parent company:** MBIA Inc.

MARSH & McLENNAN COMPANIES, INC.
1166 Avenue of the Americas, New York NY 10036-2274. 212/345-5000. **Fax:** 212/345-4838. **Contact:** Human Resources. **World Wide Web address:** http://www.mmc.com. **Description:** Provides consulting services worldwide through an insurance brokerage and risk management firm, reinsurance intermediary facilities, and a consulting and financial services group, to clients concerned with the management of assets and risks from offices in over 100 countries. Specific services include insurance and risk management services, reinsurance, consulting and financial services, merchandising, and investment management. Founded in 1871. **Corporate headquarters location:** This location. **Other U.S. locations:** Nationwide. **International locations:** Worldwide. **Subsidiaries include:** Sedgwick Group; Guy Carpenter & Company, Inc.; Seabury & Smith; Marsh & McLennen Capital; mercer Consulting Group, Inc.; Putnam, LLC; Marsh, Inc. **Listed on:** New York Stock Exchange. **Stock exchange symbol:** MMC. **Chairman/CEO:** Jeffrey W. Greenberg. **Annual sales/revenues:** $10.4 billion. **Number of employees worldwide:** 59,900.

MERCK-MEDCO MANAGED CARE, L.L.C.
100 Parsons Pond Drive, Franklin Lakes NJ 07417. 201/269-3400. **Contact:** Human Resources. **World Wide Web address:** http://www.merck-medco.com. **Description:** Manages pharmaceutical benefits through contracts with HMOs. **Parent company:** Merck & Company, Inc. (Whitehouse Station NJ) is a worldwide organization engaged in research, development, production, and marketing of products for health care and the maintenance of the environment. Products include human and animal pharmaceuticals and chemicals sold to the health care, oil exploration, food processing, textile, paper, and other industries. **Positions advertised include:** Production Manager; Administrative Assistant; Application Architect; Associate Analyst; Business Manager; Clear Case Administrator; Client Auditor; Contracts Manager; Technology Director; Financial Analyst; Inventory Accountant; File Manager; Plan Manager; System Manager; Paralegal; Project Specialist; Client Auditor; Proposal Writer; Technical Consultant; Manager; Websphere Administrator. **Listed on:** New York Stock Exchange. **Stock exchange symbol:** MRK. **Number of employees nationwide:** 10,000.

METLIFE, INC.
One Madison Avenue, Corporate Staffing Area 1-F, New York NY 10010-3690. 212/578-2211. **Contact:** Corporate Staffing. **World Wide Web address:** http://www.metlife.com. **Description:** The Metropolitan Life Insurance Company is a national insurance and financial services company that offers a wide range of individual and group insurance including life, annuity, disability, and mutual finds. **Positions advertised include:** Project Management Office Director; Budget Manager; Agency Services Consultant; Sales Director; Business Consultant; Senior Product Consultant; Communication Consultant; Financial Analyst; Secretary to Officer; Employee Relations Director; Procurement Compliance Consultant; National Sales Director. **Corporate headquarters location:** This location. **Other U.S. locations:** Nationwide. **Subsidiaries/affiliates include:** GenAmerica Financial Corporation; New England Financial; Reinsurance Group of America, Incorporated; State Street Research & Management Company; Texas Life Insurance Company. **Listed on:** New York Stock Exchange. **Stock exchange symbol:** MET. **Chairman/President/CEO:** Robert H. Benmosche. **Annual sales/revenues:** $33.1 billion. **Number of employees:** 48,500.

METROPOLITAN LIFE INSURANCE COMPANY (METLIFE)
501 U.S. Highway 22 West, Bridgewater NJ 08807. 908/253-1000. **Contact:** Human Resources. **World Wide Web address:** http://www.metlife.com. **Description:** A national insurance and financial services company that offers a wide range of individual and group insurance including life, annuity, disability, and mutual finds. **Positions advertised include:** Quality Consultant; Middleware Administrator; Information Systems Consultant; Sales Executive; Secretary to Officer; Managing Consultant; Financial Analyst; Training Coordinator; Market Research Consultant; Human Resources Generalist; Operations Consultant; Business Systems Administrator; Procurement Sourcing Consultant; Project Manager; Client Service Analyst; Underwriting Consultant; Director. **Listed on:** New York Stock Exchange. **Stock exchange symbol:** MET.

THE MONY GROUP
1740 Broadway, New York NY 10019. 212/708-2000. **Contact:** Human Resources Department. **E-mail address:** monyjobs@mony.com. **World Wide Web address:** http://www.mony.com. **Description:** A mutual life insurer. The MONY Group offers life insurance, disability income, and annuities. The company also operates investment subsidiaries engaged in the management of mutual funds and the distribution of securities. **Special programs:** Internships. **Corporate headquarters location:** This location. **Listed on:** New York Stock Exchange. **Stock exchange symbol:** MNY.

MUTUAL OF AMERICA
320 Park Avenue, New York NY 10022. 212/224-1045. **Toll-free phone:** 800/468-3785. **Fax:** 212/224-2500. **Contact:** Human Resources. **World Wide Web address:** http://www.mutualofamerica.com. **Description:** A life insurance company that offers pension plans, tax-deferred annuities, IRAs, deferred compensation plans, individual life insurance and thrift plans, funding agreements, guaranteed interest contracts, group life insurance, and group long-term disability income insurance to nonprofit, tax-exempt employers. Mutual of America also sells 401(k) products nationally. Services include actuarial (annual valuations, cost proposals, and reports to auditors); administrative (preparation of documents, monthly billings, maintenance of employee records, benefit payment services, development of administrative manuals, calculation of benefit estimates, and annual participant benefit statements); assistance with government filings (preparation and release of ERISA Information Bulletins and distribution of employer kits for qualifying pension plans); communications (Mutual of America Report, audio/visual presentations, and annual reports); investments (17 investment funds); and field consulting. **Corporate headquarters location:** This location. **Other U.S. locations:** Nationwide. **Subsidiaries include:** Capital Management Corporation. **Operations at this facility include:** Administration; Service. **Number of employees at this location:** 650. **Number of employees nationwide:** 1,050.

NATIONAL BENEFIT LIFE INSURANCE COMPANY
333 West 34th Street, 10th Floor, New York NY 10001. 212/615-7500. **Toll-free phone:** 800/221-2554. **Fax:** 212/213-7321. **Contact:** Human Resources. **Description:** A nationally licensed insurance firm dealing primarily in health and life insurance. **Corporate headquarters location:** This location.

NEW YORK LIFE INSURANCE COMPANY
51 Madison Avenue, Room 151, New York NY 10010. 212/576-7000. **Fax:** 212/447-4292. **Contact:** Employment Department. **World Wide Web address:** http://www.newyorklife.com. **Description:** New York Life Insurance Company, its subsidiaries, and affiliates offer a wide variety of products and services. Services include life, health, and disability insurance; annuities; mutual funds; health care management services; and commercial mortgage financing. The company's Asset Management operation (including pensions, mutual funds, and NYLIFE Securities) is located in Parsippany NJ. Founded in 1845. **NOTE:** Interested job seekers may submit resumes online. **Special programs:** Internships. **Positions advertised include:** Accounting Director; Senior Marketing Services Consultant; Media Relations Consultant; Quality Control Consultant; Senior Annuity Services Consultant; Securities Operations Consultant; Accountant; Licensing Associate; Customer Service Associate; Compliance Consultant. **Corporate headquarters location:** This location. **Other U.S. locations:** Nationwide. **Operations at this facility include:** Administration; Service. **Number of employees at this location:** 3,500. **Number of employees nationwide:** 7,185.

ONEBEACON INSURANCE GROUP
201 North Service Road, Melville NY 11747. 631/423-4400. **Contact:** Human Resources. **E-mail address:** careers@onebeacon.com. **World Wide Web address:** http://www.onebeacon.com. **Description:** A carrier of property, casualty, and life insurance, licensed in all 50 states, with offices throughout the country. **NOTE:** Resumes and cover letters may be forwarded to the Human Resources Department, One Beacon Street, Boston MA 02108, or faxed to: 617/725-6262. **Special programs:** Actuarial Professional Development Program. **Corporate headquarters location:** Boston MA. **Other U.S. locations:** ME; CT; NJ; MA. **Parent company:** White Mountain Insurance Group Limited. **Listed on:** New York Stock Exchange. **Stock exchange symbol:** WTM.

PRESERVER GROUP, INC.
95 Route 17 South, Paramus NJ 07653-0931. 201/291-2000. **Contact:** Human Resources. **E-mail address:** humanresources@preserver.com. **World Wide Web address:** http://www.preserver.com. **Description:** Provides automobile, homeowner, and commercial insurance. Founded in 1926. **Positions advertised include:** Lead Computer Operator. **Corporate headquarters location:** This location. **Listed on:** NASDAQ. **Stock exchange symbol:** PRES. **Number of employees at this location:** 95.

PRUDENTIAL INSURANCE COMPANY OF AMERICA
23 Main Street, Holmdel NJ 07733. 732/946-5000. **Contact:** Human Resources. **World Wide Web address:** http://www.prudential.com. **Description:** One of the largest insurance and diversified financial services organizations in the world. The company's primary business is to offer a full range of products and services in three areas: insurance, investment, and home ownership for individuals and families; health care management and other benefit programs for employees of companies and members of groups; and asset management for institutional clients and their associates. The company insures or provides other financial services to more than 50 million people worldwide. **Positions advertised include:** Investment Analyst. **NOTE:** Jobseekers should send resumes to the corporate headquarters located at 751 Broad Street, Newark NJ 07102. **Corporate headquarters location:** Newark NJ. **Other area locations:** Iselin NJ; Roseland NJ. **Other U.S. locations:** Woodland Hills CA; Jacksonville FL; Minneapolis MN; Philadelphia PA; Houston TX. **Listed on:** New York Stock Exchange. **Stock exchange symbol:** PRU. **Annual sales/revenues:** More than $100 million. **Number of employees worldwide:** 100,000.

PRUDENTIAL INSURANCE COMPANY OF AMERICA
751 Broad Street, Newark NJ 07102. 973/802-8348. **Fax:** 973/802-5825. **Contact:** Human Resources. **World Wide Web address:** http://www.prudential.com. **Description:** One of the largest insurance companies in North America and one of the largest diversified financial services organizations in the world. The company offers a full range of products and services in three areas: insurance, investment, and home ownership for individuals and families; health care management and other benefit programs for employees of companies and members of groups; and asset management for institutional clients and their associates. The company insures or provides financial services to more than 50 million people worldwide. **Positions advertised include:** Accounting Associate; Security Manager Associate; Audit Manager; Business Analyst; Compliance Director; Process Management Director; Executive Assistant. **Special programs:** Internships. **Corporate headquarters location:** This location. **Other area locations:** Holmdel NJ; Iselin NJ; Roseland NJ. **Other U.S. locations:** Woodland Hills CA; Jacksonville FL; Minneapolis MN; Philadelphia PA; Houston TX. **Listed on:** New York Stock Exchange. **Stock exchange symbol:** PRU. **Annual sales/revenues:** More than $100 million. **Number of employees worldwide:** 100,000.

PRUDENTIAL INSURANCE COMPANY OF AMERICA
200 Wood Avenue South, Iselin NJ 08830. 732/632-7000. **Contact:** Human Resources. **World Wide Web address:** http://www.prudential.com. **Description:** Prudential Insurance Company of America is one of the largest insurance companies in North America and one of the largest diversified financial services organizations in the world. The company's primary business is to offer a full range of products and services in three areas: insurance, investment, and home ownership for individuals and families; health care management and other benefit programs for employees of companies and members of groups; and asset management for institutional clients and their associates. The company insures or provides other financial services to more than 50 million people worldwide. **NOTE:** Jobseekers should send resumes to the corporate headquarters located

at 751 Broad Street, Newark NJ 07102. company insures or provides financial services to more than 50 million people worldwide. **Corporate headquarters location:** Newark NJ. **Other area locations:** Holmdel NJ; Roseland NJ. **Other U.S. locations:** Woodland Hills CA; Jacksonville FL; Minneapolis MN; Philadelphia PA; Houston TX. **Operations at this facility include:** This location manages health care policies. **Listed on:** New York Stock Exchange. **Stock exchange symbol:** PRU. **Annual sales/revenues:** More than $100 million. **Number of employees worldwide:** 100,000.

PRUDENTIAL INSURANCE COMPANY OF AMERICA
80 Livingston Avenue, Roseland NJ 07068. 973/716-6834. **Contact:** Human Resources. **World Wide Web address:** http://www.prudential.com. **Description:** One of the largest insurance companies in North America and one of the largest diversified financial services organizations in the world. The company's primary business is to offer a full range of products and services in three areas: insurance, investment, and home ownership for individuals and families; health care management and other benefit programs for employees of companies and members of groups; and asset management for institutional clients and their associates. With a sales force of approximately 19,000 agents, 3,400 insurance brokers, and 6,000 financial advisors, the company insures or provides other financial services to more than 50 million people worldwide. **Positions advertised include:** Accounting Associate; Investment Analyst; Process Management Analyst. **NOTE:** Jobseekers should send resumes to the corporate headquarters located at 751 Broad Street, Newark NJ 07102. **Corporate headquarters location:** Newark NJ. **Other area locations:** Holmdel NJ; Iselin NJ. **Other U.S. locations:** Woodland Hills CA; Jacksonville FL; Minneapolis MN; Philadelphia PA; Houston TX. **Listed on:** New York Stock Exchange. **Stock exchange symbol:** PRU. **Annual sales/revenues:** More than $100 million. **Number of employees worldwide:** 100,000.

RADIAN REINSURANCE INC.
335 Madison Avenue, 25th Floor, New York NY 10017. 212/983-3100. **Fax:** 212/682-5377. **Contact:** Human Resources. **World Wide Web address:** http://www.radiangroupinc.com. **Description:** Radian Reinsurance Incorporated provides financial guaranty insurance and reinsurance. **Corporate headquarters location:** Philadelphia PA. **Other U.S. locations:** Dayton OH. **International locations:** London, UK. **Parent company:** Radian Group Incorporated. **Listed on:** New York Stock Exchange. **Stock exchange symbol:** RDN. **CEO/Chairman:** Frank P. Filipps. **Sales/revenue:** $1.2 billion. **Number of employees worldwide:** Over 1,400.

ROBERT PLAN OF NEW JERSEY
200 Metroplex Drive, Edison NJ 08817-2600. 732/777-5300. **Fax:** 516/393-6592. **Contact:** Human Resources. **E-mail address:** drivein@rpc.com. **World Wide Web address:** http://www.rpc.com. **Description:** Robert Plan of New Jersey provides personal lines of insurance. **Positions advertised include:** Underwriting Technician. **Corporate headquarters location:** Bethpage NY. **Operations at this facility include:** This location houses an automobile claims office.

SELECTIVE INSURANCE COMPANY OF AMERICA
40 Wantage Avenue, Branchville NJ 07890-1000. 973/948-3000. **Fax:** 973/948-0292. **Contact:** Tom Magistro. **E-mail address:** tom.magistro@selective.com. **World Wide Web address:** http://www.selectiveinsurance.com. **Description:** Engaged in fire, marine, and casualty insurance. **Positions advertised include:** Processing Support.

TIAA-CREF
730 Third Avenue, New York NY 10017-3206. 212/490-9000. **Contact:** Human Resources. **World Wide Web address:** http://www.tiaa-cref.org. **Description:** Provides insurance and investment options for current and retired teachers. **Corporate headquarters location:** This location.

TRANSATLANTIC HOLDINGS, INC.
80 Pine Street, 7th Floor, New York NY 10005. 212/770-2000. **Contact:** Human Resources. **World Wide Web address:** http://www.transre.com. **Description:** An insurance holding company providing property and casualty reinsurance through its subsidiaries. **Subsidiaries include:** Transatlantic Reinsurance Company and Putnam Reinsurance Company provide general liability, fire, inland marine, workers' compensation, automobile liability, and medical malpractice insurance. **Listed on:** New York Stock Exchange. **Stock exchange symbol:** TRH.

TRENWICK GROUP INC.
One Canterbury Green, Stamford CT 06901. 203/353-5500. **Contact:** Human Resources. **World Wide Web address:** http://www.trenwick.com. **Description:** A holding company. **Corporate headquarters location:** Bermuda. **Subsidiaries include:** Trenwick America Reinsurance Corporation reinsures property and casualty risks primarily written by U.S. insurance companies. Virtually all of Trenwick America's business is produced by reinsurance brokers. Trenwick America divides its business into three distinct categories: facultative, treaty, and special programs. The company is authorized to write reinsurance nationwide. **Listed on:** New York Stock Exchange. **Stock exchange symbol:** TWK. **Number of employees at this location:** 70.

TRILEGIANT
100 Connecticut Avenue, Norwalk CT 06850. 203/956-1000. **Contact:** Human Resources. **E-mail address:** jobs@trilegiant.com. **World Wide Web address:** http://www.trilegiant.com. **Description:** Provider of travel, shopping, dental, health, entertainment, and consumer protection services. Company is member based. Founded in 1973. **Positions advertised include:** Director, New Product Development; Statistical Analyst, Segmentation Strategy; Financial Analyst; Senior Manager, General Accounting; Marketing Manager; Copywriter; Graphic Designer; Traffic Coordinator; Senior Art Director; IBM Mainframe Application Programmer; Interactive Coordinator. **Corporate headquarters location:** This location.

UNIVERSAL AMERICAN FINANCIAL CORP.
6 International Drive, Suite 190, Rye Brook NY 10573. 914/934-5200. **Contact:** Human Resources. **World Wide Web address:** http://www.uafc.com. **Description:** Underwrites life and accident insurance and health insurance to seniors. **Corporate headquarters location:** This location. **Listed on:** NASDAQ. **Stock exchange symbol:** UHCO. **Annual sales/revenues:** More than $100 million.

WILLIS OF NEW YORK, INC.
7 Hanover Square, New York NY 10004-2594. 212/344-8888. **Contact:** Human Resources. **E-mail address:** usemployment@willis.com. **World Wide Web address:** http://www.willis.com. **Description:** Provides insurance and risk management services to a broad range of commercial clients. Subsidiaries at this location include Willis Corroon Aerospace and Willis Corroon Americas. **Positions advertised include:** Senior Executive Assistant; Claims Assistant; Property Technical Broker; Senior HR Specialist; Account Manager.

XL RE AMERICA, INC.
Seaview House, 70 Seaview Avenue, Stamford CT 06902. 203/964-5200. **Toll-free phone:** 800/688-1840. **Contact:** Human Resources. **World Wide Web address:** http://www.xlcapital.com. **Description:** A holding company. **Corporate headquarters location:** Bermuda. **International locations:** Worldwide. **Parent company:** XL Capital Ltd. **Number of employees worldwide:** 500.

LEGAL SERVICES

**You can expect to find the following types of companies
in this section:**
Law Firms • Legal Service Agencies

AMERICAN ARBITRATION ASSOCIATION
335 Madison Avenue, 10th Floor, New York NY 10017-4605. 212/716-5800. **Fax:** 212/716-5905. **Contact:** Human Resources. **World Wide Web address:** http://www.adr.org. **Description:** A private, nonprofit organization dedicated to establishing and maintaining fair and impartial procedures of dispute resolution as an effective alternative to the court system. The association helps parties with disputes by encouraging them to settle differences through friendly negotiations, mediation, or arbitration. Founded in 1926. **Other U.S. locations:** Nationwide.

CADWALADER WICKERSHAM & TAFT LLP
One World Financial Center, New York NY 10281. 212/504-6000. **Fax:** 212/504-6666. **Contact:** Human Resources. **E-mail address:** cwtinfo@cwt.com. **World Wide Web address:** http://www.cwt.com. **Description:** A law firm specializing in corporate law, tax, real estate, trusts, and estates. **NOTE:** Lateral Hiring phone: 212/504-5650. **Positions advertised include:** Banking Regulatory Associate; Financial Products Associate; Commercial Mortgage Backed Securities Associate; Residential Mortgage Backed Securities Attorney; Financial Restructuring Attorney; Corporate Healthcare Associate; Healthcare Litigator; General Litigator; Reinsurance Litigator; Real Estate Associate; Tax Associate. **Other U.S. locations:** Washington DC; Charlotte NC. **International locations:** London, England.

CAHILL GORDON & REINDEL
80 Pine Street, 17th Floor, New York NY 10005-1702. 212/701-3000. **Contact:** Joyce Hilly, Hiring Coordinator. **E-mail address:** jhilly@cahill.com. **World Wide Web address:** http://www.cahill.com. **Description:** A corporate law firm also specializing in real estate, trusts, and estates. **Corporate headquarters location:** This location.

CARTER, LEDYARD & MILBURN LLP
2 Wall Street, New York NY 10005. 212/732-3200. **Fax:** 212/732-3232. **Contact:** Danielle T. Shannon, Recruitment Manager. **E-mail address:** recruit@clm.com. **World Wide Web address:** http://www.clm.com. **Description:** A law firm specializing in business, litigation, real estate, tax, and trust and estate law. Founded in 1854. **NOTE:** Recruitment Manager phone: 212/238-8744. **Positions advertised include:** Attorney; Paralegal. **Other U.S. locations:** Washington DC; New York NY. **Number of employees:** 250.

CERTILMAN BALIN ADLER & HYMAN, LLP
2 Wall Street, New York NY 10005. 212/238-8744. **Fax:** 212/732-3232. **Contact:** June Chotoo, Recruitment Manager & Attorney Development. **E-mail address:** recruit@clm.com. **World Wide Web address:** http://www.clm.com. **Description:** A law firm specializing in business, litigation, real estate, tax, and trust and estate law. Founded in 1854. **NOTE:** Recruitment Manager phone: 212/238-8744. **Positions advertised include:** Attorney; Paralegal. **Other U.S. locations:** Washington DC; New York NY. **Number of employees:** 250.

CLEARY GOTTLIEB STEEN & HAMILTON
One Liberty Plaza, New York NY 10006. 212/225-2000. **Fax:** 212/225-3999. **Contact:** Nancy Roberts, Director of Administration & Personnel. **E-mail**

address: nyrecruit@cgsh.com. **World Wide Web address:** http://www.cgsh.com. **Description:** One of the nation's largest law firms, focusing on a variety of different practice areas. **Corporate headquarters location:** This location. **Other U.S. locations:** Nationwide. **International locations:** Worldwide.

COUDERT BROTHERS LLP
1114 Avenue of the Americas, New York NY 10036-7794. 212/626-4400. **Fax:** 212/626-4120. **Contact:** Mary Simpson, Director of Legal Personnel. **E-mail address:** simpsonm@coudert.com. **World Wide Web address:** http://www.coudert.com. **Description:** A law firm with 650 lawyers at 30 offices in 18 countries specializing in international business transactions and dispute resolution. **Corporate headquarters location:** This location. **International locations:** Worldwide.

CRAVATH, SWAINE & MOORE
825 Eighth Avenue, New York NY 10019-7475. 212/474-1000. **Fax:** 212/474-3095. **Contact:** Employment Manager. **World Wide Web address:** http://www.cravath.com. **Description:** A corporate law firm specializing in litigation, trusts and estates, and taxation. **Positions advertised include:** Attorney; Legal Assistant; Legal Secretary. **Corporate headquarters location:** This location. **Other locations:** London, United Kingdom. **Number of employees at this location:** 1,200.

DAVIS POLK & WARDELL
450 Lexington Avenue, New York NY 10017. 212/450-4000. **Fax:** 212/450-3800. **Contact:** Recruiting Manager. **World Wide Web address:** http://www.dpw.com. **Description:** One of the nation's largest law firms, focusing in a variety of different practice areas. **Special programs:** Summer Internships.

DEBEVOISE & PLIMPTON
919 Third Avenue, New York NY 10022. 212/909-6657. **Fax:** 212/909-6836. **Contact:** Sandra Herbst, Director of Legal Recruitment. **E-mail address:** recruit@debevoise.com. **World Wide Web address:** http://www.debevoise.com. **Description:** An international law partnership specializing in corporate litigation, tax, trust, estates, and real estate law with over 500 lawyers in two U.S. offices and five overseas offices. Founded in 1931. **Corporate headquarters location:** This location. **Other locations:** Washington DC; London, United Kingdom; Paris, France; Frankfurt, Germany; Moscow, Russia; Hong Kong, China; Shanghai, China. **Presiding Partner:** Martin (Rick) F. Evans. **Annual sales/revenues:** $326 million.

DEWEY BALLANTINE LLP
1301 Avenue of the Americas, New York NY 10019. 212/259-8000. **Fax:** 212/259-6333. **Contact:** Recruiting Manager. **E-mail address:** nyrecruitment@deweyballantine.com. **World Wide Web address:** http://www.deweyballantine.com. **Description:** An international law partnership with a range of law specialties including corporate, estates groups, litigation, real estate, tax, and trust with 500 lawyers in a dozen offices worldwide. **Positions advertised include:** Attorney; Paralegal. **Special programs:** Internships; Summer Jobs. **Corporate headquarters location:** This location. **Other U.S. locations:** Los Angeles CA; Washington DC. **International locations:** Budapest, Hungary; Hong Kong, China; London, United Kingdom; Prague, Czech Republic; Warsaw, Poland. **Annual sales/revenues:** $328 million. **Number of employees at this location:** 645. **Number of employees nationwide:** 920. **Number of employees worldwide:** 950.

FRIED, FRANK, HARRIS, SHRIVER & JACOBSON
One New York Plaza, New York NY 10004. 212/859-8621. **Fax:** 212/859-8589.

Contact: Anwara Khanam, Human Resources Coordinator. **E-mail address:** resumes@friedfrank.com. **World Wide Web address:** http://www.ffhsj.com. **Description:** A law firm specializing in corporate law, litigation, real estate, estates, trusts, and pension. **Positions advertised include:** Attorney; Paralegal. **Corporate headquarters location:** This location. **Other U.S. locations:** Washington DC. **International locations:** London, England.

GREENBAUM, ROWE, SMITH, RAVIN, DAVIS & HIMMEL LLP
Metro Corporate Campus One, 99 Wood Avenue South, P.O. Box 5600, Woodbridge NJ 07095. 732/549-5600. **Fax:** 732/549-1881. **Contact:** Victoria Martignetti, Recruitment Coordinator. **E-mail address:** vmartignetti@greenbaumlaw.com. **World Wide Web address:** http://www.greenbaumlaw.com. **Description:** A law firm with practice areas including environmental, product liability, employment, white collar criminal, real estate, corporate, tax, and estate law.

KAYE SCHOLER LLP
425 Park Avenue, 12th Floor, New York NY 10022-3598. 212/836-8000. **Fax:** 212/836-8689. **Contact:** Human Resources Representative. **E-mail address:** jobs@kayescholer.com. **World Wide Web address:** http://www.kayescholer.com. **Description:** A law partnership engaged in a variety of areas including corporate, finance, real estate, and tax law specializing in anti-trust and white collar crimes from nine offices worldwide. Founded in 1917. **NOTE:** Entry-level positions, part-time jobs, and second and third shifts are offered. **Corporate headquarters location:** This location. **Other U.S. locations:** Los Angeles CA; Washington DC; West Palm Beach FL; Chicago IL. **International locations:** China; Germany; United Kingdom. **Chairman:** David Klingsberg. **Annual sales/revenues:** $272 million. **Number of employees at this location:** 600. **Number of employees nationwide:** 825.

KELLEY DRYE & WARREN LLP
2 Stamford Plaza, 281 Tresser Boulevard, 14th Floor, Stamford CT 06901. 203/324-1400. **Contact:** Personnel. **World Wide Web address:** http://www.kelleydrye.com. **Description:** An international law firm specializing in litigation, banking, labor and employment, employee benefits, bankruptcy, tax, real estate, and personal services. **Corporate headquarters location:** New York NY. **Other U.S. locations:** Los Angeles CA; Washington DC; Chicago IL; Parsippany NJ; Vienna VA. **International locations:** Belgium; Hong Kong; India; Indonesia; Japan, Thailand. **Number of employees worldwide:** 300.

LEBOEUF, LAMB, GREENE & MACRAE LLP
One Riverfront Plaza, Newark NJ 07102. 973/643-8000. **Contact:** Recruiting. **World Wide Web address:** http://www.llgm.com. **Description:** A law firm specializing in corporate law, international law, and litigation. The firm primarily serves the insurance and utilities industries.

LEBOEUF, LAMB, GREENE & MACRAE LLP
125 West 55th Street, New York NY 10019. **Contact:** Jill A. Cameron, Manager of Legal Recruiting. **E-mail address:** jcameron@llgm.com. **World Wide Web address:** http://www.llgm.com. **Description:** One of the nation's largest law firms, focusing in a number of different practice areas. **Corporate headquarters location:** This location. **Special programs:** Summer Associates; Summer Internships.

MILBANK, TWEED, HADLEY & McCLOY LLP
One Chase Manhattan Plaza, 56th Floor, New York NY 10005. 212/530-5000. **Fax:** 212/530-5219. **Contact:** Personnel. **E-mail address:** info@milbank.com. **World Wide Web address:** http://www.milbank.com. **Description:** A law firm specializing in litigation, corporate law, trusts and estates, and tax law.

Corporate headquarters location: This location. **Other U.S. locations:** Los Angeles CA; Washington DC. **Chairman:** Mel Immergut. **Annual sales/revenues:** $360 million. **Number of employees at this location:** 600.

MORGAN LEWIS & BOCKIUS
101 Park Avenue, New York City NY 10178-0060. 212/309-6000. **Fax:** 212/309-6001. **Contact:** Michele A. Coffey, Hiring Partner. **World Wide Web address:** http://www.morganlewis.com. **Description:** One of the nation's largest law firms, focusing in various practice areas. **Number of employees worldwide:** 1200.

PATTERSON, BELKNAP, WEBB & TYLER LLP
1133 Avenue of the Americas, New York NY 10036. 212/336-2867. **Fax:** 212/336-2222. **Contact:** Donna M. Abramo, Director of Human Resources and Operations. **E-mail address:** dmabramo@pbwt.com. **World Wide Web address:** http://www.pbwt.com. **Description:** A law firm offering services in a variety of practice areas.

PAUL, HASTINGS, JANOFSKY & WALKER LLP
1055 Washington Boulevard, Stamford CT 06901. 203/961-7400. **Contact:** Human Resources. **World Wide Web address:** http://www.paulhastings.com. **Description:** A law firm specializing in real estate, tax, litigation, and corporate law. Founded in 1951. **Corporate headquarters location:** San Francisco CA. **Other U.S. locations:** Los Angeles CA; Orange County CA; Washington DC; Atlanta GA; New York City NY. **International locations:** London, England; Tokyo, Japan.

PILLSBURY WINTHROP LLP
695 East Main Street, P.O. Box 6760, Stamford CT 06904-6760. 203/348-2300. **Contact:** Personnel. **World Wide Web address:** http://www.pillsburywinthrop.com. **Description:** A law firm specializing in estates, real estate, litigation, and corporate law. **Corporate headquarters location:** New York NY. **Other U.S. locations:** Nationwide. **International locations:** Australia; England; Hong Kong; Singapore; Tokyo.

PILLSBURY WINTHROP LLP
One Battery Park Plaza, New York NY 10004-1490. 212/858-1000. **Contact:** Human Resources. **E-mail address:** staff_ny@pillsburywinthrop.com. **World Wide Web address:** http://www.pillsburywinthrop.com. **Description:** An international law firm with a broad-based practice including corporate law, litigation, real estate, and tax law. **Positions advertised include:** Word Processing Operator; Marketing and Practice Support Manager; Paralegal; Help Desk Analyst; Technical Services Specialist; **Corporate headquarters location:** This location. **Other U.S. locations:** CA; CT; VA; DC. **International locations:** Australia; Tokyo; England; Singapore.

PROSKAUER ROSE
1585 Broadway New York NY 10036-8299. 212/969-3000. **Fax:** 212/969-2900. **Contact:** Diane M. Kolnik, Recruiting Manager. **E-mail address:** dkolnik@proskauer.com. **World Wide Web address:** http://www.proskauer.com. **Description:** One of the nation's largest law firms, focusing in a variety of different practice areas. **Special programs:** Summer Associate Program.

SHEARMAN & STERLING LLP
599 Lexington Avenue, New York NY 10022-6069. 212/848-4000. **Fax:** 212/848-7179. **Contact:** Suzanne Ryan, Professional Recruiting Manager. **E-mail address:** sryann@shearman.com **World Wide Web address:** http://www.shearman.com. **Description:** One of the nation's largest law firms, focusing in a variety of different practice areas. **Corporate headquarters location:** This location.

SIMPSON THATCHER & BARTLETT LLP
425 Lexington Avenue, New York NY 10017-3954. 212/455-2000. **Fax:** 212/455-2502. **Contact:** Dee Pifer, Director Legal Employment. **E-mail address:** dpifer@stblaw.com. **World Wide Web address:** http://www.stblaw.com. **Description:** One of the nation's largest law firms, focusing in a number of different practice areas. **Corporate headquarters location:** This location. **Other U.S. locations:** Palo Alto CA; Los Angeles CA. **International locations:** England; China; Japan.

SKADDEN, ARPS, SLATE, MEAGHER, & FLOM, LLP
Four Times Square, New York NY 10036. 212/735-3000. **Fax:** 212/735-2000. **Contact:** Wallace Schwartz. **World Wide Web address:** http://www.skadden.com. **Description:** One of the nation's largest law firms, focusing in many different areas of practice. **Corporate headquarters location:** This location

SQUIRE SANDERS & DEMPSEY
350 Park Avenue, 15th Floor, New York NY 10022-6022. 212/872-9800. **Fax:** 212/872-9815. **Contact:** Nancy Christopher, Office Manager. **World Wide Web address:** http://www.ssd.com. **Description:** A law firm whose areas of practice include corporate, environmental, and tax law.

WEIL GOTSHAL & MANGES
767 Fifth Avenue, New York NY 10153. 212/310-8000. **Fax:** 212/310-8007. **Contact:** Pat Bowers, Human Resources Director. **World Wide Web address:** http://www.weil.com. **Description:** A law firm specializing in corporate, real estate, and tax law. **Other U.S. locations:** DC; FL; TX. **International locations:** London, England.

WHITE & CASE LLP
1155 Avenue of the Americas, New York NY 10036-2787. 212/819-8200. **Fax:** 212/354-8113. **Contact:** Human Resources Director. **World Wide Web address:** http://www.whitecase.com. **Description:** A general law firm specializing in international law, as well as 30 other practice areas.

WILENTZ, GOLDMAN & SPITZER
90 Woodbridge Center Drive, Suite 900, Woodbridge NJ 07095. 732/636-8000. **Contact:** Kimberly Curtis, Personnel Director. **E-mail address:** kcurtis@wilentz.com. **World Wide Web address:** http://www.newjerseylaw.com. **Description:** A law firm specializing in corporate, employment, environmental, and tax law.

WILSON ELSER MOSKOWITZ EDELMAN & DICKER LLP
150 East 42nd Street, New York NY 10017-5639. 212/490-3000. **Fax:** 212/490-3038. **Contact:** Recruiting Manager. **World Wide Web address:** http://www.wemed.com. **Description:** One of the nation's largest law firms, focusing in a number of different practice areas. **Special programs:** Summer Internships.

MANUFACTURING: MISCELLANEOUS CONSUMER

You can expect to find the following types of companies
in this section:
Art Supplies • Batteries • Cosmetics and Related Products • Household
Appliances and Audio/Video Equipment • Jewelry, Silverware, and Plated Ware •
Miscellaneous Household Furniture and Fixtures • Musical Instruments • Tools •
Toys and Sporting Goods

AGFA CORPORATION
100 Challenger Road, Ridgefield Park NJ 07660-2199. 201/440-2500. **Contact:** Human Resources. **World Wide Web address:** http://www.agfa.com. **Description:** Produces polyurethane raw materials, polymer thermoplastic resins and blends, coatings, industrial chemicals, and other related products. **Operations at this facility include:** This location manufactures photographic imaging equipment and film.

ADVANCE INTERNATIONAL INC.
1200 Zerega Avenue, Bronx NY 10462. 718/892-3460. **Fax:** 718/409-2385. **Contact:** Human Resources. **Description:** Produces, imports, and exports holiday lighting sets, craft items, and other plastic products. **Positions advertised include:** Collections Agent; Customer Service Representative; Data Entry Clerk.

AMERTAC
25 Robert Pitt Drive, Monsey NY 10952. 845/352-2400. **Fax:** 845/425-3554. **Contact:** Human Resources. **E-mail address:** jobs@amertac.com. **World Wide Web address:** http://www.amertac.com. **Description:** Formerly American Tack & Hardware Company Inc., AmerTac manufactures a broad range of decorative hardware and electrical items. Founded in 1937. **Positions advertised include:** Senior Staff Accountant; Quality Control Inspector; Electrical Engineer; Machinist; Mechanical Engineer; Tool and Die Maker. **Corporate headquarters location:** This location. **Operations at this facility include:** Administration; Manufacturing; Marketing; Sales. **Number of employees at this location:** 225.

ART LEATHER
GROSS NATIONAL PRODUCT
45-10 94th Street, Elmhurst NY 11373. 718/699-9696. **Fax:** 718/699-9621. **Contact:** Julio C. Barreneche, Human Resources Director. **World Wide Web address:** http://www.artleather.com. **Description:** A manufacturer of photo albums, displays, and folios. Partnered with Art Leather, Gross National Product manufactures photo image box display cases. Founded in 1925. **Positions advertised include:** Advertising Clerk; Clerical Supervisor; Customer Service Representative. **Corporate headquarters location:** This location. **Operations at this facility include:** Administration; Manufacturing; Sales; Service. **Number of employees at this location:** 540.

ATARI, INC.
417 Fifth Avenue, 8th Floor, New York NY 10016. 212/726-6500. **Fax:** 212/726-6533. **Contact:** Human Resources. **E-mail address:** recruiter@atari.com. **World Wide Web address:** http://www.infogrames.com. **Description:** Creates, wholesales, and markets a wide variety of software including interactive games. **Positions advertised include:** Policies & Procedures Manager; Associate Buyer. **Corporate headquarters location:** This location. **Other U.S. locations:** CA; MA; MN; VA; WA. **International locations:** France. **Listed on:** NASDAQ. **Stock exchange symbol:** ATAR.

BLYTH INDUSTRIES, INC.
One East Weaver Street, Greenwich CT 06831. 203/661-1926. **Contact:** Jane Casey, Vice President of Organizational Development. **World Wide Web address:** http://www.blythindustries.com. **Description:** Designs, manufactures, markets, and distributes an extensive line of home fragrance products including scented candles, outdoor citronella candles, potpourri, and environmental fragrance products. The company also markets a broad range of candle accessories and decorative gift bags. Its products are sold under various brand names including Colonial Candle of Cape Cod, PartyLite Gifts, Carolina Designs, Ambria, Canterbury, Florasense, and FilterMate. The company is also a leading producer of portable heating fuel products sold under the brand names Sterno and Handy Fuel. **Corporate headquarters location:** This location. **Listed on:** New York Stock Exchange. **Stock exchange symbol:** BTH.

BROTHER INTERNATIONAL CORPORATION
100 Somerset Corporate Boulevard, Bridgewater NJ 08807. 908/704-1700. **Contact:** Human Resources. **World Wide Web address:** http://www.brother.com. **Description:** One of America's largest manufacturers and distributors of personal word processors and portable electronic typewriters. Brother also markets many industrial products, home appliances, and business machines manufactured by its parent company. Founded in 1954. **Corporate headquarters location:** This location. **Parent company:** Brother Industries, Ltd. (Nagoya, Japan). **Number of employees nationwide:** 1,300.

BULOVA CORPORATION
One Bulova Avenue, Woodside NY 11377-7874. 718/204-3384. **Fax:** 718/204-3300. **Contact:** Human Resources. **World Wide Web address:** http://www.bulova.com. **Description:** Manufactures and sells a wide variety of watches, clocks, and jewelry for the consumer market. **Corporate headquarters location:** This location. **Operations at this facility include:** Administration; Divisional Headquarters; Manufacturing; Regional Headquarters; Service. **Listed on:** Over The Counter. **Stock exchange symbol:** BULV. **Chairman:** Andrew H. Tisch. **Number of employees at this location:** 400. **Number of employees nationwide:** 560.

CASIO INC.
570 Mount Pleasant Avenue, Dover NJ 07801. 973/361-5400. **Fax:** 973/537-8910. **Contact:** Personnel Manager. **E-mail address:** casioincjobs@casio.com. **World Wide Web address:** http://www.casio.com. **Description:** Manufactures consumer electronics and computer-based products. **NOTE:** Entry-level positions are offered. **Office hours:** Monday - Friday, 9:00 a.m. - 5:00 p.m. **Corporate headquarters location:** This location. **Other U.S. locations:** Glendale Heights IL; Little Ferry NJ. **International locations:** Worldwide. **Parent company:** Casio Computer Company, Ltd. (Tokyo, Japan). **Listed on:** Privately held. **Annual sales/revenues:** More than $100 million. **Number of employees at this location:** 150. **Number of employees nationwide:** 325.

CLAIROL INC.
1 Blachley Road, Stamford CT 06922. 203/357-5000. **Contact:** Human Resources. **World Wide Web address:** http://www.clariol.com. **Description:** A worldwide marketer and manufacturer of hair care products for home and salon use. The company also manufactures beauty and personal care appliances. **Special programs:** Internships. **Corporate headquarters location:** This location. **Parent company:** Procter and Gamble.

COLGATE-PALMOLIVE COMPANY
191 East Hanover Avenue, Morristown NJ 07962-1928. 973/631-9000. **Contact:** Human Resources. **World Wide Web address:** http://www.colgate.com.

Description: Colgate-Palmolive Company manufactures and markets a wide variety of products in the United States and around the world in two business segments: Oral, Personal, and Household Care; and Specialty Marketing. Oral, Personal, and Household Care products include toothpastes, oral rinses and toothbrushes, bar and liquid soaps, shampoos, conditioners, deodorants and antiperspirants, baby and shaving products, laundry and dishwashing detergents, fabric softeners, cleansers and cleaners, and bleach. Specialty Marketing products include pet dietary care products, crystal tableware, and portable fuel for warming food. Principal global trademarks and brand names include Colgate, Palmolive, Mennen, Ajax, Fab, and Science Diet, in addition to various regional brand names. **Corporate headquarters location:** New York NY. **Other U.S. locations:** Kansas City KS; Cambridge MA; Piscataway NJ. **Operations at this facility include:** This location manufactures baby products and deodorant.

COLGATE-PALMOLIVE COMPANY
TECHNOLOGY CENTER
909 River Road, P.O. Box 1343, Piscataway NJ 08855-1343. 732/878-7500. **Contact:** Human Resources. **World Wide Web address:** http://www.colgate.com. **Description:** Colgate-Palmolive Company manufactures and markets a wide variety of products in the United States and around the world in two business segments: Oral, Personal, and Household Care; and Specialty Marketing. Oral, Personal, and Household Care products include toothpastes, oral rinses and toothbrushes, bar and liquid soaps, shampoos, conditioners, deodorants and antiperspirants, baby and shaving products, laundry and dishwashing detergents, fabric softeners, cleansers and cleaners, and bleach. Specialty Marketing products include pet dietary care products, crystal tableware, and portable fuel for warming food. Principal global trademarks and brand names include Colgate, Palmolive, Mennen, Ajax, Fab, and Science Diet, in addition to various regional brand names. **NOTE:** When submitting resumes, please include appropriate mail codes, for engineering or research positions, use Mail Code JHO and for secretarial or administrative positions, use Mail Code MG. **Positions advertised include:** Junior SAP Security Analyst; Scientist; Senior Engineer; Account Business Manager; Professional Sales Representative. **Special programs:** Internships. **Corporate headquarters location:** New York NY. **Other U.S. locations:** Kansas City KS; Cambridge MA; Morristown NJ. **Operations at this facility include:** This location houses a research and development facility. **Number of employees at this location:** 1,000.

COLGATE-PALMOLIVE COMPANY
300 Park Avenue, New York NY 10022. 212/310-2000. **Fax:** 212/310-2475. **Contact:** Human Resources. **World Wide Web address:** http://www.colgate.com. **Description:** Colgate-Palmolive Company manufactures and markets a wide variety of products in the United States and around the world in two distinct business segments: Oral, Personal, and Household Care; and Specialty Marketing. Oral, Personal, and Household Care products include toothpastes, oral rinses, toothbrushes, bar and liquid soaps, shampoos, conditioners, deodorants and antiperspirants, baby products, shaving products, laundry and dishwashing detergents, fabric softeners, cleansers and cleaners, and bleach. Specialty Marketing products include pet dietary care products, crystal tableware, and portable fuel for warming food. Principal global trademarks and tradenames include Colgate, Palmolive, Mennen, Ajax, Fab, and Science Diet. **Positions advertised include:** Cost Analyst; Legal Accountant; Home Care Buyer; Internet Marketing Associate Manager; Human Resources Information Systems Specialist. **Special programs:** Internships. **Corporate headquarters location:** This location. **Other locations:** Worldwide. **Subsidiaries include:** Hill's Pet Nutrition, Inc. **Listed on:** New York Stock Exchange. **Stock exchange symbol:** CL. **Chairman/CEO:** Reuben Mark. **Annual sales/revenues:** $9.3 billion. **Number of employees:** 37,700.

COMBE INC.
1101 Westchester Avenue, White Plains NY 10604. 914/694-5454. **Fax:** 914/694-1926. **Contact:** John Alberto, Employee Relations Manager. **World Wide Web address:** http://www.combe.com. **Description:** A manufacturer of over-the-counter personal care products including hair care and color products, feminine hygiene products, lotions, and creams. Brand names include Just for Men, Odor Eaters, and Sea Bond. Combe also manufactures some dog care and veterinary products. Founded in 1949. **Corporate headquarters location:** This location. **Other locations:** IL; PR. **Chairman/President/CEO:** Christopher (Chris) Combe. **Annual sales/revenues:** $250 million. **Number of employees:** 620.

CONAIR CORPORATION
One Cummings Point Road, Stamford CT 06902. 203/351-9000. **Fax:** 203/351-9134. **Contact:** Human Resources. **World Wide Web address:** http://www.conair.com. **Description:** Manufactures and distributes a wide range of personal and health care appliances. **Positions advertised include:** Regional Sales Manager; Sales Operation Administrator; Marketing Manager; Administrative Assistant; Electronics Engineer; Financial Manager. **Corporate headquarters location:** This location. **Listed on:** Privately held. **Number of employees at this location:** 270. **Number of employees nationwide:** 1,100.

DEL LABORATORIES, INC.
178 EAB Plaza, West Tower, 8th Floor, Uniondale NY 11556. 516/844-2020. **Fax:** 631/293-7091. **Contact:** Patty Tramposch, Human Resources. **E-mail address:** resume@dellabs.com. **World Wide Web address:** http://www.dellabs.com. **Description:** A fully integrated manufacturer and marketer of packaged consumer products including cosmetics, toiletries, beauty aids, and proprietary pharmaceuticals. Products are distributed to chain and independent drug stores, mass merchandisers, and supermarkets. Divisions include Commerce Drug Company, Del International, Natural Glow, La Cross, La Salle Laboratories, Nutri-Tonic, Naturistics, Rejuvia, and Sally Hansen. **NOTE:** Entry-level positions and second and third shifts are offered. **Positions advertised include:** Administrative Support; Business Account Manager; Category Development Manager; Operations; Regional Account Manager; Scientific Affairs; Space Management Administrator. **Corporate headquarters location:** This location. **Other area locations:** Farmingdale NY. **Other U.S. locations:** Rocky Point NC. **Operations at this facility include:** Administration; Divisional Headquarters; Manufacturing; Regional Headquarters; Research and Development; Service. **Listed on:** American Stock Exchange. **Stock exchange symbol:** DLI. **Chairman/President/CEO:** Dan K. Wassong. **Annual sales/revenues:** $350 million. **Number of employees:** 1,800.

DOMINO SUGAR
One Federal Street, Yonkers NY 10705. 914/963-2400. **Fax:** 914/963-1030. **Contact:** Human Resources Manager. **World Wide Web address:** http://www.dominosugar.com. **Description:** Refines raw sugar and distributes it to major national clients in the soft drink, confectionery, and baking industries. **Parent company:** The American Sugar Company (Moorhead MN).

DURACELL, INC.
Berkshire Corporate Park, Bethel CT 06801. 203/796-4000. **Contact:** Human Resources. **World Wide Web address:** http://www.duracell.com. **Description:** Manufactures a line of batteries sold worldwide under the Duracell trademark. Battery types include alkaline, zinc, rechargeable, and lithium. The company also manufactures batteries used in hearing aids and photographic and communications equipment. A subsidiary conducts marketing operations for a line of lighting products under the Durabeam name. **Corporate headquarters**

location: This location. **Other U.S. locations:** Alpharetta GA; Boston MA. **Parent company:** The Gillette Company.

EMPIRE SCIENTIFIC CORPORATION
87 East Jefryn Boulevard, Deer Park NY 11729. 631/595-9206. **Toll-free phone:** 800/645-7220. **Fax:** 631/595-9093. **Contact:** Personnel. **World Wide Web address:** http://www.empirescientific.com. **Description:** Empire Scientific manufactures and distributes batteries, chargers, and accessories to retailers, wholesalers, and original equipment manufacturers in the cellular, video, cordless telephone and other electronics industries. **Corporate headquarters location:** This location. **Other locations:** Tampa FL; Chicago IL.

ESSELTE AMERICAS
48 South Service Road, Suite 400, Melville NY 11747. 631/675-5700. **Fax:** 631/675-3456. **Contact:** Personnel. **E-mail address:** rpalen@esselte.com. **World Wide Web address:** http://www.esselteamericas.com. **Description:** Manufactures and distributes filing and marking systems, storage systems, and other office materials. Primary products are paper-based filing products, mainly suspension filing systems. The company operates production and sales facilities in the United States and Canada. **Positions advertised include:** Customer Service Representative; Sales Associate; Marketing Assistant; Administrative Assistant; Finance Clerk; Information Technology Specialist. **Special programs:** Internships. **Corporate headquarters location:** This location. **Other U.S. locations:** Moonachie NJ; New York NY. **Parent company:** Esselte AB (Solna, Sweden). **Operations at this facility include:** Administration; Manufacturing; Research and Development; Sales. **Number of employees worldwide:** 6,500.

THE ESTÉE LAUDER COMPANIES INC.
767 Fifth Avenue, New York NY 10153. 212/572-4200. **Fax:** 212/572-6633. **Contact:** Human Resources. **World Wide Web address:** http://www.elcompanies.com. **Description:** Manufactures, markets, and distributes cosmetics, fragrances, and skin and hair care products. Founded in 1946. **Corporate headquarters location:** This location. **Listed on:** New York Stock Exchange. **Stock exchange symbol:** EL. **Chairman:** Leonard A. Lauder. **Annual sales/revenues:** $4.7 billion. **Number of employees:** 20,400.

EVERLAST WORLDWIDE, INC.
1350 Broadway, Suite 2300, New York NY 10018. 212/239-0990. **Fax:** 212/239-4261. **Contact:** Human Resources. **World Wide Web address:** http://www.everlast.com. **Description:** Everlast Worldwide, Inc. designs, manufactures, and sells activewear and sportswear. **Corporate headquarters location:** This location. **Listed on:** NASDAQ. **Stock exchange symbol:** EVST. **Chairman/President/CEO:** George C. Horowitz. **Annual sales/revenues:** $65.5 million. **Number of employees:** 269.

EX-CELL HOME FASHIONS INC.
295 Fifth Avenue, Suite 612, New York NY 10016. 212/213-8000. **Contact:** Human Resources. **Description:** Manufactures and distributes home furnishing products including shower curtains, pillows, tablecloths, and bathroom accessories. **NOTE:** Resumes should be sent to: Human Resources, P.O. Box 1879, Goldsboro NC 27533; fax: 919/731-7209. **Corporate headquarters location:** Goldsboro NC. **Operations at this facility include:** Showroom and Sales.

FEDDERS CORPORATION
505 Martinsville Road, P.O. Box 813, Liberty Corner NJ 07938. 908/604-8686. **Fax:** 908/604-8576. **Contact:** Human Resources Department. **E-mail address:** customerservice@fedders.com. **World Wide Web address:** http://www.fedders.com. **Description:** Manufactures room air conditioners.

Brand names of the corporation include Airtemp, Emerson Quiet Kool, and Fedders. **Positions advertised include:** Administrative Assistant; Human Resources Assistant; Sales Manager; Traffic Manager. **Corporate headquarters location:** This location. **Listed on:** New York Stock Exchange. **Stock exchange symbol:** FJC.

GARY PLASTIC PACKAGING CORPORATION
1340 Viele Avenue, Bronx NY 10474-7124. 718/893-2200. **Toll-free phone:** 800/221-8150. **Fax:** 718/378-2141. **Contact:** Personnel Director. **World Wide Web address:** http://www.plasticboxes.com. **Description:** Manufactures plastic display and storage boxes for collectibles. Founded in 1963. **Corporate headquarters location:** This location.

GEMINI INDUSTRIES INC.
215 Entin Road, Clifton NJ 07014. 973/471-9050. **Fax:** 973/574-7215. **Contact:** Human Resources. **E-mail address:** hr@gemini-usa.com. **World Wide Web address:** http://www.gemini-usa.com. **Description:** Manufactures PC and cellular telephone accessories, remote controls, and cable. **Positions advertised include:** Test Engineer; Security Guard.

GREAT NECK SAW MANUFACTURERS, INC.
165 East Second Street, Mineola NY 11501. 516/746-5352. **Contact:** Mr. Sydney Jacuff, President. **World Wide Web address:** http://www.greatnecksaw.com. **Description:** Manufactures a wide range of consumer and shop-quality hand tools. Founded in 1919. **Corporate headquarters location:** This location. **Other locations:** Nationwide. **Subsidiaries include:** Mayes Brothers.

HARTZ MOUNTAIN CORPORATION
400 Plaza Drive, 4th Floor, Secaucus NJ 07094. 201/271-4800. **Fax:** 201/271-0164. **Contact:** Human Resources. **E-mail address:** jobopps@hartz.com. **World Wide Web address:** http://www.hartz.com. **Description:** Engaged in the manufacture, packaging, and distribution of consumer products including pet foods, pet accessories, livestock feed and products; chemical products; home carpet-cleaning products; and equipment rentals. **Positions advertised include:** Company Website Marketing Manager; EPA Specialist; FDA Director of Regulatory Affairs; Planner. **Corporate headquarters location:** This location. **Other area locations:** Bloomfield NJ. **Subsidiaries include:** Cooper Pet Supply; Permaline Manufacturing Corporation; Sternco-Dominion Real Estate Corporation; The Pet Library Ltd.

HOME CARE INDUSTRIES
One Lisbon Street, Clifton NJ 07013. 973/365-1600. **Contact:** Human Resources. **World Wide Web address:** http://www.homecareind.com. **Description:** Manufactures vacuum cleaner bags.

INTER PARFUMS, INC.
551 Fifth Avenue, Suite 1500, New York NY 10176-0198. 212/983-2640. **Fax:** 212/983-4197. **Contact:** Michelle Sharno, Corporate Controller. **E-mail address:** msharno@interparfumsinc.com. **World Wide Web address:** http://www.interparfumsinc.com. **Description:** Formerly Jean Philippe Fragrances, Inter Parfums develops manufactures and distributes a variety of perfumes and fragrances to department stores, wholesalers, and drugstores as well as personal care products and cosmetics including Aziza eye color products under license from Unilever. The company's brands include Burberry, Christian Lacroix, Celine, Diane Von Furstenberg, Molyneux, Paul Smith, S.T. Dupont and FUBU. Founded in 1983. **Subsidiaries include:** Inter Parfums, S.A. (Paris, France). **Listed on:** NASDAQ. **Stock exchange symbol:** IPAR.

Chairman/CEO: Jean Madar. **Annual sales/revenues:** $130 million. **Number of employees:** 103.

JLM COUTURE, INC.
525 Seventh Avenue, Suite 1703, New York NY 10018. 212/921-7058. **Fax:** 212/921-7608. **Contact:** Human Resources. **World Wide Web address:** http://www.jlmcouture.com. **Description:** Designs, manufactures, and markets bridal gowns, bridesmaid gowns, veils, and related accessories for department stores, bridal boutiques, and sells through several Websites. **Listed on:** NASDAQ. **Stock exchange symbol:** JLMC. **Chairman:** Daniel M. Sullivan. **Annual sales/revenues:** $25 million. **Number of employees:** 70.

JOHNSON & JOHNSON
One Johnson & Johnson Plaza, New Brunswick NJ 08933. 732/524-0400. **Contact:** Human Resources. **World Wide Web address:** http://www.jnj.com. **Description:** A health care products company. Products include pain relievers, contact lenses, pharmaceuticals, bandages, toothbrushes, and surgical instruments under brand names including Reach, Band-Aid, and Acuvue. **NOTE:** Resumes should be sent to Johnson & Johnson Recruiting Services, Employment Management Center, Room JH-215, 501 George Street, New Brunswick NJ 08906-6597. **Corporate headquarters location:** This location. **International locations:** Worldwide.

JOHNSON & JOHNSON CONSUMER PRODUCTS, INC.
199 Grandview Road, Skillman NJ 08558. 908/874-1000. **Contact:** Employment Management Center. **World Wide Web address:** http://www.jnj.com. **Description:** A large and diverse health care products company. Products include pain relievers, contact lenses, pharmaceuticals, bandages, toothbrushes, and surgical instruments under brand names including Reach, Band-Aid, and Acuvue. **NOTE:** Search and apply for positions online. **Positions advertised include:** Pension Administrator; Auditor; Financial Analyst; Executive Director, Health Care Compliance-Consumer. **Corporate headquarters location:** New Brunswick NJ.

KREMENTZ & COMPANY
P.O. Box 94, Newark NJ 07101. 973/621-8300. **Contact:** Grace Reed, Human Resources Director. **World Wide Web address:** http://www.krementzgemstones.com. **Description:** A manufacturer and distributor of fine jewelry and related items.

LIFETIME HOAN CORPORATION
One Merrick Avenue, Westbury NY 11590. 516/683-6000. **Fax:** 516/683-6116. **Contact:** Sally Mogavero, Director of Human Resources. **World Wide Web address:** http://www.lifetime.hoan.com. **Description:** Lifetime Hoan Corporation designs, markets, and distributes household cutlery, kitchen tools and gadgets, and other houseware products. The company manufactures a variety of carving knives under the Hoffritz, Tristar, Old Homestead, and LC Germain brand names. Lifetime Hoan Corporation also produces a deluxe line for Farberware, and operates 60 Farberware outlet stores. **Other locations:** Chicago IL; Elmsford NY; Robbinsville NJ. **International locations:** Hong Kong, China. **Listed on:** NASDAQ. **Stock exchange symbol:** LCUT. **Chairman/President/CEO:** Jeffrey (Jeff) Siegel. **Annual sales/revenues:** $131 million. **Number of employees at this location:** 300. **Number of employees worldwide:** 657.

L'OREAL USA
222 Terminal Avenue, Clark NJ 07066. 732/499-2838. **Contact:** Human Resources. **World Wide Web address:** http://www.loreal.com. **Description:** Manufactures personal care products including hair dyes and shampoo.

MAGLA PRODUCTS INC.
P.O. Box 1934, Morristown NJ 07962-1934. 973/377-0500. **Physical address:** 159 South Street, Morristown NJ 07962. **Contact:** Human Resources. **World Wide Web address:** http://www.magla.com. **Description:** Manufactures kitchen and domestic household products including ironing-board covers, dish towels, oven mitts, rubber gloves, disposable wipe cloths, and cling sheets. **Corporate headquarters location:** This location.

MARCAL PAPER MILLS, INC.
One Market Street, Elmwood Park NJ 07407. 201/796-4000. **Fax:** 201/798-0670. **Contact:** James H. Nelson, Director of Human Resources Department. **World Wide Web address:** http://www.marcalpaper.com. **Description:** Manufactures and distributes a broad range of nationally advertised paper products including paper towels, toilet tissue, and napkins. **Corporate headquarters location:** This location. **Operations at this facility include:** Administration; Manufacturing; Research and Development; Sales.

MICHAEL ANTHONY JEWELERS, INC.
115 South MacQuesten Parkway, Mount Vernon NY 10550. 914/699-0000. **Fax:** 914/699-9869. **Contact:** Human Resources. **E-mail address:** recruit@michaelanthony.com. **World Wide Web address:** http://www.michaelanthony.com. **Description:** A designer, manufacturer, and distributor of gold jewelry. The company sells its jewelry directly to retailers, wholesalers, mass merchandisers, discount stores, catalogue distributors, and television home shopping. Michael Anthony Jewelers' largest product line is an extensive selection of gold charms and pendants that include religious symbols; popular sayings (talking charms); sport themes and team logos; animal motifs; nautical, seashore, western, musical, zodiac, and other thematic figures; initials; and abstract artistic creations. The manufacturing division manufactures gold rope chain and designs gold tubing and bangle blanks used in the production of gold bracelets. The Jardinay product line consists of gold chains, earrings, and watches. **Listed on:** American Stock Exchange. **Stock exchange symbol:** MAJ. **CEO:** Michael W. Paolercio. **Annual sales/revenues:** $119 million. **Number of employees:** 742.

MONARCH LUGGAGE COMPANY INC.
475 Fifth Avenue, 3rd Floor, New York NY 10017. 212/686-6900. **Contact:** Human Resources. **Description:** Manufactures and distributes a wide range of luggage products including briefcases, tote bags, athletic bags, attaché cases, and related accessories. **Corporate headquarters location:** This location.

MR. CHRISTMAS INC.
41 Madison Avenue, 38th Floor, New York NY 10010. 212/889-7220. **Contact:** Terry Hermanson, Office Manager. **World Wide Web address:** http://www.mrchristmas.com. **Description:** Manufactures and imports Christmas items including light sets, artificial Christmas trees, and many other Christmas novelties. **Corporate headquarters location:** This location.

MYRON MANUFACTURING CORPORATION
205 Maywood Avenue, Maywood NJ 07607. 201/843-6464. **Fax:** 201/587-1905. **Contact:** Human Resources Department. **World Wide Web address:** http://www.myron.com. **Description:** Manufactures a line of custom-made vinyl products including pocket calendars for the office and business markets. This location also hires seasonally. Founded in 1949. **NOTE:** Entry-level positions and second and third shifts are offered. **Special programs:** Internships; Training. **Office hours:** Monday - Friday, 8:00 a.m. - 5:00 p.m. **Corporate headquarters location:** This location. **Operations at this facility include:** Administration; Manufacturing; Sales; Service. **President:** Marie Adler-Kravecas. **Facilities Manager:** Dan Hurtubise. **Information Systems Manager:** Bruce Kalten.

Purchasing Manager: Jim Ragucci. **Sales Manager:** Terrence Flynn. **Annual sales/revenues:** More than $100 million. **Number of employees at this location:** 600.

NIELSEN & BAINBRIDGE
40 Eisenhower Drive, Paramus NJ 07652. 201/845-6100. **Contact:** Dorothy Uhler, Personnel Director. **E-mail address:** info@nielson-brainbridge.com. **World Wide Web address:** http://www.nielsen-bainbridge.com. **Description:** Produces and distributes picture frames. **Operations at this facility include:** Administration; Divisional Headquarters; Service.

NORELCO CONSUMER PRODUCTS COMPANY
1010 Washington Boulevard, Stamford CT 06912. 203/973-0200. **Fax:** 203/967-9881. **Contact:** Jamie Guerrero, Director of Human Resources. **Description:** Markets electric razors and accessories for men and women, full-size irons, travel irons and steamers, air purifier systems and filters, and travel adapters and converters. **Parent company:** Philips Electronics North America Corporation is one of the larger industrial companies in the United States. The company concentrates its efforts primarily in the fields of consumer electronics, consumer products, electrical and electronics components, and professional equipment.

OLYMPUS AMERICA INC.
2 Corporate Center Drive, Melville NY 11747-3157. 631/844-5000. **Fax:** 631/844-5930. **Contact:** Human Resources. **E-mail address:** staffing@olympus.com. **World Wide Web address:** http://www.olympus.com. **Description:** Olympus America manufactures and markets cameras and imaging equipment as well as a variety of surgical and medical instruments. **Positions advertised include:** Staff Accountant; Staffing Specialist; Corporate Training Manager; Senior e-Commerce Programmer/Analyst; Staff Attorney; Digital Technology Associate Manager; Assistant Contract Specialist; Product Manager; Clinical Monitor; Software Products Technical Trainer; Loaner Retrieval Representative; Accounts Payable Administrator; Receptionist/Switchboard Operator. **Corporate headquarters location:** This location. **Other U.S. locations:** Nationwide. **International locations:** Worldwide. **Operations at this facility include:** This location houses administrative offices only. **President/CEO:** F. Mark Gumz.

PERFECT FIT INDUSTRIES, INC.
303 Fifth Avenue, New York NY 10016. 212/679-6656. **Contact:** Human Resources. **Description:** Manufactures bedding products such as mattress pads, decorative products, and related accessories.

POWER BATTERY COMPANY
25 McLean Boulevard, Paterson NJ 07514-1507. 973/523-8630. **Fax:** 973/523-3023. **Contact:** Human Resources. **E-mail address:** custserv@powbat.com. **World Wide Web address:** http://www.powerbattery.com. **Description:** Manufactures batteries for use in automobiles, computers, and small electronic appliances.

QUEST INTERNATIONAL FRAGRANCES COMPANY
400 International Drive, Mount Olive NJ 07828. 973/691-7100. **Contact:** Human Resources. **World Wide Web address:** http://www.questintl.com. **Description:** Develops cosmetic fragrances. **Positions advertised include:** Marketing Manager; Graduate Trainee; Regional Marketing Manager; Process Development Manager; Sales Manager; Account Manager. **Corporate headquarters location:** This location. **Operations at this facility include:** Administration; Manufacturing; Marketing; Sales.

RAND INTERNATIONAL
51 Executive Boulevard, Farmingdale NY 11735. 631/249-6000. **Fax:** 631/249-6015. **Contact:** Eileen Singer, Director of Human Resources Department. **World Wide Web address:** http://www.randinternational.com. **Description:** Manufactures a complete line of bicycles, from tricycles to racing bikes, for international distribution. **Corporate headquarters location:** This location.

RECKITT BENCKISER
Mars Corporate Center IV, 399 Interpace Parkway, Parsippany NJ 07054. 973/633-3600. **Toll-free phone:** 800/333-3899. **Fax:** 973/404-5700.**Contact:** Staffing Supervisor. **E-mail address:** human.resources@reckitt.com. **World Wide Web address:** http://www.reckitt.com. **Description:** Manufactures cleaning and specialty food products including the brand names Easy-Off oven cleaner, French's mustard, Lysol, and Woolite detergent.

REVLON, INC.
IMPLEMENT DIVISION
196 Coit Street, Irvington NJ 07111-1490. 973/373-5803. **Contact:** Personnel Manager. **World Wide Web address:** http://www.revlon.com. **Description:** Manufactures nail files, scissors, tweezers, and other manicure and pedicure products. **Positions advertised include:** Store Clerk; Warehouse Assistant. **Corporate headquarters location:** New York NY. **Listed on:** New York Stock Exchange. **Stock exchange symbol:** REV.

REVLON, INC.
625 Madison Avenue, 8th Floor, New York NY 10022. 212/527-4000. **Contact:** Human Resources. **E-mail address:** jobs.mail@revlon.com. **World Wide Web address:** http://www.revlon.com. **Description:** Manufactures and distributes a line of skin care products, fragrances, and other cosmetics internationally. **Positions advertised include:** Financial Analyst; Strategic Information Analyst; Public Relations Associate; Category Management Director; Package Development Director; Assistant Product Manager; Senior Product Manager; Trade Marketing Manager; Executive Secretary; Legal Secretary. **Corporate headquarters location:** This location. **Listed on:** New York Stock Exchange. **Stock exchange symbol:** REV.

RUSS BERRIE & COMPANY, INC.
111 Bauer Drive, Oakland NJ 07436. 201/337-9000. **Contact:** Human Resource Department. **E-mail address:** careers@russberrie.com. **World Wide Web address:** http://www.russberrie.com. **Description:** Designs and markets a line of more than 10,000 gift items in the United States and abroad. Products include toys, stuffed animals, novelties, and cards. A diverse customer base includes florists, pharmacies, party shops, and stationery stores, as well as hotel, airport, and hospital gift shops. **Positions advertised include:** Product Development Representative; Design Art Representative; Customer Service Representative; Credit & Collections Representative; Finance Representative; Information Technology Representative. **Corporate headquarters location:** This location. **Operations at this facility include:** Administration. **Listed on:** New York Stock Exchange. **Stock exchange symbol:** RUS. **Number of employees nationwide:** 2,000.

SIMPLICITY PATTERN COMPANY INC.
2 Park Avenue, 12th Floor, New York NY 10016. 212/372-0500. **Contact:** Personnel Manager. **World Wide Web address:** http://www.simplicity.com. **Description:** A manufacturer of clothing patterns. **Positions advertised include:** Illustrator; Instruction Writer. **Special programs:** Internships. **Corporate headquarters location:** This location. **Operations at this facility include:** Administration.

SONY ELECTRONICS, INC.
One Sony Drive, Park Ridge NJ 07656. 201/930-1000. **Contact:** Human Resources. **World Wide Web address:** http://www.sony.com. **Description:** Sony's U.S. operations include manufacturing, engineering, design, sales, marketing, product distribution, and customer services. **Positions advertised include:** Database Marketing Manager; Account Manager; Sales Support Engineer. **Other area locations:** Moonachie NJ; Paramus NJ; Teaneck NJ. **Other U.S. locations:** New York NY. **Operations at this facility include:** This location houses the U.S. headquarters for the international electronics manufacturer. **Number of employees nationwide:** 24,000.

SPRINGFIELD PRECISION INSTRUMENTS
76 Passaic Street, Wood-Ridge NJ 07075. 973/777-2900. **Contact:** Personnel Manager. **Description:** Manufactures thermometers and barometers for consumer use. **Corporate headquarters location:** This location.

STEINWAY & SONS
One Steinway Place, Long Island City NY 11105. 718/721-2600. **Contact:** Michael Anesta, Director of Personnel. **World Wide Web address:** http://www.steinway.com. **Description:** A manufacturer and distributor of pianos.

SWANK INC.
90 Park Avenue, 13th Floor, New York NY 10016. 212/867-2600. **Contact:** Office Manager. **World Wide Web address:** http://www.swankaccessories.com. **Description:** Swank is a manufacturer and distributor of men's and women's jewelry. **Corporate headquarters location:** This location. **Operations at this facility include:** This location houses the executive, national, and international sales offices.

UNILEVER HOME & PERSONAL CARE USA
33 Benedict Place, Greenwich CT 06830. 203/661-2000. **Contact:** Human Resources. **World Wide Web address:** http://www.unilever.com. **Description:** Manufactures personal products and health and beauty aids including Vaseline Intensive Care Lotion and Pond's Cold Cream. **Listed on:** New York Stock Exchange. **Stock exchange symbol:** UN.

VICTORIA & COMPANY
385 Fifth Avenue, 4th Floor, New York NY 10016. 212/725-0600. **Contact:** Office Manager. **Description:** Manufactures costume jewelry. **Corporate headquarters location:** This location.

WOMEN'S GOLF UNLIMITED
18 Gloria Lane, Fairfield NJ 07004. 973/227-7783. **Contact:** Personnel. **E-mail address:** eforce@wguinc.com. **World Wide Web address:** http://www.womensgolfunlimited.com. **Description:** Manufactures and markets a proprietary line of golf equipment including golf clubs, golf bags, golf balls, and accessories. The company markets these products under the trademarks Square Two, S2, PCX, XGR, ZCX, ONYX, Totally Matched, and Posiflow. Square Two Golf is also the exclusive golf club licensee of the LPGA. **Corporate headquarters location:** This location. **Listed on:** NASDAQ. **Stock exchange symbol:** GOLF.

MANUFACTURING: MISCELLANEOUS INDUSTRIAL

You can expect to find the following types of companies in this section:
Ball and Roller Bearings • Commercial Furniture and Fixtures • Fans, Blowers, and Purification Equipment • Industrial Machinery and Equipment • Motors and Generators/Compressors and Engine Parts • Vending Machines

AMERICAN STANDARD COMPANIES INC.
P.O. Box 6820, Piscataway NJ 08854. 732/980-6000. **Physical address:** One Centennial Avenue, Piscataway NJ 08855. **Contact:** Human Resources. **World Wide Web address:** http://www.americanstandard.com. **Description:** A global, diversified manufacturer. The company's operations are comprised of four segments: air conditioning products, plumbing products, automotive products, and medical systems. The air conditioning products segment (through subsidiary The Trane Company) develops and manufactures Trane and American Standard air conditioning equipment for use in central air conditioning systems for commercial, institutional, and residential buildings. The plumbing products segment develops and manufactures American Standard, Ideal Standard, Porcher, Armitage Shanks, Dolomite, and Standard bathroom and kitchen fixtures and fittings. The automotive products segment develops and manufactures truck, bus, and utility vehicle braking and control systems under the WABCO and Perrot brands. The medical systems segment manufactures Copalis, DiaSorin, and Pylori-Chek medical diagnostic products and systems for a variety of diseases including HIV, osteoporosis, and renal disease. **Corporate headquarters location:** This location. **International locations:** Worldwide. **Listed on:** New York Stock Exchange. **Stock exchange symbol:** ASD. **Chairman/CEO:** Frederic M. Poses. **Number of employees worldwide:** 57,000.

ARKWIN INDUSTRIES, INC.
686 Main Street, Westbury NY 11590. 516/333-2640. **Contact:** Personnel Manager. **E-mail address:** humanresources@arkwin.com. **World Wide Web address:** http://www.arkwin.com. **Description:** Designs and manufactures fluid power control components, including hydraulics, for a wide range of industries. Founded in 1951. **Positions advertised include:** Aerospace Engineer; Draftsperson; Industrial Engineer; Mechanical Engineer; Operations Manager; Systems Analyst. **Number of employees:** 300.

ARROW FASTENER COMPANY
271 Mayhill Street, Saddle Brook NJ 07663. 201/843-6900. **Contact:** Plant Manager. **World Wide Web address:** http://www.arrowfastener.com. **Description:** Produces stapling machines and similar products.

BMH CHRONOS RICHARDSON INC.
2 Stewart Place, Fairfield NJ 07004. 973/276-3692. **Contact:** Human Resources. **World Wide Web address:** http://www.bmhchronosrichardson.com. **Description:** Manufactures bagging equipment and batching systems for the food, chemical, rubber, and minerals market. **Office hours:** Monday - Friday, 8:30 a.m. - 5:00 p.m.

BELCO TECHNOLOGIES, INC.
7 Entin Road, Parsippany NJ 07054. 973/884-4700. **Contact:** Joseph Stehn. **E-mail address:** stehn@belcotech.com. **World Wide Web address:** http://www.belcotech.com. **Description:** A worldwide manufacturer of processes and equipment for the removal of air and water pollutants. Pollution control equipment includes electrostatic precipitators and related components. **NOTE:**

Applications may be sent to above address attention: Mr. Joseph T. Stehn. **Corporate headquarters location:** This location.

BOBST GROUP, INC.
146 Harrison Avenue, Roseland NJ 07068. 973/226-8000. **Contact:** Personnel. **World Wide Web address:** http://www.bobstgroup.com. **Description:** Produces a line of equipment for the converting, printing, and publishing industries. The company operates in the United States through three groups: Bobst, Bobst Champlain, and Bobst Registron. Products include die cutter/creasers, folder/gluers, flexo and gravure presses, electronic controls, and other sheet and web-fed equipment. The company is also a manufacturer of converting equipment for the folding carton industry. **Parent company:** Bobst S.A. (Lausanne, Switzerland).

BRANSON ULTRASONICS CORPORATION
41 Eagle Road, Danbury CT 06813. 203/796-0400. **Contact:** Human Resources. **World Wide Web address:** http://www.bransoncleaning.com. **Description:** A manufacturer of ultrasonic welders and cleaning equipment. **Corporate headquarters location:** This location. **Parent company:** Emerson Electric Company. **Number of employees at this location:** 500.

CSM WORLDWIDE, INC.
ENVIRONMENTAL SYSTEMS DIVISION
269 Sheffield Street, Mountainside NJ 07092. 908/233-2882. **Fax:** 968/233-1064. **Contact:** Human Resources. **World Wide Web address:** http://www.csmworldwide.com. **Description:** Markets, designs, manufactures, and installs air pollution control systems containing catalysts, blowers, burners, analyzers, heat exchangers, and other treatment and monitoring components. These air pollution control systems for hydrocarbon oxidation and nitrogen oxides reduction are used in a wide variety of industrial manufacturing and chemical processing applications. Environmental regulatory compliance, turnkey installation, and after-sale maintenance services are also provided. The company is a leader in supplying controls for commercial bakeries, chemical plants, the pharmaceutical industry, and can and metal coating operations. The company also sells to worldwide markets through the combination of a direct sales force and manufacturer representatives. **Positions advertised include:** Field Engineer; Sales Engineer; Project Engineer Manager.

CVD EQUIPMENT CORPORATION
1881 Lakeland Avenue, Ronkonkoma NY 11779. 631/981-7081. **Fax:** 631/981-7095. **Contact:** Human Resources. **E-mail address:** hr@cvdequipment.com. **World Wide Web address:** http://www.cvdequipment.com. **Description:** CVD manufactures chemical vapor deposition equipment, customized gas control systems, and hydrogen annealing and brazing furnaces. These products are primarily used to produce semiconductors and other electronic components. **Positions advertised include:** Electrical Engineer; Mechanical Draftsperson; Mechanical Engineer; Electrical and Systems Engineer; Manufacturing Buyer/Planner; Inventory Control Manager; Parts Kitting Clerk; Shipping/Receiving Clerk; Mechanical Machine Assembler; Electrical Machine Assembler; Harness Wirer. **Listed on:** American Stock Exchange. **Stock exchange symbol:** CVV. **President/CEO/Director:** Leonard A. Rosenbaum. **Annual sales/revenues:** $9.2 million. **Number of employees:** 80.

CANON U.S.A., INC.
One Canon Plaza, Lake Success NY 11042-1198. 516/328-5000. **Fax:** 516/328-4669. **Contact:** Human Resources Administrator. **World Wide Web address:** http://www.usa.canon.com. **Description:** A manufacturer of consumer and business imaging systems products including copy machines, facsimiles, printers, computers, cameras, camcorders, broadcasting lenses, and medical

equipment. **NOTE:** To be considered for positions job seekers are requested to access the company's online application through the company Website. **Positions advertised include:** Planning Analyist; Credit Representative; Marketing Programs Specialist; Bid Specialist; Software Development Engineer; Staff Auditor; Advertising Associate; Marketing Programs Specialist; Sales Administrative Assistant; Technical Marketing Analyst. **Special programs:** Internships. **Corporate headquarters location:** This location. **Other U.S. locations:** Nationwide. **International locations:** Worldwide. **Parent company:** Canon Inc. (Tokyo, Japan). **President/CEO:** Kinya Uchida. **Annual sales/revenues:** $7.5 billion. **Number of employees at this location:** 800. **Number of employees nationwide:** 12,000.

CERTIFIED LABORATORIES INC.
34 Stouts Lane, Monmouth Junction NJ 08852. 732/329-8117. **Contact:** Human Resources. **World Wide Web address:** http://www.certifiedlabs.com. **Description:** Manufactures and sells industrial and maintenance supplies.

COOPER ALLOY CORPORATION
201 Sweetland Avenue, Hillside NJ 07205. 908/688-4120. **Contact:** Personnel. **Description:** Manufactures and distributes a line of plastic pumps to OEMs.

COX & COMPANY, INC.
200 Varick Street, New York NY 10014. 212/366-0265 ext. 509. **Fax:** 212/366-0284. **Contact:** Human Resources. **E-mail address:** hrresources@coxandco.com. **World Wide Web address:** http://www.coxandco.com. **Description:** Manufactures heating and cooling temperature control systems. **NOTE:** Human Resources telephone extension: x509. **Positions advertised include:** Electrical Engineer; Manufacturing Engineer; Composite Manufacturing Engineer; Production Control Planner.

CRANE CO.
100 First Stamford Place, 4th Floor East, Stamford CT 06902. 203/363-7300. **Contact:** Human Resources. **E-mail address:** careers@craneco.com. **World Wide Web address:** http://www.craneco.com. **Description:** Manufactures fiberglass-reinforced panels, vending machines, water filtration and conditioning systems, pumps, valves, and coin machines for a variety of industries. **Subsidiaries include:** Hydro-Aire develops and manufactures brake systems, fuel pumps, and other products primarily for the aerospace industry; Huttig Sash & Door operates 47 branch warehouses across the United States. **Listed on:** New York Stock Exchange. **Stock exchange symbol:** CR.

CURTISS-WRIGHT CORPORATION
1200 Wall Street West, Lyndhurst NJ 07071. 201/896-9886. **Contact:** Human Resources. **World Wide Web address:** http://www.curtisswright.com. **Description:** A diversified, multinational manufacturing and service company that designs, manufactures, and overhauls precision components and systems and provides highly-engineered services to the aerospace, automotive, shipbuilding, oil, petrochemical, agricultural equipment, power generation, metal working, and fire and rescue industries. Curtiss-Wright's principal operations include five North American manufacturing facilities; several metal improvement service facilities located in North America and Europe; and four component overhaul facilities located in Florida, North Carolina, Singapore, and Denmark. **Positions advertised include:** Senior Sub Contracts Administrator; General Accountant; Senior Buyer. **Corporate headquarters location:** This location. **Subsidiaries include:** Curtiss-Wright Flight Systems, Inc.; Curtiss-Wright Flow Control Corporation; Metal Improvement Company, Inc. **Listed on:** New York Stock Exchange. **Stock exchange symbol:** CW. **Number of employees worldwide:** 2,350.

DOVER CORPORATION

280 Park Avenue, Suite 34-W, New York NY 10017-1292. 212/922-1640. **Fax:** 212/922-1656. **Contact:** Human Resources. **World Wide Web address:** http://www.dovercorporation.com. **Description:** Dover is a diversified producer of specialized industrial equipment and components for the petroleum, aerospace, construction, and electronics markets. Divisions include: Dover Technologies, which manufactures electronic circuitry assembly equipment, radio frequency filters, microwave filters, and other equipment; Dover Resources, which makes pumps, compressors, rods, valves, fittings, liquid filtration systems, and gas nozzles; Dover Industries and Dover Diversified manufacture products such as auto lifts, food preparation equipment, solid waste compaction systems, and electromechanical actuators. **Corporate headquarters location:** This location. **Subsidiaries include:** Vitronics Soltec. **Listed on:** New York Stock Exchange. **Stock exchange symbol:** DOV. **Annual sales/revenues:** $4.2 billion. **Number of employees:** 25,000.

JOHN DUSENBERY COMPANY INC.

220 Franklin Road, Randolph NJ 07869. 973/366-7500. **Contact:** Connie Krupa, Controller. **Description:** Manufactures machinery for the paper, film, and foil industries. **Corporate headquarters location:** This location.

FALSTROM COMPANY

P.O. Box 118, One Falstrom Court, Passaic NJ 07055. 973/777-0013. **Contact:** Human Resources. **Description:** Manufactures steel cabinets for various clients including the defense industry.

FOSTER WHEELER CORPORATION

Perryville Corporate Park, Clinton NJ 08809-4000. 908/730-4000. **Fax:** 908/713-3315. **Contact:** Tom Cucchiara, Personnel. **E-mail address:** us_staffing@fwc.com. **World Wide Web address:** http://www.fwc.com. **Description:** Foster Wheeler has three business segments: Process Plants segment designs, engineers, and constructs process plants and fired heaters for oil refiners and chemical producers; the Utility and Engine segment designs and fabricates steam generators, condensers, feedwater heaters, electrostatic precipitators, and other pollution abatement equipment; the Industrial segment that supplies pressure vessels and internals, electrical copper products, industrial insulation, welding wire, and electrodes. **Positions advertised include:** Senior Programmer. **Corporate headquarters location:** This location. **International locations:** Worldwide. **Listed on:** New York Stock Exchange. **Stock exchange symbol:** FWC.

GENERAL BEARING CORPORATION

44 High Street, West Nyack NY 10994. 845/358-6000. **Fax:** 845/348-9016. **Contact:** Ms. Fran Garner, Director of Human Resources. **E-mail address:** fran_garner@gbc.gnrl.com. **World Wide Web address:** http://www.generalbearing.com. **Description:** Manufactures bearing components and bearing products including ball bearings, tapered roller bearings, spherical roller bearings, and cylindrical roller bearings under The General and Hyatt trademarks. **Positions advertised include:** Sales Representative; Advertising Clerk; Computer Programmer; Customer Service Representative; Draftsperson; Industrial Engineer; Mechanical Engineer. **Listed on:** NASDAQ. **Stock exchange symbol:** GNRL. **Chairman:** Seymoure I. Gussack. **Annual sales/revenues:** $60 million. **Number of employees:** 1,001.

GENERAL ELECTRIC COMPANY

3135 Easton Turnpike, Fairfield CT 06828. 203/373-2211. **Contact:** Human Resources. **World Wide Web address:** http://www.ge.com. **Description:** Operates in the following areas: aircraft engines (jet engines, replacement parts, and repair services for commercial, military, executive, and commuter aircraft);

appliances; broadcasting (NBC); industrial (lighting products, electrical distribution and control equipment, transportation systems products, electric motors and related products, a broad range of electrical and electronic industrial automation products, and a network of electrical supply houses); materials (plastics, ABS resins, silicones, superabrasives, and laminates); power systems (products for the generation, transmission, and distribution of electricity); technical products and systems (medical systems and equipment, as well as a full range of computer-based information and data interchange services for both internal use and external commercial and industrial customers); and capital services (consumer services, financing, and specialty insurance). **NOTE:** Apply online only. **Corporate headquarters location:** This location. **Listed on:** New York Stock Exchange. **Stock exchange symbol:** GE. **Number of employees worldwide:** 230,000.

STEPHEN GOULD CORPORATION
35 South Jefferson Road, Whippany NJ 07981. 973/428-1500. **Contact:** Executive Assistant. **E-mail address;** j.sales@stephengould.com. **World Wide Web address:** http://www.stephengould.com. **Description:** Designs, produces, and supplies packaging including plastic, paper, and metal for a variety of materials industries. **Corporate headquarters location:** This location. **Other U.S. locations:** Nationwide.

GRIFFIN CORPORATION
100 Jericho Quadrangle, Jericho NY 11753. 516/938-5544. **Fax:** 516/938-5644. **Contact:** Edward I. Kramer, VP of Personnel. **World Wide Web address:** http://www.griffincorp.com. **Description:** Operates through four business segments: garage doors; installation of garage doors and manufactured fireplaces; specialty plastics, diapers, medical garments, and surgical drapes; and advanced electronic communications and aerospace information systems for air-traffic control and radar systems. **Corporate headquarters location:** This location. **Subsidiaries include:** Buildex Inc.; Lightron Corporation; Telephonics Corporation. **Listed on:** New York Stock Exchange. **Stock exchange symbol:** GFF. **Chairman/CEO:** Harvey R. Blau. **Annual sales/revenues:** $1.2 billion. **Number of employees:** 5,600.

GUSSCO MANUFACTURING INC.
5112 Second Avenue, Brooklyn NY 11232. 718/492-7900. **Fax:** 718/492-0886. **Contact:** Arlene Thomashow, Human Resources Director. **World Wide Web address:** http://www.gussco.com. **Description:** A manufacturer of office filing supplies, cabinets, and systems. **Corporate headquarters location:** This location. **Other locations include:** Garfield NJ.

HANOVIA/COLITE, INC.
825 Lehigh Avenue, Union NJ 07083. 908/688-0050. **Contact:** Rosemary McCann, Director of Human Resources. **World Wide Web address:** http://www.hanovia-uv.com. **Description:** Designs, develops, produces, and markets plasma arc lamps and related equipment including commercial and industrial ultraviolet products and accessories; produces various phosphorescent pigments, compounds, and films; and designs, develops, manufactures, assembles, and markets high-intensity lighting equipment. **Corporate headquarters location:** This location.

HAYWARD INDUSTRIES
900 Fairmount Avenue, Elizabeth NJ 07201. 908/351-5400. **Fax:** 908/351-0604. **Contact:** Human Resources. **World Wide Web address:** http://www.haywardnet.com. **Description:** Manufactures swimming pool equipment. The company is engaged in all aspects of production including design and sales. Clients use equipment in the construction, repair, and maintenance of private and commercial swimming pools. The company also

manufactures and distributes a standard line of industrial pipeline strainers and valves. **Positions advertised include:** National Technical Service Manager; Product Engineer; Marketing Product Manager; Associate Product Manager; Call Center Supervisor; Marketing Communications Manager. **Corporate headquarters location:** This location. **International locations:** Belgium.

HEXCEL CORPORATION
281 Tresser Boulevard, Two Stamford Plaza, 16th Floor, Stamford CT 06901-3261. 203/969-0666. **Contact:** Human Resources. **World Wide Web address:** http://www.hexcel.com. **Description:** Hexcel Corporation is a manufacturing firm with two primary business segments: structural materials (including aerospace products, nonaerospace honeycomb, resin-impregnated industrial fabrics, nonimpregnated fabrics) and specialty chemicals (including bulk pharmaceuticals, custom and special purpose chemicals, specialty resins, and industrial maintenance chemicals). **Other U.S. locations:** Nationwide. **International locations:** Worldwide. **Operations at this facility include:** This location houses administrative offices. **Listed on:** New York Stock Exchange. **Stock exchange symbol:** HXL. **Number of employees nationwide:** 5,000.

HOLOPAK TECHNOLOGIES, INC.
15 Cotters Lane, East Brunswick NJ 08816. 732/651-2292. **Fax:** 732/238-3018. **Contact:** Bonnie Eichel, Human Resources Director. **Description:** HoloPak, through its subsidiaries Transfer Print Foils, Inc. and Alubec Industries Inc., is a producer and distributor of hot stamping foils, holographic foils, metallized paper, and technical coatings. Hot stamping foils are elements of the graphics and packaging industries, and are used to decorate a wide variety of products. Holographic foils are high-precision images embossed into specialized coatings, which are used to discourage counterfeiting and provide specialty decorative effects. **Parent company:** Foilmark Inc. **Corporate headquarters location:** Newburyport MA. **Other U.S. locations:** Nationwide. **International locations:** Canada.

HONEYWELL
1525 West Blancke Street, Linden NJ 07036. 908/862-9551. **Contact:** Human Resources. **World Wide Web address:** http://www.honeywell.com. **Description:** Honeywell is engaged in the research, development, manufacture, and sale of advanced technology products and services in the fields of chemicals, electronics, automation, and controls. The company's major businesses are home and building automation and control, performance polymers and chemicals, industrial automation and control, space and aviation systems, and defense and marine systems. **Operations at this facility include:** This location manufactures plastic inserts for pill bottles. **Listed on:** New York Stock Exchange. **Stock exchange symbol:** HON.

HOSOKAWA MICRON POWDER SYSTEMS
20 Chatham Road, Summit NJ 07901. 908/273-6360. **Contact:** Human Resources Administrator. **World Wide Web address:** http://www.hosokawa.com. **Description:** Develops and manufactures air pollution control and process equipment. Products are used by the primary metals, nonmetallic minerals, powder, protective coatings, paper, fertilizer, chemical, pharmaceutical, and food processing industries. **Corporate headquarters location:** New York NY. **Parent company:** Hosokawa Micron International Inc.

INGERSOLL-RAND COMPANY
200 Chestnut Ridge Road, Woodcliff Lake NJ 07677. 201/573-0123. **Contact:** Human Resources. **World Wide Web address:** http://www.ingersoll-rand.com. **Description:** Manufactures compressors, pumps, and other nonelectrical industrial equipment and machinery. Ingersoll-Rand Company's products include

air compression systems, antifriction systems, construction equipment, air tools, bearings, locks, tools, and pumps. **Positions advertised include:** Human Resources Manager. **Corporate headquarters location:** This location. **Other U.S. locations:** Nationwide. **Subsidiaries include:** IR Torrington Company. **Listed on:** New York Stock Exchange. **Stock exchange symbol:** IR.

KYOCERA MITA AMERICA, INC.
225 Sand Road, Fairfield NJ 07004. 973/808-8444. **Contact:** Human Resources. **World Wide Web address:** http://www.kyoceramita.com. **Description:** One of the world's largest manufacturers of copy machines. Kyocera MITA also offers computer peripherals such as fax machines, imaging systems, and laser printers. **Corporate headquarters location:** This location.

G.W. LISK CO., INC.
dba CLIFTRONICS INC.
2 South Street, Clifton Springs NY 14432. 315/462-2611. **Fax:** 315/462-7611. **Contact:** Barbara Criblear, Director of Human Resources. **E-mail address:** marketing@gwlisk.com **World Wide Web address:** http://www.cliftronics.com. **Description:** The company manufactures solenoids, valves, and flame arresters used in aircraft, fuel lines, and fuel storage. Subsidiary Cliftronics specializes in engineering, design, and manufacture of custom solenoids, valves and flame arresters for aerospace and military applications. **Corporate headquarters location:** This location. **Other locations:** Gort, Ireland; Essex, United Kingdom.

MAGNETIC TICKET & LABEL CORPORATION
151 Cortlandt Avenue, Belleville NJ 07109. 973/759-6500. **Fax:** 973/450-4703. **Contact:** Human Resources. **World Wide Web address:** http://www.magticket.com. **Description:** Manufactures plastic and paper airline baggage tags. **Other U.S. locations:** Los Angeles CA; San Francisco CA; Nashville TN; Dallas TX. **Operations at this facility include:** Manufacturing. **Listed on:** Privately held. **Number of employees at this location:** 80. **Number of employees nationwide:** 4,000.

MAROTTA SCIENTIFIC CONTROLS INC.
P.O. Box 427, Montville NJ 07045-0427. 973/334-7800. **Fax:** 973/334-1219. **Physical address:** 78 Boonton Avenue, Montville NJ 07045. **Contact:** Robert Cooper, Personnel Manager. **E-mail address:** bcooper@marrota.com. **World Wide Web address:** http://www.marotta.com. **Description:** Manufactures high-pressure valves for pneumatic and hydraulic equipment. The company is also a custom manufacturer of fluid control products. **Positions advertised include:** Technician; Assembler. **Corporate headquarters location:** This location.

MIKRON INSTRUMENT COMPANY, INC.
16 Thornton Road, Oakland NJ 07436. 201/891-7330. **Toll-free phone:** 800/631-0176. **Fax:** 201/405-6090. **Contact:** Human Resources. **World Wide Web address:** http://www.mikroninst.com. **Description:** Develops, manufactures, markets, and services equipment and instruments for noncontact temperature measurement. The company's products are typically used to measure the temperature of moving objects; of stationary objects in environments or situations where contact temperature measurement would be difficult, hazardous, or impractical; and wherever rapid temperature changes must be accurately tracked instantaneously. The company also manufactures and/or markets calibration sources and a variety of accessories and optional equipment for its infrared thermometers. **Listed on:** NASDAQ. **Stock exchange symbol:** MIKR.

MINOLTA CORPORATION
101 Williams Drive, Ramsey NJ 07446. 201/825-4000. **Fax:** 201/825-7567. **Contact:** Human Resources. **World Wide Web address:** http://www.minoltausa.com. **Description:** Markets, sells, and distributes

photographic and business equipment, as well as document imaging systems. **Positions advertised include:** Asset Inventory Administrator; Special Events Assistant. **Corporate headquarters location:** This location. **Parent company:** Minolta Co., Ltd. (Osaka, Japan). **Operations at this facility include:** Administration; Sales; Service. **Listed on:** Privately held. **Number of employees at this location:** 500.

OHAUS CORPORATION
29 Hanover Road, Florham Park NJ 07058. 973/377-9000. **Contact:** Human Resources. **E-mail address:** hr@ohaus.com. **World Wide Web address:** http://www.ohaus.com. **Description:** One of the world's largest manufacturers of precision weighing equipment for use in laboratory, education, and specialty markets. **Corporate headquarters location:** This location.

OMEGA ENGINEERING, INC.
One Omega Drive, P.O. Box 4047, Stamford CT 06907-0047. 203/359-1660. **Contact:** Human Resources. **World Wide Web address:** http://www.omega.com. **Description:** A manufacturer and worldwide distributor of process measurement and control instrumentation. Products include temperature, pressure, strain, and flow devices; pH equipment; and a large selection of instrument and control tools. OMEGA Engineering also provides related consulting and engineering services. **Positions advertised include:** Client/Server Programmer Analyst; Electronic Design Engineer; Export Administrative Assistant; Industrial Product Manager; Manufacturing Engineer; Mechanical Design Engineer; Network Engineer; Planner; Buyer; Software/Systems Support; Sales-Quotations Engineer; Staff Accountant; Technical Customer Service; Technical Sales and Application Engineer. **Corporate headquarters location:** This location.

OTIS ELEVATOR COMPANY
625 Eight Avenue, New York NY 10018. 212/947-9269. **Contact:** Human Resources. **World Wide Web address:** http://www.nao.otis.com. **Description:** Produces and distributes a line of elevators and escalators for commercial and industrial use. **Corporate headquarters location:** Farmington CT. **Other U.S. locations:** Nationwide. **International locations:** Worldwide. **Parent company:** United Technologies Corporation. **Listed on:** New York Stock Exchange. **Stock exchange symbol:** UTX. **Sales/revenue:** $6.3 billion. **Number of employees worldwide:** Approximately 61,000.

P & F INDUSTRIES, INC.
dba EMBASSY INDUSTRIES, INC.
300 Smith Street, Farmingdale NY 11735-1114. 631/694-1800. **Fax:** 631/694-1836. **Contact:** Human Resources. **E-mail address:** info@pfina.com. **World Wide Web address:** http://www.pfina.com. **Description:** Through its subsidiaries, the company manufactures power tools, machine tools, hydraulic cylinders, and other construction and hardware products. The Embassy Industries subsidiary imports radiant heating systems and manufactures baseboard heating equipment, hardware, and sheet metal contracting. **Corporate headquarters location:** This location. **Other U.S. locations:** Boynton Beach FL; New Hyde Park NY. **Subsidiaries include:** Berkley Tools; Embassy Industries, Inc; Florida Pneumatic Manufacturing Company; Franklin MFG; Green Manufacturing, Inc.; Countrywide Hardware. **Listed on:** NASDAQ. **Stock exchange symbol:** PFIN. **Chairman/President/CEO:** Richard A. Horowitz. **Annual sales/revenues:** $76.5 million. **Number of employees:** 305.

PALL CORPORATION
2200 Northern Boulevard, East Hills NY 11548-1289. 516/484-5400. **Contact:** Rita DiStefano, Human Resources. **World Wide Web address:** http://www.pall.com. **Description:** Pall Corporation is a leader in filtration

technology, specializing in fluid clarification and high-end separation. The company's overall business is organized into three segments: Health Care, Aeropower, and Fluid Processing. **Corporate headquarters location:** This location. **Other area locations:** Cortland NY; Glen Cove NY; Hauppauge NY; Port Washington NY. **Other U.S. locations:** Putnam CT; Fort Myers FL; New Port Richey FL; Pinellas Park FL. **Subsidiaries include:** Pall Gelman Sciences Incorporated. **Operations at this facility include:** Administration; Manufacturing; Research and Development; Sales. **Listed on:** New York Stock Exchange. **Stock exchange symbol:** PLL. **Sales/revenue:** Approximately $1.3 billion. **Number of employees nationwide:** 6,500. **Number of employees worldwide:** 10,700.

PALL CORPORATION
25 Harbor Park Drive, Port Washington NY 11050. 516/484-3600. **Contact:** Human Resources. **World Wide Web address:** http://www.pall.com. **Description:** A world leader in filtration technology, specializing in fluid clarification and high-end separation. The company's overall business is organized into three segments: Health Care, Aeropower, and Fluid Processing. In the fluid clarification market, Pall sells disposable cartridges that fit into filter houses it has sold to clients. In the separations market, the company sells complete systems, which include both semi-permanent filters and systems that regularly consume disposable cartridges. **Corporate headquarters location:** East Hills NY. **Other area locations:** Cortland NY; Glen Cove NY; Hauppauge NY. **Other U.S. locations:** Putnam CT; Fort Myers FL; New Port Richey FL; Pinellas Park FL. **Subsidiaries include:** Pall Gelman Sciences Incorporated. **Listed on:** New York Stock Exchange. **Stock exchange symbol:** PLL. **Sales/revenue:** Approximately $1.3 billion. **Number of employees nationwide:** 6,500. **Number of employees worldwide:** 10,700.

PALL CORPORATION
225 Marcus Boulevard, Hauppauge NY 11788. 631/273-0911. **Contact:** Rita DiStephano, Human Resources Director. **World Wide Web address:** http://www.pall.com. **Description:** A world leader in filtration technology, specializing in fluid clarification and high-end separation. The company's overall business is organized into three segments: Health Care, Aeropower, and Fluid Processing. **Corporate headquarters location:** East Hills NY. **Other area locations:** Cortland NY; Port Washington NY; Glen Cove NY. **Other U.S. locations:** Putnam CT; Fort Myers FL; New Port Richey FL; Pinellas Park FL. **Subsidiaries include:** Pall Gelman Sciences Incorporated. **Listed on:** New York Stock Exchange. **Sales/revenue:** Approximately $1.3 billion. **Stock exchange symbol:** PLL. **Number of employees nationwide:** 6,500. **Number of employees worldwide:** 10,700.

PARKER HANNIFIN CORPORATION
300 Marcus Avenue, P.O. Box 9400, Smithtown NY 11787. 631/231-3737. **Contact:** Human Resources. **World Wide Web address:** http://www.parker.com. **Description:** Manufactures motion control products including fluid power systems, electromechanical controls, and related components. The Motion and Control Group makes hydraulic pumps, power units, control valves, accumulators, cylinders, actuators, and automation devices to remove contaminants from air, fuel, oil, water, and other fluids. The Fluid Connectors Group makes connectors, tube and hose fittings, hoses, and couplers that transmit fluid. The Seal Group makes sealing devices, gaskets, and packing that insure leak-proof connections. The Automotive and Refrigeration Groups make components for use in industrial and automotive air conditioning and refrigeration systems. Principal products of the aerospace segment are hydraulic, pneumatic, and fuel systems and components. **Special programs:** Education Reimbursement Program; Accounting Management Training Program. **Corporate headquarters location:** Cleveland OH. **Other U.S. locations:**

Nationwide. **International locations:** Worldwide. **Operations at this facility include:** As part of the Electronic Systems Division, this location manufactures and distributes aerospace instrumentation and equipment including fuel flow instruments. **Listed on:** New York Stock Exchange. **Stock exchange symbol:** PH. **Sales/revenue:** Over $6 billion. **Number of employees worldwide:** 48,000.

PERMACEL
671 US Highway 1, North Brunswick NJ 08902. 732/418-2550. **Fax:** 732/418-2457. **Contact:** Human Resources Department. **E-mail address:** human_resources@permacel.com. **World Wide Web address:** http://www.permacel.com. **Description:** Manufactures pressure-sensitive tape. **Positions advertised include:** Financial Account Manager. **Corporate headquarters location:** This location. **Operations at this facility include:** Administration; Manufacturing; Research and Development; Sales; Service. **Listed on:** Privately held. **Number of employees at this location:** 500.

PITNEY BOWES, INC.
One Elmcroft Road, Stamford CT 06926-0700. 203/356-5000. **Fax:** 203/351-6293. **Contact:** Human Resources. **World Wide Web address:** http://www.pb.com. **Description:** Pitney Bowes operates within two industry segments: Business Equipment and Services, and Financial Services. The Business Equipment and Services segment includes the manufacturing of postage meters; mailing, shipping, and facsimile systems; copiers and copier supplies; and mailroom reprographics. The Financial Services segment includes the worldwide financing operations of the company. This segment provides lease financing for the company's products, as well as other financial services for the commercial and industrial markets. Founded in 1920. **NOTE:** Apply online only. **Positions advertised include:** Accounting Analyst; Administrative Assistant; Benefits Administrator; Associate Engineer; Associate III, Payroll; Corporate Strategy Analyst; Customer Master SME; Customer Service Manager; Director, Corporate Accounting and Financial Reporting; Executive Secretary; Project Leader; Team Leader; Senior Financial Planner. **Corporate headquarters location:** This location. **International locations:** Worldwide. **Listed on:** New York Stock Exchange. **Stock exchange symbol:** PBI. **Number of employees worldwide:** 32,000.

PRECISION VALVE CORPORATION
700 Nepperhan Avenue, Yonkers NY 10703. 914/969-6500. **Fax:** 914/966-4401. **Contact:** Industrial Relations Manager. **E-mail address:** jobs@precision-valve.com. **World Wide Web address:** http://www.precision-valve.com. **Description:** An international manufacturer of aerosol valves. **NOTE:** Jobseekers may search for job opportunities on http://www.hotjobs.com. **Positions advertised include:** Warehouse Manager; Accounts Receivable Clerk; Industrial Maintenance Mechanic; Safety Manager; Facility Manager; High Speed Machine Mechanic; Machine Operator. **Corporate headquarters location:** This location. **Other U.S. locations:** Greenville SC. **International locations:** Worldwide. **Operations at this facility include:** Administration; Manufacturing; Research and Development; Sales; Service. **Number of employees at this location:** 390. **Number of employees nationwide:** 2,500.

ROYAL CONSUMER INFORMATION PRODUCTS INC
379 Campus Drive, Somerset NJ 08805. **Toll-free phone:** 888/261-4555. **Fax:** 800/232-9799. **Contact:** Human Resources. **E-mail address:** info@royalsupplies.com. **World Wide Web address:** http://www.royal.com. **Description:** Manufactures and distributes a broad line of electronic office products including typewriters, calculators, word processors, cash registers, copiers, personal and small computers, business computers, complete data processing systems, teleprinters, video terminals, telephone-switching systems, minicomputers, automatic tellers, and associated equipment.

SEALED AIR CORPORATION
Park 80 East, Saddle Brook NJ 07663. 201/791-7600. **Contact:** Manager of Employee Benefits. **World Wide Web address:** http://www.sealedaircorp.com. **Description:** Sealed Air Corporation is a diversified worldwide enterprise consisting of specialty and agricultural chemicals, energy production and services, retailing, restaurants, and other businesses. The firm operates over 2,500 facilities worldwide. **Corporate headquarters location:** This location. **Other U.S. locations:** Danbury CT; Holyoke MA; Scotia NY. **Operations at this facility include:** This location produces specialized protective packaging materials and systems that reduce or eliminate the damage to products that may occur during shipping. **Listed on:** New York Stock Exchange. **Stock exchange symbol:** SEE. **Number of employees at this location:** 35. **Number of employees nationwide:** 2,000.

TEREX CORPORATION
500 Post Road East, Suite 320, Westport CT 06880. 203/222-7170. **Contact:** Human Resources. **E-mail address:** hr@terex.com. **World Wide Web address:** http://www.terex.com. **Description:** Terex develops, manufactures, and markets a variety of vehicles and related components, primarily for the lifting and earth-moving industries. Products include loaders, haulers, scrapers, cranes, trucks, tractors, and replacement parts. **NOTE:** Apply online. **Corporate headquarters location:** This location. **Other U.S. locations:** Waverly IA; Olathe KS; Baruga MI; Southaven MI; Wilmington NC; Tulsa OK; Conway SC; Huron SD; Watertown SD; Milwaukee WI. **Operations at this facility include:** Administration. **Listed on:** New York Stock Exchange. **Stock exchange symbol:** TEX. **Number of employees at this location:** 30. **Number of employees nationwide:** 4,000.

TRANSACT TECHNOLOGIES, INC.
20 Bomax Drive, Ithaca NY 14850. 607/257-8901. **Contact:** Human Resources. **World Wide Web address:** http://www.transact-tech.com. **Description:** Manufactures and sells receipt printers. **Corporate headquarters location:** Wallingford CT. **Listed on:** NASDAQ. **Stock exchange symbol:** TACT.

TRANSTECHNOLOGY CORPORATION
150 Allen Road, Liberty Corner NJ 07938. 908/903-1600. **Contact:** Human Resources. **World Wide Web address:** http://www.transtechnology.com. **Description:** Designs, manufactures, sells, and distributes specialty fasteners. **Corporate headquarters location:** This location. **Subsidiaries include:** Breeze-Eastern (Union NJ) designs, develops, manufactures, and services sophisticated lifting and restraining products, principally helicopter rescue hoist and cargo hook systems, winches and hoists for aircraft and weapon systems, and aircraft cargo tie-down systems. Breeze Industrial Products (PA) manufactures a complete line of standard and specialty gear-driven band fasteners in high-grade stainless steel for use in highly-engineered applications. Industrial Retaining Ring (Irvington NJ) manufactures a variety of retaining rings made of carbon steel, stainless steel, and beryllium copper. The Palnut Company (Mountainside NJ) manufactures light- and heavy-duty single- and multithread specialty fasteners. The Seeger Group (Somerville NJ) manufactures retaining clips, circlips, spring pins, and similar components.

VEECO INSTRUMENTS INC.
One Terminal Drive, Plainview NY 11803. 516/349-8300. **Contact:** Human Resources. **World Wide Web address:** http://www.veeco.com. **Description:** Designs, manufactures, markets, and services a broad line of precision ion beam etching and surface measurement systems used to manufacture microelectronic products. Veeco produces and sells its ion beam etching systems under the Microtech brand name. The company also sells leak detection/vacuum equipment, which is used for the precise identification of leaks in sealed

components. Leak detectors are used in a broad range of electronics, aerospace, and transportation products, ranging from air conditioning components to fiber-optic cables. Veeco's surface measurement products include surface profilers, atomic force microscopy measurement systems, and X-ray fluorescence thickness measurement systems. **Positions advertised include:** Business Analyst; Junior Accountant; Logistics Director; Quality Control Inspector; Senior Mechanical Engineer; Software Engineer; Technical Writer. **Corporate headquarters location:** This location. **Listed on:** NASDAQ. **Stock exchange symbol:** VECO.

VICTORY/YSI INC.
118 Victory Road, P.O. Box 710, Springfield NJ 07081. 973/379-5900. **Fax:** 973/379-5982. **Contact:** Personnel. **E-mail address:** veco@ysi.com. **World Wide Web address:** http://www.ysi.com/veco. **Description:** Manufactures and distributes thermistors, varistors, and specialty temperature sensing assemblies. **Corporate headquarters location:** This location. **Parent company:** YSI Incorporated.

WEISS-AUG COMPANY INC.
P.O. Box 520, East Hanover NJ 07936. 973/887-7600. **Fax:** 973/887-6924. **Contact:** Mary Dante, Director of Personnel. **World Wide Web address:** http://www.weiss-aug.com. **Description:** Manufactures stampings, moldings, insert moldings, and assemblies. Industries served include automotive, telecommunications, electronic and electrical connector, medical, and several specialty markets. Services include design, tooling, production, and quality control. Founded in 1972. **NOTE:** Part-time jobs and second and third shifts are offered. **Special programs:** Apprenticeships; Training; Co-ops. **Corporate headquarters location:** This location. **Operations at this facility include:** Administration; Manufacturing; Regional Headquarters; Sales; Service. **Listed on:** Privately held. **President:** Dieter Weissenrieden. **Annual sales/revenues:** $21 - $50 million. **Number of employees at this location:** 200.

THOMAS C. WILSON, INC.
21-13 44th Avenue, Long Island City NY 11101-5088. 718/729-3360. **Toll-free phone:** 800/230-2636. **Fax:** 718/361-2872. **Contact:** Personnel. **World Wide Web address:** http://www.tcwilson.com. **Description:** A manufacturer of tube cleaners and tube expanders for the boiler and condenser industry. **Corporate headquarters location:** This location. **Operations at this facility include:** Manufacturing; Sales.

MINING, GAS, PETROLEUM, ENERGY RELATED

You can expect to find the following types of companies in this section:
Anthracite, Coal, and Ore Mining • Mining Machinery and Equipment • Oil and Gas Field Services • Petroleum and Natural Gas

---

AMERADA HESS CORPORATION
One Hess Plaza, Woodbridge NJ 07095-1229. 732/636-3000. **Contact:** Human Resources. **World Wide Web address:** http://www.hess.com. **Description:** Extracts, refines, and markets petroleum. **Corporate headquarters location:** New York NY. **Listed on:** New York Stock Exchange. **Stock exchange symbol:** AHC.

AMERADA HESS CORPORATION
1185 Avenue of the Americas, 38th Floor, New York NY 10036. 212/997-8500. **Fax:** 212/536-8318. **Recorded jobline:** 800/947-HESS; (800/947-4377). **Contact:** Human Resources. **E-mail address:** employeerelations@hess.com. **World Wide Web address:** http://www.hess.com. **Description:** An integrated petroleum company engaged in exploration and production with oil and gas reserves in the U.S., the UK, and the North Sea, as well as North and West Africa and Southeast Asia. In addition to a refinery in Venezuela, the company has extensive storage capacity and terminals on the East Coast from Boston to Florida. The company's retail outlets, Hess Express stores, provide food service (Godfathers Pizza, Blimpies, and TCBY yogurt), its proprietary Mountain Top coffee, fountain service, and convenience items. **NOTE:** For retail positions apply at a local Hess Express location. **Positions advertised include:** Accountant; Chemical Engineer; Financial Analyst; Marketing Specialist; Mechanical Engineer; Sales Representative; Cashier; Head Cashier; General Manager; Site Manager; Manager Trainee; Food Service Supervisor; Assistant Manager; Sales Associate; Food Service Associate. **Corporate headquarters location:** This location. **Other locations:** Woodbridge NJ; Houston TX. **International locations:** Worldwide. **Subsidiaries include:** Premier Oil; United Kingdom Energy. **Listed on:** New York Stock Exchange. **Stock exchange symbol:** AHC. **Chairman/CEO:** John B. Hess. **Annual sales/revenues:** $13 billion. **Number of employees:** 11,700.

AMERIGAS PARTNERS, L.P.
dba AMERIGAS PROPANE
69 Denton Avenue South, New Hyde Park NY 11040. 516/352-6500. **Contact:** Employment Manager. **E-mail address:** hr1@amerigas.com. **World Wide Web address:** http://www.amerigas.com. **Description:** Formerly the Columbia Propane Corporation, AmeriGas serves over one million customers from 650 locations in 46 states distributing throughout the U.S. and Canada as well as selling supplies and equipment, and exchanging empty tanks for full ones. **NOTE:** For consideration, contact Human Resources at the company's headquarters: Robert Brantley, AmeriGas, 2250 Butler Pike, Suite 150, Plymouth Meeting PA 19462; phone: 610/337-1000; fax: 610/768-7647; e-mail: brantley@amerigas.com. **Positions advertised include:** Industrial Sales Representative. **Corporate headquarters location:** King of Prussia PA. **Other locations:** Nationwide. **Parent company:** UGI Corporation (King of Prussia PA). **Listed on:** New York Stock Exchange. **Stock exchange symbol:** APU. **Annual sales/revenues:** $1.3 billion. **Number of employees:** 6,300.

BEL-RAY COMPANY, INC.
P.O. Box 526, Farmingdale NJ 07727. 732/938-2421. **Physical address:** 1201 Bowman Avenue, Wall NJ 07719. **Fax:** 732/938-4232. **Contact:** Personnel. **E-mail address:** employment@belray.com. **World Wide Web address:** http://www.belray.com. **Description:** Manufactures lubricants used in the aerospace, automotive, food, marine, mining, steel, and textiles industries. **Positions advertised include:** Research & Development Specialist; Sales Representative.

CASTROL NORTH AMERICA, INC.
1500 Valley Road, Wayne NJ 07470. 973/633-2200. **Fax:** 973/633-5305. **Contact:** Mary Thompson, Director of Human Resources. **E-mail address:** hrjobs@cnacm.com. **World Wide Web address:** http://www.castrolna.com. **Description:** Manufactures and markets lubricants and petroleum products. **NOTE:** Apply online. **Corporate headquarters location:** This location. **Parent company:** Burmah Castrol USA, Inc. **Number of employees at this location:** 200. **Number of employees nationwide:** 2,500.

CHEVRON CORPORATION
1200 State Street, Perth Amboy NJ 08861. 732/738-2000. **Contact:** Human Resources. **World Wide Web address:** http://www.chevron.com. **Description:** An international oil firm with operations in more than 90 countries. Chevron Corporation is engaged in worldwide integrated petroleum operations including the exploration and production of crude oil and natural gas reserves; the transportation of crude oil, natural gas, and petroleum products by pipeline, tanker, and motor equipment; the operation of oil-refining complexes; and the wholesale and retail marketing of petroleum products. **Operations at this facility include:** This location operates as part of the asphalt division. **Parent company:** ChevronTexaco Corporation. **Listed on:** New York Stock Exchange. **Stock exchange symbol:** CVX.

EXXONMOBIL CORPORATION
1545 US Highway 22 E, Annondale NJ 08801. 908/730-0100. **Contact:** Human Resources. **World Wide Web address:** http://www.exxonmobil.com. **Description:** An integrated oil company engaged in petroleum and chemical products marketing, refining, manufacturing, exploration, production, transportation, and research and development worldwide. Other products include fabricated plastics, films, food bags, housewares, garbage bags, and building materials. The company also has subsidiaries involved in real estate development and mining operations. **Corporate headquarters location:** Irving TX. **Listed on:** New York Stock Exchange. **Stock exchange symbol:** XOM.

GETTY PETROLEUM MARKETING INC.
1500 Hampstead Turnpike, East Meadow NY 11554. 516/832-8800. **Fax:** 516/832-8272. **Contact:** Carolann Gaites, Human Resources Manager. **E-mail address:** hrdept@getty.com. **World Wide Web address:** http://www.getty.com. **Description:** A large, independent wholesaler and retailer of gasoline and petroleum products. The company also stores and distributes petroleum and gasoline products. Service stations operate under the names Getty and Power Test. Principal products for resale include gasoline, oil, diesel fuel, and kerosene. **NOTE:** Entry-level positions are offered. **Positions advertised include:** Mechanic; Gasoline Driver. **Corporate headquarters location:** This location. **Other U.S. locations:** CT; ME; MD; NJ; PA; RI. **Parent company:** OAO LUKOIL (Moscow, Russia). **President/CEO:** Vadim Gluzman.

PETROLEUM HEAT AND POWER CORPORATION
2187 Atlantic Street, Stamford CT 06902. 203/325-5400. **Recorded jobline:** 877/325-5400. **Contact:** Human Resources. **E-mail address:** greatjobs@petroheat.com. **World Wide Web address:** http://www.petro.com.

Description: Petroleum Heat and Power Corporation is one of the nation's largest retail distributors of home heating oil. The company serves 26 Northeast and Mid-Atlantic markets including the metropolitan areas of Boston, New York, Baltimore, and Washington DC. In addition to the delivery of home heating oil, the company also installs, repairs, and services heating equipment. Founded in 1903. **Subsidiaries include:** Star Gas Corporation is one of the largest retail propane gas distributors in the country. **Number of employees at this location:** 2,400.

PHILLIPS PETROLEUM COMPANY
1400 Park Avenue, Linden NJ 07036. 908/523-5000. **Contact:** Professional Employment. **World Wide Web address:** http://www.phillips66.com. **Description:** Refines oil. **NOTE:** Mail employment correspondence to: Professional Employment, 180 Plaza Office Building, Bartlesville OK 74004.

RESOURCE ENERGY, INC.
6165 Plank Road, Mayville NY 14757. 716/269-7665. **Contact:** Human Resources. **Description:** Resource Energy, Incorporated has concentrated its activities in two industries: energy and real estate finance. In energy, REI produces and transports natural gas and oil from properties it owns and/or operates. In real estate, the company owns a portfolio of 12 mortgages with an aggregate face value for $30.7 million. **Corporate headquarters location:** Philadelphia PA.

SCHLUMBERGER LTD.
153 East 53rd Street, 57th Floor, New York NY 10022. 212/350-9400. **Fax:** 212/350-9457. **Contact:** Human Resources. **World Wide Web address:** http://www.schlumberger.com. **Description:** Schlumberger provides oil field services including logging, testing, seismic, MWD, LWD, drilling, cementing, and stimulation; CAD/CAM; automatic test equipment; electricity, water, and gas metering and measurement; and fuel dispensing and monitoring systems. **Special programs:** Internships. **Corporate headquarters location:** This location. **Other U.S. locations:** TX; NJ. **Listed on:** New York Stock Exchange. **Stock exchange symbol:** SLB. **President/CEO/Chairman:** Andrew Gould. **Sales/revenue:** Over $13 billion. **Number of employees worldwide:** 78,500.

SITHE ENERGIES, INC.
335 Madison Avenue, 28th Floor, New York NY 10017. 212/351-0000. **Fax:** 212/351-0800. **Contact:** Human Resources. **E-mail address:** info@sithe.com. **World Wide Web address:** http://www.sithe.com. **Description:** Develops, builds, owns, and operates electricity-generating facilities throughout the United States and Canada. Revenues are derived primarily from the sale of electricity produced by natural gas-fired cogeneration plants under long-term agreements with major electric utilities. The company also sells thermal energy to the government, industries, and other users. **Corporate headquarters location:** This location. **International locations:** China; France; Philippines; Thailand. **Sales/revenue:** Approximately $1 billion. **Number of employees at this location:** 220.

WILSHIRE OIL COMPANY
921 Bergen Avenue, Jersey City NJ 07306. 201/420-2796. **Contact:** Human Resources. **Description:** A diversified corporation engaged in oil and gas exploration and production, real estate operations, and investment activities. **Corporate headquarters location:** This location.

PAPER AND WOOD PRODUCTS

You can expect to find the following types of companies in this section:
Forest and Wood Products and Services • Lumber and Wood Wholesalers • Millwork, Plywood, and Structural Members • Paper and Wood Mills

BALTEK CORPORATION
P.O. Box 195, 10 Fairway Court, Northvale NJ 07647. 201/767-1400. **Fax:** 201/387-6631. **Contact:** Personnel. **World Wide Web address:** http://www.baltek.com. **Description:** Manufactures wood panels and other balsa wood products for marine and industrial use. **Corporate headquarters location:** This location.

BERLIN & JONES COMPANY, INC.
2 East Union Avenue, East Rutherford NJ 07073. 201/933-5900. **Fax:** 201/933-4242. **Contact:** Human Resources. **Description:** Manufactures envelopes. **Corporate headquarters location:** This location.

CENVEO
25 Linden Avenue East, Jersey City NJ 07305. 201/434-2100. **Toll-free phone:** 800/526-3020. **Fax:** 201/434-4048. **Contact:** Human Resources. **World Wide Web address:** http://www.cenveo.com. **Description:** Manufactures and prints envelopes and tags. Primary customers are publishing houses, insurance agencies, banks, direct mail companies, pharmaceutical companies, brokers, and jobbers. **NOTE:** A college education is required of all applicants. Sales experience with industrial accounts is preferred.

HOBOKEN FLOORS
70 Demarest Drive, Wayne NJ 07470. 973/694-2888. **Contact:** Personnel. **World Wide Web address:** http://www.hobokenfloors.com. **Description:** Manufactures hardwood flooring. **Corporate headquarters location:** This location.

IMPERIAL PAPER BOX CORPORATION
252 Newport Street, Brooklyn NY 11212. 718/346-6100. **Fax:** 718/346-0400. **Contact:** Personnel Director. **World Wide Web address:** http://www.imperialpaperbox.com. **Description:** A manufacturer of paper containers including boxes and packaging materials. Since 1902.

INTERNATIONAL PAPER COMPANY
400 Atlantic Street, Stamford CT 06921. 203/541-8000. **Contact:** Human Resources. **World Wide Web address:** http://www.internationalpaper.com. **Description:** International Paper Company manufactures pulp and paper, packaging, wood products, and a range of specialty products. The company is organized into five business segments: Printing Papers, whose principal products include uncoated papers, coated papers, bristles, and pulp; Packaging, which includes industrial packaging, consumer packaging, and kraft and specialty papers; Distribution, including the sale of printing papers, graphic arts equipment and supplies, packaging materials, industrial supplies, and office products; Specialty Products, which includes imaging products, specialty panels, nonwovens, chemicals, and minerals; and Forest Products which includes logging and wood products. **Corporate headquarters location:** This location. **Subsidiaries include:** Champion Papel e Celulose (Brazil); Weldwood of Canada. **Listed on:** New York Stock Exchange. **Stock exchange symbol:** IP. **Number of employees worldwide:** 72,500.

INTERNATIONAL PAPER COMPANY

3 Paragon Drive, Montvale NJ 07645. 201/391-1776. **Contact:** Personnel. **World Wide Web address:** http://www.internationalpaper.com. **Description:** International Paper Company manufactures pulp and paper, packaging, wood products, and a range of specialty products. The company is organized into five business segments: Printing Papers, whose principal products include uncoated papers, coated papers, bristles, and pulp; Packaging, which includes industrial packaging, consumer packaging, and kraft and specialty papers; Distribution, including the sale of printing papers, graphic arts equipment and supplies, packaging materials, industrial supplies, and office products; Specialty Products, which includes imaging products, specialty panels, nonwovens, chemicals, and minerals; and Forest Products which includes logging and wood products. **Corporate headquarters location:** Stamford CT. **Operations at this facility include:** This location houses sales offices for paperboard and paper products. **Number of employees worldwide:** 72,500.

KNOX ENTERPRISES

33 Riverside Avenue, 5th Floor, Westport CT 06880. 203/226-6288. **Contact:** Human Resources. **World Wide Web address:** http://www.knoxandco.com. **Description:** A holding company. **Corporate headquarters location:** This location. **Subsidiaries include:** Jackburn Manufacturing, Inc. (PA) manufactures fabricated steel parts; Setterstix Corporation (DE) manufactures rolled paper products for the confectionery and health care industries. **Number of employees nationwide:** 145.

MAFCOTE, INC.

108 Main Street, Norwalk CT 06851. 203/847-8500. **Contact:** Human Resources. **E-mail address:** jobs@mafcote.com. **World Wide Web address:** http://www.mafcote.com. **Description:** Paper Manufacturer. **Positions advertised include:** Sales/Marketing Trainee; Financial Analyst; Operations Manager; Administrative Assistant; Customer Service Representative. **Corporate headquarters location:** This location. **Other U.S. locations:** Nationwide.

MARCAL PAPER MILLS, INC.

One Market Street, Elmwood Park NJ 07407. 201/796-4000. **Fax:** 201/798-0670. **Contact:** James H. Nelson, Director of Human Resources Department. **World Wide Web address:** http://www.marcalpaper.com. **Description:** Manufactures and distributes a broad range of nationally advertised paper products including paper towels, toilet tissue, and napkins. **Corporate headquarters location:** This location. **Operations at this facility include:** Administration; Manufacturing; Research and Development; Sales.

MEADWESTVACO

299 Park Avenue, New York NY 10171. 212/318-5000. **Contact:** Human Resources. **World Wide Web address:** http://www.meadwestvaco.com. **Description:** A producer of forestry products, paper packaging, and specialty chemicals. Worldwide, MeadWestvaco operates 50 facilities in 29 countries including paper and paperboard mills, converting plants, chemical plants, lumber mills, research and development laboratories, and real estate operations. **Corporate headquarters location:** Stamford CT. **Operations at this facility include:** Administration; Sales. **Listed on:** New York Stock Exchange. **Stock exchange symbol:** MWV. **Chairman/CEO:** John A. Luke Jr. **Annual sales/revenues:** $7.2 billion. **Number of employees:** 30,700.

NATIONAL ENVELOPE CORPORATION

2910 Hunters Point Avenue, Long Island City NY 11101. 718/786-0300. **Contact:** Human Resources. **World Wide Web address:** http://www.nationalenvelope.com. **Description:** Manufactures a wide range of envelopes for distribution to wholesalers. Founded in 1957. **Corporate headquarters location:** This location. **Other U.S. locations:** Nationwide.

SCHIFFENHAUS INDUSTRIES
2013 McCarter Highway, Newark NJ 07104. 973/484-5000. **Fax:** 973/268-4908. **Contact:** Human Resources. **World Wide Web address:** http://www.schifpack.com. **Description:** Manufactures corrugated boxes and flexographic, preprinted liner board. **Positions advertised include:** Sales Representative. **Corporate headquarters location:** This location. **Number of employees at this location:** 165.

STANDARD FOLDING CARTONS
85th Street & 24th Avenue, Jackson Heights NY 11370. 718/335-5500. **Fax:** 718/507-6430. **Contact:** Human Resources. **Description:** A manufacturer of folding boxes. **Corporate headquarters location:** This location.

PRINTING AND PUBLISHING

You can expect to find the following types of companies
in this section:
Book, Newspaper, and Periodical Publishers • Commercial Photographers •
Commercial Printing Services • Graphic Designers

AOL TIME WARNER, INC.
75 Rockefeller Plaza, New York NY 10019. 212/484-8000. **Fax:** 212/489-6183.
Contact: Human Resources. **World Wide Web address:**
http://www.aoltimewarner.com. **Description:** Publishes and distributes books
and magazines including the weekly *Time* magazine. Time Warner also
produces, distributes, licenses, and publishes recorded music; owns and
administers music copyrights; produces, finances, and distributes motion pictures
and television programming; distributes videocassettes; produces and distributes
pay television and cable programming; and operates and manages cable
television systems. **Positions advertised include:** Executive Secretary;
Marketing & Business Development Manager; Ad Operations Manager;
Associate Finance Manager; Human Resources Director; Articles Editor;
Research Analyst; National Account Executive; Advertising Sales Assistant;
Sales Assistant; Financial Analyst; Team Assistant; Network Specialist; Manager
of Sales; Brand Manager; Technician; International Artist Promotion Assistant;
Ad Sales Assistant; High Speed Online Sale Engineer; Manager of Licensing;
Business Associate; Accounts Payable Clerk; Financial Operations and
Reporting Manager; Bilingual News Assistant; Contract Administrator;
Promotions Marketing Director; Special Book Sales Manager; Financial Capital
Analyst. **Corporate headquarters location:** This location. **Subsidiaries
include:** America Online, Inc.; AOL Time Warner Interactive Video; Columbia
House Company; CompuServe; Time Inc.; Time Warner Cable; Time Warner
Entertainment Company, L.P.; Time Warner Telecom Inc.; Turner Broadcasting
System, Inc.; Warner Bros.; Warner Music Group. **Listed on:** New York Stock
Exchange. **Stock exchange symbol:** AOL. **Chairman/CEO:** Richard (Dick) D
Parsons. **Annual sales/revenues:** $41 billion. **Number of employees:** 89,300.

ADVANCE PUBLICATIONS INC.
950 Fingerboard Road, Staten Island NY 10305. 718/981-1234. **Fax:** 718/981-
1456. **Contact:** Human Resources. **World Wide Web address:**
http://www.advance.net. **Description:** A media publishing company that owns
over 25 daily newspapers nationwide including *The Star Ledger*, *The Cleveland
Plain Dealer*, and *Staten Island Advance* – a local New York daily newspaper.
Advance has interests in cable television and Internet sites related to its
publications and the company's subsidiaries publish 41 weekly newspapers as
well as magazines including *Allure*, *Glamour*, *Vanity Fair*, *Parade Magazine*
Sunday insert, and *Women's Wear Daily*. Founded in 1886. **Positions
advertised include:** Marketing Coordinator; Account Executive; Internet
Advertising Coordinator. **Corporate headquarters location:** This location.
Subsidiaries include: American City Business Journals, Inc.; Condé Nast
Publications Inc.; Discovery Communications, Inc.; Fairchild Publications, Inc.;
Parade Publications; The Golf Digest Companies. **Chairman/CEO/Owner:**
Samuel (Si) I. Newhouse Jr. **Annual sales/revenues:** $4.2 billion. **Number of
employees at this location:** 450. **Number of employees nationwide:** 22,785.

ALEXANDER HAMILTON INSTITUTE, INC.
70 Hilltop Road, Ramsey NJ 07446. 201/825-3377. **Toll-free phone:** 800/879-
2441. **Fax:** 201/825-8696. **Contact:** Personnel. **World Wide Web address:**

http://www.ahipubs.com. **Description:** Publishes newsletters and manuals focused on employment law.

AMERICAN BANK NOTE HOLOGRAPHICS, INC.
399 Executive Boulevard, Elmsford NY 10523. 914/592-2355. **Fax:** 914/592-3248. **Contact:** Susan Herbert. **World Wide Web address:** http://www.abnh.com. **Description:** Produces laser-generated, three-dimensional images that appear on credit cards and products requiring proof of authenticity. The company operates 10 active mastering labs with the ability to create a variety of holograms including 3-D models, flat art, computer-generated animation, cinematography, dot matrix, Microline, and diffractive mercurial. **Corporate headquarters location:** This location. **Other locations:** Elmsford NY; Huntingdon Valley PA. **Operations at this facility include:** Corporate administration; Production. **Listed on:** Over The Counter. **Stock exchange symbol:** ABHH. **President/CEO:** Kenneth H. Traub. **Annual sales/revenues:** $26.5 billion. **Number of employees:** 120.

AMERICAN BIBLE SOCIETY
1865 Broadway, 6th Floor, New York NY 10023. 212/408-1200. **Contact:** Human Resources. **E-mail address:** hrinbox@americanbible.org. **World Wide Web address:** http://www.americanbible.org. **Description:** Translates, publishes, and distributes the Bible and portions of the Scriptures, without doctrinal note or comment, in more than 180 nations. Founded in 1816. **Positions advertised include:** Acquisition & Renewal Projects Manager; Marketing Fullfillment Assistant; Latino Affairs Distribution Representative; Editor; Production Manager. **Corporate headquarters location:** This location. **Other locations:** CO; FL; MO; NJ; VA. **Operations at this facility include:** Administration; Manufacturing; Sales; Service. **Number of employees at this location:** 300.

AMERICAN SOCIETY OF COMPOSERS, AUTHORS & PUBLISHERS (ASCAP)
One Lincoln Plaza, New York NY 10023. 212/621-6000. **Fax:** 212/724-9064. **Contact:** Human Resources Services. **E-mail address:** jobline@ascap.com. **World Wide Web address:** http://www.ascap.com. **Description:** An international service organization serving the music, publishing, and other creative industries. The organization provides a wide range of services to members including the supervision and enforcement of copyrights. **Positions advertised include:** Radio Analyst; Cable/PBS Analyst; Assistant Area Licensing Manager; International Services Representative; International Distribution Analyst; Executive Assistant; TV Service Representative.

APPLIED GRAPHICS TECHNOLOGIES (AGT)
One Kero Road, Carlstadt NJ 07072. 201/933-8585. **Fax:** 201/935-5108. **Contact:** Human Resources. **World Wide Web address:** http://www.agt.com. **Description:** Applied Graphics Technologies (AGT) is one of the largest providers of integrated graphic communications services to advertising agencies, magazine and catalog publishers, and corporate clients in various industries. The company's services include commercial printing, color separation and retouching, facilities management, photo CD and digital image archiving, electronic imaging services, flexo/packaging services, publication and catalog services, satellite transmission services, creative design services, technical support and training services, and black and white ad production. **NOTE:** All of the hiring is conducted through the corporate headquarters. Interested jobseekers should address all inquiries to Applied Graphics Technologies, 450 West 33rd Street, 11th Floor, New York NY 10001. 212/716-6600. **Corporate headquarters location:** New York NY. **Operations at this facility include:** This location offers publication and catalog services, satellite transmission services, a desktop service bureau, four-color facsimile or digital transmittal, and packaging services.

APPLIED GRAPHICS TECHNOLOGIES, INC.

450 West 33rd Street, 11th Floor, New York NY 10001. 917/339-7320. **Fax:** 212/716-6776. **Contact:** Human Resources. **World Wide Web address:** http://www.agt.com. **Description:** Applied Graphics Technologies, Inc. along with its subsidiaries is one of the largest providers of integrated graphic communications services to advertising agencies, magazine and catalog publishers, and corporate clients in various industries worldwide. The company's services include commercial printing, color separation and retouching, facilities management, photo CD and digital image archiving, electronic imaging services, flexo/packaging services, publication and catalog services, satellite transmission services, creative design services, technical support and training services, and black and white ad production. **Corporate headquarters location:** This location. **Other area locations:** Rochester NY. **Other U.S. locations:** Nationwide. **Parent company:** Kohlberg & Company. **Subsidiaries include:** Black Dot Graphics, Inc.; Seven Worldwide, Inc. (also at this location). **Listed on:** American Stock Exchange. **Stock exchange symbol:** AGD. **Chairman/CEO:** Fred Drasner. **Annual sales/revenues:** $507 million. **Number of employees:** 4,000.

APPLIED GRAPHICS TECHNOLOGIES

1775 Broadway, 12th Floor, New York NY 10019. 212/333-4111. **Fax:** 212/333-7921. **Contact:** Human Resources. **World Wide Web address:** http://www.agt.com. **Description:** This location provides publication and catalog services, four-color facsimile or digital transmittal, desktop service bureau, satellite transmission services, and advertising agency services. Overall, Applied Graphics Technologies (AGT)/Seven is one of the largest providers of integrated graphic communications services to advertising agencies, magazine and catalog publishers, and corporate clients in various industries worldwide. The company's services include commercial printing, color separation and retouching, facilities management, photo CD and digital image archiving, electronic imaging services, flexo/packaging services, publication and catalog services, satellite transmission services, creative design services, technical support and training services, and black and white ad production. **NOTE:** All hiring is conducted through the corporate headquarters. Interested jobseekers should address all inquiries to Applied Graphics Technologies/Seven, 450 West 33rd Street, 11th Floor, New York NY 10001. 212/716-6600. **Corporate headquarters location:** New York NY. **Listed on:** American Stock Exchange. **Stock exchange symbol:** AGD.

APPLIED GRAPHICS TECHNOLOGIES
AGT – SEVEN ASSET MANAGEMENT SERVICES

450 West 33rd Street, 11th Floor, New York NY 10001. 212/716-6600. **Fax:** 585/277-1776. **Contact:** Human Resources. **World Wide Web address:** http://www.agtseven.com. **Description:** One of the largest providers of integrated graphic communications services to advertising agencies, magazine and catalog publishers, and corporate clients in various industries worldwide. Applied Graphics Technologies/Seven's services include commercial printing, color separation and retouching, facilities management, photo CD and digital image archiving, electronic imaging services, flexo/packaging services, publication and catalog services, satellite transmission services, creative design services, technical support and training services, and black and white ad production. **Corporate headquarters location:** This location. **Listed on:** American Stock Exchange. **Stock exchange symbol:** AGD.

APPLIED PRINTING TECHNOLOGIES

77 Moonachie Avenue, Moonachie NJ 07074. 201/896-6600. **Fax:** 201/896-1893. **Contact:** Personnel. **World Wide Web address:** http://www.appliedprinting.com. **Description:** Offers commercial printing services, bindery services, a desktop service bureau, and advertising agency services. **Corporate headquarters location:** This location.

THE ASBURY PARK PRESS
3601 Highway 66, P.O. Box 1550, Neptune NJ 07754. 732/922-6000. **Contact:** Human Resources. **E-mail address:** hr@app.com. **World Wide Web address:** http://www.app.com. **Description:** Publishes a daily local newspaper. **Special programs:** Internships. **Corporate headquarters location:** This location. **Other U.S. locations:** Orlando FL. **Listed on:** Privately held. **Number of employees nationwide:** 1,900.

THE ASSOCIATED PRESS
50 Rockefeller Plaza, 7th Floor, New York NY 10020. 212/621-1500. **Fax:** 212/621-5447. **Contact:** Human Resources. **E-mail address:** apjobs@ap.org. **World Wide Web address:** http://www.ap.org. **Description:** One of the largest independent news-gathering organizations in the world. Founded in 1848. **Corporate headquarters location:** This location. **Other U.S. locations:** Nationwide. **International locations:** Worldwide.

BP INDEPENDENT REPROGRAPHICS
853 Broadway, New York NY 10003. 212/777-1110. **Fax:** 212/777-0880. **Contact:** Human Resources. **World Wide Web address:** http://www.bpirepro.com. **Description:** Provides blueprinting services, blueprint supplies, printing services, and photo services. **Other locations:** Elmsford NY; New York NY; White Plains NY. **Subsidiaries include:** B&B Independent. **Parent company:** American Reprographics Company (Glendale CA).

BAKER & TAYLOR
1120 Highway 22 East, Bridgewater NJ 08807-0885. 908/541-7000. **Contact:** Human Resources. **World Wide Web address:** http://www.btol.com. **Description:** A leading full-line distributor of books, videos, and music products. Customers include online and traditional retailers and institutional customers. Baker & Taylor also provides customers with value-added proprietary data products and customized management and outsourcing services. Founded in 1828. **NOTE:** Entry-level positions and second and third shifts are offered. **Positions advertised include:** Adaptive Cataloger; Collection Development Librarian; Publisher Services Supervisor; Support Center Representative. **Corporate headquarters location:** Charlotte NC. **Listed on:** Privately held. **Number of employees worldwide:** 2,500.

BOOKAZINE COMPANY INC.
75 Hook Road, Bayonne NJ 07002. 201/339-7777. **Fax:** 201/239-7778. **Contact:** Richard Kallman, Vice President. **E-mail address:** staff@bookazine.com. **World Wide Web address:** http://www.bookazine.com. **Description:** A general trade book wholesaler serving retail bookstores with an inventory of over 100,000 titles. Founded in 1928. **Corporate headquarters location:** This location. **President/CEO:** Robert Kallman.

BOWNE & CO., INC.
345 Hudson Street, 10th Floor, New York NY 10014. 212/924-5500. **Fax:** 212/229-3400. **Contact:** Ellen McLynch, Human Resources Manager. **E-mail address:** jobs.bowne@bowne.com. **World Wide Web address:** http://www.bowne.com. **Description:** Provides nationwide information management and compliance documentation services through principal business segments. Printing activities are divided into four segments: financial, corporate, commercial, and legal printing. Services in the legal printing segment include the typesetting and printing of compliance documentation relating to corporate and municipal financing, mergers, and acquisitions; the dissemination of information by companies through annual and interim reports and proxy material; and the printing of materials unrelated to compliance such as business forms and reports, newsletters, promotional aids, market letters, sales literature, and legal printing products. Founded in 1775. **NOTE:** Entry-level positions and second and third

shifts are offered. **Company slogan:** Empowering your information. **Positions advertised include:** Account Operations Manager; Project Manager; Administrative Assistant; Manager Human Resources; Assistant Controller; Learning Development Manager. **Special programs:** Internships; Training; Co-ops; Summer Jobs. **Corporate headquarters location:** This location. **Other U.S. locations:** Nationwide. **International locations:** Worldwide. **Listed on:** New York Stock Exchange. **Stock exchange symbol:** BNE. **CEO:** Robert M. Johnson. **Annual sales/revenues:** $1 billion. **Number of employees at this location:** 1,000. **Number of employees nationwide:** 6,000. **Number of employees worldwide:** 8,000.

BUTTERICK MCCAL PATTERN COMPANY
11 Penn Plaza, New York NY 10001. 212/465-6800. **Contact:** Human Resources. **World Wide Web address:** http://www.butterick.com. **Description:** Manufactures two lines of clothing patterns for the home sewing market and produces related fashion publications including *Weddings, Butterick Home Catalog, Vogue Patterns Magazine, and Vogue Knitting Magazine.* **Positions advertised include:** Editorial Assistant; Fashion Designer; Public Relations Specialist. **Special programs:** Internships. **Corporate headquarters location:** This location. **Operations at this facility include:** Administration; Financial Offices; Research and Development; Sales; Service.

CMP MEDIA LLC
600 Community Drive, Manhasset NY 11030. 516/562-5000. **Fax:** 516/562-5993. **Contact:** Maria Huddleston, Staffing Department. **E-mail address:** mhuddleston@cmp.com or careers@cmp.com. **World Wide Web address:** http://www.cmp.com. **Description:** Publishes high-tech, computer-related magazines and trade publications. **NOTE:** Unsolicited resumes are not accepted. **Positions advertised include:** Editorial Assistant; Audience Development Manager; Senior Writer; Associate Editor; Director of Research; Financial Analyst; Tax Accountant. **Special programs:** Internships. **Corporate headquarters location:** This location. **Other U.S. locations:** CA; GA; KS; MA; NH. **Subsidiaries include:** CMP Publications; CMP Websites. **Parent company:** United Business Media (London, United Kingdom). **Operations at this facility include:** Sales. **President/CEO:** Gary Marshall. **Annual sales/revenues:** $530 million. **Number of employees at this location:** 1,000. **Number of employees nationwide:** 1,400.

CAMBRIDGE UNIVERSITY PRESS
40 West 20th Street, New York NY 10011-4211. 212/924-3900. **Fax:** 212/691-3239. **Contact:** Deborah Chick, Personnel Associate. **E-mail address:** jobs@cup.org. **World Wide Web address:** http://www.cup.org. **Description:** Cambridge University Press publishes an average of 1,300 nonfiction books a year. **Positions advertised include:** Journals Acquisitions Editor; Journals Assistant; Development Editor; Production Manager; Project Editor.

THE CHALLENGE GROUP
1195 Atlantic Avenue, Brooklyn NY 11216. 718/636-9500. **Fax:** 718/857-9115.**Contact:** Thomas H. Watkins, Publisher. **E-mail address:** challengegroup@yahoo.com. **World Wide Web address:** http://www.challenge-group.com. **Description:** Publishes several nationally distributed, weekly newspaper (circulation of 130,000) primarily covering cultural, political, and social news of interest to African Americans. Publications include *The New American, Afro Times,* and *The Daily Challenge.* **Special programs:** Internships. **Corporate headquarters location:** This location.

COLOR OPTICS, INC.
216 Midland Avenue, Saddle Brook NJ 07663. 973/772-1007. **Fax:** 973/772-8991. **Contact:** Margaret Sapinski, Human Resources. **E-mail address:**

psapinski@coloroptics.com. **World Wide Web address:** http://www.coloroptics.com. **Description:** Commercial printing company. **Positions advertised include:** Customer Service Representative; Estimator/Print Production; Machine Operators; Outside Sales; Prepress; Proofing; Scanner Operators.

COMTEC, INC.
6 Just Road, Fairfield NJ 07004. 973/882-3050. **Fax:** 973/808-4302. **Contact:** Human Resources. **E-mail address:** hr@comtecnet.com. **World Wide Web address:** http://www.comtecnet.com. **Description:** Provider of customized printing, inserting, and mailing services including graphic design, custom application programming, high-speed printing, intelligent inserting and automated mailing. **Positions advertised include:** Creative Director; Production Printer Technician.

CONDE NAST PUBLICATIONS INC.
4 Times Square, New York NY 10036. 212/286-2860. **Fax:** 212/286-5960. **Contact:** Human Resources Department. **World Wide Web address:** http://www.condenast.com. **Description:** Publishes a broad range of nationally distributed award-winning lifestyle-oriented magazines covering food, travel, fashion, and more which include: *Mademoiselle*, *Glamour*, *House & Garden*, *Vogue*, *Self*, *Gentleman's Quarterly*, *Allure*, *Wired*, *Modern Bride*, *The New Yorker*, *Vanity Fair*, and *Lucky Magazine*. **Subsidiaries include:** Ideas Publishing Group, Inc.; Epicurious; Concierge; Swoon. **Parent company:** Advance Publications (Staten Island NY).

CREST OFFICE PRODUCTS
448 West 16th Street, 5th Floor, New York NY 10011. 212/271-2065. **Contact:** Human Resources. **Description:** Provides commercial printing services and offset lithography.

DSA COMMUNITY PUBLISHING
250 Miller Place, Hicksville NY 11801. 516/393-9300. **Contact:** Human Resources. **World Wide Web address:** http://www.dsapub.com. **Description:** A regional publisher involved in the publishing, printing, and distribution of weekly free-circulation newspapers, as well as circulars and other promotional and printed material. DSA's publications include *The Pennysaver*, *Shoppers Guide*, *Yankee Trader*, *Marketeer*, *Pocket Mailer*, and *Value Mailer*. **Operations at this facility include:** Administration; Manufacturing; Sales; Service.

THE DAILY RECORD INC.
800 Jefferson Road, Parsippany NJ 07054. 973/428-6200. **Fax:** 973/884-5768. **Contact:** Mike Owen, Personnel. **E-mail address:** mowen@morristo.gannett.com. **World Wide Web address:** http://www.dailyrecord.com. **Description:** Publishes a morning newspaper, the *Daily Record*. Circulation is approximately 63,000 on weekdays and 72,000 on Sundays. **Corporate headquarters location:** Arlington VA. **Parent company:** Gannett Company. **Listed on:** New York Stock Exchange. **Stock exchange symbol:** GSI. **Number of employees at this location:** 300.

DELUXE FINANCIAL SERVICES
105 Route 46 West, Mountain Lakes NJ 07046-1645. 973/334-8000. **Fax:** 973/334-4292. **Contact:** Russ Perry, Personnel Director. **World Wide Web address:** http://www.deluxe.com. **Description:** Engaged in the printing and selling of checks, deposit tickets, and related forms to banks and other financial institutions. The company also manufactures documents printed with magnetic ink. Printing operations are carried out at more than 15 plants throughout the United States. **Corporate headquarters location:** Shoreview MN. **Parent company:** Deluxe Corporation provides check printing, electronic funds transfer

processing services, and related services to the financial industry; check authorization and collection services to retailers; and electronic benefit transfer services to state governments. Deluxe Corporation also produces forms, specialty papers, and other products for small businesses, professional practices, and medical/dental offices; and provides tax forms and electronic tax filing services to tax preparers. Through the direct-mail channel, Deluxe sells greeting cards and gift wrap. **Listed on:** New York Stock Exchange. **Stock exchange symbol:** DLX.

DOW JONES & COMPANY, INC.
World Financial Center, 12th Floor, 200 Liberty Street, New York NY 10281. 212/416-2000. **Fax:** 212/416-4348. **Contact:** Human Resources. **E-mail address:** djcareers@dowjones.com. **World Wide Web address:** http://www.dowjones.com. **Description:** A highly diversified publishing and communications firm. Publishing operations include *The Wall Street Journal*, an international business daily newspaper; *The Asian Wall Street Journal*; and the weekly investor's newspaper, *Barron's*. The company offers a wide range of information services including an online library of news and financial information, an online sports information service, a real-time financial market data service, and a newswire service. Since 1882. **Positions advertised include:** Art Director; Classified Ad Sales Representative; Interactive News Assistant; Interactive News Writer; Senior Category Manager. **Corporate headquarters location:** This location. **Other U.S. locations:** Nationwide. **Subsidiaries include:** *Wall Street Journal*; Dow Jones Reuters Business Interactive LLC; Ottaway Newspapers; The Wall Street Journal Online. **Listed on:** New York Stock Exchange. **Stock exchange symbol:** DJ. **Chairman/CEO:** Peter R. Kann. **Annual sales/revenues:** $1.6 billion. **Number of employees:** 6,816.

THE ECONOMICS PRESS, INC.
12 Daniel Road, Fairfield NJ 07004-2565. 973/227-1224. **Toll-free phone:** 800/526-2554. **Fax:** 973/227-3558. **Contact:** Human Resources. **World Wide Web address:** http://www.epinc.com. **Description:** A publisher of books, audio and video programs, and computer programs focused on employee training, motivation, and business information.

FACTS ON FILE, INC.
132 West 31st Street, 17th Floor, New York NY 10001. 212/967-8800. **Fax:** 212/896-4383. **Contact:** Human Resources. **E-mail address:** resumes@factsonfile.com. **World Wide Web address:** http://www.factsonfile.com. **Description:** A reference book publisher that specializes in books for public and school libraries. **Positions advertised include:** Copy Editor.

FAIRCHILD PUBLICATIONS, INC.
7 West 34th Street, 6th Floor, New York NY 10001. 212/630-4000. **Fax:** 212/630-4295. **Contact:** Human Resources. **E-mail address:** hr@fairchildpub.com. **World Wide Web address:** http://www.fairchildpub.com. **Description:** A business and professional magazine publisher. Fairchild Publications' primary focus is on the fashion industry. Founded in 1892. **NOTE:** Human Resources phone: 212/630-4300. **Positions advertised include:** Junior Financial Reporter; Media Reporter; Senior Editor; Business Manager; Administrative Assistant; Account Executive. **Special programs:** Internships. **Corporate headquarters location:** This location. **Other U.S. locations:** Los Angeles CA; Washington DC; Chicago IL; Boston MA; Dallas TX. **Subsidiaries include:** *Children's' Business; Details; DNR; Executive Technology; Footwear News; Home Furnishings News; Jane; Salon News; Supermarket News; W; Women's Wear Daily*. **Parent company:** Advance Publications. **Operations at this facility include:** Administration; Divisional Headquarters; Sales. **Number of employees at this location:** 550. **Number of employees nationwide:** 750.

FARRAR, STRAUS AND GIROUX
19 Union Square West, New York NY 10003. 212/741-6900. **Contact:** Human Resources. **World Wide Web address:** http://www.fsgbooks.com. **Description:** A general trade book publisher known for its international list of literary fiction, nonfiction, poetry, and children's books. Founded in 1946. **Parent company:** Verlagsgruppe Georg von Holtzbrinck GmbH (Stuttgart, Germany).

FORBES INC.
60 Fifth Avenue, New York NY 10011. 212/620-2200. **Fax:** 212/206-5105. **Contact:** Human Resources. **E-mail address:** jobs@forbes.com. **World Wide Web address:** http://www.forbes.com. **Description:** Publisher of biweekly business periodical, *Forbes*, as well as other custom publications and magazines including *Forbes FYI, American Heritage*, and *American Legacy*. The company also operates the Forbes.com Website and produces business conferences. Founded in 1917. **Special programs:** Internships. **Corporate headquarters location:** This location. **Subsidiaries include:** American Heritage; Forbes Global; Forbes media. **Operations at this facility include:** Administration; Sales. **Chairman:** Casper W. Weinberger. **President/CEO:** Malcolm S. (Steve) Forbes Jr. **Annual sales/revenues:** $410 million. **Number of employees:** 750.

SAMUEL FRENCH INC.
45 West 25th Street, 2nd Floor, New York NY 10010-2751. 212/206-8990. **Fax:** 212/206-1429. **Contact:** Personnel Director. **World Wide Web address:** http://www.samuelfrench.com. **Description:** A publishing firm engaged in the production and distribution of plays and books relating to the theater. **Other U.S. locations:** Hollywood CA. **International locations:** Toronto, Canada; London, England.

GANNETT COMPANY, INC.
535 Madison Avenue, New York NY 10022. 212/715-5300. **Contact:** Human Resources. **World Wide Web address:** http://www.gannett.com. **Description:** Gannett Company, Inc. is one of the largest news and information organizations in the United States. Gannett Company is involved in newspaper publishing, radio and television broadcasting, cable television, television entertainment programming, and outdoor advertising. The company owns and operates 15 television stations, 7 FM radio stations, and 6 AM radio stations. The company's cable division provides service to 458,000 subscribers. Gannett Outdoor Advertising operates in 19 major U.S. markets, as well as in Canada. The company has also diversified into areas such as alarm security services; commercial printing; data services; marketing; news programming; and newswire service, with operations in 44 states, as well as Washington DC, Canada, Guam, and the U.S. Virgin Islands. Average circulation of Gannett's 92 U.S. daily and nondaily newspapers and publications is approximately 6.6 million. Founded in 1906. **Corporate headquarters location:** McLean VA. **Other U.S. locations:** Nationwide. **International locations:** Canada. **Subsidiaries include:** CareerBuilder; Gannet Broadcasting on the Web; Gannett Community Newspapers; Gannett Media Technologies International; Gennett Newspapers on the Web; Gannett Television Stations; Newsquest plc. **Listed on:** New York Stock Exchange. **Stock exchange symbol:** GCI. **Annual sales/revenues:** $6.5 billion. **Number of employees at this location:** 250. **Number of employees nationwide:** 51,000.

GARLAND PUBLISHING
29 West 35th Street, 10th Floor, New York NY 10001. 917/351-7100. **Contact:** Human Resources. **World Wide Web address:** http://www.garlandscience.com. **Description:** Publishes scholarly books in the areas of science textbooks, literary manuscripts, architecture, music, and encyclopedias. **Positions advertised include:** Assistant Editor; Science Editorial Assistant; Reference

Production Assistant. **Parent company:** Taylor & Francis Group (also at this location).

GENERAL MEDIA INTERNATIONAL, INC.
11 Penn Plaza, 12th Floor, New York NY 10001. 212/702-6000. **Fax:** 212/702-6262. **Contact:** Carmela Monte, Human Resources Director. **Description:** Engaged in the publication and sale of men's and automotive magazines and produces various entertainment products. The publishing segment publishes *Penthouse* magazine and six other affiliated men's magazines. The company also publishes four domestic automotive titles, *Four Wheeler*, *Stock Car*, *Open Wheel*, and *Super Stock and Drag Illustrated*, which have a combined average monthly circulation of approximately 700,000 copies. The entertainment segment produces a number of adult-oriented entertainment products including pay-per-call telephone lines, videocassettes, pay-per-view programming, and CD-ROM interactive products. **Corporate headquarters location:** This location. **Subsidiaries include:** Penthouse Magazine. **Chairman/CEO:** Robert (Bob) C. Guccione. **Annual sales/revenues:** $65.4 million. **Number of employees:** 107.

GOLDEN BOOKS FAMILY ENTERTAINMENT, INC.
888 Seventh Avenue, 40th Floor, New York NY 10106. 212/547-6700. **Contact:** Human Resources. **World Wide Web address:** http://www.goldenbooks.com. **Description:** A publisher of children's books and family entertainment products. Titles include *The Poky Little Puppy*, *Pat the Bunny*, and *Little LuLu*. **Parent company:** Random House, Inc.

HARCOURT, INC.
15 East 26th Street, New York NY 10010. 212/592-1000. **Contact:** Human Resources. **World Wide Web address:** http://www.harcourt.com. **Description:** A publishing company. The operations are divided into Elementary and Secondary Education, and University and Professional Education. Elementary and Secondary Education publishes textbooks and other instructional materials, publishes and scores achievement and aptitude tests, and manufactures and markets school and office supplies and equipment. University and Professional Education publishes textbooks and other instructional materials for higher education, scientific and medical books and journals, and general fiction and nonfiction; publishes books and conducts courses and seminars for law, accounting, and business; and provides outplacement counseling services. **Corporate headquarters location:** Orlando FL.

HARPERCOLLINS PUBLISHERS INC.
10 East 53rd Street, New York NY 10022. 212/207-7000. **Fax:** 212/207-7146. **Contact:** Human Resources. **E-mail address:** jobs@harpercollins.com. **World Wide Web address:** http://www.harpercollins.com. **Description:** HarperCollins Publishers is one of the largest book publishers in the world. Titles include fiction, nonfiction, and children's books. **Corporate headquarters location:** This location. **Other U.S. locations:** San Francisco CA. **Subsidiaries include:** Cliff Street Books; HarperAudio; HarperAustralia; HarperCanada; HarperCollins UK; Regan Books; Zondervan Publishing; HarperCollins Children's Books. **Parent company:** News Corporation (Sydney, Australia). **President/CEO:** Jane Friedman. **Annual sales/revenues:** $1.1 billion. **Number of employees at this location:** 600. **Number of employees worldwide:** 3,000.

THE HEARST CORPORATION
224 West 57th Street, New York NY 10019. 212/649-3660. **Fax:** 212/765-3528. **Contact:** Human Resources. **World Wide Web address:** http://www.hearstcorp.com. **Description:** A family-owned media company with operations in the publishing, broadcasting, and entertainment industries including 12 daily newspapers, 14 weekly newspapers, 15 consumer magazines, and TV and radio stations as well as interests in cable television networks and online

services. The company is divided into six divisions: Newspapers, Magazines, Broadcasting, Entertainment/Syndicates, Interactive Media, and Business Media. **NOTE:** The company does not maintain a centralized listing of available job opportunities across all divisions and advises jobseekers to contact individual properties of interest directly. For the advertised Magazine positions, resumes should be mailed to: Hearst Magazines, Human Resources Department, 224 West 57th Street, 10th Floor, New York NY 10019. Jobseekers can also see http://www.hotjobs.com for employment listings. **Positions advertised include:** Good Housekeeping Institute - Assistant to the Technical Director; Esquire - Fashion & Retail Director; Good Housekeeping Institute - Chemist. **Corporate headquarters location:** This location. **Subsidiaries include:** A&E Television Networks; ESPN, Inc.; Hearst Magazines; Hearst Newspapers; Hearst-Argyle Television, Inc.; iVillage Inc.; King Features Syndicate, Inc.; Lifetime Entertainment Services. **Chairman:** George R. Hearst Jr. **Annual sales/revenues:** $3.3 billion. **Number of employees:** 17,170.

HIPPOCRENE BOOKS INC.
171 Madison Avenue, Suite 1602, New York NY 10016. 718/454-2366. **Fax:** 718/454-1391. **Contact:** Human Resources. **E-mail address:** contact@hippocrenebooks.com. **World Wide Web address:** http://www.hippocrenebooks.com. **Description:** Publishes foreign language dictionaries, ethnic cookbooks, Jewish and Polish interest books, and military history books. **Corporate headquarters location:** This location. **Other locations:** Jamaica NY.

HOME NEWS TRIBUNE
35 Kennedy Boulevard, East Brunswick NJ 08816. 732/246-5500. **Contact:** Personnel Department. **World Wide Web address:** http://www.injersey.com/hnt. **Description:** A daily newspaper with a weekday circulation of more than 51,000. **Parent company:** Gannett Company, Inc.

HOWARD PRESS
450 West First Avenue, Roselle NJ 07203. 908/245-4400. **Fax:** 908/245-1139. **Contact:** Michelle Kaplan, Human Resources. **World Wide Web address:** http://www.howardpress.com. **Description:** A large commercial printing company. **Positions advertised include:** Production Planner.

THE JERSEY JOURNAL
30 Journal Square, Jersey City NJ 07306. 201/653-1000. **Contact:** Managing Editor. **World Wide Web address:** http://www.nj.com/jjournal/today. **Description:** Publishes a daily morning newspaper with a circulation of more than 55,000. **Parent company:** Newhouse Newspapers Group.

LAWRENCE ERLBAUM ASSOCIATES, INC.
10 Industrial Avenue, Mahwah NJ 07430–2262. 201/258–2200. **Toll-free phone:** 800/9-BOOKS-9. **Fax:** 201/236–0072. **Contact:** Human Resources. **E-mail address:** hr@erlbaum.com. **World Wide Web address:** http://www.erlbaum.com. **Description:** A publishing company specializing in higher education books in communication, education and psychology. **Positions advertised include:** Desktop Formatter; Graphic Designer.

LEBHAR-FRIEDMAN, INC.
425 Park Avenue, 5th Floor, New York NY 10022. 212/756-5000. **Contact:** Human Resources Department. **E-mail address:** ssmith@lf.com. **World Wide Web address:** http://www.lf.com. **Description:** A publisher of retail business publications, magazines, and retail directories including *Chain Store Age, Drug Store News, National Restaurant News*. **Positions advertised include:** Associate Creative Director; Executive Editor. **Corporate headquarters**

location: This location. **Other locations:** Boston MA; Chicago IL; Los Angeles CA; Tampa FL.

LIPPINCOTT WILLIAMS & WILKINS HEALTHCARE GROUP
345 Hudson Street, 16th Floor, New York NY 10014. 212/886-1200. **Fax:** 215/367-2140. **Contact:** Human Resources. **World Wide Web address:** http://www.lww.com. **Description:** Publishes the *American Journal of Nursing*. **Positions advertised include:** Associate Publisher; Manufacturing Coordinator; Production Editor; Senior Clinical Editor; Clerical Assistant. **Corporate headquarters location:** Philadelphia PA. **Other U.S. locations:** Baltimore MD; Hagerstown MD; Skokie IL; Springhouse PA. **International locations:** Australia; China; United Kingdom. **Operations at this facility include:** Administration; Sales; Service. **Number of employees at this location:** 75.

MARCEL DEKKER, INC.
270 Madison Avenue, New York NY 10016-0602. 212/696-9000. **Fax:** 212/685-4540. **Contact:** Human Resources Recruiter. **E-mail address:** careers@dekker.com. **World Wide Web address:** http://www.dekker.com. **Description:** A family-owned, international publisher of scientific, technological, and medical books, journals, and encyclopedias in the following fields: agriculture; biology; food science; chemistry; engineering; environmental science and pollution control; library information science and technology; material science and physics; mathematics; statistics; medicine; social science; business and economics; packaging and converting; and technology. Marcel Dekker distributes to libraries, societies, public institutions, hospitals, colleges, universities, and professionals. **Positions advertised include:** Administrative Assistant to Acquisitions; Graphic Artist; Book Production Editor; Editorial Assistant; Journal Production Editor; Production Assistant; Marketing Assistant; Promotions Assistant. **Corporate headquarters location:** This location. **Other locations:** Monticello NY. **International locations:** Switzerland. **Founder/Chairman:** Marcel Dekker.

MARVEL ENTERPRISES, INC.
10 East 40th Street, 9th Floor, New York NY 10016. 212/576-4000. **Fax:** 212/576-8517. **Contact:** Mary Sprowls, Human Resources Director. **E-mail address:** msprowls@marvel.com. **World Wide Web address:** http://www.marvel.com. **Description:** Marvel Enterprises is a youth entertainment company. Operations and products include Marvel Comics, one of the largest comic book publishers in North America; Marvel character-based consumer products licensing; Fleer, a marketer of sports picture cards; Dubble Bubble confectionery products; and ToyBiz. **Corporate headquarters location:** This location. **Subsidiaries include:** Marvel Publishing. **Listed on:** New York Stock Exchange. **Stock exchange symbol:** MVL. **Chairman:** Morton E. Handel. **Annual sales/revenues:** $299 million. **Number of employees:** 369.

McBEE SYSTEMS, INC.
205 US Highway 46, Totoway NJ 07512. 973/256-6047. **Fax:** 973/263-8165. **Contact:** Personnel. **World Wide Web address:** http://www.mcbeesystems.com. **Description:** Manufactures business forms designed specifically for small businesses and professional offices. **Corporate headquarters location:** This location. **Parent company:** Romo Corporation. **Operations at this facility include:** Administration. **Number of employees nationwide:** 530.

THE McGRAW-HILL COMPANIES, INC.
1221 Avenue of the Americas, New York NY 10020. 212/512-2000. **Contact:** Human Resources. **E-mail address:** career_ops@mcgraw-hill.com. **World Wide Web address:** http://www.mcgraw-hill.com. **Description:** McGraw-Hill is a

publisher and a provider of information and services through books, magazines, newsletters, software, CD-ROMs, and online data, fax, and TV broadcasting services. The company operates four network-affiliated TV stations and also publishes Business Week magazine and books for the college, medical, international, legal, and professional markets. McGraw-Hill also offers financial services including Standard & Poor's, commodity items, and international and logistics management products and services. **NOTE:** Resumes may be submitted online, by email, or regular mail to: The McGraw-Hill Companies, Human Resources Service Center, 148 Princeton-Hightstown Road, Hightstown NJ 08520-1450. **Positions advertised include:** Administrative Assistant; Institutional Equity Research Services Vice President; Investor Relations Account Manager; Business Development & Strategic Marketing Vice President; Compliance Manager; Internet Director; Fulfillment Administrator; Database and Spatial Products Sales Executive; Operations Manager; Marketing Assistant; Customer Service Representative; Financial Production Assistant; Sales Development Coordinator; Risk Solutions Group Associate Director; Taxable Pricing Product Manager; Prepub Cost Analyst; Product Management Vice President; Recruiting Specialist; Structured Finance Associate Director; Finance Manager. **Corporate headquarters location:** This location. **Subsidiaries include:** AviationNow.com; *BusinessWeek;* Construction.com; MH Education; Platts; Standard & Poor's. **Listed on:** New York Stock Exchange. **Stock exchange symbol:** MHP. **Chairman/President/CEO:** Harold (Terry) W. McGraw III. **Annual sales/revenues:** $4.8 billion. **Number of employees:** 16,500.

METRO CREATIVE GRAPHICS INC.
519 Eighth Avenue, 18th Floor, New York NY 10018. 212/947-5100. **Toll-free phone:** 800/223-1600. **Fax:** 212/967-4602. **Contact:** Human Resources Department. **World Wide Web address:** http://www.metrocreativegraphics.com. **Description:** Through its subsidiaries, the company provides camera-ready graphics, editorial, and professional production services to the newspaper and graphic communication industries. **NOTE:** When submitting a resume, computer illustrators and artists should include nonreturnable samples of computer artwork. Some testing may be required. **Corporate headquarters location:** This location. **Number of employees at this location:** 60.

MONTCLAIR TIMES
114 Valley Road, Montclair NJ 07042. 973/233-5000. **Fax:** 973/233-5031. **Contact:** Human Resources. **E-mail address:** contactus@montclairtimes.com. **World Wide Web address:** http://www.montclairtimes.com. **Description:** A newspaper serving northern New Jersey.

NYP HOLDINGS, INC.
1211 Avenue of the Americas, New York NY 10036. 212/930-8000. **Contact:** Human Resources. **World Wide Web address:** http://www.nypostonline.com. **Description:** Publishes the *New York Post* newspaper. **Positions advertised include:** Database Marketing /CRM Analyst. **Special programs:** Internships. **Parent company:** News America. **Operations at this facility include:** Administration; Divisional Headquarters; Research and Development; Sales. **Number of employees at this location:** 710.

NATIONAL REVIEW INC.
215 Lexington Avenue, 4th Floor, New York NY 10016. 212/679-7330. **Contact:** Human Resources. **World Wide Web address:** http://www.nationalreview.com. **Description:** Publishes a nationally distributed conservative magazine focusing on current political issues. **Corporate headquarters location:** This location. **President:** Thomas L. Rhodes.

NEW YORK MAGAZINE

444 Madison Avenue, 14th Floor, New York NY 10022. 212/508-0700. **Contact:** Sarah Jewler, Managing Editor. **World Wide Web address:** http://www.newyorkmetro.com. **Description:** Publishes a features-oriented weekly magazine, with primary emphasis on stories of interest to New York City residents. **Special programs:** Internships.

NEW YORK TIMES COMPANY

229 West 43rd Street, New York NY 10036. 212/556-1234. **Contact:** Human Resources. **World Wide Web address:** http://www.nytco.com. **Description:** Publishes *The New York Times*, one of the largest newspapers in the world (daily circulation exceeds 887,000 weekdays and 1.4 million on Sundays). In addition to *The New York Times*, this diversified, publicly owned communications firm publishes 30 dailies and weeklies in various cities; publishes three national magazines; and owns and operates three television stations, two radio stations, and a cable television system. The company also publishes syndicated news and features worldwide. The company also has interests in paper and newsprint manufacturing mills, and a partial interest in *the International Herald Tribune*. Newspaper subsidiaries are located throughout the country and have an average daily circulation of 272,000. **NOTE:** To contact the Recruiting Department directly, call 212/566-4080. **Special programs:** Summer Internships; Tuition Reimbursement Program; Training. **Corporate headquarters location:** This location. **Listed on:** New York Stock Exchange. **Stock exchange symbol:** NYT. **President/CEO/Director:** Janet L. Robinson. **Sales/revenue:** $3 billion. **Number of employees nationwide:** Over 12,000.

NEWSDAY, INC.

235 Pinelawn Road, Melville NY 11747. 631/843-2020. **Contact:** Employment Services. **E-mail address:** jobs@newsday.com (journalist and editorial applicants) or careers@newsday.com (business applicants). **World Wide Web address:** http://www.newsday.com. **Description:** One of the largest daily newspapers in the United States with a circulation of 750,000. **Positions advertised include:** Part-time Inserter. **Special programs:** Internships. **Corporate headquarters location:** This location. **Operations at this facility include:** Administration; Divisional Headquarters; Manufacturing; Sales; Service. **President/CEO/Publisher:** Ray Jansen. **Number of employees at this location:** 600.

NEWSWEEK MAGAZINE

251 West 57th Street, New York NY 10019. 212/445-4000. **Fax:** 212/445-4575. **Contact:** Human Resources. **World Wide Web address:** http://www.newsweek.com. **Description:** One of the most comprehensive weekly news magazines in the world. The company operates a global network of more than 60 correspondents and numerous stringers, reporting on important developments in politics, national and international affairs, business, technology, science, lifestyles, society, and the arts. In addition to its English language editions, the company also publishes two foreign language editions: *Newsweek Nihon Ban* in Japanese, and *Newsweek Hanuk Pan* in Korean and operates 23 bureaus throughout the United States and abroad. Weekly circulation is more than 4 million internationally, and more than 3 million in the United States. Founded in 1933. **Corporate headquarters location:** This location. **Parent company:** The Washington Post Company. **Listed on:** New York Stock Exchange. **Stock exchange symbol:** WPO.

NOTICIAS DEL MUNDO

3842 9th Street, Long Island City NY 11101. 718/786-4343. **Contact:** Maria Perez, Human Resources Director. **Description:** Publishes a daily Spanish newspaper. **NOTE:** Entry-level positions and part-time jobs are offered. **Special programs:** Internships; Apprenticeships. **Corporate headquarters location:**

This location. **Parent company:** News World Communications Inc. **Operations at this facility include:** Administration; Regional Headquarters; Sales; Service. **Number of employees at this location:** 60.

OXFORD UNIVERSITY PRESS
198 Madison Avenue, New York NY 10016-4314. 212/726-6000. **Fax:** 212/726-6458. **Contact:** Human Resources. **E-mail address:** personnel@oup-usa.org. **World Wide Web address:** http://www.oup-usa.org. **Description:** Publishes a diverse line of scholarly books. **Positions advertised include:** Reference Marketing Assistant; Editor; Online Publishing and Business Development Assistant; Development Editor. **Special programs:** Summer Internships. **Other U.S. locations:** Cary, NC; Bethesda MD. **Operations at this facility include:** This location houses the Editorial, Design, Manufacturing, Marketing, and Sales departments.

PANTONE
590 Commerce Boulevard, Carlstadt NJ 07072. 201/935-5500. **Fax:** 201/804-9219. **Contact:** Human Resources. **World Wide Web address:** http://www.pantone.com. **Description:** Produces color charts and color specification materials. **Positions advertised include:** Sales Representative; Marketing Assistant. **Corporate headquarters location:** This location. **Operations at this facility include:** Administration; Manufacturing; Research and Development; Sales.

PARADE PUBLICATIONS INC.
711 Third Avenue, New York NY 10017. 212/450-7000. **Fax:** 212/450-7200. **Contact:** Carol Unger, Vice President/Director of Human Resources. **E-mail address:** carol_unger@parade.com. **World Wide Web address:** http://www.parade.com. **Description:** Publishes weekly magazines, including *Parade* and *React*. **Corporate headquarters location:** This location. **Operations at this facility include:** Administration; Manufacturing; Sales; Service. **Number of employees at this location:** 200.

PEARSON EDUCATION
PRENTICE HALL INC.
One Lake Street, Upper Saddle River NJ 07458. 201/236-7000. **Contact:** Human Resources. **World Wide Web address:** http://www.pearsoneducation.com. **Description:** Pearson Education publishes consumer, educational, and professional books. Prentice Hall (also at this location) specializes in business and professional books, as well as college-level resource materials. **Positions advertised include:** Administrative Coordinator; Change Management Director; Editorial Assistant; Human Resource Manager; Image Coordinator; Accounting Manager; Staff Accountant. **Operations at this facility include:** This location houses corporate offices. **Subsidiaries include:** Macmillan. **Parent company:** Viacom. **Number of employees nationwide:** 4,000.

PENGUIN PUTNAM INC.
375 Hudson Street, New York NY 10014. 212/366-2000. **Fax:** 212/366-2930. **Contact:** Human Resources. **E-mail address:** jobs@penguingroup.com. **World Wide Web address:** http://www.penguinputnam.com. **Description:** One of the nation's largest publishers of trade fiction books. Penguin Putnam is a division of Penguin Group. **NOTE:** Entry-level positions are offered. **Special programs:** Internships. **Internship information:** Internship candidates should send resumes to the attention of the Internship Coordinator in Human Resources. **Corporate headquarters location:** This location. **International locations:** Worldwide. **Parent company:** Pearson plc. is an international media group whose subsidiaries include Penguin Group. **Listed on:** New York Stock Exchange. **Stock exchange symbol:** PSO. **CEO:** David Shanks.

PERMANENT LABEL

790 Bloomfield Avenue, Clifton NJ 07012. 973/471-6617. **Contact:** Human Resources. **Description:** Engaged in decorating and printing labels for plastic products, primarily bottles. **Corporate headquarters location:** This location.

PRIMEDIA BUSINESS MAGAZINES & MEDIA

P.O. Box 4949, Stamford CT 06907. 203/358-9900. **Physical address:** 11 Riverbend Drive South, Stamford CT 06907. **Fax:** 203/358-4194. **Contact:** Human Resources. **World Wide Web address:** http://www.primediabusiness.com. **Description:** A publisher of business-to-business newsletters concerning the information technology and online industries. The company also publishes information on the World Wide Web, and in CD-ROM and Yellow Pages formats. Founded in 1886. **NOTE:** Part-time jobs are offered. **Special programs:** Internships. **International locations:** Worldwide. **Parent company:** PRIMEDIA. **Listed on:** New York Stock Exchange. **Stock exchange symbol:** PRM. **Number of employees at this location:** 300. **Number of employees nationwide:** 2,000.

QUALEX, INC.

16-31 Route 208, Fair Lawn NJ 07410. 201/797-0600. **Contact:** Karen Mergenthaler, Senior Personnel Manager. **World Wide Web address:** http://www.kodak.com. **Description:** A photofinishing company providing processing services for print and reversal type films. **Corporate headquarters location:** Durham NC. **Parent company:** Eastman Kodak Company. **Operations at this facility include:** Administration; Customer Service; Sales; Service.

RANDOM HOUSE, INC.

1745 Broadway, New York NY 10019. 212/782-9000. **Fax:** 212/782-9054. **Contact:** Staffing Manager. **World Wide Web address:** http://www.randomhouse.com. **Description:** One of the largest trade publishers in the United States. Trade divisions include Villard Books, Vintage, Times Books, Pantheon/Schocken, and Knopf. Crown Publishing Group includes Crown Adult Books, Clarkson N. Potter, Fodor's Travel Guides, and Orion Books. Ballantine, Fawcett, Del Rey, and Ivy are mass-market imprints. **Positions advertised include:** Category Management Director; Publicity Director; Marketing Manager; Sub Rights Assistant Manager; Designer; Business Analyst; Subsidiary Rights Contract and Rights Administration Assistant; Art/Design Associate; **Special programs:** Summer Internship Program; Associates Program. **Corporate headquarters location:** This location. **Other U.S. locations:** Chicago IL; Westminster MD. **International locations:** Worldwide. **Parent company:** Bertelsmann, AG. **Number of employees at this location:** 900. **Number of employees nationwide:** 1,200.

THE READER'S DIGEST ASSOCIATION, INC.

Reader's Digest Road, Pleasantville NY 10570. 914/238-1000. **Contact:** Human Resources. **World Wide Web address:** http://www.rd.com. **Description:** A publisher of magazines, books, music, and video products. The flagship publication, *Reader's Digest*, is a monthly general interest magazine published in 17 languages with a circulation of approximately 100 million worldwide. Special interest magazines include *American Woodworker*, *The Family Handyman*, *New Choices,* and *Walking.* **Special programs:** Internships. **Corporate headquarters location:** This location. **Other area locations:** New York NY. **Subsidiaries include:** Joshua Morris Publishing, Incorporated; QSP, Incorporated is a U.S. fundraising organization that works with schools and youth groups to raise money for educational enrichment programs. **Operations at this facility include:** Administration; Manufacturing; Regional Headquarters; Research and Development; Sales; Service. **Listed on:** New York Stock Exchange. **Stock exchange symbol:** RDA. **CEO/Chairman:** Thomas O. Ryder.

Number of employees at this location: 1,500. **Number of employees nationwide:** 5,000.

THE RECORD
NORTH JERSEY MEDIA GROUP
150 River Street, Hackensack NJ 07601-7172. 201/646-4000. **Contact:** Human Resources. **World Wide Web address:** http://www.bergen.com. **Description:** A daily newspaper with a circulation of 150,000 and 203,000 for the Sunday edition. **Positions advertised include:** Post Press Production Coordinator; Press Operator; Sales Representative; Classified Sales Representative; Editorial Assistant; Reporter; Staff Accountant; Administrative Assistant; Help Desk Operator; Technical Support Supervisor; Purchasing Agent; District Manager; Customer Service Specialist; Account Executive; Receptionist; Sales Associate; Sales Support.

REED BUSINESS
1234 Summer Street, 6th Floor, Stamford CT 06905. 203/326-5161. **Contact:** Human Resources. **World Wide Web address:** http://www.reedbusiness.com. **Description:** Provider of a variety of communication mediums. **Positions advertised include:** Account Executive. **Parent Company:** Reed Elsevier Group PLC.

REED BUSINESS INFORMATION
360 Park Avenue South, New York NY 10014. 646/746-6400. **Fax:** 646/746-7433. **Contact:** Director of Human Resources. **World Wide Web address:** http://www.reedbusiness.com. **Description:** Reed Business Information is a leading business-to-business magazine publisher with more than 80 specialty publications serving 16 major service and industry sectors including media, electronics, research and technology, computers, food service, and manufacturing. **Corporate headquarters location:** This location. **Other U.S. locations:** Nationwide. **International locations:** Worldwide. **Parent company:** Reed Elsevier Group plc. **Operations at this facility include:** This location publishes several magazine titles including *Broadcasting & Cable*, *Childbirth*, *Daily Variety*, *Graphic Arts Monthly*, *Library Journal*, *Modern Bride*, *Motor Boat*, and *Publishers Weekly*. **Listed on:** New York Stock Exchange. **Stock exchange symbol:** ENL; RUK. **Number of employees at this location:** 500. **Number of employees worldwide:** 12,000.

REED ELSEVIER NEW PROVIDENCE
121 Chanlon Road, New Providence NJ 07974. 908/464-6800. **Contact:** Human Resources. **World Wide Web address:** http://www.reed-elsevier.com. **Description:** A reference publisher of marketing, advertising, and corporate directories. **Subsidiaries include:** LexisNexis Business Information Services; Marquis Who's Who; Martindale-Hubbel.

RESEARCH INSTITUTE OF AMERICA GROUP
395 Hudson Street, New York NY 10014. 212/367-6300. **Contact:** Manager of Human Resources. **World Wide Web address:** http://www.riahome.com. **Description:** Publishers of tax and other professional services publications designed for attorneys, accountants, and the business community through print, electronic, and online media. Founded in 1935. **NOTE:** Interested job seekers may apply online. **Positions advertised include:** Finance Manager; Lead Software Engineer; Associate Copy Editor; Senior Software Engineer; Senior Oracle Database Administrator; UNIX System Administrator; Software Engineer. **Corporate headquarters location:** This location. **Other area locations:** Rochester NY; Valhalla NY. **Other U.S. locations:** Washington DC; Alexandria VA; Deerfield IL; Carrollton TX. **Parent company:** Thomson Tax & Accounting. **Number of employees at this location:** 300.

ROUTLEDGE INC.
29 West 35th Street, 10th Floor, New York NY 10001-2299. 212/216-7800. **Fax:** 212/244-4561. **Contact:** Human Resources. **E-mail address:** employment@taylorandfrancis.com. **World Wide Web address:** http://www.routledge-ny.com. **Description:** A progressive, international book and journal publisher focused on the humanities and social sciences. **Positions advertised include:** Acquisitions Editor; Dissertations Editor; Editorial Assistant, Humanities/Reference. **Special programs:** Internships. **Office hours:** Monday - Friday, 9:00 a.m. - 5:00 p.m. **Other U.S. locations:** Independence KY. **Parent company:** Taylor & Francis Group. **Operations at this facility include:** This location houses the editorial and marketing offices.

WILLIAM H. SADLIER, INC.
9 Pine Street, New York NY 10005-1002. 212/227-2120. **Contact:** Francis Marsh, Personnel Director. **World Wide Web address:** http://www.sadlier.com. **Description:** Publishes textbooks and related workbooks, teachers' guides, and other supplementary materials principally in the subject areas of religion, mathematics, language arts, and social studies. Founded in 1832. **Corporate headquarters location:** This location.

ST. IVES INC. AVANTI
75 9th Avenue, 2nd Floor, New York NY 10011. 800/833-3807. **Contact:** Emma Medcalf, Human Resources. **World Wide Web address:** http://www.st-ives-usa.com. **Description:** the company is a commercial printing company specializing in annual reports and catalogs. **Positions advertised include:** Pressperson; Customer Service Representative. **Other U.S. locations:** Hollywood FL; Cleveland OH. **Parent company:** St. Ives Group. **Operations at this facility include:** Administration; Manufacturing; Sales. **Annual sales/revenues:** $51.4 million. **Number of employees at this location:** 276.

ST. MARTIN'S PRESS
175 Fifth Avenue, New York NY 10010. 212/674-5151. **Contact:** Human Resources Manager. **E-mail address:** employment.opportunities@hbpub.com. **World Wide Web address:** http://www.stmartins.com. **Description:** A national trade and scholarly book publisher. Founded in 1952. **Positions advertised include:** Editorial Assistant. **Corporate headquarters location:** This location. **Parent company:** Holtzbrinck Publishers. **Number of employees nationwide:** 930.

SCHOLASTIC, INC.
90 Sherman Turnpike, Danbury CT 06816. 203/797-3500. **Fax:** 203/797-3284. **Recorded jobline:** 203/797-3776. **Contact:** Human Resources **E-mail address:** danburyjobs@scholastic.com. **World Wide Web address:** http://www.scholastic.com. **Description:** Publishes a variety of books ranging from encyclopedias to children's books. Founded in 1896. **NOTE:** Entry-level positions are offered. **Corporate headquarters location:** New York NY. **International locations:** Worldwide. **Listed on:** NASDAQ. **Stock exchange symbol:** SCHL.

SCHOLASTIC INC.
557 Broadway, New York NY 10012-3999. 212/343-6912. **Fax:** 212/343-6934. **Contact:** Human Resources. **E-mail address:** jobs@scholastic.com. **World Wide Web address:** http://www.scholastic.com. **Description:** Publishes and distributes children's books, classroom and professional magazines, software, CD-ROMs, and other educational materials. Products are generally distributed directly to both children and teachers in elementary and secondary schools. **Positions advertised include:** Database Marketing Analyst; Sales Support Specialist; InSchool Marketing Sales Manager. **Special programs:** Internships. **NOTE:** Resumes submitted via e-mail must be formatted in Microsoft Word or

Adobe PDF. **Corporate headquarters location:** This location. **Other U.S. locations:** Nationwide. **International locations:** Australia; Canada; France; Mexico; New Zealand; United Kingdom. **Operations at this facility include:** Administration; Divisional Headquarters; Manufacturing; Research and Development. **Listed on:** NASDAQ. **Stock exchange symbol:** SCHL. **Sales/revenue:** $434 million. **Number of employees at this location:** 1,400. **Number of employees nationwide:** 5,000.

SCIENTIFIC AMERICAN, INC.
415 Madison Avenue, New York NY 10017. 212/754-0550. **Contact:** Human Resources. **World Wide Web address:** http://www.sciam.com. **Description:** Publishes an international monthly magazine dealing with recent scientific research. **Special programs:** Internships. **Corporate headquarters location:** This location.

SIMMONS-BOARDMAN PUBLISHING CORP.
345 Hudson Street, 12th Floor, New York NY 10014. 212/620-7200. **Contact:** Human Resources. **Description:** Publishes trade magazines and books. **Special programs:** Internships. **Corporate headquarters location:** This location. **Operations at this facility include:** Administration; Sales.

SIMON & SCHUSTER, INC.
1230 Avenue of the Americas, New York NY 10020. 212/698-7000. **Fax:** 212/698-7640. **Contact:** Human Resources Department. **E-mail address:** ssjobs1@simonandschuster.com (for positions in the Sales, IS&T, Audio/Interacitve, Online, HR/Facilities, Finance, General, and Administrative departments), ssjobs2@simonandschuster (for positions in the Children's, Production, and Supply Chain departments) and ssjobs3@simonandschuter.com (for positions in the Adult Trade and Legal departments). **World Wide Web address:** http://www.simonandschuster.com. **Description:** Publishes consumer, educational, and professional books. **Positions advertised include:** Associate Manager of Premium Sales; Editorial Assistant; National Account Manager; Online Technical Support Coordinator; Online Customer Data Coordinator; Director of Creative Services; Sales Communication Manager; Associate Producer; Senior Editor; Subsidiary Rights Assistant; Marketing Assistant. **Corporate headquarters location:** This location. **Other U.S. locations:** CA; MA; NJ; OH. **Subsidiaries include:** Macmillan; Prentice-Hall. **Parent company:** Viacom. **Operations at this facility include:** Administration; Marketing; Sales. **Listed on:** New York Stock Exchange. **Stock exchange symbol:** VIA. **Number of employees nationwide:** 4,000.

SPRINGER-VERLAG NEW YORK, INC.
175 Fifth Avenue, New York NY 10010. 212/460-1500. **Fax:** 212/473-6272. **Contact:** Human Resources. **World Wide Web address:** http://www.springeronline.com. **Description:** An international publisher of scientific, technical, and medical books, journals, magazines, and electronic media. Founded in 1842. **Special programs:** Internships; Co-ops. **Corporate headquarters location:** This location. **Parent company:** BertelsmannSpringer.

STANDARD & POOR'S CORPORATION
55 Water Street, 37th Floor, New York NY 10041. 212/438-2000. **Contact:** Human Resources. **World Wide Web address:** http://www.standardandpoors.com. **Description:** Publishes the Standard & Poor's Register and a number of other financial information products. **Parent company:** McGraw-Hill, Inc. **Listed on:** New York Stock Exchange. **Stock exchange symbol:** MHP.

THE STAR-LEDGER
One Star Ledger Plaza, Newark NJ 07102. 973/877-4141. **Contact:** Human Resources. **World Wide Web address:** http://www.nj.com/starledger. **Description:** Publishes a large circulation daily newspaper covering local news. **Positions advertised include:** Recruitment Category Specialist.

STATEN ISLAND ADVANCE
950 Fingerboard Road, Staten Island NY 10305. 718/981-1234. **Contact:** Richard Diamond, Publisher. **World Wide Web address:** http://www.silive.com/advance. **Description:** Publishes the *Staten Island Advance,* a daily local newspaper. The paper has a weekday circulation of 80,000 and a Sunday circulation of 95,000. Founded in 1886. **Corporate headquarters location:** This location. **Parent company:** Newhouse Newspapers Group. **Number of employees at this location:** 450.

STERLING PUBLISHING COMPANY
387 Park Avenue South, New York NY 10016. 212/532-7160. **Contact:** Human Resources. **World Wide Web address:** http://www.sterlingpub.com. **Description:** Publishes a wide variety of how-to books.

TV GUIDE
1211 Avenue of the Americas, 4th Floor, New York NY 10036. 212/852-7500. **Contact:** Human Resources. **World Wide Web address:** http://www.tvguide.com. **Description:** Produces a national publication for television viewers. **Corporate headquarters location:** Radnor PA. **Parent company:** Gemstar-TV Guide International. **Listed on:** NASDAQ. **Stock exchange symbol:** GMST.

L.P. THEBAULT COMPANY
249 Pomeroy Road, P.O. Box 169, Parsippany NJ 07054. 973/884-1300. **Toll-free phone:** 800/848-1702. **Contact:** Human Resources. **E-mail address:** jobs@thebault.com. **World Wide Web address:** http://www.thebault.com. **Description:** One of the largest commercial printing companies in the United States. The company specializes in the print-buying market, with projects ranging from annual reports to promotional pieces. **Positions advertised include:** Sales Executive. **Special programs:** Internships. **Corporate headquarters location:** This location. **Other U.S. locations:** Detroit MI; New York NY. **Subsidiaries include:** LPT Express Graphics. **Operations at this facility include:** Administration; Manufacturing; Sales. **Number of employees nationwide:** 400.

THOMAS PUBLISHING COMPANY
5 Penn Plaza, New York NY 10001. 212/560-1887. **Contact:** Human Resources. **World Wide Web address:** http://www.thomaspublishing.com. **Description:** Publishes a directory of manufacturers, wholesalers, and distributors. **Corporate headquarters location:** This location. **Operations at this facility include:** Administration; Divisional Headquarters; Sales; Service.

THOMSON MEDICAL ECONOMICS COMPANY
5 Paragon Drive, Montvale NJ 07645. 201/358-7500. **Fax:** 201/722-2668. **Contact:** Human Resources. **E-mail address:** hr_postings@medec.com. **World Wide Web address:** http://www.medec.com. **Description:** Publishes medical books and journals. **Positions advertised include:** Human Resources Generalist; Program Manager; Customer Service Representative; Business Unit Advocate; Program Director; Marketing Director. **Special programs:** Internships. **Corporate headquarters location:** This location. **Other U.S. locations:** DC; IL; KS. **Operations at this facility include:** Administration; Divisional Headquarters; Research and Development; Sales; Service. **Number of employees at this location:** 425. **Number of employees nationwide:** 510.

THE TIMES-HERALD RECORD
40 Mulberry Street, P.O. Box 2046, Middletown NY 10940. 845/346-3112.
Contact: Human Resources. **World Wide Web address:** http://www.th-record.com. **Description:** Publishes a daily newspaper, with a circulation of more than 80,000. **Corporate headquarters location:** Campbell NY. **Other area locations:** New Paltz NY; Newburgh NY; Port Jervis NY. **Parent company:** Ottaway Newspapers, Inc.

USA WEEKEND
535 Madison Avenue, New York NY 10022. 212/715-2100. **Contact:** Human Resources. **World Wide Web address:** http://www.usaweekend.com. **Description:** Publishes a general interest national weekly magazine, sold in syndication as a Sunday newspaper supplement. USA Weekend has approximately 31.6 million readers every weekend. Features include national affairs, sports, personal care, and other subjects. **Special programs:** Internships. **Parent company:** Gannett Company, Inc. (Arlington VA). **Operations at this facility include:** Divisional Headquarters. **Listed on:** New York Stock Exchange. **Stock exchange symbol:** GCI.

UNIMAC GRAPHICS
350 Michele Place, Carlstadt NJ 07072. 201/372-1000. **Fax:** 201/372-1241. **Contact:** Personnel. **E-mail address:** info@unimacgraphics.com. **World Wide Web address:** http://www.unimacgraphics.com. **Description:** Provides a full range of commercial printing services.

VNU INC.
770 Broadway, New York NY 10003-9595. 646/654-5000. **Contact:** Human Resources. **World Wide Web address:** http://www.vnu.com. **Description:** VNU offers marketing information, media measurement information, business information and directory information. VNU publishes 67 business publications, stages 52 trade shows and conferences, and operates more than 75 business-to-business electronic media sites. **Positions advertised include:** Executive Assistant; Associate Publisher; Databases Developer. **Corporate headquarters location:** This location. **Other U.S. locations:** Nationwide. **International locations:** Worldwide.

VNU BUSINESS PUBLICATIONS, INC.
770 Broadway, New York NY 10003-9595. 646/654-5270. **Contact:** Human Resources. **E-mail address:** bmcomm@vnuinc.com. **World Wide Web address:** http://www.vnubusinessmedia.com. **Description:** Publishes a weekly trade periodical covering newspapers and an annual yearbook for the newspaper industry. **Positions advertised include:** Executive Assistant; Associate Publisher; Databases Developer. **Corporate headquarters location:** This location. **Parent company:** VNU, Inc.

JOHN WILEY & SONS, INC.
One Wiley Drive, Somerset NJ 08875. 732/469-4400. **Toll-free phone:** 800/225-5945. **Contact:** Human Resources. **World Wide Web address:** http://www.wiley.com. **Description:** This location houses the U.S. distribution center. Overall, John Wiley & Sons, Inc. is an international publishing house that publishes in four categories: Educational; Professional; Trade; and Scientific, Technical, and Medical (STM). In Educational, Wiley publishes textbooks and instructional packages for undergraduate and graduate students in the United States and internationally. Publishing programs focus on the physical and life sciences, mathematics, engineering, and accounting, with an increasing emphasis on economics, finance, business, MIS/CIS, and foreign languages. In Professional, Wiley publishes books and subscription products for lawyers, architects, accountants, engineers, and other professionals. In Trade, Wiley publishes nonfiction books in areas such as business, computers, science, and

general interest. In STM, Wiley publishes approximately 260 scholarly and professional journals, as well as encyclopedias, other major reference works, and books for the research and academic communities. Major subject areas include chemistry, the life sciences, and technology. **Corporate headquarters location:** New York NY. **Other U.S. locations:** Colorado Springs CO. **Number of employees nationwide:** 1,200.

JOHN WILEY & SONS, INC.
605 Third Avenue, New York NY 10158. 212/850-6000. **Fax:** 212/850-6049. **Contact:** Human Resources. **E-mail address:** info@wiley.com. **World Wide Web address:** http://www.wiley.com. **Description:** An international publishing house. Wiley publishes in four categories: Educational; Professional; Trade; and Scientific, Technical, and Medical (STM). In Educational, Wiley publishes textbooks and instructional packages for undergraduate and graduate students worldwide. Publishing programs focus on the physical and life sciences, mathematics, engineering, and accounting, with a growing business in economics, finance, business, MIS/CIS, and foreign languages. In Professional, Wiley publishes books and subscription products for lawyers, architects, accountants, engineers, and other professionals. In Trade, Wiley publishes nonfiction books in areas such as business, computers, science, and general interest. In STM, Wiley publishes approximately 260 scholarly and professional journals, as well as encyclopedias, other major reference works, and books for the research and academic communities. Major subject areas include chemistry, the life sciences, and technology. Founded in 1807. **Special programs:** Internships. **Office hours:** Monday - Friday, 8:30 a.m. - 4:30 p.m. **Corporate headquarters location:** This location. **Other U.S. locations:** Colorado Springs CO; Somerset NJ. **International locations:** Asia; Australia; Canada; Europe. **Operations at this facility include:** Administration. **Listed on:** New York Stock Exchange. **Stock exchange symbol:** JW. **Number of employees at this location:** 800. **Number of employees nationwide:** 1,200. **Number of employees worldwide:** 2,000.

THE H.W. WILSON COMPANY
950 University Avenue, Bronx NY 10452. 718/588-8400. **Toll-free phone:** 800/367-6770. **Contact:** Human Resources. **E-mail address:** eoflynn@hwwilson.com. **World Wide Web address:** http://www.hwwilson.com. **Description:** A publisher of indexes and reference works for libraries covering a broad range of the arts and sciences.

WORRALL COMMUNITY NEWSPAPERS INCORPORATED
P.O. Box 3109, 1291 Stuyvesant Avenue, Union NJ 07083. 908/686-7700. **Fax:** 908/686/4169. **World Wide Web address:** http://www.localsource.com. **Contact:** Human Resources. **Description:** A publisher of 18 weekly newspapers in Union and Essex Counties with a total circulation of over 40,000.

ZIFF-DAVIS MEDIA INC.
28 East 28th Street, New York NY 10016. 212/503-3500. **Contact:** Human Resources. **World Wide Web address:** http://www.ziffdavis.com. **Description:** A magazine publisher whose periodicals are primarily computer related. Ziff-Davis also has minor broadcasting operations. **Corporate headquarters location:** This location.

REAL ESTATE

**You can expect to find the following types of companies
in this section:**
Land Subdividers and Developers • Real Estate Agents, Managers, and
Operators • Real Estate Investment Trusts

AMREP CORPORATION
641 Lexington Avenue, 6th Floor, New York NY 10022. 212/705-4700. **Fax:** 212/705-4740. **Contact:** Andrea Passes, Human Resources. **Description:** AMREP Corporation is a real estate developer and housing builder; a national distributor of magazines; and a provider of subscription fulfillment services for publishers with businesses operated by subsidiaries. AMREP Southwest Inc. is a real estate company in New Mexico and Kable operates the fulfillment services and magazine distribution company. **Corporate headquarters location:** This location. **Subsidiaries include:** Kable News Company, Inc.; Kable Distribution Services, Inc.; AMREP Southwest Inc. **Listed on:** New York Stock Exchange. **Stock exchange symbol:** AXR. **Annual sales/revenues:** $75 million. **Number of employees:** 925.

ASHFORTH COMPANY
707 Summer Street, 4th Floor, Stamford CT 06901. 203/359-8500. **Fax:** 203/327-5610. **Contact:** Human Resources. **E-mail address:** humanresources@ashforthcompany.com. **World Wide Web address:** http://www.ashforthcompany.com. **Description:** A property management and commercial real estate construction company. **Positions advertised include:** Tax Accountant.

AVALONBAY COMMUNITIES, INC.
220 Elm Street, Suite 200, New Canaan CT 06840. 203/801-3300. **Fax:** 203/762-1240. **Contact:** Human Resources. **World Wide Web address:** http://www.avalonbay.com. **Description:** A self-administered and self-managed equity real estate investment trust that specializes in the development, construction, acquisition, and management of apartment communities in the Mid-Atlantic and Northeastern United States. AvalonBay Communities' real estate consists of approximately 10,000 apartment homes in 33 communities located in six states and Washington DC. **Positions advertised include:** Assistant Superintendent; Financial Analyst. **Corporate headquarters location:** Washington DC. **Other U.S. locations:** Nationwide. **Listed on:** New York Stock Exchange. **Stock exchange symbol:** AVB.

CB RICHARD ELLIS
61 South Paramus Road, 4th Floor, Paramus NJ 07652. 201/556-9800. **Fax:** 201/556-5100. **Contact:** Human Resources. **E-mail address:** opps@cbre.com. **World Wide Web address:** http://www.cbrichardellis.com. **Description:** A real estate services company offering property sales and leasing, property and facility management, mortgage banking, and investment management services. **Positions advertised include:** Building Engineer; Assistant Manager; Real Estate Manager; Sales Professional. **Corporate headquarters location:** Los Angeles CA. **Number of employees worldwide:** 9,000.

CENTRAL PARKING SYSTEMS
360 West 31st Street, 12th Floor, New York NY 10001. 212/502-5475. **Contact:** Human Resources. **World Wide Web address:** http://www.parking.com. **Description:** Operates parking garages and lots throughout New York. **Positions advertised include:** Area Manager; Field Auditor; Night Area

Manager; Project Manager; Paralegal; Staff Accountant. **Corporate headquarters location:** This location. **Other U.S. locations:** Nationwide. **Parent company:** Central Parking Corporation (Nashville TN).

CHELSEA PROPERTY GROUP, INC.
105 Eisenhower Parkway, Roseland NJ 07068. 973/228-6111. **Contact:** Human Resources. **E-mail address:** jobs@cpgi.com. **World Wide Web address:** http://www.cpgi.com. **Description:** A self-administered and self-managed real estate investment trust engaged in the development, leasing, marketing, and management of upscale and fashion-oriented manufacturers' outlet centers. **Positions advertised include:** Security Supervisor; Assistant General Manager. **Listed on:** New York Stock Exchange. **Stock exchange symbol:** CPG.

COLDWELL BANKER
151 North Main Street, New City NY 10956. 845/634-0400. **Contact:** Human Resources. **World Wide Web address:** http://www.coldwellbanker.com. **Description:** This location is one of the 3,500 independently owned and operated franchised brokerages engaged in residential and commercial real estate transactions with 106,000 Sales Associates worldwide. **Corporate headquarters location:** Parsippany NJ. **Other locations:** Worldwide. **Parent company:** Cendant Corporation (New York NY). **Operations at this facility include:** Sales.

CUSHMAN & WAKEFIELD, INC.
51 West 52nd Street, 8th Floor, New York NY 10019-6178. 212/841-7500. **Fax:** 212/841-5039. **Contact:** Human Resources. **E-mail address:** recruiting@cushwake.com. **World Wide Web address:** http://www. http://www.cushmanwakefield.com. **Description:** An international commercial and industrial real estate services firm with 44 offices in 20 states. The company is engaged in appraisals, financial services, project development, research services, and the management and leasing of commercial office space, as well as providing assessment services, corporate services, brokerage services, financial and general administration, research, sales, and valuation advisory services. **Positions advertised include:** Asset Services Administrator; Executive Assistant; Marketing Coordinator; Accounting Supervisor; Payroll Coordinator; Purchasing Assistant; Broker Compensation Supervisor; New York Area Operations Manager; Administrative Assistant; Hospitality Valuation Professional. **Office hours:** Monday - Friday, 8:30 a.m. - 5:30 p.m. **Corporate headquarters location:** This location. **Other U.S. locations:** Los Angeles CA; San Francisco CA; Chicago IL. **International locations:** Worldwide. **Parent company:** The Rockefeller Group Inc. **Chairman:** John C. Cushman. **Annual sales/revenues:** $870 million. **Number of employees at this location:** 500. **Number of employees nationwide:** 11,000.

DVL INC.
70 East 55th Street, 7th Floor, New York NY 10022. 212/350-9900. **Fax:** 212/350-9911. **Contact:** Human Resources. **Description:** Acquires and develops retirement and resort properties; purchases, collects, and services installment sales contacts originated by national tool companies for automobile mechanics' tools; and manages and services existing real estate properties. **Listed on:** Over The Counter. **Stock exchange symbol:** DVLN. **Chairman:** Frederick E. Smithline. **Annual sales/revenues:** $9.1 million. **Number of employees:** 11.

GRUBB & ELLIS COMPANY
55 East 59th Street, 10th Floor, New York NY 10022. 212/838-2000. **Contact:** Drew, O'Conner, Human Resources. **E-mail address:** jobs@grub-ellis.com. **World Wide Web address:** http://www.grubb-ellis.com. **Description:** A real estate management firm dealing primarily with commercial real estate including

shopping centers, office buildings, and similar complexes. **Positions advertised include:** Real Estate Administrative Assistant; Business Analyst; Systems Analyst. **Corporate headquarters location:** Northbrook IL. **Other locations:** Worldwide. **Subsidiaries include:** The Wadley Donovan Group; Landauer Realty Group; Knight Frank. **Listed on:** Over The Counter. **Stock exchange symbol:** GBEL. **Annual sales/revenues:** $313 million. **Number of employees:** 8,300.

HELMSLEY ENTERPRISES, INC.
dba HELMSLEY-NOYES COMPANY INC.
230 Park Avenue, Suite 659, New York NY 10169-0399. 212/679-3600. **Fax:** 212/953-2810. **Contact:** Human Resources. **Description:** A commercial real estate agency engaged in the management of office buildings and a wide range of other institutional buildings including department stores, hotels, and corporate office buildings. **Corporate headquarters location:** This location. **Subsidiaries include:** Helmsley Hotels. **Chairperson/CEO:** Leona Helmsley. **Annual sales/revenues:** $1 billion. **Number of employees:** 3,000.

HELMSLEY-SPEAR, INC.
60 East 42nd Street, 53rd Floor, New York NY 10165. 212/687-6400. **Contact:** Human Resources Department. **World Wide Web address:** http://www. helmsleyspear.com. **Description:** One of the largest real estate service companies in the nation offering leasing (including industrial leasing, and retail and store leasing divisions); sales and brokerage; management; development; appraisals; and financing services. Founded in 1866. **Corporate headquarters location:** This location. **Parent company:** Helmsley Enterprises, Inc. (New York NY).

K. HOVNANIAN COMPANIES
10 Highway 35, Red Bank NJ 07701. 732/747-7800. **Contact:** Human Resources. **World Wide Web address:** http://www.khov.com. **Description:** Designs, constructs, and sells condominium apartments, townhouses, and single-family homes in residential communities. The company is also engaged in mortgage banking. Founded in 1959. **Positions advertised include:** Training and Development Specialist; Training and Documentation Specialist; HRIS Coordinator; Benefits Coordinator. **Corporate headquarters location:** This location. **Other U.S. locations:** CA; FL; NC; NY; PA; VA. **Subsidiaries include:** New Fortis Homes. **Listed on:** New York Stock Exchange. **Stock exchange symbol:** HOV. **Number of employees at this location:** 90. **Number of employees nationwide:** 1,150.

INSIGNIA DOUGLAS ELLIMAN
575 Madison Avenue, New York NY 10022. 212/832-0083. **Toll-free phone:** 800/355-4626. **Fax:** 212/891-7239. **Contact:** Human Resources. **E-mail address:** inquiry@elliman.com. **Description:** A real estate firm engaged in apartment sales, rentals, and insurance. **Subsidiaries include:** Insignia/ESG, Inc.; Insignia Richard Ellis; Insignia Residential Group. **Operations at this facility include:** Administration; Sales; Service.

LEXINGTON CORPORATE PROPERTIES TRUST
315 Park Avenue South, New York NY 10010. 212/460-1900. **Fax:** 212/598-4869. **Contact:** Laura E. Ulbrandt, Human Resources. **Description:** Leucadia National is a diversified holding company with subsidiaries with interests in over 30 companies involved in the insurance, manufacturing, banking, investments, and real estate industries. The insurance business offers property, casualty, and life insurance nationwide. **Corporate headquarters location:** This location. **Subsidiaries include:** Allcity Insurance; American Investment Bank, N.A.; American Investment Financial; Charter, CPL; Empire Insurance Group; Intramerica; MK Gold Company. **Listed on:** New York Stock Exchange. **Stock**

exchange symbol: LUK. Chairman: Iam M. Cumming. Annual sales/revenues: $297 million. Number of employees: 1,066.

J.W. MAYS, INC.
9 Bond Street, Brooklyn NY 11201-5805. 718/624-7400. Fax: 718/935-0378. Contact: Frank Mollo, Personnel Director. Description: A real estate company operating seven commercial properties in Brooklyn, Jamaica, Levittown, Fishkill, and Dutchess County NY, as well as a warehouse in Circleville OH, all of which were former department store locations, which the company liquidated in 1989. Since 1924. Corporate headquarters location: This location. Listed on: NASDAQ. Stock exchange symbol: MAYS. Chairman/President/CEO/COO: Lloyd Shulman. Annual sales/revenues: $13.4 million. Number of employees: 31.

WILLIAM RAVEIS HOME-LINK
7 Trap Falls Road, Shelton CT 06484. 203/926-1090. Fax: 203/929-6523. Contact: Human Resources. World Wide Web address: http://www.raveis.com. Description: A commercial real estate agency. Founded in 1974. Corporate headquarters location: This location.

UNITED CAPITAL CORPORATION
United Capital Building, 9 Park Place, 4th Floor, Great Neck NY 11021. 516/466-6464. Contact: Human Resources. Description: United Capital Corporation invests in and manages real estate properties. Subsidiaries include: Metex Corporation provides antenna systems and knitted wire products to aviation and automotive markets worldwide. Corporate headquarters location: This location. Listed on: AMEX. Stock exchange symbol: AFP.

WEICHERT REALTORS
1625 Route 10 East, Morris Plains NJ 07950. 973/267-7777. Contact: Human Resources. World Wide Web address: http://www.weichert.com. Description: A commercial real estate agency. NOTE: Jobseekers should specify a department of interest when applying. Corporate headquarters location: This location.

RETAIL

You can expect to find the following types of companies in this section:
Catalog Retailers • Department Stores, Specialty Stores • Retail Bakeries • Supermarkets

---

ANN TAYLOR STORES CORPORATION
142 West 57th Street, New York NY 10019. 212/541-3300. **Fax:** 212/536-4410. **Contact:** Laurie David, Human Resources. **E-mail address:** recruitment@anntaylor.com. **World Wide Web address:** http://www.anntaylor.com. **Description:** Ann Taylor is a leading national specialty retailer of women's apparel, shoes, and accessories sold primarily under the Ann Taylor brand name. The company operates 585 stores nationwide. Ann Taylor stores offer a collection of career and casual separates, dresses, tops, weekend wear, shoes, and accessories. **Corporate headquarters location:** This location. **Other locations:** Nationwide. **Subsidiaries include:** Ann Taylor Stores; Ann Taylor Loft; Ann Taylor Factory Stores. **Listed on:** New York Stock Exchange. **Stock exchange symbol:** ANN. **Chairman/CEO:** J. Patrick Spainhour. **Annual sales/revenues:** $1.4 billion. **Number of employees:** 10,900.

AVON PRODUCTS INC.
1345 Avenue of the Americas, New York NY 10105. 212/282-5000. **Fax:** 212/282-5941. **Contact:** Staffing Manager. **E-mail address:** jobs@avon.com. **World Wide Web address:** http://www.avon.com. **Description:** A direct seller of beauty care products, fashion jewelry, gifts, fragrances, and decorative products, marketing its products through a network of almost three million independent sales representatives in 135 countries worldwide. **NOTE:** Salespeople are considered independent contractors or dealers and most work part-time. If you are interested in becoming a sales representative, please call 800/FOR-AVON, or visit the company's Website. **Positions advertised include:** Supply Manager; Product Manager; Business Analyst. **Corporate headquarters location:** This location. **Other U.S. locations:** Nationwide. **Listed on:** New York Stock Exchange. **Stock exchange symbol:** AVP.

BARNES & NOBLE BOOKSTORES
360 Connecticut Avenue, Norwalk CT 06854. 203/866-2213. **Contact:** Manager. **World Wide Web address:** http://www.barnesandnoble.com. **Description:** A bookstore chain. This location also has a cafe. **Corporate headquarters location:** New York NY. **Other U.S. locations:** Nationwide.

BARNES & NOBLE BOOKSTORES
1076 Post Road East, Westport CT 06880. 203/221-7955. **Contact:** Manager. **World Wide Web address:** http://www.barnesandnoble.com. **Description:** A bookstore chain. This location also has a cafe and music department. **Corporate headquarters location:** New York NY. **Other U.S. locations:** Nationwide.

BARNES & NOBLE BOOKSTORES
1400 Old Country Road, Westbury NY 11590. 516/338-8000. **Contact:** Human Resources. **E-mail address:** careerswestbury@bn.com. **World Wide Web address:** http://www.barnesandnobleinc.com. **Description:** A bookstore chain operating 900 stores nationwide. **NOTE:** Resumes may be either sent to the above e-mail address; posted on the company Website (http://www.barnesandnobleinc.com/jobs/index.html); sent to the company's headquarters address: Barnes & Noble, Inc., Human Resources, 122 Fifth

Avenue, New York NY 10011; or faxed to: 212/463-5640. **Positions advertised include:** Accounts Payables Administrator; Expense Payables Administrator; Specialty Payables Administrator; Human Resources Representative; General Accounting Manager; Staff Accountant; AJB Programmer/Analyst. **Corporate headquarters location:** New York NY. **Other locations:** Nationwide. **Operations at this facility include:** Financial offices. **Listed on:** New York Stock Exchange. **Stock exchange symbol:** BKS. **Chairman:** Leonard S. Riggio. **Annual sales/revenues:** $5.2 billion. **Number of employees worldwide:** 37,000.

BARNES & NOBLE CORPORATION
122 Fifth Avenue, 2nd Floor, New York NY 10011. 212/633-3300. **Fax:** 212/463-5640. **Contact:** Human Resources. **E-mail address:** careersnyc@bn.com. **World Wide Web address:** http://www.barnesandnobleinc.com. **Description:** A bookstore chain operating 900 stores nationwide. **NOTE:** Resumes may be either sent to the above mailing address, e-mail address, fax, or posted on the company Website: http://www.barnesandnobleinc.com/jobs/index.html. **Positions advertised include:** Director of Financial Planning and Analysis; Human Resources Manager; Store Operations Administrative Assistant; Marketing Coordinator; Database Administrator; Web Production Engineer; Product Development Engineer. **Corporate headquarters location:** This location. **Other locations:** Nationwide. **Operations at this facility include:** Corporate administration. **Listed on:** New York Stock Exchange. **Stock exchange symbol:** BKS. **Chairman:** Leonard S. Riggio. **Annual sales/revenues:** $5.2 billion. **Number of employees worldwide:** 37,000.

BARNEYS NEW YORK, INC.
575 Fifth Avenue, New York NY 10017. 212/229-7300. **Fax:** 212/450-8489. **Contact:** Human Resources. **E-mail address:** hr@barneys.com. **World Wide Web address:** http://www.barneys.com. **Description:** A national specialty retailer offering upscale men's and women's apparel collections from both American and international designers operating eight full-price stores and 12 outlets nationwide. Founded in 1923. **NOTE:** For retail positions, contact the appropriate store. **Positions advertised include:** Buyer; Customer Service Representative. **Corporate headquarters location:** This location. **Operations at this facility include:** Administration; Sales; Service. **Listed on:** Over The Counter. **Stock exchange symbol:** BNNY. **Annual sales:** $371 million. **Number of employees:** 1,300.

BLOOMINGDALE'S, INC.
1000 Third Avenue, New York NY 10022. 212/705-2000. **Fax:** 212/705-2805. **Contact:** Human Resources. **World Wide Web address:** http://www.bloomingdales.com. **Description:** Operates a chain of 25 department stores in 10 states, mostly in New York and California. Founded in 1872. **NOTE:** You may apply online. **Positions advertised include:** At-His Service Manager; Bridal Registrar/Consultant; Chanel Business Manager; Cosmetics Department Manager; Director of Technical Support; Sales Associate; Women's Shoes Associate; Fragrance Specialist; Shoes Sales Associate; Graphic Designer; Gross Margin Planner; Line Cook; Marketing Analyst; Designer Apparel Sales Associate; Vendor Selling Specialist; Fine Jewelry Sales Associate; Juniors Sales Associate. **Corporate headquarters location:** This location. **Other U.S. locations:** Washington DC; Boca Raton FL; Miami FL; Palm Beach FL; Chicago IL; Boston MA; Minneapolis MN; Philadelphia PA. **Parent company:** Federated Department Stores Inc. (Cincinnati OH). **Operations at this facility include:** Administration; Regional Headquarters; Research and Development; Sales; Service. **Chairman/CEO:** Michael Gould. **Annual sales/revenues:** $1.7 billion. **Number of employees:** 9,800.

BROOKS BROTHERS
346 Madison Avenue, New York NY 10017. 212/682-8800. **Fax:** 212/985-1854. **Contact:** BB Employment Specialist. **E-mail address:** jdesmar@brooksbrothers.com. **World Wide Web address:** http://www.brooksbrothers.com. **Description:** Operates over 160 retail stores and factory outlets in the United States and 75 in Southeast Asia. Founded in 1818. **NOTE:** Resumes may be sent to the human resources office at 100 Phoenix Avenue, Enfield CT 06083. 800/249-6947 ext. 2324. Fax: 860/741-3171. **Positions advertised include:** Advertising Clerk; Architect; Branch Manager; Buyer; Claim Representative; Computer Programmer; Customer Service Representative; Department Manager; Draftsperson; Editor; General Manager; Human Resources Manager; Management Trainee; Operations/Production Manager; Purchasing Agent/Manager; Receptionist; Reporter; Secretary; Stock Clerk; Systems Analyst. **Corporate headquarters location:** This location. **Parent company:** Retail Brand Alliance, Inc. (Enfield CT). **Operations at this facility include:** Administration; Divisional Headquarters; Regional Headquarters; Sales; Service. **Annual sales/revenues:** 635 million.

CDW
535 Connecticut Avenue, Norwalk CT 06854. 203/899-4000. **Fax:** 203/899-4242. **Contact:** Lisa Cristantiello, Director of Corporate Human Resources and Communication. **World Wide Web address:** http://www.warehouse.com. **Description:** Micro Warehouse is a specialty catalog and online retailer and direct marketer of brand name Macintosh and IBM-compatible personal computer software, accessories, and peripherals. Founded in 1987. **NOTE:** Entry-level positions are offered. **Special programs:** Internships. **Corporate headquarters location:** This location. **Other U.S. locations:** Gibbsboro NJ; Lakewood NJ; Wilmington OH. **International locations:** Canada; England; France; Germany; Mexico; Sweden; The Netherlands. **Operations at this facility include:** Administration; Sales. **Annual sales/revenues:** More than $100 million. **Number of employees at this location:** 600. **Number of employees nationwide:** 2,400. **Number of employees worldwide:** 3,500.

CACHÉ, INC.
1460 Broadway, 15th Floor, New York NY 10036-7306. 212/575-3200. **Fax:** 212/944-2842. **Contact:** Margarita Croasdaile, Human Resources Manager. **World Wide Web address:** http://www.cache.com. **Description:** Owns and operates 220 upscale women's apparel specialty stores. **Corporate headquarters location:** This location. **Other locations:** Nationwide. **Listed on:** NASDAQ. **Stock exchange symbol:** CACH. **Chairman/CEO:** Brian P. Woolf. **Annual sales/revenues:** $200 million. **Number of employees:** 2,000.

D'AGOSTINO SUPERMARKETS, INC.
1385 Boston Post Road, Larchmont NY 10538-3904. 914/833-4000. **Contact:** Human Resources. **World Wide Web address:** http://www.dagnyc.com. **Description:** A supermarket chain offering a full line of grocery, produce, and meats. The company operates more than 23 stores serving Westchester County, and New York City. Founded in 1932. **NOTE:** Employment inquiries should be directed to: Frank Tucciarone, Director of Associate Development, 257 West 17th Street, New York NY 10011; phone: 917/606-0280; fax: 917/606-0367; email: ftucciarone@dagnyc.com. **Positions advertised include:** Cashier; Department Manager; Management Trainee; Retail Sales Worker. **Special programs:** Internships. **Corporate headquarters location:** This location. **Operations at this facility include:** Corporate Administration. **Chairman/President/CEO:** Nicholas (Nick) D'Agostino Jr. **Annual sales/revenues:** $175 million. **Number of employees at this location:** 50. **Number of employees statewide:** 1,150.

THE DRESS BARN, INC.
30 Dunnigan Drive, Suffern NY 10901. 845/369-4500. **Fax:** 845/369-4829.

Contact: Human Resources. **E-mail address:** hrrecruit@dressbarn.com. **World Wide Web address:** http://www.dressbarn.com. **Description:** Operates a chain of 750 women's apparel stores nationwide. **Corporate headquarters location:** This location. **Listed on:** NASDAQ. **Stock exchange symbol:** DBRN. **Chairman:** Elliot S. Jaffe. **Annual sales/revenues:** $717 million. **Number of employees:** 8,900.

EPSTEIN, INC.
P.O. Box 902, Morristown NJ 07963-0902. 973/538-5000. **Contact:** Personnel. **Description:** A department store offering a wide range of fashions and other soft and hard goods. **Corporate headquarters location:** Cedar Knolls NJ. **Other U.S. locations:** Bridgewater NJ; Princeton NJ; Shrewsbury NJ. **Operations at this facility include:** Sales.

ETHAN ALLEN INC.
Ethan Allen Drive, Danbury CT 06811. 203/743-8000. **Contact:** Charles Farfaglia, Human Resources. **World Wide Web address:** http://www.ethanallen.com. **Description:** An international retailer of home furnishings operating approximately 350 retail locations. Founded in 1932. **Positions advertised include:** Retail Production Coordinator; Merchandise Manager, Soft Goods; Advertising Production Manager; Interior Design/Sales Professional; Designer, Store Planner. **Corporate headquarters location:** This location. **Listed on:** New York Stock Exchange. **Stock exchange symbol:** ETH.

FINLAY ENTERPRISES, INC.
529 Fifth Avenue, New York NY 10017. 212/808-2800. **Fax:** 212/557-3848. **Contact:** Personnel Manager. **E-mail address:** humanresources@fnly.com. **World Wide Web address:** http://www.finlayenterprises.com. **Description:** Operates through its subsidiary, Finlay Fine Jewelry Corporation, which sells jewelry through over 950 department store locations in the United States. **Corporate headquarters location:** This location. **Subsidiaries/affiliates include:** Thomas H. Lee; Finlay Fine Jewelry Corporation. **Listed on:** NASDAQ. **Stock exchange symbol:** FNLY. **Chairman/President/CEO:** Arthur E. Reiner. **Number of employees:** 6,500.

FOOD CITY MARKETS INC.
440 Sylvan Avenue, Suite 120, Englewood Cliffs NJ 07632. 201/569-4849. **Contact:** Barry Schwartz, Supervisor of Store Operations. **Description:** Operates a chain of supermarkets. **Corporate headquarters location:** This location.

FOODARAMA SUPERMARKETS
922 Highway 33, Building 6, Suite 1, Freehold NJ 07728. 732/462-4700. **Contact:** Human Resources. **World Wide Web address:** http://www.foodarama.com. **Description:** Foodarama operates supermarkets in the states of New Jersey, New York, and Pennsylvania. **Corporate headquarters location:** This location.

FOOT LOCKER, INC.
112 West 34th Street, New York NY 10120. 212/720-3700. **Fax:** 866/855-4510. **Contact:** Larry Haley, Regional HR Director. **E-mail address:** lhaley@footlocker.com. **World Wide Web address:** http://www.footlocker.com. **Description:** Formerly the Venator Group, Foot Locker, Inc. is a global retailer with stores and related support facilities in 22 countries. The company retails and distributes a broad range of footwear, apparel, and department store merchandise through more than 3,600 specialty stores and general merchandise stores. The company operates retail units under the following names: Eastbay, Kinney, Foot Locker, Champs Sports, Lady Foot Locker, Northern Reflections, Little Folks, San Francisco Music Box Company, Rx Place, and World Foot

Locker as well as operating the FootLocker.com Website. Founded in 1894. **NOTE:** Entry-level positions are offered. **Positions advertised include:** Finance Associate; Human Resources Specialist; Information Systems Engineer; Legal Associate; Logistics Specialist; Real Estate Analyst. **Corporate headquarters location:** This location. **International locations:** Worldwide. **Subsidiaries include:** Champ Sports; East Bay; Foot Locker; Kids Foot Locker; Lady Foot Locker. **Listed on:** New York Stock Exchange. **Stock exchange symbol:** FL. **Chairman:** J. Carter Bacot. **Annual sales/revenues:** $4.5 billion. **Number of employees at this location:** 450. **Number of employees nationwide:** 24,000. **Number of employees worldwide:** 25,000.

FORTUNOFF
70 Charles Lindbergh Boulevard, Uniondale NY 11553. 516/832-9000. **Fax:** 516/832-1999. **Contact:** Personnel Manager. **E-mail address:** westburyhr@fortunoff.com. **World Wide Web address:** http://www.fortunoff.com. **Description:** Fortunoff offers a wide range of merchandise including home furnishings, fine jewelry, and fine silver. **Positions advertised include:** Buyer; Administrative Assistant; Call Center Representative; Training Manager; Sales Associate; Warehouse Clerk. **Corporate headquarters location:** This location. **Other locations:** Nationwide. **Annual sales/revenues:** $425 million. **Number of employees:** 3,000.

THE GREAT ATLANTIC & PACIFIC TEA COMPANY
2 Paragon Drive, Montvale NJ 07645. 201/573-9700. **Contact:** Personnel. **World Wide Web address:** http://www.aptea.com. **Description:** The Great Atlantic & Pacific Tea Company maintains approximately 700 retail supermarkets throughout the East Coast, the Mid-Atlantic region, and Canada. **Positions advertised include:** Benefits Coordinator; Information Systems Auditor; Payroll Operations Clerk; Compensation Analyst; Human Resources Supervisor; Accountant; Voice Analyst; Coordinator. **Corporate headquarters location:** This location. **Operations at this facility include:** This location houses administrative offices for one of the nation's largest supermarket chains. **Listed on:** New York Stock Exchange. **Stock exchange symbol:** GAP. **Number of employees at this location:** 650. **Number of employees nationwide:** 85,000.

HANOVER DIRECT, INC.
115 River Road, Building 10, Edgewater NJ 07020. 201/863-7300. **Fax:** 201/272-3280. **Contact:** Personnel. **World Wide Web address:** http://www.hanoverdirect.com. **Description:** A direct marketing company that sells products manufactured by other companies through its 12 core catalogs structured into operating groups. **NOTE:** Entry-level positions are offered. **Positions advertised include:** Analyst. **Corporate headquarters location:** This location. **Other U.S. locations:** San Diego CA; San Francisco CA; Hanover PA; De Soto TX; Roanoke VA; La Crosse WI. **Operations at this facility include:** Administration; Divisional Headquarters; Sales. **Listed on:** American Stock Exchange. **Stock exchange symbol:** HNV. **Annual sales/revenues:** More than $100 million. **Number of employees at this location:** 250. **Number of employees nationwide:** 3,000.

KEY FOOD STORES CO-OPERATIVE, INC.
1200 South Avenue, Staten Island NY 10314. 718/370-4200. **Fax:** 718/370-4225. **Contact:** Human Resources. **Description:** A private co-operative of 115 independently owned food stores and supermarkets throughout the New York metropolitan region. Founded in 1937. **Corporate headquarters location:** This location. **Other locations:** Bronx NY; Brooklyn NY; Queens NY; Manhattan NY; Staten Island NY; Yonkers NY. **CEO:** Richard Pallitto. **Annual sales/revenues:** $445 million. **Number of employees:** 150.

KMART CORPORATION

7401 Tonnelle Avenue, North Bergen NJ 07047. 201/868-1960. **Contact:** Human Resources. **World Wide Web address:** http://www.kmartcorp.com. **Description:** One of the largest nonfood retailers in the United States. The company operates over 2,000 stores nationwide under the Kmart name, with more than 50 Kmart stores located in the New York metropolitan area. All stores offer a broad range of discounted general merchandise, both soft and hard goods. **Corporate headquarters location:** Troy MI. **Operations at this facility include:** Administration; Divisional Headquarters; Service. **Listed on:** New York Stock Exchange. **Stock exchange symbol:** KM. **Number of employees at this location:** 1,700. **Number of employees nationwide:** 330,000.

LERNER NEW YORK, INC.

450 West 33rd Street, 5th Floor, New York NY 10001. 212/736-1222. **Fax:** 212/884-2396. **Contact:** Recruitment. **World Wide Web address:** http://www.limited.com. **Description:** A specialty women's clothing retailer specializing in city-style apparel and accessories selling name-brand and private-label clothing from over 500 mall-based stores in 43 states. **Special programs:** Internships. **Listed on:** New York Stock Exchange. **Stock exchange symbol:** LTD. **President/CEO:** Richard P. Crystal. **Annual sales/revenues:** $940 million. **Number of employees at this location:** 300. **Number of employees nationwide:** 14,000.

LILLIAN VERNON CORPORATION

One Theall Road, Rye NY 10580-1450. 914/925-1200. **Fax:** 914/925-1320. **Contact:** Human Resources. **E-mail address:** bgarti@lillianvernon.com. **World Wide Web address:** http://www.lillianvernon.com. **Description:** Lillian Vernon markets gift, household, gardening, decorative, Christmas, and children's products through a variety of specialty catalogs. Catalog titles include: Lillian Vernon; Lillian Vernon Gardening; Neat Ideas; Personalized Gift; Christmas Memories; Lilly's Kids; Favorites; and Private Sale. Founded in 1951. **Office hours:** Monday - Friday, 8:30 a.m. - 5:00 p.m. **Corporate headquarters location:** This location. **Other U.S. locations:** Virginia Beach VA. **Listed on:** American Stock Exchange. **Stock exchange symbol:** LVC. **Chairperson:** Lillian Vernon. **Annual sales/revenues:** $247 million. **Number of employees at this location:** 165. **Number of employees nationwide:** 1,400.

LINENS 'N THINGS

6 Brighton Road, Clifton NJ 07015. 973/778-1300. **Fax:** 973/815-2990. **Contact:** Personnel. **World Wide Web address:** http://www.lnthings.com. **Description:** A specialty retailer selling linens, home furnishings, and domestics. Linens 'n Things operates over 230 stores nationwide. **Positions advertised include:** Analyst; Tax Analyst; Inventory Analyst; Store Support Coordinator. **Corporate headquarters location:** This location.

LORD & TAYLOR

424 Fifth Avenue, New York NY 10018. 212/391-3344. **Contact:** Human Resources. **World Wide Web address:** http://www.lordandtaylor.com. **Description:** A full-line department store operating 85 stores nationwide offering clothing, accessories, home furnishings, and many other retail items. Founded in 1826. **Positions advertised include:** General Sales Associate; Commission Sales Associate; Cosmetics Beauty Advisor. **Parent company:** The May Department Stores Company (St. Louis MO).

MACY'S EAST

151 West 34th Street, New York NY 10001. 212/695-4400. **Fax:** 212/494-1057. **Contact:** Human Resources. **World Wide Web address:** http://www.macys.com. **Description:** Macy's East, part of the Federated Department Stores family, sells family apparel, home furnishings, and other

merchandise from 115 stores in the eastern U.S. with the largest department store in the world at this location. **Positions advertised include:** Art Director; Assistant Buyer; Buyer/Merchandising Buyer; Associate Giftwrap & Extra's Buyer; Divisional Operations Director; Fire Safety Director; Macintosh Technical Support Representative; Assortment Management Planner; Publicity Coordinator; Regional Merchandise Manager; Systems Administrator. **Corporate headquarters location:** This location. **Parent company:** Federated Department Stores, Inc. (Cincinnati OH). **Chairman/CEO:** Harold (Hal) D. Kahn. **Annual sales/revenues:** $5 billion. **Number of employees:** 33,200.

MICROWAREHOUSE INC.
1690 Oak Street, Lakewood NJ 08701. 732/370-3801. **Fax:** 732/886-0567. **Contact:** Kathy Hopkins, Human Resources. **E-mail address:** careers@mwhse.com. **World Wide Web address:** http://www.warehouse.com. **Description:** A catalog retailer of brand-name Macintosh and IBM-compatible personal computer software, accessories, and peripherals. **Positions advertised include:** Account Manager. **Corporate headquarters location:** South Norwalk CT. **Other U.S. locations:** Gibbsboro NJ; Wilmington OH. **International locations:** Canada; England; France; Germany; Mexico; Sweden; The Netherlands. **Operations at this facility include:** Sales; Service. **Number of employees at this location:** 600. **Number of employees nationwide:** 2,400.

NINE WEST GROUP
Nine West Plaza, 1129 Westchester Avenue, White Plains NY 10604-3529. 914/640-6400. **Fax:** 914/640-3499. **Contact:** Melissa Tavino, Human Resources. **E-mail address:** jobs@ninewest.com. **World Wide Web address:** http://www.ninewest.com. **Description:** A manufacturer and retailer of women's shoes. **Positions advertised include:** Planner; Director of Product Development; Corporate Technical Director; Product Data Maintenance Specialist; Sample Coordinator; Merchandise Processor; Design Assistant; Allocations Manager. **Office hours:** Monday - Thursday, 9:00 a.m. - 5:00 p.m.; Friday, 8:30 a.m. - 3:00 p.m. **Corporate headquarters location:** This location. **Other U.S. locations:** Nationwide. **Parent company:** Jones Apparel Group. **Listed on:** New York Stock Exchange. **Stock exchange symbol:** JNY.

PATHMARK STORES INC.
200 Milik Street, Carteret NJ 07008. 732/499-3000. **Fax:** 732/499-4250. **Contact:** Human Resources. **E-mail address:** employment@pathmark.com. **World Wide Web address:** http://www.pathmark.com. **Description:** A diversified retailer engaged primarily in the operation of large supermarket/drug stores. The company operates one of the largest supermarket chains in the country. Its Rickel Home Center division is among the largest do-it-yourself home center chains in the nation. The company's retail stores are located in the Mid-Atlantic and New England. **Positions advertised include:** Store Clerk; Store Engineer; Store Maintenance Mechanic; Merchandiser; Cashier; Night Crew Associate; Cart People; Maintenance Clerk; Cake Decorator. **Corporate headquarters location:** This location.

PICK QUICK FOODS INC.
83-10 Rockaway Boulevard, Ozone Park NY 11416. 718/296-9100. **Fax:** 718/296-6203. **Contact:** Human Resources. **Description:** A grocery retailer. **Corporate headquarters location:** This location.

POPULAR CLUB PLAN
22 Lincoln Place, Garfield NJ 07026. 973/471-4300. **Contact:** Human Resources. **World Wide Web address:** http://www.popularclub.com. **Description:** Operates a full-service, mail-order catalog operation offering apparel, housewares, personal care products, jewelry and related items. **Office**

hours: Monday – Friday. 8:00 a.m. – 8:30 p.m. **Corporate headquarters location:** This location.

SAKS FIFTH AVENUE
611 Fifth Avenue, New York NY 10022. 212/753-4000. **Contact:** Employment Manager. **World Wide Web address:** http://www.saksincorporated.com. **Description:** Saks Fifth Avenue is a 62-store chain emphasizing soft-goods products, primarily apparel for men, women, and children. **Special programs:** Internships. **Corporate headquarters location:** Birmingham AL. **Other U.S. locations:** Nationwide. **Parent company:** Saks Incorporated is a department store holding company that operates approximately 360 stores in 36 states. The company's stores include Saks Fifth Avenue, Parisian, Proffit's, Younker's, Herberger's, Carson Pirie Scott, Boston Store, Bergner's, and Off 5th, the company's outlet store. Saks Incorporated also operates two retail catalogs and several retail Internet sites. **Operations at this facility include:** This location is a part of the nationwide specialty department store chain. **Listed on:** New York Stock Exchange. **Stock exchange symbol:** SKS. **Sales/revenue:** $5.9 billion. **Number of employees nationwide:** Approximately 55,000.

SOFTWARE ETC.
1120 Avenue of the Americas, New York NY 10036. 212/921-7855. **Contact:** Store Manager. **World Wide Web address:** http://www.software-etc.com. **Description:** Retails computer software, hardware, video games, accessories, and books. **Corporate headquarters location:** Dallas TX. **Other U.S. locations:** Nationwide. **International locations:** Worldwide. **Parent company:** Babbage's Etc.

STEW LEONARD'S FARM FRESH FOODS
100 Westport Avenue, Norwalk CT 06851. 203/847-7214. **Contact:** Recruiting Manager. **World Wide Web address:** http://www.stew-leonards.com. **Description:** One of the world's largest retail dairy and food stores. Founded in 1969. **Company slogan:** Rule 1 - The customer is always right. Rule 2 - If the customer is ever wrong, reread Rule 1. **Special programs:** Internships. **Internship information:** Culinary and bakery internships are offered. **Corporate headquarters location:** This location. **Other U.S. locations:** Danbury CT; Yonkers NY. **Operations at this facility include:** Administration; Sales. **Annual sales/revenues:** $51 - $100 million. **Number of employees at this location:** 700. **Number of employees nationwide:** 1,400.

STRAUSS DISCOUNT AUTO
9A Brick Plant Road, South River NJ 08882. 732/390-9000. **Contact:** Human Resources Administrator. **World Wide Web address:** http://www.straussauto.com. **Description:** Engaged in the retail trade of automotive aftermarket products. **Positions advertised include:** Store Manager; Assistant Store Manager; Service Department Manager; Auto Technician; Service Writer. **Corporate headquarters location:** This location. **Listed on:** Privately held. **Number of employees at this location:** 200. **Number of employees nationwide:** 2,200.

SYMS CORPORATION
One Syms Way, Secaucus NJ 07094. 201/902-9600. **Fax:** 201/902-0758. **Contact:** John Tyzbir, Personnel Director. **E-mail address:** hr@syms.com. **World Wide Web address:** http://www.syms.com. **Description:** Syms Corporation operates a chain of over 45 off-priced apparel stores located throughout the Northeast, Midwest, Southeast, and Southwest. All stores offer men's tailored clothing; women's dresses, suits, and separates; and children's apparel. **Corporate headquarters location:** This location. **Operations at this facility include:** This location houses a retail location and a distribution center.

TOYS 'R US
1 Geoffrey Way, Paramus NJ 07652. 201/262-7800. **Contact:** Director of Employment. **World Wide Web address:** http://www.toysrus.com. **Description:** One of the largest children's specialty retailers in the world. The company operates over 1,450 stores worldwide. Founded in 1948. **NOTE:** Entry-level positions are offered. **Special programs:** Training. **Corporate headquarters location:** This location. **Other U.S. locations:** Nationwide. **Subsidiaries include:** Babies 'R Us; Kids 'R Us. **Listed on:** New York Stock Exchange. **Stock exchange symbol:** TOY. **Number of employees at this location:** 1,400. **Number of employees worldwide:** 94,000.

UNITED RETAIL GROUP, INC.
365 West Passaic Street, Rochelle Park NJ 07662. 201/845-0880. **Toll-free phone:** 800/963-2744. **Contact:** Human Resources Manager. **World Wide Web address:** http://www.unitedretail.com. **Description:** A leading nationwide specialty retailer of plus-size women's apparel and accessories. The company operates 502 stores in 36 states, principally under the names The Avenue and Sizes Unlimited. New/remodeled stores will bear the name Avenue Plus. Founded in 1987. **Positions advertised include:** Regional Sales Director; District Sales Manager; Store Manager; Assistant Manager; Sales Associate. **Corporate headquarters location:** This location. **Subsidiaries include:** United Retail Incorporated. **CEO:** Raphael Benaroya.

UNITEDAUTO GROUP, INC.
One Harmon Plaza, 9th Floor, Union NJ 07087. 201/974-0869. **Contact:** Human Resources. **World Wide Web address:** http://www.unitedauto.com. **Description:** Operates car dealerships. **Corporate headquarters location:** This location. **Listed on:** New York Stock Exchange. **Stock exchange symbol:** UAG.

VILLAGE SUPERMARKET, INC.
733 Mountain Avenue, Springfield NJ 07081. 973/467-2200. **Contact:** John Jay Sumas, Personnel Director. **Description:** Operates 20 supermarkets, 17 of which are located in north central New Jersey and three of which are in eastern Pennsylvania. Village Supermarket offers traditional grocery, meat, produce, dairy, frozen food, bakery, and delicatessen departments, as well as health and beauty aids, housewares, stationery, and automotive and paint supplies. Six stores contain prescription pharmacy departments, and the company also owns and operates two retail package liquor stores and one variety store. **Corporate headquarters location:** This location. **Other area locations:** Bernardsville NJ; Chester NJ; Florham Park NJ; Livingston NJ; Morristown NJ; The Orchards NJ; Union NJ. **Parent company:** Wakefern Food Corporation.

WESTERN BEEF, INC.
47-05 Metropolitan Avenue, Ridgewood NY 11385. 718/456-3048. **Contact:** Human Resources. **World Wide Web address:** http://www.westernbeef.com. **Description:** A warehouse supermarket chain in the metropolitan New York area that provides a full-line of value-priced perishable and grocery products. In addition to operating 14 supermarkets, the company is also a meat and poultry distributor. **Positions advertised include:** Store Manager; Assistant Store Manager; Deli Manager.

WESTERN BEEF, INC.
4444 College Point Boulevard, Flushing NY 11355. 718/539-4900. **Contact:** Human Resources. **World Wide Web address:** http://www.westernbeef.com. **Description:** A warehouse supermarket chain in the metropolitan New York area that provides a full-line of value-priced perishable and grocery products. In addition to operating 14 supermarkets, the company is also a meat and poultry distributor. **NOTE:** Interested jobseekers should send resumes to 47-05 Metropolitan Avenue, Ridgewood NY 11385.

STONE, CLAY, GLASS, AND CONCRETE PRODUCTS

**You can expect to find the following types of companies
in this section:**
Cement, Tile, Sand, and Gravel • Crushed and Broken Stone • Glass and Glass
Products • Mineral Products

BARRETT PAVING MATERIALS INC.
3 Becker Farm Road, Roseland NJ 07068-1748. 973/533-1001. **Fax:** 973/533-1020. **Contact:** Chris Kirby, Director of Human Resources. **E-mail address:** bpmicorp@aol.com. **World Wide Web address:** http://www.barrettpaving.com. **Description:** Barrett Paving Materials is engaged in the manufacture of road construction materials and the construction and paving of roads, airports, parking lots, race tracks, driveways, and bike paths. Founded in 1903. **NOTE:** Entry-level positions are offered. **Positions advertised include:** Manager; Construction Support Supervisor; Project Manager; Estimator; Equipment Support Specialist; Plant Superintendent; Quality Control Technician; Sales Associate; Accounting Associate; Administrative Associate; Plant Operator; Equipment Operator; Plant Foreman; Mechanic; Welder; Laborer; Truck Driver; Clerical Associate. **Special programs:** Training; Co-ops; Summer Jobs. **Corporate headquarters location:** This location. **Other U.S. locations:** Hebron CT; Richmond IN; Bangor ME; Ypsilanti MI; Hooksett NH; Bridgewater NJ; East Syracuse NY; Norwood NY; Utica NY; Cincinnati OH; Piqua OH. **International locations:** Worldwide. **Operations at this facility include:** This location houses administrative offices. **Parent company:** Colas Inc. **Annual sales/revenues:** More than $100 million. **Number of employees at this location:** 1,000.

RALPH CLAYTON & SONS
1215 East Veterans Highway, Lakewood NJ 08701. 732/363-1995. **Contact:** Human Resources. **World Wide Web address:** http://www.claytonco.com. **Description:** Manufactures concrete. **Parent company:** The Clayton Companies.

FLORAL GLASS
895 Motor Parkway, P.O. Box 18039, Hauppauge NY 11788. 631/234-2200. **Fax:** 631/234-8866. **Contact:** Personnel. **World Wide Web address:** http://www.floralglass.com. **Description:** Manufactures specialty glass products including beveled mirrors. Founded in 1955. **Corporate headquarters location:** This location. **Other locations:** Bohemia NY; Cheshire CT; East Rutherford NJ. **Subsidiaries include:** Shapes & Surfaces.

INRAD INC.
181 Legrand Avenue, Northvale NJ 07647. 201/767-1910. **Fax:** 201/767-9644. **Contact:** Human Resources. **World Wide Web address:** http://www.inrad.com. **Description:** Manufactures and finishes synthetic crystals.

MINERALS TECHNOLOGIES INC.
The Chrysler Building, 405 Lexington Avenue, 20th Floor, New York NY 10174-1901. 212/878-1800. **Fax:** 212/878-1801. **Contact:** Human Resources Department. **World Wide Web address:** http://www.mineralstech.com. **Description:** Minerals Technologies is a resource- and technology-based company that develops and produces performance-enhancing minerals and mineral-based and synthetic mineral products for the paper, steel, polymer, and other manufacturing industries. The company's three businesses include producing and supplying precipitated calcium carbonate to the paper industry; developing and marketing mineral-based monolithic refractory materials that are

used to resist the effects of high temperatures and are usually applied as coatings to surfaces exposed to extreme heat; and mining and producing natural mineral-based products including limestone, lime, talc, calcium, and metallurgical wire products. **Corporate headquarters location:** This location. **Listed on:** New York Stock Exchange. **Stock exchange symbol:** MTX. **Chairman:** Paul R. Saueracker. **Annual sales/revenues:** $753 million. **Number of employees:** 2,400.

TRANSPORTATION AND TRAVEL

You can expect to find the following types of companies in this section:
Air, Railroad, and Water Transportation Services • Courier Services • Local and Interurban Passenger Transit • Ship Building and Repair • Transportation Equipment • Travel Agencies • Trucking • Warehousing and Storage

---

AIR FRANCE
142 West 57th Street, New York NY 10019. 212/830-4000. **Fax:** 212/830-4191. **Contact:** Air France Recruitment. **E-mail address:** mail.resume@airfrance.fr. **World Wide Web address:** http://www.airfrance.com. **Description:** An international airline serving 20 U.S. cities. Founded in 1933. **NOTE:** Part-time, seasonal, second shift and third shift jobs are offered. Electronic copies of resumes/applications are only accepted in Word format, and if the position applied for is indicated. **Positions advertised include:** Manager of National Account Sales; Account Representative; Accountant; Administrative Assistant; Sales Executive. **Office hours:** Monday - Friday, 9:00 a.m. - 5:15 p.m. **Corporate headquarters location:** Paris, France. **Other area locations:** JFK Airport NY; Newark Airport NJ. **Other locations:** Worldwide. **Number of employees at this location:** 830. **Number of employees worldwide:** 49,000.

AIR INDIA
570 Lexington Avenue, 15th Floor, New York NY 10022. 212/407-1300. **Fax:** 212/838-9533. **Contact:** Human Resources Department. **World Wide Web address:** http://www.airindia.com. **Description:** An international airline with routes to major cities throughout the world. **NOTE:** Most positions are only open to Indian citizens belonging to certain caste levels who meet the company's stated requirements. **Corporate headquarters location:** Mumbai, India. **Listed on:** Government owned.

AVANT SERVICES CORPORATION
686 Lexington Avenue, New York NY 10022. 212/755-7320. **Fax:** 212/370-1452. **Contact:** Personnel Manager. **Description:** A delivery company. **NOTE:** Entry-level positions, part-time jobs, and second and third shifts are offered. **Positions advertised include:** Administrative Assistant; Assistant Manager; Driver. **Special programs:** Summer Jobs.

CAMP SYSTEMS INC. (CSI)
Long Island MacArthur Airport, 999 Marconi Avenue, Ronkonkoma NY 11779-7299. 631/588-3200. **Toll-free phone:** 877/411-2267. **Contact:** Human Resources. **E-mail address:** careers@campsys.com. **World Wide Web address:** http://www.campsys.com. **Description:** Camp Systems Inc. (CSI) performs computerized aircraft maintenance and management services. **Positions advertised include:** Aircraft Analyst. **Corporate headquarters location:** This location. **Subsidiaries include:** CAMP Europe SAS; Daniel Systems.

CENDANT CORPORATION
1 Sylvan Way, Parsippany NJ 07054-0642. 973/428-9700. **Fax:** 973/496-5966. **Contact:** Human Resources. **E-mail address:** cendant.jobs@cendant.com. **World Wide Web address:** http://www.cendant.com. **Description:** Provides a wide range of business services including dining services, hotel franchise management, mortgage programs, and timeshare exchanges. Cendant Corporation's Real Estate Division offers employee relocation and mortgage services through Century 21, Coldwell Banker, ERA, Cendant Mortgage, and

Cendant Mobility. The Travel Division provides car rentals, vehicle management services, and vacation timeshares through brand names including Avia, Days Inn, Howard Johnson, Ramada, Travelodge, and Super 8. The Membership Division offers travel, shopping, auto, dining, and other financial services through Travelers Advantage, Shoppers Advantage, Auto Vantage, Welcome Wagon, Netmarket, North American Outdoor Group, and PrivacyGuard. **Positions advertised include;** Commercial Marketing Associate; Mortgage Processor; Staff Accountant; Financial Analyst; International Treasury Manager; Marketing Manager; Executive Assistant; Regional Business Consultant; Staff Accountant; Director; Finance Manager; Administrative Assistant; Marketing Communications Manager. **Corporate headquarters location:** New York NY. **Listed on:** New York Stock Exchange. **Stock exchange symbol:** CD. **President/CEO:** Henry Silverman. **Number of employees at this location:** 1,100. **Number of employees worldwide:** 28,000.

COURTESY BUS COMPANY
107 Lawson Boulevard, Oceanside NY 11572. 516/766-6740. **Fax:** 516/678-0253. **Contact:** Personnel Office. **Description:** Provides bus service to local school districts, as well as a range of charter services through several area locations. **Positions advertised include:** Automotive Mechanic; Driver.

DHL
120 Tokeneke Road, Darien CT 06820. 203/655-7900. **Contact:** Human Resources. **World Wide Web address:** http://www.dhl.com. **Description:** An international freight forwarder, serving customers in over 135 countries. **NOTE:** Call 954/888-7000 for Human Resources. **Corporate headquarters location:** Plantation FL. **Other U.S. locations:** Nationwide.

DPT
1200 Paco Way, Lakewood NJ 08701. 732/367-9000. **Contact:** Personnel. **E-mail address:** confidence@dptlabs.com. **World Wide Web address:** http://www.dptlabs.com. **Description:** Packages and ships pharmaceutical products manufactured by other companies. **Positions advertised include:** Scientist; Line Supervisor; Manufacturing Engineer; Lab Technician.

EL AL ISRAEL AIRLINES LIMITED
120 West 45th Street, 18th Floor, New York NY 10036-9998. 212/869-4164. **Contact:** Personnel Department. **World Wide Web address:** http://www.elal.co.il. **Description:** An Israeli government-owned international air carrier operating a route system that includes major United States cities, and destinations in Israel, Europe, and Africa. Founded in 1948. **Corporate headquarters location:** Ben Gurion Airport, Israel. **Annual sales/revenues:** $1.1 billion. **Number of employees:** 3,224.

GENESEE & WYOMING INC.
66 Field Point Road, Greenwich CT 06830. 203/629-3722. **Fax:** 203/661-4106. **Contact:** Human Resources. **World Wide Web address:** http://www.gwrr.com. **Description:** Operates 18 railroads with 4,700 miles of track in the United States, Canada, Australia, and Mexico. Founded in 1895. **NOTE:** The Human Resources Department is in the Rochester NY location. Please fax resumes to 716/328-8622. **Subsidiaries include:** Allegheny & Eastern Railroad, Inc. (Punxsatawney PA); Buffalo & Pittsburgh Railroad, Inc. (Punxsatawney PA); Illinois & Midland Railroad, Inc. (Springfield IL); Portland & Western Railroad, Inc. (Albany OR); Rail Link, Inc., which provides switching, rail freight, coal loading and unloading, and locomotive leasing in North America; Rochester & Southern Railroad, Inc. (Rochester NY); Willamette & Pacific Railroad, Inc. (Albany OR). **Other U.S. locations:** IL; NY; OR; PA. **International locations:** Australia; Bolivia; Canada; Mexico. **Listed on:** NASDAQ. **Stock exchange symbol:** GNWR. **President/CEO:** Mortimer B. Fuller III.

GLOBAL GROUND
111 Great Neck Road, Great Neck NY 11021. 516/487-8610. **Fax:** 516/498-1534. **Contact:** Human Resources. **Description:** A nationwide aviation service company providing contracting services to airlines and airports including loading/unloading, cleaning planes, fueling planes, and cargo services. **Special programs:** Internships. **Corporate headquarters location:** This location. **Subsidiaries include:** Hudson Aviation Services, Inc. **Number of employees at this location:** 45.

HARBOUR INTERMODAL LTD.
1177 McCarter Highway, Newark NJ 07104. 973/481-6474. **Contact:** Human Resources. **Description:** Provides local intermodal transportation services in the greater New York Harbor area. The company also develops and sells equipment for intermodal services including waterborne vessels and mobile and fixed heavy materials handling equipment for transporting and sorting containers, trailers, and general cargo.

THE HERTZ CORPORATION
225 Brae Boulevard, Park Ridge NJ 07656. 201/307-2000. **Fax:** 201/307-2644. **Contact:** Director of Personnel. **World Wide Web address:** http://www.hertz.com. **Description:** A large rental company that leases new and used cars and industrial and construction equipment in 130 countries worldwide. The company also sells used cars in the United States, Australia, New Zealand, and Europe. The fleet of cars consists of 283,000 automobiles, which are leased through 5,300 offices. **Corporate headquarters location:** This location.

INTTRA INC.
One Upper Pond Road, Morris Corporate Center II, Building E, Parsippany NJ 07054. 973/265-2221. **Fax:** 973/263-5969. **E-mail address:** jobs@inttra.com. **World Wide Web address:** http://www.inttra.com. **Description:** INTTRA creates efficiencies for the ocean transportation industry by standardizing and optimizing traditionally inefficient processes. INTTRA enables shippers, freight forwarders, third party logistics providers, brokers, importers, and industry portals to manage the scheduling, booking, documentation, Bills of Lading, and tracking of cargo and the negotiation of freight services across multiple shipping lines in a single integrated process. **Positions advertised include:** Business Analyst/Product Designer; Product Manager; Quality Assurance/EDI Analyst; Technical Support Manager; Technical Support Technician. **Corporate headquarters location:** This location.

LAIDLAW TRANSIT
LAIDLAW EDUCATIONAL SERVICES
3349 Highway 138, Building 1, Unit D, Wall NJ 07719. 732/556-0255. **Contact:** Human Resources. **World Wide Web address:** http://www.laidlaw.com. **Description:** Laidlaw Educational Services provides school bus transportation services. **NOTE:** Entry-level positions and part-time jobs are offered. **Company slogan:** Laidlaw - we carry the nation's future. **Special programs:** Apprenticeships; Training. **Corporate headquarters location:** Lawrenceville NJ. **Other U.S. locations:** Nationwide. **Operations at this facility include:** This location houses administrative offices. **Listed on:** New York Stock Exchange. **Annual sales/revenues:** $21 - $50 million. **Number of employees nationwide:** 60,000.

LIBERTY LINES TRANSIT INC.
475 Saw Mill River Road, P.O. Box 624, Yonkers NY 10703. 914/969-6900. **Fax:** 914/376-6440. **Contact:** Human Resources. **E-mail address:** jobs@libertylines.com. **World Wide Web address:** http://www.libertylines.com. **Description:** One of the largest and most diversified bus services in the

Yonkers/Westchester area. Services include commuter and transit bus operations. Founded in 1953. **Positions advertised include:** Bus Driver. **Corporate headquarters location:** This location. **Operations at this facility include:** Administration; Service. **President:** Jerry D'Amore.

LINDBLAD SPECIAL EXPEDITIONS
720 Fifth Avenue, 6th Floor, New York NY 10019. 212/261-9000. **Contact:** Human Resources. **World Wide Web address:** http://www.specialexpeditions.com. **Description:** A cruise line operator with destinations throughout the Pacific and the Caribbean including the Galapagos Islands, Mexico's Baja Peninsula, Alaska, Antarctica, Arctic Norway, and Costa Rica, as well as up the Colorado and Snake Rivers. **Positions advertised include:** Steward; Deckhand; Physician.

THE LONG ISLAND RAILROAD COMPANY
Sutphin Boulevard Jam, Hicksville NY 11801. 516/733-3900. **Contact:** Human Resources. **World Wide Web address:** http://www.lirr.org. **Description:** Operates one of the oldest active railroads in the United States. The company has extensive commuter passenger and freight service railroad operations, primarily between New York City and numerous points on Long Island. The Long island Railroad Company is one of the busiest passenger railroad operators in the United States. **NOTE:** Application materials should be sent to: Human Resources-SR, Mail code 1155-IT-NET, MTA Long Island Rail Road, Jamaica Station, Jamaica NY 11435. **Positions advertised include:** Assistant Conductor; Electrician. **Corporate headquarters location:** This location. **Parent company:** Metropolitan Transportation Authority. (New York NY).

MTA BUS COMPANY
128-15 28th Avenue, Flushing NY 11354. 718/445-3100. **Contact:** Kathleen O'Shea, Director of Human Resources. **World Wide Web address:** http://www.qsbus.com. **Description:** A public transportation firm providing express and local service in Queens and Manhattan with more than 270 buses operating on nearly 20 routes. **Positions advertised include:** Bus Operator; Cleaner/Shifter; Foreman. **Special programs:** Internships. **Office hours:** Monday - Friday, 8:30 a.m. - 4:30 p.m. **Corporate headquarters location:** This location. **Operations at this facility include:** Administration. **Number of employees at this location:** 700.

MAERSK-SEALAND
Giralda Farms, Madison Avenue, P.O. Box 880, Madison NJ 07940-0880. 973/514-5000. **Contact:** Human Resources Department. **World Wide Web address:** http://www.maersksealand.com. **Description:** Maersk-Sealand ships large containers. **Operations at this facility include:** This location houses the northeast regional headquarters operations. **Parent company:** A.P. Moller Group.

McALLISTER TOWING AND TRANSPORTATION COMPANY, INC.
17 Battery Place, Suite 1200, New York NY 10004. 212/269-3200. **Fax:** 212/509-1147. **Contact:** Nancy Errichiello, Director of Personnel. **World Wide Web address:** http://www.mcallistertowing.com. **Description:** A marine services firm providing ship docking, deep-sea and coastal towing, oil transportation, bulk transportation, special projects such as positioning tunnel and bridge segments and other services for the transportation industry. McAllister also offers full-service, in-house capabilities through a complete packaged transportation service provided to shippers. The company operates one of the largest fleets of tugs and barges on the East Coast and in the Caribbean, with ship docking services in New York NY, Philadelphia PA, Norfolk VA, Charleston SC, Jacksonville FL, Baltimore MD, and Puerto Rico. Marine towing and transportation services are operated along the East Coast, in the Caribbean,

through the New York State barge canal system, and in the Great Lakes and the St. Lawrence River. Founded in 1864. **Corporate headquarters location:** This location. **Other locations:** FL; MD; PR; SC. **President:** Capt. Brian A. McAllister.

METROPOLITAN TRANSPORTATION AUTHORITY (MTA)
347 Madison Avenue, New York NY 10017-3739. 212/878-7000. **Fax:** 212/878-7227. **Contact:** Human Resources Division. **E-mail address:** mtahr@mtahq.org. **World Wide Web address:** http://www.mta.nyc.ny.us. **Description:** A public benefit corporation primarily devoted to obtaining funding for mass transportation in the New York City area, as well as serving as the headquarters for the MTA's constituent agencies. **Positions advertised include:** Police Radio & Communications Specialist; Senior Executive Secretary; Summons Administrator; Business Programs Deputy Director; Financial Analyst; Facilities Manager; Facilities Operation and Support Director; Crime Analyst; Communications Operator. **Chairman/CEO:** Peter S. Kalikow. **Annual sales/revenues:** $4 billion. **Number of employees:** 64,169.

OMI CORPORATION
Metro Center, One Station Place, 7th Floor North, Stamford CT 06902. 203/602-6700. **Contact:** Human Resources. **World Wide Web address:** http://www.omicorp.com. **Description:** A large bulk shipping company with interests in 46 ocean-going bulk carriers, tankers, and gas carriers. OMI also provides logistics, crewing, technical, and commercial operations for international clients. The company has interests in OMI Petrolink Corporation and in Chiles Offshore Corporation, which operates 14 drilling rigs. **Corporate headquarters location:** This location. **Subsidiaries include:** OMI Marine Services, LLC. **Listed on:** New York Stock Exchange. **Stock exchange symbol:** OMM.

STOLT-NIELSEN TRANSPORTATION GROUP LTD.
P.O. Box 2300, Greenwich CT 06836. 203/625-9400. **Physical address:** 8 Sound Shore Drive, Greenwich CT 06836. **Contact:** Human Resources. **World Wide Web address:** http://www.stoltnielsen.com. **Description:** Operates the world's largest fleet of bulk chemical, oil, acid, and specialty liquid tankers. **Parent company:** Stolt-Nielsen S.A.

SWISSPORT USA
JFK International Airport, Building 151, East Hanger Road, Jamaica NY 11430. 718/995-8405. **Fax:** 718/244-7560. **Contact:** Human Resources Department. **World Wide Web address:** http://www.swissportusa.com. **Description:** Provides a wide range of ground-handling services for airlines and airports. Services include maintenance, inspections, spare parts inventory, into-plane fueling, cargo handling, cabin cleaning, and ramp services. Swissport USA also operates reservation centers for airlines. **Parent company:** Alpha Airports Group.

TITAN GLOBAL TECHNOLOGIES, LTD.
85 Chestnut Ridge Road, P.O. Box 617, Montvale NJ 07645. 201/930-0300. **Contact:** Human Resources. **World Wide Web address:** http://www.titan-global.com. **Description:** Designs, manufactures, and installs monorail transportation systems. **Corporate headquarters location:** This location. **Operations at this facility include:** Administration; Research and Development.

TIX INTERNATIONAL GROUP
201 Main Street, Nyack-On-Hudson NY 10960. 845/358-1007. **Fax:** 845/358-1266. **Contact:** Human Resources. **World Wide Web address:** http://www.tixtravel.com. **Description:** A full-service travel agency and ticket broker for concerts, sports, and theater events. **Corporate headquarters location:** This location.

UNITED AIR LINES, INC.
Newark International Airport, Newark NJ 07114. 973/624-6925. **Toll-free phone:** 800/241-6522. **Contact:** Human Resources. **World Wide Web address:** http://www.ual.com. **Description:** An air carrier that provides transportation of people and goods through more than 1,100 daily scheduled flights at 100 airports in the United States, Canada, and Mexico. **NOTE:** Resumes should be sent to United Air Lines-WHQES, P.O. Box 66100, Chicago IL 60666. **Corporate headquarters location:** Elk Grove Township IL. **Parent company:** UAL, Inc. **Listed on:** New York Stock Exchange. **Stock exchange symbol:** UAL.

UNITED PARCEL SERVICE (UPS)
One Clover Place, Edison NJ 08837. **Toll-free phone:** 800/622-3593. **Contact:** Human Resources. **World Wide Web address:** http://www.upsjobs.com. **Description:** UPS provides package delivery services nationwide. **Positions advertised include:** Principal; Automotive Mechanic; Regional Account Manager. **Operations at this facility include:** This location is a package-handling center.

WE TRANSPORT INC.
303 Sunnyside Boulevard, Plainview NY 11803. 516/349-8200. **Contact:** Mary Prioli, Personnel Manager. **Description:** An area school bus and van transportation company. **Special programs:** Internships. **Corporate headquarters location:** This location. **Number of employees at this location:** 70.

UTILITIES: ELECTRIC, GAS, AND WATER

**You can expect to find the following types of companies
in this section:**
Gas, Electric, and Fuel Companies • Other Energy-Producing Companies •
Public Utility Holding Companies • Water Utilities

CITIZENS COMMUNICATIONS
3 High Ridge Park, Stamford CT 06905-1390. 203/614-5600. **Fax:** 203/614-4602. **Contact:** Christy O'Brien, Human Resources. **World Wide Web address:** http://www.czn.com. **Description:** A diversified public utility providing telecommunications, electric, gas, water, and wastewater treatment services nationwide. Founded in 1935. **Positions advertised include:** Manager, Revenue Accounting; Capital Budget and Recording Manager; Director, Labor Relations; Manager, Accounting; Tax Accountant; Senior Accountant; Financial Analyst; Senior Financial Analyst; Senior Accountant Capital. **Corporate headquarters location:** This location. **Listed on:** New York Stock Exchange. **Stock exchange symbol:** CZN. **Number of employees nationwide:** 2,300.

CONSOLIDATED EDISON, INC.
4 Irving Place, Room 2215, New York NY 10003-3598. 212/460-4600. **Fax:** 212/228-9439. **Contact:** Human Resources Director. **E-mail address:** opportunities@coned.com. **World Wide Web address:** http://www.conedison.com. **Description:** Through its subsidiaries, Consolidated Edison supplies electricity to New York City and most of Westchester County; supplies gas to Manhattan, the Bronx, and parts of Queens and Westchester; and serves over 400,000 electric and gas customers in the tri-state area. The company is also engaged in energy marketing, fiber-optic telecommunications, and merchant power plant development. **Positions advertised include:** Associate Engineer; Engineer; Environmental Engineer; Instrument Controls Specialist; Junior Designer; Project Specialist; Section Manager; Senior Engineer; Technical Analyst; Production Technician; Asbestos Administrator; Safety Specialist; Scientist; Senior Scientist; Senior Environmental Engineer; Senior Specialist; Human Resource Generalist; Supervisor; Bi-Lingual Korean Customer Service Representative; Electrical Mechanic; Welder Mechanic; Operating Mechanic. **Subsidiaries include:** Consolidated Edison Communications; Consolidated Edison Company of New York; Consolidated Edison Development; Consolidated Edison Energy; Consolidated Edison Solutions; Orange and Rockland Utilities. **Corporate headquarters location:** This location. **Listed on:** New York Stock Exchange. **Stock exchange symbol:** ED. **Chairman/President/CEO:** Eugene R. McGrath. **Annual sales/revenues:** $8.5 billion. **Number of employees:** 14,300.

ELIZABETHTOWN GAS COMPANY/NUI
P.O. Box 1450, Union NJ 07207. 908/289-5000. **Physical address:** 1085 Morris Road, Union NJ 07083. **Contact:** Human Resources. **E-mail address:** hr@nui.com. **World Wide Web address:** http://www.nui.com. **Description:** Through several area locations, Elizabethtown Gas Company is engaged in the distribution of natural gas through its subsidiaries and investments in joint ventures. The company serves more than 240,000 customers. **Subsidiaries include:** Energy Marketing Exchange. **Parent company:** NUI Corporation (Bedminster NJ).

FIRSTENERGY CORPORATION
300 Madison Avenue, P.O. Box 1911, Morristown NJ 07962-1911. 973/955-8200. **Contact:** Personnel. **World Wide Web address:**

http://www.firstenergycorp.com. **Description:** An electric utility holding company with several operating subsidiaries. **Positions advertised include:** Purchasing Representative; Executive Assistant; Lineman; Law Clerk; Attorney; Associate Generation Specialist. **Corporate headquarters location:** Akron OH. **Operations at this facility include:** Administration. **Listed on:** New York Stock Exchange. **Stock exchange symbol:** FE.

KEYSPAN ENERGY CORPORATION
dba KEYSPAN ENERGY DELIVERY
One MetroTech Center, Brooklyn NY 11201-3850. 718/403-1000. **Fax:** 718/488-1782. **Contact:** Elaine Weinstein, Human Resources VP. **E-mail address:** employment@keyspanenergy.com. **World Wide Web address:** http://www.keyspanenergy.com. **Description:** Provides natural gas service and engages in gas exploration, production, and transportation. **NOTE:** Interested applicants are requested to send resumes with the job reference code to: KeySpan, Talent Management Department , 175 East Old Country Road, Hicksville NY 11801. **Corporate headquarters location:** This location. **Subsidiaries include:** Brooklyn Union Gas Company; KeySpan Energy Delivery; KeySpan Energy Development Corporation; KeySpan Services, Inc.; The Houston Exploration Company. **Listed on:** New York Stock Exchange. **Stock exchange symbol:** KSE. **Chairman/CEO:** Robert B. Catell. **Annual sales/revenues:** $6 billion. **Number of employees:** 13,000.

LONG ISLAND POWER AUTHORITY (LIPA)
333 Earle Ovington Boulevard, Suite 403, Uniondale NY 11553. 516/222-7700. **Fax:** 516/222-9137. **Contact:** Human Resources. **E-mail address:** info@lipower.org. **World Wide Web address:** http://www.lipower.org. **Description:** Supplies electric and gas service in Nassau and Suffolk Counties and the Rockaway Peninsula in Queens County. **Positions advertised include:** Rates and Pricing Manager; Marketing Assistant. **Special programs:** Internships. **Corporate headquarters location:** This location. **Other locations:** Brentwood NY; Garden City NY.

NEW JERSEY RESOURCES CORPORATION
1415 Wyckoff Road, Wall NJ 07719. 732/938-1480. **Recorded jobline:** 732/938-1000. **Contact:** Human Resources. **E-mail address:** careers@njresources.com. **World Wide Web address:** http://www.njresources.com. **Description:** A holding company for natural gas and energy companies. **Subsidiaries include:** New Jersey Natural Gas Company distributes natural gas to over 400,000 customers in Monmouth and Ocean Counties, and parts of Morris and Middlesex Counties. Other subsidiaries are engaged in exploration for natural gas and oil, real estate development, and the development of cogeneration projects.

ORANGE AND ROCKLAND UTILITIES
71 Dolson Avenue, Middletown NY 10940. 845/342-8940. **Fax:** 845/577-2958. **Contact:** J. Renella, Human Resources. **World Wide Web address:** http://www.oru.com. **Description:** Orange and Rockland Utilities and its subsidiaries supply electric service to 254,000 customers and gas service to 108,200 customers in southeastern New York, northern New Jersey, and northeastern Pennsylvania. **NOTE:** Resumes may be mailed to Human Resources, Attention: J. Renella, Orange and Rockland Utilities, Incorporated, One Blue Hill Plaza, Pearl River NY 10965, or faxed to: 845/577-2958. **Corporate headquarters location:** Pearl River NY. **Other U.S. locations:** Spring Valley NY. **Subsidiaries include:** Rockland Electric Company (NJ); Pike County Light and Power (PA). **Parent company:** Consolidated Edison, Inc. **President:** John D. McMahon. **Number of employees nationwide:** 1,000.

PASSAIC VALLEY WATER COMMISSION

1525 Main Avenue, Clifton NJ 07011. 973/349-4309. **Contact:** Jim Gallagher, Personnel Director. **World Wide Web address:** http://www.pvwc.com. **Description:** Provides water utility services. **Corporate headquarters location:** This location.

PUBLIC SERVICE ENTERPRISE GROUP (PSEG)

80 Park Plaza, Newark NJ 07101. 973/430-7000. **Contact:** Human Resources. **World Wide Web address:** http://www.pseg.com. **Description:** An electric and gas utility holding company. **Positions advertised include:** Business Continuity Planner; Power Generation Manager; Power Accounting Manager; Global Accounting Director; Staff Engineer; Administration Associate; Consultant; Lead Associate. **Corporate headquarters location:** This location. **Other area locations:** Hancock's Bridge NJ. **Subsidiaries include:** Public Service Electric & Gas Company provides nuclear, coal, gas, oil, and purchased and interchanged power to industrial and commercial customers. **Listed on:** New York Stock Exchange. **Stock exchange symbol:** PEG.

UNITED WATER RESOURCES, INC.

200 Old Hook Road, Harrington Park NJ 07640. 201/784-9434. **Fax:** 201/767-7142. **Contact:** Carol Ike, Recruiting Department. **E-mail address:** recruiting@unitedwater.com. **World Wide Web address:** http://www.unitedwater.com. **Description:** A holding company for regulated water utilities. **Subsidiaries include:** United Water New Jersey supplies water service to over 750,000 customers in 60 communities in Hudson County and Bergen County NJ.

WATER AUTHORITY OF WESTERN NASSAU COUNTY

58 South Tyson Avenue, Floral Park NY 11001. 516/327-4100. **Contact:** Janice Varley, Director of Human Resources. **Description:** The Water Authority of Western Nassau County supplies and distributes water for residential and commercial use in western Nassau County. **NOTE:** Positions are filled in accordance with Nassau County Civil Service Commission rules. **Corporate headquarters location:** This location.

MISCELLANEOUS WHOLESALING

You can expect to find the following types of companies in this section:
Exporters and Importers • General Wholesale Distribution Companies

ALLOU HEALTH & BEAUTY CARE, INC.
50 Emjay Boulevard, Brentwood NY 11717. 631/273-4000. **Fax:** 631/851-2699. **Contact:** Kathy Calzente, Personnel Manager. **World Wide Web address:** http://www.allou.com. **Description:** Distributes health and beauty products such as fragrances, cosmetics, and food items to independent retailers in the metropolitan New York area. **NOTE:** Entry-level positions and second and third shifts are offered. **Corporate headquarters location:** This location. **Listed on:** American Stock Exchange. **Stock exchange symbol:** ALU. **Chairman:** Victor Jacobs. **Annual sales/revenues:** $564 million. **Number of employees:** 300.

ATELIER ESTHETIQUE INC.
386 Park Avenue South, Suite 1409, New York NY 10016. 212/725-6130. **Contact:** Human Resources. **World Wide Web address:** http://www.aeinstitute.net. **Description:** A wholesaler of cosmetic products and equipment. This location also houses a beauty school.

CCA INDUSTRIES INC.
200 Murray Hill Parkway, East Rutherford NJ 07073. 201/330-1400. **Contact:** Human Resources Department. **World Wide Web address:** http://www.ccaindustries.com. **Description:** Distributes a wide variety of health and beauty products manufactured by other companies using CCA's formulations. The majority of its sales are made to retail drug and food chains and mass merchandisers. Nail treatment products are sold under the name Nutra Nail; hair treatment products are sold under the names Pro Perm, Wash 'n Curl, Wash 'n Tint, and Wash 'n Straight; depilatory products are sold under the Hair Off label; skin care products are sold under the Sudden Change name; oral hygiene products are sold under the Plus+White trademark; meal replacement products are sold under the trademark Eat 'n Lose; and diet products under the trademarks Hungrex and Permathene. **Listed on:** NASDAQ. **Stock exchange symbol:** CCAM.

DYNAMIC INTERNATIONAL LIMITED, INC.
58 Second Avenue, Brooklyn NY 11215. 718/369-4160. **Fax:** 718/369-2210. **Contact:** Human Resources. **Description:** Dynamic Classics sells and distributes a diverse line of exercise equipment, sport bags, luggage, and gift products, which are distributed nationwide. The majority of sales are to catalog showrooms, drug chains, sporting goods chains, distributors, chain stores, discount stores, and the premium trade.

ITOCHU INTERNATIONAL INC.
335 Madison Avenue, New York NY 10017. 212/818-8500. **Fax:** 212/818-8543. **Contact:** Recruiting, Human Resources. **E-mail address:** recruiting@itochu.com. **World Wide Web address:** http://www.itochu.com. **Description:** A diversified international trading company with markets that include textiles, metals, machinery, foodstuffs, general merchandise, electronics, chemicals, and energy. The company has import/export, distribution, finance, investment, transportation, and joint venture operations, all of which contribute to an annual business volume of over $12 billion. Itochu International is also engaged in direct investments and partnerships in many additional industries including high-technology manufacturing, retailing, fiber optics, satellite

communications, and real estate development. **Corporate headquarters location:** This location. **Other locations:** AL; CA; CO; GA; IL; MO; WA. **Parent company:** Itochu Corporation.

MARUBENI AMERICA CORPORATION

450 Lexington Avenue, 35th Floor, New York NY 10017-3907. 212/450-0100. **Fax:** 212/450-0715. **Contact:** Human Resources. **E-mail address:** info@marubeni-usa.com. **World Wide Web address:** http://www.marubeni-usa.com. **Description:** An international trading firm that provides importing and exporting services to and from Japan. Operations are conducted through seven groups: Metals & Minerals Group; Machinery Group; Petroleum Group; General Merchandise Group; Chemical & Plastics Group; Textile Group; and Grain, Marine, & Other Products Group. The New York and New Jersey operations involve all groups and offer a wide range of products. **Corporate headquarters location:** This location. **Other U.S. locations:** Nationwide. **Subsidiaries include:** Don Juan Sportswear Inc.; It Fabrics Inc. **Parent company:** Marubeni Corporation (Japan).

McMASTER-CARR SUPPLY COMPANY

473 Ridge Road, Dayton NJ 08810. 732/329-6666. **Contact:** Recruiting Department. **E-mail address:** recruiting@mcmaster.com. **World Wide Web address:** http://www.mcmaster.com. **Description:** Distributes industrial products and supplies primarily through catalog sales. Products are sold worldwide. **NOTE:** Mail employment correspondence to: Recruiting, McMaster Supply Company, P.O. Box 4355, Chicago IL 60680-4355. **Positions advertised include:** Customer Service Representative. **Corporate headquarters location:** Elmhurst IL. **Operations at this facility include:** Service.

MITSUBISHI INTERNATIONAL CORPORATION

520 Madison Avenue, 16th Floor, New York NY 10022. 212/605-2000. **Fax:** 212/605-2597. **Contact:** Human Resources. **World Wide Web address:** http://www.mitsubishiintl.com. **Description:** Mitsubishi International operates through several trading divisions and related support divisions including Petroleum, Steel, Foods, Chemicals, Machinery, Textile, Non-Ferrous Metals, Ferrous Raw Materials, Lumber and Pulp, and General Merchandise. Regional offices are located throughout the United States. **Corporate headquarters location:** This location. **Other U.S. locations:** Nationwide. **Subsidiaries include:** Mitsubishi Trust & Banking Corporation (also at this location, 212/838-7700) is a bank with diverse activities that include real estate and foreign exchange services. **Parent company:** Mitsubishi Corporation of Japan. **Annual sales/revenues:** $119 million. **Number of employees at this location:** 400. **Number of employees nationwide:** 850.

MITSUI & CO., LTD.

200 Park Avenue, New York NY 10166. 212/878-4000. **Fax:** 212/878-4800. **Contact:** Human Resources. **World Wide Web address:** http://www.mitsui.com. **Description:** An international trading firm engaged in a wide range of import and export activities. **Corporate headquarters location:** Tokyo, Japan. **Other U.S. locations:** Nationwide. **Operations at this facility include:** Administration; Divisional Headquarters; Regional Headquarters; Sales. **Listed on:** NASDAQ. **Stock exchange symbol:** MITSY. **Annual sales/revenues:** $4.2 billion. **Number of employees:** 36,116.

SAVIN CORPORATION

P.O. Box 10270, Stamford CT 06904-2270. 203/967-5000. **Physical address:** 333 Ludlow Street, Stamford CT 06904. **Contact:** Bob Manley, Human Resources Director. **World Wide Web address:** http://www.savin.com. **Description:** Distributes copiers and facsimile machines. **Corporate headquarters location:** This location.

UOP/XEROX
2344 Flatbush Avenue, Brooklyn NY 11234. 718/252-6500. **Fax:** 718/252-8585.
Contact: Human Resources. **Description:** Sells and services copiers, fax machines, laser printers, and other types of office equipment.

ACCOUNTING AND MANAGEMENT CONSULTING

AMERICAN ACCOUNTING ASSOCIATION
5717 Bessie Drive, Sarasota FL 34233-2399. 941/921-7747. **Fax:** 941/923-4093. **E-mail address:** Office@aaahq.org. **World Wide Web address:** http://aaahq.org. **Description:** A voluntary organization founded in 1916 to promote excellence in accounting education, research and practice.

AMERICAN INSTITUTE OF CERTIFIED PUBLIC ACCOUNTANTS
1211 Avenue of the Americas, New York NY 10036. 212/596-6200. **Toll-free phone:** 888/777-7077. **Fax:** 212/596-6213. **World Wide Web address:** http://www.aicpa.org. **Description:** A non-profit organization providing resources, information, and leadership to its members.

AMERICAN MANAGEMENT ASSOCIATION
1601 Broadway, New York NY 10019. 212/586-8100. **Fax:** 212/903-8168. **Toll-free phone:** 800/262-9699. **E-mail address:** info@amanet.org. **World Wide Web address:** http://www.amanet.org. **Description:** A non-profit association providing its members with management development and educational services.

ASSOCIATION OF GOVERNMENT ACCOUNTANTS
2208 Mount Vernon Avenue, Alexandria VA 22301. 703/684-6931. **Toll-free phone:** 800/AGA-7211. **Fax:** 703/548-9367. **World Wide Web address:** http://www.agacgfm.org. **Description:** A public financial management organization catering to the professional interests of financial managers at the local, state and federal governments and public accounting firms.

ASSOCIATION OF MANAGEMENT CONSULTING FIRMS
380 Lexington Avenue, Suite 1700, New York NY 10168. 212/551-7887. **Fax:** 212/551-7934. **E-mail address:** info@amcf.org. **World Wide Web address:** http://www.amcf.org. **Description:** Founded in 1929 to provide a forum for confronting common challenges; increasing the collective knowledge of members and their clients; and establishing a professional code conduct.

CONNECTICUT SOCIETY OF CERTIFIED PUBLIC ACCOUNTANTS
845 Brook Street, Building Two, Rocky Hill CT 06067-3405. 860/258-4800. **Fax:** 860/258-4859. **E-mail address:** info@cs-cpa.org. **World Wide Web address:** http://www.cs-cpa.org. **Description:** A statewide professional membership organization catering to CPAs.

INSTITUTE OF INTERNAL AUDITORS
247 Maitland Avenue, Altamonte Springs FL 32701-4201. 407-937-1100. **Fax:** 407-937-1101. **E-mail address:** iia@theiia.org. **World Wide Web address:** http://www.theiia.org. **Description:** Founded in 1941 to serves members in internal auditing, governance and internal control, IT audit, education, and security worldwide.

INSTITUTE OF MANAGEMENT ACCOUNTANTS
10 Paragon Drive, Montvale NJ 07645-1718. 201/573-9000. **Fax:** 201/474-1600. **Toll-free phone:** 800/638-4427. **E-mail address:** ima@imanet.org. **World Wide Web address:** http://www.imanet.org. **Description:** Provides members personal and professional development opportunities in management accounting, financial management and information management through education and association

with business professionals and certification in management accounting and financial management.

INSTITUTE OF MANAGEMENT CONSULTANTS

2025 M Street, NW, Suite 800, Washington DC 20036-3309. 202/367-1134. **Toll-free phone:** 800/221-2557. **Fax:** 202/367-2134. **E-mail address:** office@imcusa.org. **World Wide Web address:** http://www.imcusa.org. **Description** Founded in 1968 as the national professional association representing management consultants and awarding the CMC (Certified Management Consultant) certification mark.

NATIONAL ASSOCIATION OF TAX PROFESSIONALS

720 Association Drive, PO Box 8002, Appleton WI 54912-8002. 800/558-3402. **Fax:** 800/747-0001. **E-Mail address:** natp@natptax.com. **World Wide Web address:** http://www.natptax.com. **Description:** Founded in 1979 as a nonprofit professional association dedicated to excellence in taxation with a mission to serve professionals who work in all areas of tax practice.

NATIONAL SOCIETY OF PUBLIC ACCOUNTANTS

1010 North Fairfax Street, Alexandria VA 22314. 703/549-6400. **Toll-free phone:** 800/966-6679. **Fax:** 703/549-2984. **Email address:** members@nsacct.org. **World Wide Web address:** http://www.nsacct.org. **Description:** For more than 50 years, NSA has supported its members with resources and representation to protect their right to practice, build credibility and grow the profession. NSA protects the public by requiring its members to adhere to a strict Code of Ethics.

ADVERTISING, MARKETING, AND PUBLIC RELATIONS

ADVERTISING RESEARCH FOUNDATION
641 Lexington Avenue, New York NY 10022. 212/751-5656. **World Wide Web address:** http://www.thearf.com. **Description:** Founded in 1936 by the Association of National Advertisers and the American Association of Advertising Agencies, the Advertising Research Foundation (ARF) is a nonprofit corporate-membership association, which is today the preeminent professional organization in the field of advertising, marketing and media research. Its combined membership represents more than 400 advertisers, advertising agencies, research firms, media companies, educational institutions and international organizations.

AMERICAN ASSOCIATION OF ADVERTISING AGENCIES
405 Lexington Avenue, 18th Floor, New York NY 10174-1801. 212/682-2500. **Fax:** 212/682-8391. **World Wide Web address:** http://www.aaaa.org. **Description:** Founded in 1917 as the national trade association representing the advertising agency business in the United States.

AMERICAN MARKETING ASSOCIATION
311 South Wacker Drive, Suite 5800, Chicago IL 60606. 312/542-9000. **Fax:** 312/542-9001. **Toll-free phone:** 800/AMA-1150. **E-mail address:** info@ama.org. **World Wide Web address:** http://www.marketingpower.com. **Description:** A professional associations for marketers providing relevant marketing information that experienced marketers turn to everyday.

DIRECT MARKETING ASSOCIATION
1120 Avenue of the Americas, New York NY 10036-6700. 212/768-7277. **Fax:** 212/302-6714. **E-mail address:** info@the-dma.org. **World Wide Web address:** http://www.the-dma.org. **Description:** Founded in 1917 as a non-profit organization representing professionals working in all areas of direct marketing.

INTERNATIONAL ADVERTISING ASSOCIATION
521 Fifth Avenue, Suite 1807, New York NY 10175. 212/557-1133. **Fax:** 212/983-0455. **E-mail address:** iaa@iaaglobal.org. **World Wide Web address:** http://www.iaaglobal.org. **Description:** A strategic partnership that addresses the common interests of all the marketing communications disciplines ranging from advertisers to media companies to agencies to direct marketing firms to individual practitioners.

MARKETING RESEARCH ASSOCIATION
1344 Silas Deane Highway, Suite 306, PO Box 230, Rocky Hill CT 06067-0230. 860/257-4008. **Fax:** 860/257-3990. **E-mail address:** email@mra-net.org. **World Wide Web address:** http://www.mra-net.org. **Description:** MRA promotes excellence in the opinion and marketing research industry by providing members with a variety of opportunities for advancing and expanding their marketing research and related business skills. To protect the marketing research environment, we will act as an advocate with appropriate government entities, other associations, and the public.

PUBLIC RELATIONS SOCIETY OF AMERICA
33 Maiden Lane, 11th Floor, New York NY 10038-5150. 212/460-1400. **Fax:** 212/995-0757. **E-mail address:** info@prsa.org. **World Wide Web address:** http://www.prsa.org. **Description:** A professional organization for public relations

practitioners. Comprised of nearly 20,000 members organized into 116 Chapters represent business and industry, counseling firms, government, associations, hospitals, schools, professional services firms and nonprofit organizations.

AEROSPACE

AMERICAN INSTITUTE OF AERONAUTICS AND ASTRONAUTICS
1801 Alexander Bell Drive, Suite 500, Reston VA 20191-4344. 703/264-7500. **Toll-free phone:** 800/639-AIAA. **Fax:** 703/264-7551. **E-mail address:** info@aiaa.org. **World Wide Web address:** http://www.aiaa.org. **Description:** The principal society of the aerospace engineer and scientist.

NATIONAL AERONAUTIC ASSOCIATION OF USA
1815 N. Fort Myer Drive, Suite 500, Arlington VA 22209. 703/527-0226. **Fax:** 703/527-0229. **E-mail address:** naa@naa-usa.org. **World Wide Web address:** http://www.naa-usa.org. **Description:** A non-parochial, charitable organization serving all segments of American aviation whose membership encompass all areas of flight including skydiving, models, commercial airlines, and military fighters.

PROFESSIONAL AVIATION MAINTENANCE ASSOCIATION
717 Princess Street, Alexandria VA 22314. 703/683-3171. **Toll-free phone:** 866/865-PAMA. **Fax:** 703/683-0018. **E-mail address:** hq@pama.org. **World Wide Web address:** http://www.pama.org. **Description:** A non-profit organization concerned with promoting professionalism among aviation maintenance personnel; fostering and improving methods, skills, learning, and achievement in aviation maintenance. The association also conducts regular industry meetings and seminars.

APPAREL, FASHION, AND TEXTILES

AMERICAN APPAREL AND FOOTWEAR ASSOCIATION
1601 North Kent Street, Suite 1200, Arlington VA 22209. 703/524-1864. **Fax:**
703/522-6741. **World Wide Web address:** http://apparelandfootwear.org.
Description: The national trade association representing apparel, footwear and
other sewn products companies, and their suppliers. Promotes and enhances its
members' competitiveness, productivity and profitability in the global market.

THE FASHION GROUP
8 West 40th Street, 7th Floor, New York NY 10018. 212/302-5511. **Fax:** 212/302-
5533. **E-mail address:** info@fgi.org. **World Wide Web address:**
http://www.fgi.org. **Description:** A non-profit association representing all areas of
the fashion, apparel, accessories, beauty and home industries.

**INTERNATIONAL ASSOCIATION OF CLOTHING DESIGNERS AND
EXECUTIVES**
124 West 93rd Street, Suite 3E, New York NY 10025. 603/672-4065. **Fax:**
603/672-4064. **World Wide Web address:** http://www.iacde.com. **Description:**
Founded in 1911, with the mission to serve as a global network for the sharing of
information by its members on design direction and developments, fashion and
fiber trends, and technical innovations affecting tailored apparel, designers, their
suppliers, retailers, manufacturing executives and educational institutions for the
purpose of enhancing their professional standing and interests.

NATIONAL COUNCIL OF TEXTILE ORGANIZATIONS
1776 I Street, NW, Suite 900, Washington DC 20006. 202/756-4878. **Fax:**
202/756-1520. **World Wide Web address:** http://www.ncto.org. **Description:**
The national trade association for the domestic textile industry with members
operating in more than 30 states and the industry employs approximately
450,000 people.

ARCHITECTURE, CONSTRUCTION, AND ENGINEERING

AACE INTERNATIONAL: THE ASSOCIATION FOR TOTAL COST MANAGEMENT
209 Prairie Avenue, Suite 100, Morgantown WV 26501. 304/296-8444. **Fax:** 304/291-5728. **E-mail address:** info@aacei.org. **World Wide Web address:** http://www.aacei.org. **Description:** Founded 1956 to provide its approximately 5,500 worldwide members with the resources to enhance their performance and ensure continued growth and success. Members include cost management professionals: cost managers and engineers, project managers, planners and schedulers, estimators and bidders, and value engineers.

AMERICAN ASSOCIATION OF ENGINEERING SOCIETIES
1828 L Street, NW, Suite 906, Washington DC 20036. 202/296-2237. **Fax:** 202/296-1151. **World Wide Web address:** http://www.aaes.org. **Description:** A multidisciplinary organization of engineering societies dedicated to advancing the knowledge, understanding, and practice of engineering.

AMERICAN CONSULTING ENGINEERS COMPANIES
1015 15th Street, 8th Floor, NW, Washington DC, 20005-2605. 202/347-7474. **Fax:** 202/898-0068. **E-mail address:** acec@acec.org. **World Wide Web address:** http://www.acec.org. **Description:** Engaged in a wide range of engineering works that propel the nation's economy, and enhance and safeguard America's quality of life. These works allow Americans to drink clean water, enjoy a healthy life, take advantage of new technologies, and travel safely and efficiently. The Council's mission is to contribute to America's prosperity and welfare by advancing the business interests of member firms.

AMERICAN INSTITUTE OF ARCHITECTS
1735 New York Avenue, NW, Washington DC 20006. 202/626-7300. **Fax:** 202/626-7547. **Toll-free phone:** 800/AIA-3837. **E-mail address:** infocentral@aia.org. **World Wide Web address:** http://www.aia.org. **Description:** A non-profit organization for the architecture profession dedicated to: Serving its members, advancing their value, improving the quality of the built environment. Vision Statement: Through a culture of innovation, The American Institute of Architects empowers its members and inspires creation of a better-built environment.

AMERICAN INSTITUTE OF CONSTRUCTORS
P.O. Box 26334, Alexandria VA 22314. 703/683-4999. **Fax:** 703/683-5480. **E-mail address:** admin@aicenet.org. **World Wide Web address:** http://www.aicnet.org. **Description:** Founded to help individual construction practitioners achieve the professional status they deserve and serves as the national qualifying body of professional constructor. The Institute AIC membership identifies the individual as a true professional. The Institute is the constructor's counterpart of professional organizations found in architecture, engineering, law and other fields.

AMERICAN SOCIETY FOR ENGINEERING EDUCATION
1818 N Street, NW, Suite 600, Washington DC, 20036-2479. 202/331-3500. **Fax:** 202/265-8504. **World Wide Web address:** http://www.asee.org. **Description:** A nonprofit member association, founded in 1893, dedicated to promoting and improving engineering and technology education.

AMERICAN SOCIETY OF CIVIL ENGINEERS
1801 Alexander Bell Drive, Reston VA 20191-4400. 703/295-6300. **Fax:** 703/295-6222. **Toll-free phone:** 800/548-2723. **World Wide Web address:** http://www.asce.org. **Description:** Founded to provide essential value to its members, their careers, partners and the public by developing leadership, advancing technology, advocating lifelong learning and promoting the profession.

AMERICAN SOCIETY OF HEATING, REFRIGERATION, AND AIR CONDITIONING ENGINEERS
1791 Tullie Circle, NE, Atlanta GA 30329. 404/636-8400. **Fax:** 404/321-5478. **Toll-free phone:** 800/527-4723. **E-mail address:** ashrae@ashrae.org. **World Wide Web address:** http://www.ashrae.org. **Description:** Founded with a mission to advance the arts and sciences of heating, ventilation, air conditioning, refrigeration and related human factors and to serve the evolving needs of the public and ASHRAE members.

AMERICAN SOCIETY OF MECHANICAL ENGINEERS
Three Park Avenue, New York, NY 10016-5990. 973-882-1167. **Toll-free phone:** 800/843-2763. **E-mail address:** infocentral@asme.org. **World Wide Web address:** http://www.asme.org. **Description:** Founded in 1880 as the American Society of Mechanical Engineers, today ASME International is a nonprofit educational and technical organization serving a worldwide membership of 125,000.

AMERICAN SOCIETY OF NAVAL ENGINEERS
1452 Duke Street, Alexandria VA 22314-3458. 703/836-6727. **Fax:** 703/836-7491. **E-mail address:** asnehq@navalengineers.org. **World Wide Web address:** http://www.navalengineers.org. **Description:** Mission is to advance the knowledge and practice of naval engineering in public and private applications and operations, to enhance the professionalism and well being of members, and to promote naval engineering as a career field.

AMERICAN SOCIETY OF PLUMBING ENGINEERS
8614 Catalpa Avenue, Suite 1007, Chicago IL 60656-1116. 773/693-2773. **Fax:** 773/695-9007. **E-mail address:** info@aspe.org. **World Wide Web address:** http://www.aspe.org. **Description:** The international organization for professionals skilled in the design, specification and inspection of plumbing systems. ASPE is dedicated to the advancement of the science of plumbing engineering, to the professional growth and advancement of its members and the health, welfare and safety of the public.

AMERICAN SOCIETY OF SAFETY ENGINEERS
1800 E Oakton Street, Des Plaines IL 60018. 847/699-2929. **Fax:** 847/768-3434. **E-mail address:** customerservice@asse.org. **World Wide Web address:** http://www.asse.org. **Description:** A non-profit organization promoting the concerns of safety engineers.

ASSOCIATED BUILDERS AND CONTRACTORS
4250 N. Fairfax Drive, 9th Floor, Arlington VA 22203-1607. 703/812-2000. **E-mail address:** gotquestions@abc.org. **World Wide Web address:** http://www.abc.org. **Description:** A national trade association representing more than 23,000 merit shop contractors, subcontractors, material suppliers and related firms in 80 chapters across the United States. Membership represents all specialties within the U.S. construction industry and is comprised primarily of firms that perform work in the industrial and commercial sectors of the industry.

ASSOCIATED GENERAL CONTRACTORS OF AMERICA, INC.
333 John Carlyle Street, Suite 200, Alexandria VA 22314. 703/548-3118. **Fax:** 703/548-3119. **E-mail address:** info@agc.org. **World Wide Web address:** http://www.agc.org. **Description:** A construction trade association, founded in 1918 on a request by President Woodrow Wilson.

THE ENGINEERING CENTER (TEC)
One Walnut Street, Boston MA 02108-3616. 617/227-5551. **Fax:** 617/227-6783. **E-mail address:** tec@engineers.org. **World Wide Web address:** http://www.engineers.org. **Description:** Founded with a mission to increase public awareness of the value of the engineering profession; to provide current information affecting the profession; to offer administrative facilities and services to engineering organizations in New England; and to provide a forum for discussion and resolution of professional issues.

ILLUMINATING ENGINEERING SOCIETY OF NORTH AMERICA
120 Wall Street, Floor 17, New York NY 10005. 212/248-5000. **Fax:** 212/248-5017(18). **E-mail address:** iesna@iesna.org. **World Wide Web address:** http://www.iesna.org. **Description:** To advance knowledge and to disseminate information for the improvement of the lighted environment to the benefit of society.

JUNIOR ENGINEERING TECHNICAL SOCIETY
1420 King Street, Suite 405, Alexandria VA 22314. 703/548-5387. **Fax:** 703/548-0769. **E-mail address:** info@jets.org. **World Wide Web address:** http://www.jets.org. **Description:** JETS is a national non-profit education organization that has served the pre-college engineering community for over 50 years. Through competitions and programs, JETS serves over 30,000 students and 2,000 teachers, and holds programs on 150 college campuses each year.

NATIONAL ACTION COUNCIL FOR MINORITIES IN ENGINEERING
440 Hamilton Avenue, Suite 302, White Plains NY 10601-1813. 914/539-4010. **Fax:** 914/539-4032. **E-mail address:** webmaster@nacme.org. **World Wide Web address:** http://www.nacme.org. **Description:** Founded in 1974 to provide leadership and support for the national effort to increase the representation of successful African American, American Indian and Latino women and men in engineering and technology, math- and science-based careers.

NATIONAL ASSOCIATION OF BLACK ENGINEERS
1454 Duke Street, Alexandria VA 22314. 703/549-2207. **Fax:** 703/683-5312. **E-mail address:** info@nsbe.org. **World Wide Web address:** http://www.nsbe.org. **Description:** A non-profit organization dedicated to increasing the number of culturally responsible Black engineers who excel academically, succeed professionally and positively impact the community.

NATIONAL ASSOCIATION OF HOME BUILDERS
1201 15th Street, NW, Washington DC 20005. 202/266-8200. **Toll-free phone:** 800/368-5242. **World Wide Web address:** http://www.nahb.org. **Description:** Founded in 1942, NAHB has been serving its members, the housing industry, and the public at large. A trade association that promotes the policies that make housing a national priority.

NATIONAL ASSOCIATION OF MINORITY ENGINEERING PROGRAM ADMINISTRATORS
1133 West Morse Boulevard, Suite 201, Winter Park FL 32789. 407/647-8839. **Fax:** 407/629-2502. **E-mail address:** namepa@namepa.org **World Wide Web**

address: http://www.namepa.org. **Description:** Provides services, information, and tools to produce a diverse group of engineers and scientists, and achieve equity and parity in the nation's workforce.

NATIONAL ELECTRICAL CONTRACTORS ASSOCIATION
3 Bethesda Metro Center, Suite 1100, Bethesda MD 20814. 301/657-3110. **Fax:** 301/215-4500. **World Wide Web address:** http://www.necanet.org. **Description:** Founded in 1901 as representative segment of the construction market comprised of over 70,000 electrical contracting firms.

NATIONAL SOCIETY OF PROFESSIONAL ENGINEERS
1420 King Street, Alexandria VA 22314-2794. 703/684-2800. **Fax:** 703/836-4875. **World Wide Web address:** http://www.nspe.org. **Description:** An engineering society that represents engineering professionals and licensed engineers (PEs) across all disciplines. Founded in 1934 to promote engineering licensure and ethics, enhance the engineer image, advocate and protect legal rights, publish industry news, and provide continuing education.

SOCIETY OF FIRE PROTECTION ENGINEERS
7315 Wisconsin Avenue, Suite 620E, Bethesda MD 20814. 301/718-2910. **Fax:** 301/718-2242. **E-mail address:** sfpehqtrs@sfpe.org. **World Wide Web address:** http://www.sfpe.org. **Description:** Founded in 1950 and incorporated as in independent organization in 1971, the professional society represents professionals in the field of fire protection engineering. The Society has approximately 3500 members in the United States and abroad, and 51 regional chapters, 10 of which are outside the US.

ARTS, ENTERTAINMENT, SPORTS, AND RECREATION

AMERICAN ASSOCIATION OF MUSEUMS
1575 Eye Street NW, Suite 400, Washington DC 20005. 202/289-1818. **Fax:** 202/289-6578. **World Wide Web address:** http://www.aam-us.org. **Description:** Founded in 1906, the association promotes excellence within the museum community. Services include advocacy, professional education, information exchange, accreditation, and guidance on current professional standards of performance.

AMERICAN FEDERATION OF MUSICIANS
1501 Broadway, Suite 600, New York NY 10036. 212/869-1330. **Fax:** 212/764-6134. **World Wide Web address:** http://www.afm.org. **Description:** Represents the interests of professional musicians. Services include negotiating agreements, protecting ownership of recorded music, securing benefits such as health care and pension, or lobbying our legislators. The AFM is committed to raising industry standards and placing the professional musician in the foreground of the cultural landscape.

AMERICAN MUSIC CENTER
30 West 26th Street, Suite 1001, New York NY 10010. 212/366-5260. **Fax:** 212/366-5265. **World Wide Web address:** http://www.amc.net. **Description:** Dedicated to fostering and composition, production, publication, and distribution of contemporary (American) music.

AMERICAN SOCIETY OF COMPOSERS, AUTHORS, AND PUBLISHERS (ASCAP)
One Lincoln Plaza, New York NY 10023. 212/621-6000. **Fax:** 212/724-9064. **E-mail address:** info@ascap.com. **World Wide Web address:** http://www.ascap.com. **Description:** A membership based association comprised of composers, songwriters, lyricists, and music publishers across all genres of music.

AMERICAN SYMPHONY ORCHESTRA LEAGUE
33 West 60th Street, 5th Floor, New York NY 10023-7905. 212/262-5161. **Fax:** 212/262-5198. **E-mail address:** league@symphony.org. **World Wide Web address:** http://www.symphony.org. **Description:** Founded in 1942 to exchange information and ideas with other orchestra leaders. The league also publishes the bimonthly magazine.

AMERICAN ZOO AND AQUARIUM ASSOCIATION
8403 Colesville Road, Suite 710, Silver Spring MD 20910-3314. 301/562-0777. **Fax:** 301/562-0888. **World Wide Web address:** http://www.aza.org. **Description:** Dedicated to establishing and maintaining excellent professional standards in all AZA Institutions through its accreditation program; establishing and promoting high standards of animal care and welfare; promoting and facilitating collaborative conservation and research programs; advocating effective governmental policies for our members; strengthening and promoting conservation education programs for our public and professional development for our members, and; raising awareness of the collective impact of its members and their programs.

ASSOCIATION OF INDEPENDENT VIDEO AND FILMMAKERS

304 Hudson Street, 6th floor, New York NY 10013. 212/807-1400. **Fax:** 212/463-8519. **E-mail address:** info@aivf.org. **World Wide Web address:** http://www.aivf.org. **Description:** A membership organization serving local and international film and videomakers including documentarians, experimental artists, and makers of narrative features.

NATIONAL ENDOWMENT FOR THE ARTS
1100 Pennsylvania Avenue, NW, Washington DC 20506. 202/682-5400. **E-mail address:** webmgr@arts.endow.com. **World Wide Web address:** http://www.nea.gov. **Description:** Founded in 1965 to foster, preserve, and promote excellence in the arts, to bring art to all Americans, and to provide leadership in arts education.

NATIONAL RECREATION AND PARK ASSOCIATION
22377 Belmont Ridge Road, Ashburn VA 20148-4150. 703/858-0784. **Fax:** 703/858-0794. **E-mail address:** info@nrpa.org. **World Wide Web address:** http://www.nrpa.org. **Description:** Works "to advance parks, recreation and environmental conservation efforts that enhance the quality of life for all people."

WOMEN'S CAUCUS FOR ART
P.O. Box 1498, Canal Street Station, New York NY 10013. 212/634-0007. **E-mail address:** info@nationalwca.com. **World Wide Web address:** http://www.nationalwca.com. **Description:** Founded in 1972 in connection with the College Art Association (CAA), as a national organization unique in its multi-disciplinary, multicultural membership of artists, art historians, students /educators, museum professionals and galleries in the visual arts.

AUTOMOTIVE

NATIONAL AUTOMOBILE DEALERS ASSOCIATION
8400 Westpark Drive, McLean VA 22102. 703/821-7000. **Toll-free phone:** 800/252-6232. **E-mail address:** nadainfo@nada.org. **World Wide Web address:** http://www.nada.org. **Description:** NADA represents America's franchised new-car and -truck dealers. Today there are more than 19,700 franchised new-car and -truck dealer members holding nearly 49,300 separate new-car and light-, medium-, and heavy-duty truck franchises, domestic and import. Founded in 1917.

NATIONAL INSTITUTE FOR AUTOMOTIVE SERVICE EXCELLENCE
101 Blue Seal Drive, SE, Suite 101, Leesburg VA 20175. 703/669-6600. **Toll-free phone:** 877/ASE-TECH. **World Wide Web address:** http://www.ase.com. **Description:** An independent, non-profit organization established in 1972 to improve the quality of vehicle repair and service through the testing and certification of repair and service professionals. More than 420,000 professionals hold current ASE credentials.

SOCIETY OF AUTOMOTIVE ENGINEERS
400 Commonwealth Drive, Warrendale PA 15096-0001. 724/776-4841. **E-mail address:** customerservice@sae.org. **World Wide Web address:** http://www.sae.org. **Description:** An organization with more than 84,000 members from 97 countries who share information and exchange ideas for advancing the engineering of mobility systems.

BANKING

AMERICA'S COMMUNITY BANKERS
900 Nineteenth Street, NW, Suite 400, Washington DC 20006. 202/857-3100.
Fax: 202/296-8716. **World Wide Web address:** http://www.acbankers.org.
Description: Represents the nation's community banks of all charter types and
sizes providing a broad range of advocacy and service strategies to enhance
their members' presence and contribution to the marketplace.

AMERICAN BANKERS ASSOCIATION
1120 Connecticut Avenue, NW, Washington DC 20036. 800/BANKERS. **World
Wide Web address:** http://www.aba.com. **Description:** Founded in 1875 and
represents banks on issues of national importance for financial institutions and
their customers. Members include all categories of banking institutions, including
community, regional and money center banks and holding companies, as well as
savings associations, trust companies and savings banks.

BIOTECHNOLOGY, PHARMACEUTICALS, AND SCIENTIFIC R&D

AMERICAN ASSOCIATION FOR CLINICAL CHEMISTRY
2101 L Street, NW, Suite 202, Washington DC 20037-1558. 202/857-0717. **Fax:** 202/887-5093. **Toll-free phone:** 800/892-1400. **World Wide Web address:** http://www.aacc.org. **Description:** Founded in 1948 as an international scientific/medical society of clinical laboratory professionals, physicians, research scientists and other individuals involved with clinical chemistry and other clinical laboratory science-related disciplines. The society has 10,000 members.

AMERICAN ASSOCIATION OF COLLEGES OF PHARMACY
1426 Prince Street, Alexandria VA 22314. 703/739-2330. **Fax:** 703/836-8982. **E-mail address:** mail@aacp.org. **World Wide Web address:** http://www.aacp.org. **Description:** Founded in 1900 as the national organization representing the interests of pharmaceutical education and educators. Comprising all 89 U.S. pharmacy colleges and schools including more than 4,000 faculty, 36,000 students enrolled in professional programs, and 3,600 individuals pursuing graduate study, AACP is committed to excellence in pharmaceutical education.

AMERICAN ASSOCIATION OF PHARMACEUTICAL SCIENTISTS
2107 Wilson Boulevard, Suite 700, Arlington VA 22201-3042. 703/243-2800. **Fax:** 703/243-9650. **E-mail address:** aaps@aaps.org. **World Wide Web address:** http://www.aaps.org. **Description:** Founded in 1986 as professional, scientific society of more than 10,000 members employed in academia, industry, government and other research institutes worldwide. The association advances science through the open exchange of scientific knowledge; serves as an information resource; and contributes to human health through pharmaceutical research and development.

AMERICAN COLLEGE OF CLINICAL PHARMACY (ACCP)
3101 Broadway, Suite 650, Kansas City MO 64111. 816/531-2177. **Fax:** 816/531-4990. **E-mail address:** accp@accp.com **World Wide Web address:** http://www.accp.com. **Description:** A professional and scientific society providing leadership, education, advocacy, and resources enabling clinical pharmacists to achieve excellence in practice and research.

AMERICAN PHARMACISTS ASSOCIATION
2215 Constitution Avenue, NW, Washington DC 20037-2985. 202/628-4410. **Fax:** 202/783-2351. **E-mail address:** info@aphanet.org. **World Wide Web address:** http://www.aphanet.org. **Description:** Founded in 1852 as the national professional society of pharmacists. Members include practicing pharmacists, pharmaceutical scientists, pharmacy students, pharmacy technicians, and others interested in advancing the profession.

AMERICAN SOCIETY FOR BIOCHEMISTRY AND MOLECULAR BIOLOGY
9650 Rockville Pike, Bethesda MD 20814-3996. 301/634-7145. **Fax:** 301/634-7126. **E-mail address:** asbmb@asbmb.faseb.org. **World Wide Web address:** http://www.asbmb.org. **Description:** A nonprofit scientific and educational organization with over 11,900 members. Most members teach and conduct research at colleges and universities. Others conduct research in various government laboratories, nonprofit research institutions and industry. The Society's student members attend undergraduate or graduate institutions.

AMERICAN SOCIETY OF HEALTH-SYSTEM PHARMACISTS
7272 Wisconsin Avenue, Bethesda MD 20814. 301/657-3000. **Toll-free phone:** 866/279-0681. **World Wide Web address:** http://www.ashp.org. **Description:** A national professional association representing pharmacists who practice in hospitals, health maintenance organizations, long-term care facilities, home care, and other components of health care systems.

NATIONAL PHARMACEUTICAL COUNCIL
1894 Preston White Drive, Reston VA 20191-5433. 703/620-6390. **Fax:** 703/476-0904. **E-mail address:** main@npcnow.com. **World Wide Web address:** http://www.npcnow.org. **Description:** Conducts research and education programs geared towards demonstrating that the appropriate use of pharmaceuticals improves both patient treatment outcomes and the cost effective delivery of overall health care services.

NATIONAL SPACE BIOMEDICAL RESEARCH INSTITUTE
One Baylor Plaza, NA-425, Houston TX 77030. 713/798-7412. **Fax:** 713/798-7413. **E-mail address:** info@www.nsbri.org. **World Wide Web address:** http://www.nsbri.org. **Description:** Conducts research into health concerns facing astronauts on long missions.

BUSINESS SERVICES & NON-SCIENTIFIC RESEARCH

AMERICAN SOCIETY OF APPRAISERS
555 Herndon Parkway, Suite 125, Herndon VA 20170. 703/478-2228. **Fax:** 703/742-8471. **E-mail address:** asainfo@appraisers.org. **World Wide Web address:** http://www.appraisers.org. **Description:** Fosters professional excellence through education, accreditation, publication and other services. Its goal is to contribute to the growth of its membership and to the appraisal profession.

EQUIPMENT LEASING ASSOCIATION OF AMERICA
4301 North Fairfax Drive, Suite 550, Arlington VA 22203-1627. 703/527-8655. **Fax:** 703/527-2649. **World Wide Web address:** http://www.elaonline.com. **Description:** Promotes and serves the general interests of the equipment leasing and finance industry.

NATIONAL ASSOCIATION OF PERSONNEL SERVICES
The Village at Banner Elk, Suite 108, P.O. Box 2128, Banner Elk NC 28604. 828/898-4929. **Fax:** 828/898-8098. **World Wide Web address:** http://www.napsweb.org. **Description**: Serves, protects, informs, and represents all facets of the personnel services industry regarding federal legislation and regulatory issues by providing education, certification, and member services which enhance the ability to conduct business with integrity and competence.

CHARITIES AND SOCIAL SERVICES

AMERICAN COUNCIL FOR THE BLIND
1155 15th Street, NW, Suite 1004, Washington DC 20005. 202/467-5081. **Fax:** 202/467-5085. **Toll-free phone:** 800/424-8666. **World Wide Web address:** http://www.acb.org. **Description:** The nation's leading membership organization of blind and visually impaired people. It was founded in 1961.

CATHOLIC CHARITIES USA
1731 King Street, Alexandria VA 22314. 703/549-1390. **Fax:** 703/549-1656. **World Wide Web address:** http://www.catholiccharitiesusa.org. **Description:** A membership association of social service networks providing social services to people in need.

NATIONAL ASSOCIATION OF SOCIAL WORKERS
750 First Street, NE, Suite 700, Washington DC 20002-4241. 202/408-8600. **E-mail address:** membership@naswdc.org. **World Wide Web address:** http://www.naswdc.org. **Description:** A membership organization comprised of professional social workers working to enhance the professional growth and development of its members, to create and maintain professional standards, and to advance sound social policies.

NATIONAL COUNCIL ON FAMILY RELATIONS
3989 Central Avenue, NE, #550, Minneapolis MN 55421. 763/781-9331. **Fax:** 763/781-9348. **Toll-free phone:** 888/781-9331. **E-mail address:** info@ncfr.org. **World Wide Web address:** http://www.ncfr.org. **Description:** Provides a forum for family researchers, educators, and practitioners to share in the development and dissemination of knowledge about families and family relationships, establishes professional standards, and works to promote family well-being.

NATIONAL FEDERATION OF THE BLIND
1800 Johnson Street, Baltimore MD 21230-4998. 410/659-9314. **Fax:** 410/685-5653. **World Wide Web address:** http://www.nfb.org. **Description:** Founded in 1940, the National Federation of the Blind (NFB) is the nation's largest membership organization of blind persons. With fifty thousand members, the NFB has affiliates in all fifty states plus Washington D.C. and Puerto Rico, and over seven hundred local chapters. As a consumer and advocacy organization, the NFB is a leading force in the blindness field today.

NATIONAL MULTIPLE SCLEROSIS SOCIETY
733 Third Avenue, New York NY 10017. **Toll-free phone:** 800/344-4867. **World Wide Web address:** http://www.nmss.org. **Description:** Provides accurate, up-to-date information to individuals with MS, their families, and healthcare providers is central to our mission.

CHEMICALS, RUBBER, AND PLASTICS

AMERICAN CHEMICAL SOCIETY
1155 Sixteenth Street, NW, Washington DC 20036. 202/872-4600. **Fax:** 202/872-6067. **Toll-free phone:** 800/227-5558. **E-mail address:** help@acs.org. **World Wide Web address:** http://www.acs.org. **Description:** A self-governed individual membership organization consisting of more than 159,000 members at all degree levels and in all fields of chemistry. The organization provides a broad range of opportunities for peer interaction and career development, regardless of professional or scientific interests. The Society was founded in 1876.

AMERICAN INSTITUTE OF CHEMICAL ENGINEERS
3 Park Avenue, New York NY 10016-5991. 212/591-8100. **Toll-free phone:** 800/242-4363. **Fax:** 212/591-8888. **E-mail address:** xpress@aiche.org. **World Wide Web address:** http://www.aiche.org. **Description:** Founded in 1908 and provides leadership in advancing the chemical engineering profession; fosters and disseminates chemical engineering knowledge, supports the professional and personal growth of its members, and applies the expertise of its members to address societal needs throughout the world.

THE ELECTROCHEMICAL SOCIETY
65 South Main Street, Building D, Pennington NJ 08534-2839. 609/737-1902. **Fax:** 609/737-2743. **World Wide Web address:** http://www.electrochem.org. **Description:** Founded in 1902, The Electrochemical Society has become the leading society for solid-state and electrochemical science and technology. ECS has 8,000 scientists and engineers in over 75 countries worldwide who hold individual membership, as well as roughly 100 corporate members.

SOCIETY OF PLASTICS ENGINEERS
14 Fairfield Drive, PO Box 403, Brookfield CT 06804-0403. 203/775-0471. **Fax:** 203/775-8490. **E-mail address:** info@4spe.org. **World Wide Web address:** http://www.4spe.org. **Description:** A 25,000-member organization promoting scientific and engineering knowledge relating to plastics. Founded in 1942.

THE SOCIETY OF THE PLASTICS INDUSTRY, INC.
1667 K Street, NW, Suite 1000, Washington DC 20006. 202/974-5200. **Fax:** 202/296-7005. **World Wide Web address:** http://www.socplas.org. **Description:** Founded in 1937, The Society of the Plastics Industry, Inc., is the trade association representing one of the largest manufacturing industries in the United States. SPI's members represent the entire plastics industry supply chain, including processors, machinery and equipment manufacturers and raw materials suppliers. The U.S. plastics industry employs 1.4 million workers and provides more than $310 billion in annual shipments.

COMMUNICATIONS:TELECOMMUNICATIONS AND BROADCASTING

ACADEMY OF TELEVISION ARTS & SCIENCES
5220 Lankershim Boulevard, North Hollywood CA 91601-3109. 818/754-2800. **Fax:** 818/761-2827. **World Wide Web address:** http://www.emmys.com. **Description:** Promotes creativity, diversity, innovation and excellence though recognition, education and leadership in the advancement of the telecommunications arts and sciences.

AMERICAN DISC JOCKEY ASSOCIATION
20118 North 67th Avenue, Suite 300-605, Glendale AZ 85308. 888/723-5776. **E-mail address:** office@adja.org. **World Wide Web address:** http://www.adja.org. **Description:** Promotes ethical behavior, industry standards and continuing education for its members.

AMERICAN WOMEN IN RADIO AND TELEVISION, INC.
8405 Greensboro Drive, Suite 800, McLean VA 22102. 703/506-3290. **Fax:** 703/506-3266. **E-mail address:** info@awrt.org. **World Wide Web address:** http://www.awrt.org. **Description:** A non-profit, professional organization of women and men who work in the electronic media and allied fields.

COMPTEL/ASCENT
1900 M Street, NW, Suite 800, Washington DC 20036. 202/296-6650. **Fax:** 202/296-7585. **World Wide Web address:** http://www.comptelascent.org. **Description:** An association representing competitive telecommunications companies in virtually every sector of the marketplace: competitive local exchange carriers, long-distance carriers of every size, wireless service providers, Internet service providers, equipment manufacturers, and software suppliers.

MEDIA COMMUNICATIONS ASSOCIATION-INTERNATIONAL
7600 Terrace Avenue, Suite 203, Middleton WI 53562. 608/827-5034. **Fax:** 608/831-5122. **E-mail address:** info@mca-i.org. **World Wide Web address:** http://www.itva.org. **Description:** A not-for-profit, member-driven organization that provides opportunities for networking, forums for education and the resources for information to media communications professionals.

NATIONAL ASSOCIATION OF BROADCASTERS
1771 N Street, NW, Washington DC 20036. 202/429-5300. **Fax:** 202/429-4199. **E-mail address:** nab@nab.org. **World Wide Web address:** http://www.nab.org. **Description:** A trade association that represents the interests of free, over-the-air radio and television broadcasters.

NATIONAL CABLE & TELECOMMUNICATIONS ASSOCIATION
1724 Massachusetts Avenue, NW, Washington DC 20036. 202/775-3550. **E-mail address:** webmaster@ncta.com. **World Wide Web address:** http://www.ncta.com. **Description:** The National Cable and Telecommunications Association is the principal trade association of the cable and telecommunications industry. Founded in 1952, NCTA's primary mission is to provide its members with a strong national presence by providing a single, unified voice on issues affecting the cable and telecommunications industry.

PROMAX & BDA
9000 West Sunset Boulevard, Suite 900, Los Angeles CA 90069. 310/788-7600.
Fax: 310/788-7616. **World Wide Web address:** http://www.promax.org.
Description: A non-profit association dedicated to advancing the role and effectiveness of promotion, marketing, and broadcast design professionals in the electronic media.

U.S. TELECOM ASSOCIATION
1401 H Street, NW, Suite 600, Washington DC 20005-2164. 202/326-7300. **Fax:** 202/326-7333. **E-mail address:** membership@usta.org. **World Wide Web address:** http://www.usta.org. **Description:** A trade association representing service providers and suppliers for the telecom industry. Member companies offer a wide range of services, including local exchange, long distance, wireless, Internet and cable television service.

COMPUTER HARDWARE, SOFTWARE, AND SERVICES

ASSOCIATION FOR COMPUTING MACHINERY
1515 Broadway, New York NY, 10036. 212/626-0500. 212/626-0500. **Toll-free phone:** 800/342-6626. **World Wide Web address:** http://www.acm.org. **Description:** A 75-000-member organization founded in 1947 to advance the skills of information technology professionals and students worldwide.

ASSOCIATION FOR MULTIMEDIA COMMUNICATIONS
PO Box 10645, Chicago IL 60610. 773/276-9320. **E-mail address:** info@amcomm.org. **World Wide Web address:** http://www.amcomm.org. **Description:** A networking and professional organization for people who create New Media, including the Web, CD-ROMs and DVDs, interactive kiosks, streaming media, and other digital forms. The association promotes understanding of technology, e-learning, and e-business.

ASSOCIATION FOR WOMEN IN COMPUTING
41 Sutter Street, Suite 1006, San Francisco CA 94104. 415/905-4663. **Fax:** 415/358-4667. **E-mail address:** info@awc-hq.org. **World Wide Web address:** http://www.awc-hq.org. **Description:** A not-for-profit, professional organization for individuals with an interest in information technology. The association is dedicated to the advancement of women in the computing fields, in business, industry, science, education, government, and the military.

BLACK DATA PROCESSING ASSOCIATES
6301 Ivy Lane, Suite 700, Greenbelt MD 20770. 301/220-2180. **Fax:** 301/220-2185. **Toll-free phone:** 800/727-BDPA. **World Wide Web address:** http://www.bdpa.org. **Description:** A member-focused organization that positions its members at the forefront of the IT industry. BDPA is committed to delivering IT excellence to our members, strategic partners, and community.

INFORMATION TECHNOLOGY ASSOCIATION OF AMERICA
1401 Wilson Boulevard, Suite 1100, Arlington VA 22209. 703/522-5055. **Fax:** 703/525-2279. **Wide Web address:** http://www.itaa.org. **Description:** A trade association representing the U.S. IT industry and providing information about its issues, association programs, publications, meetings, and seminars.

INTERNATIONAL WEBMASTER'S ASSOCIATION- HTML WRITERS GUILD
119 E. Union Street, Suite F, Pasadena CA 91030. **World Wide Web address:** http://www.hwg.org. **Description:** Provides online web design training to individuals interested in web design and development.

NETWORK PROFESSIONAL ASSOCIATION
17 South High Street, Suite 200, Columbus OH 43215. 614/221-1900. **Fax:** 614/221-1989. **E-mail address:** npa@npa.org. **World Wide Web address:** http://www.npa.org. **Description:** A non-profit association for professionals in Network Computing.

SOCIETY FOR INFORMATION MANAGEMENT
401 North Michigan Avenue, Chicago IL 60611. 312/527-6734. **E-mail address:** sim@simnet.org **World Wide Web address:** http://www.simnet.org. **Description:** With 3,000 members, SIM is a network for IT leaders including CIOs, senior IT executives, prominent academicians, consultants, and others. SIM is a community of thought leaders who share experiences and knowledge, and who explore future IT direction. Founded in 1968.

SOCIETY FOR TECHNICAL COMMUNICATION
901 North Stuart Street, Suite 904, Arlington VA 22203-1822. 703/522-4114. **Fax:** 703/522-2075. **World Wide Web address:** http://www.stc.org. **Description:** A 25,000-member organization dedicated to advancing the arts and sciences of technical communication

SOFTWARE & INFORMATION INDUSTRY ASSOCIATION
1090 Vermont Avenue, NW, Sixth Floor, Washington DC 20005-4095. 202/289-7442. **Fax:** 202/289-7097. **World Wide Web address:** http://www.siia.net. **Description:** The SIIA is the principal trade association for the software and digital content industry. SIIA provides services in government relations, business development, corporate education and intellectual property protection to leading companies.

USENIX ASSOCIATION
2560 Ninth Street, Suite 215, Berkeley CA, 94710. 510/528-8649. **Fax:** 510/548-5738. **E-mail address:** office@usenix.org. **World Wide Web address:** http://www.usenix.org. **Description:** Founded in 1975 the association fosters technical excellence and innovation, supports and disseminates practical research, provides a neutral forum for discussion of technical issues, and encourages computing outreach to the community. USENIX brings together engineers, system administrators, scientists, and technicians working on the cutting edge of the computing world.

EDUCATIONAL SERVICES

AMERICAN ASSOCIATION OF SCHOOL ADMINISTRATORS
801 North Quincy Street, Suite 700, Arlington VA 22203-1730. 703/528-0700. **Fax:** 703/841-1543. **E-mail address:** info@aasa.org. **World Wide Web address:** http://www.aasa.org. **Description:** The professional organization for more than 14,000 educational leaders in the U.S. and other countries. The association supports and develops effective school system leaders who are dedicated to the highest quality public education for all children.

AMERICAN ASSOCIATION FOR HIGHER EDUCATION
One Dupont Circle, Suite 360, Washington DC 20036-1143. 202/293-6440. **Fax:** 202/293-0073. **E-mail address:** info@aahe.org. **World Wide Web address:** http://www.aahe.org. **Description:** An independent, membership-based, nonprofit organization dedicated to building human capital for higher education.

AMERICAN FEDERATION OF TEACHERS
555 New Jersey Avenue, NW, Washington DC 20001. 202/879-4400. **E-mail address:** online@aft.org. **World Wide Web address:** http://www.aft.org. **Description:** Improves the lives of its members and their families, gives voice to their professional, economic and social aspirations, brings together members to assist and support one another and to promote democracy, human rights and freedom.

COLLEGE AND UNIVERSITY PROFESSIONAL ASSOCIATION FOR HUMAN RESOURCES
Tyson Place, 2607 Kingston Pike, Suite 250, Knoxville TN 37919. 865/637-7673. **Fax:** 865/637-7674. **World Wide Web address:** http://www.cupa.org. **Description:** Promotes the effective management and development of human resources in higher education and offers many professional development opportunities.

NATIONAL ASSOCIATION FOR COLLEGE ADMISSION COUNSELING
1631 Prince Street, Alexandria VA 22314-2818. 703/836-2222. **Fax:** 703/836-8015. **World Wide Web address:** http://www.nacac.com. **Description:** Founded in 1937, NACAC is an organization of 8,000 professionals dedicated to serving students as they make choices about pursuing postsecondary education. NACAC supports and advances the work of college admission counseling professionals.

NATIONAL ASSOCIATION OF COLLEGE AND UNIVERSITY BUSINESS OFFICERS
2501 M Street, NW, Suite 400, Washington DC 20037. 202/861-2500. **Fax:** 202/861-2583. **World Wide Web address:** http://www.nacubo.org. **Description:** A nonprofit professional organization representing chief administrative and financial officers at more than 2,100 colleges and universities across the country.

NATIONAL SCIENCE TEACHERS ASSOCIATION
1840 Wilson Boulevard, Arlington VA 22201-3000. 703/243-7100. **World Wide Web address:** http://www.nsta.org. **Description:** Promotes excellence and innovation in science teaching and learning.

ELECTRONIC/INDUSTRIAL ELECTRICAL EQUIPMENT AND COMPONENTS

AMERICAN CERAMIC SOCIETY
P.O. Box 6136, Westerville OH 43086-6136. 614/890-4700. **Fax:** 614/899-6109. **E-mail address:** info@ceramics.org. **World Wide Web address:** http://www.acers.org. **Description:** Provides technical, scientific and educational information to its members and others in the ceramics and related materials field, structures its services, staff and capabilities to meet the needs of the ceramics community, related fields, and the general public.

ELECTRONIC INDUSTRIES ALLIANCE
2500 Wilson Boulevard, Arlington VA 22201. 703/907-7500. **World Wide Web address:** http://www.eia.org. **Description:** A national trade organization including 2,500 U.S. manufacturers. The Alliance is a partnership of electronic and high-tech associations and companies whose mission is promoting the market development and competitiveness of the U.S. high-tech industry through domestic and international policy efforts.

ELECTRONICS TECHNICIANS ASSOCIATION, INTERNATIONAL
5 Depot Street, Greencastle IN 46135. 765/653-8262. **Fax:** 765/653-4287. **Toll-free phone:** 800/288-3824. **E-mail address:** eta@tds.net. **World Wide Web address:** http://www.eta-sda.org. **Description:** A not-for-profit, worldwide professional association founded by electronics technicians and servicing dealers in 1978. Provides professional credentials based on an individual's skills and knowledge in a particular area of study.

FABLESS SEMICONDUCTOR ASSOCIATION
Three Lincoln Center, 5430 LBJ Freeway, Suite 280, Dallas TX 75240. 972/866-7579. **Fax:** 972/239-2292. **World Wide Web address:** http://www.fsa.org. **Description:** An industry organization aimed at achieving an optimal balance between wafer supply and demand.

INSTITUTE OF ELECTRICAL AND ELECTRONICS ENGINEER (IEEE)
3 Park Avenue, 17th Floor, New York NY 10016-5997. 212/419-7900. **Fax:** 212/752-4929. **E-mail address:** ieeeusa@ieee.org. **World Wide Web address:** http://www.ieee.org. **Description:** Advances the theory and application of electrotechnology and allied sciences, serves as a catalyst for technological innovation and supports the needs of its members through a wide variety of programs and services.

INTERNATIONAL SOCIETY OF CERTIFIED ELECTRONICS TECHNICIANS
3608 Pershing Avenue, Fort Worth TX 76107-4527. 817/921-9101. **Fax:** 817/921-3741 **Toll-free phone:** 800/946-0201 **E-mail address:** info@iscet.org **World Wide Web address:** http://www.iscet.org. **Description:** Prepares and tests technicians in the electronics and appliance service industry. Designed to measure the degree of theoretical knowledge and technical proficiency of practicing technicians.

NATIONAL ELECTRONICS SERVICE DEALERS ASSOCIATION
3608 Pershing Avenue, Fort Worth TX 76107-4527. 817/921-9061. **Fax:** 817/921-3741. **World Wide Web address:** http://www.nesda.com. **Description:** A trade organization for professionals in the business of repairing consumer electronic equipment, appliances, or computers.

ENVIRONMENTAL & WASTE MANAGEMENT SERVICES

AIR & WASTE MANAGEMENT ASSOCIATION
One Gateway Center, 3rd Floor, 420 Fort Duquesne Boulevard, Pittsburgh PA 15222-1435. 412/232-3444. **Fax:** 412/232-3450. **E-mail address:** info@awma.org. **World Wide Web address:** http://www.awma.org. **Description:** A nonprofit, nonpartisan professional organization providing training, information, and networking opportunities to thousands of environmental professionals in 65 countries.

AMERICAN ACADEMY OF ENVIRONMENTAL ENGINEERS
130 Holiday Court, Suite 100, Annapolis MD 21401. 410/266-3311. **Fax:** 410/266-7653. **World Wide Web address:** http://www.aaee.net. **Description:** AAEE was founded in 1955 for the principal purpose of serving the public by improving the practice, elevating the standards, and advancing public recognition of environmental engineering through a program of specialty certification of qualified engineers.

INSTITUTE OF CLEAN AIR COMPANIES
1660 L Street, NW, Suite 1100, Washington DC 20036. 202/457-0911. **Fax:** 202/331-1388. **World Wide Web address:** http://www.icac.com. **Description:** The nonprofit national association of companies that supply air pollution monitoring and control systems, equipment, and services for stationary sources.

NATIONAL SOLID WASTES MANAGEMENT ASSOCIATION
4301 Connecticut Avenue, NW, Suite 300, Washington DC 20008-2304. 202/244-4700. **Fax:** 202/364-3792. **Toll-free phone:** 800/424-2869. **World Wide Web address:** http://www.nswma.org. **Description:** A non-profit, trade association that represents the interests of the North American waste services industry.

WATER ENVIRONMENT FEDERATION
601 Wythe Street, Alexandria VA 22314-1994. 703/684-2452. **Fax:** 703/684-2492. **Toll-free phone:** 800/666-0206. **World Wide Web address:** http://www.wef.org. **Description:** A not-for-profit technical and educational organization, founded in 1928, with members from varied disciplines. The federation's mission is to preserve and enhance the global water environment. The WEF network includes water quality professionals from 79 Member Associations in over 30 countries.

FABRICATED METAL PRODUCTS AND PRIMARY METALS

ASM INTERNATIONAL: THE MATERIALS INFORMATION SOCIETY
9639 Kinsman Road, Materials Park OH 44073-0002. 440/338-5151. **Fax:** 440/338-4634. **Toll-free phone:** 800/336-5152. **E-mail address:** cust-srv@asminternational.org. **World Wide Web address:** http://www.asm-intl.org. **Description:** An organization for materials engineers and scientists, dedicated to advancing industry, technology and applications of metals and materials.

AMERICAN FOUNDRYMEN'S SOCIETY
1695 Penny Lane, Schaumburg IL 60173-4555. 847/824-0181. **Fax:** 847/824-7848. **Toll-free phone:** 800/537-4237. **World Wide Web address:** http://www.afsinc.org. **Description:** An international organization dedicated to provide and promote knowledge and services that strengthen the metalcasting industry. AFS was founded in 1896 and has approximately 10,000 members in 47 countries.

AMERICAN WELDING SOCIETY
550 NW LeJeune Road, Miami FL 33126. 305/443-9353. **Toll-free phone:** 800/443-9353. **E-mail address:** info@aws.org. **World Wide Web address:** http://www.aws.org. **Description:** Founded in 1919 as a multifaceted, nonprofit organization with a goal to advance the science, technology and application of welding and related joining disciplines.

FINANCIAL SERVICES

THE BOND MARKET ASSOCIATION
360 Madison Avenue, New York NY 10017-7111. 646/637-9200. **Fax:** 646/637-9126. **World Wide Web address:** http://www.bondmarkets.com. **Description:** The trade association representing the largest securities markets in the world. The Association speaks for the bond industry, advocating its positions and representing its interests in New York; Washington, D.C.; London; Frankfurt; Brussels and Tokyo; and with issuer and investor groups worldwide. The Association represents a diverse mix of securities firms and banks, whether they are large, multi-product firms or companies with special market niches.

FINANCIAL EXECUTIVES INSTITUTE
200 Campus Drive, PO Box 674, Florham Park NJ 07932-0674. 973/765-1000. **Fax:** 973/765-1018. **E-mail address:** conf@fei.org. **World Wide Web address:** http://www.fei.org. **Description:** An association for financial executives working to alert members to emerging issues, develop the professional and management skills of members, provide forums for peer networking, advocate the views of financial executives, and promote ethical conduct.

NATIONAL ASSOCIATION FOR BUSINESS ECONOMICS
1233 20th Street, NW, #505, Washington DC 20036. 202/463-6223. **Fax:** 202/463-6239. **E-mail address:** nabe@nabe.com. **World Wide Web address:** http://www.nabe.com. **Description:** An association of professionals who have an interest in business economics and who want to use the latest economic data and trends to enhance their ability to make sound business decisions. Founded in 1959.

NATIONAL ASSOCIATION OF CREDIT MANAGEMENT
8840 Columbia 100 Parkway, Columbia MD 21045. 410/740-5560. **Fax:** 410/740-5574. **E-mail address:** nacm_info@nacm.org. **World Wide Web address:** http://www.nacm.org. **Description:** Founded in 1896 to promote good laws for sound credit, protect businesses against fraudulent debtors, improve the interchange of credit information, develop better credit practices and methods, and establish a code of ethics.

NATIONAL ASSOCIATION OF REAL ESTATE INVESTMENT TRUSTS
1875 Eye Street, NW, Washington DC 20006. 202/739-9400. **Fax:** 202/739-9401. **E-mail address:** info@nareit.org. **World Wide Web address:** http://www.nareit.com. **Description:** NAREIT is the national trade association for REITs and publicly traded real estate companies. Members are real estate investment trusts (REITs) and other businesses that own, operate and finance income-producing real estate, as well as those firms and individuals who advise, study and service these businesses.

SECURITIES INDUSTRY ASSOCIATION
120 Broadway, 35th Floor, New York NY 10271-0080. 212/608-1500. **Fax:** 212/968-0703. **E-mail address:** info@sia.com. **World Wide Web address:** http://www.sia.com. **Description:** The Securities Industry Association (SIA) was established in 1972 through the merger of the Association of Stock Exchange Firms (1913) and the Investment Banker's Association (1912). The Securities Industry Association brings together the shared interests of more than 600 securities firms to accomplish common goals. SIA member-firms (including

investment banks, broker-dealers, and mutual fund companies) are active in all U.S. and foreign markets and in all phases of corporate and public finance.

WOMEN'S INSTITUTE OF FINANCIAL EDUCATION
PO Box 910014, San Diego CA 92191. 760/736-1660. **E-mail address:** info@wife.org. **World Wide Web address:** http://www.wife.org. **Description:** A non-profit organization dedicated to providing financial education to women in their quest for financial independence.

FOOD AND BEVERAGES/AGRICULTURE

AMERICAN ASSOCIATION OF CEREAL CHEMISTS (AACC)
3340 Pilot Knob Road, St. Paul MN 55121-2097. 651/454-7250. **Fax:** 651/454-0766. **World Wide Web address:** http://www.aaccnet.org. **Description:** A non-profit international organization of nearly 4,000 members who are specialists in the use of cereal grains in foods. The association gathers and disseminates scientific and technical information to professionals in the grain-based foods industry worldwide for over 85 years.

AMERICAN BEVERAGE ASSOCIATION
1101 16th Street, NW, Washington DC 20036. 202/463-6732. **Fax:** 202/659-5349. **World Wide Web address:** http://www.ameribev.org. **Description:** An association for America's non-alcoholic beverage industry, serving the public and its members for more than 75 years.

AMERICAN FROZEN FOOD INSTITUTE
2000 Corporate Ridge, Suite 1000, McLean VA 22102. 703/821-0770. **Fax:** 703/821-1350. **E-mail address:** info@affi.com. **World Wide Web address:** http://www.affi.com. **Description:** A national trade association representing all aspects of the frozen food industry supply chain, from manufacturers to distributors to suppliers to packagers; the Institute is industry's voice on issues crucial to future growth and progress.

AMERICAN SOCIETY OF AGRICULTURAL ENGINEERS
2950 Niles Road, St. Joseph MI 49085. 269/429-0300. **Fax:** 269/429-3852. **World Wide Web address:** http://www.asae.org. **Description:** An educational and scientific organization dedicated to the advancement of engineering applicable to agricultural, food, and biological systems.

AMERICAN SOCIETY OF BREWING CHEMISTS
3340 Pilot Knob Road, St. Paul MN 55121-2097. 651/454-7250. **Fax:** 651/454-0766. **World Wide Web address:** http://www.asbcnet.org. **Description:** Founded in 1934 to improve and bring uniformity to the brewing industry on a technical level.

CIES – THE FOOD BUSINESS FORUM
8455 Colesville Road, Suite 705, Silver Spring MD 20910. 301/563-3383. **Fax:** 301/563-3386. **E-mail address:** us.office@ciesnet.com. **World Wide Web address:** http://www.ciesnet.com. **Description:** An independent global food business network. Membership in CIES is on a company basis and includes more than two thirds of the world's largest food retailers and their suppliers.

CROPLIFE AMERICA
1156 15th Street, NW, Suite 400, Washington DC 20005. 202/296-1585. **Fax:** 202/463-0474. **World Wide Web address:** http://www.croplifeamerica.org. **Description:** Fosters the interests of the general public and member companies by promoting innovation and the environmentally sound manufacture, distribution, and use of crop protection and production technologies for safe, high-quality, affordable and abundant food, fiber and other crops.

INTERNATIONAL DAIRY FOODS ASSOCIATION
1250 H Street, NW, Suite 900, Washington DC 20005. 202/737-4332. **Fax:** 202/331-7820. **E-mail address:** membership@idfa.org. **World Wide Web**

address: http://www.idfa.org. **Description:** IDFA represents more than 500 dairy food manufacturers, marketers, distributors and industry suppliers in the U.S. and 20 other countries, and encourages the formation of favorable domestic and international dairy policies.

NATIONAL BEER WHOLESALERS' ASSOCIATION

1101 King Street, Suite 600, Alexandria VA 22314-2944. 703/683-4300. **Fax:** 703/683-8965. **E-mail address:** info@nbwa.org. **World Wide Web address:** http://www.nbwa.org. **Description:** Founded in 1938 as a trade association for the nations' beer wholesalers. NBWA provides leadership which enhances the independent malt beverage wholesale industry; advocates before government and the public on behalf of its members; encourages the responsible consumption of beer; and provides programs and services that will enhance members' efficiency and effectiveness.

NATIONAL FOOD PROCESSORS ASSOCIATION

1350 I Street, NW, Suite 300, Washington DC 20005. 202/639.5900. **E-mail address:** nfpa@nfpa-food.org. **World Wide Web address:** http://www.nfpa-food.org. **Description:** NFPA is the voice of the $500 billion food processing industry on scientific and public policy issues involving food safety, nutrition, technical and regulatory matters and consumer affairs.

HEALTH CARE SERVICES, EQUIPMENT, AND PRODUCTS

ACCREDITING COMMISSION ON EDUCATION FOR HEALTH SERVICES ADMINISTRATION
2000 14th Street North, Arlington VA 22201. 703/894-0960. **Fax:** 703/894-0941. **World Wide Web address:** http://www.acehsa.org. **Description:** An association of educational, professional, clinical, and commercial organizations devoted to accountability and quality improvement in the education of health care management and administration professionals.

AMERICAN ACADEMY OF ALLERGY, ASTHMA, AND IMMUNOLOGY
555 East Wells Street, Suite 1100, Milwaukee WI 53202-3823. 414/272-6071. **E-mail address:** info@aaaai.org. **World Wide Web address:** http://www.aaaai.org. **Description:** A professional medical specialty organization representing allergists, asthma specialists, clinical immunologists, allied health professionals, and other physicians with a special interest in allergy. Established in 1943.

AMERICAN ACADEMY OF FAMILY PHYSICIANS
11400 Tomahawk Creek Parkway, Leawood KS 66211-2672. 913/906-6000. **Toll-free phone:** 800/274-2237. **E-mail address:** fp@aafp.org. **World Wide Web address:** http://www.aafp.org. **Description:** Founded in 1947, the Academy represents family physicians, family practice residents and medical students nationwide. AAFP's mission is to preserve and promote the science and art of family medicine and to ensure high quality, cost-effective health care for patients of all ages.

AMERICAN ACADEMY OF PEDIATRIC DENTISTRY
211 East Chicago Avenue, Suite 700, Chicago IL 60611-2663. 312/337-2169. **Fax:** 312/337-6329. **World Wide Web address:** http://www.aapd.org. **Description:** A membership organization representing the specialty of pediatric dentistry.

AMERICAN ACADEMY OF PERIODONTOLOGY
737 North Michigan Avenue, Suite 800, Chicago IL 60611-2690. 312/787-5518. **Fax:** 312/787-3670. **World Wide Web address:** http://www.perio.org. **Description:** A 7,900-member association of dental professionals specializing in the prevention, diagnosis and treatment of diseases affecting the gums and supporting structures of the teeth and in the placement and maintenance of dental implants. The Academy's purpose is to advocate, educate, and set standards for advancing the periodontal and general health of the public and promoting excellence in the practice of periodontics.

AMERICAN ACADEMY OF PHYSICIANS ASSISTANTS
950 North Washington Street, Alexandria VA 22314-1552. 703/836-2272. **Fax:** 703/684-1924. **E-mail address:** aapa@aapa.org. **World Wide Web address:** http://www.aapa.org. **Description:** Promotes quality, cost-effective, accessible health care, and the professional and personal development of physician assistants.

AMERICAN ASSOCIATION FOR CLINICAL CHEMISTRY
2101 L Street, NW, Suite 202, Washington DC 20037-1558. 202/857-0717. **Fax:** 202/887-5093. **Toll-free phone:** 800/892-1400. **World Wide Web address:**

http://www.aacc.org. **Description:** Founded in 1948 as an international scientific/medical society of clinical laboratory professionals, physicians, research scientists and other individuals involved with clinical chemistry and other clinical laboratory science-related disciplines. The society has 10,000 members.

AMERICAN ASSOCIATION FOR ORAL AND MAXILLOFACIAL SURGEONS
9700 West Bryn Mawr Avenue, Rosemont IL 60018-5701. 847/678-6200. **E-mail address:** inquiries@aaoms.org. **World Wide Web address:** http://www.aaoms.org. **Description:** The American Association of Oral and Maxillofacial Surgeons (AAOMS), is a not-for-profit professional association serving the professional and public needs of the specialty of oral and maxillofacial surgery.

AMERICAN ASSOCIATION FOR RESPIRATORY CARE
9425 North MacArthur Boulevard, Suite 100, Irving TX 75063-4706. 972/243-2272. **Fax:** 972/484-2720. **E-mail address:** info@aarc.org. **World Wide Web address:** http://www.aarc.org. **Description:** Advances the science, technology, ethics, and art of respiratory care through research and education for its members and teaches the general public about pulmonary health and disease prevention.

AMERICAN ASSOCIATION OF COLLEGES OF OSTEOPATHIC MEDICINE
5550 Friendship Boulevard, Suite 310, Chevy Chase MD 20815-7231. 301/968-4100. **Fax:** 301/968-4101. **World Wide Web address:** http://www.aacom.org. **Description:** Promotes excellence in osteopathic medical education throughout the educational continuum, in research and in service; to enhance the strength and quality of the member colleges; and to improve the health of the American public.

AMERICAN ASSOCIATION OF COLLEGES OF PODIATRIC MEDICINE
15850 Crabbs Branch Way, Suite 320, Rockville MD 20855. **Fax:** 301/948-1928. **Toll-free phone:** 800/922-9266. **E-mail address:** aacpmas@aacpm.org. **World Wide Web address:** http://www.aacpm.org. **Description:** An organization advancing podiatric medicine and its education system.

AMERICAN ASSOCIATION OF HEALTHCARE CONSULTANTS
5938 North Drake Avenue, Chicago IL 60659. **Fax:** 773/463-3552. **Toll-free phone:** 888/350-2242. **E-mail address:** info@aahc.net. **World Wide Web address:** http://www.aahc.net. **Description:** Founded in 1949 as the professional membership society for leading healthcare consultants and consulting firms.

AMERICAN ASSOCIATION OF HOMES AND SERVICES FOR THE AGING
2519 Connecticut Avenue, NW, Washington DC 20008. 202/783.2242. **Fax:** 202/783-2255. **World Wide Web address:** http://www.aahsa.org. **Description:** The American Association of Homes and Services for the Aging (AAHSA) is committed to advancing the vision of healthy, affordable, ethical aging services for America. The association represents 5,600 not-for-profit nursing homes, continuing care retirement communities, assisted living and senior housing facilities, and home and community-based service providers.

AMERICAN ASSOCIATION OF MEDICAL ASSISTANTS
20 North Wacker Drive, Suite 1575, Chicago IL 60606. 312/899-1500. **World Wide Web address:** http://www.aama-ntl.org. **Description:** The mission of the American Association of Medical Assistants is to enable medical assisting professionals to enhance and demonstrate the knowledge, skills and

professionalism required by employers and patients; protect medical assistants' right to practice; and promote effective, efficient health care delivery through optimal use of multiskilled Certified Medical Assistants (CMAs).

AMERICAN ASSOCIATION OF NURSE ANESTHETISTS
222 South Prospect Avenue, Park Ridge IL 60068. 847/692-7050. **World Wide Web address:** http://www.aana.com. **Description:** Founded in 1931 as the professional association representing more than 30,000 Certified Registered Nurse Anesthetists (CRNAs) nationwide. The AANA promulgates education, and practice standards and guidelines, and affords consultation to both private and governmental entities regarding nurse anesthetists and their practice.

AMERICAN CHIROPRACTIC ASSOCIATION
1701 Clarendon Boulevard, Arlington VA 22209. **Fax:** 703/243-2593. **Toll-free phone:** 800/986-4636. **E-mail address:** memberinfo@amerchiro.org. **World Wide Web address:** http://www.americhiro.org. **Description:** A professional association representing doctors of chiropractic that provides lobbying, public relations, professional and educational opportunities for doctors of chiropractic, funds research regarding chiropractic and health issues, and offers leadership for the advancement of the profession.

AMERICAN COLLEGE OF HEALTH CARE ADMINISTRATORS
300 North Lee Street, Suite 301, Alexandria VA 22314. 703/739-7900. **Fax:** 703/739-7901. **Toll-free phone:** 888/882-2422. **E-mail address:** membership@achca.org. **World Wide Web address:** http://www.achca.org. **Description:** A non-profit membership organization that provides educational programming, certification in a variety of positions, and career development for its members. Founded in 1962.

AMERICAN COLLEGE OF HEALTHCARE EXECUTIVES
One North Franklin Street, Suite 1700, Chicago IL 60606-4425. 312/424-2800. **Fax:** 312/424-0023. **World Wide Web address:** http://www.ache.org. **Description:** An international professional society of nearly 30,000 healthcare executives who lead our nation's hospitals, healthcare systems, and other healthcare organizations.

AMERICAN COLLEGE OF MEDICAL PRACTICE EXECUTIVES
104 Inverness Terrace East, Englewood CO 80112-5306. 303/799-1111. **Fax:** 303/643-4439. **Toll-free phone:** 877/275-6462. **E-mail address:** acmpe@mgma.com. **World Wide Web address:** http://www.mgma.com/acmpe. **Description:** Established in 1956, the ACMPE offers board certification, self-assessment and leadership development for medical practice executives.

AMERICAN COLLEGE OF OBSTETRICIANS AND GYNECOLOGISTS
409 12th Street, SW, PO Box 96920, Washington DC 20090-6920. **World Wide Web address:** http://www.acog.org. **Description:** Founded in 1951, the 46,000-member organization is the nation's leading group of professionals providing health care for women.

AMERICAN COLLEGE OF PHYSICIAN EXECUTIVES
4890 West Kennedy Boulevard, Suite 200, Tampa FL 33609. 813/287-2000. **Fax:** 813/287-8993. **Toll-free phone:** 800/562-8088. **E-mail address:** acpe@acpe.org. **World Wide Web address:** http://www.acpe.org. **Description:** A specialty society representing physicians in health care leadership. Provides educational and career development programs.

AMERICAN DENTAL ASSOCIATION
211 East Chicago Avenue, Chicago IL 60611-2678. 312/440-2500. **World Wide Web address:** http://www.ada.org. **Description:** A dental association serving both public and private physicians. Founded in 1859.

AMERICAN DENTAL EDUCATION ASSOCIATION
1400 K Street, NW Suite 1100, Washington DC 20005. 202/289-7201. **Fax:** 202/289-7204. **World Wide Web address:** http://www.adea.org. **Description:** A national organization for dental education. Members include all U.S. and Canadian dental schools, advanced dental education programs, hospital dental education programs, allied dental education programs, corporations, faculty, and students.

AMERICAN DENTAL HYGIENISTS ASSOCIATION
444 North Michigan Avenue, Suite 3400, Chicago IL 60611. 312/440-8900. **E-mail address:** mail@adha.net. **World Wide Web address:** http://www.adha.org. **Description:** Founded in 1923, the association develops communication and mutual cooperation among dental hygienists and represents the professional interests of the more than 120,000 registered dental hygienists (RDHs) in the United States.

AMERICAN HEALTH INFORMATION MANAGEMENT ASSOCIATION
233 North Michigan Avenue, Suite 2150, Chicago IL 60601-5800. 312/233-1100. **Fax:** 312/233-1090. **E-mail address:** info@ahima.org. **World Wide Web address:** http://www.ahima.org. **Description:** Represents more than 46,000 specially educated health information management professionals who work throughout the healthcare industry. Health information management professionals serve the healthcare industry and the public by managing, analyzing, and utilizing data vital for patient care -- and making it accessible to healthcare providers when it is needed most.

AMERICAN HOSPITAL ASSOCIATION
One North Franklin, Chicago IL 60606-3421. 312/422-3000. **Fax:** 312/422-4796. **World Wide Web address:** http://www.aha.org. **Description:** A national organization that represents and serves all types of hospitals, health care networks, and their patients and communities. Approximately 5,000 institutional, 600 associate, and 27,000 personal members belong to the AHA.

AMERICAN MEDICAL ASSOCIATION
515 North State Street, Chicago IL 60610. **Toll-free phone:** 800/621-8335. **World Wide Web address:** http://www.ama-assn.org. **Description:** American Medical Association speaks out on issues important to patients and the nation's health. AMA policy on such issues is decided through its democratic policy-making process, in the AMA House of Delegates, which meets twice a year.

AMERICAN MEDICAL INFORMATICS ASSOCIATION
4915 St. Elmo Avenue, Suite 401, Bethesda MD 20814. 301/657-1291. **Fax:** 301/657-1296. **World Wide Web address:** http://www.amia.org. **Description:** The American Medical Informatics Association is a nonprofit membership organization of individuals, institutions, and corporations dedicated to developing and using information technologies to improve health care. Founded in 1990.

AMERICAN MEDICAL TECHNOLOGISTS
710 Higgins Road, Park Ridge IL 60068. 847/823-5169. **Fax:** 847/823-0458. **Toll-free phone:** 800/275-1268. **World Wide Web address:** http://www.amt1.com. **Description:** A nonprofit certification agency and

professional membership association representing nearly 27,000 individuals in allied health care. Provides allied health professionals with professional certification services and membership programs to enhance their professional and personal growth.

AMERICAN MEDICAL WOMEN'S ASSOCIATION
801 North Fairfax Street, Suite 400, Alexandria VA 22314. 703/838-0500. **Fax:** 703/549-3864. **E-mail address:** info@amwa-doc.org. **World Wide Web address:** http://www.amwa-doc.org. **Description:** An organization of 10,000 women physicians and medical students dedicated to serving as the unique voice for women's health and the advancement of women in medicine.

AMERICAN NURSES ASSOCIATION
8515 Georgia Avenue, Suite 400 West, Silver Spring MD 20910. 301/628-5000. **Fax:** 301//628-5001. **Toll-free phone:** 800/274-4ANA. **World Wide Web address:** http://www.nursingworld.org. **Description:** A professional organization representing the nation's 2.6 million Registered Nurses through its 54 constituent state associations and 13 organizational affiliate members. Fosters high standards of nursing practice, promotes the economic and general welfare of nurses in the workplace, projects a positive and realistic view of nursing, and by lobbies Congress and regulatory agencies on health care issues affecting nurses and the public.

AMERICAN OCCUPATIONAL THERAPY ASSOCIATION
4720 Montgomery Lane, PO Box 31220, Bethesda MD 20824-1220. 301/652-2682. **Fax:** 301/652-7711. **Toll-free phone:** 800/377- 8555. **World Wide Web address:** http://www.aota.org. **Description:** A professional association of approximately 40,000 occupational therapists, occupational therapy assistants, and students of occupational therapy.

AMERICAN OPTOMETRIC ASSOCIATION
243 North Lindbergh Boulevard, St. Louis MO 63141. 314/991-4100. **Fax:** 314/991-4101. **World Wide Web address:** http://www.aoanet.org. **Description:** The American Optometric Association is the acknowledged leader and recognized authority for primary eye and vision care in the world.

AMERICAN ORGANIZATION OF NURSE EXECUTIVES
325 Seventh Street, NW, Washington DC 20004. 202/626-2240. **Fax:** 202/638-5499. **E-mail address:** aone@aha.org. **World Wide Web address:** http://www.aone.org. **Description:** Founded in 1967, the American Organization of Nurse Executives (AONE), a subsidiary of the American Hospital Association, is a national organization of nearly 4,000 nurses who design, facilitate, and manage care. Its mission is to represent nurse leaders who improve healthcare.

AMERICAN ORTHOPAEDIC ASSOCIATION
6300 North River Road, Suite 505, Rosemont IL 60018-4263. 847/318-7330. **Fax:** 847/318-7339. **E-mail address:** info@aoassn.org **World Wide Web address:** http://www.aoassn.org. **Description:** Founded in 1887, The American Orthopaedic Association is the oldest orthopaedic association in the world.

AMERICAN PHYSICAL THERAPY ASSOCIATION
1111 North Fairfax Street, Alexandria VA 22314-1488. 703/684-2782. **Fax:** 703/684-7343. **Toll-free phone:** 800/999-2782. **World Wide Web address:** http://www.apta.org. **Description:** The American Physical Therapy Association (APTA) is a national professional organization representing more than 63,000

members. Its goal is to foster advancements in physical therapy practice, research, and education.

AMERICAN PODIATRIC MEDICAL ASSOCIATION
9312 Old Georgetown Road, Bethesda MD 20814. 301/571-9200. **Fax:** 301/530-2752. **Toll-free phone:** 800/FOOTCARE. **World Wide Web address:** http://www.apma.org. **Description:** The American Podiatric Medical Association is the premier professional organization representing the nation's Doctors of Podiatric Medicine (podiatrists). The APMA represents approximately 80 percent of the podiatrists in the country. APMA includes 53 component societies in states and other jurisdictions, as well as 22 affiliated and related societies.

AMERICAN PSYCHIATRIC ASSOCIATION
1000 Wilson Boulevard, Suite 1825, Arlington VA.22209-3901. 703/907-7300. **E-mail address:** apa@psych.org **World Wide Web address:** http://www.psych.org. **Description:** With 35,000 members, the American Psychiatric Association is a medical specialty society recognized worldwide.

AMERICAN PUBLIC HEALTH ASSOCIATION
800 I Street, NW, Washington DC 20001. 202/777-2742. **Fax:** 202/777-2534. **E-mail address:** comments@apha.org. **World Wide Web address:** http://www.apha.org. **Description:** The American Public Health Association (APHA) is the oldest and largest organization of public health professionals in the world, representing more than 50,000 members from over 50 occupations of public health.

AMERICAN SOCIETY OF ANESTHESIOLOGISTS
520 N. Northwest Highway, Park Ridge IL 60068-2573. 847/825-5586. **Fax:** 847/825-1692. **E-mail address:** mail@asahq.org. **World Wide Web address:** http://www.asahq.org. **Description:** An educational, research and scientific association of physicians organized to raise and maintain the standards of the medical practice of anesthesiology and improve the care of the patient. Founded in 1905.

AMERICAN SPEECH-LANGUAGE-HEARING ASSOCIATION
10801 Rockville Pike, Rockville MD 20852-3226. **Toll-free phone:** 800/638-8255. **E-mail address:** actioncenter@asha.org. **World Wide Web address:** http://www.asha.org. **Description:** The professional, scientific, and credentialing association for more than 110,000 audiologists, speech-language pathologists, and speech, language, and hearing scientists with a mission to ensure that all people with speech, language, and hearing disorders have access to quality services to help them communicate more effectively.

AMERICAN VETERINARY MEDICAL ASSOCIATION
1931 North Meacham Road, Suite 100, Schaumburg IL 60173. 847/925-8070. **Fax:** 847/925-1329. **E-mail address:** avmainfo@avma.org. **World Wide Web address:** http://www.avma.org. **Description:** A not-for-profit association founded in 1863 representing more than 69,000 veterinarians working in private and corporate practice, government, industry, academia, and uniformed services.

ASSOCIATION OF AMERICAN MEDICAL COLLEGES
2450 N Street, NW, Washington DC 20037-1126. 202/828-0400. **Fax:** 202/828-1125. **World Wide Web address:** http://www.aamc.org. **Description:** A non-profit association founded in 1876 to work for reform in medical education. The association represents the nation's 126 accredited medical schools, nearly 400

major teaching hospitals, more than 105,000 faculty in 96 academic and scientific societies, and the nation's 66,000 medical students and 97,000 residents.

ASSOCIATION OF UNIVERSITY PROGRAMS IN HEALTH ADMINISTRATION
2000 North 14th Street, Suite 780, Arlington VA 22201. 703/894-0940. **Fax:** 703/894-0941. **E-mail address:** aupha@aupha.org. **World Wide Web address:** http://www.aupha.org. **Description:** A not-for-profit association of university-based educational programs, faculty, practitioners, and provider organizations. Its members are dedicated to continuously improving the field of health management and practice. It is the only non-profit entity of its kind that works to improve the delivery of health services throughout the world - and thus the health of citizens - by educating professional managers.

HEALTH INFORMATION AND MANAGEMENT SYSTEMS SOCIETY
230 East Ohio Street, Suite 500, Chicago IL 60611-3269. 312/664-4467. **Fax:** 312/664-6143. **World Wide Web address:** http://www.himss.org. **Description:** Founded in 1961 and provides leadership for the optimal use of healthcare information technology and management systems for the betterment of human health.

HEALTHCARE FINANCIAL MANAGEMENT ASSOCIATION
2 Westbrook Corporate Center, Suite 700, Westchester IL 60154-5700. 708/531-9600. **Fax:** 708/531-0032. **Toll-free phone:** 800/252-4362. **World Wide Web address:** http://www.hfma.org. **Description:** A membership organization for healthcare financial management professionals with 32,000 members.

NATIONAL ASSOCIATION FOR CHIROPRACTIC MEDICINE
15427 Baybrook Drive, Houston TX 77062. 281/280-8262. **Fax:** 281/280-8262. **World Wide Web address:** http://www.chiromed.org. **Description:** A consumer advocacy association of chiropractors striving to make legitimate the utilization of professional manipulative procedures in mainstream health care delivery.

NATIONAL MEDICAL ASSOCIATION
1012 Tenth Street, NW, Washington DC 20001. 202/347-1895. **Fax:** 202/898-2510. **World Wide Web address:** http://www.nmanet.org. **Description:** Promotes the collective interests of physicians and patients of African descent with a mission to serve as the collective voice of physicians of African descent and a leading force for parity in medicine, elimination of health disparities and promotion of optimal health.

HOTELS AND RESTAURANTS

AMERICAN HOTEL AND LODGING ASSOCIATION
1201 New York Avenue, NW, #600, Washington DC 20005-3931. 202/289-3100.
Fax: 202/289-3199. **World Wide Web address:** http://www.ahla.com.
Description: Provides its members with assistance in operations, education, and communications, and lobbies on Capitol Hill to provide a business climate in which the industry can continue to prosper. Individual state associations provide representation at the state level and offer many additional cost-saving benefits.

THE EDUCATIONAL FOUNDATION OF THE NATIONAL RESTAURANT ASSOCIATION
175 West Jackson Boulevard, Suite 1500, Chicago IL 60604-2702. 312/715-1010. **Toll-free phone:** 800/765-2122. **E-mail address:** info@nraef.org. **World Wide Web address:** http://www.nraef.org. **Description:** A not-for-profit organization dedicated to fulfilling the educational mission of the National Restaurant Association. Focusing on three key strategies of risk management, recruitment, and retention, the NRAEF is the premier provider of educational resources, materials, and programs, which address attracting, developing and retaining the industry's workforce.

NATIONAL RESTAURANT ASSOCIATION
1200 17th Street, NW, Washington DC 20036. 202/331-5900. 202/331-5900. **Fax:** 202/331-2429. **Toll-free phone:** 800/424-5156. **World Wide Web address:** http://www.restaurant.org. **Description:** Founded in 1919 as a business association for the restaurant industry with a mission to represent, educate and promote a rapidly growing industry that is comprised of 878,000 restaurant and foodservice outlets employing 12 million people.

INSURANCE

AMERICA'S HEALTH INSURANCE PLANS
601 Pennsylvania Avenue, NW, SOuth Building, Suite 500, Washington DC 20004. 202/778-3200. **Fax:** 202/331-7487. **World Wide Web address:** http://www.ahip.org. **Description:** A national association representing nearly 1,300 member companies providing health insurance coverage to more than 200 million Americans.

INSURANCE INFORMATION INSTITUTE
110 William Street, New York NY 10038. 212/346-5500. **World Wide Web address:** http://www.iii.org. **Description:** Provides definitive insurance information. Recognized by the media, governments, regulatory organizations, universities and the public as a primary source of information, analysis and referral concerning insurance.

NATIONAL ASSOCIATION OF PROFESSIONAL INSURANCE AGENTS
400 North Washington Street, Alexandria VA 22314. 703/836-9340. **Fax:** 703/836-1279. **E-mail address:** piaweb@pianet.org. **World Wide Web address:** http://www.pianet.com. **Description:** Represents independent agents in all 50 states, Puerto Rico and the District of Columbia. Founded in 1931.

PROPERTY CASUALTY INSURERS ASSOCIATION OF AMERICA
2600 South River Road, Des Plaines IL 60018-3286. 847/297-7800. **Fax:** 847/297-5064. **World Wide Web address:** http://www.pciaa.net. **Description:** A property/casualty trade association representing more than 1,000 member companies, PCI advocates its members' public policy positions at the federal and state levels and to the public.

LEGAL SERVICES

AMERICAN BAR ASSOCIATION
321 North Clark Street, Chicago IL 60610. 312/988-5000. **E-mail address:** askaba@abanet.org. **World Wide Web address:** http://www.abanet.org. **Description:** A voluntary professional association with more than 400,000 members, the ABA provides law school accreditation, continuing legal education, information about the law, programs to assist lawyers and judges in their work, and initiatives to improve the legal system for the public.

FEDERAL BAR ASSOCIATION
2215 M Street, NW, Washington DC 20037. 202/785-1614. **Fax:** 202/785-1568. **E-mail address:** fba@fedbar.org. **World Wide Web address:** http://www.fedbar.org. **Description:** The professional organization for private and government lawyers and judges involved in federal practice.

NATIONAL ASSOCIATION OF LEGAL ASSISTANTS
1516 South Boston, #200, Tulsa OK 74119. 918/587-6828. **World Wide Web address:** http://www.nala.org. **Description:** A professional association for legal assistants and paralegals, providing continuing education and professional development programs. Founded in 1975.

NATIONAL FEDERATION OF PARALEGAL ASSOCIATIONS
2517 Eastlake Avenue East, Suite 200, Seattle WA 98102. 206/652-4120. **Fax:** 206/652-4122. **E-mail address:** info@paralegals.org. **World Wide Web address:** http://www.paralegals.org. **Description:** A non-profit professional organization representing more than 15,000 paralegals in the United States and Canada. NFPA is the national voice and the standard for excellence for the paralegal profession through its work on the issues of regulation, ethics and education.

MANUFACTURING: MISCELLANEOUS CONSUMER

ASSOCIATION FOR MANUFACTURING EXCELLENCE
380 Palantine Road West, Wheeling IL 60090-5863. 847/520-3282. **Fax:** 847/520-0163. **World Wide Web address:** http://www.ame.org. **Description:** A not-for-profit organization founded in 1985 consisting of 6000 executives, senior and middle managers who wish to improve the competitiveness of their organizations.

ASSOCIATION FOR MANUFACTURING TECHNOLOGY
7901 Westpark Drive, McLean VA 22102-4206. 703/893-2900. **Fax:** 703/893-1151. **Toll-free phone:** 703/893-2900. **World Wide Web address:** http://www.amtonline.org. **Description:** Supports and promotes American manufacturers of machine tools and manufacturing technology. Provides members with industry expertise and assistance on critical industry concerns.

ASSOCIATION OF HOME APPLIANCE MANUFACTURERS
1111 19th Street, NW, Suite 402, Washington DC 20036. 202/872-5955. **Fax:** 202/872-9354. **World Wide Web address:** http://www.aham.org. **Description:** Represents the manufacturers of household appliances and products/services associated with household appliances.

SOCIETY OF MANUFACTURING ENGINEERS
One SME Drive, Dearborn MI 48121. 313/271-1500. **Fax:** 313/425-3401. **Toll-free phone:** 800/733-4763. **World Wide Web address:** http://www.sme.org. **Description:** Promotes an increased awareness of manufacturing engineering and helps keep manufacturing professionals up to date on leading trends and technologies. Founded in 1932.

MANUFACTURING: MISCELLANEOUS INDUSTRIAL

ASSOCIATION FOR MANUFACTURING EXCELLENCE
380 Palantine Road West, Wheeling IL 60090-5863. 847/520-3282. **Fax:** 847/520-0163. **World Wide Web address:** http://www.ame.org. **Description:** A not-for-profit organization founded in 1985 consisting of 6000 executives, senior and middle managers who wish to improve the competitiveness of their organizations.

INSTITUTE OF INDUSTRIAL ENGINEERS
3577 Parkway Lane, Suite 200, Norcross GA 30092. 770/449-0460. **Fax:** 770/441-3295. **Toll-free phone:** 800/494-0460. **World Wide Web address:** http://www.iienet.org. **Description:** A non-profit professional society dedicated to the support of the industrial engineering profession and individuals involved with improving quality and productivity. Founded in 1948.

NATIONAL ASSOCIATION OF MANUFACTURERS
1331 Pennsylvania Avenue, NW, Washington DC 20004-1790. 202/637-3000. **Fax:** 202/637-3182. **E-mail address:** manufacturing@nam.org. **World Wide Web address:** http://www.nam.org. **Description:** With 14,000 members, NAM's mission is to enhance the competitiveness of manufacturers and to improve American living standards by shaping a legislative and regulatory environment conducive to U.S. economic growth, and to increase understanding among policymakers, the media and the public about the importance of manufacturing to America's economic strength.

NATIONAL TOOLING AND MACHINING ASSOCIATION
9300 Livingston Road, Fort Washington MD 20744-4998. 800/248-6862. **Fax:** 301/248-7104. **World Wide Web address:** http://www.ntma.org. **Description:** A trade organization representing the precision custom manufacturing industry throughout the United States.

SOCIETY OF MANUFACTURING ENGINEERS
One SME Drive, Dearborn MI 48121. 313/271-1500. **Fax:** 313/425-3401. **Toll-free phone:** 800/733-4763. **World Wide Web address:** http://www.sme.org. **Description:** Promotes an increased awareness of manufacturing engineering and helps keep manufacturing professionals up to date on leading trends and technologies. Founded in 1932.

MINING, GAS, PETROLEUM, ENERGY RELATED

AMERICAN ASSOCIATION OF PETROLEUM GEOLOGISTS
P.O. Box 979, Tulsa OK 74101-0979. 918/584-2555. **Physical address:** 1444 South Boulder, Tulsa OK 74119. **Fax:** 918/560-2665. **Toll-free phone:** 800/364-2274. **E-mail address:** postmaster@aapg.org. **World Wide Web address:** http://www.aapg.org. **Description:** Founded in 1917, the AAPG's purpose is to foster scientific research, advance the science of geology, promote technology, and inspire high professional conduct. The AAPG has over 30,000 members.

AMERICAN GEOLOGICAL INSTITUTE
4220 King Street, Alexandria VA 22302-1502. 703/379-2480. **Fax:** 703/379-7563. **World Wide Web address:** http://www.agiweb.org. **Description:** A nonprofit federation of 42 geoscientific and professional associations that represents more than 100,000 geologists, geophysicists, and other earth scientists. Provides information services to geoscientists, serves as a voice of shared interests in the profession, plays a major role in strengthening geoscience education, and strives to increase public awareness of the vital role the geosciences play in society's use of resources and interaction with the environment.

AMERICAN NUCLEAR SOCIETY
555 North Kensington Avenue, La Grange Park IL 60526. 708/352-6611. **Fax:** 708/352-0499. **World Wide Web address:** http://www.ans.org. **Description:** A not-for-profit, international, scientific and educational organization with a membership of 10,500 engineers, scientists, administrators, and educators representing 1,600 corporations, educational institutions, and government agencies.

AMERICAN PETROLEUM INSTITUTE
1220 L Street, NW, Washington DC 20005-4070. 202/682-8000. **World Wide Web address:** http://www.api.org. **Description:** Functions to insure a strong, viable U.S. oil and natural gas industry capable of meeting the energy needs of our Nation in an efficient and environmentally responsible manner.

GEOLOGICAL SOCIETY OF AMERICA
3300 Penrose Place, P.O. Box 9140, Boulder CO 80301. 303/447-2020. **Fax:** 303/357-1070. **Toll-free phone:** 888/443-4472. **E-mail address:** gsaservice@geosociety.org. **World Wide Web address:** http://www.geosociety.org. **Description:** The mission of GSA is to advance the geosciences, to enhance the professional growth of its members, and to promote the geosciences in the service of humankind.

SOCIETY FOR MINING, METALLURGY, AND EXPLORATION
8307 Shaffer Parkway, Littleton CO 80127-4102. 303/973-9550. **Fax:** 303/973-3845. **Toll-free phone:** 800/763-3132. **E-mail address:** sme@smenet.org. **World Wide Web address:** http://www.smenet.org. **Description:** An international society of professionals in the mining and minerals industry.

SOCIETY OF PETROLEUM ENGINEERS
P.O. Box 833836, Richardson TX 75083-3836. 972/952-9393. **Physical address:** 222 palisades Creek Drive, Richardson TX 75080. **Fax:** 972/952-9435. **E-mail address:** spedal@spe.org. **World Wide Web address:** http://www.spe.org. **Description:** SPE is a professional association whose

60,000-plus members worldwide are engaged in energy resources development and production. SPE is a key resource for technical information related to oil and gas exploration and production and provides services through its publications, meetings, and online.

PAPER AND WOOD PRODUCTS

AMERICAN FOREST AND PAPER ASSOCIATION
1111 Nineteenth Street, NW, Suite 800, Washington DC 20036. **Toll-free phone:** 800/878-8878. **E-mail address:** info@afandpa.org. **World Wide Web address:** http://www.afandpa.org. **Description:** The national trade association of the forest, pulp, paper, paperboard and wood products industry.

FOREST PRODUCTS SOCIETY
2801 Marshall Court, Madison WI 53705-2295. 608/231-1361. **Fax:** 608/231-2152. **E-mail address:** info@forestprod.org. **World Wide Web address:** http://www.forestprod.org. **Description:** An international not-for-profit technical association founded in 1947 to provide an information network for all segments of the forest products industry.

NPTA ALLIANCE
500 Bi-County Boulevard, Suite 200E, Farmingdale NY 11735. 631/777-2223. **Fax:** 631/777-2224. **Toll-free phone:** 800/355-NPTA. **World Wide Web address:** http://www.gonpta.com. **Description:** An association for the $60 billion paper, packaging, and supplies distribution industry.

PAPERBOARD PACKAGING COUNCIL
201 North Union Street, Suite 220, Alexandria VA 22314. 703/836-3300. **Fax:** 703/836-3290. **E-mail address:** http://www.ppcnet.org. **World Wide Web address:** http://www.ppcnet.org. **Description:** A trade association representing the manufacturers of paperboard packaging in the United States.

TECHNICAL ASSOCIATION OF THE PULP AND PAPER INDUSTRY
15 Technology Parkway South, Norcross GA 30092. 770/446-1400. **Fax:** 770/446-6947. **Toll-free phone:** 800/332-8686. **World Wide Web address:** http://www.tappi.org. **Description:** The leading technical association for the worldwide pulp, paper, and converting industry.

PRINTING AND PUBLISHING

AMERICAN BOOKSELLERS ASSOCIATION
828 South Broadway, Tarrytown NY 10591. 914/591-2665. **Fax:** 914/591-2720.
Toll-free phone: 800/637-0037. **E-mail address:** info@bookweb.org. **World Wide Web address:** http://www.bookweb.org. **Description:** A not-for-profit organization founded in 1900 devoted to meeting the needs of its core members of independently owned bookstores with retail storefront locations through advocacy, education, research, and information dissemination.

AMERICAN INSTITUTE OF GRAPHIC ARTS
164 Fifth Avenue, New York NY 10010. 212/807-1990. **Fax:** 212/807-1799. **E-mail address:** comments@aiga.org. **World Wide Web address:** http://www.aiga.org. **Description:** Furthers excellence in communication design as a broadly defined discipline, strategic tool for business and cultural force. AIGA is the place design professionals turn to first to exchange ideas and information, participate in critical analysis and research and advance education and ethical practice. Founded in 1914.

AMERICAN SOCIETY OF NEWSPAPER EDITORS
11690B Sunrise Valley Drive, Reston VA 20191-1409. 703/453-1122. **Fax:** 703/453-1133. **E-mail address:** asne@asne.org. **World Wide Web address:** http://www.asne.org. **Description:** A membership organization for daily newspaper editors, people who serve the editorial needs of daily newspapers and certain distinguished individuals who have worked on behalf of editors through the years.

ASSOCIATION OF AMERICAN PUBLISHERS, INC.
71 Fifth Avenue, 2nd Floor, New York NY 10003. 212/255-0200. **Fax:** 212/255-7007. **World Wide Web address:** http://www.publishers.org. **Description:** Representing publishers of all sizes and types located throughout the U.S., the AAP is the principal trade association of the book publishing industry.

ASSOCIATION OF GRAPHIC COMMUNICATIONS
330 Seventh Avenue, 9th Floor, New York NY 10001-5010. 212/279-2100. **Fax:** 212/279-5381. **E-mail address:** info@agcomm.org. **World Wide Web address:** http://www.agcomm.org. **Description:** The AGC serves as a network for industry information and idea exchange, provides graphic arts education and training, promotes and markets the industry, and advocates legislative and environmental issues.

BINDING INDUSTRIES OF AMERICA
100 Daingerfield Road, Alexandria VA 22314. 703/519-8137. **Fax:** 703/548-3227. **World Wide Web address:** http://www.bindingindustries.org. **Description:** A trade association representing Graphic Finishers, Loose-Leaf Manufacturers, and suppliers to these industries throughout the United States, Canada, and Europe.

THE DOW JONES NEWSPAPER FUND
P.O. Box 300, Princeton NJ 08543-0300. 609/452-2820. **Fax:** 609/520-5804. **E-mail address:** newsfund@wsj.dowjones.com. **World Wide Web address:** http://djnewspaperfund.dowjones.com. **Description:** Founded in 1958 by editors of The Wall Street Journal to improve the quality of journalism education and the pool of applicants for jobs in the newspaper business. It provides internships and scholarships to college students, career literature, fellowships for high school

journalism teachers and publications' advisers and training for college journalism instructors. The Fund is a nonprofit foundation supported by the Dow Jones Foundation, Dow Jones & Company, Inc. and other newspaper companies.

GRAPHIC ARTISTS GUILD
90 John Street, Suite 403, New York NY 10038-3202. 212/791-3400. **World Wide Web address:** http://www.gag.org. **Description:** A national union of illustrators, designers, web creators, production artists, surface designers and other creatives who have come together to pursue common goals, share their experience, raise industry standards, and improve the ability of visual creators to achieve satisfying and rewarding careers.

INTERNATIONAL GRAPHIC ARTS EDUCATION ASSOCIATION
1899 Preston White Drive, Reston VA 20191-4367. 703/758-0595. **World Wide Web address:** http://www.igaea.org. **Description:** An association of educators in partnership with industry, dedicated to sharing theories, principles, techniques and processes relating to graphic communications and imaging technology.

MAGAZINE PUBLISHERS OF AMERICA
810 Seventh Avenue, 24th Floor, New York NY 10019. 212/872-3746. **E-mail address:** infocenter@magazine.org. **World Wide Web address:** http://www.magazine.org. **Description:** An industry association for consumer magazines representing more than 240 domestic publishing companies with approximately 1,400 titles, more than 80 international companies and more than 100 associate members.

NATIONAL ASSOCIATION FOR PRINTING LEADERSHIP
75 West Century Road, Paramus NJ 07652-1408. 201/634-9600. **Fax:** 201/986-2976. **E-mail address:** information@napl.org. **World Wide Web address:** http://www.napl.org. **Description:** A not-for-profit trade association founded in 1933 for commercial printers and related members of the Graphic Arts Industry.

NATIONAL NEWSPAPER ASSOCIATION
P.O. Box 7540,, Columbia MO 65205-7540. 573/882-5800. **Fax:** 573/884-5490. **Toll-free phone:** 800/829-4662. **World Wide Web address:** http://www.nna.org. **Description:** A non-profit association promoting the common interests of newspapers.

NATIONAL PRESS CLUB
529 14th Street, NW, Washington DC 20045. 202/662-7500. **Fax:** 202/662-7512. **World Wide Web address:** http://npc.press.org. **Description:** Provides people who gather and disseminate news a center for the advancement of their professional standards and skills, the promotion of free expression, mutual support and social fellowship. Founded in 1908.

NEWSPAPER ASSOCIATION OF AMERICA
1921 Gallows Road, Suite 600, Vienna VA 22182-3900. 703/902-1600. **Fax:** 703/917-0636. **World Wide Web address:** http://www.naa.org. **Description:** A nonprofit organization representing the $55 billion newspaper industry.

THE NEWSPAPER GUILD
501 Third Street, NW, Suite 250, Washington DC 20001. 202/434-7177. **Fax:** 202/434-1472. **E-mail address:** guild@cwa-union.org. **World Wide Web address:** http://www.newsguild.org. **Description:** Founded as a print journalists' union, the Guild today is primarily a media union whose members are diverse in their occupations, but who share the view that the best working conditions are achieved by people who have a say in their workplace.

TECHNICAL ASSOCIATION OF THE GRAPHIC ARTS
200 Deer Run Road, Sewickley PA 15213. 412/259-1813. **Fax:** 412/741-2311. **E-mail address:** jallen@piagatf.org. **World Wide Web address:** http://www.taga.org. **Description:** A professional technical association founded in 1948 for the graphic arts industries.

WRITERS GUILD OF AMERICA WEST
7000 West Third Street, Los Angeles CA 90048. 323/951-4000. **Fax:** 323/782-4800. **Toll-free phone:** 800/548-4532. **E-mail address: World Wide Web address:** http://www.wga.org. **Description:** Represents writers in the motion picture, broadcast, cable and new technologies industries.

REAL ESTATE

INSTITUTE OF REAL ESTATE MANAGEMENT
430 North Michigan Avenue, Chicago IL 60611-4090. 312/329-6000. **Fax:** 800/338-4736. **Toll-free phone:** 800/837-0706. **E-mail address:** custserv@irem.org. **World Wide Web address:** http://www.irem.org. **Description:** IREM, an affiliate of the National Association of Realtors, is an association of professional property and asset managers who have met strict criteria in the areas of education, experience, and a commitment to a code of ethics.

INTERNATIONAL REAL ESTATE INSTITUTE
1224 North Nokomis, NE, Alexandria MN 56308. 320/763-4648. **Fax:** 320/763-9290. **E-mail address:** irei@iami.org. **World Wide Web address:** http://www.iami.org/irei. **Description:** A real estate association with members in more than 100 countries, providing media to communicate on an international basis.

NATIONAL ASSOCIATION OF REALTORS
30700 Russell Ranch Road, Westlake Village CA 91362. 805/557-2300. **Fax:** 805/557-2680. **World Wide Web address:** http://www.realtor.com. **Description:** An industry advocate of the right to own, use, and transfer real property; the acknowledged leader in developing standards for efficient, effective, and ethical real estate business practices; and valued by highly skilled real estate professionals and viewed by them as crucial to their success.

RETAIL

INTERNATIONAL COUNCIL OF SHOPPING CENTERS
1221 Avenue of the Americas, 41st floor, New York NY 10020-1099. 646/728-3800. **Fax:** 732/694-1755. **E-mail address:** icsc@icsc.org. **World Wide Web address:** http://www.icsc.org. **Description:** A trade association of the shopping center industry founded in 1957.

NATIONAL ASSOCIATION OF CHAIN DRUG STORES
413 North Lee Street, PO Box 1417-D49, Alexandria VA 22313-1480. 703/549-3001. **Fax:** 703/836-4869. **World Wide Web address:** http://www.nacds.org. **Description:** Represents the views and policy positions of member chain drug companies accomplished through the programs and services provided by the association.

NATIONAL RETAIL FEDERATION
325 7th Street, NW, Suite 1100, Washington DC 20004. 202/783-7971. **Fax:** 202/737-2849. **Toll-free phone:** 800/NRF-HOW2. **World Wide Web address:** http://www.nrf.com. **Description:** A retail trade association, with membership that comprises all retail formats and channels of distribution including department, specialty, discount, catalog, Internet and independent stores as well as the industry's key trading partners of retail goods and services. NRF represents an industry with more than 1.4 million U.S. retail establishments, more than 20 million employees - about one in five American workers - and 2003 sales of $3.8 trillion.

STONE, CLAY, GLASS, AND CONCRETE PRODUCTS

THE AMERICAN CERAMIC SOCIETY
PO Box 6136, Westerville OH 43086-6136. 614/890-4700. **Fax:** 614/899-6109. **E-mail address:** info@ceramics.org. **World Wide Web address:** http://www.acers.org. **Description:** An organization dedicated to the advancement of ceramics.

NATIONAL GLASS ASSOCIATION
8200 Greensboro Drive, Suite 302, McLean VA 22102-3881. 866/342-5642. **Fax:** 703/442-0630. **World Wide Web address:** http://www.glass.org. **Description:** A trade association founded in 1948 representing the flat (architectural and automotive) glass industry. The association represents nearly 5,000 member companies and locations, and produces the industry events and publications.

TRANSPORTATION AND TRAVEL

AIR TRANSPORT ASSOCIATION OF AMERICA
1301 Pennsylvania Avenue, NW, Suite 1100, Washington DC 20004-1707. 202/626-4000. **Fax:** 301/206-9789. **Toll-free phone:** 800/497-3326. **E-mail address:** ata@airlines.org. **World Wide Web address:** http://www.air-transport.org. **Description:** A trade organization for the principal U.S. airlines.

AMERICAN SOCIETY OF TRAVEL AGENTS
1101 King Street, Suite 200, Alexandria VA 22314. 703/739-2782. **Fax:** 703/684-8319. **World Wide Web address:** http://www.astanet.com. **Description:** An association of travel professionals whose members include travel agents and the companies whose products they sell such as tours, cruises, hotels, car rentals, etc.

AMERICAN TRUCKING ASSOCIATIONS
2200 Mill Road, Alexandria VA 22314. 703/838-1700. **Toll-free phone:** 888/333-1759. **World Wide Web address:** http://www.trucking.org. **Description:** Serves and represents the interests of the trucking industry with one united voice; positively influences Federal and State governmental actions; advances the trucking industry's image, efficiency, competitiveness, and profitability; provides educational programs and industry research; promotes highway and driver safety; and strives for a healthy business environment.

ASSOCIATION OF AMERICAN RAILROADS
50 F Street, NW, Washington DC 20001-1564. 202/639-2100. **World Wide Web address:** http://www.aar.org. **Description:** A trade associations representing the major freight railroads of the United States, Canada and Mexico.

INSTITUTE OF TRANSPORTATION ENGINEERS
1099 14th Street, NW, Suite 300 West, Washington DC 20005-3438. 202/289-0222. **Fax:** 202/289-7722. **E-mail address:** ite_staff@ite.org. **World Wide Web address:** http://www.ite.org. **Description:** An international individual member educational and scientific association whose members are traffic engineers, transportation planners and other professionals who are responsible for meeting society's needs for safe and efficient surface transportation through planning, designing, implementing, operating and maintaining surface transportation systems worldwide.

MARINE TECHNOLOGY SOCIETY
5565 Sterrett Place, Suite 108, Columbia MD 21044. 410/884-5330. **Fax:** 410/884-9060. **E-mail address:** mtsmbrship@erols.com. **World Wide Web address:** http://www.mtsociety.org. **Description:** A member-based society supporting all the components of the ocean community: marine sciences, engineering, academia, industry and government. The society is dedicated to the development, sharing and education of information and ideas.

NATIONAL TANK TRUCK CARRIERS
2200 Mill Road, Alexandria VA 22314. 703/838-1960. **Fax:** 703/684-5753. **E-mail address:** inquiries@tanktruck.org. **World Wide Web address:** http://www.tanktruck.net. **Description:** A trade association founded in 1945 and composed of approximately 180 trucking companies, which specialize in the nationwide distribution of bulk liquids, industrial gases and dry products in cargo tank motor vehicles.

UTILITIES: ELECTRIC, GAS, AND WATER

AMERICAN PUBLIC GAS ASSOCIATION
201 Massachusetts Avenue, NE, Suite C-4 Washington DC 20002. 202/464-2742. **Fax:** 202/464-0246. **E-mail address:** website@apga.org. **World Wide Web address:** http://www.apga.org. **Description:** A nonprofit trade organization representing publicly owned natural gas local distribution companies (LDCs). APGA represents the interests of public gas before Congress, federal agencies and other energy-related stakeholders by developing regulatory and legislative policies that further the goals of our members. In addition, APGA organizes meetings, seminars, and workshops with a specific goal to improve the reliability, operational efficiency, and regulatory environment in which public gas systems operate.

AMERICAN PUBLIC POWER ASSOCIATION (APPA)
2301 M Street, NW, Washington DC 20037-1484. 202/467-2900. **Fax:** 202/467-2910. **World Wide Web address:** http://www.appanet.org. **Description:** The service organization for the nation's more than 2,000 community-owned electric utilities that serve more than 40 million Americans. Its purpose is to advance the public policy interests of its members and their consumers, and provide member services to ensure adequate, reliable electricity at a reasonable price with the proper protection of the environment.

AMERICAN WATER WORKS ASSOCIATION
6666 West Quincy Avenue, Denver CO 80235. 303/794-7711. **Fax:** 303/347-0804. **Toll-free phone:** 800/926-7337. **World Wide Web address:** http://www.awwa.org. **Description:** A resource for knowledge, information, and advocacy to improve the quality and supply of drinking water in North America. The association advances public health, safety and welfare by uniting the efforts of the full spectrum of the drinking water community.

NATIONAL RURAL ELECTRIC COOPERATIVE ASSOCIATION
4301 Wilson Boulevard, Arlington VA 22203. 703/907-5500. **E-mail address:** nreca@nreca.coop. **World Wide Web address:** http://www.nreca.org. **Description:** A national organization representing the national interests of cooperative electric utilities and the consumers they serve. Founded in 1942.

MISCELLANEOUS WHOLESALING

NATIONAL ASSOCIATION OF WHOLESALER-DISTRIBUTORS (NAW)
1725 K Street, NW, Washington DC 20006-1419. 202/872-0885. **Fax:** 202/785-0586. **World Wide Web address:** http://www.naw.org. **Description:** A trade association that represents the wholesale distribution industry active in government relations and political action; research and education; and group purchasing.

INDEX OF PRIMARY EMPLOYERS

Washington Mutual, Inc./103
Water Authority of Western Nassau
    County/341
Waterview Nursing Care Center/244
Watson Pharmaceuticals, Inc./119
We Transport Inc./338
Webster Bank/103
Wegmans/226
Weichert Realtors/321
Weight Watchers International
    Inc./244
Weil Gotshal & Manges/267
Weiss-Aug Company Inc./290
Welsbach Electric Corporation/81
Jane Wesman Public Relations/62
West Point Stevens, Inc./74
Westchester Community Opportunity
    Program/137
Westchester Library System/130
Western Beef, Inc./330
Western Connecticut State
    University/184
Western Union Corporation/155
George Weston Bakeries, Inc./227
Westside Veterinary Center/244
White & Case LLP/267
Wildlife Conservation Society
    (WCS)/Bronx Zoo/91
Wilentz, Goldman & Spitzer/267
John Wiley & Sons, Inc./316, 317

William Morris Agency, Inc./91
William Paterson University of New
    Jersey/184
Willis of New York, Inc./261
Wilshire Oil Company/293
The H.W. Wilson Company/317
Thomas C. Wilson, Inc./290
Wilson Elser Moskowitz Edelman &
    Dicker LLP/267
Winfield Security/130
Winston Resources, Inc./130
Women's Golf Unlimited/278
Woodbridge Developmental
    Center/244
World Wrestling Federation
    Entertainment, Inc./91, 155
Worrall Community Newspapers
    Incorporated/317
Wunderman/130
Wyeth Corporation/119
Wyeth/120

X, Y, Z
XL Re America, Inc./262
Xerox Corporation/198
YWCA/138
Yonkers Raceway/92
Young & Rubicam, Inc./62
Ziff-Davis Media Inc./317